ASPEN

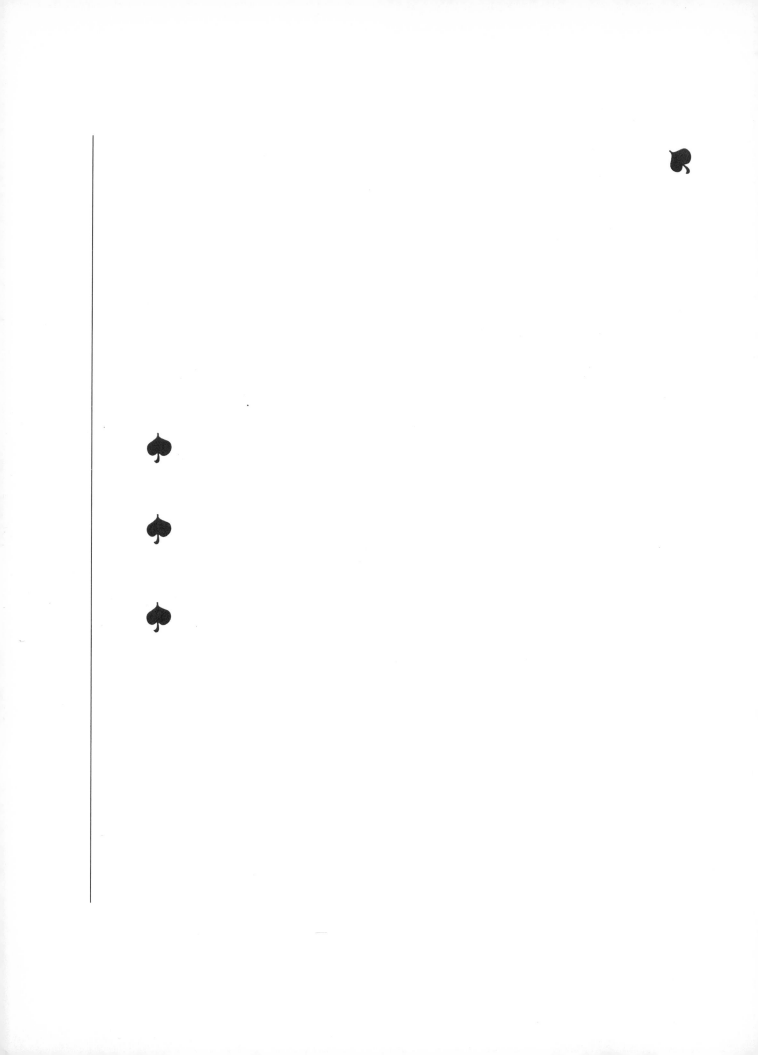

ASPEN

The Quiet Years

BY

KATHLEEN KRIEGER DAILY

AND

GAYLORD T. GUENIN

Red Ink Inc.
Aspen, Colorado

Aspen: The Quiet Years

Copyright © 1994 by Red Ink Inc.

ISBN: 0-9641399-0-1

Library of Congress Cataloging-in-Publication Data

Daily, Kathleen Krieger, 1947-
  Aspen: the quiet years / Kathleen Krieger Daily and
Gaylord T. Guenin. — 1st ed.
      p.   cm.
  Includes bibliographical references (p.).
  ISBN 0-9641399-0-1
  1. Aspen (Colo.) — History. 2. Aspen (Colo.) — Social life
and customs. I. Guenin, Gaylord T.   II. Title.
  F784.A7D35   1994
  978.8'43—dc20   94-23231
                                                                CIP

Cover and Interior Design:
Dianne Borneman, Shadow Canyon Graphics
and Kathleen Krieger Daily
Editors: Kathleen Krieger Daily and Dianne Borneman

First Edition
1 2 3 4 5 6 7 8 9

Printed in the United States of America

CONTENTS

ACKNOWLEDGEMENTS

We would like to acknowledge these people for their assistance:

Berry Roper
Arthur Daily
Richard Cowling
Dorothy Portner
Francis Kalmes
Walnut House Lab
Kathy Strough Foote
Aspen Historical Society
Pitkin County Library

A thank you
from the heart
to George and Patti Stranahan,
who still believe
in the community of Aspen
and the Roaring Fork Valley.

To my parents,
who always believed
in me,
And to Art, Tanner, and Shea,
who forever love me.

♠

Kathy

For my father,
who encouraged me to open
as many of life's doors
as possible,
and by example,
taught me to respect
and to attempt
to understand
those drawn
to other doors.

♣

Gaylord

Introduction

Mill Street in the mining days.
Courtesy Aspen Historical Society

Reminders of Aspen's rich heritage as a silver-mining town are as abundant as the aspen trees that grace so much of this magnificent valley. That heritage is celebrated in the names of local businesses and in the hundreds of old photographs that adorn the walls of restaurants, bars, lodges, hotels, and banks. There are many books that detail Aspen's formative years, as well as an occasional lawsuit involving disputed ownership of an ancient mining claim. And then there are the cries of protest that reverberate from one end of the valley to the other whenever it appears that someone might actually attempt to once again mine in Pitkin County.

The pick and shovel may have given birth to Aspen, but the credit card and abundance of disposable income are what sustain it today. The silver and gold imported into the community by tourists and new residents are what fuel the valley, not the remains of minerals still hidden beneath the mountains. And visitors are not really attracted to the Aspen area because of its past — they come to play in the present. It is not the solid foundation so laboriously set in place by the early settlers that draws today's visitor — it is the finished and expensive veneer of the twentieth century, coupled with a pace that often has the exhilarating feel of the twenty-first century. It is not the promise of experiencing yesterday, but the possibility of tasting tomorrow that gives Aspen so much of its unique appeal today.

Growth has become a major concern in Aspen and the surrounding valleys, but it most certainly was what the majority of valley residents sought in the late 1800s. Each increase in the local population and in the production of silver ore was applauded by the citizenry and celebrated by local editors, even though the Roaring Fork River was becoming polluted, herds of deer and elk were being diminished, and timber was being stripped from the local mountains at an accelerating rate. Aspen was a boom town, and the people who lived there wanted only to encourage growth. In 1887, the year the two railroads began serving the community, one editor proclaimed that Aspen was now "the most prosperous city in Colorado." In 1893, another editor was stirred to write,

"Aspen is the greatest silver mining camp in the world today if indeed, it is not the most wonderful in history." Alter that sentence slightly so that it reads, "Aspen is the greatest winter and summer resort in the world today, if indeed, it is not the most wonderful in history," and few would be shocked by the claim.

The endless parade of private jets at Sardy Field alone offers the most convincing testimony to Aspen's status in the modern world. It is hard to believe that 113 years ago, men and women walked from Leadville and Buena Vista to begin populating this valley. In the 1960s and 1970s, a new population arrived. Many drove ancient Volkswagen buses and bugs painted in bizarre ways, yet this group was as diverse and as intent upon settling in Aspen as were the early miners. Then, in the 1980s, a new breed of Aspenite began to immigrate into the valley, arriving in private jets or driving the finest of imported luxury cars. That immigration continues to this day.

The changes in Aspen since the late 1940s have continued to escalate with each decade, filling the valley with new controversies. None of this comes gently or slowly. Yet through it all, Aspen's mining heritage has remained intact and reasonably free from the threat of ever being forgotten completely. No matter how limited our knowledge of that period may be, it marks the birth of Aspen.

There is a period of Aspen's history, however, that could easily be forgotten, a period when the lights of Aspen began to dim and softly flicker for almost fifty years. Still, the lights never went out. These were the years between prospecting and prosperity. We call them the Quiet Years.

✦

The Quiet Years

A town without a tomorrow.
At one time, Aspen was such a town.
For a period of years from about 1893 to 1947,
Aspen's only future lay in its past.
All of its dreams were trapped in its
memories of yesterday.
In 1893, when the United States repealed
the Sherman Silver Purchase Act of 1890 and
returned to a gold standard,
Aspen slipped into that netherworld,
into that strange room with a single door
that opened only into the past.

Homesteaders, about 1900.
Courtesy Robert Zupancis.

CRYSTAL CITY OF THE ROCKIES

It was a stark about-face for a community that was built and sustained by dreams of a brighter and more prosperous future. Such dreams had fueled the creation of endless mining camps and boom towns across the West, communities that exploded onto the scene, then abruptly vanished and were forgotten. In Aspen, however, the promise of a better tomorrow seemed well founded. In only fourteen years, from 1879 to 1893, Aspen and the Roaring Fork Valley went from an empty wilderness — one the Ute Indians had only recently been forced to leave — to the third largest city in Colorado, behind Denver and Leadville. Aspen was, for a brief period, the largest producer of silver in North America and with unabashed pride referred to itself as the Crystal City of the Rockies. Aspenites, many of whom were immigrants fresh from Europe, had caught a glimpse of a future that was more spectacular than anything most of them could have imagined. After the events of 1893, there was only the diminishing hope that tomorrow would bring a return to that brief and shimmering time.

The first prospectors who trudged across the Continental Divide from Leadville to the Roaring Fork Valley in the summer of 1879 surely believed that a brighter tomorrow awaited them. During 1873-74, Frederick V. Hayden and his surveying party had been allowed by the Ute Indians to map the geographic and geologic features of the region. Once copies of Hayden's surveys began to circulate in Denver and Leadville, it became obvious to knowledgeable miners that the Roaring Fork Valley was rich in the features associated with mineral deposits such as silver and gold.

Two different prospecting parties arrived in the Aspen area in the summer of 1879, and in all likelihood they were among the first white men to have ever visited the area other than Hayden and his surveying party. A group of three, consisting of Phillip W. Pratt, Smith Steele, and William Hopkins, departed

*Construction of the
Mesa Store, about 1888.
On far left in straw hat
is Edward Grover,
Charley Grover's
grandfather.
Courtesy
Charley Grover.*

Leadville in late June to explore this new area. Approximately one week later, four more prospectors from Leadville arrived in the valley of the Roaring Fork. They were Charles E. Bennett, Walter S. Clark, A. C. Fellows, and S. E. Hopkins. The two groups shared an evening together, and the following day the Pratt party began the trek back to Leadville, where the three men registered their claims and spread the word about the new bonanza. The creation of a place to be called Aspen had begun.

The Bennett party spent five days in the valley staking claims and then returned to Leadville to file on those claims, generating even more interest among the miners, prospectors, and entrepreneurs who had poured into Leadville during the past two years. In 1877, the population of Leadville was estimated to be less than 200, yet by 1880 it was approaching 15,000 and was Colorado's second largest city, testimony to the enormous attraction of successful mining camps and the promise of sudden wealth. Now, as word of the Bennett and Pratt findings spread, men who had barely settled into a life in Leadville prepared to pursue yet another dream in the Roaring Fork Valley. In a matter of weeks after the Bennett party returned to Leadville, groups of prospectors were heading back to the valley of the Roaring Fork, and some thirty to thirty-five men observed Christmas and the arrival of the New Year in their newly adopted home.

Aspen began life as a place called Ute City (the name was changed to Aspen in the summer of 1880), and for a brief time it was forced to take a back seat to a pair of other nearby mining camps — Independence, essentially a gold camp, and Ashcroft. By 1882, however, Independence was on the verge of becoming a ghost town, and Ashcroft eventually followed in its footsteps. But Aspen was beginning to stir. It was estimated that as many as 150 miners were employed in Aspen in 1883. The total resident population was believed to be in excess of 1,000, and the local papers spoke of a housing shortage. The following year, 1884, 500 miners were said to be working in Aspen. Those numbers increased steadily until 1893, when a peak population of perhaps 3,000 miners was reached. In approximately fourteen years, the tiny mining camp became a prosperous and permanent city, and Aspenites were not the least bit shy about describing their community in the most glowing of terms.

B. T. Pearce and Company, Aspen, 1898. Courtesy Del Gerbaz.

Hotel Jerome,
early 1900s.
Courtesy Aspen
Historical Society.

If the residents of Aspen were boastful about their community, they were not without justification. Aspen's mining-camp days were already a part of history. Aspen was a modern city, one that could claim almost all of the amenities available in the most progressive cities of the day. Two railroads, the Denver & Rio Grande and the Midland, offered daily freight and passenger service to Aspen. As if to emphasize its permanence, Aspenites put great stock in the fact that most of its downtown area and two of its major churches were constructed of brick and stone. The community pointed with pride to the Jerome Hotel, considered one of the finest hostels in the West; to the Wheeler Opera House, the third largest in Colorado; to its magnificent courthouse and city armory; and to its hospital and public-school system. Aspen had a municipal water system, two electric light and power companies, a streetcar system, and approximately a half-dozen newspapers, including two dailies. It is estimated that in 1893, 227 mines were operating in Pitkin County, and, in the Mollie Gibson, Aspen had the largest producing silver mine in the United States.

DOWN, BUT NOT OUT

The repeal of the Sherman Act initiated Aspen's downward spiral. President Benjamin Harrison had signed the Sherman Act into law in 1890 to offer some protection to the price of silver. It required the government to buy 4.5 million ounces of silver each month and to pay for it with U.S. Treasury certificates. Its repeal effectively collapsed the price of silver, which was already in decline. Silver sold at $1.32 an ounce in 1872, seven years prior to the discovery of silver in Aspen; it was $1.10 an ounce in 1887, $0.93 in 1888, and $0.82 in 1892. It was predicted that most Colorado silver mines would close if silver dropped below the ninety-cent mark, and indeed, Aspen's mines were in serious trouble in 1892. With the repeal of the Sherman Act, silver dropped to $0.60 an ounce, and it appeared that the final curtain was about to fall on Aspen, just as it had fallen on so many mining camps throughout the American West.

The nation's return to the gold standard was not an isolated event by any means. The U.S. economy had steadily worsened since 1890, when panic struck Wall Street as a result of the failure of a major London banking firm and the dumping of U.S. securities by English investors. By 1892, America was in an economic depression as more and more European investors turned their backs on the United States. Less than two months after celebrating the New Year of 1893, the Philadelphia and Reading Railroad went into receivership with debts of $123 million, followed shortly by the Northern Pacific, the Erie, the Union Pacific, and the Santa Fe. Wall Street experienced a sudden drop in prices in May, and the market collapsed on June 27. Some 600 banks closed, 15,000 businesses failed, and 74 railroads went into receivership in a depression that continued for four more years.

President Grover Cleveland was convinced that the economic depression facing the nation was tied directly to "free silver." He successfully lobbied Congress to repeal the Sherman Act, which it did in special session on October 31, 1893. Almost overnight, the Crystal City of the Rockies was threatened with becoming just another down-and-out mining camp, if not another ghost town.

The events of 1893 knocked Aspen to its knees, and perhaps unbeknownst to its citizens, that awesome punch also managed to trap Aspen in its own past. Here was a community that knew only one thing — silver. Silver would dominate the dreams of Aspenites for the better part of another thirty years, but the realization of those dreams was never to be fulfilled. Aspen would boom once more, but not as a result of mining or silver. The decline brought on by the

Lobby of Hotel Jerome, about 1890. Courtesy Aspen Historical Society.

events of the 1890s would only worsen, until by the 1930s, Aspen's population was estimated to be 750, a figure more than one citizen of the period considered to be 200 to 300 residents too many. In fact, one resident was quite emphatic about Aspen's population, saying, "I can tell you that in the 1930s there weren't more than 350 in this town. I knew everybody in town. Hell, I knew the name of every damn dog in town, too."

No matter how desperate or hard the times were to become after the 1893 bust, those who chose to remain in the valley did not give up their community. Aspen simply refused to die, although death certainly lingered nearby for almost half a century. One Aspen native, recalling his childhood, compared his hometown to a boxer: "Aspen was like a prize fighter — down, but it wasn't out. Like Jack Dempsey said, 'The champion is one who gets up when he can't.' I don't think Aspen was ever out. It was down, but not out."

Nowhere is this attitude better recorded than in the two local papers, where the most insignificant of mining news was reported with a flourish and always with the possibility that "this event" might be the one that would elevate Aspen to its former glory. An "editorial" that appeared in the *Aspen Democrat Times* on January 2, 1926, is representative of Aspen's state of mind for the better part of forty years. Under a headline that read "New Year's Day in Aspen," the editor wrote:

> The New Year was ushered in here in Aspen with many watch parties and gatherings at homes where the radio furnished the chief amusement . . .
>
> Many homes were thrown open to friends and guests and the feasts that were spread furnished proof that Aspen was indeed a City of happy homes filled with happy, prosperous people.

Episcopal Church, West End, 1901. Courtesy Peggy Rowland.

Jacks on Hyman Avenue,
1898.
Courtesy
Peggy Rowland.

Nineteen Twenty-six has great things in store for Aspen and before the year is out we will have taken our old place as the leading Silver Camp in the World. Just remember this, please.

In the face of the cancerous decline of Aspen since the repeal of the Sherman Act in 1893, it would have been impossible in 1926 for the editor to substantiate such an optimistic claim, yet apparently most Aspenites shared the editor's confidence that their community might once again become recognized as the Crystal City of the Rockies. This was a near-to-impossible dream, not only because of the repeal of the Sherman Act, but because another force was complicating mining operations in the valley and making it increasingly difficult and expensive to reach and to remove the precious silver. This force was water. As the early miners inched their way deeper and deeper into the bowels of the mountains surrounding Aspen, water began to flood and close the deep tunnels.

In 1910, an attempt was made to pump the water from a rich shaft that intersected the Smuggler and Mollie Gibson claims. The operation was successful enough that approximately $2 million worth of ore was removed. Even that amount could not cover the costs of the operation, however, and in 1911, the pumps were turned off.

The same year that these pumps were silenced, a shaft was started on the Castle Creek side of Aspen Mountain under Richmond Hill. This was the Hope Tunnel, and the intent of the operation was to drive a shaft under the Little Annie Mine, drain the mine of water, then remove the ore via this new entrance. Here was another example of the confidence Aspenites had in themselves and in their future. Thanks to an engineer by the name of Frederick W. Foote, a resident of New York City who was hired to assist with the engineering of the tunnel, we have a first-hand and often poignant portrait of Aspen during this time. Foote came to Aspen in 1917, and in addition to his professional duties as an engineer, he maintained a private journal in which he detailed his most personal reactions to a community that had known far better times. The following passages are from his journal.

HOPE STORY
Frederick W. Foote
Aspen, 1911

The trip was one of several-fold appeal to me. I was getting back to Colorado, which I dearly loved, for a short visit and I was to see a gripping silent drama. I was to see a town in its old age fighting for its life. As a cub surveyor I had seen a town in its youth being carved out of the inhospitable wilderness of the inaccessible British Columbia coast — a town possible because of the copper in the hills behind it. I was now to see a town thirty-five years of age, founded and owing its life to silver mines in the surrounding hills fighting for its continued existence. In its heyday almost a million dollars a month passed through its gates. It was now fighting poverty and a steady dwindling population. In my younger days I had seen some of the ghost towns of Colorado — silent eerie places, merely assemblages of tumbledown cabins inhabited by rats and memories only. The immense waste dumps were silent witnesses to the exhausted mines. Unless

Hope Mine, 1936.
Courtesy Del Gerbaz.

Aspen could find another mine that would pay on low-price silver, it must ultimately die — die of starvation.

The evening we left Denver, we soon started a steady climb that culminated at Tennessee Pass at an elevation of over 10,000 feet. The D. and R.G. probably crosses the Rockies at the highest elevation of any of the lines making through connections. We asked the conductor if he knew Aspen.

"Oh sure, Aspen — that old-time mining camp — about forty miles up the Roaring Fork from Glenwood. Everyone in the state knows it. Used to be the biggest silver camp in Colorado — hit might hard in '93. Used to be 14,000 people there, 1,800 now. All 'old timers' though. It's a game old town — hoping for dollar silver twenty-five years. They have it now. It's looking up some. Wouldn't be surprised to hear of it again these next few years, the way we used to when they got the big nuggets in the Smuggler. One of them weighed 1,850 pounds — solid silver. Funny place in the winter time. Sun rises and sets twice every day. Saw-tooth mountains to the south."

Having completed this thumbnail sketch, the conductor passed on, leaving us to our own resources. My appetite was whetted to see this town that refused to die.

An early morning change to a local train composed of an engine, two freight cars and a baggage-passenger car and a short run along the Roaring Fork took us through a valley of rather poor

Hope Tunnel, 1917. Courtesy Aspen Historical Society.

Hope Tunnel, 1917.
Courtesy Aspen
Historical Society.

looking ranches. The valley narrowed to the ultimate exclusion of the ranches until we reached a park surrounded on all sides by rugged mountains. This was so manifestly a place for a town that Ashcroft had been moved thereto house by house in the early days to become the nucleus of Aspen. The train took a loop around the town and then drew up at the station. We were met by two officials of the company and taken to the Hotel Jerome. This was a large four-story red brick building strong with the earmarks of the "gay nineties" coupled with more than a faint aroma of cabbage. We were escorted up a long flight of stairs to Parlor "B" — an immense, high-ceilinged room equipped with two double beds (which were dwarfed to insignificance), a large, marble-topped central table and a battery of radiators sizzling and booming contentedly.

Subtly the Hotel Jerome conveyed an impression of a brave fight against time. One could easily envisage the bustle and activity of its lobby in days of yore. One could see its barn-like dining room guileless of curtains or rugs, the walls covered with bearskins, as the setting for large boisterous dinners. At present it contained a number of small tables, one occupied by school teachers and several of the others as the individual headquarters of grass widowers — men whose wives had gone down from the High Country to escape some of the rigors of winter. Conviviality and cheerfulness was not one of its keynotes.

Upon our return from an afternoon at the office, our host — a small elderly man with ice blue eyes and a walrus moustache — by long habit led us into the bar. Here one could feel the presence of the old timers in the very mahogany of the bar itself and brass of the footrail. One could see the long row of vari-colored and vari-shaped bottles on the back shelf and frosted designs in soap on the mirrors. The photographs on the walls were of groups of men with big moustaches against a background of mountains, or a tunnel entrance, or a mill building, or a shipment of silver bricks — all stern, hard-eyed men. The large, broad-shouldered barkeeper in his white apron leveling off the foam with his ivory spatula was replaced by a youth in white apron and cap. We three edged up to the bar and placed our feet familiarly on the brass rail and an elbow on the smooth mahogany.

Aspen has rather consolidated its waning business to one main block of substantial brick buildings. Several of these were vacant and those at the end of the street appeared ghostlike and eerie. Their windows were guileless of glass and the wind howled mournfully through their vacant interiors. They were forerunners of the death that seemed to be creeping slowly upon Aspen from the hills that had formerly given it life. One noticed the preponderance of middle-aged to elderly men on the streets — the almost complete absence of young men. They were too old and too deeply rooted to seek a newer camp, and besides, they had lived so long in Aspen they had forgotten how to live elsewhere. It had been their home since youth.

Hope Tunnel, 1917.
Courtesy Aspen
Historical Society.

The people of Aspen, one and all, realized that the ultimate life of the community as such depended on finding another mine — a mine rich enough to pay on any price silver. The dream of bi-metallism returning was growing dim after twenty-five years of hoping. The surrounding country unwillingly gave a precarious foothold to a few ranches. The mountains attracted their quota of tourists, campers and lovers of the majesty and beauty of the Rockies — but a new mine was needed to hold the town together, yield a steady payroll and stop the slow but sure drift of men to other places where they could wrest a living from the mines.

The townspeople formed a cooperative company and the merchants agreed to subscribe certain amounts a month for stock. Others agreed to work, taking part of their pay in stock and just enough in cash to provide the bare necessities of life. They agreed to keep as much of the money as possible in Aspen, to buy their supplies locally, use machinery from the old mines and employ Aspen labor. They made a careful study of the possibilities in the region and decided that the best bet was to drive a deep level tunnel under Richmond Hill and catch the veins therein at depth. On top of Richmond Hill, at nearly 12,000 feet altitude, there had been a rich little mine in the old days. It had followed a narrow but profitable vein of silver ore down a hundred-two hundred feet. At this depth these doughty pioneers had been driven out by water. Work at this altitude under the primitive conditions must have been heartbreaking literally and life at the Little Annie must have tried men's souls. Some forgotten early settler with more vision than perseverance had come down from the hill to the waters of Castle Creek and started a tunnel with the idea of reaching under the Little Annie, draining it, and mining from the comparative comfort of this lower entrance. He had accomplished 900 feet and stopped.

In 1911, the Hope Company, as it was fittingly called, started to lengthen this tunnel, hoping to gain the riches of the Little Annie. Six self-confident men and the wife of one as cook moved to Castle Creek, built cabins, moved in an air compressor from another mine, and, backed by the subscriptions and Godspeed of the town, started their long fight against nature — but with an all-powerful incentive behind them.

We spent a week studying the array of rock formations exposed in the tunnel, measuring and recording their dips and strike and the evenings plotting plans and sections until exhaustion claimed us — and then I was too tired to sleep. The tunnel was a living laboratory of nature's chemistry. Water working down a fault zone ran over pyrite and dissolved some of the iron. This redeposited in the tunnel as ferric hydroxide — the catsupy material familiar to all high school chemists. Waters running over copper-bearing minerals took the copper into solution and deposited green and blue copper salts — as delicate and intricate in form and color as the pinnacle of the lacemaker's art.

Little Annie, on the back of Aspen Mountain, 1917.
Courtesy Aspen Historical Society.

Acid waters dissolved the iron pipes and rails to skeletons — plaguing the tunnel drivers with a mischievous insistency. Beds of gleaming white gypsum were undercut by the acid waters, as ice is rotted by spring sunshine. The movement in fault planes had ground the rock to the purest clay. These features held my interest the first few days, but as our work took us further and further from the portal and the walk in and out became longer and longer, my aching neck and shoulders claimed all my surplus attention. On the last day, it was just a damn long wet hole that we had to go into once more. But those six men had plugged along six days a week for six years, but they at least could walk upright where I had to bend and in places take over six inches from my height. Try walking two or three miles a day shrinking six inches from your frame. . . .

We returned to Aspen, prepared our report, dined at the homes
of several of the citizens of the game town and departed for the
low country and the east. I returned another March, when the
snow was hard and deep, to study the added exposure of rocks
revealed within the mountain. I again departed for Boston and
later for Europe. I lost track of the Hope. In Africa, in 1921, I
read in a month-old technical paper that the Hope had shipped
two carloads of ore running several thousand dollars each.

I would that I could end this chapter of a long fight well fought
at this point — but truth requires that I record the anticlimax:

> News item in technical paper in 1929: "Fire
> completely destroyed the new mill and practi-
> cally all the surface property. . . The new mill
> had not been in operation over two hours . . .
> when fire, thought to be caused by defective
> wiring, put a complete end to work of the com-
> pany. Loss, estimated at $100,000, not covered
> by insurance. Rebuilding unlikely at present."

The 1930 census showed even a greater drop in the population
of Aspen. My hat is off, however, to those six men. They were
real miners!

Times were tough for Aspenites during the Quiet Years, yet among all the
individuals who lived through those years and were interviewed for this book,
there is not a suggestion in their memories of hopelessness, or bitterness, or of
surrendering to the disruption in their lives. Thousands of residents abandoned
the community following those disastrous days in 1893, and the exodus continued over the years as individuals and families left the valley in search of better
lives elsewhere. In time, the community came to be dominated by abandoned
homes, boarded-up businesses, and collapsing mine shafts. Nature slowly
reclaimed the mountains. Many of those interviewed talked about entire blocks
in which there was not a single occupied house and about buildings that stood as
bare skeletons, their siding, shingles, and interior fixtures carted off by neighbors intent upon improving their own homes or by industrious children and

Aspen's Athletic Park, 1895. Courtesy Aspen Historical Society.

adults who cannibalized vacant buildings and mining structures in search of material they might be able to sell to junk dealers. Copper tubing and pipes became prized treasures during World War II, and during the 1930s, local youngsters removed hardwood flooring from some of the abandoned buildings in town, material that they converted into homemade skis. It is impossible to estimate just how many miners' shacks and other structures simply vanished from the scene, slowly becoming nothing as bits and pieces were hauled away by residents who put them to better use.

The once vibrant, progressive, and proud city slowly became a skeleton perched high in the Rockies, its bones exposed to scavengers and to relentless seasonal storms. A community in such a state of deterioration should have left a dark impression. Yet those who spoke of the hard times did so in a matter-of-fact manner, as if all of the abandoned homes, businesses, and mines were nothing more than a fact of life, simply another aspect of their hometown. Perhaps the vacant structures reminded residents that no matter how hard the times were for them, there were many others who had suffered as much, if not more. Despite the decay and so much evidence of failure, Aspenites saw something that would escape the majority. They saw a much-loved hometown. One resident explained, "When I grew up, there was a presence in the whole town. It was so ramshackley . . . I want to emphasize that. As latercomers to Aspen

*Aspen's Athletic Park,
1895.
Shadow Mountain
in the background.
Courtesy Aspen
Historical Society.*

uttered things like Aspen was a dump, I never had that feeling. Maybe Aspen was down in the dumps, but it was never a dump. And in those worst so-called hard times, with ramshackled houses and vacant lots, there was something always there — a presence or resurging of the aspen trees coming back. Nature sort of took over. And where there was a cabin, there might be an aspen tree starting up through the floorboards . . . growth came back."

Although Aspen would experience a partial recovery in 1894 and would valiantly attempt to restore its earlier brilliance well into the 1900s, the forces set in motion in 1893 were not to be reversed. Those at the bottom of the economic ladder — miners and laborers — were the first to exit Aspen in search of work elsewhere. They were followed by merchants who did not need to be reminded of the futility of stocking their shelves, and by tradesmen whose services were no longer needed.

Aspen's elite, the investors and promoters who had helped create the Crystal City of the Rockies, maintained their optimism until the early 1900s. But one by one, they, too, came to realize that there was little or no return to be made on their investments and no possibility of attracting fresh money to the valley. In 1890, the official census of Pitkin County reported 8,929 residents, 5,108 of whom lived within the existing city limits of Aspen. By 1920, however, twenty-seven years after silver was left unprotected, the county claimed only 2,707 residents, a figure not to be exceeded again until the 1960s.

*Hunter Creek Bridge,
South Trail, 1901.
Courtesy Peggy Rowland.*

Although Aspen was forced to shed the glitter of its Crystal City days and concentrate on survival, a community was created in which neighbor helped neighbor. Hardship was not the burden of a single group but something that was shared by all. As the population of Pitkin County and Aspen dwindled, those who remained came to recognize that, despite differences in ethnic background, religion, and political beliefs, they needed to band together as friends and neighbors. Most residents of the Quiet Years recalled that period as a time when there were no locked doors and when a man's word was all anyone needed to do business.

If one theme seemed to dominate during the Quiet Years, it was the unfailing pride exhibited by the people of the Roaring Fork Valley. An Aspen newspaper editor wrote in December 1929: "Christmas Day in Aspen was an ideal winter day. . . . And there was the Christmas spirit that reigned supreme — everyone glad and happy and full of the spirit of doing good unto others. Not a selfish thought or act bobbed up in this beautiful mining camp situated amidst the snow-capped peaks of the Rockies. Not a family that went without their Christmas dinner; not a child that Santa didn't remember; not an empty stocking — all well filled. And that's Aspen!" Yet, the Great Depression had begun just two months earlier. For Aspenites, this simply meant tightening their belts another notch and continuing with the business of life. What the nation experienced in 1929, Aspen had already gone through thirty-six years earlier.

Aspen became a community operating on a zero-based economy. Residents raised as much of their own food as possible, merchants extended credit whenever they could, and neighbors shared with neighbors. Aspenites found much to enjoy even during the hardest of times. Money may have been short, but enthusiasm abounded. On weekends, there were dances at the Armory Hall, at Woody Creek, at Gerbazdale, and at many of the ranches in the valley. Two fraternal organizations, the Elks and Eagles, were active in sponsoring dances, as well as numerous community picnics and outings. The annual flower show was a community event, as were Fourth of July horse races.

Wagon road to Maroon Bells, 1905. Courtesy Peggy Rowland.

Whist Club, 1901.
Courtesy Peggy Rowland.

There was roller-skating in Armory Hall and, in the winter, sledding, skiing, sleigh rides, and ice-skating on Hallam Lake and Sullivan's Pond. Summer months were a time for picnics in Hunter Creek Valley, and people would get together year-round for playing cards. And no matter whose home you visited, there was the real possibility of being treated to homemade jams, preserves, cheeses, and sausages, and a wondrous variety of homemade wines. During Prohibition, there was an abundance of bootleggers to provide even stronger substances. The woods were thick with deer and elk and the streams and lakes were full of trout. Families spent fair-weather days in the mountains collecting wild berries, mushrooms, and other edibles. The emphasis on community and family was dominant.

THE QUIET YEARS BEGIN TO FADE

The Quiet Years did not last long. Interest in Aspen as a potential ski resort began in 1936 with a focus on Mount Hayden near Ashcroft — not on Aspen Mountain. In 1937, however, the Roaring Fork Winter Sports Club (later to become the Aspen Ski Club), with assistance from Works Projects Administration (WPA) crews, cut the first run, designed by Andre Roch. Aspen's famous boat tow was then constructed to carry skiers up Aspen Mountain for ten cents per ride. Recreational skiing was still in its infancy in the 1930s, but two skiers who would have a profound effect on Aspen's future arrived in town in 1939. Lowell Thomas, the NBC and CBS news broadcaster who would become one of radio's most famous voices, visited Aspen after a ski trip to Idaho and became an immediate and long-time booster of the community and its excellent skiing.

Flag at half-mast, about 1900. Courtesy Aspen Historical Society.

Ellie's Building, 1910.
Courtesy Aspen
Historical Society.

The other visitor was Elizabeth Paepcke, the wife of Walter Paepcke, president of the Container Corporation of America.

Aspen's fame as a ski resort grew, and in 1941, many of the finest racers in the nation, as well as Austria's famed downhill racer, Toni Matt, spread the word after participating here in the National Alpine Championships, one of Aspen's first major ski competitions. While skiers from around the country were discovering Aspen and Aspen Mountain, the Mount Hayden project also was being pursued. As Christmas neared, it seemed as if good fortune finally was smiling on Aspen. And then the Japanese bombed Pearl Harbor on December 7, 1941, and the United States was at war.

For the next four years, Americans were unified in a single, national effort to win the war. There would be little time to worry about frivolous projects such as the development of ski areas. Yet even in the tragedy of a world war, good fortune remained at Aspen's side. In 1942, the army's 87th Mountain Infantry Regiment,

Aspen, 1905.
Courtesy
Peggy Rowland.

soon to become the famed 10th Mountain Division, began training at Camp Hale near Leadville, and the troops quickly discovered Aspen, about eighty miles away. Some of the men were so taken by the valley and the potential it offered as a ski resort that they returned to Aspen after the war to live.

Germany surrendered to the Allies in May 1945, and Japan followed in August. Suddenly, thousands of young men and women returned to an America bursting with new energy and confidence in the future that had an immediate impact on Aspen. The stories of the development of Aspen skiing and of Walter Paepcke's vision are told in a number of books, but it is wise to be reminded of the swiftness with which the face of Aspen changed at war's end.

Elizabeth Paepcke returned to Aspen in 1945 accompanied by her husband Walter. They purchased a Victorian home on their second day in Aspen and formulated a plan to improve Aspen's economy and to make the community an international center for intellectual and cultural activity.

*Hyman Avenue and
Galena, about 1907.
Courtesy
Peggy Rowland.*

     The Aspen Skiing Corporation was formed in 1945, and that winter, Freidl Pfeifer opened his ski school on Aspen Mountain. The summer of 1946 was devoted to cutting new trails and building lifts, and on January 11, 1947, Aspen's new ski area celebrated its grand opening. On November 9, 1948, the first airplanes landed at Aspen Airport, which eventually became Sardy Field. Nine days later, the Aspen Times wrote on its front page that the Goethe Bicentennial, honoring Johann Wolfgang von Goethe, would be conducted in Aspen with a two-week celebration beginning in June 1949. This observance brought the famed humanitarian Albert Schweitzer to the valley. Sharing the front page was an announcement by Dick Durrance, then mountain manager for the Aspen Skiing Corporation, that the Federation Internationale de Ski (FIS) World Championships would be held in Aspen in 1950.

Another front-page story in 1948 detailed the filming of "Red Stallion of the Rockies," one of the first movies shot in the Aspen area. It was produced by Eagle Lion Studios on the T-Lazy-7 Ranch in Maroon Creek. The hype had arrived in the Crystal City and the glitz would eventually follow as Aspen shed the isolation of the Quiet Years and slowly gained international fame. Even with these events, the Roaring Fork Valley managed to retain vestiges of its small-town existence. Immediately adjacent to the front-page story about the movie company was the headline "Horse and Mule Auction At Carbondale August 12."

The postwar years did not mark a boom period like the one of 1879, but there is no question that a new era had begun. For the first time in fifty-some years, the citizens of Pitkin County were not glancing over their shoulders and dreaming of another silver boom. Paepcke and skiing created the potential for an entirely new future for the Roaring Fork Valley. The Quiet Years were about to take their place in history.

◆

Hannibal Brown

(1876-1952)

Hannibal Brown.
Courtesy Aspen Historical Society.

Hᴀɴɴɪʙᴀʟ Bʀᴏᴡɴ died long before work began on this book. In truth, we never heard of Hannibal Brown until we began talking to people who were born and raised in Aspen. Our involvement in this project gave us the opportunity and privilege of getting to know this very special man.

If Hannibal were alive today, we would enjoy spending summer days listening to him chat about "his" Aspen. We would go for a ride with Hannibal in his pride and joy, a huge Hudson that was one of Aspen's only automobiles, certainly its largest, for a number of years. We would urge him to talk about his many hunting and fishing trips, one of which was an outing with Teddy Roosevelt, and we would beg for an invitation to his home to sample one of the many exotic cocktails for which he enjoyed unchallenged local fame. Above all, we would be proud to call him our friend.

After only a few interviews, it became apparent to us that in the hearts of those who lived in Aspen during the Quiet Years, a special place was reserved for Hannibal Brown. Without exception, everyone interviewed knew Hannibal one way or another. When people reminisced about him, two noticeable things occurred — a smile immediately appeared on their faces at the mention of his name, and suddenly their voices took on a softer, gentler tone. There is an abundance of evidence to support the contention that Hannibal was a man loved and respected by his neighbors.

Enough of our own conclusions about Hannibal. Far better to let you hear from those who shared Aspen with him. The quotations that follow include comments from individuals who knew Hannibal but were not interviewed by us, and comments from Hannibal's granddaughter (by marriage), Muriel Patterson, who now lives in Oakland, California, and her mother, Myrtle Smith, who lives in Memphis.

Old Hannibal was a real good guy. He wasn't above breaking the law either. He had a little house right across from the Catholic Church. Han was running a bootleg business when the country was dry. Gawd, I drank a lot of booze at his house — never any beers, always booze. He was a pretty great guy, old Hannibal — I liked him. When he was bootlegging, a bunch of us would go to his house, and he'd give away more booze than he would sell. We'd get drunk and raise hell around town, pester people — you know, like kids will do — just any ol' thing to make them mad.

◆

Hannibal kept a bar down at his house, and it was nice. It was very small, and only a few of his very good friends and elite got in there. Hannibal had all of these drinks posted up on the wall that he'd make. Oh Jesus, I wouldn't want to repeat a couple of them. He had Wasp's Flight, Horse's Neck, Goose's Neck. Then he had a Yellow Dandelion. Hannibal was smart. He cooked up those names and remembered them real good.

◆

Hannibal Brown used to live right next door to me. I remember him because they were neighbors of ours and used to cater to the rich people — serve drinks, you know. Also, he worked up in the Elks Club — used to bartend there. I know he made Tom and Jerrys, Eggnog, and I guess he had other drinks, too. Willa Mae was his second wife. His first wife died. She was a very wonderful person and so was Willa. Do you remember Dedrick Britenum who was here? His mother was married to Hannibal and Han was his stepfather. They lived here for awhile. The Britenums came from Tennessee and had four children. He ran a cleaning outfit for awhile here. They all had names that started with a "D" — Debra, Dedrick, Denise, and Demore. I know Han used to have one of those fancy horse carts that you see racing, with the one seat. They used to race out at the race tracks where the tent is — the Meadows. There was a house next door to Hannibal Brown's that belonged to some people by the name of Boars. They left here and then Warren Conner was born in that house.

◆

Tom & Jerry

12 eggs, separated
3 ½ pounds bar sugar
½ teaspoon ground nutmeg
½ teaspoon ground cinnamon
¼ teaspoon ground cloves
¼ teaspoon cream of tartar

Beat egg yolks with 3 pounds of sugar, nutmeg, cinnamon, and cloves until thick and light. Beat egg whites with cream of tartar until soft peaks form. Gradually beat in remaining ½ pound of sugar in the egg whites until soft. Gently fold egg whites into yolks.

Preheat Tom & Jerry mugs in hot water. To each mug add ½ ounce dark Jamaican rum. Fill half of mug with boiling water; add 2 tablespoons of Tom & Jerry batter to boiling water.

"

Han ran a bootleg business when the country was dry. Gawd, I drank a lot of booze at his house.

"

I remember old Han. He was the only Negro that I ever saw. He was up in Aspen. Everybody knew Hannibal, and he was kind of the town chauffeur. He could drive a car . . . a wild old driver. You could hire Han and he'd take you to Glenwood, or if the doctor had to make a night call, why he'd get Han. He was a big old man, nice old guy. He always had a long car. He used to go to Denver lots — somebody's business or something. He had several cousins. Brought back a different cousin about every few weeks when it was necessary. I think that's the way it worked. I never saw any of the cousins, but I heard that he had them. He was a real fine old gentleman.

✦

Hannibal Brown lived across from the church. Us kids would always go by there, and Mrs. Hannibal Brown always gave us an apple. Mary Stallard and I, we'd go by there all the time. That was really nice.

✦

He was the only black person I ever saw until I went to college, I think. He would be up at the post office — he cleaned the post office at that time. They used to pour sawdust on the floor and sweep it. He always chatted with all the old boys that came to town. Before my time, when his wives were still living, he used to have special parties at Christmas for the whole town. Everyone would drop by. One at Christmas and one at New Years. Each time he had something special. I was told that Hannibal Brown came from Leadville with Tagert. I've heard that for a hundred years.

✦

Hannibal, he was liked by everybody. He was the Brown's chauffeur. He would get up very early in the morning to fire up the furnaces, which was no small chore in those days. Coal-fired furnaces. During the midday while the sun was shining in the garage door facing the east, there was a captain's chair and Hannibal would sit and take a snooze. Nothing bothered him. People would come by and he was sound asleep. In the Aspen Building — the garage was Dummer and Hansen at one time but prior to that it was Rader and Rule. They had a Ford garage in Glenwood and had the branch garage in Aspen. Hannibal spent a lot of time in there.

✦

Han would often go out fishing, but he'd watch out for the bears. He was scared of bears. He used to like to go fishing down at Hook's Bridge down by

" Han would often go out fishing, but he'd watch for bears. He was scared of bears. I think most of his fishing was snoozing on the bank, worm in the water. "

the Snowmass trailer court. I think most of his fishing was snoozing on the bank, worm in the water. He was good-natured.

◆

Hannibal was a big man and a generous one. Thanksgiving, Christmas, and New Years he always had an open house. People would drop in, and he was a pretty good bartender — made very good Tom and Jerrys.

◆

Was there any kind of prejudice in Aspen at that time? None whatsoever. It didn't matter. There was no prejudice. Everybody liked Hannibal.

◆

Dummer and Hansen Garage, 1930s. Courtesy Aspen Historical Society.

Bleeker Street, West End,
May 19, 1911.
Courtesy Del Gerbaz

Hannibal didn't age much. His face stayed about the same. In the 1930s he was, I would say, in his early fifties. When he was old, he had dropsy. He had bad circulation and his legs would hurt.

✦

Han would have company a lot of times, but they were always cousins and always from Denver. I thought he was a bachelor at the time. There was never any wife when I knew him. He kept to himself pretty much. He didn't talk about his background. The only affiliations he had were with people from Denver. I have no idea where he was from. When you talked to Hannibal, you thought he would be around forever, and you didn't think about getting any background or even taking a picture. I took a lot of pictures around town, but I never did get one of him. I'm not even sure where he was married — I think in Denver. He used to have people come, and they would stay for a few days. He didn't let anybody interfere with his duties. He had his obligations and duties and nobody interfered — very conscientious.

✦

Hannibal Brown

◆◆◆◆◆◆◆◆◆◆◆◆◆◆◆

Hannibal would clean up and dress well, especially when he would get in his Hudson and take the Browns somewhere. They didn't want to drive, so he had to drive them everywhere. I'm not sure whether it was his own car or whether it was their car. He probably had the use of it because he was the only one that could drive. It may have been his own car. He would dress up very nicely. He'd wear a hat or a cap with a bill.

◆

Was Hannibal every deputized as a marshall? I think he might have been. He may have had a badge. He did have a permit to carry a side arm. He was a deputy when they needed him.

◆

I just know one story that they used to tell at the hardware store. Dynamite comes in tubes and they're eight inches long. Occasionally, to fill up a space in the box, instead of putting dynamite in, they'd fill it with sawdust just to fill in that space. There were usually one or two in each box. They got several fake ones together and tied them in a bundle. One day Hannibal walked into the hardware store — walked toward the back, where he came across them. They had this big pretend bundle of dynamite and said, "Here Hannibal, catch." They tossed it at him. Hannibal went out the door just like that! He didn't pick it up or catch it. He just ran out the door. He didn't come back for a long time.

◆

Hannibal. I only remember one time when we were kids, Tony Maddalone and I blackened our faces. We were walking down by the Armory Hall, and Hannibal was coming up from his house. He ran right into us. Han said, "Where did you two men come from? I thought all my relatives had gone." I was about eleven. I'll always remember that. Really nice man.

◆

Hannibal Brown. He was just something else. He was the kindest, gentlest man, and the only Negro in Aspen. I can't remember the name of the drink, but it's the kind that is poured in layers, and if you do it right, every layer will be

" Hannibal was everywhere. He took care of everybody's furnaces in the buildings, businesses, houses, and stuff. He did so many things. He was everybody's friend — a very fine man. "

separate. Hannibal could do that to perfection. Everybody thought the world of him, and he'd help anybody out that needed it.

✦

At one time here in Aspen you'd get the chilblains from the cold. My kids all had them. Your feet would itch. I don't know whether it was from frost or getting your feet wet. Your feet would itch so bad it would drive you crazy. Our oldest son, Jimmy, on his sixteenth birthday, killed a bear and rendered the lard out. Hannibal said, "Use the rendered lard for chilblains." And you know, my kids used it and they never had chilblains again. You just rub it on your feet before you put on your socks. I think we all had a little doctor in us when we had to do it the old-time way. Hannibal used to make some awfully good meals. Good cook. He cooked for different people. One time he come to the house and was talking to Jimmy and John and he said, "Elsie, if you'll drive that car around the block I'll give it to you." John says, "Don't tell her that because she *can* drive! You'd better be careful, Hannibal." So I never took him up on it. He

*Hannibal Brown,
late 1930s.
Courtesy
Myrtle Smith.*

Jerome Hotel.
Catholic Church.
Main St. Aspen Colo.

Main Street in Aspen, about 1918. Gebhardt Collection, Courtesy Aspen Historical Society.

had a big car. I'll tell you, he had a lot of cousins, too. They were all girlfriends — my cousin this, my cousin that — there were so many of them.

Hannibal Brown was a wonderful man. Every New Years and Christmas Eve, he would always have us for drinks. The one drink that sticks in my mind . . . he had a big punch bowl full of fruit. Then he would pour alcohol all over it and set it on fire. It would be the most wonderful centerpiece. Alcohol makes a beautiful light. After the alcohol burned out, he would serve the drinks. It was like a fruit punch. He would see to it that nobody got really drunk. He also loved to fish. He fished at Woody Creek and he was a good fisherman.

Hannibal Brown used to be one that drove us on our American Legion base-ball trips. Stuck the whole baseball team in his car. He had a green Hudson. It was him, and Bill McCugh had a Model A, and they'd haul us. Han also worked at the bank. Tended it all these years here as a janitor. I liked old Hannibal.

✦

Hannibal Brown. I do know that Joe Lewis, they said, was a credit to his race — the heavyweight champion. Hannibal thought a lot of Joe Lewis, and so the whole town would be invited for drinks if Joe felled his next opponent. They'd all crowd around Hannibal's celebratory table. I heard the older guys talking about it. "Joe Lewis had another victim last night so Hannibal had a celebra-tion." Hannibal Brown always took care of friends.

✦

I remember my Grandmother Pearce chuckling at me because in my youth (I was tiny then), I didn't have the language down. I called him "Animal Brown."

✦

Hannibal Brown taught me to skate when I was in high school. You know where the Isis Theater is? If you're going up toward city hall, there was a big empty lot. They used to flood it and have a town skating rink. Later on, we skated across the river. There was a man that put up ice that he sold in the sum-mer. He'd put up great chunks of ice and would cover it all with sawdust when it was real cold in the winter. Well, until he started to cut the blocks, he had a skating rink there. He was a good skater himself. His name, I think, was Nel-son. I forgot his first name.

✦

Hannibal was everywhere. He took care of everybody's furnaces in the build-ings, businesses, houses, and stuff. He did so many things. They'd call on Han-nibal. He was everybody's friend — a very fine man.

✦

"

When Han put my little paw inside of his when I was maybe six or seven, why, he'd have most of my lower arm, my wrist, and hand in his huge hand all together flying up the street.

"

46

Hannibal and Willa Mae Brown,
about 1944.
Courtesy Myrtle Smith.

He was my neighbor next door. He was the only black man that was in Aspen. Hannibal worked all the time. He was good looking. I got used to being around him when I was little because he used to drag me all over everywhere. And I mean he *drug* me with those great big hands he had. He'd put my hand in his and, goddamn, we'd go flying up the street.

◆

*Coming down
Independence Pass
into Aspen, about
1921.
Courtesy
Ruth Perry.*

Hannibal Brown was a great guy. He never missed one of our baseball games. He used to drive those big Hudsons. He was a real fine guy, such a polite man. He used to drive up there on the right-field line and sit with that big green — he had kind of a light green Hudson — he'd sit there and watch that ball game. Big man. Good size. Really a gentleman, but I think he could be real tough if he wanted to be. Nice.

✦

Hannibal Brown used to have the old Terraplane. It was a forerunner made by the Hudson Motor Car Company. My gawd, if you had one of those now, it would probably be worth $75,000.

✦

I think Han was one of the first ones to have a car in Aspen. He used to have the old Terraplane. Then he had a Hudson, and we'd ride in that damn Hudson. We

took my sister to Glenwood a couple of times with Hannibal driving the car . . . down to catch the darn train to go to California. You'd get about four bucks together and Hannibal'd take you to Glenwood. Dad would always say, "Keep talking on the road coming back," because Hannibal used to fall asleep. He'd go off the damn road and wreck that car.

✦

He hit a horse down over by Cozy Point one night. Knocked a hole under the car and they had to drag it into the garage. Poor Hannibal. I never did know where he came from, maybe Denver.

✦

I shot a bear when I was sixteen, and Hannibal Brown come up to see the doings, but he wouldn't come inside the door. He was scared of bears. He just stayed outside the door. Course, when he seen the bear, he jumped back. Finally

Hannibal Brown's house on East Main Street, 1930s. Now the Courthouse Plaza Building. Courtesy Myrtle Smith.

49

*Hannibal and
Willa Mae Brown,
about 1944.
Courtesy
Myrtle Smith.*

he says, "You know, I'm going to leave you guys. You're teasing me too much, but I'd sure like to have some of that lard that I can render out." When you render it out, you cook it on the stove and squeeze it so that it separates. After that, you squeeze the fat to get the liquid out of it. He said, "That's good for chilblains and stuff like that." So my mother used it, too. Me and Lucas had chilblains something terrible. Do you know what chilblains are? A lot of people don't. It's worse than frostbite. It burns and it tingles, I'll tell you. We used to go run in crusted snow barefoot. We'd take the good old dutch brushes and rub each other's feet, put ice on them. It was terrible. You don't even hear of them anymore. We put some of the bear grease on our feet and that stopped them. Put it on in the morning and then put our socks on. Of course, those colored people, they had a lot of ideas us whites never even heard of. Oh god, everybody wanted a chunk of the bear meat, too. It's just like pork, only it's real sweet. The bear was kind of a tan and cream colored, cinnamon colored. You seldom see them. In those years, you saw either brown or black.

✦

Hannibal Brown

❖❖❖❖❖❖❖❖❖❖❖❖❖❖❖

Hannibal Brown. For five dollars he'd take someone that had to go to Glenwood to see a special doctor or something down there in those days. Kind of a taxi business. If a guy was down and out, why he would take them and not charge, not even for the gas.

❖

Han was a real gentleman. You know, he wouldn't come in my house. He'd come to the back door, but he wouldn't come in. When Claude was a baby, after we brought him home from the hospital, Han came to the back door to see Claude, and I said, "Come in." Han said, "No," and I had to take Claude, the little baby, out there to show him. He wouldn't come in. And then when Claude was growing up, he was playing in the yard all the time, and Hannibal would go by, back and forth, and talk to him. One day I guess Claude looked at him and saw he was a little different. He went over and took Hannibal's hand and said, "God, Hannibal, why don't you go home and wash your hands."

❖

I don't think Han had any children. He had a step grandchild that I went to school with by the name of Muriel. I can remember his wife, Willa Mae Brown. She was kind of a timid little thing. I can't remember her ever going out very much. I don't know where Han came from before Aspen.

❖

Back in those days, Hannibal would go to Denver and would cut quite a swath because, I guess, he was thought to be very good looking. I'm sure that he was when he was forty-five to fifty. He'd go down there to Five Points and "holy comoly." They'd have some good parties, and a lot of times he'd bring back a load of booze in the Hudson.

❖

The names of Hannibal's drinks? Oh, gawd, I can see them. Someone that was a friend of his would paint them on a wood panel in white, oh gawd. Certainly he had the Pink Lady; let's see, I think there was Hannibal's Delight. Yes, he had one that was a Main Street Special. One called the Roaring Fork, and that's

" Hannibal would go to Denver and would cut quite a swath because, I guess, he was thought to be very good looking. He'd go down to Five Points and holy comoly. They'd have some good parties, and a lot of times he'd bring back a load of booze in the Hudson. "

all it said was just Roaring Fork, because Hannibal was a good fisherman. He must have had twenty different drinks.

✦

As I said, when Han put my little paw inside of his when I was maybe six or seven — I don't know where we'd go — up to one of the grocery stores or something — why, he'd have most of my lower arm, my wrist, and hand in his huge hand all together flying up the street. I think he was six feet, two or six feet, three. In those days, you weren't used to seeing very many giants around. Judge Shaw was six feet, three or thereabouts. Manford Smith, he was big. Hannibal was right up there amongst them.

✦

Top of Mill Street, late 1930s. Courtesy Aspen Historical Society.

Hannibal Brown

✦✦✦✦✦✦✦✦✦✦✦✦✦✦✦

When Hannibal put the white jacket on, it would be spotless. He was pretty darn good looking, but as he got older, like all the rest of us, you start falling apart. When he was old, Hannibal's legs and ankles used to swell up. When I was working in the courthouse, I used to go by and say, "Hannibal, is there anything I can do for you? I've got plenty of coal and everything like that." And I think that he probably had dropsy [heart trouble]. Eventually, he went to Denver to seek some medical help. Somebody took him over. He died in Denver, and they buried him there.

✦

Oh, was I ever excited about the first black baby I seen! Hannibal always had cousins come, and one time this lady had a baby with her. Ardith and I was coming home from school one day. Han lived there by the courthouse. And we heard about this baby, so new. None of us had seen a black baby, so we went over there and knocked on the door. We asked the lady if we could see. She let us in and was so sweet. The baby was in a bassinet. He was so clean and with those white eyes! Of course, we all stared at that baby. Then I came home and I said, "Oh momma, momma, you can't believe what I seen today!" She said, "What?" and I said, "Oh, a black baby!" I thought she was going to die laughing. We were still going to grade school then.

✦

I can remember when Hannibal (the first time I'd ever seen this) froze fresh flowers in a big block of ice. He froze the ice outside, of course. We didn't have the deep freezes then (this was for special occasions like New Years and Christmas). Beautiful. And then he'd bring it in for the party and put it in a punch bowl. I've always threatened to try it.

✦

I went to a party at Hannibal's, a New Years party or something. Han fixed all these different drinks. Every drink would be different, they claim. I didn't drink that much, but they claimed he could tell if somebody was getting too loaded. He'd fix them a drink and they'd sober up.

✦

"Han fixed all these different drinks. Every drink would be different, they claim. He could tell if somebody was getting too loaded. He'd fix them a drink and they'd sober up."

You know that a lot of these people around Aspen — I guess me included — are inclined to BS a little bit, no doubt about it. I think about half of what you hear is accurate. When there was an occasion in town, the turkey roll was the big deal. Well, the turkey roll was sponsored by the Elks Club. I think they still do that. They would have a big party and a dance and would play bingo. This would be before Thanksgiving. They would play bingo, and the winners would get turkeys. I mean, this was a big occasion. It started at four in the afternoon and would go all night long. They would dance and drink. Hannibal Brown would provide the drinks. In those days, there was maybe one bar in town. Han was a bartender for the Elks. Hannibal's house was painted green and white, and he had that Hudson. I think it was blue. Wait, let me think about that Hudson. Gees, it seems to me like that was green and white, too. The one that I remember was about a 1939 Hudson.

✦

> *Father McSweeney, our priest, liked to drink, too, and I think he spent a lot of time over at Hannibal's.*

I was Catholic, and Han lived right across the street from the Catholic Church. Father McSweeney, our priest, liked to drink, too, and I think he spent a lot of time over at Hannibal's. Father McSweeney used to come into church when we were at sister school in the spring. You could hear him a mile off. He would walk in the door and we'd say, "Good morning, Father," and he'd say, "Good morning, children." He would talk to us, you know. He was really humorous; he was old Irish. One time he was talking to us about matrimony — he used to give us little lectures about religion and matrimony. He'd say, "And of course you can't be like Hannibal Brown over here across the street." Someone new every year.

✦

I remember one time when we were at sister school, and there was a young colored lady over at Hannibal's. She had a small black baby. You know, we had never seen one. We used to see Hannibal, of course, and we never thought anything about Hannibal — he was just, you know, part of the town. We had no prejudice toward him, or thought he was different. But we all had to run over and see that baby. We all ran across the street during our free time, and the mother was out there with that marvelous baby. We all loved it! Han used to go to Denver all the time, and I think everybody thought he was originally from Denver. But I don't really know.

✦

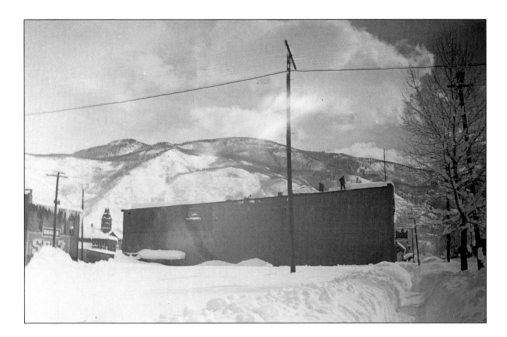

The Isis Theater,
1920s.

Hannibal Brown came from — he did mention Memphis an awful lot. I really don't think he knew who his mom and dad were, because he never definitely said. He would have otherwise. I was his confidante for years and years. He learned all his trade — he was a good cook and a good bartender — from the people who took him. Usually they were connected to banks, and he worked as a servant for them. But he only worked for the very rich. He didn't work for peasants.

◆

Hannibal Brown. Hell, I was only about ten or twelve. I went down there by the Hotel Jerome and I said, "Hey Hannibal, how 'bout a white spot on ya." I hit him right in the back of the neck and I ran like heck. When he caught me, I said, "Honest, Han, I didn't mean it." He went to my daddy, and my daddy raised heck with me.

◆

I don't know who bought Han's house for him, but it was a nice home, very comfortable. It had everything in it and a beautiful dining room to serve his drinks. Everything was catered around what he could do.

◆

"

In my youth
(I was
tiny then),
I didn't have
the language
down. I called
him
Animal Brown.

"

The first day I was in Aspen I had to go to the store for my mother. Well, we had quite a fighter of a dog. I was about fourteen years old. He was a beautiful big collie, and the people by the name of Jewett, who had the grocery store, had a big collie, too. My Laddie and I went — he always carried for me. He was taught to carry your bag in his mouth. Anyway, when we walked up on the steps, this big dog jumped out at him, and they had a horrible dog fight. Around the building comes Hannibal — the first time I ever saw him. He came from the back and separated them. He said, "I tell you, little girl, you better take this dog away, because he's going to get killed." I said, "No, it's the other way around. My Laddie is the killer." And he said, "I better call the Jewetts and ask them to put the dog away." I said, "Until after I get my groceries, and then I'll be on my way." That's how I met him. I didn't know whether he was black or what. I don't see people's color.

✦

E.W. Jewett Grocery, about 1925. Courtesy Aspen Historical Society.

Hannibal Brown

✦✦✦✦✦✦✦✦✦✦✦✦✦✦✦

We're friends from way back. As far as him coming out from behind the bank that day, I just clung to him. I just loved him. He was such a dear man to me. Hannibal Brown sing? No. But oh, he loved music. We would always arrange to have a group play at his home around the big table when he served drinks. Anybody who was a musician at all was glad to get a chance to play. There were lots and lots of good times. I just don't remember anyone who ever said anything bad about him. And they won't. You can't find anyone.

✦

Hannibal Brown was our only black for years and years in Aspen. He had a little white house, and I don't know when he died or when he moved away. He kind of bootlegged drinks during dances and stuff. The people would go over there for intermission and he would mix drinks. Of course, he wouldn't set a price — you had to just leave a donation. In other words, you would know what he normally would charge, and you left something. I think you paid, when I was a young fellow in the 1940s, fifty cents a drink. I used to order a Pink Lady. I don't even know what he mixed it with.

✦

Hannibal would follow my brother, Fletcher, and myself when we went on our ponies. I think he had to watch my sister for a year. Then we were on our own as far as where we went on a horse. And that's all I can remember about Hannibal.

✦

We would go to town in a wagon, don't ya see. Hannibal would push my baby buggy all over town while I did my shopping. He took care of that. He would push it all over, and everybody said, "Oh Hannibal, where did you get that baby?"

✦

In my earliest memories, Hannibal was always old. He was thirty years older than my grandmother Willa Mae. I lived with my grandma off and on. The first time I went to live with her and Hannibal in Aspen I was in the third or fourth grade. I lived with her about two years in a white house on Main Street.

✦

"

The old Whispering Swede used to say that Hannibal was real tight-lipped. He said that Hannibal went away one day and came back with a wife. And how he got back was in a carriage that looked like a deer.

"

57

*Post office in
Aspen, 1941.
Photo by
Marion Post
Wolcott.
Courtesy
Lee Wolcott.*

Hannibal was an avid hunter. He had some trophies on the wall that just terri-fied me when I was little. He had this big stuffed moose head, and I was always afraid of that. It was bigger than I was. He also had a stuffed bear, a standing one. And a mountain lion. It looked like it was getting ready to spring. I really didn't like that one. I don't think there was a room in the house that didn't have those stuffed animals, except the kitchen. The bedroom and the kitchen were about the only rooms that did not have some kind of stuffed dead animal in it.

People came over to drink in the dining room. They would sit around. There was a huge dining table. About ten people could sit around it in comfort. That's where they'd be, in the dining room or the living room. Hannibal had the bar

58

set up in the one corner of the dining room, and that's where he would make drinks. He would stand around there and talk. One drink that he had I loved to look at he called Puey Foosay. It was a layered drink, different colors. He would light it, and I always liked that. One time somebody forgot to blow it out, and it went up in flames. Everybody thought that was hysterical. In the wintertime around Christmas there would always be Tom and Jerrys. That was the main thing.

◆

Pousse Café (Puey Foosay)

Note: Ingredients must go in the order listed.

1 part raspberry syrup
1 part anisette
1 part parfait amour
1 part yellow chartreuse
1 part green chartreuse
a part curaçoa
1 part cognac

Serve in a cordial glass.

Light the cognac if desired.

Other ingredients may have been used, such as dandelion wine and lord only knows what else.

"

Hannibal was an avid hunter. He had some trophies on the wall that just terrified me when I was little. He had this big stuffed moose head, and I was always afraid of that. It was bigger than I was.

"

Maroon Creek Bridge, Aspen Colo.

Old Maroon Creek Bridge about 1920 (hooked into now Silverking Drive along the Red Butte), dismantled after World War I. Courtesy Del Gerbaz.

Hannibal didn't talk a lot, and I don't know if he didn't like children, but he would talk if you asked him about his photographs. He was very, very proud of that picture of Teddy Roosevelt — it was of him and Teddy Roosevelt — a large photo with several people in it. Hannibal was on one end of the line, but he was standing by Roosevelt. Han was the only black man in the party. The rest of them were just kind of lined up. He had a typical hat, kind of cowboyish. They all had big, oversized hats. Hannibal was looking very proud.

◆

My grandma was working in Denver when Hannibal got sick. He could have had dropsy. I remember Hannibal saying he didn't feel well. He contacted my grandmother in Denver, and she had him brought down to her. He died in Denver, and he's buried there.

◆

After he died, someone broke in his house. A lot of Hannibal's stuff — guns and things — were missing. I don't think anybody wanted those stuffed animals. I know when we went back the moose was still there. My grandmother finally took the moose down. She took down all of the stuffed animals. I think she did leave one elk . . . kind of a mascot.

◆

All of Hannibal's photographs were stolen. They say whoever it was had plenty of time to go through the house. They broke into his locked strong box that he had various bank notes in and stuff like that. They went through that. They were scattered all over, which made it very difficult to establish exactly what was missing, other than the obvious. We figured the thieves were people passing through Aspen, not local people.

◆

The old Whispering Swede used to say that Hannibal was real tight-lipped. He said that Hannibal went away one day and came back with a wife. And how he got back was in a carriage that looked like a deer. That was his first wife, about 1913. It was a fancy carriage — a black two-seater. It was upholstered and all that good stuff. And he'd take her out for Sunday rides. They would ride around Aspen. When I lived there, Hannibal had it covered up in the back yard. I peeked under there, and the upholstery was cracked and the paint was coming off, but I could tell that at one time it was real fancy.

◆

I don't know what his wife died of. All I heard was that she was pretty young. He bought a piano for her, so she must have played piano. I don't think he played any musical instruments.

◆

Hannibal was an old colored fellow. He was the only one here that I ever remember. I believe he was the custodian at the Elks. He had a little white house down there, east of the courthouse. Han was pretty well known for mixing drinks. He didn't sell it; he would just invite people down and fix them whatever they wanted.

◆

"

Hannibal was very, very proud of that picture of him and Teddy Roosevelt. Hannibal was on one end of the line, but he was standing by Roosevelt. He was the only black man in the party.

"

Hannibal Brown was a great old guy. I was kind of young when he was around, but he was a dark black man. He was just as kind and good as anybody you ever knew. He was always doing something good for somebody else. He always had a cousin that was here to live with him — all lady cousins. It was really cute. Later on, Han had a wife named Willa. People would have parties, and he would be the bartender. He was a great cook, too.

✦

Hannibal Brown was quite a character. He was well integrated, and everybody accepted him. He used to be a janitor and would cater a lot of the parties. He was quite a bartender. And on Christmas and Easter, he would make his famous eggnog and everybody would go to his house. He took the boys in my graduating class, when we went on our sneak day, to Grand Junction. It was during the war, and they were rationing gas. So he saved all his gas ration stamps. That was the spring of 1944. He was pretty elderly then. The car was an old Hudson. He was supposed to be our chaperone in Grand Junction, and he says, "Well, you boys be careful and we'll meet you later" — days later.

✦

Hannibal would take Father McSweeny down to Basalt once a month so Father could have mass down there. They stopped in at Bioneys on the way back. The Lazy Glen was their ranch. They would stop in for a little wine. When women came to visit, he said they were his cousins.

✦

Hannibal used to also clean up the post office. He used to take care of that big lemon tree over where the bank is. It looked like he had some lemons on there. He took care of the Isis Theater for a long time, too.

✦

Hannibal was the only dark man in Aspen at that time. We had no Mexicans, or Chinese. He used to make drinks in his house. You would take booze over there, and he would mix up drinks. Hannibal used to take care of furnaces in buildings.

Hannibal Brown

✦✦✦✦✦✦✦✦✦✦✦✦✦✦✦

When I was working at the hotel, he was always so polite — more polite than a lot of white people that I know. He was so nice you had to like him.

✦

I knew Hannibal Brown very well — the old D.R.C. Brown's janitor. He was more than a janitor — he served and welcomed people. He'd dress up, and we'd go over to his place. He knew how to mix drinks. He didn't drink on duty. After all the bars were closed, what is now Mrs. Paepcke's house (that was the Brown house), she'd throw some big parties in there. When that party ended, we'd go over to Hannibal's and then carry on till morning. Some of the drinks he'd set on fire. His brandy would be glowing. He just knew the right touch to put on it. The favorite drink in town a little later on was right at the Jerome Hotel. They still sold malted milks. Prohibition had ended. You'd go in there and see these people giggling and carrying on drinking a malted milk. We'd say, "What the hell goes on here?" And we were going to find out. They put one, two, three, four shots of booze in it. and called it the Aspen Crud. So we'd get drunk on that.

✦

At Hannibal's house, Han wasn't allowed to charge anything — prohibition you know — so we just donated. He didn't charge because it was against the law. He was great with his eggnogs. When they put the tunnel through — the diversion tunnel up Independence Pass — they had a big party when it was finished in the Armory Hall. Hannibal Brown was in charge of the bar, and he made a huge block of ice with roses frozen in it. It was a popular spot, that block of ice. The punch got a little stronger all the time, because the ice didn't melt fast enough and they had to keep pouring liquor in . . . very popular punch.

✦

Hannibal Brown and I were real good friends. He had a great big car. He liked big cars. A gray Hudson. The first date I ever had I was trying to fix my uncle's car. Hannibal came in and said, "What's the problem?" I told him that I had a date and I had to go to the West End and pick the girl up. Hannibal said, "Take my car." So he let me use his car, and from then on, I used to take care of his car for him.

✦

> "
> When they put the tunnel through — the diversion tunnel up Independence Pass — they had a big party. Hannibal was in charge of the bar, and he made a huge block of ice with roses frozen in it. It was a popular spot, that block of ice. The punch got a little stronger all the time, because the ice didn't melt fast enough and they had to keep pouring liquor in . . . very popular punch.
> "

Hannibal Brown at the Elk's Club, 1910. Courtesy Warren Conner.

He was a chauffeur to David R.C. Brown, Sr., who owned the bank. If Han brought a lady friend to town, it was always his cousin. I always went to the dances with my folks, and I can remember going to Hannibal's house after a dance and he'd make all these fancy drinks. He had a big moose head on the wall when I was in high school — don't remember what year. His wife, Willa . . . at that time, her granddaughter Muriel lived with them. She was the only black girl in school.

♦

I used to go out to his home. Han had a room we would drink in. He had these little plates that hung on the wall with every type of drink that you could think of written on them. He had like a Red Rose cocktail, or Bull Moose cocktail. He asked you what kind of drink you wanted. You just mentioned one and he'd fix it. Han worked for the bank, where Ute City Banque is now. He was the janitor for years.

♦

Hannibal Brown

✦✦✦✦✦✦✦✦✦✦✦✦✦✦

Before that, years ago — course that was before my time — he used to be a bartender in a saloon downstairs in the Brand Building. Everybody liked him. Not very many people had cars in those days. If you needed to take the train to Denver, Hannibal used to drive people down to Glenwood to catch the train or pick people up.

✦

Han was married early on, but she died and he was alone for quite awhile. His wife lived here, too, and stayed in the house. He was one of the most well-liked coloreds, and he would do anything for you. I don't think there was racism in Aspen. But one thing that was different in Aspen was that the churches didn't get along so well. The Catholic children or the Catholics weren't allowed to go to the Community Church. We were allowed to go to Catholic Church if we wanted, and we used to take in the Easter services sometimes, but they weren't allowed to come to our church.

✦

Hannibal had on his wall plaques of different names of drinks, and the two that appealed to me were Bull Moose cocktail and Red Rose cocktail. My cousin and I were leaving for the service. Hannibal was a good friend of mine, so he wanted me to come down and have a drink. I had a Bull Moose and a Red Rose.

✦

Hannibal was the janitor for the Bank of Aspen. Yep, he was the only colored person in Aspen for years. He would have some parties though — he was kind of a caterer. He could make drinks that you couldn't believe. I drank some of them the day before I went into the service. There was five of us that went into the service at the same time, so Hannibal invited us down to his house to give us a going-away party. He would mix some of the most exotic drinks you ever seen. I don't remember any of the names of his drinks . . . heck, we were too busy drinking!

✦

> "
> *Hannibal was a chauffeur to David R.C. Brown, Sr., who owned the bank. If Han brought a lady friend to town, it was always his cousin.*
> "

65

*Hyman Avenue
in Aspen,
1940s.
Courtesy
Francis Kalmes.*

The old post office was in the Elks Building on the corner there. Han used to sit all day long and sun himself right on the sidewalk against the building. He also took care of the furnaces and maintenance over at the bank.

◆

Hannibal Brown was one of the most well-liked people in town. He loved big cars. He had this great big light green Hudson. We used to go down to Hannibal's between dances from the Armory Hall. I know a lot of people used to go down there. He was not supposed to sell or anything like that, so it was under the table. You ordered what you wanted. He had a little bar. Han would give you the drink and you could put in whatever money you wanted. I know at the dances they would always say, "Let's go down and get a couple of drinks at Hannibal's place." That was just between locals. Frank Bruin was the sheriff and he had this sidekick, Jakey Reynolds, and they used to go over there. Jakey was supposed to be the deputy sheriff.

◆

Hannibal Brown

◆◆◆◆◆◆◆◆◆◆◆◆◆◆◆◆

I think he had one drink they called Angel Tits. Hannibal came down one time to hunt with us; we were in Starwood. Han went on a little ways and suddenly came back. Apparently he saw a bear track. I don't think you ever saw anybody that was so frightened. He didn't like bears.

◆

Hannibal Brown was a great guy. He was a Negro — I think the only Negro they ever let in town. He lived close to where Liz Callahan lives, right in there. You would go to the post office and he'd be there. He would talk to everybody that would come in.

◆

I heard a story about Hannibal coming home drunk one night with a friend. He hit a horse on the Maroon Creek Bridge. They got out of the car and his friend said, "I better put it out of its misery," and he went and got his gun. Well, he was so drunk that when he shot the horse, he completely missed. The loud noise startled the horse so much that it jumped up and ran away.

◆

I remember he used to wash windows at the bank and post office. One of his sayings was, "There never was, and there never will be, a constipated fly." He was the only black guy in town.

◆

Hannibal came to Aspen with some rich people associated with the banks. The Browns didn't bring him. There were the Cowenhovens. She was the wife of the first D.R.C. Brown. The women had the money. He was a servant of theirs. Han did every kind of a job, odds and ends, keeping the fires in the furnaces and everything else going. He was a very thorough man, very dependable. Cowenhoven came from Blackhawk, but I doubt if Hannibal was over there with him. I never heard him mention it.

◆

"I heard a story about Hannibal coming home drunk one night with a friend. He hit a horse on the Maroon Creek Bridge. They got out of the car and his friend said, 'I better put it out of its misery,' and went and got his gun. Well, he was so drunk that when he shot the horse, he completely missed. The loud noise startled the horse so much, it jumped up and ran away."

His first wife, Laura, died in 1913. He never said anything that wasn't nice about her. They married in Denver. Hannibal is buried in Denver. His body just wore out. Some people wear out sooner than others. I saw pictures of his horses and black buggy he used to have. I don't know what he did with that buggy. Anyway, he was proud that he could give her that to show off. He also bought her a piano. I used to play it.

✦

Hannibal's first wife died very young. I don't know how young. Don't know what she died of. I know she had bad lungs. It could have been TB or something like that. He never mentioned it. He never mentioned her being incapacitated in any way. As far as he was concerned, she was just perfect. He got married very young. He cared more for her health than he did having children. He always put her first.

✦

"

One of his
sayings was,
'There never was,
and there never
will be, a
constipated fly.'

"

His was a charming little old house. All you saw on the walls were stuffed things looking down at you. He talked to me about being Teddy Roosevelt's fishing guide. He had photos of them together. I guess Willa would be the only one who would inherit pictures from him. Someone broke in his house after he died. Stole everything, even the pictures. I don't know who's got them or who destroyed them.

✦

He had a slight southern accent. Yes, he did. He had very southern manners. Like me, no matter what, how many years he knew me, "Miss Louise" always. I said, "Please don't use Miss Louise. I'm not Miss Louise." He said, "No, you're my friend so you are Miss Louise and your children, Miss Louise's children." My Gary, my David, my Darlene. He had pictures of them.

✦

Hannibal married Willa Mae Brown many years later. He was in his seventies. Willa was a very aristocratic lady. She would take my boys away from me and take them to her home. They would have little tea parties and would know how

to handle a fork and a knife. They'd know how to do this and that when they came home. My little one got so bad he'd say, "Okay, I don't like you no more. I'm going to go live with Willa." Muriel, Willa's grandchild, came here to go to school. She was the only black child in the school system at the time.

Main Street in Aspen, 1938. Sheriff Frank Bruin is on the right. Courtesy Robert Zupancis.

✦

Hannibal, my very beloved person. I loved him. He was everything a friend could be. He must have come to Aspen when he was in his twenties. He worked at the Elks. He was very fastidious about his appearance. His ring and his clothing was absolutely spotless. I respected him that much. He would always ask, "Miss Louise, how do I look?" I said, "Just fine." I booked parties for him after awhile. He said, "Miss Louise, you know these people from the hotel. Would you tell me the ones that really deserve something special." I would always say, "Well, the Gary Coopers are here and the Ray Millands," and way on down the list — Robert Taylor and Barbara Stanwyck. He also served for them. But it was extra-special. It was just a little more because they enjoyed it. They said, "Can we bring our friends when they come to see us?" Honey, it don't take you years to learn how to make beautiful drinks and put them on with a flair. He didn't learn in Aspen. He learned from all the people he ever served, and they were so glad to show him every secret they had.

◆

Hannibal's cooking was exquisite. Better than any woman's I have ever tasted. His favorite dish? Anything barbecued and anything that would be along with it — baked beans, and salads, and potato salads especially. All the good things that could ever go with anything. It was perfect. His elk stew had to be cooked one and one-half days. Not any less, not any more. It was beautiful.

◆

At Christmas, Han made Tom and Jerrys for everybody in town. That's right. Only by appointment. You couldn't just walk in. Of course, he had a phone. He was not listed in the phone book. I knew. It was private. So nobody could call him that shouldn't be calling him and bothering him. Whatever was good for him, I saw to it.

◆

I remember his photos of Teddy Roosevelt — the two of them standing, with Roosevelt's hand on Hannibal's shoulder. Han had made beautiful drinks for his party. Hunting guide . . . mostly hunting. Han was a fishing person; he could tell you good places to hunt or fish.

◆

As far as I know, everyone was always very nice to Willa. Everybody loved her. She was a very intelligent, beautiful person. She and Hannibal went to Denver to socialize. Willa had all kinds of relatives, and Hannibal had all kinds of friends who would never think of going through Aspen without stopping at Han's. Never. As far as just going out together, no. Not unless they were invited to a party to serve. They always put them in that classification of serving.

◆

Hannibal Brown

◆◆◆◆◆◆◆◆◆◆◆◆◆◆◆◆

As for me, I'd say, "Come down to dinner. Let's have dinner." Did he come to my house? Honey, he was mad if I didn't ask him every week. And he would come in and say, "Miss Louise, you need a night out. Please bring the children here or let me come over and take care of them. Let me put them to bed." He'd be my babysitter. Now, most people don't know that, and I never did say anything about it because he was so dear. I could have stayed away for a year and I would have known they were safe because they didn't want to come home. It wasn't his cooking. It was just his storytelling and doing little things.

◆

Lots of people lived for the chance to go and sit at Han's big table and be served. Snowy white napkins, little plaques on the wall that had names of drinks — lots of them, every place. He had Pink Julep for little kids and he had this and that. He'd doll them up. Oh, he could tell a kid anything . . . funny names for the drinks — Giggly Gooses and some things like that. He'd just make them up as he went along. Bless his heart. He always had something going for children. He didn't have any, but he loved children.

◆

Hannibal was a chauffeur for the D.R.C. Browns. He chauffeured for Brown's first wife, Kate Cowenhoven. They were there at the D.R.C. Brown's home. Not often, but he did chauffeur and the Browns had a chauffeur of their own, too.

◆

I don't think the Cowenhovens bought the house for Han. I don't think so. Hannibal wasn't exactly poor. He made good money. Are you kidding? He made better money than most people. You know what I mean. People were very anxious coming from other places to have him preside over the meal and all that good stuff — cocktails. He was very elegant.

◆

In those days, I found less prejudice than I do today. I never saw anything like it is now. People have gone back into stupidity. I don't understand. Everybody was just beautiful as far as I was concerned. You heard the words once in

> " *Hannibal married Willa Mae Brown many years later. He was in his seventies. Willa was a very aristocratic lady. She would take my boys away from me and take them to her home. They would have little tea parties and would know how to handle a fork and a knife. They'd know how to do this and that when they came home.* "

*Hyman Avenue
looking west,
1905.
Courtesy
Peggy Rowland.*

awhile, like a spick, Jewish, etc. I would always say to them, "Please don't talk like that about my people." And I'm Scotch. That would stop them. "Oh, I'm so sorry," they'd say, and I'd say, "Be sorry because you don't say that." I'd make a good Spaniard, too, and I'd make a good Wop. In those days you had your Slovenians in certain parts of town and your Irish — Swedes, Italians downvalley. How about at my end, all Italians lived there. Caparella's down to you know who. That was fun. I went to all their parties. When they had parties up at Stillwater, I didn't know that there was any difference at all. I didn't see it.

✦

Hannibal Brown was a janitor around the Elk's building and he had a deal down at his house. He would mix drinks there. He had a little bar and everything. I think the only drink I remember was one where he poured a little

Hyman Ave., Aspen, Colo.

Hyman Avenue, 1938. From the Gebhardt Collection; Courtesy Aspen Historical Society.

liquor in a glass, then he poured some more of a different kind. There would be half a dozen different colors. Then he lit it on fire. He had a house right across the street from the Catholic Church. He was an old man then, but he looked the same to me all the time. He would mainly have the bar open for the dances. The Armory Hall was right up the street from him. He never had a license or anything, but you could go in and he'd serve you drinks — whatever you wanted — but he couldn't charge for it. If you wanted to pay him, you could. If you didn't, why, he couldn't charge because he didn't have a license. I don't even know how he could operate the outfit. But back then you could have pretty much anything. We used to go to the liquor store when we were only about fourteen years old and get liquor. Charged it and everything.

My dad had me start sweeping the post office floor, which was in the Elk's building. I came up every night, and Hannibal Brown was always there. That was kind of the local hangout for the city marshall, Hannibal, and some of the old bums around town. The old winos stood in there because it was warm in the winter and they could talk. I got to know a lot of them because I was in sweeping the floor every night. Hannibal was there, and that's how I knew him.

✦

My first memory of Hannibal Brown is from my mother. When I was a little kid, she said, "Now don't say anything. This person's skin is different. This is Hannibal Brown." He was real friendly. She met him on the street and he said, "Hello," and was very nice. She warned me not to ask why his skin was a different color. Of course, they told us in those days to say colored instead of nigger or Negro. I went to a sister school — the Catholic parochial school — in the summer for a couple of weeks, and we were always across the street from Hannibal Brown's house. You'd see him going in and you'd say, "Who's that girl?" Han would say, "Oh, my cousin's visiting me from Minnesota." Later there'd be another cousin. Another after that. He was a very, very nice man.

✦

> "
> *In those days, I found less prejudice than I do today. I never saw anything like it is now. People have gone back into stupidity. I don't understand. Everybody was just beautiful as far as I was concerned.*
> "

Prejudice in Aspen at that time? No. I remember hearing that in previous years the older kids had fought back and forth, but it was gone by the time we were here. We were from the center of town. Some of the West Enders and the East Enders had problems. A lot of the East Enders were Catholic and Austrian — mostly miners. The West Enders were not necessarily any richer or any poorer, but they were Protestant in general — came from Irish, Norwegian, or other extractions. I would say there was more of a division on religious lines because there was a Catholic Church, St. Mary's, and the Community Church. All Protestant religions went to the Community Church. It made a division in that respect. We were Catholic, so we were part of that group. We also lived in the center of town, so we kind of belonged to both sides. There was not any real prejudice.

✦

Prejudice? Down on the ranch and different places they talked about dumb Italians, or something like that. Not so much the East Enders, but Italian farmers.

Hannibal Brown

✦✦✦✦✦✦✦✦✦✦✦✦✦✦

A lot of the old folks barely spoke English. The women didn't have to learn, but the men did because they worked in the mines. You couldn't talk to them, so you didn't know them as well. Like one old lady, she had these goats up by the Glory Hole. When you saw her, she would come out in these long old gowns with a stick, because we would be bothering her goats or something. We thought she was crazy, because she would be yelling in some strange language. I can remember the relatives always talking about that "dumb old so and so, can't even speak English yet. Been here for forty years." And that kind of thing. I lived overseas, and I often thought how hard it is to learn a foreign language and how Americans never do.

✦

I liked Hannibal. Sometimes his latest cousin would come on the train. I guess he went through three or four. He was great. He would visit with you and tell you about New Orleans and everything. I don't know where he was from, but he would talk about New Orleans. Evidently that's where he tended bar. "I believe in the better hotels." That's what he told me.

✦

"

Sometimes his latest cousin would come on the train. I guess he went through three or four. He was great. He would visit with you and tell you about New Orleans and everything.

"

I remember Hannibal real well. He lived in the house just east of the courthouse. It was a little white house. He was one of the only colored folks in Aspen at the time. They were real good folk. We were well acquainted with them, and Hannibal was sort of a caterer. That was part of his business. He would cater parties and serve drinks. That was how he made his living. Plus he had an old Hudson and was the town taxicab driver. If you needed to get a ride to Glenwood or go down and catch the train, Hannibal would take you down in his car. He would really make good drinks, too. We never got to have any, but I remember that he was quite a guy. He had the only taxicab in Aspen.

✦

Hannibal Brown. Just loved him. Nobody thought of him as being a different color. The thing I remember about him is all the beautiful serving hutches he made. He catered a lot.

✦

Galena Street looking toward Ajax Mountain, 1905. Courtesy Peggy Rowland.

Hannibal Brown could mix the most difficult drinks I knew of. He'd just lay the liquor in perfect layers. He always had a different cousin every two or three years and always had a Hudson. It was a steel-roofed car and Han was always turning it over on Independence Pass. He was one of the elite of the colored people. He used to throw some wingding parties for colored people from Denver, Grand Junction, and everywhere. He used to have some beautiful dancing parties across from the Aspen Drug, right in the middle of the Hyman Avenue block. Hannibal was the host. He and his cousin at the time. We used to go up there and hang around the door trying to get a peak in but we couldn't get past the door. About once a year, I think it was. I liked Hannibal very much.

◆

Hannibal Brown

✦✦✦✦✦✦✦✦✦✦✦✦✦✦

✦

AS WELL KNOWN AS HE WAS, Hannibal's story remains incomplete, and there are some things about him that we will never know. We do know that for many years, Hannibal Brown was Aspen's only black, its only African-American resident outside of his immediate family.

There was no apparent racial prejudice in Aspen. Residents of the city, including the newspaper editors, took pride in Aspen's cosmopolitan makeup. Germans and Irish dominated the early population, with another dozen or so European nations represented, plus men and women from all over the United States. Early Aspen also had a small black community, although it probably never consisted of more than a few dozen members (the 1885 census recorded twenty-nine blacks and nineteen mulattos). Although we do not know what most did for employment in Aspen, a few early residents recalled their fathers talking about the black "gangs" that worked the mines. Some of Aspen's wealthier white families had blacks in their service, and this was the path that led Hannibal Brown to Aspen.

Hannibal was born in Kansas in August 1876 and apparently set out on his own when he was about fourteen years old. He was extremely reticent about his past. Although he often spoke of Memphis, Tennessee, it is believed that he spent some time in New Orleans working in hotels, which may explain his celebrated status as a bartender. At some point, he may have settled in Denver, because after moving to Aspen, Hannibal made frequent trips to Denver to visit friends, and he had a variety of female "cousins" from Denver who often came to Aspen to visit him.

In 1880, a year after silver was discovered in the Roaring Fork Valley, H. P. "Grandpap" Cowenhoven, a merchant from Black Hawk, Colorado, his wife, Margaret, his daughter, Katherine, and his clerk, David R. C. Brown, made the arduous journey with two wagons from Leadville to Buena Vista, then across Taylor Pass to Ashcroft and finally into Aspen, where Cowenhoven bought a corner lot at Cooper Avenue and Galena for seventy-five dollars and began constructing a house and a general store.

D.R.C. Brown married Katherine Cowenhoven in 1883 and became a full partner in the already thriving Cowenhoven enterprises. It is believed that Hannibal arrived on the scene perhaps as early as 1884 and probably no later than 1885 to work in Kate Cowenhoven Brown's household. Kate Cowenhoven Brown died in 1898, and in 1900, her grieving widower moved to Paris to assist in the education of his two daughters.

For his own private reasons, Hannibal remained in Aspen when so many others were leaving. As early as 1900, his may have been the only black family in town. The population had dropped from an estimated 17,000 residents and transients in 1893 to 3,303 in 1910, and that decline was to continue well into the 1940s. There is no reason to believe, however, that Hannibal was "stuck" in Aspen. As an employee of the Browns, it is possible that his income was greater than that of most of the miners and other laborers in town, and it certainly wasn't subjected to the many variables faced by the miners, such as sudden mine closures and fluctuations in the price of silver. It would seem that Hannibal was reasonably secure. He owned one of the first cars in town; by 1910, he owned a home on East Main Street, which was immediately east of the Pitkin County Courthouse, across from the Catholic Church; he entertained extensively; and he had a reputation for being a kind and generous man, one who would help out anyone in trouble.

Nor was Hannibal stuck in Aspen in the sense that he had nowhere else to go. He apparently had many friends and relatives in Denver, including his infamous "female cousins," so it seems that he could have left Aspen for greener pastures whenever he wanted. He loved to hunt and fish, and those pleasures may have had a major influence on his decision to remain in Aspen. Yet Hannibal was undoubtedly attracted to Aspen by much more than just the hunting and fishing. The Aspen residents were open and friendly. It seems as if that holds true today. The Roaring Fork Valley has always attracted exceptional people who are drawn to its beauty. The valley seduces some to stay forever. Perhaps Hannibal Brown simply fell in love with the valley and its people and could not leave.

Mill Street, looking toward Smuggler Mountain, 1905. Courtesy Peggy Rowland.

HANNIBAL BROWN

1900 Pitkin County Records:
> Hannibal Brown, 23 years old (saloon porter)
> Married to Anna, 29 years old
> Hannibal Brown born August 1876; Anna born June 1870
> Both listed as first marriage
> No children dead or living claimed by either
> She could read and write, but he could not
> They rented a house
> Hannibal was employed all year
> Both listed as black (not mulatto)

1900 Census: etc.
> Hannibal Brown, born in Kansas in 1876
> Father from North Carolina
> Mother from Arkansas
> In 1900 he is registered as a saloon porter
> In 1910 he is registered as porter at Elks
> Married Mary Parker between 1901 and 1909?
>> Children born:
>>> 1903 Male Child   }
>>> 1904 Male Child   } don't know what happened
>>> 1905 Male Child   } to wife or children

In 1900 Hannibal lived next door to two blacks:

May W. Hawkins, born January 1875, 25 years old, single, from Missouri

William McGruder, born September 1864, 35 years old, single, from Missouri. William was saloon porter. Both could read and write, and she rented the house.

1910 Pitkin County Census:
> Hannibal Brown, 33 years, Elks porter
> Married to Laura Brown, 37 years (she died in 1913)
> Her father from Scotland
> Her mother from Arkansas
> Laura was mulatto.
> Both married seven years, she married once before
> Both could read and write
> He owned house on East Main Street, debt free

1920 Pitkin County, etc. & Census:
> Hannibal Brown, 42 years, Elks janitor
> Listed as married, but no woman on census

Taken from Marriage Records:
> Hannibal Brown married Kellie Campbell August 10, 1921, in Denver
> Hannibal Brown married Mary Johnson September 15, 1926, in Denver

Hannibal Brown married Willa Mae Rubin (1900-1958) October 14, 1944, Hannibal was 67 years old; Willa was 37 years old.

Hannibal died around 1952.

Tough People, Hard Times

Not long after mining declined, thousands of people left Aspen
to find work elsewhere. A small number remained.
Some men knew nothing but mining and chose
to keep on searching for the mother lode.
Others chose to stay because Aspen was home.

Most of the people in the following interviews
are the children of the Aspenites who stayed on after mining
and through the Depression. Like their parents before them,
these people remained in Aspen during the Quiet Years
and on into the era of skiing.
They are the wisdom keepers of the Quiet Years.

Hildur spent most of her life teaching young children. She is still a very determined woman who will never stop learning.

Photo by Kathy Daily

Hildur Hoaglund Anderson

I was born June 28, 1907, at home in Aspen. My sisters were quarantined with scarlet fever at the time, and the doctor came to deliver me. My dad had taken too much time when he went after the doctor. Mother got one of the girls out of bed to go up to the neighbor — Mrs. Roman — and ask her to come down. She came down and delivered me. About the time the doctor arrived, I was already born. According to my mother, Dr. Lof was running around wringing his hands and saying, "There's a mistake here, some big mistake. I was supposed to deliver that baby and the baby's already here." So my mother always called me her mistake. My sisters were ten and twelve. I know that because my sister Selma was ten years older than I, and Rose was two years older than Selma. I had three brothers, Paul, Henry, and Ralph. My brother Ralph is still living in Fruita. I'm the youngest — the mistake. My mother decided that was enough — six of us.

My father's name was Charles Hoaglund. He came to Aspen with two brothers in 1882. The three brothers came from Sweden on a cattle boat. They slept in the hay that was used for the cattle to keep warm at night. There were some people on the boat who knew they were there and would save food from the kitchen, so they had plenty to eat. When they got to New York, they got off before the ship landed at Ellis Island. They skipped ship. I've never figured out why they came to Aspen except that there was supposedly work here. Aspen was getting to be a name to lonely immigrants — the place to go for work with friendly people. That's the reason they came to Aspen, I guess. One of my father's brothers went to DeBeque and the other one went to Kansas. Only my father stayed here. Aspen was one of the biggest silver booms in the country at that time. One brother married someone from DeBeque. She was in Aspen and then they went to DeBeque and lived. My uncle John married a girl from Kansas, and she wanted to go back to Kansas, so they went back.

My mother's name was Marie Hennrietta Beck (not related to Anton Beck of Aspen). She ended up at Cocamo. It's close to Leadville. It was probably an old mining camp. She worked as a maid and then transferred to Leadville, where she worked. Mother loved to be perfect. And she wanted to be American. The lady she lived with was Irish. She evidently had a friend who was a dentist who was not getting much trade. Mother said this woman convinced her that to be American, you had your teeth pulled out and wore dentures. Mother said, well that would be okay except she was going to a Swedish picnic the following Sunday — about a week and a half away. She wouldn't let this dentist touch her teeth until he promised he could make her a set of dentures right away. At that time, the thought was that if you pulled your teeth, you waited six months for your gums to settle to get dentures. My mother would not allow him to pull her teeth until he promised he would immediately make dentures, which is what they do now. He pulled all of her teeth and left her with the teeth. Then he went home to clean up. He didn't give her gas, I guess. He gave her something that put her out. When she woke up, there were teeth all over the floor. There was blood that needed to be cleaned up, and that was her job. In less than a week, he gave her temporary teeth. In six months, he was going to make a permanent set.

The Smuggler Mine,
1892.
Courtesy Del Gerbaz.

He did a good job on the first temporary set and they fit perfectly. She wore them for fourteen years. So the dentist didn't get to make her another set. She came out fairly good in the deal. That was hard on us children, especially when I had a toothache. I'd be crying as a small child and mother would say, "Oh quiet that. Nothing can be that bad." Because she never experienced a toothache. Her teeth were fine!

My father and his two brothers didn't go through Ellis Island. I think they got their citizenship later in Aspen. Dad did get his citizenship because he voted. I don't think it was so difficult at that time like now. He was a miner; he worked in the Smuggler. He was a boss in the Smuggler and kind of bossed getting the ore out of the ore cars. The Smuggler shut down in 1892, but my dad was left on the payroll until 1910. He got all of the ore cars out and cleaned up the mess there. He locked the door to the Smuggler in 1910 and then immediately moved to Brush Creek on what is now the Anderson Ranch. We had

380 acres — took in all of the pasture land way back to the forest — all of the land that you go through now. I was three years old when I moved to the ranch. I think dad paid less than a thousand dollars.

Tom Kearns lived on a ranch just above us. He had an accident and limped. He always said he'd go down one side of a hill because his legs were just right, and go back up the other side. He was a great man, Tom Kearns.

Everyone put cattle up on the forest. Our place stretched back about a mile. Tom would stop by and I'd ride with him. We'd go back into the forest land and ride over where Burnt Mountain is now. The cattle had access to all of that land. I always had a little cowdog. I'd take him and go with Tom, and he'd stay on the path. Tom would say, "Hilder, there's a cow back up there. Go get it." So I'd be on my horse, of course, and I'd say, "Come on Buster. Let's get this cow." So I rode through the brush. I didn't mind. It was a wonderful experience. When we weren't herding cattle, Tom would be telling me stories about Ireland and his trip to America. I was quite fascinated with his stories. Tom is Pat Maddalone's grandfather. Pat's always been a very good friend of mine. I had a picture where Pat was in the Brush Creek school. There were about ten pupils. When my oldest son was born, I'd take him to school and the kids all babied him. One of the pictures that I have shows Pat holding Bert. It was a very wonderful school.

I went to high school in Aspen and at first all you needed was to take a county superintendent test. If you passed that test you got a teacher's certificate, so that's what I did. When I graduated in 1925, they were giving a course in Glenwood. I figured that after ten years, some teachers wanted a little extra cash. So they planned this two-week teacher's course in Glenwood. We went to school from eight o'clock to noon. The teachers did also, so they could have the afternoon off to do what they wanted. That lasted two weeks. After that, in summers, I started going to Gunnison. I went to Gunnison for twelve weeks, which was the equivalent of a quarter of college.

Why did I want to be a teacher? I always loved my eighth grade teacher — her name was Margaret Watt. Her father lived up Castle Creek. He was one of the big people up there at the time. I don't know what they did, but they were very instrumental in the valley. Margaret Watt boarded at our place, and of course farmhouses didn't have that much space, so she slept in my bedroom. I was very close to her. She loved animals, and my favorite cat always wanted to sleep with me, and Margaret thought that was fine. We always had Tom in bed and my mother would hear him purring and she'd say, "I thought I heard a cat purr." Margaret would put her hand over his mouth to keep him quiet. She was just wonderful. She inspired me. Her brother worked at the Glendale stock farm.

Jack Brunton owned the Glendale. Their family did a lot of things for the school, even put in a telephone. We were the only school in the country at that time with a telephone. The teacher could call home if a student decided he had a tummyache or something. Kenneth Watt (Margaret's brother) would come and get him. That really was great for the kids on Brush Creek. On the boy's birthday, the Bruntons had a wonderful birthday party and invited all of we poor wilderness folks to this elegant party. They had three housemaids that prepared games, food, and elaborate stuff for all the Brush Creek kids. That was wonderful. He had hired men — eight or ten. The foreman was Ralph Kemper. They built a house just below where the Bruntons lived for this foreman, and they had two children that went to the Brush Creek school. We had us some very nice people. In my estimation, all the people who came were especially nice. I don't know if the country itself influenced them or what. The Bruntons were great, even being millionaires. All the other people were great, too.

The school I taught in is still there — the little red schoolhouse in Snowmass. Somehow or another they dubbed it Hilder Anderson's little red school, I think because there was a time when it wasn't a school — it was an empty building. Where we lived, it was on our property and we claimed it. Our hired man and his family lived in the schoolhouse. Our ranch now is called Anderson Ranch. They give art classes there.

I married Bill Anderson. He was born in Utah in 1898. They lived in Silt and Bill was raised there. His profession was shearing sheep and he sheared for the Williams families. The Williams are still instrumental just this side of Capitol Creek. There was a house way back in there — a schoolhouse — and it was used primarily for dances. I always played for the dances from nine o'clock at night until six or seven in the morning. At that time, Bill was shearing sheep. Bill always liked music. The people he was shearing for told him about the dance. There would be someone playing the accordion. So he went to the dance, and there I was playing the accordion. We got very well acquainted. Bill played the violin, self-taught. I think a couple of times he would go to the dances and take me home to Brush Creek. Bill always sheared from California through to Aspen, up through Wyoming and Montana. Eventually he asked me to marry him. School was out the twenty-first of May and we were married May 23, 1927. I was twenty I think. We went up through Wyoming, Montana, through Yellowstone Park for a honeymoon. I just loved it.

Then Bill took over the ranch. Dad was getting up in years. My dad loved the ranch. He wanted to live there. My mother didn't care much for it. She was in Rifle with me when I taught there. After I married Bill, he and I moved to the ranch and my dad was very ill. We put his bed in the livingroom and somebody sat with him all night, every night. A neighbor boy, Pete Roberts, was very good. He'd come sit with him until 2:00 A.M. or 3:00 A.M. and then either I'd wake up or Bill would take over so that he was never alone. We always had either Pete Roberts, one of the Kearns, or one of us. He had emphysema from the early mining days. If you don't smoke, don't do it. My father did. Took up smoking late in life.

It was odd. We had transferred sheep one day. We put them up on Smuggler Mountain way back to Independence. Art Roberts had sheep up there. Once in a while, one or two of our sheep would mix with Art's. He was herding his sheep into the depot out there east of the mountain. They did what they call "stray the sheep," which meant that they looked for any that were ours that had mixed with theirs. I hadn't been away from the ranch for a long time. Mrs. Kearns, who was a nurse, Patty's mother, came down to watch over my dad. My mother was there so I could leave, and I went with Bill. He went through Art Robert's sheep and people came running and told him, "You're wanted at home. Get home as fast as you can." So we jumped into the car. On the way home, we met the doctor. My mother and Mrs. Kearns had called him because dad had taken a bad spell. He told us that my dad had died. We hurried home. It was ironic, because for months, I'd not left my dad's bedside, only to be in the next room. The minute I was gone, he died. But mother and Mrs. Kearns were there. They got the doctor. So he died quickly and peacefully. All I cared about was that he was being cared for.

I loved that ranch. I certainly did. The only reason we left the ranch was because our kids were in school and it got to be a difficult situation. Our neighbors, the Meltons, bought it and we bought property in Aspen.

We had three boys — Bert, Ed, and Jim — and the girl Margie. All the boys played basketball and football. Bert was outstanding in football. He learned how to run on the ranch and he was the fastest runner on the team. One of the kids from the T Lazy 7, Buck, kept telling people that Bert was the fastest one on the team in football. They all laughed at him. I went up there one time on a Friday afternoon. Some of the girls saw me coming and said, "Hurry, hurry, hurry. You've got to watch Bert!" He'd get the ball at the far end and take off. The other guys would just stand there and watch him. They didn't follow him because they knew they couldn't catch him.

I taught school for forty-eight years. I taught in Rifle and I taught in Crested Butte. I was probably a little ahead of my years in teaching. Having gone to a country school, I often let the kids decide what they wanted to do, what they wanted to learn. I would say, "Well, you plan your schedule and, if it's agreeable, I'll back you. You can ask the questions when you get stuck." So the kids sort of planned their own schedules, and even now when I think of having forty kids or more, how I could keep up with all of them? When I hear all this new stuff I melt and say, "That's not new. That's my way of teaching." I taught first grade through eighth. Sometimes a first-grader would work with a fourth-grader, a sixth-grader worked with a third-grader. Whatever level they were, that's where they worked. I didn't just say, "Well, here's the book. We'll do sixteen through nineteen."

What do I think of Aspen changing? We have to accept change. When I go downtown, I go to places like the Hickory House and the post office. It hasn't changed for me because I see people I've known for a long time.

✦

Photo by Kathy Daily

Jennie Arlian and Palmira Arlian Favre

Our parents' names were Josephine and Laurent Arlian. They were both born in Italy in 1876. We grew up at the mouth of Little Woody Creek. That big, red, four-gable house on the left — our dad built that in 1928. Mike Arlian was a cousin of our dad's. He came to Aspen first. He bought the ranch from Clavel in about 1908. Our dad came from St. Barthlema, Italy, in about 1910, to work for Mike Arlian. Mother came later with Jennie, Margaret, and Brice about 1913.

Jennie:

I was born in Italy on January 1, 1906. Palmira was born on the ranch December 18, 1914. We had five children in our family, Linda, Jennie, Brice, Palmira, and Margaret. I came to the United States with my mother in about

Palmira Arlian Favre is Jennie's younger sister, and I think that Jennie took pretty good care of her. She thinks before she speaks.

Photo by Kathy Daily

1913, when I was about seven. I remember my brother was awful sick on the boat. We came directly to Aspen; my dad was already here. He came because Mike Arlian, his cousin, had that ranch in Woody Creek, so my dad came to work for him in 1911. Mike Arlian and his brother first worked somewhere in Colorado. Then they worked in Leadville, and then they came down to Woody Creek. In 1920 we bought that place. I think dad paid about twenty thousand dollars, which was like a million dollars is now.

When I was growing up on the ranch, I did everything — worked hard from hog feeding to milking cows for twenty-five years without missing a day. And when I gave that up, I said that's it. Haven't milked a cow since we sold the place. That was in 1945. Then we moved down here, where Blue Lake is. My brother bought Blue Lake. You should have known our dad. He used to ride the horse from where the high school is now. He owned all that property of Duroux (James E. Moore now). He would ride down by the cemetery all the way to the Stein Ranch — he owned all of that.

We had phones in later years. We built our new house in 1928, and then we had a telephone — a party line with four to eight people. We didn't have electricity. We left Woody Creek with no electricity. We had water to start with. We had a ditch and we went and carried water.

Palmira:

There was an old Woody Creek school down off of the railroad track, down off that hill. It's still there — the red house just at the end of the pond. One of the Walter's kids drowned in that pond. And you know we walked. Now kids ride on the bus to go two steps. Isn't that awful? Back then it was all grades, first grade to the eighth grade, one teacher.

We wore dresses to school. There wasn't such a thing as slacks. In the winter, well, I suppose you had these long cotton socks, and then shoes. The dresses weren't long — three-quarters length. We walked to school. The Natals rode horses because they were three miles from school. The house was plenty warm because we had a kitchen stove and a big heater. And in school they had these great big stoves that you could go put logs in . When we got there, the school was already warm. George Vagneur used to ride from his ranch from up on McLain Flats, and sometimes when he would get to school, he would be crying because he was so cold. He was riding a horse, and his feet would get so cold that when they would warm up, they hurt.

In my fondest memories, it just seemed like you worked hard, and when you came home there was a dance. And you weren't tired anymore. There were dances just up above us in a family home and up where Mr. Stranahan is. Mr. and Mrs. Bionaz were there and they had a dance quite often — music on the accordion. If you want music, you got to have the accordion. Tony Antinelli played and Amy Blanc played the violin.

We didn't get off the ranch much. Our brother did, by horse and buggy, every week. My brother would go to Aspen with the horse and buggy to buy the groceries. There was a stable where you tied up your horse. He would go and buy the groceries, go to the bank, and do a little business. And when he come home, the horse was anxious to come. Boy, he took no time down McLain Flats — fast as lightning.

Tough People, Hard Times

Jennie:

I don't think when I went to school we did too much mischief, just fun. We used to play run sheep run. One was the herder and then he would cover his eyes. That's when we went clear up on McLain Flats. The nice part of it was we had a man teacher, Mr. Byers, and we got him to go with us clear up on top of the flats, so when the bell rang, he was with us.

The church was down in Basalt and Aspen. That's where we had communion, confirmation — St. Mary's Church with Father McSweeny. Elizabeth Callahan was our sponsor when we took confirmation in about 1928. Mother would read the Bible and all those things. I learned more from her than you do now. My dad's Bible is about worn out. Dad would read that Bible and then he would just recite it — he knew it by heart. You would see him start reciting it before it was all the way open.

Palmira:

Those were hard times. At Christmas we barely got gifts because we were so poor. Hard times. There was no place to go because all we had was the horse and buggy. We couldn't go to Aspen too much, only once in awhile. Those early years were hard years — you don't know how hard. Jennie knows more than I know because I was younger. As we were growing up, we had to do everything — work in the fields and all that kind of stuff. The days were so hot. I remember weeding the potatoes when I was just knee high to a grasshopper. Oh yes, it wasn't easy. But we never went hungry; we always had food on the table.

Then the Depression came in the 1930s, so once again, hard times. But we kind of had our place paid for between 1920 and 1930. During the Depression we just struggled along. We sold a hundred pounds of potatoes, you know for how much? Twenty-five cents. One hundred pounds for twenty-five cents. After that, don't you know, we were selling them for twenty-five cents and the government came in and paid for them. You couldn't sell them; there were no buyers. So the government gave us twenty-five cents per hundred pounds. They would come in and paint them purple so you couldn't resell them to anybody. You had a bin and then they kind of measured them and figured, well maybe there are five hundred pounds or whatever. Later on, we sold a lot of potatoes for fifty cents per hundred pounds. It was hard even when we got married; we had to struggle in 1934. The best price, I think — I don't know what year it was — we had just about sold all our potatoes by May. The price

Shale Bluffs,
Midland Railroad,
1903.
Courtesy Del Gerbaz.

jumped to seven dollars per hundred pounds, but we were out of potatoes by that time. All I remember is we had very few left. So we only got two dollars per hundred pounds.

Jennie:

We sometimes had four or five dairy cows. In the morning we had to get up at 4:00 A.M. and go irrigate in the summertime, then come home and milk. I was the only one to go and milk those cows. Then I'd eat breakfast, then take off again and work. I know how to milk, I mean, I still can. We raised beef cattle also — Herefords. We must have always had at least a hundred of them. We used to chase them on the highway up there by Shale Bluffs.

I'll never forget the Shale Bluffs — never. We were chasing the cows there and Albert Duroux had a few of his cattle on the road. They got in with ours, so we tried to head them back. One of those cows climbed up the bluff. When she got up to the top, she couldn't go any further, and she jumped down on the road. I thought, oh my gosh! But she got up. Mr. Duroux was coming to get the others, so he just got her and put her back. But when I saw her jump off there down on the road, I thought she was dead.

Palmira:

I met Vinance Favre at one of those country dances when I was eighteen. Got married at nineteen. Now it's been fifty-seven years together. Then we moved right down here at El Jebel over where Crawford is after we were married. We worked that ranch from 1938 to 1960. We were just by ourselves, so we sold it.

I suppose in the last ten, fifteen years there has been such a change in the whole valley. I hate to say this, but it was nice when there weren't so many people. They are all over the place now.

What can you learn from all this? That we had hard times and then better times. Always hang onto the hope that it is always going to be better times again. I think that is what my mother used to say. After the hard times, you have to break into better times. Some of these people now are too demanding. They want everything, all at once. A young couple who gets married, they want to start with everything I got in this house today, which isn't a lot, but they want that and more. They start at the top. We started at the bottom. I don't know what we would have done if it hadn't been for my mother, because she helped us. Anytime that we needed money for something, she would let us have it without much interest — just pay it back, which we always did. About the time we got married, we had a little better going then. After the ranch was paid, we made a couple of dollars. So mom helped us buy a little old Model A Ford. I wish we had it now. We had it until about 1960, and then we traded it off for a Chevrolet pickup.

✦

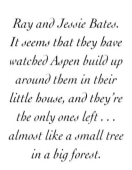

*Ray and Jessie Bates.
It seems that they have
watched Aspen build up
around them in their
little house, and they're
the only ones left . . .
almost like a small tree
in a big forest.*

Ray Bates

 I was born March 7, 1911, in Denver and I came to Aspen in 1933. My mother came from Norway and my father from Ireland. I am married to Jessie Sparovic. Jessie was born and raised here.

Jessie's parents came from Austria. Their names were John and Mary Sparovic. Her mother had a sister that was already here in the United States. Jessie's parents met in Europe. Her dad came to the United States and then sent for her mom. They had more stuff. Jess has her mama's sewing machine. It still sews. And beautiful dishes. They came to the United States in 1905. That was when they got married in Pueblo. Jessie's dad worked in the steel mills in Pueblo, and her mom worked, too. They had a boardinghouse. Her mom said she had six boarders and she would buy fifty cents worth of steak and the whole bunch of 'em was able to eat.

Jessie's dad was a miner in the Smuggler and Durant. There is a lot of silver down there still, but it is all flooded with water.

I came to Aspen for the work — driving that tunnel through over at Twin Lakes. The water diversion is down in the Arkansas and goes to the southeastern corner of the state for irrigation. It is private. They said they were going to take the spring runoff. Instead, they took everything that was not adjudicated. Smart people.

I came to Aspen when I was twenty-two. There were a few people coming for work; none of 'em knew how to do that particular kind of work anyway. Even if they got the job, they couldn't handle it.

I wasn't qualified. That's a story in itself, how I got the job. I had heard about it in Denver. My boss in Denver had told us we were gonna cut down one day. I told Jessie we can't make it. Her sister who lived in Leadville had heard about this job hiring men. I said, "Well, I'm going." So I grabbed a boxcar on the train and come up here — went to Leadville, over the pass. This was in October, and the boss doing the hiring was staying down at the Jerome Hotel. He would leave in the morning and drive up there. There was an old-way station cabin. They drove coaches over. They would pick up a lunch there. Anyway, I asked him at the hotel and he said "No, maybe later on." And I said, "I need a job now." He said, "Later." Then he went into the hotel. They had a candy wagon out front, a panel truck. I climbed in the back and rode on up there. These guys got out. I went in and got into line with them and picked me up a sack, too. They came out and he saw me and he said, "I guess, by God, you *do* want to go to work." So he took me up there and dumped me off. Handed me a damned railroad pick. That was work! I wasn't dressed for it and I didn't know how to swing a pick. You hit that frozen ground — ugh! I got four dollars a day to begin with, and when I got underground, I still got four dollars as a chuck tender. When I got on a machine, I got six dollars for an eight-hour day.

Before I met her, Jessie worked for the Hotel Jerome as a waitress for five years. She went to Denver and we met there. We came back here together in 1933.

During the Depression it was nice, quiet, and decent in town. There was an Elks and an Eagles. I miss the quiet, yes I do. This isn't Aspen like it was.

You knew everybody and his dog. It never posed any problems. The horses didn't pose any problems, and the streets weren't paved. Nobody had a key to their front door. You could leave your door open, go to Denver, and everything would be there when you got back. We were just one big family, the whole town. The streets had all been named at one time, but the signs were all torn down.

We bought our property in 1952. Used to live on King Street where No Problem Joe lives now. He's the guy that used to be the mechanic for the Aspen Ski Corporation. He still lives over there.

I went to work for the Ski Company until 1966 setting machinery and towers. Since then I've been struggling to make ends meet on social security. It isn't easy; you got to buy groceries, too. Over there at City Market, if you start down the aisle, before you get to the counter, they've already raised the prices.

I still drive but don't go downvalley — too scared of the highway. Not so afraid of my driving, I'm afraid of what the other fool is going to do. A lot of people moved downvalley to Carbondale. Carbondale is getting so full now, too. They have these condos here across the alley; they tore down all the houses. When we moved here, this house and the little one next door were the only houses that were here. This was an empty lot over here. Now I can't see a damned thing. I used to be able to sit here and see the elk cross over in the fall of the year . . . come around Smuggler, cross down into Hunter Creek, and go behind Red Mountain.

Aspen was good then; we didn't have all these danged condos and other things. When we bought this house, they were renting it for $45 a month. The first year we bought it, the taxes were $45. And now we pay damn near $2,000.

Have I considered moving? If Jessie goes, I'll sell, and if I go, she'll sell. Could have sold, but I stopped it 'cause Jessie won't move out of Aspen. Jessie told me one time if she ever got a home of her own, she's never gonna leave it. I think she meant it.

We used to belong to Eagles. There used to be people our age and all. We used to go down there and now it is all young kids and we're too old to go around with young kids.

When we first bought this place you couldn't have paid me enough money to move out. Hunting was good, fishing was good, you knew everybody. You'd go skiing and go have a couple of beers and leave your skis. You'd go back the next day and your skis would still be there. Now you can lock them up and people will still steal them.

We used to go camping every weekend up to Ruby toward Independence Pass. There was a two-story cabin. A bunch of us would go up there and stay overnight. When Jessie was a little kid, the neighbors would get together and buy a little pig. The men would get up at two o'clock in the morning and go and barbecue it down at the ice pond. The pond is gone now. The womenfolk would do the baking and come there about noon. You could smell it — the Yugoslavs would make wonderful sausage.

What would I want for Aspen now? To put it back like it was. Regardless of what the answer would be, it would be wrong. It's like saying you got too many people. Who is the first one you are going to kick out? You don't want to go yourself. Are you going to kick the other guy? If they could have done it different — if everyone had been like Gary Cooper when he

Ray Bates loading Gary Cooper on the top of Aspen Mountain, 1948. Courtesy Ray Bates.

came. He was just as plain and nice. I was working for the Ski Corporation. The chipmunks would come in the work shack. I had peanuts and those little guys would open up your fingers to get the peanuts. And ol' Cooper, he couldn't get over that. He said, "I sure would like to have one to take home to my daughter." And I said, "I'll get you one." The next time he come up I had one for him. Coop sent me a picture of the house he had made for that chipmunk. It was better than houses in Aspen. It had wheels on it.

✦

Paul Beck —
I bet all
of the Beck boys
were a
bunch of rowdies.
They shoot
straight from
the hip.

Photo by Kathy Daily

Paul and Glenn Beck

Paul:

I was born June 7, 1933, in the old hospital in Aspen. Glenn was born June 2, 1930. We don't know when my great-grandfather Beck came to Aspen, but we have a newspaper clipping that says my great-grandfather John Stuart Stewart on my mother's side came to Leadville in 1881, from Nova Scotia, Canada. In 1884, he came to Snowmass Creek. He either homesteaded or bought the Gateway

*Glenn Beck.
None of the Becks
seem like they
would take any guff
from anyone.
They are as honest
as the day is long.*

Photo by Kathy Daily

Ranch. They were starting to mine in Aspen, and there were a few things going on. He wasn't a miner or a rancher and must have had a little money. He was an older man, fiftyish by then. His wife didn't come with him at first, supposedly. Her maiden name was Katherine McClean. They were married in Nova Scotia and she was his second wife. He had two children by her that also lived in this area later.

There's an old directory in the Aspen Historical Museum that talks about prominent men in the area, and in approximately 1901 Stewart was the county commissioner. It speaks of Commissioner Stewart and said he had mining interests in Hunter Creek. Can't tell that he ever really worked.

*Railroad on
Castle Creek, 1905.
Courtesy Peggy Rowland.*

Our great-uncle was a Midland Railroad stationmaster and postmaster in old Snowmass around 1900. His name was John Henry Stewart. He never married and was a prospector. We called him uncle, but he was actually our great-uncle. John Henry Stewart lived at Center Street (Garmisch) and Hopkins Avenue in a little miner's cabin, you'd call it nowadays. Both he and his father alternately were postmasters at Snowmass. John Henry Stewart, the son, built the Snowmass store and house that were there. Originally he had a little cabin right by the river on the edge. John, the son, was also the Midland Railroad agent for a period of time — 1888 through 1904, or something like that. His job was to check the passengers on and take off the freight at Snowmass. All we really know is that our Uncle Hubert Chisholm has a number of identification cards that say "John Henry Stewart, Midland Railroad" — a pass for he and his family to go anywhere they wanted. He was the agent of both the Midland and the Denver and Rio Grande Western. He has cards for both of them. John Henry Stewart never married. He was a good-looking, tall, thin man.

Glenn:

Tom Beck was our great-grandfather. He came around 1891 and opened a grocery store in the Wheeler Opera House. It was called Beck and Quail's. Thomas Beck and Thomas Quail had it. The opera house had just been built two years before. A newspaper clipping said that Beck came from Galena, Illinois, where he had been a grocery-man for twenty-five years. My guess is

John Stuart Stewart,
age 92, 1925
(1852-1927).
Photo taken near
Snowmass Creek.
Courtesy Bert Chisholm.

that all the Becks came from the town of Laxy on the Isle of Man. The Isle of Man had a big lead mine. They seem to have gone to Galena, Illinois, also a lead-mining town. A number of people came to Aspen from Galena, probably because the mining there was going down. Although he was always a groceryman, if you look in the *Aspen Times* a few years later, it just says "Thomas Beck." It doesn't say Beck and Quail, so I don't know what happened to Quail. Then it was "Thomas Beck's," the great-grandfather, until the early 1900s, maybe 1905 or 1910.

Our grandfather, John Alton Beck, was born in this country. There were Altons all the way. My father was Charles Alton. I'm Glenn Alton Beck. Back before that, there was a woman named Barbara Alton. So that's where it became a family name, apparently back on the Isle of Man, where "Alton" came from. There were many Becks here. There were two families in those early histories. There was a Henry Beck that had a distillery that's not related to us — a legal distillery. It was over by the old hospital at the base of Red Mountain. That was Hilder Anderson's uncle. We would find all these jugs that said "Henry Beck, Aspen." Old crocks. It wasn't beer — it was whiskey.

The store went from Thomas to John Beck. John had that store until around 1940. Thomas had it probably until 1905. Almost went broke according to my father. Thomas disappeared — we don't know where. He's not buried here — maybe back in Galena. John A., who had worked at the grocery store as a clerk, took over. These old registers of Aspen show that they lived on Mill Street up from the store. John A. Beck was a resident of that same house and a clerk in the Beck grocery store. Bill Beck (our great-uncle) was a clerk in Shiller's dry goods.

According to my dad, the store practically went broke, and then John (our grandfather) took over and paid off everybody. Then the store did well for all those years. It was a good-sized store, too. When Mrs. Paepcke came here, that

*Glenn and Paul Beck,
about 1939.
The Sardy House is
in the background.
Courtesy Bert Chisholm.*

store had at least six or seven people working in it all the time. John had it until around 1940, and then the two sons, my father, Alton, and Uncle Henry, bought the store with some agreement between them, and so it became "Beck Brothers."

It was Beck Brothers, but the grandfather, John A., continued to go work there. He never changed. He was always there working. His brother, Bill, had worked there for years. Bill took care of produce. John A. did the book work. His son, Alton, my father, worked there. His other son, Henry, worked there, too. My Uncle Hughie Chisholm (Edie Chisholm's husband) worked for a couple of years. It was Beck Brothers until after World War II, around 1945. Albert Bishop then came back from the merchant marines and bought Alton Beck's house and the business. From then on the store was "Beck and Bishop." Al Bishop bought our house on 101 East Hopkins, where Paul and I grew up. He lives there now. My dad became the postmaster. His uncle was Thomas Beck and had been postmaster for many years. He lived on First and Hopkins.

Beck and Bishop sold out to City Market; they did not operate long in the opera house at all. In fact, I don't think they did. They moved it. It was called Alpine Market. They moved it up to where City Market is now. It went from Beck and Bishop to Alpine Market in the 1960s. I remember in the newspaper it said that it was the longest continuing business from 1891 until 1968, or whenever it was. It's kind of neat that we can go over to Albert's house, and when he says, "Come on in," everything's the same as when we left it — same furniture and same light fixtures.

That little house of Albert Bishop's was kind of notorious in that my mother always said, "Every room had an outside door." Kind of common for these Victorians to have outside doors. Every room in that house of Bishop's had a door. From the time we were born until now, people were redoing the interior of the houses. They hated the Victorian look — the old people. So they were constantly changing them, trying to make them modern. That house had a dining room and a living room with the wall in between with pocket doors. One of the first things our parents did was tear out that wall and make it one big room. Then they started putting closets in.

We had a coal stove in the kitchen and another one down in the basement that heated the front part of the house. When my dad got up early in the morning, the first thing he did was go out and put newspapers and kindling in that coal stove and get it going. Then he put a little coal on top and shifted the ashes down from the night before. We had these coal scuttles that were kind of pointed. The coal was brought in trucks in the alley, and they would throw it into the coal shed in big chunks. We had a big hammer and broke it into little pieces to put in the coal scuttle. In that kitchen stove, they had to be fairly small. And it went all day.

When I was little, I didn't do my first chore at home very well. I was supposed to chop kindling and bring the coal in every day. The houses were heated entirely by coal in those days.

We have three children in our family. We have a sister, Sandra Hernandez. She lives in Bisbee, Arizona. We lived in our house until Paul was eleven. Then we moved to Fourth and Main, across the street from the Mesa Store. It belonged to Francis Kalmes when our folks bought it. My dad sold the store and the house to Albert Bishop and at the same time bought Kalmes's house because Kalmes went off to war. That's kind of an interesting thing because Kalmes, when we were talking to him, said that my mother wouldn't buy the house and she turned down the deal almost to the end because she didn't want to live that far out of town (Fourth and Main). Finally she said they had to have his car, too. It was an old 1939 Ford woody station wagon. He threw the car in and all the furniture. They left all our furniture that we had in Albert Bishop's house. Pearl says, "That stain on the wall back there you kids put on is still there." We went back and sure enough. You'd recognize everything in there.

Paul:

My first job as a kid was cutting the lawn. When we were a little older, we got to work in the grocery store. At the house we didn't have any chores other than cutting the lawn. We didn't have any animals like our grandmother down on the ranch. She lived out on the ranch down in Snowmass where I am now. Grandmother Beck had a big garden. Grandfather Beck lived right across the street. There were relatives everywhere. The house next store belonged to our cousins, the Johnsons. John A. Beck originally owned that house. He owned all of those on two blocks of Hopkins.

Our parents were married in 1929. My mother's maiden name was Alma Chisholm. That comes from the Stewart side. John Stewart's daughter, Annie Stewart, married a fellow from Nova Scotia. She came here when she was a very

Stuart Chisholm
about 1920.
Courtesy
Bert Chisholm.

small girl. He was a miner named Dan Chisholm. That's Hubert and Hugh Chisholm's father. My mother is their sister. There were eight in the family. Grandmother Chisholm was on the ranch, and Grandmother Beck was in town.

Glenn:

My father had produce trucked in. He didn't get much of it locally. When I was little, I remember making trips with dad. At one time, Uncle Bill Beck had had a fruit ranch down in Clifton, and I can still remember going on a trip in the pickup down and over the hill to DeBeque. He knew the various fruit ranchers, and we bought pears and peaches. Milk came from a local dairy right up on Mill Street. The dairy delivered the bottles to your house. The eggs were local, too. When we were quite small, in the 1930s, the normal thing in your house would be an ice man, who brought ice for the ice box every day from the ice pond. They came to your door, right in, and put it in the ice box.

My fondest memory of childhood is playing in the Wheeler Opera House. Our grandfather had the only business in the building, and all the upstairs was vacant. The top floor windows were broken out and the pigeons lived in there. We could go up the back stairway of the store and finally crawl out right under the stage. The pigeons were all over, and the old balcony was up high where it had been burned. All of it was vacant. We played cops and robbers. It was a wonderful place to play. It was kind of charred, and there was a rope from the top of the ceiling. We could get on the balcony and swing clear over to the stage. It was a long way across. My friend Gail Jones would climb up and walk on those beams. I was afraid to do it. There were big square beams way up on the top. He lived right where the ice rink is. His folks moved out of town when he was little. He was a small kid but very brave.

What I remember most about that opera house is almost every office had a safe — a big, built-in safe. It had been part of the bank below. The safes always had beautiful paintings on the outside door. We opened those and then got into the big thick vault door, and I kept thinking that it would have been nice to have one of those. They were open when we played in there. Were we afraid we

Wheeler Opera House, 1905.
Courtesy
Peggy Rowland.

would get locked in? Never gave it a thought. People couldn't really get in the building. We got in from the grocery store. You had to get in the grocery store to get to the back stairway. The pigeons were wild.

Paul:

There were a hundred old houses around that we played in. You could go into any of the old buildings in town. Did we ski? Oh yes. They had the boat tow. They have a picture of Paul and our cousin, Neil Beck, at the Highland Bavarian Lodge when they were five years old. The first place that we really skied was Highlands. We rode up in the truck to the Midnight Mine. We probably shouldn't have even been up there, because that was a pretty good trek to the top and then ski down. I didn't ski well enough. It was a chore to get down at first. It was all deep snow. There weren't enough people to ever pack it. It was a pretty good walk to the top because it was never packed much. We skied the face. Roch Run was cut. There was the rope tow and the boat tow. Glenn raced a lot until he went to college. I didn't race much.

Glenn:

From left to right, back row: Bert Chisholm, Annie Chisholm, Hugh Chisholm, Stuart Chisholm, Alton Beck. Front row, left to right: Paul Beck and Glenn Beck. About 1938. Courtesy Bert Chisholm.

I went to college in 1948 at the University of Colorado. I basically quit skiing then. They had many races for the kids when we were growing up. They'd race from what we call the second road to the end of the old boat tow. I remember many races where you could win gloves or a certificate to go into Mike Magnifico's and get gloves or socks. Frank Willoughby was very supportive of kids, too. He was the president of the ski club. He held it together. It was just the local men in town. All these men in town — Laurence Elisha, Mike Magnifico, the Willoughbys, the Dolinseks — all cut Roch Run in 1937. At that time, we still skied out at the Highlands. The city dump was out there at that time, and there was a nice little slope which was just right for beginners. Also, we used to ski at

the Watson Divide going down to Snowmass. Our whole family would go down to the Chisholm Ranch. We'd all get out at the top and ski on that little flat there, in the early days. Then when they got the boat tow, we really got going on Roch Run. Donny Elisha was a really good skier. Chido Popish was pretty good, too.

Paul:

When I first started sweeping the post office, John Loushin, who was the city marshall, was in there all the time, and he would talk to me. He had a Slovenian accent. I remember I would just say yes and no hopefully at the right point. Then I went to my dad, because my dad talked easily to him, and I said, "Dad, how do you understand a word old John says?" He says, "Sure, no problem." About a year later, all of a sudden, I could start understanding John.

Today, everybody says, "How come you let everybody come in?" Dad, Laurence, and all these people were tickled. Things were in sad shape in those years. It was getting worse and worse all the time. They'd do anything that brought a few people in. Everyone was doing their banking in Glenwood. All the businessmen got together, and once a week one of them would take all the money and go down to Glenwood. They put the pistol in the glove box and away they went. They were just barely going. Aspen is carried away now, but I didn't think so until a few years ago. My biggest complaint is always the politicians — all the dumb things that they're doing, from screwing up the parking to fouling up the West End. There are no sidewalks, no nothing. They let everybody just crowd it to death. Things like that just drive you crazy. If you watch the city and county, they'll plant $10 million worth of trees over here, and two years later they're digging them up to put a tennis court in. I could show you a zillion things like that. Just kills you to watch them.

Glenn:

I keep seeing Aspen change over the years. If there is one thing, it's the sidewalks. It just drives me nuts. When we grew up, you could ride a bicycle or walk on sidewalks anywhere. When you go to the West End, they build a house too big and then crowd out to take some of the street. It's not a major catastrophe, but it's kind of the essence of what's wrong. These people come, build an enormous house, and then hardly ever come back. They really aren't part of the community except to get onto some cause.

✦

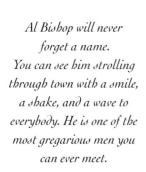

*Al Bishop will never
forget a name.
You can see him strolling
through town with a smile,
a shake, and a wave to
everybody. He is one of the
most gregarious men you
can ever meet.*

Albert Bishop

I was born July 22, 1915, in Aspen. My mother, Georgia Healy, was born in Aspen in 1892. On my mother's side, my grandmother, Lenora Buffehr, was born in Leadville, and my grandfather, Mike Healy, was born in Kansas. They were married in Leadville, as I understand it, and drove a herd of cattle from Leadville to Aspen. They started a dairy farm two miles up the pass; the house is still there on the left. It's been added onto a lot. My father, Joseph Bishop, was born in Fruita in 1891, but don't ask me how he got there!

Joe Bishop,
Albert Bishop's father,
March 1914, in
Groschurth Grocery
Store.
Courtesy
Albert Bishop.

My father's father's name was Ernest Bishop. He was married to Anne Bishop, but I don't know about his mother because they were getting along in years before I was even born.

During the Depression, I was going to school and I had a younger brother, Martin. We didn't have any money, but we seemed to get along pretty well. I played basketball in high school. They had a nice tennis court down by the red brick school. Summers were good. We did a lot of swimming in some of the ponds and rivers. It wasn't bad. We didn't have any money but it didn't seem to matter — everybody was in the same boat.

My parents had a grocery store next to Sardy's Hardware. Sabbatini had a sports shop there in the 1930s, and so forth. My dad died in 1928 and my mother continued to run it. Her brother, Martin Healy, worked for her. He finally bought it. I got out of high school in 1933 and spent a year in Denver. When I came back, there were several small jobs around. I worked at the Lincoln Gulch tunnel for a year and worked in the forest service. I got in the garage business for a couple of years — Brand's Garage.

I went into the service in 1945 and came back and bought Alton Beck's partnership in Beck Brother's Grocery Store in the Wheeler Opera House. He was in with his brother, Henry. We had the Beck and Bishop store for twenty-three years. After we sold it in 1967, I continued to work there for a year. Chuck Sheehy built the City Market building. It was called Alpine Market. He had an accident in the store one day. He fell down, hit his head, and cracked his skull and died from it a couple days later. At that time the City Market group bought the business and building from his widow. I stayed and worked for them for thirteen more years, then retired.

There were several grocery stores. My partner's father, John A. Beck, had a store. In fact, I think his father had a store before him up in the same building, in the opera house. There was another grocery called the Mesa Store on Main Street run by Julius Zupancis [brother of Elizabeth Callahan]. Another fellow named Jewett had a store where Andre's Building is now. Ed Groschurth had a store up catty-corner from City Market. There were several grocery stores around. Back then, I think, we shopped at Kalmes Clothing Store and we bought our groceries in Aspen. But going to Glenwood was a treat for the ladies. Beck & Bishop did some trading — eggs, potatoes, and grain. A lot of the people had chickens in their backyard so they bought wheat and grain to feed those chickens.

When Hugh Chisholm and I were sophomores in high school, our biggest deal was to raid fruit trucks that came into town. The farmers from down around Grand Junction would come up with watermelons, cantaloupes, and so forth. We'd sneak in the back and toss them out to each other, then hide them until the fruit truck was gone. Never got caught.

Aspen had more get-togethers. They had dances in country schools almost every other week and the Armory Hall always had dances. The Armory was really the center point of all social activities — basketball games, roller-skating.

Celebrations in Aspen? Fourth of July, picnics. We always went to Mike and Opal Marolt's and then to a dance. We also had other family picnics.

Times have changed in Aspen. I'm not going to give you a price, but we bought this house in the fall of 1945 and two years ago we bought curtains. They cost within a hundred dollars of what we paid for the whole house. They were a hundred dollars more!

The most memorable Christmas we had with our children in Aspen was 1951 or 1952. The kids were probably three or four years old. We had a nice

*Hyman Avenue
fire, 1941.
Courtesy
Warren Conner.*

Christmas tree and we bought an electric train. I mounted the track on a big board and set it in the middle of the room. We had a movie camera. The next morning when the kids got up we had the train going around. We also bought them a couple of little cars that you pump. One was a racer and one was a fire truck. And Tinker Toys . . . the kids come up and looked at the cars and said, "Oh boy, more tinker toys." Paid no attention to those darn cars at all.

Tom's Market was in the Elks Building. It was a grocery store owned by a fella named E. L. Paige. It changed hands several times. Frank Sparovic bought it, Tom McFaden bought it, and then Curt Baar. That was after the war, probably the 1950s. At first, it was called Paiges.

We bought ice from a guy named Arthur Ives when we had the grocery store. He would cut ice in the winter at what they called the ice pond. It was just below Gary Cooper's house. I think the pond is still there. He cut ice in the winter and stored it about where Cap's Auto is now. There was a big barn there. He would store and cover all his ice with sawdust. In the summer, he would distribute it.

✦✦✦✦✦✦✦✦✦✦✦✦✦✦✦

At one time every Saturday night we played cards. Once when we were at Jimmie and Alberta Moore's we got through about eleven o'clock. We started home and saw these flames in town. They were on Hyman Street on Halloween in 1941. Well, that fire sure wiped out half a block there. There was one old guy that had a barbershop. They called him the goat barber because he raised a lot of goats. He lived out in the West End of town and went to work the next morning and the shop was gone. He didn't even know there was a fire.

I noticed a change in the late forties. Walter Paepcke came in and things began to pick up and look better. As far as Aspen now, I like it the way it is. I like to walk uptown and see people. When I was a kid, we'd look up the street and there was nobody around.

Aspen has changed a lot now. I think it should slow down a little bit — about 30 percent. Then it would be a little easier living. We're living pretty good right now. We're both retired and we're eating three meals a day and doing what we want, but I think it was a little nicer town ten or fifteen years ago.

✦

Photo by Kathy Daily

Pearl Peterson Bishop

I was born September 17, 1918, in Aspen. My father's name was Andrew (Riley) Peterson. He came to Aspen in 1900 from Sweden. My mother's maiden name was Alma Holmstrom, and she was born in Leadville of Swedish parents. They were married in Aspen in 1909.

My mother was a cook at the Citizens Hospital and a homemaker. Father was a miner.

After I graduated from high school in 1936, I worked at the *Aspen Times* office for three years. I was a reporter. I did the "Around About Aspen" and was society editor. I got the names of people who entertained at bridge. I was also a proofreader.

After I married Albert in 1939, I took up housekeeping and raised two sons, Gary and Barney. When Albert had the grocery store, I worked part-time taking orders over the phone. They had grocery delivery at that time. When Albert went into the service in 1945, I stayed with my parents.

I had a brother, also named Riley, who died in 1986, and a brother, Elmer, who lives in Denver. When I was a reporter for the *Times*, Elmer also worked there after school as the "printer's devil" — one who melted down the lead and cleaned up. He later became a general printer for sixteen years when he moved to Denver and was a linotype operator for the *Denver Post* for thirty-three years. My sister is Opal Marolt, who a few years ago sold her property to the city of Aspen for the Marolt Museum and moved to Boulder.

The house east of us sold for a million and a half. We have never met them. A lot of people from Aspen have moved to Carbondale and some to Glenwood.

What was the biggest change in Aspen for me? I think the number of people and cars in town. There were times in the 1940s and 1950s when you'd walk uptown and wouldn't see a soul. Now you walk uptown and you never know anybody. Not much difference. I liked it better about ten years ago.

✦

Photo by Kathy Daily

D.R.C. (Darcy) Brown

I was born in San Francisco, December 20, 1912. My mother, Ruth McNutt, had gone back to San Francisco from Aspen to have her first child because that's where she was from. Her father was a physician there. Shortly after I was born, they brought me back to Aspen. My parents had been living in Aspen and Denver, I guess.

David R.C. Brown,
about 1881.
Courtesy Ruth Perry.

My dad's name was David R.C. Brown. I don't know exactly when he was born — about 1856 — in New Castle, New Brunswick. I wish I could tell you what brought him to Aspen, but I don't know. He came as a very young man in 1877 to Colorado, and just how he got to Colorado, I don't really know. He was working in a grocery store for Mr. Henry Cowenhoven in Blackhawk, Colorado, when they decided to pull up stakes and look for greener pastures. And you've heard, I'm sure, how they got to Aspen from Blackhawk — over Cottonwood Pass and Taylor Pass — and reached Aspen in 1880. My father drove one of the wagons, and he said at one point it took two weeks to go ten miles. I don't remember father telling me any old stories about when he first got here and

Kate Cowenhoven Brown,
about 1890.
Married in 1881.
Courtesy Ruth Perry.

what it was like. I know very little about my parents' background. My father died when I was seventeen. He was fifty-eight when I was born. Mother was thirty. I was the first child.

My father was married once before to Kate Cowenhoven, and she died in 1898. Father was living in France when he met my mother, who was on a trip around the world. They eventually married in 1907 in Paris. He took her back to Colorado to show her where he had made his fortune in the Rockies. She liked it so well she persuaded him to get back into business in Colorado. This would have been about 1908. There are a lot of questions I would like to ask now, but it's too late.

D.R.C. Brown mansion, 1st and Hallam, in the 1920s. Courtesy Helen Zordel.

My father worked for the Cowenhoven Company, H.P. Cowenhoven. He married Cowenhoven's daughter, Kate, in about 1881. He either purchased, or staked, or a little of both, mining claims. Some of them proved to be quite rich. He did quite well in the mining business and then he branched out later into cattle. He also owned the power, water, and light companies here in Aspen.

My mother had four children in a rather rapid order after 1912. It kept her pretty busy running the household both here and in Denver. She had a home in Denver where we kids spent all our winters. We came up here for the summer. Aspen, I imagine by 1907, was pretty well on the skids. The first couple of years we spent a good time between here and San Francisco. Then, in about 1915 or 1916, my father bought a house in Denver and we started spending all our winters there. After I was old enough to go to school, we were in Denver during the school year, which was from September to June.

When we came up to Aspen in the summers, we had saddle horses and pack horses. We used to do a lot of riding. We had a tennis court. Our house was the house that Mrs. Paepcke lives in now. The Aspen Center for Environmental Studies — we had that for a horse pasture. We kept it drained in those days. Will Shaw lived next door. We used to go on a lot of camping trips, pack trips all over the country, fishing. We used to go over to cow camp — my father had a big cow outfit. That was a big deal in our lives, getting to go to cow camp and help the cowboys. Mostly get in their way . . . just enjoyed being with them — Dave Dove, Charlie Childress, Rowland, Islin maybe. He is still alive up near Crystal. They are really the only names I can remember.

Red Rowland lived across the street, and he was just a little bit older than I. I had a cousin, Clarkson Brown, who was also a little older, and there weren't really too many local kids. Peggy Rowland was Peggy Lamb. She was a great friend of my sister.

My first recollection was that we used to come to Aspen every summer, and we had an English gardener. I used to know his name. He died during that winter. My father hired someone else to take over the care of the garden and everything, because it was a pretty good size. One time we arrived from Denver and things were in a mess. The garden grass hadn't been properly cut. Everything

First wood building in Aspen, built by Cowenhoven and David R. C. Brown about 1908. David R. C. Brown in front. Courtesy Ruth Perry.

*David R.C. Brown, Sr.
and Three-Finger
Atchinson, about 1911.
Burt Brown in the back.
Courtesy Ruth Perry.*

seemed to be screwed up, and my father was not very easygoing in those mat-
ters. He fired the guy on the spot. But then he suddenly realized that he had two
milk cows to take care of down in the barn. I don't think he had ever milked a
cow in his life. The Caparella family lived in a shack down behind the barn, so
he went down to see old man Cap to ask him if he could milk a cow. Cap said
sure, and he came over and milked the cows. He worked for us for the next
thirty years. Cap worked for us fulltime from then on 'til the day he died. His
boys would help him mow the lawn and take care of the garden. We had a big
vegetable garden. He was a damn good employee, a good man. His son Jessie
worked for me. He was lift superintendent at Snowmass, one of the best. He's
been lift superintendent at Snowmass since the day we built the first lifts there.

My father enjoyed being here. He owned the bank, the water company,
and the power company. And he walked to work; he had an office in the bank.
As a child, I worked there sometimes counting money. I'd help one of the
cashiers count money or something. I never got paid for that!

*From left to right:
Fletcher, Darcy,
Gordon, Ruth, and
D.R.C. Brown, Sr.,
about 1923.
Courtesy Ruth Perry.*

At that time, there weren't rich or poor. It didn't really make that much difference. On the 4th of July, a former partner of my father used to send us two tremendous boxes of fireworks, and we always had a great fireworks display. We shot them out over Hallam Lake, and the whole town came in the alley behind the tennis court. The tennis court is no longer. It was half a block east of the present house. We had a block and a half. Did anybody ever play tennis? Yes. Red Rowland was our neighbor, but he wouldn't have been caught dead on a tennis court. My cousin, Mary Louise Potter, was a ranked tennis player at one time, and she was older than we were, about ten years. She used to kind of play with us and coach us a little. My mother played tennis. In the 1920s, there weren't many people here. The only person I really remember is Red Rowland, and then the Walters brothers, who lived right across the street from us.

After high school, I went to Yale. After Yale, I went to work for Continental Oil Company in Lance Creek, Wyoming. I was in Lance Creek for a little less than a year when they moved me down to Denver, and I had a pretty good job in the land office of Continental Oil Company. I worked for them for several years. This would have been 1935 to 1938. In those days you didn't get time off from work. You worked 8:00 to 5:00, five days a week, and 8:00 to 12:00 on Saturday. We still owned the house here. My mother was alive for some years after dad. She would come up with the younger children. I went in the navy in early 1943. I got out Thanksgiving of 1945. My first wife and three children were living here during the war in that house. I came back to Aspen then. We divorced shortly after that.

I never had a vision about skiing. I got started skiing right after I got out of college, and my youngest brother talked me into it. That's when I came to Aspen. Of course, I was working then and I skied Berthoud and Winter Park and places outside Denver. I came up here to race a few times. I had quit Continental in 1940 and was out on my own in the oil business and I got a little more time to ski. I raced in the nationals in 1941. And then the war came along and I was in the South Pacific. My father had a ranch near Carbondale. There was a much larger operation, but he sold the rest of it off.

My brother-in-law, Bob Perry, is married to my sister, and we decided, just before the war, that we'd get in the cattle business together. We both liked horses and cattle. He stayed on and ran the ranch during the war years. Afterward, I came back and started to build a house down in Carbondale. Bob's father ran a coal mine over at Oak Creek near Steamboat. They also lived in Denver in the winter. Bob's sister was one of my sister's closest friends. They went to school together. They were married in 1940 and moved down to Carbondale shortly thereafter. Bob and I bought my two brothers' interest in the ranch.

Ruth and I were married in September 1947. I had known her for a long time. Was I a cowboy? Well, pretty much; I'd do a little bit of rodeoing on the side. I stayed in the cattle business for, I don't know, four or five years with Bob. Then my father-in-law had a big bunch of mining claims and some other land near Vernal that he didn't know what to do with. I very stupidly said, "Well, I'll put up my share of the money to see what we can do with this thing," and I tried to make like Brigham Young and make the desert bloom. We bought a big beautiful summer range up on what they call Blue Mountain. I ran cattle over there sort of by proxy. I had an airplane and a little landing strip at Carbondale. I'd just throw my saddle in the airplane and take off to go over there. I had three strips on the ranch, different places where I wanted to go. It was a big ranch. I ran that for several years. I was also state senator at the time, and that was keeping me busy. We had an opportunity to sell out for a little profit, and we sold it in 1956.

That's when I came to run the Aspen Skiing Corporation. I had been a director of the company all along and helped lay out some of the trails. I was the only director that was close to it that also knew a little about skiing. Ruth bought this house before we were married for $500. The house next door went for $200. All the kids were raised on the ranch.

What would I wish for Aspen? They need to simplify the whole, not only the people's life-style, but particularly the governmental life-style. I think the local government has gotten out of control.

♦

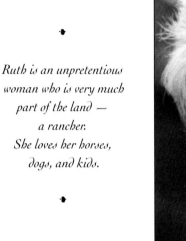

Ruth is an unpretentious woman who is very much part of the land — a rancher. She loves her horses, dogs, and kids.

Photo by Kathy Daily

Ruth Brown Perry, Gordon Brown, Bob Perry

Ruth:

I was born November 28, 1918 and Gordon was born October 1, 1917. Our father, D.R.C. Brown, was born in Canada on November 27, 1856. His full name was David Robinson Crocker Brown. His mother's maiden name was Mary Crocker, and his grandmother's maiden name was Mary Robinson. He came West as a young man and went to work in Blackhawk for H.P. Cowenhoven for

*Gordon Brown,
had kind eyes and a
sweet, gentle soul.
(October 1, 1917 –
August 11, 1993)*

Photo by Kathy Daily

a few years. The Cowenhovens decided in 1880 it was time to move. They started out thinking they might even go to Arizona. Along the way, they met someone that told them they thought Aspen was the place to go. It was just starting. So they thought they would try Aspen. It was then called Ute City.

They had a very difficult trip. It took months and the roads were nonexistent. They had wagons and arrived at Ashcroft in July 1880. They came down over Taylor Pass but there was no road. They had to take the wagon apart and lower it over cliffs. It was a very difficult approach into Ashcroft. They came on down the valley and arrived in Aspen.

H.P. Cowenhoven ran a general store in Blackhawk. It was something that was very necessary in a mining town. This was a new start in Aspen. There were no buildings, only tents. They proceeded to build the first wooden building for a store and living quarters. I presume it was to live in. My father, Dave Brown, was twenty-four years old. He traveled with the Cowenhovens and their one daughter, Kate. He married Kate the following year in 1881. One of my papers showed that my father left Canada at twenty-one. We don't know how or why he came to Blackhawk. He went to school in New Castle, Nebraska. He married Kate and had two daughters. They were seven years apart.

They had a lovely home in Aspen. Kate died in 1898. Dave gave their house to be used for the high school. It was a wonderful old house, and it was a school through the forties and then it was torn down. It stood where the old red brick school building is now.

The old high school, formerly the D.R.C. Brown, Sr. mansion, with a 1932 Chevrolet and a Model T Ford in front. Courtesy Robert Zupancis.

My parents met on board a ship going from San Francisco to South America on their way to France in 1907. Mother had gone to school in Germany and had stayed there several years.

Gordon:

I have an entirely different story. I was told and always thought that they met when they were crossing the Andes. They went from Valparaiso by horseback over the Andes, where they took a train to Buenos Aires. Then they took a ship to Europe and were married in Paris. Back in the early days, people didn't like to go around the Horn because it was so rough, so there was a regular arrangement to take horses over the Andes and take the train to Buenos Aires. Then they could catch another ship and go on to Europe.

*Ruth McNutt Brown,
camping, about 1910.
Courtesy Ruth Perry.*

Ruth:

Mother's name was Ruth McNutt. Her father was Dr. William Fletcher McNutt, who had his own hospital in San Francisco. She was twenty-five years younger than my father. In 1907, after they were married, they came to Colorado and onto Aspen. He loved the country. It was their home. They had many San Francisco friends come and visit them in Aspen. Mother loved horses and she loved dogs. She arrived in Aspen with three or four dogs and two horses and she loved the outdoors. They rode to Leadville, the Flat Tops, and all the

Ruth McNutt Brown with Fletcher, Gordon, Ruth, and Darcy, 1919. Courtesy Ruth Perry.

high-country lakes — Cathedral Lake. They went on camping trips for weeks. They went to Snowmass Lake and then over Trail Rider Pass to what we used to call West Snowmass Lake, and it's now called Geneva Lake. They rode all through this country. They loved it dearly.

My father really wanted Aspen to progress and did a great deal for Aspen. In the beginning, he helped get the power plant. It was the first town to have electric lights in the state of Colorado in 1885. Dave had four brothers. Burt and Harry were both active in the bank. Harry ran the water office. And Burt was a commissioner. Aspen State Bank was the only bank when we were children. It was where the Ute City Banque is now. Burt was president after dad died. Billy left Aspen. Billy is another uncle. He had an office in the bank and he was head of an insurance company in Aspen. Jim never came to Aspen. He was the only one. He went to Mexico and never married. He was in the silver mining business. There were five brothers and a half-brother, Osburn Nickelson. My brother, Fletcher, lived with him when he went to Magill University in Montreal. Osburn (they called him O.N.) taught math.

David R.C. Brown, Sr.
on the right.
Mrs. Mary Louise
Potter, sitting.
About 1911.
Courtesy Ruth Perry.

Dad died in 1930. He was seventy-three. I was eleven. My brother, Darcy, was seventeen. Mother died very shortly afterwards in 1936. I was seventeen. My fondest memories of Aspen are those pack trips and family trips.

Gordon:

I remember we were trying to round up the horses at the Snowmass beaver dams. We used to camp at the beaver dams because of the lake. I would say this is about 1928. The horses started to run back to camp in my direction. I started to run and fell on the ground, and all of the horses ran over me. Every one of them jumped and missed me. I didn't have a scratch. I must have been about ten. We always had Mugsy Wilson along on our camping trips. He was the camp cook.

Ruth:

And Charlie Olson. Charlie was wonderful. Charlie went to work for my father in 1916. Dad sent him to St. Louis to a mechanic's school because my father didn't

Fletcher,
David R.C. Brown,
and Darcy, with
Judge Shaw's house in
the background.
About 1918.
Courtesy Ruth Perry.

drive, and he wanted somebody that could look after the cars. Charlie came back and worked for my father until my father died. After that he went to work for us at the power plant. When we moved to Carbondale, he said he would like to move down with us. If he didn't have a mechanical part, he made it. There was nothing he couldn't fix. He was marvelous. He died May 18, 1973. He was seventy-eight. He was a wonderful, wonderful man.

Gordon:

Ditty (Ruth) says that Dad never drove, but he did. I remember once he took me out to the ranch in Broomfield in the Cadillac. Our home in Denver was above the street level. There was a terrace coming down five feet and the driveway cut through it to the street. Dad turned into the driveway when we were coming back and forgot to turn the steering wheel back. The car tilted on its side and we tipped over. I think that's the last time he ever drove.

*Camping, 1927.
Charlie Olson in the
front, along with
David R. C. Brown,
Darcy, Gordon, and
Fletcher (with the hat).
Courtesy Ruth Perry.*

Ruth:

Why didn't he ever learn to drive? He just didn't. My mother drove everywhere. She even drove over Independence. He preferred horses. He rode an
army saddle. It took me a long time to figure out why, but now I know why.
They have a free-swinging stirrup, and when you get older your knees bother
you a bit. That's my theory. A Ditty theory. I rode one last summer and liked it a
lot. What was my dad's favorite horse? I can tell you what all the boys rode
when I rode, but I couldn't possibly tell you who my father rode. I rode Buster, I
rode Socks, I rode Nut, I rode Denver, and Sophie. Gordon rode Straight Edge,
Ribbon, and I rode Jingles. Jingles was a good horse. We bought Jingles after
Bob and I were married. School Zone was Gordon's, long after the school days.
Bob grew up on Grant, practically back to back. His family kept horses on
Grant Street in Denver.

Bob Perry:

Why was I scared of Ditty's father? I called him Mr. Brown and the Aspen people called him Dave. He and my grandfather were contemporaries. They leased Barr Lake just northeast of Denver with ducks on it. They went every Wednesday and Saturday to Barr Lake. If we wanted to go, we had to sit in the car and be quiet and not fool around or throw things at each other — no noise. I wanted to go duck hunting and didn't want to rock the boat, so I sat friendly on the seat and said nothing all the way out and all the way back. It was all of eighteen miles and it took about thirty-five minutes. No horseplay over here. Not when Mr. Brown was there.

When we got there, they all had their own blind and away they went. Blinds are boxes that are sunk in the sand so you can get down in. They had decoys around and a man that rowed a rowboat up and down the lake stirring the ducks up. You couldn't shoot him. He was sometimes a mile away. You only shot the ducks that flew over. Later I had a blind by myself.

I suppose at first I probably had a blind with my father. Mr. Brown would always have first choice of the blinds, then my grandfather, and so on. So the blinds that we got weren't always in the greatest spots. I was about eight when I started using a gun. My father taught me how to handle it.

Gordon:

I don't think I sat in the same blind with dad most of the time, just one day. The next season I shot with Chuck Olson and then the next season I got my own blind. Was dad real patient with us? He wasn't very autocratic. He didn't bawl us out or anything. He was real conscious about getting us into the outdoors. We'd go camping by the time we were seven or eight years old.

Ruth:

None of us children had summer birthdays. We were in Denver. In the winter, dad would have to come up to Aspen once in a while to do business and come back. Why did mother want us in Denver? Because of the schools. But we couldn't wait to get up here and start riding. We came up the day school was out. Peggy Rowland and I were great friends. We enjoyed the same things. I remember it took us a long time to catch the horses.

Up Independence Pass.
Charlie Olson, driver;
David R.C. Brown,
passenger.
Courtesy Ruth Perry.

Gordon:

My best friend in Aspen was Bud Cooper, Peggy's brother. We'd hike up to the top of Aspen Mountain once in a while and went camping a couple of times. We didn't take him too often because at night he would scream and holler. He'd have these terrible dreams and talked in his sleep. Peggy stayed up there at her grandfather's house. The Lamb house — I remember Al Lamb. He used to drink near-beer on picnics. — This was Prohibition.

Ruth:

We had our own lake. We loved to go down and catch fish. Hallam Lake was full of fish. It wasn't deep enough to swim. I liked catching pollywogs.

Bob Perry and I were married in 1940. We grew up together in Denver. We lived in Steamboat for a year and then we moved to Carbondale to our family ranch. My father bought it in 1924. It was on the Colorado state maps as the Grubb Ranch. Now it's called Mt. Sopris Hereford Ranch. It's probably called the Perry Ranch by the majority of the people in Carbondale. We started raising cows and horses here. We had 400 head. How many horses? We never counted them. We bought Kate Lindvig's ranch in Old Snowmass. She homesteaded there. We had horses. We didn't have horse trailers then. We just let them out and they'd come home. We did that probably for three years. In the fall we'd put the horses out, and then in a couple of days they'd show up down in Carbondale. We didn't think a thing about it — five, or seven horses, horses that were raised here and knew the place. They just went back and forth. The point being that there was nobody on the road. You could turn them loose then. Until 1952, we used to drive the cattle up 82. It took us two days. We don't do that anymore. We took them up there for the summer grass.

Darcy and Fletcher Brown at the Glenwood hot springs pool, about 1918. Courtesy Ruth Perry.

We had seven children. Two were born in Denver, two were born in Glenwood, and three were born in Aspen. All the children helped out on the ranch. We were moving cattle one time up 82, and there was getting to be a little more

traffic. One man rolled down his window and shook his fist at Bob and said he was going to report him for child labor laws!

My father never lived here in Carbondale. He had several ranches. He ran cattle and sheep here. He had cattle at Hotchkiss, Crawford, and Broomfield.

Gordon:

I have four children. I raised them all over the place. I married my wife in San Francisco and lived there. She passed away a couple of years ago, and her name was Leila Boskoi. She was actually born in China. Her father worked in Peking. I was working for Pan American Airways in San Francisco when I met her. We got married there and spent a year together, and then I was sent overseas in the navy. Afterwards we came back to Denver for a little while. I was in the real estate business in Denver and then decided to go back to California. I was in real estate there for many years. That's where we raised our children. Then we decided, what the heck, we'd come back to Colorado. Our youngest boy, Bernie, lived with Bob and Ditty for a couple of years, working on the ranch here and going to Rocky Mountain School. Then he wanted to go to CSU. He got into CSU, so we moved back to Denver to spend time with him.

When do I think the best years in Aspen were? I loved it when we were growing up — the 1920s.

Ruth:

Wish something for Aspen now? I know what we *did* wish for. And I don't know *why* now. When we were climbing up Aspen Mountain to ski down, we would think, "Wouldn't it be nice to have a tow." The year that Aspen really changed? It started in the 1960s and kept going. I think it got out of hand here in the 1980s. Aspen politics? The reason I don't take the papers is, all they do is have one big fight over something. And I don't like the language. I wrote the paper and I said I thought they should clean up their language.

Is there anything Aspen could have done a long time ago to prevent the situation now? Less interference. With all the rules and regulations they have now, we can't change the progress or whatever you want to call it. That isn't what I object to as much as somebody like our son-in-law. He bought the ranch next to us and it's taken them two years to go through all the regulations to build. It's unnecessary. When you've got the climate, the snow, and the people with the kind of money they've got today for recreation, it's inevitable. If you're going to live in a pretty place, you're going to have people.

✦

*Liz Callahan
was an independent,
strong woman and a
die-hard Bronco fan.
She was ninety-six years
old and could remember
more about her past
than I can remember
about last week.*

Photo by Kathy Daily

Elizabeth Zupancis Callahan
(November 11, 1896 – November 6, 1993)

 I was born in a barn in Rock Vale, Colorado, on November 11, 1896. I was eighteen months old when my parents came to Aspen. It must have been about 1898.

Tough People, Hard Times
◆◆◆◆◆◆◆◆◆◆◆◆◆◆◆◆◆

My parents, John Zupancis and Mary Obester, were born (at that time) in Austria, but after the First World War, they called it Yugoslavia. The emperor was Prince Joseph. You've heard of Prince Joseph and his wife, Empress Elizabeth? My parents were married in Austria, and I had three brothers that were born there — my oldest brother, Peter, the second, Blaise, and the third, Julius. Julius was only two years old when he came over with my mother. She left the two oldest there. They didn't have money enough to bring them all over here at once. So my brothers stayed with her parents, Grandmother and Grandfather Obester. They were twelve and fifteen years old when they finally came over here.

My father came first to the United States and worked in the coal mines. Mama came later. First he went to Cleveland, Ohio, and then to Colorado. He went to Crested Butte and worked up there before I was born. Then from Crested Butte, he went to Pueblo and worked in the steel mill. They heard about Aspen when they were in Pueblo. In Aspen, dad worked at the smelter first. And then he went into the Smuggler, the Silver Shack, and the Molly Gibson.

There were nine of us in our family, seven boys and two girls. Only one child was born in Aspen. He was only about one month old when he died. You know, there was so many babies passed away in those days. His name was Louis. He's buried out in the cemetery. I still remember the old mining town — from about 1903 to the early 1920s. They had three eight-hour shifts. They had the day shift, the four o'clock men would come down, and the night shift. Then they did not have flashlights. They had a can light with a candle in it with a handle. I think every two weeks they would change their shifts and the day shift would go on four o'clock and the four o'clock would go to graveyard shift. They mined silver, lead, and zinc. I had three brothers that died working in that dust — black lung, silicosis. They all got it and all died. None of my brothers and sisters lived to be very old. My mother lived to pretty near ninety and dad was lacking of being ninety-five. But I'm the oldest of the children. I'm ninety-six.

The miners in the Smuggler had a band. They called it the Smuggler Tin Band. Every Saturday night up on Durant Street they'd have a dance. There was a hall there. It was upstairs and wasn't very big.

The Depression started in Aspen in 1920 and the town went down. I think there was only a population of 750 left here. People moved and they just left their houses; didn't even sell them. You could buy a house for taxes for five dollars. That's how Paepcke got here. He bought a lot of this property. I remember Mr. and Mrs. Paepcke when they were here and lived in Pioneer Park. They were really good customers of ours at the Mesa Store. When I sold the store, Mr.

Hallam Lake, City Park, about 1907. David R.C. Brown bought the lake in 1907. Courtesy Ruth Perry.

Paepcke wrote me the nicest letter telling me how much they enjoyed me. I still have it around someplace. Then Mrs. Paepcke wrote me a nice letter, too. She said, "When I'm working the garden, I want you to come down and sit by the big shady tree there."

On the 4th of July they had parades. It was all dirt roads and the sidewalks were boards. My dad would put me on his shoulder to watch the parade. People would crowd up and you couldn't see. I was in many floats they had. On the 4th of July, years ago . . . Hallam Lake had quite a park down there. They had a dance pavilion and a place where a big organization could give parties. On the 4th of July, the Catholic ladies would serve big luncheons.

For fun, we used to go sleigh riding. We had Tally Ho parties, we used to call them. Especially on New Years Eve. We used to go around singing Christmas carols and we had fur blankets over our legs to keep warm. They had a New Years dance in the Armory Hall. That was a good dance floor there and we had a good time. Men had to have shirts, ties, and a dress suit. Formal ladies

140

would wear their long dresses. And then at Christmas and Thanksgiving the Eagles gave the dance.

The opera house was set on fire twice. It was arson. The first time it was damaged terribly. They had a beautiful curtain — the curtain that had the Silver Queen on it. They had the boxes on one side in red velvet for the special people that had a little money. Way back under the balcony there were bleacher seats. We used to go there to the shows. They called it the pig pen. We sat in the pig pen. The whole town watched it burn. Oh yes, it was a night. They had the wagon firehouse; they had different fire companies. We always knew where the fire was because when the fire whistle blew once it was the east end of town. When they blew twice it was the center of town, and the west end was three times. When it was out they blew four times. It was all volunteer.

When they first started skiing in 1937 they had this slope boat that they pulled on a rope — oar boat. We had a study club — the Catholic Ladies — and

Fire bell tower (on the left) in Aspen, 1905. Courtesy Peggy Rowland.

we used to meet. This one night we decided to go skiing on the hill. I had never been on skis before and I've never been on them since. But we didn't use the tow that night. We just kind of went where there was a slope. I borrowed a suit, ski shoes, and skis. The ski poles had a round wheel and a point on the end. Doris Willoughby was a pretty good skier, so she said, "Elizabeth, let me give you my skis," and I said, "Alright." I put one ski on ahead of the other and I took off. I fell, sat on the pole, and broke the head off. I couldn't get up we got to laughing so hard. They had to lift me and take the skis off, and I've never been on them since.

My first job was — you know where that ol' Elisha house is on Main Street? The people there were wealthy people by the name of Thatcher, Cap Thatcher. If I remember, I think they built that house. After I was in the seventh or eighth grade, I used to go out there on Saturdays and Sundays and kind of help out. I used to scrub the floor and polish it. I was about fourteen. In the summertime — I didn't work when I went to school — I got $3.50 per week. Oh, at that time I was wealthy.

I went to the Catholic school. I graduated from the parochial school here in Aspen — Saint Mary's. I finished the sixth grade, and then in the seventh grade I went to public school. Margaret Conner went to school with me. She's two years younger than I am. Her sister, who was two years older than her, her name was Nora — we went to school and graduated together. She's passed away. I think Margaret Conner is the only one left in her family, and I am, too.

When I got a little older, they used to have the Colorado Midland up on Durant Street. See, we had two trains coming into Aspen, the D and RG and the Colorado Midland. They had a boardinghouse there and they called it the Bird House, 'cuz I guess the lady that run it had a lot of parrots and birds. Her name was Mrs. Burke and they called her "the Bird Lady." When I worked there I kind of washed dishes and then I got so I waited tables. They served family style. Her husband had a garden in the summertime and he raised lettuce, green onions, radishes, and fresh vegetables. And those things were put on family style. I was about fifteen or so.

I've always lived in this area. We built that garage in the back of my house later on, in the 1920s. And that old cabin that's down there was called the McMurchery entry. A man by the name of McMurchery had it. He was a prospector and built that cabin. The cabin is still there. We're the fourth owners of this property here. People came here and bought from Bob McMurchery, people by the name of Sprat. They built on that cabin that is still there. The next people that bought from Sprats was Ennis. Then my folks bought it. You know

where Sears Roebuck built that building? We lived down there. We built this house in 1960.

My first marriage was in 1922. I had one child, but she was a stillborn, so then I didn't have any more. I married Floyd Callahan January 22, 1959. Floyd was born September 20, 1884, in Gunnison County. He was only about eighteen months old when his parents came to Aspen. He was about twelve years older than me. They lived way down at the end of town; that house is still standing. He had five sisters and he was the only boy in the family. His father was a cement builder and bricklayer. He also stored ice to sell in the summer. We had ice boxes. They used Hallam Lake when it was frozen. They cut ice in blocks. Floyd died December 16, 1963.

I used to help Dr. Twining in the hospital and was a registered nurse. I graduated from St. Josephs-Denver Hospital on June 7, 1921, but that's torn down. Floyd mined in the early days, too, and later on he worked for the Tompkin's

Hardware Store. Then he bought the building. The original building was down. It caved in because the guys didn't keep the snow shoveled off.

What is missing in Aspen today is that good old friends have died or moved away. Don't get me wrong, I have many new friends, too. I also love the new conveniences, services, and stores. You see, I lived through the hard times here. I'm not too much bothered by the changes in Aspen. I like the traffic lights. I understand they are discussing putting in traffic meters and I am horrified at the cost of one dollar for an hour!

✦

Photo by Kathy Daily

Martin and Virginia Wagner Cerise
(Martin: April 25, 1926 – March 9, 1993)

Martin:

I was born April 5, 1926, at the end of Little Woody Creek on my parents' ranch. An uncle of mine came into Leadville in the late 1880s or early 1900s. He went back to Italy and told about the silver out in the mountains and being able to get jobs; it was pretty desolate for jobs back in Val d'Aosta, Italy. He told everyone about Leadville, but he never did come back to the United States.

Virginia Cerise is a soft but strong woman. It seems as though she could bend like a young tree in the wind.

Photo by Kathy Daily

My father, Albert D. Cerise, came over as a fourteen-year-old boy in 1904, and at the age of eighteen he decided to go back to Italy and see his folks. He hadn't become a citizen of this country yet, so when he got back to Italy they said he was a deserter because he hadn't registered for the army at eighteen. They threw him in the army for four years. After he got out of the army, he come back to Leadville.

Leadville and Aspen were pretty much the same on jobs — they could work up there a year or two and come over here a year or two. He worked in the smelters, processing ore. He learned that when he got here. I think the reason he came here from Italy was partly because he was born in the Alps — the mountains. They come here for the mountains, and in that part of Italy they weren't miners, but they dug a lot of tunnels for trains and stuff. So they had a background in drilling and making tunnels in hard rock. After his experience of going over there and being stuck in the army for four years, he would never go back. He had a number of brothers and one sister. His folks were still living, but he had no hankering of ever going back there. I mean, we're talking about a pretty rowdy period in history. Italy was in wars all the time. He said the United States was his country. He never lost anything in the Italian Alps, and he would never go back. He never did.

He never married until he was rather older. He was probably thirty-five years old when he met my mother. She was from northern Italy, but not up in

Up Independence Pass, 1905. Courtesy Peggy Rowland.

Independence Highway, 1919.
Courtesy Del Gerbaz.

the Alps. She was from the other side of the Alps. Her name was Onorina Milanesio. In those days, if you had a horse or a team of horses, you could find work just about anywhere. He met her when he was working building the new Independence Pass road. It used to just be kind of a cowpath down in the bottom, and there was lots of bridges going up. Well, they built this new road, and he was hired like you would hire a bulldozer or anything else. That's how it was done, with dynamite, scrappers, and fresnos with teams of horses. He boarded with this family, the Barraillers, up on Stillwater. That's where he met my mother. She had just come over to this country. She come over because a sister of hers was already living here. She was from a town probably twenty or thirty miles from where my father was born.

After they were married, a son was born but he died not long after birth — like when I was born, about six or twelve hours later the doctor showed up. My mother was by herself; dad was out working that day. It's hard to say what the problem was. But there's quite a difference in the ages between my mother and my father. When she got married, she was only about nineteen years old and my dad was probably about thirty-five. When my sister Amelia was born, my dad was probably over forty years old.

Afterward, the mining just disappeared. So he went to Woody Creek in about 1916 and bought a ranch up at Little Woody Creek with his brother. Neither one of them was married at the time, and my uncle never did get married. They were still both bachelors and they bought this ranch up at the end of the valley. Later on, I moved our family house down across from the Little Woody Creek Road when I got married. It's still there. Our kids were born there. We bought that big red house later from the Arlians. We bought that in about 1946, right after World War II. Those houses were all on our ranch. The Aspen Community School up on the mesa was all part of that ranch. That is the second ranch we bought. We owned all of Little Woody Creek — all of it — from the mouth clear on up.

When I was a small boy on the ranch, I tell you, we didn't have time to fool around. We had to learn to work early. It was the type of work in the early days when you didn't have tractors. You put up hay with an overshot stacker, and when you're real small, you led what we call the stacker horse. You pulled up the stacker to dump the hay on a stack. After I got a little bit older, my day started about five in the morning and ended up about eight at night. We raised cattle. Ranches back in those days had chickens and pigs, just enough for their own use, and milk cows. My dad made cheese in Italy before he came over. Even in the Italian Alps they made Swiss cheese. My father had to teach my mom how to make it, because she wasn't up in that part of the country. Nothing was very scientific, so you had anywhere from Limburger, Gargonzola, to plain old Munsters. It was just a variety. You never knew exactly. You could have almost a Swiss cheese with the holes. Amelia helped more around the house. She did do some outdoors, but not as much as a boy would have done.

I went eight years to Little Woody Creek School. As a matter of fact, a lot of kids back in those days — me included — didn't know how to speak English. So they let you start at five years old. Incidently, I learned enough English and all to pass the first grade at five. They put you in the class so you could listen. You'd just sit around and usually you'd have a big sister or a big brother. The kids did real well, and by the end of the year they knew how to speak English. I don't think there was anybody that I went to school with that wasn't one of the French Italians. After I started into school, I hardly ever spoke that French dialect. I spoke English. Which was kind of a curse, too, because I lost a lot of it.

When I was a little boy, I had the best place in the neighborhood for entertainment. We had an old buggy. From that upper ranch, it's all downhill to the road. Anyway, I'd stripped it, except the running gear. We did have a brake on it. They all had brakes. We put ropes to steer the thing, and we'd load up a bunch of guys and go clear on down. We'd ride about two miles. We lost it a time or two and went through the fences and tore up the wires at Arlian's. It's a good thing Jennie [Arlian] wasn't there to see us or she'd have made us fix fences. Well, I think she knows who did it for the simple reason that the last ride we had, we went off and the fence didn't hold us. The buggy ended up down there in their yard. We left it. We just left it. We didn't dare have Jennie catch us with that.

When I went to high school, we didn't have buses, so we boarded in town. I used to ride a horse into town sometimes, but we would stay in town. We'd stay for the whole winter, but we'd come home on the weekends. I think we paid about ten or fifteen dollars a month for rent, but then, being on a farm, we'd furnish most of the food. We'd haul up the milk and the eggs and everything else. We never did have a phone at the upper ranch. And then, like I say, in 1946 we bought that lower ranch. I paid $19,000 and 3 percent interest. About that period, it was right after the war, ranches were doing real well. Of course, I borrowed the money just strictly on my name. They were trusting enough that I didn't have to sign anything but the notes. My half was $1,000 notes I had to pay off in a year, and that was pretty simple to do because at that time we still raised potatoes for a cash crop. Once in awhile, we'd get three or four dollars for 100 pounds of potatoes, which was big bucks in those days. You could purt' near pay a ranch off in two years.

On Halloween when we were kids, all of these little country schools would have their little country dances and parties. We put on a little play for Halloween, and all the people would come. For pranks, we would take tumbleweeds and put them in the hole of the ladies' privy. We had a two-seater out at Woody Creek. And, of course, there were no lights out there. Then we put some nettle-weeds on top of it. You could always tell the ladies . . . they couldn't sit down. They also used to catch the ladies in there, close the door, and then upset the house on top of the door so they couldn't get out. Most of them had floors. I got in a lot of jams; used to get the sheriff on me. I can't remember all of the mischievous things!

Virginia:

I was born April 17, 1927. My mother's name was Bertha Heuschkel and my father's name was William Wagner. I met Martin in about 1951, and we got married when we were twenty-five and twenty-six years old. I was born in Glenwood

*Eva and Irma Cerise,
about 1925,
up Woody Creek.
Courtesy
Robert Zupancis.*

Springs. Glenwood was a very active town. It was the hub where everybody had to come for supplies — the farmers, the ranchers. From Eagle, all this area went to Glenwood for all their supplies. My father was born in Glenwood. My mother moved there when she was two. She was born in Leadville. My grandfather was a teamster. He rode between Leadville and Aspen; brought stuff back and forth. He had a small ranch in Leadville. I don't know what they had — just a few milk cows, I think. And then he went to Cattle Creek, between Carbondale and Glenwood, up on Missouri Heights. He had to have black dirt; red dirt wasn't any good. He came from Germany and he could have any place that he wanted. He was one of the first ones in Glenwood. He could have had any of that land, but it wasn't any good to him. He had to go clear back to get to the black dirt. Just to carry that a little bit further, the Italians had the red sandy slope on this side of the Roaring Fork. The other side was the Germans, which we're talking about. The German families were on the other side of the mountain. That again was the black dirt. The soils over there are dark.

I have no idea how they came to Leadville from Germany. My grandfather and grandmother met on the boat coming over. She was from England and he was from Germany. He was a seaman at one time. My mother was related to the Haskall family. There were a lot of them down around Carbondale. I think he was one of the first ones to come in here. Leadville was a huge town, one of the first with electricity in Colorado. Denver wasn't even known, as a matter of fact. Gunnison was originally supposed to be the capital of Colorado. See, these little mining towns existed long before Denver ever became a town. They found gold up around Central City, but Denver itself, it's just kind of out there in the plains. Farming wasn't profitable back in those days.

Martin:

I met Virginia at a country dance. There were dances in Carbondale, Basalt, Glenwood, and Aspen. There were no ladies in Aspen. A lot of Aspen women went to Glenwood to work. They worked in the telephone office and other jobs because there wasn't anything really for them to do in Aspen. There was still a little bit of mining going on, and then all the young boys from the farms. As soon as a girl got out of high school, she left. This was in the late 1930s. They went to Grand Junction or Denver.

There were old stories about brothels in Aspen. Old-timers, a generation ahead of me, would tell them. They said there was whole rows of them over there at Little Nells. That's where the Midland Railroad used to go. And at the end of the line where the people would get off the trains, was where all the brothels were. That would be Durant Street, where the gondola is now. Right there used to be the Glory Hole. Alongside the tracks were the brothels. Women did not go into bars. My dad used to take me in as a little kid. I was probably eight or ten years old. I'd go in, but never would a woman be seen in the Red Onion. The Hotel Jerome was the fountain place — more or less the social place for the kids and all. If you had a dime, I remember these great big milkshakes, ten cents. I used to go around shoveling the roofs to make enough money. Shoveled all the roofs for these ladies that didn't have husbands. I'd get twenty-five cents. Of course, the snow would be so deep and you had to shovel the walks, you'd shovel the sheds, you'd shovel the roof, and you got twenty-five cents. Well, that was a couple times at the Hotel Jerome. You could go in there and spend two or three hours sipping on one dime.

For music, there was Sis McCugh. She had an orchestra. There were the Harrington brothers. They'd stand on the street corner and drink. They were Buck Parson's uncles, and they were real good musicians. At dances, we didn't

The Buffet in the Jerome Hotel, early 1920s. Mansor Elisha behind the counter. Courtesy Ingrid Elisha.

wear suits. Being on the ranch, I always wore western gabardine pants and western shirts. We'd never date for the simple reason that you never did want to get stuck with just dancing only with your date. Like Virginia said, we'd stag the dances. Girls stagged, boys stagged, and everybody just met there. Five or six girls would go in one car.

Like I said, I met Virginia at a country dance. I drove down to Glenwood to take her out. We went to most of the dances. Aspen had a few at the Armory Hall, but not too many. Most of the dances were at Carbondale, Basalt, and Glenwood Springs. And, of course, being a rancher, we bought all of our equipment down at Glenwood and so we done most of our dealings there. I'd just go to town to maybe go to the bar and have a few drinks or every once in awhile to dance. I really knew more people downvalley, because all of our business transactions were done there. We got married in 1952, then moved to Woody Creek.

Virginia:

When I grew up, we lived in town. I knew nothing about ranching. And I didn't know how to cook, let alone milk the cows. Our son Jim was born in 1953 in Glenwood, and then Carolyn was born in 1954 in Aspen. We moved into Aspen when the kids were four.

Martin:

I sold the ranch in 1956. My dad was old at that time. See, there was quite a difference. When I moved, I was probably only thirty-two, somewhere in there, but my dad was already up around seventy years old. I think I sold it for about $90,000 without cattle, somewhere in there. I put my money back into Aspen and started a business, so it was kind of an exchange. It was kind of a move. I went in with my brother-in-law and we started Herald Motors in Aspen.

The way I got my name Martin was a story in itself. Most of these Europeans, when they come over, loved cowboys. Cowboys were a fantasy; they still are. European people love cowboys. The Japanese have grown to like cowboys, too. When my dad bought that little ranch up at Little Woody Creek, there wasn't hardly a ranch there at all. My dad cleared most of it. More or less, you'd say he homesteaded. These other people, their business was horse stealing. Horses always sold for a lot of money, even back in those days. A team of horses was $500. That was a lot of money, and a good riding horse sold for good money. So what they'd do, they'd go around Meeker and all with some of the wild horses they'd round up over there. They'd also round up from people's ranches. They'd take these wild horses and put them on this ranch up Little Woody Creek, and they were regular horse thieves. Anyway, my dad knew them because they were really rough-and-tough cowboys. I remember them as a kid — people with few words and just as rough and hard as nails. My dad kind of knew these two guys, and one of them's name was Martin. That's what he named me — from Martin Scott. He was a horse thief. As a matter of fact, my first brother had exactly the same name, and he died, and dad just took the name and give it to me. He had to have a Martin because of this Martin Scott and John Scott. That's who we bought the ranch from. Dad bought it from them. It wasn't a ranch — it was just a good out-of-the-way place to rustle horses. You'd never find one up in that little neck of the woods.

Logging also figured into the history of the Woody Creek area. There was a lot of logging for the mining industry. All these props, timbers — that's the reason they cut all the timbers off of Aspen Mountain. When they couldn't get them there anymore, they would go somewhere else. A timber in a mine is what they call a set. I'm not a real miner, but I think it's something like eight-by-four is what they call a set. In other words, it holds the roof of the mine. They had to have a tree of certain width. They'd use spruce. It had to be tough, because what you're talking about, you had to hold Mother Earth up and all those big boulders — keep them from coming down and crushing you.

When I was still small, the timber men were mainly Swedes. The loggers would come down back of the ranch, and in those days, you didn't have trucks. You had to haul the trees out with teams of horses. What they would use is the front end of a sleigh — just the front bobs, and then the logs would drag on the back end. They'd drag on the snow.

We had a fellow that was in back of our ranch, and he'd always make a lot of moonshine up there. He'd buy raisins, and everybody knew he had moonshine. Fred Adams was his name. Buy cases of raisins, dried raisins. It was good. After he passed away — well, to tell you how he passed away, to show you how tough these people were — he'd come down to the ranch on a cold winter day. Fred lived in town, but he had this cabin up here back of Little Woody up on the flats. He come down there one day and he wasn't feeling well. It was probably about ten o'clock when he got to the ranch. Mom said, "Well, if you aren't feeling well, leave your horses here and your load." "No, I got to go on in." He says, "I'll just take it on in." You're talking about horses on their way into town. See, they'd sell their logs to a sawmill. They'd find out how many board feet the log would make, squared out. Anyway, he'd loaded his load, got sick during the night at his cabin, and although he was sick, he didn't want to go in empty. He had a ruptured appendix and he did make it all the way into town. Of course, he died in town. I think they put him in the hospital that evening, but gangrene had already set in.

These were tough characters. I always remember him by his great big handlebar mustache. You know what happens in the wintertime? With that mustache, he had icicles hanging all the way down. My mother would always make him stop and give him hot coffee or something. It was a cold jaunt to our ranch from all the way up there, probably eight or nine miles, then all the way into town. One thing my mother couldn't stand was when them icicles would start thawing! Another thing I remember is that most people chewed tobacco in those days, either pipe smoke or tobacco, and he could hit the gold bucket I'll bet eight feet away. Mother felt sorry for him in the winter.

There was a big sawmill in what they call Kobey Park. It was named after Ben Kobey. They used to haul logs down Little Woody, and there was a little transfer station. They'd have horses there and they'd transfer them — bring them down that far and then leave a set of horses in the barns. There were cabins. The workers lived there. There were the haulers and the timber cutters. In the winter they did most of it with sleds. You couldn't haul the timber out in the summer hardly at all. Couldn't use wagons coming off of those steep hills; the horses couldn't hold them back. Dragging in the snow acted like brakes. If you dragged the timber on the dry ground, they'd just grind up on rocks and stuff. Anyway, there were always piles of logs that stayed there for years.

There was an old boiler at the sawmill. They used to saw right there in Kobey Park and haul out the lumber. That way they didn't have to take out the waste, like the slabs and all. I often wondered why they didn't do all these logs. There were just piles of them around there. Well, there was a labor dispute back in them days, just like there is now. This is just a hand-me-down story, but he wouldn't give these people any pay, and so they spiked the logs — drove nails in them. They were big spikes, so you couldn't cut them, like people are doing in the forest now. They put in nails and the loggers couldn't come in and cut the trees because it would just ruin the saw. You can get spikes and drive them in pretty far. Sawing across wouldn't be bad, but sawing a log into lumber lengthwise — if you ever hit a nail with a saw, the teeth would just kill you because you're standing right behind. That was the end of Ben Kobey. I don't know why he wouldn't pay his people — probably because times were tough and he wasn't making any money. They didn't pay much wages back in those days. They never went back in that country to log anymore, because they spiked the living trees. And it wasn't only the piles of logs that were already cut — they went in and spiked the trees. I suppose that a lot of those spikes are still up there in those trees. Of course, Flogus went in there and cut a lot of them, but by that time, I suppose that a lot of the old trees were dead and fallen over.

One time a boiler blew up. That was in Bob Set. They call it Bob Set, which is Cow Camp. A set is a sawmill that was set there. Of course, everything was powered by steam back in those days, and they would just bring in a boiler and they'd fire it up. Then they'd get the power to run a belt with it. This again is my dad talking about it, because you can find pieces of heavy boiler plate up there all twisted. They went to lunch and didn't drain out the steam and stuff, and the valve stuck. That thing blew wide open and just blew pieces of steel all over. No one was hurt.

There are also good stories about old farm equipment in Woody Creek. I had to improvise and invent a lot of it. There wasn't a lot of equipment for farmers. It was very basic — mower or reaper. We'd plant potatoes and we had a planter, which we bought. Then you'd hill the potatoes. You've probably never seen it done, but the machine would make a trench and then you'd sit back. You had a little wheel that went around, and these potatoes had to be spaced just so. If there was a potato missing, you had to put one in. If there were two in one spot, you had to take one out. When you got through, you had these hills, and they were loose so the potatoes would dry. So to pack these things down, we would improvise our own, because we couldn't buy a lot of these kinds of parts. So we'd go out and find a good round tree and then drive two rods on the end. Then we'd make hitch to the horses and the thing would roll. People would take an old culvert and fill it with cement and do the same thing — just improvise their own. It was just like dragging the fields after cows. You'd have to drag all the droppings from the cows to make a field look good. You'd just go out and cut a bunch of scrub oak and put a deal out in front with a chain. But you'd leave all the branches on it so that this would spread. You had to improvise a lot of your own equipment.

At Woody Creek, about 1925. Back row: Pete Letty, Kelley Cerise, Flavian Cerise, Major Chano, Eva Cerise, Gena Cerise, Irma Cerise. Middle row: Eugene Chaterin, Casnire Bick. Front row: Pete Rosette, Mila Cerise, John Cerise, and another Cerise family member. Courtesy Robert Zupancis.

The Italians did not have a national unity in Woody Creek. They would fight. I think the Italians fought more. You know how Italians are — they fight more amongst each other than they do with anybody else. No, we were very good neighbors. Us and the Arlians were very good, close neighbors. Their brother, Brice, had bought the ranch from his parents. Brice come up one winter day about 1944 and said, "I'd like to give you first chance at buying my ranch." He said, "I'll sell it to you for the payments I have left." So he'd already made some payments. We bought it for $19,000, but I think he paid around $25,000 for it. He wanted to get out of the valley and go down and buy another ranch at 3 percent interest. He said, "I'd like to give you first chance." My gosh, I couldn't resist.

Woody Creek has always been a very scrappy place for water. Water was scarce, and your livelihood depended on the water. There was a lot of feuding and fighting, and they carried guns. Natal was pretty much severed. We're talking about a little further downvalley. The ones way up there at the end of the valley were kind of disassociated. But we're talking about Little Woody Creek on up to the ranch above — the Vagneur ranches and all of them included. They were feuding at the time about water. They handled water disputes with guns, more or less to scare people. Like I say, I got picked up on assault and battery. Once in awhile we'd get into it. I didn't hit anybody with a shovel, but I kind of battered him up a little bit. I got taken in for assault and battery. That was all part of the deal. The thing of it was, you're talking about guns. Most of the water come down off of Little Woody Creek and then split over different ditches, so somebody would want to irrigate their potatoes. They were getting dry, and you'd have maybe a second water right or a third water right, which meant when it got low there wouldn't be any water right for him. Well, that's kind of tough to sit there and see your potatoes dry up. So what they'd do, they'd go up at night and they'd hire some old wino out of Aspen or something like that and give him a double-barrel shotgun. They'd tell him, you go up there and don't let anybody turn that water down. Well, in one night and one day, they'd irrigate a lot of their potatoes and then they'd do that again in a week or two. There was just a lot of feuding around, and Brice's family finally just didn't want to take it. His sisters all left, and he wasn't as good a scrapper as Jennie. If they couldn't do anything else, they could do it verbally. Brice just didn't have to fight for what normally was his.

Now that we got on that subject — Italians would order grapes, make their wine, and then they'd make their grappa after the wine. So they'd order two or three train cars of wine grapes from California. They didn't just make it out of anything. All these people would come down in whatever they had — a

Model T, a pickup truck, or team of horses — and get their quota of grapes. That was in the fall, about October, about thrashing time. They'd have their barrels and they'd make all this wine. It was legal. After the wine, there was still a lot of alcohol. They'd ferment this with sugar and then they'd make their grappa. There weren't very many would sell that stuff — they'd give it away. They were very free and generous. These Italians, if you walked into their house, even if you were a total stranger, you were offered a glass of wine. That was the hospitality. You were offered a meal, too. If you were there around mealtime you were always invited for a meal. Always had plenty to eat. It might have been the same stuff everyday, depending on the season, but food was plentiful.

Aspen, for being a mining town, was fairly peaceful. Oh, we'd go to dances, and if there wasn't a fight or two for entertainment, that was a poor night. You had to have that.

In the old days, everybody had a nickname. The thing is, you didn't ask a lot of questions in those days. Just an example of how you didn't ask questions, there were a lot of bums, railroad bums. You'd have them almost every day, and they'd come to your place and ask for handouts. Nobody ever turned them away. They'd offer to do work and so forth. We had one fellow that come in and he asked for a handout, and then he said he kind of liked the valley. This is when we lived at the upper end of Little Woody Creek. They used to come clear up, away from the railroad. A lot of them would. Anyway, he said he liked the valley and if we had a place for him to stay. We did. We had a sawmill at the upper end of our ranch with a little cabin and my dad said, "Well, yeah, there's a vacant cabin up there. Why don't you make yourself at home?" You know, no rent, no nothing. That's the way people were in those days. This fellow was named Shorty, and when he left, I don't know if anybody knew anymore than his name was Shorty.

As it turned out, Shorty was a great mechanic. So he was the mechanic for Woody Creek and all around Basalt. He went and made himself some ramps where he could drive a car on top. He put clutches in and whatever. He never told you where he was from. These people — you didn't ask questions. If they volunteered advice, you accepted. You never asked any questions. All of a sudden, he decided he wanted to change territory, so he packed up his tools and left. My dad never collected a nickel's worth of rent, although he did make things for us. These drifters were pretty tight-lipped. I think it goes as far back as the Civil War. There was a lot of displaced people. Families were displaced. Maybe he was just a kid at the time and there were hard feelings. You just didn't ask questions where they were from. Aspen was North, I think. I'm not sure. Those drifters just never talked about themselves.

I forgot to tell you about the old sawmill. Anyway, the sawmill fellow had a big Avery steam engine for belt power, and he didn't know how to run a steamer. Of course, my dad, in the army, that was part of the job, learning how to run steam engines. He wouldn't drive a car, but he could drive any type of steam engine in the world. This fellow was on his own. He just had a piece of land up there and set up his sawmill. He'd come up and get trees, and when he'd got enough, he'd get my dad to fire up the Avery steam engine. He'd run the saw for making the lumber. Anyway, how he passed away: Hunting season he would take hunters up on a wagon to Fly Camp and Cow Camp. This was a great hunting area up toward Lenado. Erickson was his name. He was typical of the Swedes — they like their booze. He was pretty drunk, and somebody shot a deer close by him. It scared his horses, and he had running gear. He didn't have boxes of any sort on top of the wagon. When the horses took off, he got both legs caught in the spokes of the wagon, and it just beat him to death.

In about 1939, I finally found a still that this one fellow had over here in the woods. I looked for it for years after he died, and I knew he had one. I knew he kept it up here below Kobey, down toward Cow Camp. Every time I'd go back up there, I'd go out in the woods. His cabin was right in the middle of heavy woods. I'd look and look, and there was a spring. One day, I happened to look up the tree, and there it was, way up there. He must have used a long pole to get it up and down. He hung it way up there in the trees to hide it. It was a copper deal — looked like a milk can. It was a small still. He put it on a limb. He'd take a long pole, put it up there, and hook it on. But I never did find the coils or the cap.

The history of Woody Creek goes way back. There was a fellow by the name of Clavel that owned a lot of Woody Creek, and he would get these families to come to the United States and then he'd work them for nothing. He'd give them food and stuff like that, maybe enough to buy cigarettes or something, and then he'd work them three or four years. Kind of like, I hate to say it, but kind of like Guido did in Aspen. You know what I mean. By paying their way, I think Guido more or less just used them on visas. And then someone would finally tell them, "Gee, you're foolish. Working all that time for just paying your way." That's how Jennie and her family come over here. He paid their way, and they would stay and eventually buy him out. Mind you, there's a class act. You're a hired hand and you buy the boss out. That's how a lot of these ranches got started up there, and even downvalley. The Clavels owned a nice big mansion right down by Glenwood, and that's the last I remember of them. Virginia's uncle owned it later on.

Tough People, Hard Times

❖❖❖❖❖❖❖❖❖❖❖❖❖❖❖❖❖❖

Virginia:

When I was just two or three, I can just barely remember going in the house when they owned it. It was a mansion then, but not by today's standards. Not even in those days, really, but it was a nice big house.

Martin:

Medical assistance was pretty scarce back in the hard times. In the twenties and thirties, there was a lot of flu, strep throat, and heart conditions. Most of my friends, guys my age, die from heart conditions. I had problems with it, and I link it back to strep throats — scarlet fever, rheumatic fever — weakens your heart. They didn't really know that they had it. They were just sick and never treated it.

I was probably about fourteen years old in 1930 and my sister got appendicitis. It was in the spring of the year; of course, there were no roads oiled. Roads were muddy as could be and no doctors in Aspen. The closest doctor was in Glenwood Springs. My mother didn't drive at the time. She learned later. My father didn't drive. He drove a steam engine and that was all. He wouldn't have anything to do with cars. So it was up to me. No phones to call, and there were no ambulances. So anyway, I took my sister — never drove a car in my life. My mother went with me, and I took her to the hospital in Glenwood Springs. We had a car, but my uncle would drive us. I think, at that time, my sister Amelia was three years older and she would have been driving, but being sick, she couldn't. By the time we got there, she did have a ruptured appendix. The big killer back in those days was really pneumonia. It was a flu that would start and then turn into pneumonia later. Half a family would die within one year from flu. People were pretty sturdy and there was nobody bringing diseases in because nobody moved.

When I was going to high school in Aspen, everybody knew each other's car. One guy would run an old GMC pickup to deliver groceries. He had a grocery store, and Beck & Bishop was another grocery store up there. They delivered with a team of horses and a sleigh. I remember walking down Main Street, and there was never a car that you had to walk off the side for. They never even plowed. My gosh, the snow was two or three feet deep. And this went for the ranchers, too. Out there on the farms in the country when I was a young guy going to school down there, there were no snowplows to come in there for the simple reason the ranchers didn't want it. When they had to haul their potatoes, hay, grain, or whatever to the railroad — everything went by rail in those days

Deep snow in 1935, 300 block of Hopkins and Mill Street. Courtesy Kathy Daily.

— the ranchers didn't want you to plow. They would have their own makeshift deal to plow. They'd take boards and make an A-frame. They'd take a team of horses and hitch it to them. They'd plow enough so it would pack, but they wanted to run their sleigh on there. If you plowed it down to the dirt, it melted a little, and boy, those ranchers would have a fit.

I always rode a horse to school. We rode a horse unless he bucked you off, and then the horse would come home and we walked. Also, once we had a teacher we didn't like. She lived up at George and Ellen Vagneurs — Louis Vagneur's place. We went out there one day and took a knife and cut the cinch just purt' near in two. She went down the road and the saddle come off and plopped her off. Now that was only the teacher we didn't like. It was kind of tough. I'll tell you, these country boys out there in school were hard to handle. Kids were tough. Finally, we had one man. He brought order, but the women had an awful time. We had a pretty big school at Woody Creek. We had about thirty kids and one teacher handling it.

It was cold riding to school in those days. We didn't have the clothes you have nowadays — rubber overshoes over a light pair of shoes. You'd practically freeze to death.

I grew up with cowboy boots. I still have them. But we didn't wear those to go to school. We used them for riding in the hills. We didn't have these walking boots like you have now. We had these high-heeled cowboy boots. Cowboy boots always come with a high, spiked heel slanting in. It's just been recently you can buy flat walking boots.

Definitely it was cold back in those days. We had colder winters back then than you do now. Of course, we had that great big house. We had bunkhouses for our hands. That's a tremendous house. Don Henley has it now. It's got seven bedrooms and they're all good-sized. We had a big kitchen. The kitchen was that portion out there in front. We had a kitchen stove and we practically lived there, outside of going to bed. We had one of these combination wood and coal stoves in the dining area and then what they used to call the parlour in the back. The parlour was always kept closed off. Then we had five bedrooms upstairs. Never any heat. If you brought up a glass of water, it froze in December, and if you didn't bring it down, it would be frozen for months. We just got used to it. We used a lot of covers. Our house was comfortable because we lived in it. We were able to separate the kitchen from the rest of the house.

My mother used to make all of our comforters. Don't ask me the process, but she'd take the sheep and card the wool and make filling. She would fill them. When we were younger, she would raise ducks just for the down and made down comforters. Later she sent it through the woolen mill and had blankets made. The Mormons in Utah and Salt Lake made beautiful blankets. We were self-sufficient. We didn't need anything. We raised a little bit of wheat, and that went for making flour and breakfast cereal. We kept our bran and stuff, and my mother would sift it out. That would take the hull out and that was our cracked-wheat type. We had a store there at Woody Creek, and then we used to trade a lot with his family there in Aspen. At that time you could exchange. Our grocery bill hardly ever ran over $125 a year. We'd butcher a hog and exchange it for groceries. We took the wheat to Glenwood and had it ground into flour and bran. There were a lot of mills back in those days. There were several in Glenwood.

As a matter of fact, my wife has still got a lot of these old flour sacks that have the emblem and the name of the mill. We used the flour sacks to dry dishes. We would store up a couple of hundred pounds of sugar and coffee and baking soda. We didn't care if it snowed all winter for the simple reason my mother could can about 400 quarts of fruits, vegetables, soups, and meats. There was no way to keep meat. We didn't have electricity, so she would can all of this stuff. She would make on the average about forty cartwheels of cheese. We had our chickens and eggs. We didn't mind if we were stranded. We made sausage every fall. It was good sausage — not Italian, but more like French.

The people up there weren't of Italian background and their cooking was French. Pastas and stuff were not our specialty at all. We ate French more than Italian. A good common meal was a good big bunch of polenta with chicken, chicken and noodles or fried chicken, mashed potatoes and gravy. My mother was the world's greatest cook. Of course, with eggs and all, we had the sweetest cream. Made our own butter and cream. It tasted better then, when you used all the eggs in butter and cream. Nobody told you it was going to kill you.

It's like my wife here. After I got married, Virginia would come and cook at the big house for me and my dad or the thrashing or potato crew. My mom had decided it was time for her to have a little fun. She'd been hidden up there. She learned how to drive, so she'd take off.

Virginia made jello one day with our meal, and we always had jello as a dessert. We didn't eat it with our meal. So it come down to the jello. We were sitting there looking it. They'd look at me and then look at the jello. My dad and I, we weren't the greatest talkers. I learned to talk later in life, I guess, but at that time I wasn't a good talker. Pretty soon she noticed we wouldn't eat our jello. Finally, I think I told Virginia, "We don't eat jello here without whipped cream." We never ate anything without whipped cream. You know, that good old country cream. So she learned how to cook for us. Well, that's all we had those cows for. We didn't ship any milk or anything like that. My mother used good thick cream and homemade butter, and we made our own noodles with lots of eggs. There's no question about it. The diet was special. That twelve hours of work a day took care of staying thin. I was a bean pole. When I got married I weighed 170 pounds at six-foot, two. Now if that isn't a bean pole! Well, I imagine back then cholesterol wasn't going to kill you. There was lots of exercise going on. I still don't have a cholesterol problem. I never did get lazy. I finally got ill with a heart condition and couldn't work.

Some of my favorite times were in the fifties. The town was still small and nice and people that came in back in that era, you know, being in business, I knew all of them. In the fifties and sixties they were swell people. About the funniest thing I remember is when I owned the garage. Mrs. Marge Stein came in one day. She had an old Willys which she drove for years and years. We always kept the big doors open — there were two doors lined up in the building, straight through. She came in and had it in a real low gear. As she drove in, creeping along, we thought she was going to stop sooner or later. The back door was closed. Anyway, she went on and crashed through that door and about half the car was in and half of it was out through the door. She was able to get out and she says, "I think I got brake trouble." She forgot to turn the key off. They started it in low gear so she came all the way up into town in low gear. She'd driven a lot before, but that was the first time she'd ever driven with no brakes. If she'd turned off the key it would have been fine. Anyway, we had a door with a big hole in it out the back end. There were others. Mrs. French drove around for a day without a tire. The tire had gone flat and it finally fell off. She didn't realize it and she came into town one day on the rim and you could hear her coming from five blocks away. Anyway, she come up and she'd always say "Mautin." You know, she had that real English brogue. "Mautin, I think I have some noise in my car. Could you tell me what it is?"

Tough People, Hard Times
◆◆◆◆◆◆◆◆◆◆◆◆◆◆◆◆◆◆◆◆◆

Virginia:

Later on, the changes were good. Now don't get me wrong — of course, it went a little further than it probably would have been necessary, but the area was very depressed.

Martin:

Aspen was nothing. There were no jobs. All the girls had to leave and most of the boys did, too. Only a few of them stayed. In 1946 was when it started to change, and we needed an extra dollar around because there were no dollars coming into Aspen. Now Aspen's so highly known, but back at that time, when we'd ship cattle into Denver, they'd say, "Well, where are you from?" We'd say Carbondale because everybody knew where Carbondale was because it was a kind of industrial place. They shipped a lot of cattle and potatoes — it was a very good agricultural area. If you said Aspen, people would look at you and go, "Why I never heard of the place."

In about 1946 Paepcke started making changes. I think they did real well. We'd all go to the bars and we were respected as much as the Paepckes. There was no class distinction at all. I would have said for thirty years there people really fit in well. There was Harold Paps, which was a different class than we were. I always remember going into the Golden Horn and there was the ambassador to Italy. Clair Booth Lewis was in there with a few dignitaries, and there was also Harold Paps. I was in there, too, and they always put on a little show. Bob Knight would put on a little skit. Anyway, one night, he come up and said, "Also, we have two of the biggest bull shippers in the valley — Paps and Martin Cerise." There was no class distinction. I was never in Harold Paps' class, but that didn't matter. That's kind of how it was.

When skiing started, we didn't have the time. Raising a family was about all the time you had. Don't get me wrong, I enjoyed the crowd at that time and I enjoyed the skiing part. In the real early days, my dad used to go up and buy houses for back taxes — twenty-seven dollars for a house. My dad would then strip down the house for lumber and take it down to Little Woody Creek and build what we needed. That was probably back in the twenties and thirties. And then he'd let it go back to taxes, because who wanted that worthless land in Aspen. He bought it for the houses. Twenty-seven dollars was pretty cheap lumber. There were a lot of old buildings around. People just boarded up, and there was a lot of furniture inside of these houses. Everything was left inside those old buildings, and during World War II metal became valuable and there was a fellow

165

in town — he was a junk dealer — and he'd go into these places. I don't know if he had permission or not, but I'd see him taking rifles that were hanging in there. They were old antiques. He'd break the wood stock off. Duff was the junk man's last name. He was also the town marshall for some time. Aspen was really the first city that got started, before Carbondale or Glenwood Springs. After things slowed down in the mining in the early 1900s, the migration went down.

My dad was about seventy when he retired. He and my mother lived in Aspen. He died a couple of years after he got to town. Retirement wasn't probably the best thing for him, but he got to the point to where he couldn't do too much. He sure missed the cows and the ranch. Mom lived maybe ten years longer. She was known for her gardens and flowers. She lived on the West End.

In the sixties, Aspen was still a great town — great people. The hippies didn't frighten me. I had one of them helping me build this hunting cabin — Roy Forge. Still around. He's really a hippie. At the time, he was living in a tepee up Hunter Creek. He had a beard down to here. He has a wood-cutting company. He used to be really one of the genuine hippies, and he's still that way. I mean, their way of life is kind of similar to mine. I was never a hippie, but I probably would have been. That's the thing about Aspen. There was really no class structure. Nobody judged you for what you were wearing. Your kids would go to school, the rich ones and the poor ones, and basically they were all friends and they always did their things together and nobody paid any attention.

And people dressed the same. Take Edgar Stanton and all those people. I knew them all because we did work for them and they would never tell you who they were. You'd have to find out through the grapevine maybe ten years after they were here who they were. They didn't flaunt anything. As a matter of fact, I remember he had Development Electric. That was the company that he and his brother owned, and it took me years before I found that out. I was rewiring a car that had got burnt. We had the NAPA store there in Aspen, too, and NAPA had billed him for wires and so forth. Edgar come over and asked me what I was doing, and he always called me, like the rest of these English, "Mautin." That was my name, "Mautin, whatcha doin'?" "Well", I says, "I'm wiring this burned out car. If I had some good wire, this job would be a hell of a lot easier." He looked at it — it was belted. He looked it all over and he said, "What's wrong with this?" He didn't say, "I own the company," he said, "What's wrong with this?" And I said, "It just isn't worth a darn. It's all we have, but it just isn't worth a darn." He kind of took it seriously. I couldn't keep from laughing anymore, and he said, "Why you son of a so and so." This is the way these people were. It was great. Even during the sixties, people were great. I didn't mind the growth. The town needed it. It really did.

The change I didn't like was in the mid-seventies. I'll tell you, the big change happened. I got out of the garage in 1965. I leased the building and everything out, and the big change was really when Snowmass went in. Now that was big. Then the people moving in were different. We moved out to Gunnison in 1975 or 1976. I missed the cows, and I'd rather see the cows than the people. Gunnison was still a cow town. Don't have any cows now; I don't even have a dog anymore. I never did get the country boy out. I still love the country. If there was a road around Aspen, I'd drive around it. If I didn't have to go into town to see my kids, I don't think I'd probably ever come over to Aspen, because it's just not my style. I don't fit in with the people or the town itself anymore.

How do I feel about Aspen now? Well, I would say there was a time when you didn't have doctors; you didn't have dentists in the area. They talk about the "good old days;" they weren't good old days. It was hard. I would say if I had a wish, I'd like to have stopped Aspen about 1965. And the same kind of people who were here at the time. That would have been the answer for me.

Virginia:

I would agree with that. I think that was a beautiful time in Aspen. Business was going. People were friendly. Even the new people coming in were very nice. Everybody helped each other. Everybody knew everybody.

Martin:

People never locked their doors, even these wealthy people. They'd come in and say, "Martin, my car don't start. It's in the garage, the keys are on the kitchen table, and I won't be home." So you walked up there and sure enough, the house was unlocked and you'd walk in.

I think there was a time when Aspen did have a bad reputation for drugs and so forth. Knowing other areas, I think Aspen, even right now, outside of some of the weird people, is still a good place. You have these people anywhere you go anymore. There's still a lot of nice people in Aspen, though. I don't think I've ever met nicer people than I have in Aspen, and a lot of them are still there. I would tell my kids, "Stay right in Aspen. You're just as well off as you are anywhere else." It's still a small enough town. They make fair money. Through our kids, we meet young people, and I find that Aspen has always been a young town. The kids meet wonderful people. But then I think there's some of them older ones down there that could just as well be eliminated. They're real wealthy. I think now they could be eliminated and still make a better town. The old philosophy of Walter Paepcke was that the rich kept very simple. Oh, they had a little bigger houses than we did, but I remember all these older people, I worked on their cars — they run the oldest cars in town. Not the junkiest, don't get me wrong. They kept them up, but they had the oldest Jeeps. Naturally, they'd fly a lot. You'd never know the wealthy from the poor. Of course, now it's a matter of flaunting. They would invite you to their homes and treat you just like anybody else. That's what was so nice about back then.

I think Aspen is still a great area. I don't come over here from Gunnison to see Aspen. The one thing that I like about it is that all these wilderness people, these outdoors people, they walk up and down the streets and on the Rio Grande right-of-way. They're not bothering me at all. Soon as I step four miles out of town there isn't a soul out there. They really don't bother me, and like I say, I don't have anything harsh to say about Aspen.

✦

Photo by Kathy Daily

*Amelia, being the
hairdresser in Aspen
for I don't know
how many years,
must know everybody's dirt.
She is strong and likes to
dance. She goes out and
tackles things.*

Amelia Cerise Kopp

I was born June 28, 1923, in Woody Creek. My mother's name was Onorina Milanesio and was from Torno, Italy. My father was from Val d'Aosta, Italy, and his name was Albert Cerise. I was born at the end of Little Woody Creek, and later we lived in that big red house on the right where you turn to go up Little Woody Creek. Mrs. Barrailler was a relative of my mother. She had the dairy for quite a few years, and my mother and dad met at her place. Dad was working on Independence, helping with the road. He had his horses boarded at my aunt's, and they met there. Mother was going to go back to Europe. She wasn't going to stay. But they got married, and that's when they moved on the ranch.

My earliest memory of childhood up Woody Creek was when I was two or three years old. Mostly I remember taking care of my brother Martin. He is three years younger than me. We both were out in the fields when mother helped dad. Dad was a miner first when he came over, and then he went into farming.

The Woody Creek School was the red house down after the Woody Creek Tavern. That was our schoolhouse. When we were young, the winters were tough. We'd get up before daylight with cold stoves in the house and no lights. We walked and rode horseback to school. We went pretty much by ourselves from way up Little Woody down to the Arlian's Ranch. It took us probably thirty-five minutes. Martin and I rode the same horse. I don't remember the horse's name, but I do remember he was ornery. If he didn't want to go, he'd just throw us off. Never hurt us, though. The schoolhouse was one room. Attendance went up to thirty or thirty-five with one teacher. She taught eight grades, all classes — reading, writing, arithmetic, history, music, etc. We had one teacher by the name of Mrs. Mahoney, and, of course, Hilder Anderson taught most of my years at Woody Creek.

We were happy around here when we were little. We had a simple life. For shopping we'd go to Glenwood about every six months. It took you all day to go to Glenwood and back with the old cars, no paving, and rough roads. For fun on the ranch, all the neighbor kids got together. We had this buggy. Martin fixed it somehow so that it had brakes and he could guide it. He was always doing stuff like that. He fixed it all up. We'd push it all the way back up the hill and ride down, lickety-split. One time we went through Jennie Arlian's fence. It was a wonder we didn't kill ourselves. We just left it in her yard.

When we went to high school, we stayed in town all week and then our neighbors, the Vagneurs, used to give us a ride back on Friday. I stayed with Anna Borgeson. That's right when you go into town where the Villas are. She had a little house right there. I felt very grown up to be away from home.

We used to do a lot of dancing in the valley. Saturdays were always taken up. The dances were at the Armory Hall. We had a seven-piece orchestra that was really good. Then we would go to Basalt, Carbondale, and Glenwood. They had nice halls. We did a lot of dancing in our lives. There was Sis McCugh's band — a beautiful band. We were lucky. We had our own built-in band. We had a big family, a lot of Cerises. My dad had five brothers. So we'd all get together and have big family gatherings on holidays. Then we'd have picnics in the summer. We didn't sit around. We had a good time.

I'm finally a little bit more carefree. I had forty-five years of working in my beauty shop. Now I'm doing a little bit for myself. I wanted to be a hairdresser since I was little. I used to always fix people's hair and enjoyed it. I started working when I was nineteen.

I went to the Western Slope in Grand Junction to get licensed in 1946. I came back here and got married to Louis Zupancis and was married five years. I had my son Bob. Later on, in about 1952, I married Robert Kopp and had Stan. I worked for Marge Clifford in Glenwood for about six months, and then I worked where the Hotel Jerome bar is now for her. There was a hair salon there. And then I went on my own. My shop was always Amelia's. I was on the ground floor of the Hyman Mall and then moved upstairs. I built the downstairs, and I was down there five years and then after I found a renter, I went up. I started Amelia's in 1962. At one time or another, I was all over town. I was where the Cantina is — a big place, and we fixed it all up. That was my first salon, probably the early 1950s. Terese David took it over when I was going to have Stan. Then I went to where my son Bob lives now, on Walnut. There was an old house there then. It burned down. I went from there down to where the Bank of Aspen is. There was a long building which they tore down. Doing people's hair, I have heard everybody's story in town. I cut most everybody's hair off in my day. Everybody wore long hair, and all of a sudden it was short.

One time, when I was in the Cantina Building, which was then the Chitwood Building, I had a lady come in, diamonds, rubies, etc., and she rented Parlor A at the Hotel Jerome. She came over with her maid and sat down. It was a nice salon — it was big and clean but nothing fancy. Back in those days you didn't have the money. She looked around and said, "Oh God, what a dive." I had a little lady, Mrs. Earl Jackson, whose hair I'd just got through doing, and she wouldn't leave. I thought, "What's the matter with her?" Afterwards I asked her, "Why did you stick around?" She said, "I wouldn't leave you with that old bag for nothing!" After awhile, I get this phone call. In those days I did everything myself. I didn't hire anybody for a few years. Evidently, this fancy lady took all her jewelry off and put it under the towel on the manicuring table. I got a call from her maid. "Oh my god. Have you got her jewelry over there?" I said, "Gosh, I don't know. I didn't look for jewelry." Thank god it was all sitting there on the table.

All kinds of crazy things happened in my salon upstairs. I had one lady — I won't mention her name, because she still comes to me — used to always bring

Rio Grande water tank at the old Woody Creek site, about 1958. Old Woody Creek post office and store in the background. Courtesy Del Gerbaz.

her lap dog. Finally I told her, "You're going to have to leave that dog at home." She never would leave it at home, so this one day there was another lady in there and she just hated dogs. I had a good fight on my hand — the two of them right in the salon. I won, I guess. I told the one with the dog if she ever brought that dog back, they were both going. I should have had a tape recorder. You can't believe what goes on in a salon!

When I look back, I ran a business by myself and raised two kids. *I* did it. It was tough, but you got used to it. Now I wonder how I did it.

I've seen Aspen go through a lot of changes, some good, some bad. I liked it much better before. What's changed the most is the amount of people. I don't think the town's done bad with the changes. I hate to see some of the old houses torn down, but most of them were no good anyhow. I think the changes to me are in the people, even through my business. When I started out hairdressing, I had people about my age from all over the world, and they were much friendlier, nicer people. They all mingled with the locals. They were part of the locals, whether they were tourists or not. In the last ten years, that's been lost. Locals feel it more, and that's why they're moving. They just feel left out. I think the whole thing has changed. I noticed my last year in business I wasn't enjoying it anymore.

In the last four years, I've kind of gotten away from it. We do a lot of things downvalley because most of the people up here have left. We still have friends in Aspen, but most of the older people are leaving. I don't know what it is, but I think it's because the town's growing. I think you lose something once the town grows. There's a lot of good people, don't take me wrong. The town has lost a sense of community in the last ten years. To me, there's more of a community feeling down the valley.

What Aspen needs is a big place where they can hold a lot of social activities, like dancing. We tried to get a square-dance club going up here. Square dancing is something the young and the old can do together. All the young people are beginning to get back into the mood of the dancing of the 1940s, 1950s, and 1960s. It's all coming back. It would be nice, because a lot of older people — I for one — love young people. That's why I work. I don't want to quit, because I'm around young people. I love the old, but I like to be with young people, too. I think young people are missing out a lot by not mingling with the older people. This is what I miss in Aspen.

This could be a better community if we'd get to know each other better. In the old days, the young danced with the old and you got to knowing everybody. As a young lady, you wouldn't have thought of not dancing with an older man. He would have been insulted. It kept the community together. But now you have to go to bars, or spend a lot of money on eating, and I don't get a kick out of that. I just don't get a kick out of sitting and sipping on a drink. I'd rather go and have fun doing something like dancing. I think Aspen's lacking that.

I'd like to see something for the young, too. Even when my kids were growing up, a lot of that was lost. It would have been nice if my children could have had a little bit more of what I had, because it makes you appreciate older people more. Now, to me, it's totally gone. That's what I like about it downvalley. There's still square dancing, round dancing, polka dancing, and western dancing. The young and the old are still getting together. But I'm afraid that's going to be lost before long down there, too.

◆

*Edie is organized.
When she says
she's going to do
something, she does it.
I see Edie walking
all over town.
She walks fast.
She's in shape.*

Edie Skiff Chisholm

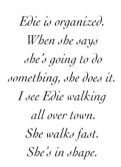

I was born in the early 1920s in Aspen. Dr. Twining was in attendance and I was born on our ranch. We lived where Marge Stein lives now, which was the Skiff Ranch for years and years. My parents both immigrated from Yugoslavia. Their names were Anton Skiff and Margaret Yartz. They met in Pueblo and were married in the church that still stands in Pueblo — St. Mary's Catholic Church. My father immigrated to America and my mother came later. He moved to Pueblo because the smelter was really booming. That was a good job, and he knew a lot of people. But my mother had family. Her older sister and husband lived in Pueblo and immigrated many years before that. Three children were born in Pueblo, seven in Aspen. They moved to Aspen after the silver rush in about the early 1900s. My father worked in the mines for awhile. Later he was able to accumulate enough money to buy the ranch. After that, we were farmers most of our lives.

As a child, I loved horses. My favorite horse was Poor Old Betty, I guess. She was a little old swayback bay, really old. I guess she was the one that Dad would trust me, my younger sister, Lois, and brother, Jimmie, to ride. So the three of us would all pile up on Betty and go bring in the milk cows, if we could get her going. But later, as I grew up, my brothers would let me ride their horses. I did like horses.

I went to school when I was five years old. Ours was the only class in the Lincoln School that year because it was practically condemned, but there wasn't room for our class yet at the Washington School.

In the winter, when the weather was really bad, my father would bring us to school on a sleigh. Other times we walked. Yes, that was nothing — I walk that much now. But when the weather was really really bad, we could not walk. Probably by the time we got home we were frozen and had to thaw our poor little feet. We really did get chilblains. In the wintertime, when it was really harsh, we had two homes. I mean, my oldest sister usually would be in charge, and we rented a house in Aspen. For two or three winters we rented the house that Lucille Price lives in now on Main Street. There were so many of us in our family going to school — five brothers and five sisters — we had a nice little sleigh with strong horses.

My sister, Lois, brother, Jimmie, and I were the three youngest. We really didn't have any big specific jobs, but we all helped pull weeds out of the potato patch in the spring. There was a holiday from school for the first two weeks in October when people were harvesting because they needed their children to help pick potatoes, or help cook. I always liked cooking, so I spent a lot of time in the house with my mother. Cooking is one of my favorite hobbies. My memories are mainly on the ranch, you know, because my father moved there long before I was born.

My dad was a hero to me. My parents were wonderful people. I guess having a large family and having an opportunity to move to an acreage and a farm — he knew that it would probably be easier to support a family. And we did. We raised our own food; we never went hungry. I can never remember a day that I went without shoes. We were poor by today's standards. That was not the priority in my father's life. It was that we were happy, well cared for, and went to school. I wouldn't give my childhood for any of the childhoods I see today.

We had a great time, we really did. So many of our friends from town would come over on Sundays and we would crank up the ice-cream freezer and make ice cream. Mother always did her own baking, so there was plenty to eat. We worked hard and raised wonderful things to eat. Like I said, when you talk about fancy jewelry, the best furniture, and all this and that, we didn't have it. We had all that we needed, really. You might say we want something better for our children. Well, I don't know.

I went on to school. I was able to work for the original Aspen Company, which was through the Hotel Jerome at that time. And then I went on with the Aspen Skiing Corporation and worked there for twenty-one years. You know, for my generation, I have no regrets. I can't remember that anyone was hungry in Aspen, and there was sort of a barter system. We had friends in Palisade. They would bring up fruit, grapes, and everything from their harvest. In turn, my father would send home wheat and potatoes. So if you couldn't pay with money, you exchanged. My father brought in lots of potatoes, hogs, beef, and everything. I'm sure to this day, he never was paid for some of them. If anybody needed anything, he took them in. My father was very meticulous. He paid his bills and taxes on time. Cattle, potato crops — our crops were magnificent. That's what we did — worked real hard. We were real farmers. Absolutely.

After high school, I attended Blair Business College and Colorado College in Colorado Springs. I received a small high-school scholarship. Lois Nicholson, one of my very best friends, was the valedictorian and I was the salutatorian, and listen to this: There were only eight of us in our graduating class. We each received a scholarship, and so I used my two years at Blair Business College and I went an additional year on my own.

After high school I wanted to leave. I wanted to go away to school. After college I worked at the Broadmoor for a year and then decided I would take the civil service exam, which I passed. At that point in time, war broke out in Europe and the government was converting Pando, Colorado, to the 10th Mountain Division site known today as Camp Hale. I worked at Camp Hale the summer before troops were sent in for training.

My job was finished in late November and I transferred to the Treasury Department downtown in Denver. My job there was to help proofread Colorado state checks that came in before being mailed to recipients — welfare checks, payroll checks, most any kind of checks that the state government issued

*Hotel Jerome
about 1951.
Courtesy
Martin Garfinkel.*

at that time. So one day, I just looked around and I thought, ooo . . . if I stay here this long, I'm going to look like the rest of these little old gray-haired ladies, which I am now!

I thought joining the navy would be exciting, so I took the exam. I received my orders in three months to report to Hunter College in New York City for boat training. I was in the navy almost three years. About three months before I was discharged and the war was over, I had acquired the necessary points. I could have gone on to Honolulu. They needed additional personnel out there to help discharge the naval personnel. But my father had a coronary, a very serious heart attack, and survived. He left the hospital and was at home for about six weeks. So my brother and I flew home to visit him. We knew from the diagnosis that he would not be living long. I had been gone so much that I thought I'd go home for awhile and spend some time with my mother. So I didn't accept the offer to go to Honolulu. I accepted my discharge and flew home. My father passed away a month later in March 1946. He was sixty-nine.

At that point in time, Walter Paepcke was already looking at Aspen and moving in. It was Tom Sardy that came to me one day and said, "Mr. Paepcke needs a secretary and I know you would be good. You just came home from the navy and you have done that kind of work. Why don't you go see him — he really is looking for someone." I said, "No, I have been gone for too many years. I went to school, I was at Camp Hale, I was here, I was there, I just want to take some time off, spend some time with my mother," and so my mother and I planned a little trip. We went East to visit some of her relatives after my father passed away, and I was in no hurry to go back to work.

When I came back, Tom Sardy was still waiting for me and he says, "Well, you have had a good vacation and I know you are not going to loaf anymore. You better go to work. The job is still available." Well, I debated and I thought, oh dear, and I didn't know at that point in time if I really wanted to stay in Aspen. But I knew Aspen was making a turn and it would be different. Because I had been quite a few places, I thought, okay, I'll do it for the summer. And I did it for eighteen years. My good friend, Luetta Kearns Whitson, and I basically closed the Hotel Jerome. From there we both went to work for the Aspen Skiing Corporation.

I did a lot of work for Walter Paepcke. At first my office was up in Parlor B where they were remodeling the Hotel Jerome. Plaster would fall down on my typewriter and on my head. Then we moved across the hall. Actually, the first manager that I worked under was Ferdinand Sperl, and later for Charles Bishop. It was the Ski Corporation, and then it was the Ski Company, and now it's the present Aspen Skiing Corporation. I went to work for them in October 1965.

In the meantime, Hugh Chisholm came back after the war, too. Hugh worked as the postal clerk. He worked for the post office for thirty years. Hugh

Hugh and Bert Chisholm, about 1927, Snowmass Creek. Courtesy Bert Chisholm.

lived at Snowmass when he was young; I didn't know him too well then. He went to country schools most of the time. I really knew Hughie best after the war. That's when I met him and started dating him. He would come out to the house to visit my father and mother. The Chisholms knew the Skiffs and so he would come out, and pretty soon it was, "Would you like to go to the movie tomorrow night? Would you like to do this, would you like to do that? Now would you like to get married?" So that's it. One thing led to another. We were married October 2, 1948. We had two children; Heather was born in 1953 and Karen in 1956.

When did Aspen change? You know, the world is full of changes. I suppose if I had come home and turned around and moved to Denver, or moved back out to San Francisco, think of the changes I would have seen out there. I was out there about three years ago and it is nothing at all like it was when I was there in the navy — all the skyscrapers and everything. Well, you are not going to stop change and you are not going to stop progress. You may not say it's what you want, but I certainly wouldn't be living in Aspen today if it was like it was when I left here. See, there are good things and there are bad things.

Of course, I think politics always enters in any place. People that are here for about maybe a whole two years think they know exactly what the town needs. And I don't begrudge them; I'm sure we have some very intelligent people coming into the town. But I don't think they do enough research; I don't think they do enough groundwork. I wish I knew a lot of the things that the young people do today. I can compare my own daughters and what they know. But when I was growing up, I was very thankful that I could go on to college from such a large family.

✦

Bert Chisholm was a fun man. I can just tell that he liked to sow his oats and eat them, too. He played hard, worked hard, and partied hard. What a neat guy.

Photo by Kathy Daily

Bert Chisholm
(August 11, 1914 – December 18, 1993)

 I was born August 11, 1914, across the Watson Divide on Snowmass — the real Snowmass, not that phony Snowmass [ski area]. We had a ranch over the Watson Divide, the first ranch, called Williams Hill. My parents came from Nova Scotia, Canada. Mother's father, Johnny Stewart, came to Aspen around 1885. My mother was seventeen then. Her name was Anne Stewart. Johnny Stewart was very interested in geology and, to a certain extent, in the mines, but he didn't do much mining.

My dad's half-brother also came from Nova Scotia and bought a claim up in Montezuma. He made about $350,000, and at that time it was quite a bit of money. It was rich silver and that gave him the interest to go into the Klondike. His name was Big Alec McDonald. Those first two claims that he bought were the two richest that were ever discovered in the Klondike. Later, he kept on buying and buying, and stayed in his cabin. He didn't go down to the water truck down in Dawson, where the miners were spending all their money on these wild women, booze, and stuff like that. He just stayed out in the cabin there — he was a businessman. Then he owned the shipway from Skagway to Kinoa, coming up the other way. He had a lot of property. He never stopped buying and he made millions, but then he lost most of it before he died.

My grandfather, Johnny Stewart, first took up a ranch down near Snowmass, and I still have pictures of it. It had an old sod roof, and boy, it was primitive. Later, my uncle, John Henry Stewart, was the agent on the Midland Railroad, which is now Killer Highway 82. He owned the store at the original Snowmass. He had just a frame building and hitch rail for the horses.

Bert Chisholm, about 1925. Courtesy Bert Chisholm.

My grandpa designed a chicken house so that we had eggs sooner than anyone else in the valley. It was laid out so neat, and it cut off the cold west wind. It was enclosed so the chickens could start laying their eggs sooner because it was so warm and sunny. We went out there even in February. My mother was a great judge of horses, and she knew every horse that came down the road. Boy, she could look out the window and know whether it was a good horse or a bad one, and how a person could ride. She also was a photographer. We still have some glass plates. She developed her own film.

When I was a kid, I went to the Capitol Creek schoolhouse. We all rode horses there. Every kid had his own horse, and the school had a barn with stalls that faced to the east to cut off the wind. By the time we were six, we had to push that saddle up and over the horse by ourselves. My dad says, "Yep, you gotta push that saddle over." And I'll tell you, a kid didn't lie around in the morning either. Boy, I loved to read in that old bunkhouse, listening to the stream go by.

I think my dad met my mom first in Cripple Creek. His name was Dan Chisholm. It was later that they were married here in Aspen. He was from Nova Scotia, too.

My mother was very young — she was only about seventeen when she married Dad. He was quite a bit older, probably in his early thirties. Well, look what they are doing right here in Aspen — you see these old bald-headed guys with plenty of money going around with these nice chicks, about twenty-one. I've seen them walking right around up at the mall there — crazy! My mom had eight children. Hugh and I were twins, the last. We were the babies. She started having babies early on. By that time, Dad had bought the ranch over the Watson Divide.

Bert Chisholm, about 1935. Courtesy Bert Chisholm.

In the 1920s, my grandfather, John Stuart Stewart, was very progressive and started the first telephone in the valley. He bought the equipment. First he hooked up the phone from his place down at Snowmass to my uncle. He ran it up the valley and then hooked it up to the Williams, then he jumped over to our place. And that's as far as they ran it. It had the old ringer-type telephone. At that time, my mother, grandpa, and my Uncle Henry all talked Gaelic. Boy, these people — it was like radio. They liked to listen and they'd get all the gossip. But of course, they would listen in on other people's calls and you'd hear the ringers the minute you called anyone. I remember our phone was one long and two shorts. You'd hear every phone on the whole line. The receivers would go up and they were listening. They wanted to get the gossip more than anything else. This was before the 1920s. And then Ma Bell came in and we still had the same phones. As I said, they talked Gaelic, but everyone still kept listening.

When I was little, first thing in the morning, I ran down to the spring. We had a beautiful spring with water cress in it. We would bring the water up, because we didn't have a modern plumbing system, water pipes, or anything like that. When I was about three years old, I'd run down and get a fresh bucket of water for drinking. It had to be absolutely fresh for my dad when he would come in. He'd sprinkle oatmeal in the water. We had a little spring house down there. This spring water came out into a little v-shaped trough and then went into another barrel. We cut that barrel in half. It would never freeze — it would come right out. It was cold, but the temperature was much warmer than the water in the river, so it would freeze over but never freeze up.

Daniel William Chisholm (1865 – 1944) and Bert Chisholm, at Snowmass Lake. Courtesy Bert Chisholm.

When we were stacking hay, we'd stack with a bull rig — overstock stackers. The first thing we learned was to lead the stack horse. The bull rig had teeth, and the stacker had similar teeth — there were different types of stackers. The stacker horse would pull and drop the hay on the stack you started. You started small and gradually went up. There was one or two men on the stack. Some of the hay we would sell, but mostly we'd use it. Then we grazed alfalfa for the milk cows and timothy for the cattle that you'd ship to market. The milk cows did better on alfalfa.

Our ranch had cattle, hogs, turkeys — anything — we were self-sufficient. We made our own butter and cheese. We had deer all over the place — that was free food. With venison, we made sausage. We also canned it and put it in jars.

Oh, boy, it made wonderful gravy. The sausage came out like wieners when we put it on the grinder. Put lots of garlic in it.

All the way down the valley from Aspen, you could go to dances. We used to go over and dance at Basalt and around El Jebel. A lot of Italians would bring their dago red wine. Boy, they'd have dago red, and they'd dance and dance, I tell ya. They would want to spice it up a little and had a certain name for it. It was the bottom of the wine — grappa. It was just like drinking champagne or something bubbly like that. Boy, they would get everybody to get that dance going. They'd have the dance over where Gerbaz is now. They had a schoolhouse there, too. I remember as a kid, they would let us go to the Italian

Bert Chisholm,
about 1935.
Courtesy Bert Chisholm.

dances and we would stand there looking because we knew we would get big bologna sandwiches or something like that. They had big old pickles real long. After a few drinks and a few dances, they'd get up and fight. They didn't want someone to dance with their girl. I still remember as a kid, someone would say, "You called my girl a brockelface" — you know, a brockelface cow. It's got spots of red and different colors. Anyway, it wasn't exactly a compliment. So they would get in a fight — get drunk and carry on. Oh, there always had to be two or three fights or it wasn't a good dance.

When I was little, there were a lot of ranch hands, or cowboys, that I wanted to be like. I was a good rider myself, but I didn't go in for getting rolled on. I had a mare that was just wonderful and sure footed. We had an irrigation ditch. A bunch of horses were loose and running around in a hayfield. Well, we didn't want them running around in a hayfield, so I got on my horse. Right in the middle of that road, she was so sure footed you'd never believe it, but that road was so dry and hard, she rolled right over the top of me and I could feel the whole weight of her. I thought sure she was going to break my back, but I was face down and somehow the saddle had turned sideways. It would have otherwise put the horn through my back. Her name was Lucky. We called her Lucky because she was lucky. Her mother died and she was lucky she made it.

Anyway, the Light Ranch was not too far away. There was a guy that used to work up there — Bill Sievers was his name. He actually was from Carbondale.

Stuart Chisholm
and Paul Beck,
about 1939.
Courtesy Bert Chisholm.

Sievers, by gawd, he could ride a horse. One time the crazy horse stuck its head between the rails in the fence and I thought he was going to kill Bill, but he hung in there and came out of it. Later on he went to different rodeos. It ended up he was the first from this area to get to Madison Square Garden. He won first in the rodeo.

We made our own cheese on our ranch. The big job was to separate the milk. I'd hate those milk cows 'cuz you had to get up and milk them every morning. Then you'd take the milk and put it through the cream separators. I have one in the barn out here.

To separate the milk, I sat on a spindle, and when it got up to speed (the cream is actually lighter than the milk, so it rises), there was one spout where the cream came out, and through the lower spout, the milk came out. This was because the specific gravity was lower in there. It would just wind and wind around, and once it got up to top speed, I would turn the spicket and let the milk drain down into the spout.

Right down here on Smuggler Avenue, I owned this whole half-block at one time. Had a barn down there on the end, all vacant. I bought it soon after the war. I always base everything on the war. I bought it in about 1950 from Mack McKinley. He came from up Capitol Creek. He had a homestead up there. Finally, he sold his homestead out, came down, and bought this property. He had a barn in the alley. He had one light bulb hanging from the ceiling and an old Majestic range like the one we had on the ranch. Mother would bake bread, cornbread, and every other kind. She put out more stuff out of that

Majestic. The picture on the stove was of the *Great Majestic* (a sailing ship). That's why they named it. So anyway, I was looking around for property to buy. Ol' Mack was sitting in there and had his feet up on the stove. He had one big old barrel stove that had nickel curled around her. It curled around the bottom so you could put your feet up and get them warm. So he said, "This is the best house I've ever lived in." He didn't have any switches on the wall, but he did have electric current and one light bulb hanging down. That's all he needed.

Finally I bought the place. I think I paid him about $4,000. And everybody then said, "You're a damn fool — you are paying too much." My own brother-in-law said, "You are paying too much," and Laurence Elisha, the family that owned the hotel, said, "Oh, you're paying too much for that." I bought the whole half-block and I wanted it intact as much as possible. Ikey Mogan was a fire bug, and he burned the barn down later on. No one could ever prove it. Oh, he burned property all over town. He burned my Uncle Henry's house down. Ikey'd be the first one to come around and grab the fire hose and put the fire out. He was probably seventeen when he did this. He was old enough to know better. He burned his own grandmother's house down. It was right across east of the Jerome Hotel. They were Irish and very nice people. His aunts and all were schoolteachers and everything. Oh, he was just wacky, that's all.

I went to the Capitol Creek School. First we had a little log schoolhouse up Snowmass. My brother, Stuart, was about fourteen years older, oldest in the family. He taught school in a little log building. It is a shame it's not there anymore — it was a landmark. It was a nice little log house with a bell on top. It was a big school and there was only Popish kids, the one Reed, and so on — probably about ten kids in all. In the first grade I went to the Lincoln schoolhouse in Aspen. It was a dangerous place, and it was torn down later. The Lincoln School was a fire trap. Anyway, I went to first grade there and then second grade was in this little place up Snowmass. From there on through the sixth and seventh grade, I went to Capitol Creek. That's when we rode our horses to school. And then after that, when we reached about the seventh grade, we went to the Washington School in Aspen.

I enlisted in the navy in 1942. I returned to Aspen in 1945. Even though the war had given people jobs, mostly, Aspen hadn't changed. I went back to the ranch for awhile, and then I got interested in real estate. I started college in Pomona, California. So I left again and, as it turned out, I was very interested in aeronautical engineering. I didn't complete college because it was expensive. There was still a depression and money was not available. Then I bought this block around 1950 and I built this house in 1954. I met my wife along about then. She had come out from Chicago and I would have been better off if I hadn't met her at all — she cost me a fortune.

I had three children — Chris, Dan, and Stuart. After my divorce, I didn't marry again.

I had cabins right over next to the number-one lift. I had a second cabin camp license in Aspen. I called them Roch Run Cabins. I had a pair of Andre Roch's skis, and damned if somebody didn't come in and steal them. They had the continuous binding, the old Groswell — the first ski that came here out of Groswell.

If I could give Aspen one wish right now, it would be to go back to the way it was thirty years ago. You knew a lot more people. You'd go in the Red Onion and know everybody that come in. And later on I used to go to the Cooper Street Pier, where it was more like the Red Onion used to be. There were young people, old geezers, and kind of a mix.

✦

*Jens Christiansen is a
man of the land.
I would imagine he's
more comfortable
in the saddle
than on the ground.
All guts and eyebrows.*

Jens Christiansen

I was born May 4, 1902, in Denmark. I came to Aspen in 1914. My father's name was Mads Christiansen and my mother's was Sophia. My aunt, Kate Lindvig, was already living here in Snowmass. Lindvig is my middle name and was the name of our ranch in Denmark. It's all generations, you know. She lived on the very last ranch in Snowmass where you go up to Snowmass Lake. My parents rented the ranch from my Aunt Kate.

Hyman Avenue, 1905.
Courtesy Peggy Rowland.

I went to school out in Snowmass with a cousin that came with us from Denmark. She taught us. She was there four years. That's the only schooling I had. I learned English living on the ranch. My parents came for my mother's health. She had several sisters and brothers who died of tuberculosis in Denmark because of the climate, so they came to Colorado.

Gladyce and I met at a country dance in 1929 at the Cozy Point Ranch. Our ranch, the Glendale, was up Owl Creek — 640 acres. Eventually we sold off part in 1967 and kept the ten acres with the house and barn. We lived there until a year or two ago.

I started working for Jack Brunton in 1918. He originally owned the Glendale. We ran cattle and that's nothing but work, work, work — every day of the year, twelve to fourteen hours a day. For hay we'd use stackers and buckers. In the wintertime, we'd drive out and put a load on the sled for the cattle. I didn't know anything else. High-school kids would come out and work on our ranch in the summer. I had about eight or nine of them who picked potatoes and stayed with us.

In the 1930s we didn't have a dime and people had no jobs. They'd come from Aspen to Glenwood just to see the train go by that had people sitting on top of it — terrible, terrible.

I had a still one time. The sheriff had one he confiscated from somebody and I gave him a gallon of wine for it. So he gave me the still. He was a Swede — Otto Johnson. It was a very good still. I loaned it to the Strongs and never got it back. I ran something through it only one time. It was good. I put my wine through it. Red Rowland used to borrow the still from the Strongs.

I fished for eighty years. I started when I was about nine years old. I loved to fish Snowmass Creek. We lived up there four years when I was a kid. There were lots of fish — lot of them cutthroat. We rode horseback to get there. I rode a horse for years and fished off the horse. The horse would just stand still. We'd go up and camp for a week at a time at Snowmass Lake. Fished at Willow Lake quite a few times.

Aspen started changing when that guy came in from Chicago. I could have bought a hundred lots in town for five dollars per lot. And the house where Sardy used to live — he offered that to me for $500. I didn't have the $500. At the time it was empty. No one paid taxes. The only ones who paid taxes were farmers. All the farmers down the Roaring Fork, they're Italians. They would come up and buy a house, tear it down, move it, and build a shed. Then they'd give the lot back to the county — they didn't want to pay taxes on it. It was cheaper to do it that way than to go to the lumberyard.

We were all thrilled to death when the first lift was put in. That was in 1946, and then Snowmass Village opened in 1967. I wasn't too excited about that. When they started building that ski area, I laughed. I said that won't last, it will be like these little golf courses — some two or three years, that will be all. I didn't know — I was too damn dumb. Like when they first started selling those lots in Brush Creek in Snowmass Village, they wanted $15,000 a lot, and I thought, who will buy them? Robert McNamara bought one of the first. He built a house.

I loved Aspen before all the people started coming in. We parked our car in the middle of the street and left it. Everything was just wonderful. Nobody stole a thing. We never locked any door.

◆

Photo by Kathy Daily

Gladyce Hart Christiansen

I was born November 25, 1911, in Aspen. My maiden name is Hart. My father, Fred Hart, came from Iowa to Aspen when he was eight years old in 1888. He came on the Midland train with his parents. His family came for the mining. My mother, Ella Colby Hart, came with her mother and father when she was seven years old on the Midland. That would have been in 1891. My mother's mother was born in Minnesota, and it was for her health that they came here

Aspen, about 1900.
Courtesy Del Gerbaz.

also — tuberculosis. My father's father had a grocery store in Aspen. He was also a miner. It was where Andre's Building is now. I think it was Hart's Grocery, or Hart's Merchandise.

When I was born, my father was county assessor in Aspen. When I was two years old, we moved to Capitol Creek to the Hart Ranch, which my grandfather owned. After I moved there I rode horseback to grade school. I went to Capitol Creek School. I knew Ann Wieben. She and my brother were in the same grade in high school. She married Chris Wieben; they were our neighbors. When I went to high school, I stayed with my grandparents, who lived in Aspen. They had a house where the Grog Shop is now.

My mother's uncle was Henry Staats, who was one of the first prospectors in Aspen. He homesteaded a ranch on Capitol Creek, and that was where my mother and her mother lived. Henry Staats's wife was a sister to my mother's mother. Henry Staats came over Independence Pass in 1879 and was one of the first prospectors in Aspen. He was one of the first thirteen men to winter over in

Aspen. The governor warned the prospectors not to stay in Aspen the first winter, because they thought there would be an Indian uprising. But there were thirteen who stayed, and he was one of the thirteen. They lived in tents that winter of 1879 up Hunter Creek. When I was real young, I was told a story that the thirteen ran out of food during that long winter. So Staats skied over Independence Pass, pulling a boat sled, to go to Leadville and get supplies. In Leadville, he got bacon, flour, and supplies. He put it in this boat sled, and on the way back to Aspen, he had an eerie feeling. He looked back, and a mountain lion was stalking him. He really didn't know what to do, so he let out a blood-curdling scream, and the lion ran away. And that supposedly is a true story. My mother told me that one. When Henry got the homestead over in Capitol Creek, he traded five dollars and a pair of rubber boots for his homestead. That's the monastery now.

Jens and I met at a country dance at Cozy Point Ranch. It was called True Smith Ranch at that time — where that big barn is. It was really called Rath Bone, because it was a stop on the Midland Railroad. And then the other stop at Shale Bluffs was called Cozy Point. Then everybody knew it as the True Smith place, because True Smith and his family lived there for many, many years. We were married in 1932 — I was twenty, he was thirty. We got married at my parents' home on Capitol Creek, July 17, 1932. We had one child, Joyce, in 1934. Jens and his father, Mads Christensen, bought the Glendale in 1925.

In the 1930s everybody moved to Denver — a lot of them wanted relief. The farmers and ranchers didn't suffer too much, because they had their own produce and cattle for food.

The Williams Brothers Ranch was up Snowmass Creek, just at the beginning of Snowmass Creek. They'd have these parties and ride horses up and down the road. People would shoot their hats off. That's true. One of the boys shot someone right in their mouth, in the cheek, with a .22. Well, it didn't hurt him. He didn't do anything about it. This must have been the 1920s.

After every dance, which was held in the Armory Hall, one of the Gerbaz boys would go out and get drunk. He'd go out from the dance and kick all the headlights out of the cars. One night, he made a mistake. He didn't realize it was Bill Tagert's car, and he kicked them out. I guess Bill never knew who it was. And if he didn't do that, going home he'd knock all the road signs down. Another time, Jens and a friend were riding horseback. I guess it was a spooky new horse. In the spring there was a lot of mud. The horse was prancing, and this Mrs. Hamilton, she was a little bitty short woman; her husband was the marshall. She and another woman were going along and Jens splattered mud on them. They were going to church — it was Easter Sunday morning. She had a little hat on, and the horse splattered mud all over it. So, they had Jens there in police court. They let him off — just got a little reprimand. Jens was maybe twenty-one or twenty-two at the time.

Jens's aunt, Kate Lindvig, was known as the cattle queen of Snowmass. She ran cattle. They just named her that, I guess, because she was the only single woman who homesteaded over there and all of that. She was a maiden lady. She was a virgin, too, she said. She ran a boardinghouse in Aspen first, for the miners. I think it was called Kate's. When she came to this country, she loved it here. After she became an American citizen, she just worshipped the American flag — the stars and stripes. She didn't have any yen to go back to Denmark at all.

I guess there were no drugs in the old days — no drugs at all. It seemed like life was real simple. We knew everybody. Go to dances and they were clean. We'd get drunk, of course. But everyone knew everyone else and life was good.

✦

Photo by Kathy Daily

*Joyce Kearns is a tomboy
and a good horsewoman.
She is honest and a bit shy,
with a dry sense of humor.*

Joyce Christiansen Kearns

I was born August 19, 1934, at the Citizen's Hospital in Aspen. One of my first chores on the Glendale Ranch was getting the horses into the corral from the pasture. I'd lead the slacker horse when I was six years old. Always rode horseback. When I got bigger, I raked hay some. I was a regular tomboy. My fondest memories were riding my horse and helping my dad with the cattle. I rode a lot alone. I helped drive the cattle down to Woody Creek to be loaded on the train

195

Anita Roberts and Joyce Christiansen, 1944. Courtesy Anita Smades.

to be shipped to the Denver stockyards. This was an important annual event for the ranch kids, as we skipped school to help our dads with the cattle and then drank pop at the Woody Creek store run by Mr. and Mrs. Bogue. Occasionally, I rode to school down to Owl Creek School, that pink building at the bottom of the Stapleton Hill that's been added onto.

I remember when I was in high school, there was this girl — I probably shouldn't name names — but I said to her, "Well, what do you do in the summer?" She said she got up about ten, had breakfast, walked downtown, went to Aspen Drug and had a Coke, then went home. And I thought, "My God, what a boring life that must be!" This was in the early 1950s. I'd get up about 5:00 A.M. and go get the horses, cook breakfast, and go out and work in the fields all day.

There was a lady that lived over in Brush Creek where the Snowmass Club is now. Her name was Emma Burke. She married Leo Kearns. One time my dad (Jens) kept Emma engaged in conversation. She had a car and she liked to come see my dad. She was kind of a local butterfly type. But anyway, while he engaged her in conversation, another fellow tied a dead rabbit on the back of her car. She drove all over town with that rabbit on the bumper of her car. She was so mad that she didn't speak to my dad for a year after. They used to go ice skating and she didn't know how to skate. Jens and another fellow got her between them and got her going fast and then turned her loose.

Tough People, Hard Times
◆◆◆◆◆◆◆◆◆◆◆◆◆◆◆◆◆◆◆

When I was little, my dad and I drove out of town one day. We got to that corner by the Hickory House, and the front wheel of our truck came off and rolled across the lawn and through the sweet-pea bed. The truck just sort of settled down and we went chasing the tire. We weren't going fast, 'cuz it was this old Chevy truck. For some reason, the front wheel came off — the whole wheel, not just the tire. That was excitement in Aspen in those days. Wish we had those times back.

My favorite years in Aspen were through the fifties, because it was small and you knew everybody. I would probably stop it in the fifties. Gary Cooper used to fit in to Aspen. He'd go up to the Jerome bench and visit with the old-timers. Aspen needs to face reality — it's not a small town anymore. They have to live with stoplights and a four-lane highway. The land-use codes have driven up prices on land so the average person cannot afford to house in Aspen. Government should not be involved in employee housing. The government puts such restrictions on land use. Transportation is a mess.

I'm glad I grew up here when I did. I wouldn't want to be growing up here now. About five hundred people were here then, and we knew everybody. We all had parties together. It's a billionaire town now. You have to be a billionaire to do anything. I don't trust them anymore. In the old days, we'd shake hands to make a deal. We didn't sign anything — we trusted people. I don't trust them anymore.

◆

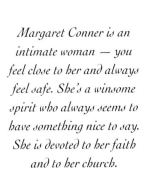

*Margaret Conner is an
intimate woman — you
feel close to her and always
feel safe. She's a winsome
spirit who always seems to
have something nice to say.
She is devoted to her faith
and to her church.*

Margaret Harrington Conner

I was born January 12, 1899, in Aspen. I grew up here and my name was Margaret A. Harrington. My mother came from Ireland when she was nineteen years old. My dad was born in Ireland and came to this country when he was an infant. He was raised in Massachusetts. Silver mining brought him to Aspen in 1887. He was in the grocery business — had a grocery store on Cooper Avenue.

*Aspen Fire Department
in 1897.
Mr. Harrington is
in the photo.
Courtesy
Warren Conner.*

The store's name was Harrington and Holland. Holland was my uncle. Dad first came to Leadville, then later by wagon to Aspen.

My mother, Abbey Harrington, came to Aspen because her aunts owned the hotel up in Wagner Park, the Clarendon. She came to work. The Clarendon was built about 1885. It was a big old thing — about 100 rooms. There are a lot of pictures of it in the historical society. Good-looking old place, too. A lot of the miners lived there. They used to have on the key rings a big star like a sheriff would wear, made out of brass. The Clarendon Hotel had that so the miners wouldn't put them in their pocket and carry them off to work. They had to turn them in at the desk after locking the room and going to work. I used to have one of those Clarendon stars. My mom and dad were married at St. Mary's Catholic Church here in 1889.

I went to school with Ann Wieben and Elizabeth Callahan. We attended St. Mary's Grade School. I went to fermer class. That's what they called it. I guess it was kindergarten then, but they called it fermer — first grade, second grade, and third grade. Then the school closed. I guess when the town went down they couldn't support a Catholic school, so I went out to the Lincoln School up to sixth grade, then to the Washington School, where I graduated from the eighth grade, and then into high school. I graduated from Aspen High School in 1918. The high school was where the red brick school is now. The west end of it was the high school. It was a beautiful building. D.R.C. Brown, Sr. donated that mansion for a school. It was different, I'll tell you, because they didn't have the inside toilets. We had to go to the toilets which were on the outside — one division for the boys and one division for the girls. And that's what I remember about school. I remember it was a pretty cold walk.

I had five brothers and four sisters. I'm the last remaining of the Patrick Harrington family. I was the second daughter and the fifth child. My family lived on Riverside. We lived in the area called the Riverside Irish — that's where they all were. There weren't any school buses then. You walked in your leggings, and I don't ever remember taking lunches — we walked home for lunch. Because of mining, we had a pretty good-sized class in grade school. I believe that the average class was in the neighborhood of forty-five.

My original home was right over on Riverside Avenue, right as you cross the Cooper bridge and go down Riverside Avenue. My dad died about 1946. He had contracted silicosis from working so long in the mines. My mom lived in that house for another year or two, and then we moved down here on Galena and Hopkins to the third house down below us in this block — the little one. Mom lived there, and that's where she died. That would have been in 1952.

We bought this house at 534 East Hopkins in 1924. We didn't buy it right off the bat, because we rented from the man that owned the old Tompkins Hardware. Andy Weber was the one that we bought the house from in 1927. I think the price then was somewhere around $550, and that was right before the stock market went haywire and my husband was working in the mine. My husband paid for our house down here — somewhere in the neighborhood of $1,000. Remember, that was in the 1940s, about the time Mr. Paepcke started doing stuff. It don't sound like much, but it was a heck of a price then when you're only making three dollars a day.

My first chores at home were washing the dishes and making my bed. After I graduated from high school, I didn't go to college. Around 1920, I worked for the Buffet at the Hotel Jerome. I guess we got about a dollar a day.

In high school, they had a women's basketball team and tennis. I guess I was a coward. I didn't go in for any of that stuff. All I did was cook. When I was growing up, my oldest sister would say, "Dad's got her rotten spoiled."

Always said I was rotten spoiled. When I got married, why Grandma Conner lived over near us, and they used to kind of spoil us. Was I rotten spoiled? I guess I was. She always said I was rotten spoiled. Maybe I am still.

After high school, there were dances at the Armory Hall — the 4th of July and all those big dances. There was always something going around, like playing cards. That was the big thing over at the Harrington house. We played cards — casino and hearts.

I married Milton Conner. I knew him for a long time — we were in school together. He was an Aspen boy and he didn't finish high school. He enlisted in the army and was in the First World War — served over in France. He came back in 1917. We were married in 1919. Milton wasn't a Catholic then, so we were married in the rectory by the priest. Now, you can be married in the church if you're not Catholic, but not then. They've changed, you know. After I graduated from high school, I worked as the desk girl at the Hotel Jerome. I answered the phone and all that stuff. I was also the bookkeeper for the Conner Chevron Station for about twenty-two years.

I was twenty years old when I married. I had four children, two boys and two girls. Warren is the oldest, Jerry's the next, then Margie Ann and Claude. Claude's my baby, and he was rotten spoiled.

4th of July, 1936, tail end of parade. Warren Conner in the tall hat. Courtesy Warren Conner.

After we were married, for social activities in Aspen, we had friends to visit with. There was the movie; it was called the Isis. There were family or church picnics, and friends and Sunday dinners. We had a lot of fun. We weren't poor; we had enough to get along. Everybody was about in the same boat, I suppose. There was a candy store down there where Ellie's is now. They used to call it Bunk's. That's where we'd hang out for an hour or two for ice cream and coffee.

The Depression, I can remember that. It was hard on a lot of people. They used to give the stamps. You'd go to the courthouse and get stamps for groceries. We never did it, but I remember some people did. The WPA came in here. They worked on the county road system. The WPA started the Willoughby jump up here on Aspen Mountain. That was one of their projects. They started the projects to cut the logs and build the first ski lodge — that was the old ski lodge up where the Caribou Condominium is. That was a WPA project.

I remember the races were all in Glenwood — the road races and all that. Down to Glenwood and Strawberry Days. That was a long time ago, too. They used to run a train special — the Strawberry Days railroad. You'd go down for Strawberry Days and come back in the night. There was the racetrack out in the Meadows. I can remember going up there to races. I remember the Tagerts; they had the horses.

Even when we had hard times, I never thought of leaving Aspen. Nope. I never, ever had any intention or any desire. I've traveled in every state in the union — Hawaii and all of them. Never found any place that I liked better.

Warren was always a pretty good boy. He worked, helped down at Mike Brand's Garage. Dad worked down there and Warren worked there, too. He did a lot of little jobs. Then he got sick. He had a bad valve in his heart, and he sat in the house for a few years. He had to take all that medicine. But he's still doing good.

All my memories here are special. It's all special. It's all good. I've had a good life, and I'm very thankful for it. I'm ninety-four years old and have good health. That's what Dr. Witcomb said to me the last time I was in. Last October he said, "Well, you must be doing something right, because you stay pretty good."

Right now, Aspen is a changed town, I'll tell you that. I don't know many people here now, very, very few. People passing by every time of the day. But it's all right. You have to go along with progress. I remember that's what Granddad Conner said once when we'd have to walk to the post office — they didn't deliver mail. He used to go every day. They lived down in that little house where the Main Street Bakery is. One day he met somebody. They invited him to go into the hotel and have a glass of beer. He come home and I think they charged twenty-five cents or something like that for a beer. It used to be a nickel or something. He was telling about it. He said, "Well, I guess we have to go along with progress." That's it. When I see all of these buildings, everything changed, well, it's all right — we have to go along with progress.

Would I change Aspen if I could? I don't know. I'm not a person to find fault with people. If they're making their living that way and they have the money and the power to do it, more power to them. That's the way I see it. I don't want to condemn anybody. Sometimes you hate to see people move in here, but you can't do anything about it.

♦

Photo by Kathy Daily

Warren Conner is the nicest man around. I just love him. I feel like I've made a friend for life.

Warren Conner

I was born July 25, 1920, right next to the courthouse in a little tiny house next to Hannibal Brown.

My father's name was Milton Conner. His father, my grandad, John, was a miner at first but then worked in the courthouse. He was county clerk and recorder for awhile. Grandad Conner came to Aspen about 1888 looking for work in the mines because there wasn't any good work elsewhere. Everything

204

*Making Independence
Pass for autos,
about 1909.
Courtesy Ruth Perry.*

in Ohio and Iowa and places like that had no employment opportunities. Grandad Conner was from Henry County, Ohio. That's where he was born, and his father before him was born there. Great-grandfather used to be county assessor in Henry County, Ohio, in 1830 or thereabouts. Before that they came from Hagerstown, Maryland, and before that, Ireland. Some of those relatives served with General Washington in the Irish Battalion back in the Revolutionary War. I don't know just exactly the dates that they left, but they came from Ireland about the time the Revolutionary War was about to start.

Anyway, they settled in Hagerstown and then they went into Henry County, Ohio. He decided he didn't like it, and so they moved from there to Mount Pleasant, Iowa. They were there for awhile, and that's where he met my grandmother, Phoebe Olinger. Her family had come from Maryland and moved into Iowa. They were married in Iowa. They heard about all of the good silver strikes in Colorado and arrived in 1887.

Independence Pass,
about 1910.
Courtesy Ruth Perry.

Granddad, Patrick Harrington, came in a wagon from Leadville in 1888. He met Alex Brown on the road to Aspen coming over the pass. He got here and went right to work. Grandma Harrington, Abbie Leahy, was already here when granddad came and they met each other. Although they both came from the same part of Ireland, their families never knew one another. That's kind of the early history of the Milton Conner family.

Grandfather Conner came to Aspen before the water lines were in. They lived on Main Street and used to have to buy water from the water wagon, so it must have been 1885 or 1886. Granddad Harrington came probably a couple of years later. I know Grandma Conner used to tell me that they'd have to buy water from the water wagon every morning. It would go out on Main Street. They lived right across from the Mountain Rescue cabin. Right across the street on the corner is where some of the Conner kids were born. That's where my dad was born. They also remembered the old horse-drawn streetcars —

hooking a ride downtown, getting on for a nickel, getting off at Tompkins Hardware or one of those places like that. It was Main Street. I know it was sort of a general loop in town someplace, then it would go back on Main Street.

My granddad, John Milton Conner, was the court bailiff, undersheriff, jailor, and custodian of the courthouse for almost twenty-nine years, from about 1915 to 1934 when Hod Nicholson became sheriff. When I was growing up, hell, I was down in the bottom of the courthouse as much as I was over here at the house. He did everything. He took care of the prisoners. Grandma cooked for them — that was back in the bootleg time and stuff like that. There were many confiscated stills stored as evidence.

I can remember dragging the stills in from some of the places where they'd have a raid. Those beautiful things would come in and the revenue officer would be there inventorying everything. The law confiscated them. If I'd had any brains, I would have got some of the copper from the condensers or whatever they were, but I never did. I should have, I guess, because there were three or four lying around.

Granddad had to keep track of all of the prisoners. Not that there were a lot of them at any one time, but since they were right in the courthouse — right

Bootleg from Leadville, 1926. From left to right: revenue officer and son in front, Earl McPhee, Kenneth Hanson, a Ms. Roughbar, Charlie Wagner, Mary Mellor, Dr. McKee, Frank Bruin, Amos Bourquin, and John Milton Conner. Courtesy Warren Conner.

in the bottom of the darn place — he'd have to listen to all of their problems. Just before that, he was county clerk and recorder for four years, 1908 to 1912. There was always a lot of connections with the courthouse in my family. That's why I started to work there back when I was pretty young. I always pretty much knew where all the loose bricks were, if there were any. I worked in every office in the courthouse from 1946 to 1990.

Mother's two brothers, John Harrington and Bill Harrington, had a dance band here in Aspen called the Roamer's Rhythm Kings. They used to play for all the dances. We were always connected with a lot of music. They played at the Armory Hall. They also used to go over to Redstone and play a couple of times in the summer. They'd go over the pass to Twin Lakes to the pavilion on the other side of the lake and play and maybe take a trip to Glenwood and play for a summer dance down there. They always had a lot of music going.

I learned to play the clarinet at an early age from Uncle John. We were all in the Elk's band and had about twenty-two members. We used to play concerts all over. I started playing in the Elk's band when I was about fifteen. We'd go over to Buena Vista to Lettuce Day celebrations, go to Glenwood for Strawberry Days, and I think we may have gone to one Carbondale Potato Day celebration. We gave concerts in the old bandstand most every Thursday night in the summertime. We had to practice hard. We never got a dollar for it. It was just for fun. Used to wear those old green uniforms that had the tight necks on them. I played in a high-school orchestra, too. There aren't very many people left that were in any of the old bands. Louis Zupancis and I played in the Elk's band together. Louis played saxophone; he sat right behind me. He blew the tenor sax. We used to go tromping up to those practices on the third floor of the Elks building.

After my mom and dad were married in 1919, Dad started to work. They were improving Independence Pass. That's one of the first jobs he had. He worked with Mona Frost's husband Paul (Frosty) and Mr. Frost. They lived up in the town of Independence in what they call Lincoln's cabin. Dad told me that the mountain lions were thick up there at that time. He said they couldn't leave anything out. They had to bring their damn stuff in at night or the lions would come by and get up on their haunches and tear the stuff off of the trees or the clotheslines — wherever they'd have it stashed. In those days, I don't think they had deer season like they do now, so you could kill a deer the first part of September. The nights would be cool enough so you'd leave it out, but the cougar'd come along and get it. Dad worked up there six or seven years.

After that, my father went to work in the Durant and Veteran mines. When I was growing up, I used to go in and carry samples down to the assay

Hyman Avenue fire,
1941.
Courtesy Warren Conner.

office for him. He worked with some interesting people. He also worked on the county road system for awhile with some interesting people. I think he more or less leased in all the Aspen mines. Leasing was a hell of a job. It was almost worse, because you got it all. You had to pay the company that owned the mine a large percent of the value of the ore, you had to ship the powder, and had to pay for the air to run the jackhammers — everything. So it was almost harder than working for pay. Mighty poor pay, too. They worked for what they could make. And they didn't make an awful lot — enough for us to get by in the manner of the day. Dad was elected to the school board in 1936 and served for twenty years.

Before Dad had the station, he had a bulk gasoline distributorship. He took fuel oil and gas to every ranch in Woody Creek, Old Snowmass, and Capitol. So that was a billing task that Mom had to keep with. The gasoline used to come in on the railroad car, and they'd unload it down by the Rio Grande park. Then there was a bunch of huge tanks from which to fill the truck up. We'd go up to Natal's Ranch, Vagneur's, or out to Light's Ranch on Sopris Creek. In town here, when a lot of the lodges started up, they all had fuel oil because that was the rage before natural-gas lines were installed. They were getting away from coal so they wouldn't be mucking coal in during the cold time of the year.

I started school in Lincoln School and then I went to Washington School. Lincoln School had stoves in the classroom. We had to carry wood in to help the teachers. Maybe it was for demerits. I don't remember, but I do remember the wood and coal detail. When we got to Washington School, it had central heating. I thought that was pretty good because the punishment there was walking up the stairs from the bottom. They'd assign you one hundred times from the bottom to the top because you laughed or hit somebody in line. God, those old teachers — they were rascals for sure. They wanted you to mind every minute. So you got plenty of trips up the stairs. Mona Frost's dad was the janitor at the Washington School, and I can remember him looking and laughing because he knew that I was a Conner. He had been a miner with my Granddad Conner up in the Bonny Belle Mine and some more of the mines up in Tourtelotte Park. He would always be laughing at me and shaking his finger. If they caught the kids smoking in the toilet or something, the teachers were really strict. They met you with a damn great big razor strap and beat the hell out of you. You'd have to lean over one of the tables and they'd whack you on the behind or right up on the back of your back. They'd never draw blood or anything like that, but you sure as hell knew you got a good whacking. You'd better shut up and keep in line.

They had an NYA project along about that time, and I was old enough to get in on it. That was National Youth Administration. I remember the bosses and how you'd have to make your slips out to get paid. We could only make fifteen dollars a month. I think we had to work seven days to make the fifteen dollars. The CCC was here also. They had a camp on Woody Creek and another camp over on the Frying Pan.

We used to have our track meets out at the meadows back in grade school. You could run the mile around the track, the quarter, the half, or the hundred-yard dash. I remember going out there and racing. I think that was the last thing that ever happened there. Because probably around 1934 or so, they tore the grandstand down.

I noticed a change in Aspen when I was asked to come to work in the treasurer's office. They assigned me to the vault in the basement of the courthouse to look for tax-sale certificates of purchase for Walter Paepcke. Boy, it was dirty down there. My salary was twenty-five cents an hour. That was about 1946.

✦✦✦✦✦✦✦✦✦✦✦✦✦✦✦✦✦

As far as Aspen today, one of my heartfelt wishes would be for people who live and work here to be able to afford to live here and not go banging down the highway to go home. Another wish would be to have people slow down and watch for others in the crosswalks. People are always in such a hurry nowadays. Also, Aspen should either have a leash law that they enforce or let them all run free. Why not?

✦

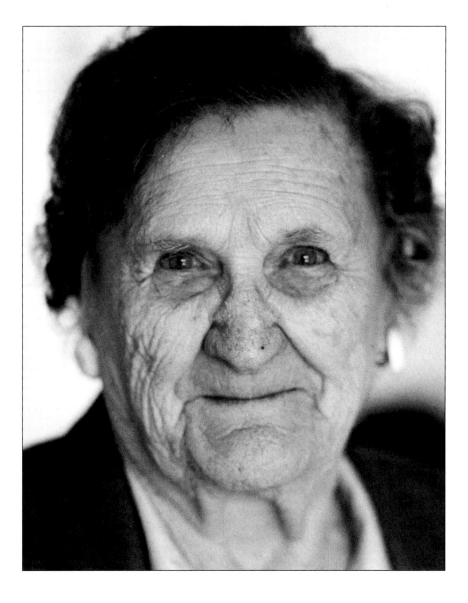

*Jennie Cowling is
easygoing and takes it
a day at a time.
She's very kind.*

Jennie Miklich Cowling

I was born on September 17, 1907, in Aspen. In the early days they didn't go to
the hospital. I was born at home. My parents came from Yugoslavia. My father,
John Miklich, was a miner. I don't know how my mother came here. Her name
was Johanna Erchul. She had three or four brothers in Minnesota, and all my
cousins were up there. My parents met in Aspen, I think, but I don't know
much about that history. I was born in 1907, so I think they came to Aspen

sometime before 1905. I was the first child — there were three kids in our family. One died at birth. My brother died a couple of years ago. My mother worked at the boardinghouse; I think that's where she met Dad. I don't know anything about it, because my mother died when I was just sixteen and I never thought to ask my dad anything. Mother died of a burst tumor. Dad raised we two children on his own. He taught me how to cook. And he made me go to school. I went to the Aspen school there on Bleeker. That's my high school. I graduated from Aspen High School and went to school, all grades, in Aspen.

Our ranch was up in White Horse Springs. The white ranch house and red barn are still there. Tom Moore lives there now. On the ranch we raised chickens and hogs, and we grew potatoes — a lot of potatoes. Then we had pickers pick them because potatoes were a good price and they kept pretty good. Dad died of that miner's disease, black lung — emphysema from the mines. He died in 1947. I was forty years old.

It was a nice ranch. Later on, Chris Karde owned it and my husband worked for him. Chris got killed under a tree there by lightning. Then my husband, Earl, took over for Karde's sister, Dorothy Lippert. We bought the ranch from the Lipperts in the early 1940s. We had some land under on a bench where we put our cattle in the spring before they went on the range. I wasn't a cowgirl. I didn't even milk cows. We sold milk and cream. What was my job on the ranch? Everything. We ran the ranch until the 1980s, when we sold it to Moore.

For fun when I was little, I loved to fish. I fished up Roaring Fork, not too much at Woody Creek. I walked. Everybody walked in the early days. The only car — I remember Judge Shaw had one. He had a big red one.

The big red barn was ours. Our big, white house was ordered from Sears, Roebuck. I don't know how they did it — I guess it came in parts. It was all up when we moved in.

If you talk to Art Trentaz, they lived right up above us, and I knew him when he was a little kid in Aspen. When they lived out there, our families were great friends. Every weekend we'd play cards at one place or the other — poker. Is Arthur a good poker player? I guess he is. And mean, too, in the meantime. Penny ante. I don't think the maximum was very much — maybe ten, fifteen cents. You know we were lucky to get a penny.

My dad had a still. My son, Richard, has it now, but he doesn't make any. He doesn't even drink, but he has a still. First he made wine. I remember with my bare feet I used to stomp those damn grapes. My feet would be purple. They got the wine, and I don't know how they did the rest of it. They distilled it some

*Jennie Cowling and
Mary Stallard,
early 1920s.
Courtesy Helen Kralich.*

way and made whiskey. My folks made good wine. In the early days, I think almost everybody from the old country did.

We made cheeses, sausages, things like that. We used to butcher hogs, and then we'd have the whole gang come, neighbors and all, and they'd cut up the pork and make meat sausage. They made those and we hung them out in a little shed we had and we'd smoke them. We made blood sausage. Cooked a lot of rice and mixed it with the blood and spices and then cooked that. We had sausage fillers; somehow they filled them in the intestines. You bought those and cleaned them, too. They were good.

When we were young, Mary Stallard and I used to play on the paddy cars — those little cars that the train used to move their cars and stuff. They weren't too big — about half as big as my kitchen. They were kind of like flatbeds on the railroad. We'd go up to the tunnel and we'd steal it. They were on the railroad tracks. And we went across that big trestle by Mike Garrish's house. One day, Chuck Hannon was down at the other end, and the train was coming. The depot was down below that big trestle in the early days. It wasn't where it is now. We took that paddy car, and we saw the train coming. We knew we couldn't make it, so we got Chuck Hannon to push the paddy car off the tracks.

They used to have parties up at Stillwater. The Mautz family owned the property. We'd go up there and they'd have accordion music. Martin Mishmash, the father, usually played. And then Pete Vidmar used to come from Leadville, I think, and played. This is when they had the outdoor pavilion. I was a kid then, before 1920. We had a clog dance. I don't know what they called it. It was beautiful. And the polkas were a good dance. Dances ran sometimes until morning. Depends on how they felt. There were fights all the time. I guess they got too much to drink and they'd start. Any little thing would upset them.

I taught school at Snowmass and Aspen. After that I met my husband, Earl Cowling, in southeast Colorado. We got married in New Mexico in 1932 and returned to Aspen that year. We had three children, Larry, Joann, and Richard.

Earl was born May 13, 1904, in Indian Territory. He was the son of George Cowling and Harriet Boren Cowling of Texas. His family moved around Indian Territory and the Texas Panhandle, finally ending up at Vilagreen, Colorado, in 1916.

There was a brewery in Aspen. I think that's where Hilder Anderson's relatives had a brewery, but somebody must have bought it from them. They had those five-pound buckets and so we went down one day to get our parents some beer at the brewery. Every night when they came home we had to have the beer there for them. So we went down and it was cold as could be. They had a hitching post — pipes out there for people to tie horses on — so we stuck our tongues on that. Boy, did we stick. We pulled and pulled until we got all bloody. We were all bloody. Our tongues almost came out. We couldn't scream for help with our tongues stuck. We were just kids. I wouldn't do that now.

In the early days, Dad was working in Park City, Utah, and he'd send the money home to my mother. We didn't take it to the bank. We wadded it up in a handkerchief and put it under the pillow. When my mother got sick, they took her to the hospital and Mary Stallard and I took everything — the money and everything — and burned it up. We didn't know the money was there. We burned the mattress because of germs. And the money burned up. In those days, oftentimes the husband was working someplace else.

I was talking to a lady in Leadville. Leadville must have a hundred people over eighty. She said, "How can we worry about all this lead and stuff when everybody we know is eighty years old." All of those people that used to live in Aspen, if they didn't die from miner's consumption, they lived way old. It might have been stuff like sauerkraut. You grew it and you ate it. It might be the stuff they ate, but they ate a lot of fat stuff, too. Lots of cream and lots of wine. The women did everything. The women did the garden, too, usually. They did their own garden if they lived alone. They were tough.

Farmers at that time raised potatoes, wheat, oats, hay, and cattle. A few had sheep. Some of the busiest times on the farm, aside from regular plowing, irrigating, and maintenance, were threshing time, potato picking time, taking the cattle to range, and sorting potatoes.

When the grain became ripe in the fall, it was cut with a binder (first pulled by horses, later pulled by tractor). The grain was then shucked, usually by family members. When it was time for threshing (the shucks were dry), the farmers would decide in what order (by farm) the grain would be threshed. Some people had their own thresher, but most relied on a thresher that went from farm to farm. When the day for threshing had come, the farmers had all arranged to trade services — going from farm to farm until completion. Benny Smith would arrive with his threshing machine and iron-wheeled tractor. Everyone would bring their wagons and pitchforks and the work began.

The two best jobs were loading the wagons and pitching the bales onto the wagon. The worst job, because it was so dusty, was sacking the grain as it was separated from the straw.

The women of these farms also went from farm to farm to cook for the threshers, sometimes as many as twenty-five. That was hard work, considering some of the farms didn't have electricity. Most farmers had large tables, but when they were filled, threshers ate wherever they could find a place to sit. The women and nonworking children ate after workers returned to field. This process continued until all the farms had finished threshing.

After the first hard frost and the potato tops had dried, it was potato-picking time. School was suspended for a week so the students could work at picking potatoes.

Potatoes were dug with a potato digger — a machine pulled by horses or tractor which plowed the potatoes out of the ground and ran them through a series of shakings to separate the old greenery and the potatoes. When the potatoes fell out the back, they were picked and put in sacks.

Each farmer had a potato cellar — a partial underground dugout with a heavy dirt roof. This kept the potaoes until farmers thought prices were good. Potatoes were sorted and sacked in hundred-pound sacks. When a farmer (or several farmers) got enough to fill a freight car, they were sold and shipped.

A man from Silt named Vallet was the usual agent. The cars we loaded were usually parked on the railroad line near the Albert Duroux place.

Most people didn't have many cattle but usually grazed them on public land in summer. Several people used the same range. When grass was good on the range, farmers combined their cattle into a group and drove them to range — Snowmass, Lenado, whatever range was designated. In those days, cattle and sheep were driven right down the only real paved street in town.

In the fall, the cattle were rounded up and returned to home farm. Those to be sold were (at appointed time) shipped by train to Denver. When cattle were combined from more than one ranch farm, a person was designated to ride the train with them to Denver. They rode in the caboose. Their job was to keep track of the cattle and sell them at the stockyards. Nino Trentaz often went with Cowlings' cattle.

Haying was a summer-long process from July 4 to snow. Most early hayings involved piling the hay into stacks. These stacks had to be carefully fenced to keep deer out in winter. When automatic balers became popular, most people baled their hay.

It was not unusual for women to participate in the farmwork. Some irrigated, some mowed hay, some stacked hay, etc. There are at least two women living today who handled 100-pound sacks of potatoes. Those who didn't work in the fields milked the cows, tended the gardens, and cooked for the rest.

✦

*John Dolinsek
was a man of few words
when I first met him.
But I was surprised
after a little while.
John started telling
great stories.*

John and Frank Dolinsek

John:

I was born August 26, 1925, and Frank was born August 31, 1923. Mother, Nellie Plasic Dolinsek, is ninety years old now. She was born and raised here also. She was born in about 1901 at the bottom of Roam Hill, down there by Herron Park and No Problem Bridge. There were twelve children in our mother's family. Six died in the flu epidemic of 1918. Her dad was a miner. He owned

Frank Dolinsek really told a life story. Both Frank and John worked for the Ski Company for a long time and didn't get a lot of credit. When I see Frank walking to the post office, I love to stop and say hi.

Photo by Kathy Daily

Mehle's Saloon. There was a boardinghouse above. The saloon was where Les Chefs store is now, across the street from Boogie's. Our mom, as a little girl, helped out in the boardinghouse. Our dad, Frank Dolinsek, Sr., was born about 1890. In 1913, he came over here from Yugoslavia. Our parents got married about 1918. Mom was about sixteen years old. She had five children. I'm the baby and Frank is the third born.

Our family lived on this property [619 South Monarch] and raised vegetables, hogs, and one cow. No need for a horse. We walked to school. Grade school was the Washington School, in back of the security building [used to be Mesa

Store]. The high school was down on the corner where the red brick school is now. When they rebuilt that, they used brick and whatever material they could salvage out of the grade school [the old Washington School] and the old high school to build it. The old high school was an old house of D.R.C. Brown. One Halloween, some of the bigger kids hoisted a wagon up on top of the roof of Washington School. They probably disassembled it and pulled it up piece by piece and then put it back together again.

The only dances were held on Saturday night. They used to be at the Armory Hall — City Hall now — we'd go and watch. Like all boys, it was too much trouble to go dance. We used to watch the people get drunk and sometimes fight. Blaine Bray used to have a dance hall up where we call Stillwater. Blaine tore the dance hall down way back, 1935 or 1936. He then built his fishing cabins.

Frank:

I did ski. We tied boards on our feet and went for it. We would slide off a pile of snow from the shed roof. There were some cow paths up on Aspen Mountain that we would follow. It's surprising, even after they cut Roch Run, there weren't any accidents. For bindings, we had a toe strap from an old innertube, and we'd slip it over the heel. We used to ski on this side of Aspen Mountain, and the East Enders used to ski over on Smuggler Mountain on the old mine roads.

Our first chore around here was chopping wood. We skied wood down from the hill, sawed, and chopped it. Took care of the livestock. We'd let the grass grow long; we didn't mow it. We would dry it for feed instead of buying hay. We also worked for Albert Bishop at the garage. We were janitors. On weekends, we would go down and work on cars or something — washed and waxed them. The average kid's salary at that time was about ten cents an hour. So a whole day's work was like a dollar. We sawed wood for Mrs. Bowman. The younger people watched out for the older people, too, at that time. It was a donation thing about every two weeks.

Were we good skiers? Oh I don't know, we could hold our own. Never competed — not officially. They started a skiing team with the ski club, but the school never did have a team. Nobody had the means to go anywhere. The only place you could compete would be here. The main race they had was on Roch Run once a year. They used to ski, the last run usually on Sunday or Saturday as a challenge race. They would challenge somebody to a race off the hill and race to the Hotel Jerome. They would just keep skiing right across town. Usually their skis and equipment was scattered from the Hotel Jerome all the way on up, but the first one to get to the hotel didn't have to buy — everybody else had

Roch Run, Mill Street,
1937.
Gebhardt Collection.
Courtesy Aspen
Historical Society.

to buy. Laurence Elisha, the owner, was also the chaperone, because he could watch and make sure the kids sat on their side of the bar and ice-cream parlor. The bar was on one side of the main lobby, and there was a place for the kids to gather. So kids were more or less chaperoned.

The class of skier changed probably in the 1960s. They went from the rugged macho skier to the destination resort skier: "I have to have my trail groomed like a billiard table." And that costs. Then they come into the syndrome of, "Let's sue them. I can be going down a hill looking backwards, hit a tree, and I'll sue." And that costs. So somebody has to pay. Even with all the stuff, as far as I'm concerned, with a daily ticket, you get your money's worth. I can remember when I skied. On my day off, I really wanted to go out and go gung-ho. That was when we just had Number One Lift to take you up the hill and Number Two. It was nothing to make four or five runs. So you figure at that kind of price, making a run was pretty darn cheap for awhile. And now

*Old Roch Cup Trail,
Aspen Mountain,
with the old jail
on the left,
late 1930s.
Courtesy
Robert Zupancis.*

with the high-speed gondola, I imagine a guy could make at least ten or twenty runs. When we skied Spar Gulch, if you missed and got off on the wrong spot, you wound up in the rocks. Later they filled all that in with trash and bulldozed the dirt clear from Tourtelotte all the way down.

Between the dam and Tourtelotte, where Number Six is now, on down to the junction, they called it Grand Junction. We filled all that in with dirt, old stumps, cable, and a lot of the old cable cars that were hauling ore from the mines — tram cars, ore cars. A lot of the old towers that fell over and were rotting, all went down under to make that nice big bowl. When we went in to clear, we'd run across these old cabins that had old newspapers. We'd use that old newspaper and pile all the old wood on top and around it to burn the trail cuttings. We used to stack it, and then when the snow came, we'd burn the piles. We used to pop old bottles with a rock — dishes and all that kind of stuff. They left everything in their cabins up there. The same in town here.

222

A lot of people figured they were going to come back to Aspen some day. They left the houses just as they were living in them — curtains on the windows and beds made up. The windows were broken and the doors were open when I was growing up. But you would walk into a house and you would find all the original stuff there.

We both worked for the Ski Corporation. John worked off and on for about eight years; he was trail boss on all the mountains. I worked for the Ski Corporation, too. I was maintenance man, and when Red Rowland wasn't around, I was assistant boss. Then I worked for the City of Aspen in the Street Department until I retired two years ago.

Ninety percent of Aspen's history was hauled out in trucks to the Maroon Creek dump where Iselin Park is now. I imagine if you went down by the river, you could still find some tin cans that were pushed into Maroon Creek. Later they brought dirt in and covered it. Then they moved the dump to where it is

223

now. When they went in these old buildings to renovate, the people they hired didn't care. They went in and took everything out, and it went to the dump.

The Park Tunnel tram had buckets that were a good size. On each side the round things came out — the part that hung from the cable came down and had a hook. The knob would fit in this hook. On the hook arm there was a catch, so when it came down they tripped a lever and it would release from the traveling cable. It would go off just exactly like the gondola. The modern engineers copied the old-timers.

We played around the mine shafts when we were little, but our parents took a weekend and stuck with us and told us what we could and couldn't do. And you learned. We never went down in the shaft; we would crawl on our bellies to look over the edge. A lot of those shafts were open right to the very surface, and the surface would cave in. It was dangerous.

Wish something for Aspen now? Where would we have stopped it? The later part of the 1950s. The town was not too big or too small. In other words, people here say, "Well, if you was smart you would have bought all this land, and this and that." If we owned all the land, nobody could even come in, so where would we be then? Right back fighting the free war. Of course, nobody had any money. Nobody had money to buy. Who would have known? People bought these old houses and then would fix up their homes. They bought those old houses that was up for taxes and tore them down to save the lumber. What they couldn't save, they burned for firewood. And then they let the lots go back for taxes.

What do we think about Aspen politics now? Politics is politics. It started way back when politics first originated. I think if you had recordings of the old-timers doing their bitching about politics, I'm sure it was the same kind of bull as right today. The only thing was, a lot of it back in the good old days, you could settle with a forty-five.

♦

Photo by Kathy Daily

Uno is a modest,
quiet man.
He says what he feels.
He seems content
and relaxed.
He is easy and fun
to talk to.

Uno Elder

I was born in Aspen on September 12, 1916. My father came to this country in 1901. In 1906 or 1907, my father, John J. Elder, came to Aspen because two of his brothers were already here. He operated the jig tables in the silver-concentrating mill. The jig table jiggled the fine crushed ore. It had ridges in it — the different weights of the metals ran off and separated the gold, silver, and lead.

225

Sullivan's Pond,
July 4, 1936.
Martin Mishmash on the
diving board; Mautz
house in the background.
Courtesy Ed Gregorich.

Water ran through the ore and then ran over the top of it. The mill was back of our house and up the river.

My mother's maiden name was Ingrid Oberg. My parents were friends in Sweden, but they didn't come to the United States married. Dad came to the United States first and then went back to Sweden and got her in 1907. They married in Denver in May 1907. My Uncle Swan was a miner in Aspen. Later on he got consumption and had to quit the mines. Uncle Swan went down to Greeley — flatlands and dry. Uncle Ben worked in a biscuit factory in Aspen in 1910 and was probably a miner early on. Ben's wife was the widow of Ben's brother, Nick, who was killed in a mine accident.

There were four kids in our immediate family. I was the last born. My brothers and sisters were Svea Fredrica, John Bernard, Nels Reinhard was next, and I was the last.

We moved uptown from Oklahoma Flats to our present house — the blue house right back of the Hotel Jerome — when I was real little. It wasn't blue then. When I was in high school, I worked in the hotel, taking care of the pool room on Saturdays and Sundays. I swept and mopped up, brushed the tables, and collected the money from the players.

As children we played cops and robbers down on the trestle — Indians and cowboys. We swam in the old Salvation Ditch up there, at the ice pond, and at Sullys. After my sister Svea got married to Laurence Elisha, I worked for Laurence a lot as a bartender and soda fountain man in the Buffet.

✦✦✦✦✦✦✦✦✦✦✦✦✦✦✦✦✦✦✦

One day a week my shift was from seven o'clock in the morning until noon. Then it was from three 'til six, three days a week. The other shift was from noon until three o'clock and then six until closing time. We had no set closing time — anywhere from ten-thirty until midnight.

Aspen now? I can't stand it. I miss knowing everybody — seeing everybody. I don't know a person here. Maybe I know five people. Aspen is a modern development. The little town I live in in New York is years behind Aspen. We're still going at a slow pace. All my life here, up until the time I left, Aspen was just a little town of 500 people, maybe only 250 people at times — very quiet, sleepy town. Everybody knew everybody, and everybody had a good time. I left here in 1940 before the big boom. At that time I was enjoying the change because the skiers were coming in, and there were more people.

✦

Photo by Kathy Daily

Don Elisha and Ingrid Elisha Stuebner

 I was born in Aspen, Colorado, on November 24, 1928, at the Aspen Hospital over on Smuggler Mountain. My grandfather came to Aspen prior to 1900. His name was Mansor S. Elisha (1872–1935). His naturalization papers renounced allegiance to the Sultan of Turkey, but he came from Beirut. It was apparently under Turkish domination then. That particular area has changed nationalities

Left:
Ingrid Elisha Stuebner.
When I met her,
I felt that I had
known Ingrid before.
She is a truthful being.

Photo by Kathy Daily

Below:
The Elisha family,
about 1910.
Ella, LuLu, Lila,
Mansor, and Laurence.
Courtesy Ingrid Elisha.

Mansor Elisha
(1872 – 1955)
Courtesy Ingrid Elisha.

many many times. It's been Syrian, Lebanese, and Turkish. Mansor was naturalized in Aspen on March 17, 1894.

He came to Aspen, and one of his first jobs in Colorado was selling newspapers. I don't know just what year he got to Aspen. I don't know why he came. I think that he was first either in New York or in New Orleans. I've heard two or three different stories. He arrived in New Orleans in 1888. He probably came because of the silver. He came here a single man and met my grandmother here. My grandmother's name was Lulu (1884-1945). Lulu was the eldest daughter of Michael J. and Lenora (Buffehr) Healy. They had a dairy in Aspen in the early part of the century up until Mike's death in 1925. (Georgia Healy Bishop is the mother of Albert Bishop). The Healy family was related to the Buffehr family. The Buffehr family is very significant in the Minturn/Vail area. John and Georgia Healy were twins and they were my grandmother's brother and sister. My grandparents had three children, Ella, Lila, and my father, Laurence (1907-1961).

Dorothy Portner (daughter of Lila Elisha Portner) wrote a book on *Lulu Nell (Healy) Elisha*, and in that book, she mentions that the Elishas enjoyed many social activities with their neighbors, the Everetts. In 1909, Mansor and Everett also undertook a business relationship. In addition to his bus, baggage, and transfer business, Everett was serving one of his three terms as sheriff of Pitkin County, and in that capacity he became involved in the Hotel Jerome's financial affairs. Jerome B. Wheeler, the owner of the Hotel Jerome, was bankrupt and unable to keep his hotel operating. Thus, to keep the hotel open, he entered into an unusual agreement on October 6, 1909, involving Irving Everett, sheriff of Pitkin County (and representing the Board of County Commissioners), Charles Kane, member of the city council (and representing the council), Mansor Elisha, and Mrs. M. B. Brown. He agreed to lease the Hotel Jerome, free of all rent for two years, to Mrs. M. B. Brown, who was to supply, at her own expense, fixtures, furniture, and bedding that might be needed. Mansor Elisha agreed to rent the Hotel Jerome's amenities (the bar, billiard, and card rooms) for $100 per month but free of all liquor-license fees for a two-year period. He was to provide the necessary fixtures and supplies at his own expense. Charles Kane, on behalf of the city council, agreed to remit the fifty-dollar-per-month liquor-license fee for the Hotel Jerome bar for two years. Irving Everett agreed to collect the $100-per-month rental fee from Mansor Elisha and expend the same in payment of the hotel's water and electric bills and use any balance for repairs to the hotel.

With this agreement, the luxurious Hotel Jerome, which was considered an asset to Aspen, was allowed to continue operating for another two years. It also offered

Laurence and Mansor Elisha, about 1918. Courtesy Ingrid Elisha.

Wheeler hope that his financial welfare would improve during the two-year period. For Mansor, it meant a livelihood to provide for his family. He bought the Jerome Hotel for back taxes in 1911.

On August 28, 1918, the pandemic entered Boston via a sailor on a transport ship. It killed 15,000 civilians in four months. The transfer of the sailors on

*Laurence Elisha
(1907 – 1961)
Courtesy Ingrid Elisha.*

the Boston transport ship to Michigan and Illinois became the nucleus for the spread of influenza in the Midwest. In September/October, one out of five soldiers stationed in the United States was stricken with the illness. It spread rapidly in the civilian population for one to two weeks. Then high morbidity and mortality prevailed for two to three weeks, whereafter the epidemic rapidly subsided.

The pandemic influenza hit Aspen in October. After a twenty-four- to forty-eight-hour incubation period, morbidity was first noted in school children, then in young adults, and finally in older adults.

The Aspen hotel was filled to capacity with patients ill with the flu. Parlors A and B, the largest guest rooms in the Hotel Jerome, also became hospital wards to care for some flu patients. Both of Lulu's daughters, Lila (fifteen years old) and Ella (thirteen years old), and her sister, Georgia (twenty-six years old), and her father, Mike Healy (sixty-one years old), were stricken. Nursing duties, in addition to cooking three meals a day for hotel guests, became part of Lulu's daily routine.

Lila and Georgia had severe symptoms: high fever, sore throat, nonproductive cough, headache, malaise. The remedy prescribed was bed rest, fluids, aspirin, mouth washes, warm baths, and a heating pad.

Ella's flu symptoms were so slight that she was not bedridden. She sat by the window, writing a letter to her Uncle Martin overseas and talking to Lila, who wanted to know who was in the hearse that went up Main Street each day.

Then simultaneously both girls became very sick. Ella caught bacterial pneumonia and died Friday, October 25, 1918, at 5:35 A.M. Ella's death occurred at the height of the epidemic in Aspen. The day she died the newspaper reported five deaths and four funerals. Lila was moved to a side room the day of her sister's funeral so she would not see the hearse procession.

JEROME HOTEL AT ASPEN, COLO.

Hotel Jerome, 1930s.
Courtesy Helen Zordel.

Lila, who also was given the sacrament, Extreme Unction, was not informed of her sister's death for fear that the news would be too shocking to her weakened system. It was a very difficult time for Lulu and Mansor to ignore Lila's inquiries about Ella as they tried to comfort her.

Years before, in September, Mansor gave up the agency of the *Rocky Mountain News* to devote all his efforts to the proprietorship of the Hotel Jerome. He was a courageous and bold man to venture into the hotel business without any sustaining funds. Under such circumstances, most business enterprises will become bankrupt within a year. However, Mansor and Lulu were able to successfully manage their hotel enterprise because they both were resourceful, well-organized persons and were able to raise the necessary sustaining funds through chattel mortgage loans. On August 9, 1912, they raised $400 by mortgaging all their personal property in their new house which they were to pay back in eight monthly installments at an interest rate of 1½ percent per month. On June 24, 1913, they obtained another $400 by mortgaging the Hotel Jerome property.

The lengths to which people had to go in the Quiet Years are fascinating. They had to mortgage everything down to the teaspoons.

*Svea Elisha, about 1946.
Courtesy Ingrid Elisha.*

My grandparents on my mother's side came over from Sweden. My grandfather, John Elder, came first in 1901. You're going to find some discrepancies in the things that I'm telling you because both grandparents changed their names. My mother's name was Svea Elder (1908-1979). Her parents came to Aspen in 1901 and 1907. I think they came because there was a significant group of inhabitants in the Swedish village, Oklahoma Flats. I'm not sure there were any relatives here, but there were relatives elsewhere in Colorado, and why they came to Aspen, I don't know.

My parents went to Aspen High School together. My dad grew up in the hotel. Svea was the girl next door. I grew up there, too. We did not have a usual childhood, growing up in a hotel. We lived up in one of the rooms. My mother and father had two rooms, #19 and #20, and I had the room next to them. The other room next to them was Grandfather Mansor's room, and the room next to it was Grandmother Lulu's. The corner room was her livingroom. We had the whole back side of the first floor of the Jerome Hotel. All meals were consumed in the dining room or at a table in the kitchen. We're talking about the early 1940s. Skiing started about 1935. I carried Lowell Thomas's skis to his room in 1935 or 1936. That was a thrill for me. I skied with him, as a matter of fact.

We always had to service what was then called the Buffet Room. We had to make sure that there was plenty of ice and enough of the items that were necessary to run the fountain. We also carted a little beer in for the beer taps. My brother (Lowell) and I janitored every morning before school. We had to sweep and mop out the Buffet Room and get it ready for opening that day. In our family, there was my older brother Lowell, myself, and then a long time later came M.J. and Ingrid.

My memory of my Grandfather Mansor is very limited. I'm particularly fond of a birthday — it was probably his last birthday. He was sitting at the family table at the Jerome and I handed him a box of cigars — he

Svea and Laurence Elisha, about 1946. Bud Shehan in window. Courtesy Ingrid Elisha.

loved his cigars — and the center cigar was a fake cigar, and I kept nudging him to take it. Grandpa knew that he was being tricked because it was so obvious. One looked like a licorice cigar. But he was playing the part. My wonderful grandpa reached down and grabbed the cigar and somehow switched it. He lit it and I kept waiting for the thing to explode. I can remember that.

The Buffet, about 1932.
Laurence Elisha
and Clarence "Kance"
Johnson.
Courtesy Ingrid Elisha.

All of the people who lived in Aspen hung out at the hotel — Sardys, Popishes, Atchisons. Everyone came to the Jerome Hotel either for a shot and a beer or for Sunday dinner. Sunday dinner was served in the dining room and we had music — Sis Ritchie played the violin and Mona Frost played the piano. We had tea music during the meal hour. Prime-rib dinner was, I think, sixty-five cents. My Grandmother Lulu was the cook and we had local people that were our wait staff. Everyone pitched in and helped. I think half the people in Aspen must have worked at the hotel at some time. When they cleared out my mother's house and the carriage house/barn, we found all the canceled checks from thirty-five years of the hotel, and there were so many names of people who had worked there!

I think all my old memories were great. I had a wonderful childhood. I had lots of friends. I grew up with a great group of people, and the Jerome was something that was significant to me. I enjoyed it. That's why I stayed in the business. I'm retired now.

236

I noticed Aspen changing after the chairlift was built and after the Aspen Company moved in. Everyone kept saying, "Wow, when is the bubble going to break?" The Aspen Company leased the Hotel Jerome from my father and he was retained as maintenance manager. The hotel just changed overnight to a sophisticated hotel operation. Prior to the Aspen Company moving in, the only way my parents were able to survive was to maintain a residential-type hotel. There were so very few transient people coming to Aspen. There was no reason for them to come. The residents paid by the month and that included meals. We had the man who ran the hardware store, schoolteachers, and the doctor and his wife. During the Depression, the Elishas hoped to get enough summer vacationers in the hotel to pay for the coal

Laurence Elisha in front of Hotel Jerome, 1960. Courtesy Ingrid Elisha.

there in the winter. Miners who lived in the hotel through the winter went back to their digs in the summer, so tourists took their place. They came to Colorado to cool off! We leased the Jerome in 1946 and my mother sold it in 1967. I managed the Jerome from 1960 to 1965. We sold the hotel because my father had passed away and my mother had very little income — she needed to be taken care of.

I've been away from Aspen for so many years. I can't go back into the past and look at what it was when I was a child, though wouldn't it be great! But you can't do that. Change is important and is necessary in the development of everything. I think the change in Aspen was needed. Aspen would have crumbled, as did many towns, if the Ski Corporation and the Aspen Ski Company hadn't moved in. Aspen became a resort and had an income. I think controlled growth is important, and I would only ask that this be considered.

Ingrid Elisha Stuebner

I think I would want to stop Aspen right before I left in 1967. There was a lot of the influence of the new and still the influence of the old, before the *big* money boom. That is the time I felt most comfortable. I think that there is still a lot of communal feeling, growth, and change. It's harder for those of us not living here, because we don't have that sense of belonging anymore. The most recog-

nizable element I see is that Aspen has changed. It's a big city now, and every inch of space is being used.

Aspen is a difficult place to move away from. I still feel that it is my hometown. As soon as I drove in, I felt like I was home. But it's bittersweet, because it's the people that count and they are no longer here. I have wonderful memories of growing up here.

Photo by Kathy Daily

Delbert Gerbaz

I was born March 30, 1919, in Denver, Colorado. My grandparents, Jeremy and
Cecile Mary Gerbaz, came here from a little village called Doues in Val d'Aosta,
in the mountains of northern Italy just over the hill from Chamonix in the
shadow of Mount Blanc. They had neighbors who had come previously and

they wrote back what a great country this was. They didn't come directly to the Roaring Fork Valley. They came by way of Detroit, Michigan. My grandfather worked in a glass factory in Del Rey, Michigan, which is a suburb of Detroit. That's where my father, Auzel, was born in 1893. Auzel came to Woody Creek with his parents when he was seven years old. My grandfather purchased the old A.B. Foster Ranch in 1896. In later years, they purchased additional land adjacent to them until the ranch was finally full size, about 1,200 acres.

My grandfather supported himself with cattle, hay, and potatoes. Much of it was shipped out. They were fortunate to live adjacent to two railroads, and most of their produce was shipped out on the Colorado Midland. There was a siding called Watson, which was about ten miles downvalley from Aspen. They would load out the livestock and their produce at that particular location. My grandparents had nine boys, no girls. So they had plenty of ranch hands. One of the boys died in infancy and another when he was sixteen. They all survived the flu epidemic of 1918. They seemed to have been away from the centers. Maybe

Opposite page, top: Stacking hay, about 1915. Mike and Edmond Gerbaz (boys); Auzel Gerbaz on hay stacker. Courtesy Del Gerbaz.

Opposite page, bottom: Old Woody Creek Bridge, 1935, now Gerbaz Road. Looking toward Highway 82. Courtesy Del Gerbaz.

Below: Four generations of Gerbaz: Cecilie, Delbert holding Larry, Auzel, 1948. Courtesy Del Gerbaz.

good outdoor living helped. None of them got sick, to my knowledge. Auzel grew up on the ranch. He met my mother through correspondence. My mother's maiden name was Claudia Ree Corbin. She lived in the southern part of Indiana in a hilly area, near Bloomfield and Bedford.

Grandfather and grandmother learned English very rapidly. Of course, all the boys were taught their dialect, which was called *Patois*. The Gerbaz family never changed their name, which is an interesting fact. People say that it isn't Italian, even though they came from northern Italy. A cousin of mine, Flavian Arbaney, who was born and raised in Val d'Aosta, did some research of the family and found out that they immigrated from Germany back during the time of Charlemagne, during the Holy Roman Empire. Perhaps other people that are fair complected had ancestors who came from Germany or the northern part of Europe.

My father proposed to mother by mail and she accepted. They were married in 1917. I think they exchanged pictures. They lived at the ranch, in the old

Opposite page, top: Auzel Gerbaz, 1928, with a steam tractor. Courtesy Del Gerbaz.

Opposite page, below: Threshing on the Gerbazdale Ranch about 1930. Courtesy Del Gerbaz.

Below: Gerbaz moving truck in Denver, about 1917. Courtesy Del Gerbaz.

Ashby house where the Watson post office was. That building is still standing and is occupied as a dwelling. A number of families have lived there. They stayed there a short time and then went to Denver, where he worked as a baggage handler with a truck. He left the ranch because my mother wanted him to get away, for one thing. He thought he could make it over in Denver. That's where I was born. He came back to the ranch in 1922. My mother never got along with ranch life such as it was. In 1923, she took me and went back to Indiana. She divorced him, and I never saw my father again until 1932.

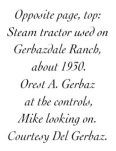
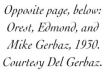

Opposite page, top: Steam tractor used on Gerbazdale Ranch, about 1930. Orest A. Gerbaz at the controls, Mike looking on. Courtesy Del Gerbaz.

Opposite page, below: Orest, Edmond, and Mike Gerbaz, 1930. Courtesy Del Gerbaz.

Left: Auzel Gerbaz in bunkhouse, 1937. Photo by Del Gerbaz.

Gerbaz House on Highway 82, 1935. Courtesy Del Gerbaz.

Dad arranged for me to come out and visit that summer. I was thirteen years old. I came to Denver alone on the Burlington Railroad, and he met me in Denver. I didn't recognize him, but he recognized me. He had driven over, and we drove back together. I was the only child. Incidentally, the morning he went over to get me, he left the ranch at 4:30 A.M. and got to Denver at 2 P.M. He said it took him nine hours of driving time. During that era, you can understand why people traveled by rail. They didn't drive to Denver. They took the train. It was very exciting for me. The Depression hit extremely bad in the Midwest and in the area of Indiana that I lived. It was like going to heaven almost, visiting Colorado.

I rode horseback, and we made a lot of trips into the high country. We camped out at Conundrum hot springs. I was between my grade at high school, and school started in September, so back to Indiana I went. I graduated from high school in 1936, and then I came back to Woody Creek that spring, after school. During 1936 to 1941, I lived and worked on the ranch and went to the

University of Colorado in the wintertime during the school year. My mother never came out. I visited her. She later moved to Fort Worth, Texas, and my father visited her once when we ourselves were living in Fort Worth. She remarried in 1928, and I have a half-brother and a half-sister.

I made Woody Creek my permanent home during the late thirties. In the spring of 1941, I hadn't finished school yet. I lacked about two quarters of finishing CU, but I thought the opportunity for working in the aerospace industry was pretty good, so I applied to General Dynamics in San Diego, California. Lo and behold, they made me an offer of $125 a month and I couldn't turn it down. I went to work for them while I was 1-A in the draft. I thought surely I would be drafted into the service, but they deferred me and I stayed with General Dynamics for twenty-nine years.

In early 1971, my father was getting up in years, and he and his brothers had agreed to sell the ranch. They had already contracted to sell the ranch but were still operating it. I had expressed a lot of displeasure in working under the conditions in California. I was an avid anti-smoker, and the area where I worked, people smoked at will and it was getting to me. So I thought it was a good time to pull up stakes and go back. Dad said, "Come on back to the ranch and we'll work out something." So that I did in 1971.

During that era, we didn't run to town every time we thought something was going on. Only went on Saturday afternoon or Sunday. One of the high-

*Watson Hall,
on Watson Divide,
a community center
for dances, 1935.
Last dance held
in 1931.
Courtesy Del Gerbaz.*

lights was the old dances at the Armory, City Hall. Everybody went. You didn't take a date, you just went to meet the gals and dance. If you wanted to take someone home, okay. That's one of the things that sticks in my memory.

I used to go after the mail when I was up at the ranch. We got our mail up Woody and I'd ride horseback. One time I felt a little aggressive, I guess, so I raced the train and beat it. They didn't travel very fast. The engineer gave me the devil for running the horse so much. The old Woody post office was about three-quarters of a mile downvalley from the present one. I remember Jess and Prue Bogue, she was postmistress. They had a few things in their store. It wasn't very much, but it was always a pleasure going to Woody Creek to see if you got any mail.

I used to go up to Aspen sometimes on a Saturday evening with my uncle Edmond Gerbaz and visit with him when he was courting Albina Tekoucich. All of my uncles' names, in order — Olice, Orest, Homer, Edmond, and Harvey. Harvey is the only one that is still living. His initials are H.F. — Harvey Flavian. He is eighty-four. He goes by the name of Mike. There is another Mike Gerbaz, but they call him Little Mike. His name is actually Michael.

I got married in 1945 to Janie Marie Lowe. We have four children, Larry, Molly, Janice Marie, and Cecile, all born in Fort Worth.

I worked for the Ski Company for thirteen seasons. One year I worked summer and winter. I was a lift operator on the bottom of No. 6 lift. During that time, it was quite a contrast to what I had been doing as an aerospace engineer. It was a lot of fun. I had always enjoyed skiing and being with people who did ski. During that time, I met an awful lot of people who I still have casual contact with. In fact, we were in Alaska the summer of 1992 on a trip, on the Alaskan marine ferry *Columbia*. We were in the dining room, and a fellow kept looking at me, and I looked at him, and later we had to go down in the hold to move our vehicles. It turned out to be a fellow that I had loaded on the lifts at Aspen Mountain. His father lived in Carbondale. We had quite a chat. I run into people all over who remember me at the bottom of No. 6 lift.

I saw dramatic changes in Aspen and the Roaring Fork Valley from the time that I left in 1941. Of course, I would come back here on vacations. Actually, there have probably been more far changes since 1971. What is missing from Aspen today is the old kindred spirit. Anybody you met on the street, you'd wave at them. You knew practically everybody. There were no strangers in town. There was more of a sense of permanence.

It would be hard to say what I would do now to change it. I'm afraid they've gone beyond the point of no return. If I could stop Aspen in any year, it would be about 1940. Skiing had started. They had the old boat tow on Aspen Mountain, and that was a great addition. Skiing actually started up at Highlands at the Highland Bavarian Lodge at the junction of Castle and Conundrum creeks. If World War II hadn't come along, the skiing activity probably would be in that general area, because there had been promoters that had already obtained enabling legislation for bonds to build a tram up Mount Hayden. That disappeared with World War II. The economy was picking up, and there was no congestion. You didn't have to worry about a place to park.

✦

Photo by Kathy Daily

*Vic is a good ol' guy.
Nothing riles Vic too much.
He has a hearty laugh and
a good sense of humor.*

Vic Goodhard

I was born in Elkhorn, Nebraska, September 11, 1926. I went to school at Creighton University. That's where I met Eileen [Vagneur]. She was born and raised in Aspen. Eileen was working in Denver as a secretary for Central Electric. She went to Barnes Business School. We got married in Denver in 1949, and Eileen wanted to come back to Woody Creek, where she grew up. I liked it over here, too. Ben Vagneur, her dad, was a widower, so we moved in with him for a year on his ranch. It is now Carol Craig's ranch up Woody Creek.

Eileen's grandfather, Jeremie Vagneur, homesteaded back in the 1880s. At one time, I think it was the 1920s or 1930s, the Vagneurs owned the whole Woody Creek Valley. Then it didn't seem to work out. There were five boys — Jim, Louis, Dellore, Ben, and Sullivan.

I was a greenhorn on the ranch, very green. I felt like a city slicker. Like stacking hay. They had balers at the time, but Ben didn't have any, so we stacked hay in haystacks. I was real sore after all that work! 'Specially when you don't know what you're doing. There's a trick to it, believe it or not. You moved the hay with a pitchfork. You made your haystack so you could get to it, then put it on a wagon to feed. I didn't even know how to ride a horse. They used to run cattle up in Kobey Park. There weren't any roads up there at that time. We went up through Collin's Creek. There were about four or five of us working on the ranch at that time. There used to be a house up above, that cabin of Carol Craig. You know that log cabin? That next driveway, about a half-mile up the road, there used to be a house where the hired help lived, but it burned down years and years ago.

I was in the navy, the Seabees. It was 1943. I got out in 1945 or 1946. I was on Okinawa. I guess I got shot at, but I didn't stick my neck out to find out what was going on. I was shot at a few times, but we were behind the lines more or less. I was working in the construction end of it — carpenter and painting. That's what Seabees did. We built the NAHA airstrip and the Gung communication center.

Back then, we'd go into Aspen go to the Elks and the Eagles. That's about all there was. Laurence Elisha had the hotel then. He was just in the process of leasing it.

I bought a ranch up Woody Creek in 1952. It now belongs to George Stranahan. Oliver Bionaz had that land. They bought it in 1912, I think. And I can't remember who they bought it from. I paid $20,000.

We had cattle; season is too short for potatoes, it's iffy. You can still grow great potatoes — same as Idaho potatoes, if you hit them good. And then if you don't have water, well then you're dead. George's place doesn't have a lot of good water rights because Collin's Creek is not a good watershed — it's limited. It just goes back up. It was pretty tough, and so we finally sold out, I think in 1958. It just wasn't working. I wasn't making a living out there. I had thirty head of cattle and could graze on BLM land then. I had a permit up Red Mountain, up Hunter Creek. I only had thirty because that's about all the ranch would support. It's just not that big of a ranch. There's a lot of timber. One hundred ninety acres are farmable. There was always fighting over water. That's the life blood of these ranches. At that time it was. They were all working ranches.

Aspen: The Quiet Years

❖❖❖❖❖❖❖❖❖❖❖❖❖❖❖

I bought the trash company in, I think, 1961 — bought it from a guy by the name of Allen Bimbo. Aspen Ash and Trash. There used to be a lot of ashes from coal. There was one small truck. It wasn't quite modern — wasn't much packing to it. It was closed with a flap tailgate. It only had one door. Bimbo was in trouble because he was always in front of the city council. Eileen and I were trying to decide what we could do to stay in Aspen, because we liked it here. So the chance come up to buy him out. He just didn't run it right. He had a cleaning service and the trash service hand in hand. He could have done great, but he didn't work. He kind of was the manager type, but he just didn't manage it quite right. He'd break down and there wouldn't be trash picked up for days. I drove the truck myself and had one other guy working with me. There was a door gone on the other side of the truck. It had come off and Bimbo didn't bother to put it back on.

In those days, the dump was out at the high school. One time this guy was gone for the weekend and his kids threw out all of his sterling silver. He called me. I said, "Hey, I'll tell you where I dumped it." He went out and it had been burnt. They burned at the time. He went out and found all of it. They'd dig a pit and bury it. Another time, some gal was heading out of town with guests and she had about $15,000 worth of this silver and turquoise jewelry. That was pretty hot at one time. So the gal put it in the bottom of her wastepaper basket so nobody'd steal it. There weren't really any thieves or much burglary at that time. So anyhow, the maid come along and dumped it. She found all of it.

I loved to hunt. In the 1950s there weren't too many elk around here. They were hunted in the early 1900s because of the miners. And then they shipped in two boxcar loads of them here in Aspen in 1919 and dumped them up there on the Rio Grande Park where the parking garage is. That was the depot. Then they turned them loose. Good game management, really. Now there are more up there than there's ever been.

That cabin about a mile up from Natal's place in Woody Creek was the old ranger's station. There is one that is gone completely except for remnants of the chimney. That used to be what they called the Pitkin County pest house. They used to put sick people in there years and years ago — people who had scarlet fever and stuff like that. That's what I heard. The old road used to go along there. It was isolation — to get them away from other people, I think. You go past Natal's. There's a side road that goes to the right, and people camp there. There's a fenced area, right below the road. You know that big house that sits there by Natal's? Well, Lee and Virginia Jones bought that from the government. That was government land up there. It was the old ranger station, as they used to call it. There used to be a flume that came across Stanley's property where the Salvation Ditch is. The flume is underground now. That's as far as they could get, so there set the house. They moved it down to the flume, and that was it. It was never used. I always call that the old ranger station trail. It sits right on the road. Another ten years it will collapse, if not sooner.

The changing of Aspen was kind of gradual until the 1960s, and then it really started popping. I couldn't keep up buying garbage trucks because I had Snowmass and Aspen at the same time. Just trying to keep up. You didn't know what to plan for. All of a sudden, there were new places, bigger places that demanded more service, more people. I'd say the Sixties and Seventies are when it really exploded. From 1949 to 1959, essentially, things were changing, but not fast. It was a slow process. Like I say, everybody left because they couldn't afford to live here for the prices they paid for things. That's progress, I guess. I think that's true in all resort towns. Eventually the people that started these businesses left town. It was kind of hard living in the 1960s because there wasn't a lot of income. Aspen was a smaller place, and then it got bigger, and then all of a sudden we attracted the people with money. And it still turns over today.

Every year there's a different turnover. I think about every four or five years all the businesses just churn. That's just part of the resort town, I guess. In the 1950s, I think there were only seven hundred cars registered to the whole county. You'd go in the courthouse anytime in the 1950s and you'd know everybody. There wasn't anything going on. Really, Aspen to me is a town, but it's not what you call a hometown, because everybody left. There's a few left, but that whole East End, there still are Ray Bates and Jessie. They're still hanging in there. All the Strongs and Loushins used to live there.

✦

Aspen Eddie — what a sweet man. Eddie makes beautiful knives. He is an excellent craftsman. Eddie is giving, and I can tell that when he was young, he certainly had fun.

Ed Gregorich

I was born October 9, 1917, in Aspen. My mother came to the United States from Yugoslavia before the turn of the century — 1898 or 1899. She came with Mike Garrish's mother. Her name was Helena Smole. I don't think she was over sixteen at the time. She came over here to work for Mr. Marolt when he had the saloon on Cooper Street. She met Mike's mother on the boat. My mom used to tell me they wouldn't eat the bologna — they threw it overboard. They didn't know what it was. My mother came from Ljubljana, Yugoslavia. That used to be Austria Hungary. At one time, we weren't recognized as Yugoslavs; we were recognized as Austrians. She was a housekeeper.

My father's name was Frank Gregorich. He came to Aspen in the late 1880s from Yugoslavia. They met here. I guess he just wanted to get away from the old country. Aspen was something like the terrain where he used to live. I think he stopped in Cleveland and then went to Leadville. He walked over from Leadville to Aspen.

My daddy didn't talk too much when I was a boy. He was a hard worker. I assume my parents met in the saloon. When mother got married, she was probably about eighteen. Dad was about ten years older than my mom. There were eleven kids in our family, but three of them passed away in the flu epidemic of 1918.

When we were growing up in Aspen, our first chores were to get our winter supply of wood. As soon as school would get out, we would go out and start chopping wood, right in back of the house. I worked for the forest service when I was about fifteen; we used to go out and thin timber. We would have to cut out the school marms and the professors. The school marm has two forks way up where they branch out — only two of them. The professor has three where they branch out on top. Three or more — they were professors. Up on the Frying Pan, when I was a kid, I worked about four years. I worked on trails, grubbing larkspur, game survey.

When I was small, they had all kinds of old buildings around here — the Slamper and all the Crown houses. We used to play tag on old buildings. We used to play tag on the tramways, too. We used to go hand-over-hand on those cables that went across. Mama used to tell me about the Glory Hole. She and Mrs. Vedic were picking dandelions when all of a sudden they saw a great big cloud of smoke. The train whistled and some of the boxcars went down in the huge hole. The earth just fell in. There were mine tunnels underneath. It was right close to high noon when it happened. Mama saw the train and everything. When I was a kid, I used to see those railroad tracks sticking up there. They stuck up out of the hole from the bottom. We used to go down there and dig around. They used that as the city dump for years. They filled it in when I was gone. I guess somebody wanted to commercialize it or something. It was a sore spot with the city. It's where Glory Hole Park is now.

We lived in that four-room little house with eleven kids — never did have a store-bought mattress. We slept on straw mattresses. Mom made them. My brothers and I slept in one big bed. All three heads were together at the same end.

Aspen Mountain,
May 1, 1923.
Denver & Rio Grande
Railroad
Courtesy
Robert Zupancis.

My dad worked the mines around here and then worked on Independence Pass. He used to take us kids fishing all the time. He taught me to fish. The Roaring Fork River was my favorite place, in the dead waters. Up at Stillwater there used to be an ice house. Before Sparky was up there, a fellow by the name of Blaine Bray owned it. He bought the land and put up a dance hall. They used to have wild dances when I was about eight years old. My brother Joe was the one that helped build that dance hall. Bray later tore it down, put little cabins in, and rented them out. Then Sparky bought it from Bray.

There used to be an animal pound right by the opera house, between there and Koch's Lumber Yard. They had bulls, cows, horses, or any loose animal. They would pick them up and then I think they would charge a dollar to get them out. The marshall collected them. That was in the 1920s. Charlie Wagner was the city marshall. He was an ornery so and so. But he was a good marshall. He meant discipline. Frank Hamilton, he was the marshall. Panhandle Pete was a marshall, too.

SLAVONIC CATHOLIC UNION SOCIETY of St. BARBARA, Nº 47.

Slavonic Catholic Union Society, about 1900. Top row, fourth from left, Gregorich; eighth from left, Snyder; middle row, eighth from left, Tony Gregorich; bottom row, seventh from left, Marolt; sixteenth from left, Skiff. Courtesy Jim Snyder.

Did my dad make whiskey? No, Mama used to make the whiskey. She would make it out of apricots and prunes. It was more like brandy. We would distill it. It was grappa.

Our meals at home were simple. For breakfast we didn't have much — a cup of coffee and bread. My mom made bread out of rye. She would bake bread, I think on Friday. It was a big round loaf. She would put egg on top of it. At lunchtime, we would have about the same thing. And then at night, we could have soup and maybe a lot of wild meats. Dad was quite a hunter. He taught me. The first thing I ever shot was a rabbit. I must have been about seven or eight.

I left Aspen about 1938. I was about eighteen. I hoboed on the train and went to Silverton. I knew where I was going. I already had a job. I met a fella fishing who was a master mechanic. And he said, "Hey, would you like to go to work for me?" And I said, "Yes." So he put me to work in Silverton.

After I left Silverton, I went and worked in the navy yard; then I went to Honolulu. I went over there as a civilian. When they had all the ships repaired, I went in the navy in 1942. After they got all the fleet out, I worked for the bureau ships and dock, repairing submarines, building submarines. I used to be in charge of the watertight integrities to see if the ship was watertight. I used to come home to Aspen all the time — just about every year.

Mother was getting on in years. That's one reason I came home. I wasn't going to come home. Mother used to call me Cadet when I was a kid. I don't know why, but she called me Cadet, and she said, "Cadet, why don't you come home?" And I said, "No, I don't want to come home." "Aw, come on." That was in 1969 and she passed away in 1971.

When I came back from Pearl Harbor in 1942, all these soldiers from the Tenth Mountain Division went down to Tim Kelleher's. I got in a hell of a beef. I had three of them down — had them stacked up just like cords of wood. Tim Kelleher got the baseball bat after me.

In 1970, the town was full of hippies, long hairs, crazies. It was lots of fun. Oh, I loved it, I'll tell ya. I like them people. I like the young ones. I like kids. Who wants to go around associating with the old. In 1970, I couldn't wait until the bars would open up. I had a fella staying with me by the name of John Trip. He and I used to go out and raise hell. We would go to the Eagles, Cooper Street Pier, and the Roaring Lion.

1937 trip to Denver to play in American Legion Baseball Tournament. Courtesy Warren Conner.

Tough People, Hard Times

♦ ♦ ♦ ♦ ♦ ♦ ♦ ♦ ♦ ♦ ♦ ♦ ♦ ♦ ♦ ♦ ♦ ♦ ♦

The funniest thing happened one time. I went in the Ute City Bank; ah hell, I got drunk. I got in a fight with the bartender and we went outside. Trip was coming up the street and I said, "Hey, Trip, I need some help." I had one bartender down. Boy, he came up there, picked that guy up, and he threw him clear out in the middle of the street. He said, "Let's get the hell out of here, Eddie." So we left there and we hid in Little Annie's. And sure enough, the cops came up. They couldn't find us. That was a long time ago. Did you ever hear the tale of Trip picking me up? He was a big man. He put me on his arm. It was twenty-three below zero. I had my shorts and bedroom slippers on, and he took me out to the Hickory House. Twenty-three below zero at six in the morning, waiting for the bar to open up so we could drink beer. I didn't want to go, but he put me under his arm and took me — carried me. Then we passed out.

I saw a big difference in Aspen right after World War II, about 1948 when I got out of the service. The people were a lot different. I could remember every cat and dog in town when I left here. People started coming in and changing the town. I figured there were about three hundred people in town when I moved. But I didn't know what the population in the whole valley was. I doubt if the population in the city limits of Aspen was over three hundred. In 1930, it was seven hundred-two, and that's the county. But the city limits, I don't know. After I worked, all I wanted to do was come home to live. This was home. I'm just like an elephant — I come home to die. I retired from the government in 1968 and I've been idle ever since. I worked for Jimmy Snyder and Del Mars plumbing for awhile.

I like Aspen today. I like these young kids. Who the hell wants to look back? Never mind what you did twenty years ago — look for tomorrow. Aspen is too big — too much money. When you find money, what do you find? Corruption, it has a lot of it. Same way with gambling. When they get gambling in this state, you are going to find a lot of corruption. Maybe I'm wrong on it, but that's my feeling.

♦

*Angie still has her parents'
original house on her
property. When I look
back there at that old house
beyond her clothesline, I see
a part of the past that
wasn't mine.
It's wonderful.*

Angeline (Angie) Muhich Griffith

I was born in Aspen on May 23, 1923. My parents came from Yugoslavia. His name was Joe Muhich and her name was Johanna Blatnik. My father came to Leadville about 1907, and Mom came in 1909. She worked in Leadville in a boardinghouse for seventy-five cents a week. She cooked for fifteen miners and washed their long underwear and hung them out. She cooked on a coal wood stove and made bread — everything was from scratch. She got up at 4 A.M. Mother made

*Joe and Johanna
Blatnik Muhich,
Angie Griffith's parents.
Married in Leadville
in 1911.
Courtesy Angie Griffith.*

their breakfasts, their lunches, and dinner. Then she worked in the saloon at night until about 1 or 2 A.M. She waited on people. She was about thirty-two.

My mom and dad married in Leadville in 1911. They met in Leadville, at the boardinghouse, I imagine. They were from different villages in Slovenia.

They came to Aspen in 1919. My father walked over Independence Pass because the doctor told him he had to go to a lower climate. He heard about Aspen, and he liked it because it was like their home in Yugoslavia. He went back and he told my mom, "Boy, it's just beautiful, just like home." My mom really liked Leadville because she knew a lot of Slovenians that settled there. She had two sisters that came before her, so she liked it. I could never understand why she would like Leadville. When my dad walked over, it was more or less just a path. That was 1919. Then he walked back, of course. They both came together on the railroad — the Midland. I had one brother and two sisters that were born in Leadville. One sister was born in 1918, my brother in 1914. The other sister was born in Aspen in 1920. Both girls passed away in 1927 from appendicitis, four months apart. They were seven and nine years old. I was four.

My parents spoke broken English when they came. See, my mom never went anywhere. Of course, my dad worked at the mines. He worked for the county. That was it. We just had to provide, you know.

I went to the Washington School. It was right behind the Mesa Store. I walked all the way and even came home for lunch a lot of times. It was a two-story house with many rooms. I went until eighth grade. The high school was the D.R.C. Brown mansion where the red brick building is now.

I was a pretty good girl in high school. Oh, we did go out on Halloween. One couple lived there on Main Street. I think they owned the water works. Well, we would go to the door and they wouldn't even come and answer. They were very rich and we were very poor. We just wanted a little tiny piece of candy or something. If they would have just come to the door. But she sat there knitting, and he sat reading the paper like nothing was going on. There was maybe twenty kids on the porch. Then we just got angry with them and soaped all their windows. I'll tell you, their windows were so soaped every Halloween they couldn't even see out. I think we went there first before we ran out of soap. Then the bigger boys would take their gate — they had a nice picket fence — and the boys would take it and hang it up in a tree.

When I walked to school, the snow was clear up above my knees and there were no snowplows. We walked down the old railroad trestle and the snow would build up. Ice would be in clumps on the ties. The ties were about a foot apart, and you just had to keep going; otherwise your foot would go between. Then at noon we'd come home for lunch. The train would come into the depot, and sometimes we'd have to run across the railroad trestle before the train started coming. It would go over to the Durant to pick up the ore cars. Then it came all the way up here to Smuggler Trailer Park. The trestle was located right there by Mike Garrish's. The tracks went across to the Eagle's Club. There was a trestle from where the Eagles is over to Mike Garrish's on the west side of Mike's house. Then it would come up around where the trailer park is, over by the Cooper Bridge, then over to Durant.

The Washington School was behind the red Mesa Store, one block north of Main Street. There were a lot of kids walking to school. My brother used to come home from school and shovel the walk all the way up to the alley. He'd shovel all the way down there so we'd have a path. We always made it to school. You know what? I had several perfect attendances. In fact, I'd get certificates for perfect attendance. Yup, living on this lead. I never got sick living on this lead in the soil.

After high school, I went to work for Mr. Kalmes at the Kalmes Store. That was my first job. Then I went to work for Edie Rader in her restaurant at night. At that time, it was the Silver Grill. I worked there from about 6 to 10 P.M. I helped clean up for my lunch the next day. That was my pay. When I worked for Francis Kalmes, I started at twenty-five cents an hour in 1942. He sold shoes and clothes. He closed because he went to war.

I married Newt Klusmire in 1945. We were married eight years. I opened up the White Kitchen in 1947. Then I married my second husband, Roy, in 1956. He was a state patrolman in this area. He was transferred out of here in 1957. So we leased the White Kitchen.

When I was young, we had everything in our garden. This was for the family, and my folks would always go out to the farm and get a couple of little pigs. We'd raise all the vegetables, wash them good, and chop them up. My dad had a mining car fixed so he could build a fire under it. It was an ore car that they used up here in the tram. They'd wash the vegetables real good, chop them up, and boil them like a stew. They had turnips and everything in there, even

Opening date,
March 27, 1946.
Courtesy Angie Griffith.

the tops. Then my mom would put two buckets of warm water in and mash it all. We had a trough for the pigs, so she'd dump it in the trough and they'd slurp slurp.

We had seven lots here . . . still have the original land. That back there was my brother's. It was a railroad bed that would come over to the Cowenhoven Tunnel. They sold it and my brother bought it in the 1940s. He passed away in 1987. We had a root cellar here under the house. My folks would make sauerkraut in a fifty-gallon barrel and we'd eat sauerkraut and potatoes, lots of potatoes. In fact, I'm still raising potatoes.

On my birthday, which is May 23, we'd have a big party. I'd help plant all the potatoes. My mom would make the holes with the hoe, and I would go along and put all of the potatoes in. That was my birthday — planting potatoes. My aunt, Mrs. Frances Miklich, would help my mother. Then my mom would help my aunt plant hers. They would do their visiting, work hard, talk, and laugh.

We had two cows, and they would roam all over along the ditches. When I came home at night after school I'd have to go bring them home so my mom could milk them. After supper, I'd have to go deliver milk. We never pasteurized. We charged ten cents a quart. We used to carry it in little lard buckets. At first, I could only carry one. When I got stronger, I could carry two. That was pretty heavy. We had one customer that lived up by the ski lift. They're still up there — the Dolensiks. I had to go across the trestle with the milk, even in the wintertime. I also helped with the yard by pulling the vegetables for the pigs.

We butchered the hogs in the fall, and all the neighbors and friends would come to help. Six or eight couples would come. We'd start early in the morning and catch the blood and make blood and meat sausage. Then we'd smoke the ham and the bacon. That's what we ate all winter. We usually had one or two calves that we'd butcher, and we always had plenty to eat. We never lacked for eating, because we worked and saved.

My folks would go out and cut hay with a sickle and put it up. That's what this old house was for — to store the hay in. They would put up hay for the cows in the winter.

We had a sled. We used to sleigh ride and ice skate. I don't know where we got the skates. Somebody probably gave them to us. We used to go up here and sled on the crust. We ice skated down at the ice pond. We'd have to shovel off the snow and skate — down by Red and Peggy Rowland's, down in that area. There was another pond up here as you go up the pass — Sullivan's pond.

In high school, I played basketball at the Armory Hall. I played guard. I loved that. We played against Basalt, Carbondale, Eagle, and Gypsum. We were

Hyman Avenue, 1954.
Courtesy Angie Griffith.

pretty good. We didn't have tournaments like they have now. I was thrilled to get to wear shorts. We weren't allowed to wear them to school or at home. We wore dresses to school. We had this long underwear and cotton socks with big garters. No wonder I've got varicose veins! Then, in the spring — I couldn't wait for spring to come — we rolled them down and pulled our underwear up. Well, my mom wouldn't let me do that because it was a long walk. But I'd do it when I was downtown and then put them back when I got near home. In my class, there were only four boys. There were only sixteen in my class when I graduated.

We would go dance. I'd dance two or three times a week. We went to country dances. They'd have dances at Brush Creek School, Owl Creek School, and Woody Creek School. We'd hit them just about every weekend. My parents didn't go, but I'd go with other people and my brother. He always went. He'd always dance with me. Hilder Anderson and her husband used to play. She played accordion, and he played the fiddle. The Stallards had a band too [Roman Roamers]. My folks used to walk all the way up to Stillwater for a dance. There was a big building there. They'd walk up there to dance and then walk home. That was good exercise. My mom lived to be ninety-nine and she worked hard. She lived here with me until she died. My mom and my brother both lived with us.

Roy and I were gone from Aspen for fifteen years, from 1959 on. I came back to a strange town. Roy had retired in 1975, so he went to work. He set up Starwood Security. He worked from '75 to '80 there.

I bought the White Kitchen Restaurant from my ex-husband. We bought it in 1949 for $5,000. I still own the building. It's right on the Hyman Street Mall. It was just a little tiny thing when we started, and then I built an apartment over the top.

I have a wine press. My parents made grape wine. They would buy some grapes when someone from downvalley would bring in a railroad carload from California. My folks ordered 500 pounds of grapes at two-and-a-half cents a pound. We used to make chokecherry wine. That's good stuff. I'd come home for lunch from school and have tea with a little wine in it. It kept you warm. If you ever have tea, put a little red wine in there — it's good.

Marge Fisher worked for me at the White Kitchen. When her daughter Joanie was pregnant, Irene Tagert, who had Louie's Spirit House, Marge, Joan, and I went to Denver to do a little shopping. Irene and I bought Joanie some new little baby things. We came back through Colorado Springs and Leadville. Of course, we stopped in Leadville in the afternoon and had a few drinks. They started a band, so we danced a little, even Joanie. Her baby was due any minute. And then all at once the band stopped, and they said, "Well, we've got an announcement. Has anybody found any teeth?" Somebody had lost their false teeth! Anyway, we started home, never thinking about gas. I had a brand new car — a 1954 Buick. We couldn't come over the pass, so we had to go all the way through Glenwood. We got just below Basalt, at about El Jebel, and run out of gas. This was about midnight. There weren't very many cars then, so who was to walk to Basalt? Irene said, "Well, I'm not going to stay with Joanie, because she's about to have her baby." Her mother wouldn't, either, so I had to stay with Joanie and they started walking up the highway — no cars, no nothing. Luckily, the fellow who owned the Basalt Drugstore with the gas pumps come down the road and picked them up. They got some gas and brought it back. We didn't get home probably until 2 or 3 A.M.

Oh, we had a good time in the White Kitchen. Everybody would come there and have coffee and pie. One day Jim Hayes came in about four in the afternoon and he said, "Angie, do you have a whole pie?" And I said, "Well,

◆◆◆◆◆◆◆◆◆◆◆◆◆◆◆◆◆◆◆

Jim, I don't have a whole one, but I've got a couple pieces of coconut, apple, cherry, blueberry, and whatever." He said, "Okay, just make it a whole pie." So I put it all together and started to wrap it and he said, "Oh no, you don't have to wrap it." So he sat at the end stool looking out. Otis Gaylord, who always wore a black overcoat, came out of the liquor store. Jim went out there and pushed that pie right in his face. Then they started fighting. Jim Hayes couldn't fight his way out of a paper bag. Old Gaylord wasn't much of a fighter either. They were just kind of going down the street. Then, of course, everybody's getting off work, stopping, and looking. Finally somebody went up to them and said, "Okay guys, you don't want to fight." They stopped. You know, they didn't even hit one another. See, Jim went to Alaska on that pipeline. In fact, he went away owing me $200 because I used to charge to these guys — all of them — because they didn't have any money. Even if coffee was only a nickel a cup, they'd run a tab. It was quite a big tab for Jim, and I thought I'd lost that one. Well, Jim went up and worked on the pipeline. First thing, when he come back to town, he came into the White Kitchen and paid me. It was great. So anyway, Jim would go out and could pick up any girl that he wanted. He'd go to the Red Onion and the Golden Horn. They had a band — Steve Knowlton. It was good. I'd go there every night, too. Anyway, Jim would get these gals and wine and dine them. Then this Gaylord, he'd start dancing with them about the time it came to take them home. Well, this happened quite a few times to poor Jim. This was the way he had his revenge. It was in the *Aspen Times*. This was before Roy and I were married, so it must have been around 1954.

We had a good time in the Kitchen. It was fun. If anyone went anywhere, they'd always come in and say, "Well, now when so and so asks where I'm at, why you tell them I'm somewhere." So I had to keep track of everybody. I was a messenger service, too. The White Kitchen was the news center — all the gossip had to go through there. Oh yes, there was lots of gossip. There was some good stuff going on.

From the late 1930s to the 1950s, the sheriff was real mellow. There was Johnson and then Herwick. It was pretty quiet. I know my friend Irene, who had the liquor store, would always go to council if anyone would come in to get another liquor license. Of course, that was cutting in on her business. But I said, "It's alright for everybody to come and put restaurants in. So what difference does it make? Competition's competition."

I noticed the change in Aspen after World War II. Being in business in the White Kitchen, I thought it was pretty nice to have some business, because hamburgers were thirty cents. And they were the real thing — not sawdust. And I had to make pies from scratch. We didn't have any frozen stuff. So I was happy to see the business. But when I came back in 1975, I didn't know people. I'd go to town or the grocery store and I didn't know anyone.

Aspen now, well, I don't know. I guess it's all right. It would have been bad if we had just said, "Well, we'll just put a gate here and not let anybody in." It upsets me because the people that's been here twenty years, they say, "Well, I've been here twenty years and don't want you new guys here." I don't think they've got any right to say that. People came here because they enjoy what's here. But so many come to reap the harvest, vote all the unnecessary taxes in, then they are long gone and we are holding the bill.

I've just been so used to hard work, and a lot of people now don't want to work too hard. I know a lot of businesses that come into Aspen don't want to work and expect somebody else to take care of it. Well, it doesn't happen. If you have a job, hold on to it and work hard.

Did I ever consider leaving here? Well, yes, I'm at the point now where I'm going to have to think about that. I do go to California and Phoenix in the wintertime. But I still love the valley. It's home. I've got all of my roots here, but it's coming to the point where I don't like the cold weather and it bothers me. I like the Western Slope. I've lived on the Eastern Slope, and I have a lot of friends over there, too, but I like it on the Western Slope.

✦

Photo by Kathy Daily

Charley never stops laughing. He's a good photographer and takes time in the darkroom. I have a lot of respect for him.

Charley Grover

I was the last of the Grovers to be born up over the Mesa Store. First was my father in 1896, followed by his brothers, Willard and Albert. Dr. Lof delivered me on February 11, 1914.

My father's full name was Edward Jake Grover. Some say he was born over the Mesa Store, but I understand he was born in Leadville in 1896. My mother's name was Charlotte Louise, and she was a daughter of Mr. and

*Isaac Grover
(1829 – 1908)
Courtesy Charley Grover.*

Mrs. Charles Feist. It's kind of interesting because her mother was a Koch. Back in the middle 1840s, the Koch family was a large, diverse group. Interestingly enough, parents, grandparents, aunts, uncles, cousins, etc. were all in one way or another professionals. However, in this period of German history, revolution was a sign of the times. It was in this time frame that one of the Koch family members fell out of favor with the ruling powers because of his political support for the democratic movement.

Ernst Wilhelm Edward Koch and family left Lower Saxony (later Germany) and emigrated to the United States, living first in Philadelphia, Pennsylvania, next in Buffalo, New York, then Bowling Green, Kentucky, and finally settling in the young city of Toledo, Ohio. During his young years in Germany, E.W.E. Koch had received an excellent education, had become conversant in five languages, and was very much interested in the sciences. After his move to Toledo, Ohio, E.W.E. Koch became connected with the Toledo public schools. During this period, he founded the first gymnasium and started the first physical education program in the United States. He became an instructor of German and art in the high school. Other accomplishments included being president of the Toledo Horticultural Society and a member of the National Science Society of America. In 1869, he severed his connections with the Toledo schools to become an instructor of fine arts and languages at the University of Kentucky at Lexington. After about two or three years at the university, E.W.E. Koch resigned.

In 1880, at the request of the Vanderbilts, and accompanied by his friend Henry Gillispie and son Will Koch, E.W.E. Koch journeyed out West to a young mining camp at the site that later became known as Aspen, Colorado. Vanderbilt was looking for a good mineral investment, which they found in the Spar and Galena claims on Aspen Mountain. Henry Gillispie apparently saw a good future for the mining camp and wanted to call it by some official name. He suggested Ute City, because the spot where they were camping was known as Ute Springs. However, the name was voted down in favor of Aspen. Gillispie had E.W.E. Koch survey and make a plat of the town. After spending a year in Aspen, Koch returned to his home in Toledo. Sometime later, his son Harry returned to Aspen with his wife. They had two children, Edward and Dorothy. Harry Koch at one

time had four sawmills operating around here. One was up in Lenado. The Kochs helped lay out Aspen. Everett didn't stay. He went up into Washington. That was all pioneer country. He stayed around there and became somewhat of a wheel. The town of Everett, Washington is named after him. That's the story of the Koch family.

Above:
Anna M. Koch
(1836 – 1944)
Courtesy Charley Grover.

Left:
Ernst Wilhelm
Edward Koch,
about 1903
Courtesy Charley Grover.

Charley Feist had what you call roaming feet developing early in his life. At the tender age of thirteen, he ran away from home and joined the Union Army as a drummer boy. When the military brass made a check of his age, they told him to go home and grow up a little. At sixteen he left home for good. This time it was west and south down into Texas, where he hired on as a cowboy. One day during an Indian raid on the cattle, Charley took an arrow in one of his ankles. Next, he rode the rail as an express messenger on the MK&T Railroad, running from Sedalia, Missouri, down to Dennison, Texas. Charley used to tell stories about the old railroad days, for they were pretty exciting. When the train went through Indian Territory (now Oklahoma), they had to barricade their express car, for the Indians used the train for target practice. Later on, he was an express agent for the Denver & Rio Grande Railroad at Granite, Colorado, in the 1880s.

In 1897, Charles met Bertha Koch on her way to visit her brother Harry Koch, who was living in Aspen. Between 1887 and 1889, they corresponded with each other and in 1888 were married. They moved to Granite.

Aspen in the years 1887 and 1888 was a booming town. However, they had a small problem in Aspen — they were mining silver in huge quantities, and the only way they could get it to Leadville and the smelter was by way of wagon or pack train over Hunter Pass (later called Independence Pass), an expensive, labor-intensive, time-consuming chore. For the railroads — the D&RG and the Colorado Midland — the prize was the one that got to Aspen first. The D&RG won, arriving in Aspen in October 1887, the Colorado Midland arriving February 8, 1888. The arrival of the railroad in Aspen put all the pack and wagon trains operating between Aspen and Leadville out of business.

Shortly after arriving back in Granite, Charles transferred to Glenwood Springs as the station agent from 1888 to 1893. In February 1893, my mother, Charlotte Louise Feist, was born. Then came disaster — the silver crash of 1893. Glenwood Springs was not a happy place after that event. Charles and his little family left Glenwood and moved to Aspen. In spite of silver's low cost, the mineral being mined in Aspen was of such high quality it was still profitable to mine it, making many other job opportunities related to mining.

Charles Feist, my grandfather, had the bakery in Glenwood. That's where Mother was born. When they moved up to Aspen, he started a bakery. He just called it C.J. Feist or something. It was right next door to where they lived. They bought this old house and converted it into a bakery on Third and Francis. Edward G. and Fannie Grover were my father's parents.

The Grover family worked around Leadville in the mines. I have a picture of him and some other people. They were going out hunting, and boy, he was a tough-looking character. He had his hand on his hip and a rifle in the other. They came over to Aspen back around the beginning of the century, maybe a little before. Now Charley was one of the sons. He was born over in Lenado. His name was Charles Lenado Grover. That was my uncle. Grandpa Grover was running a boardinghouse when Charley was born. That's the story.

Dad had a commission downtown. Dad would buy hides from ranchers and bundle them up and send them down to Denver for tanning. He'd sell hay and grain and stuff like that. I have a diary of his telling about it. He never finished high school. They said they needed him at the store. He worked hard.

There was an old "batch" (as unmarried men around Aspen were called) by the name of Calvin Miller. Originally from Pennsylvania, he came West at an early age and prospected around various places, finally settling in Ashcroft and later Aspen. Cal, in those early years, spent most of his time in Ashcroft, coming down only in the early winter and going back up to Ashcroft as soon as the snow would allow.

As we boys grew up and got to know Cal better, we found him to be a kind, gentle person, but a bit of an eccentric in some ways. He always wore his hair very long. In later years, he had long flowing hair falling down over his shoulders. Asked why he didn't cut his hair, his explanation was, "It would weaken my strength." Another peculiarity was, as you passed his house at night, there he would be, sitting near his stove with the door to the stove wide open and the room full of smoke. His explanation for doing this was that the magnetic heat from the flame was good for you. Somewhere in his past he had learned to read palms. Often as you passed by his house, there he would be, door to the stove open and a group of high-school girls clustered around his table. He would be reading their palms. He enjoyed it and the girls did, too.

About 1937, old Cal reached that point in life where he could no longer go back to Ashcroft. Mother and Dad began to look after Cal — meals and such. Finally, one day in the middle of the summer, he passed away. It had been rumored around Aspen the old man had a lot of money stashed away in his house. It wasn't 'til his death and Dad had been appointed administrator of his estate that Cal's secret was revealed. Piled up to the ceiling in two of his rooms were wood boxes — cardboard boxes of various sizes with a narrow passageway between. The boxes held a treasure in old newspapers from many of the old mining camps around the area, old books, brochures on the railroads in Colorado, and mine-equipment catalogs. He even saved the paper wrappings that came around fruit. Much of the good stuff Dad took down to Denver. It now resides in the Western History section of the Denver Public Library.

First residence of Bertha and Charley Feist when they moved to Aspen in about 1893.
The woman standing in the doorway is Bertha Koch Feist, Charley Grover's grandmother. The small one-story building was owned by John Hollister, who came from Omaha, Nebraska. This building was later converted into an ice house for the Mesa Store. Partially shown on the right is the Mesa Store, at that time known as Gould Brothers Store, on Main Street.

Down on the corner from Millers' place, a couple by the name of Short lived there. He was Uncle Harry's right-hand man in the Koch Lumber Company.

Across the alley on the north side of the block lived an older couple by the name of Saunders who worked for the city of Aspen. Then there was the Hanson family with two boys, George and Roy, and a girl, Hildur. In another block north lived the Hendricks boys, Melvin and Ray. Mother and Dad, when we were younger, tried to shield us boys from playing with the Hendricks. Their father had a draying business and used pretty rough language on his horses.

However, when I started school, all of us were thrown into the same pot. So Mom and Dad must have realized they were fighting a losing battle. Going to school allowed us more freedom. Gram's house was where we usually went first after school. Gram always had cookies left over from baking. In the summertime, we boys were always up to something. We'd get up early, somewhere about 4:30 or 5:00 A.M., and go down to Gram's. She would have oatmeal for breakfast and usually well-watered coffee for us. The neighbors always had unkind words for us because we weren't very quiet at that hour.

Winters weren't too much fun then. By the time we got home from school, there was always wood and coal to bring in, and we had to shovel the sidewalk before nightfall. Saturdays in the winter were usually pretty kultzy days for us. The only thing to do was sleigh riding. Our sled was the laughingstock of the neighborhood — about as glamorous as a post. All the other neighbor boys had big Flexible Flyer sleds. I was never able to figure out why my dad refused to get us boys one of those sleds.

Christmastime was always exciting. Days before Christmas, we boys would pore over the wish books (catalogs), making up a list of things we would like to have. Then the packages would come in. Mother would hide them from us. We in turn would look into everything trying to find them. The holidays started on Christmas Eve. Dad had a horse and sleigh and would hitch up the horse to the sleigh. Then he'd put on sleigh bells, and off we'd go to Uncle Harry's (Harry Koch). It would be dark and cold, and we'd hear the snow squeak under the sleigh runners and the jingle of the bells. It was so wonderful. Uncle Harry had a large house. There would be a big tree all decorated with real candles, a burning fire in the fireplace, and all warm and cozy. There would be some refreshments, presents for us all, then back home. Christmas day started at our house with presents and a big breakfast for all. By the time this was finished, it was well into morning. Late afternoon we'd all end up down at Gram's house. There was a very large dinner, and all the Grovers would be there — Uncle Harry and Aunt Anna — a very large crowd.

We didn't know it 'til later, but the uncles had been doing a lot of talking and planning about leaving Aspen. Uncles Willard and Albert were getting tired of mining. Things at the Mesa Store were not going well. So it was decided some time in the late spring of 1924 they would all go out to California. The Mesa Store was sold to Julius Zupancis, and in the summer, Willard, Charlie, and Albert, along with their wives and children, all left for the coast. It would be some time before we'd see them again. My father's mother and dad stayed on for awhile, but eventually they, too, left for California.

There were two events that seemed to change Aspen. In 1918, the west end of Castle Creek Bridge was burned, forcing everyone to go down around the power house on Castle Creek and up the other side to Cemetery Lane. I was just a small boy, but Dad took me out to see it. Then later, November 16, 1919, a fire destroyed a part of the downtown business section. I remember about 7:30 that evening they called for Dad to come help. We all went upstairs in our house, and we could see the flames shooting high into the sky. Sometime later in the early part of the next morning, about 4:30 A.M., Dad came home awfully tired. I can remember hearing his cuffs on his overalls, which were frozen and swishing against each other as he came in the house after the fire had been put out. This event was pretty frightening to me, and afterwards it seemed to take the punch out of the townspeople. They weren't as upbeat about things as they had been before these fires.

Photo taken in front of Mesa Store, about mid 1920s, shortly before part of group left Aspen for California.
The old Model T was used to transport part of the group out West.
Left to right, bottom row: Kathren Grover, holding son Barney, Albert Grover holding son Buddy G., Mr. Atkinson
(friend of family), Florence Gould, Claire Grover in front, Atkinson boy, Helen Grover (with big hat), Donald Grover and
son E.J. Grover, E.J. Grover holding daughter Lois, Kenneth Grover (behind father).
Seated on right of photo: Helen Grover, Willard Grover, Fannie Grover (mother of four Grover boys), Emmett Gould
(Fannie Grover's brother) Charles Grover.
Standing in the back: Jim Gould, Charlotte Grover, Mrs. Herron (mother of Johnny and Bill Herron), Edward G. Grover
(husband of Fannie Grover), lady in white dress unknown, Mrs. Atkinson, and Molly Gould (wife of Emmett Gould).

However, for my brothers and I, things continued much the same. It seemed we always were getting into trouble. Somehow it would pass over 'til we got into trouble again. There were events that we'll always remember, like the time we went to the old town of Independence. Dad was a county commissioner at that time. Also, they were building the present automobile road over Independence Pass, working from both sides of the pass. Dad wanted to see how much of the road they had done on the east side. They were having slow going over on the east side because of having to build the road through rock cliffs. So this particular day after lunch at the old town, Dad and I hiked up the west side over the top and down to where they were working. They were working seven days a week and were about two thirds of the way through the cliffs — not too far from Mountain Boy Park. Once they got through the rock, it would be pretty easy going from then on. Dad chatted with the workmen for awhile, then we started back.

We had a .44 Winchester rifle with us, and when we got on top of Independence we stopped and Dad let me shoot the gun. After getting back to the old town, Uncle Duff La Plante (husband of my mother's sister) had been fishing and had seen a couple of nice fish he wanted to try and catch. We went downstream a ways from the old town but didn't get any fish.

Another day while they were building that road, the folks let me ride up to Lost Man Gulch with a fellow by the name of Tom Workman. He was driving an old four-wheel-drive truck hauling supplies for the road-building crews. The truck had solid rubber tires, so you can imagine what a bumpy ride that was.

South of Aspen near the top of Richmond Hill there is a particular and unusual piece of ground known as a fault block — a fairly large area surrounded on all four sides by faults. It was very rich in silver ore. Sometime in the early days of Aspen, my grandfather acquired title to this fault block. The story told to me begins with Grandfather Grover leasing the property to several prospectors with the proviso that the lease would terminate on a certain day at midnight. Luck was with the group, and they struck ore not too many feet down the shaft. Time was not with them. Frantically from then on they worked three shifts a day. The fateful day arrived. Grandfather Grover had pitched a tent close by, with a group of miners ready to take over. Midnight arrived. The miners were wondering what to call the mine. Someone pulled out his watch, looked at it, and said, "Well, it's midnight." Another man exclaims, "Hey, that's it. Let's call it the Midnight." From then on the mine was always known as the Midnight.

The Midnight Mine was given to my father by Grandpa Grover. Each one of the four Grover boys was given one-sixth of the mine. Then the Goulds got into the act, but I don't remember how. They wanted to develop it up on the top

*John Strong's
lumber truck
with Mesa Store
in background on
Main Street, 1947.
Courtesy Bud Strong.*

where the mine was. The original mine was a shaft. Driving a shaft is an expensive way of doing things because you've got to pump the water out and all kinds of extra junk. So they decided that they would go over Queen's Gulch and drive a tunnel through and intercept the fault block. Way back as far as I can remember, they were working on that tunnel, then they would run out of money. But anyway, they'd get a few bucks and they'd go up and work for awhile and then run out again. Back and forth so many times. This is the way it was done. Somehow the Willoughbys got a major interest in the Midnight. Fred Willoughby Senior was elected president.

Trips to the Midnight Mine were always fun. We boys would get the little timber car and play with it, pushing each other around on the track. Once in awhile the muck train would come out and we'd get to see them empty the cars. The train was pulled by a mule coming out of the tunnel. It was easy pulling on a slight downhill grade, but going back in the tunnel was quite a bit

278

different, all uphill. There were other things that always drew our attention, like the compressor house. The big air compressor pumped air into the tunnel to run the rock drills. Then there was the blacksmith shop, where they would sharpen the drill steel. There was one special time that Dad took my brother and I up to the mine. This was in wintertime on a Saturday. We rode up in a sleigh pulled by a team of horses. During the day, the weather turned bad and started snowing. It was decided by midafternoon we should stay overnight. Grandpa Grover had a cabin to himself. It had a couple of bunks in it, so we got to stay with him. This was all very exciting to two small boys. The following day, Sunday, it was still snowing. They thought we shouldn't try to go down because of a bad snowslide area further down the gulch. Monday it started to clear — but it was still no go. Tuesday, late in the afternoon, we started out. It was tough, slow going breaking trail in the deep snow, so it was about 8:00 P.M. before we were almost down to town. There was a full moon that night, flooding the valley to the west in a soft light. It was so beautiful, the magic of it all with the fresh new snow so quiet and peaceful. It was at that moment I wished I could bring a scene like that to the people so they could enjoy what we were seeing.

My first chores as a little boy were mainly getting in the wood and coal and shoveling snow off the walks. But we never shoveled walks for any money. In 1926, my dad, my youngest brothers, sister, and mom all went to Denver. They left my brother Ken and I in Aspen. We needed some bucks for Christmas presents, so we went around to the neighbors and took orders for Christmas trees. That's the way we made our money. Cut them up on Aspen Mountain.

We went up Aspen Mountain one Saturday to cut the trees. We started down this trail and here was these paw prints — big. These darn paw prints in the trail really intrigued me. I don't know why, but they did. I mentioned them to my grandfather and he said, "Are you sure that wasn't a mountain lion that was following you? I think it was. You guys be careful." Grandpa told us boys that cats had a streak of curiosity and they would often follow you.

Was there prejudice between the West Enders and the East Enders? Oh yes. You can say that again. Mother always told us boys that we shouldn't be playing with any of those kids because she always thought we were a little better than they were. I told her it was nonsense. When I was bigger, if she wanted me to quit seeing some girl, I said, "Hey, I'm not going to. She's as American as I am and I'm not going to stop." The neighborhood kids all played together. Mother didn't want us to do it. They tried to protect us to a certain degree. But we were always sneaking around.

What about Halloween? We'd do anything we could think of! I can remember going to the old Lincoln School after Halloween one year and there was a mowing machine — a big old pathetic mowing machine — sitting up on the roof. Who put that there? I don't know, but I think from the few remarks that were said, Red Rowland was one of them. They had a heck of a time getting it down. They had to take it apart. It took them about two days to do it. We tipped over outhouses, cut clotheslines with wirecutters, and swiped gates. If you had a gate on your yard, why that would disappear.

Our whole family went to California in 1927. We were there for about seven years and then we came back in 1934. Then Dad got involved with the Highland Mine up in Castle Creek. Here again, the Midnight was going gung-ho and they were doing very well. My Uncle Emmett and I don't know who else conceived the idea of driving a tunnel from the Castle Creek side and intersecting a body of ore in there. It was a great idea. Dad and Grandpa used their welding money from the Midnight to finance this property. We drove it back in there. I did an awful lot of it — about a thousand feet. Then I got tired of it. All the old holes were deep enough for me as far as I was concerned. So I went to work for the Highland Bavarian up Castle Creek Road.

The Highland Bavarian was started by a group from California, and the East Coast was involved in it. They wanted to put lifts up at Ashcroft. Tom Flynn was the one that showed them where. Tom used to live in Aspen. He was the one that really brought skiing to Aspen.

When I worked for the Bavarian Lodge, I started as a driver for a bus that they had. People would come on a train. I'd meet the train and haul them up. The original thinking on the lodge was that they would put up a cabin big enough for the guy staying, maybe he and his wife, and they could do the cooking. They'd have engineers to look the country over and see where to put in all the lifts. Somebody said, "Hey, let's make it a little bigger and get some guests up there and see what their reaction is." So as a result, the building up there now is a result of their thinking. It's right at the mouth of Conundrum over on the east end of the property, right on the edge where the old road used to be. They put in two rooms and bunkbeds. One was for the women and one was for the men. They each had a bathroom and shower. They had a maid's room down in a kind of a garage or stable or what-have-you, and that's where we stayed.

I married Genevieve in 1945 when I was thirty-one. We had two boys, Ralph and Dana.

I knew the change in Aspen was coming years and years ago. Like everything else, it grew in spite of itself. My favorite years were probably when I was a small boy. My father and mother went to Denver to visit my grandmother, and my brother and I had quite a bit of freedom. I guess I was around eleven or twelve years old — about 1924 or somewhere in that range. After we moved to Denver, all that stopped.

Bubby has good intuition about people. He's enthusiastic and handsome. I just don't know why some woman hasn't grabbed him right out of his saddle.

Bubby Light

I was born March 12, 1922, in Capitol Creek. In 1882, my grandfather, Fred Light, came from New York and homesteaded. His mother-in-law, who was my great-grandmother, Agnus Climont, homesteaded, too. That was done about 1882, when they built the ditch and things. The mines brought him to Aspen, but he was not a miner. He didn't like the mines, and he staggered around awhile. He wanted to get in the livestock business, so that's where he got. Grandfather built what's called the Fred Light Ditch. He started and adjudicated it in 1881. Adjudicated means he built the ditch and then validated the water right. He also built a ditch up here called the Green Meadow Ditch.

My grandparents had eight children, four boys and four girls. My father, Leo, was the third child but the oldest boy, and then I'm not too sure how they came. Some of them died young. The little boy, Howard, died of diabetes when he was twelve years old. Ray was about eighteen when he was killed by lightning in the cellar — right down in the basement. There was a hell of a storm. Lightning struck him when he was standing in the doorway by his two sisters. It knocked them down and the girls got over it, but he never got up. It killed him. The others all lived until they were grown. One brother, Frederick — they called him Fritz — lived here and died in 1931. He was thirty-six years old. He died of diabetes, just like the little boy did. When the little boy died, they didn't have insulin. There was nothing to do but get him on a diet. It got away from him and killed him. So my father outlived all the boys. He died around 1970. He was a big eighty-three when he died.

I haven't always lived here on the ranch. It's a long story. My dad owned Mrs. Wieben's property at one time. See, he left the nest and wanted to get married and there was the one boy, his brother, Fritz, still on grandfather's ranch. So dad bought a place from a man named Orvil Eib. Dad lived there and bached a while and then got married in 1917. In due time, my sister Betty came along. Before I came along, they moved onto a piece of land that Daniel Fealy homesteaded. We called it the Fealy and it was part of our ranch. I was born on the Fealy. Then they acquired more land. Then my folks bought more from a man by the name of Joe Montever. Uncle Fritz lived here in this white house. Later Fritz got married and lived here on this ranch with his family.

My father assumed the whole outfit from his father. So my dad had it all. We had 2,000 acres. This place up here was a homestead. For a while it was out of the family, and then we got it back. We lost it due to finances, I think. I don't know. That was before I was born.

My father, Leo, was born in a log house. I lived in it for twenty-nine years myself. I've just been down here at my mother's house for about two years. I lived in that log house, baching it by myself. Then I moved down here. The house was empty. My mother was sick and in a home for six years, and the house just laid empty. It's always been in the family. Grandfather must have bought this place right about 1890. It was just a log cabin with a dirt roof. That's the way he bought it, and then it's belonged to some of the Lights continually

283

ever since. They tore the log cabin down and built the house. Later they built the barn, and others were added to it as time went on.

My father never left the valley. I've hardly been out of this valley, either — never been anyplace. I've been to Denver maybe four times, Grand Junction, six. That's the only place I've ever been. Ranching has been our whole life for the whole family. That's how we were raised. Never sold anything off the ranch except what we drove off with livestock. We never sold hay or anything. Everything was put back to the cattle. Then we sold the cattle. We raised oats for our own use. In other words, if you'd have sold grain, you'd have had to haul it with a team and wagon to someplace. Well, the cattle could be driven to the railroad, so it was less work. That's what we've always done. We've always been the cattlemen.

I started working on the ranch as soon as I got out of high school. I was eighteen. I came home and never left. Of course, I was here in the summers. I went to a little white school right over here in Elk Creek Village for years. That's the Lower Capitol Creek School. In fact, the first teacher in Lower Capitol Creek was my Aunt Edith Light, the one that lived until she was ninety-three years old. She taught some of the locals.

When I was a kid, we had damn few neighbors. We owned up this valley. There were no close ones. There were a few up here about two miles who had a little place. We might call them little nesters. They homesteaded, too. I don't know what time. I went to school with some of the kids. It was just a little place to make a living.

There might have been fifteen in my school, some in every grade. Only three graduated from eighth grade with me — two girls and myself.

After school, I came home every night. I got the coal and wood and fed the skim-milk calves. When you milk the cows, you put them on the bucket — you cut the good milk with skim milk so you have more cream to sell. So you called them skim-milk calves. They were too little to feed just hay, so they were put on a little bucket. Every night I had to feed them. The men milked the cows, separated the milk, and sold the cream. The bigger I got, the more I could do. I started out early with chores. When I was little, I could drag in the wood. We all had coal-fired stoves and wood. After eighth grade, my parents sent me to Glenwood and boarded me down there. We should have gone either to Aspen or to the school in Basalt. I could come home on Friday. Sometimes I'd ride the train and they'd meet me; sometimes they'd come down after me. Once a week they got to go to town, so to speak.

See, when I was going down to Glenwood, Aspen was kind of a dead spot. You had to go to Glenwood for the bank. You couldn't buy a car upvalley; you

Bubby Light,
Willard Grover, and
Leo Light, 1942,
Box L Ranch,
East Sopris Creek.
Courtesy Bubby Light.

had to buy it down there. In Aspen, I think the bank was closed up for awhile
— hard times. Then later it opened up and, of course, now there's a lot.

   We always had a lot of ranch hands. Dad had about 400 head of cattle, and
they had to be fed all winter. He hired three men in the winter that worked all
the time. In the summer, sometimes dad would have six or seven hired men.
They stayed in the bunkhouse and mother fed them. Some would come in from
Missouri — they were good ol' hard-working boys! Some of them come in from
Kansas. Sometimes locals would come.

   When I was little they used a thrasher with a steam engine that took coal
and water, just like a locomotive. I got a shine on the guy that owned it. His
name was Gus Hotz. He was as old as my dad, and I was Gus Hotz for years.
He'd always give me his greasy gloves to play with. It was a greasy old hot
smoker from Basalt. They'd go around the country doing contract thrashing,
charging so much a bushel. You had to furnish them coal that they'd get from
Mrs. Bradshaw down here.

285

I never palled around. I guess my folks kept me busy, and it was quite a ways to go. These two girls were my age in the same class, and of course there were boys older and younger, but for some reason I didn't pal around. I was raised alone, so to speak. They never let me off. I could do anything I wanted on the ranch. I went into Aspen very seldom. Years ago, before my father was married, they'd go with the team and buggy and would get in on the holidays and things to celebrate a little. So they said. Of course, I wasn't born yet. But we stayed pretty close to home after I was born.

I heard after I was grown up that they used to have a red-light district and a lot of saloons in Aspen, probably before my dad was married. I think he got into town a lot on horseback. They were young and didn't think anything about riding in. And Steve Marolt's father had a saloon. They were closed up when I was big enough to know. The ranch where the golf course is now was the Marolt Ranch. As I get it, the saloon business was bad or the town went dead, and Mr. Marolt bought that ranch. It was called the Midland Ranch due to the Midland Railroad. I've heard my dad tell about those Marolt kids — little fellows. The little guys would play on the wood sidewalk. There was quite a large family, I gather.

A long time ago, there was lots of bootlegging in Aspen. Of course, I knew pretty much what it was. A lot of times they would get bootleg, or so I heard from the hired men. They'd get it and hide it in the bunkhouse, because mother didn't think too much of drinking. There were several people that made and sold hooch up in Aspen. I guess it wasn't too bad. They brought it in on pack-horses from Wyoming, too. Apparently it was legal up there. The guys would get something to drink, always. I suppose a few made their own.

A lot of Italians settled down here, and they always made wine. They'd buy grapes. They'd ship them into Glenwood on the railroad. Then they would brew the pulp and called it grappa. It was clear and it would knock you down. The first jolt I ever got, my God — it was something else. My dad always offered me a drink, so I didn't have to sneak it. If he had any, he offered it to me. The ranch hands would give it to me if I wanted it, but I never craved it. Oh, you get a little bit snooty as you grow up. I never had to sneak it so that it got to be a habit or anything, but it was always available. I can remember when Prohibition was over. An underage person could go in the bar and buy it, but you had to be accompanied by an adult, and he had to buy it for you. The kid couldn't. But if we ever went in, dad always said, "You want a beer or something?" and he'd get me one or he'd give me some of his. I never did care much for it, though — maybe a sip or two. But I never craved it.

Tough People, Hard Times

+ + + + + + + + + + + + + + + + + + +

I think my mother, Mary Epperson, was born in New Castle. She later moved to where the post office is — that was old Kelly's Saloon. Her daddy tended bar for old Kelly when she was a little girl. They migrated to Aspen when she wasn't too old. I think the younger sister was born here. They had a small dairy up above Aspen — Epperson's Dairy, I guess. She had an older sister, a brother, and a younger sister. The younger sister just died, I think, ninety-three years old. But anyway, they grew to adulthood and she went to school and somewhere along the line poppa met her. They got married in 1917.

My father raised horses, and so did grandfather. When he first started out, that's all he raised. He'd sell them clear up and down the valley — saddle horses. The miners would buy them and use them to haul from the sawmills and the mines. He had several stallions, mostly Belgian. I think he had some horses first in Leadville. Aspen hadn't busted open at the seam yet. They come over Independence, and I think he hauled over Independence with work horses. Then he come down and finally settled in the valley. He probably had some mares and got a stallion, then started raising them and grew hay. Then, as the horse business goes, they got cars and trucks, and this and that, and it petered out. So then he commenced to buy more cattle.

I helped break horses, too. I never got hurt, though. One fell on me one time and cracked the bone in my ankle, but that was all. Oh, I would get bucked off, but hell, that never hurts you. Long before I was here they had rodeos, but it was all business when I remember it. They broke them to ride.

I guess you could call me a real cowboy. But anymore, the riding's gone. It's all irrigating and things like that. I haven't got a motorcycle. I've still got two good horses to irrigate. I have two or three and I got the team. I feed and water with a team of horses. My neighbor is after me every day, "You ought to have a motorcycle. You ought to have one." I says, "Naw. I got two horses. That's enough for me, and I don't want one." And I don't feed in the winter with a pickup like some do.

To take the cattle to the railroad, you had to get them in a day or two before, down this road. It's about four miles. At one time we used to go by Snowmass, but you had to go across the highway. When they black-topped it, the cows wouldn't walk on it because they were scared. They'd never been off dirt. So then we went dirt road most of the time. Way down in Emma there was a stockyard and railroad, but we'd have to get them in the day before and cut them out. We'd separate the shippers from the mother herd. We didn't ship calves. The mother was the cow, see, and they would have a calf in the spring. Then in the fall, the calves were weaned so they were weaners. In the spring,

The Light family with the overshot stacker on the Box L Ranch, 1910. Courtesy Bubby Light.

they were yearlings and mom would have a new one. We run them until fall so they were a year and a half old. Then we went to market. We'd keep the mother until she got old or was no good anymore. We just sold the children. It's a good thing to do. Every so often you would have to ship older cows and keep a heifer in her place. We raised our own replacements so that you didn't have to buy them. As soon as we thought we'd split off all of the drys, which are the steers, the heifers, and anything that didn't have a calf suckling, they were put in another field and were considered beef. Then you'd pick what you wanted.

All the steers went to market, and you'd pick what you thought were the tops. Then you'd count them up — so many head to the carload. You'd keep them here. When you decided to ship, you had to go down to Carbondale. There was a depot and a man there to order your cars. They might bring the cars from Denver and you'd tell him what day. It had to be on a Saturday because you wanted to get them in Denver to sell by Monday. They would generally bring them up on Friday, because the train didn't run Sunday.

Well, we'd get ready and so many counted, and then we left here as soon as it was light enough. Sometimes one would get away and we'd lose it, but generally we'd ride fast. There were no fences. They'd wander anyplace. We'd get them in there and then they were counted, so many per load. The train would go up and they'd send section hands to move the cars for us. They had their own little telephone. Then they'd say, "The train's ready to leave Aspen. Better load." So they'd move them down and we'd load them and pretty soon the train would come down. They'd couple up, and then we'd go to Carbondale and bill them out. You got a pass. You could ride the caboose over and they'd give you a paper so if you would go down to the railroad yard, they would let you come back as a passenger with this pass.

They'd take 'em to Glenwood, and they'd switch them on the main line. The night train came through. Generally all they hauled in the fall was cattle. Otherwise they'd have anything on there. Generally, they'd put them up next to the engine and then snap them together, and you better get in the caboose. When you went to Denver, you'd have to ride her all night long. You'd get into Denver about seven in the morning. It was an all-night trip. Sometimes the whole valley would go. Sometimes the Aspen branch would have twenty cars of cattle. Then maybe they'd only have one. It took four or five of us to drive them down. We'd have cowboys and neighbors help us. Two men couldn't just take them, because they'd get away from you. We had over a hundred head. They had men that would unload them and then put them in a pen. Monday morning they sold. They had to feed and water them.

I never married. I just never got the job done. I've been a bachelor all the time. I thought I was going to get rich ranching. I don't know. It just seems like you get busy, and there's lots of fun on the ranch. I just didn't I guess.

It's been a good life. I like it. I'm glad I stayed here with it. I turned seventy in March. Maybe it's my haircut. I used to have to go to the barber occasionally; it would get out on my ears and bother me. Then it got a little thinner. My horseshoer cuts my hair. He comes up to shoe my horses, and we got an old pair of dog clippers and he clips. Doesn't charge me anything for the haircut.

There were always rivalries about water around here. I've listened to that all my life. I don't think grandfather ever had a gun, but by God, he could get to them otherwise. Damn right. He fought all of his life for water.

In those days, there were claim jumpers, too. They'd just squat on the land, and if you didn't kick them off, they could claim an interest. It was illegal, but they could pull it if you couldn't run them off. Some of them bristled. I mean, they were ornery, trying to get something for nothing.

In those days, the men wore red wool underwear. That was all grandfather would buy. Anyway, it was dark when he come home, and I guess he went to bed. For some reason, he roused up and looked out his cabin window and saw this little campfire and he knew what the hell it was because nobody camped in those times. They'd come in and stay with you in your cabin. You know, "Come on in." So he put on his pants and suspenders and went up to see. Here was this bozo, and the fight was on. I guess he was a pretty big man and they got to scuffling up there in the moonlight. Finally they staggered in the creek, and grandfather held him under until he kind of quit kicking a little bit. When grandfather let him up, the squatter had the fight taken out of him.

The land office was in Glenwood. Grandfather got some dry underwear, saddled a horse, and lit out in the night. When they opened up in the morning, he went in and filed his claim. He went in the saloon because he knew that guy wasn't going to give up. He waited in the saloon, and here come the stage. There was this guy all wet. Pretty soon he come in, and it was "Oh feathers and Willoughby." It was too late. Grandfather'd beat him by about four hours. It was a homestead claim. So it was his, and he got on his horse and went home and he never saw the guy again.

We had no doctors around. If you couldn't doctor yourself, you went to Glenwood. Dr. Hopkins brought us into the world and took care of us all until he got too old. I guess when the Light kids were born, you just had them. You know what I mean. They were pretty tough old people. I suppose some might have been born in Aspen, but some of them were born right on the ranch.

This house was built in 1902. Never been a door locked here, not that I know of. I don't have any keys — the windows are painted shut. They never did work. I never locked a door in my life. I still don't. Some of these people are raised different than we were. They will lock their gates. In the old days there were short cuts. Nowadays people call it trespass. I don't think they mean bad but there's too many of them. You never locked anything in the old days. It was a disgrace to see a man's ranch with a lock on it. You were welcome to come in. You know what I mean.

My Grandfather Light had a sawmill up at Lenado many years ago. He got up there with a team and wagon. And they had to haul the lumber down and put it on the railroad. He'd sell it. That was when mining was going on. The mines were hot up there. When my dad was real small, there was no school here, and they'd have to move the mother and the little kids into Aspen to go to school. Grandfather just kept an old hired man here to feed the horses and the stock. In the summer, they'd come back. He had two businesses going, lumber and raising horses.

My dad wouldn't go to school. He only went to the fourth or fifth grade. He just wouldn't go. He come down and bached with this old guy and lived down here all of his life. He wouldn't stay up in Aspen. "Baching" meant you were a bachelor. There were lots of old bachelors. The old men would come and work for you, hole up, trap, and things. They just didn't have a woman.

I wasn't a good cook. I've lived on it and did all right, but it wasn't too good. I still do my own cooking. I used to make a kind of God-awful sour-dough biscuits. That was pretty good stuff if I had a good batch of it. It's a little bit soggy, but it's good food. It'll stay with you. You can do hard work on it. Get a bellyful of that and meat, and you can make it. I still eat off of my cows. I had to get on a little diet and had to kind of shape up. I had to cut down on the meat and sweet stuff. Boy, it bothered me for awhile. I've been on it for four years. I had a hell of a time, but I stayed with it. I finally pulled off about thirty pounds, and it's a good thing I did. I turned into a diabetic. I had two uncles die of diabetes and I don't want to.

I rode my horse to school. There was a shed right behind it, and you tied your horse in there. Some of the kids closer walked but we rode across horse-back. You allowed thirty minutes — we didn't take too long. We went every day. We'd cut across the neighbor's — a man named Williams owned it. The snow would drift, but the old horse would make it through. You'd just get up on him and he'd go. We had a lot of saddle horses. Grandpa had a lot of them, but my dad must have kept fifty or sixty. We'd have all the horses you wanted.

We went to school no matter what the weather. It didn't make any difference. You got up, you got on the horse, and you went. The horse took you. In bad storms, you just let the horse go. If you let him alone he'd take you home. It was awful with that wind blowing. We each had a horse. We didn't ride double. There were three kids that rode one horse. He was a big saddle horse, kind of a

The Honorable Frederick Light, member of the Colorado House of Representatives from Pitkin County, 1894. Courtesy Bubby Light.

Morgan. You read in old times where people got lost in blizzards. Well, if they'd just have left their horses alone, they'd have made it. But they thought they could find the way. Of course, sometimes I guess they got in drifts they couldn't get through.

Several of the horses my dad sold would get away from the new owners and, by God, you'd be standing out here and they'd come back home. The old guy would call up and say, "You got my horse?" And we'd say, "Yeah, come get him." And they'd come over and get him. Well, we sold one to Albert Cerise — that's not very far. It was a working mare and she got away from him. She was here one morning. Pa called him and said, "Albert, old Flax is here." He said, "Well, I'll get over there after her. I'll send Martin over." Albert was mad.

People don't realize the amount of work on a ranch. It was all hard work, and they think the fences were here when grandpa moved in. There wasn't a god-damn thing but a bunch of willows. That's all that was here. When my dad was little, my grandfather didn't have a drill to drill grain, and they plowed it with a walking plow. He'd make my dad drive a buggy and sit in the back and run it through his fingers, then throw it out and take the harrow crossways. It was just as even if you drilled it. I've got a mechanical butter mixer in the cellar. You turned the crank. It looks kind of like a clothes wringer. You'd work it and it was built on an incline so the buttermilk would run out and down in a container. When they bought it, it was really modern, because they used to milk cows and take the butter clear to Aspen. I've got some of the cartons — Box L Butter.

A lot of the old people did find the gold or silver and turned it into a mine, but I guess my grandfather went in the mines a little bit but didn't like it. He said, "I want to stay outside and to hell with the damned mine. I'll make it some way." I've never been in one, but when I looked back and saw that much daylight, man, I'd break and run. That's the way I am. I don't want to be in no damn hole. Might end up in a hole. I think we're all going to. But then I ain't going to have that light when I go. It's going to be solid.

I think Aspen started to change about the time of World War II — the early 40s. The Tenth Mountain Division came over to ski and people came from other countries.

We didn't go up to Aspen much, but we knew everyone in town in the 1930s. Things were slow and relaxed. Good times then. I don't fit in up there in Aspen. It's not a rural man's town anymore — it's a city man's town.

◆

Frank was the pharmacist who knew everyone in town. His nickname was Doc. He is proud of his past and of Aspen.

Photo by Kathy Daily

Frank Loushin

I was born October 24, 1918, in Aspen. My mom was also born in Aspen, in 1900. Her name was Mary Vedic. My dad, John Loushin, was born in Slovenia in 1889. They lived up there on Riverside Addition. My mother, Mary Vedic, was born here, but her mother and dad came from Slovenia. They must have come early because my mom was born here in 1900 — must have come in the 1880s. Her father was a miner. Her mother, at that time, ran a boardinghouse.

My grandmother's maiden name was Antona Gregorich. She married Anton Vedic. Anton first went to Leadville, and then from Leadville they came over and got a place in Aspen.

My mom would help around the house when she was small. Of course, they used to have her go to school at the Catholic convent. But during the summer, she helped at home. They had a little place, and they used to take care of the garden and the rest of the kids. They would take the cows and range them around where the old Aspen Grove cemetery is. There were nine of them in that family. In Austria and Slovenia, the government was forcing all the young men to be in the military — they couldn't get out of it. Most of them decided to come to America. That's how my dad came over. His brother was here first. Then my grandfather came and settled over in Leadville for awhile. When the money started getting good in Aspen, he settled and lived the rest of his life here. He died young — in middle age — 'cause he had cancer. They didn't know at that time about cancer.

At first, my dad stayed with his brother because his brother got my dad over here. He used to have friends at the boardinghouse, so that is where he met my mother. I think my mom was sixteen years old when they got married and my dad was around twenty-six. He was ten years older than she was. They didn't go out on dates. My mom said that he went up and asked my granddad or grandma if he could marry my mom and they said sure. And that was that. Mom said she never had a choice. That's how a lot of them did it. She was seventeen when she had her first child, my brother John. I was born next, and my other brother, Bill, after that. The youngest brother, Ludvick, was born ten years later. There's four in our family — she had her hands full.

When my dad first came here, his profession was a blacksmith. The only reason he got a job was 'cause the company wanted him to sharpen all the drills for mining. Then they gave him a lease in the mine. Dad worked in the mine awhile. After the war, he became the city marshall until he finally retired. I guess that was about five or six years. He coughed quite a bit and then had heart failure. The Durant, the Smuggler, and the Cowenhoven mines were going full blast. When we were small, we'd go every Sunday over to that area 'cause my dad was working outside.

At that time, my parents would try to speak English to us when we were growing up. The only ones who would talk to us in Slovenian were my grandmother and some of the people around the area. A lot of Slovenians were here in the East End of town. The neighbors always looked up to my dad 'cause he got to speaking English pretty good and so they always came around. They'd come over and get information from my dad, especially during the elections. He knew

about the city and would tell them who he thought was the best candidate. At that time, the East End was the workers' part of town. The Italians were out in Woody Creek and also in the West End. The English were on the other side of the East End and kind of central. There were a few Irish, but the English ran 'em out of town.

Hyman Avenue and West End Street, 1942. Snyder, Popish, Loushin, and Strong kids. Courtesy Jennie Popish.

My parents never spoke Slovenian except with close friends. Years ago, across Cooper Avenue, my uncle and aunt had a house with a great big long porch. All the neighbors close by would come and congregate right there. They sang songs every night. And, of course, they would speak the language. I can understand it, but I can't really speak it real good. So I would speak to my grandmother and try to learn. I forgot a lot of it, too. Years ago, everybody spoke it, and then everybody died. Then no one spoke it at all. So it was forgotten.

There was a German marshall — Charlie Wagner. Wagner Park is named after him. He was the marshall a long time until he finally passed away. One minute he was on the West End of town and the next minute he was on the East End. He traveled all over and he didn't sit home. He was on the go all the time. He didn't have an office. He was a very good marshall.

I graduated from Aspen High School in 1937 and went to pharmacy college in Denver. I started working at the Lamb Drugstore first, and then it burned down. Mr. Lamb died, then Mr. Lamb's daughter sold the Lamb Drugstore to Aspen Drugstore. Lamb's Drug was in the middle of the Hyman Mall.

Hyman Avenue fire,
October 30, 1941.
Courtesy Helen Kralich.

The Lamb Drugstore had on one side a big case of imported perfumes — some as high as one hundred dollars. He had a lot of these cosmetics. He knew that was a big draw, and of course, he had his pharmacy in there, too. His pharmacy was in the back of the store with a separate door so it would not interfere with anything out in front. In the front, he had his cosmetics, different tonics, aspirins, and all that stuff. They used to have these great big jars with sticks and little squares of cherry and root beer candy. We used to buy that.

I was going home the day they sold out, and they loaded me up with some cigarettes 'cause I was smoking a little bit. Mr. Hanson was out by the drugstore and said, "Where the heck are you going?" I said, "Home," and he said, "Why?" I didn't know that he had bought the drugstore. He said, "You get your butt in here. You are working for us. We bought you, too." So I asked him if I could have the weekend off. I worked for him from 1940 until his death in 1980. Then I worked for James Parson, Mr. Long, and a couple of years for Steve Wickes. I resigned in 1980. After 1980, I worked for Magnifico Liquors until it sold out. Then I worked for Aspen Hardware & Supply.

Tough People, Hard Times

◆◆◆◆◆◆◆◆◆◆◆◆◆◆◆◆◆◆◆

I did everything at the drugstore. In the Fifties, I filled prescriptions if somebody needed it. The doctors would get called out and they didn't have a pharmacy in the hospital. They'd call the doctor over and regardless of where it was, he would call and get me up at any time of night, and I would deliver. The worst deliveries were when I had to walk up to McLaughlins. He had that place out there about three miles by Difficult Campground. I delivered that in a blizzard. His wife was really sick, so I walked all the way up there and back. Half the time I didn't know where I was. But I kind of had an idea, and I walked by the bank of the river. I never was so cold in all my life.

Medicine changed through the years. People in the 1930s and 1940s didn't take medicine for anything. My grandma never took an aspirin until the very last years of her life. Some of them would take some kind of herbs and tonics.

Back when we were younger was a slower time, and there was not all this rush. Now it's hustle bustle. We worked hard and our work came first. Of course, on the Fourth of July, we worked in the morning, then in the afternoon we would go to the parade. At that time, people didn't have too much money. We would

Aspen Drug after fire, November 15, 1919. Courtesy Aspen Historical Society.

297

save and buy a ten-cent package of a hundred and fifty firecrackers. Never shot them in town. We used to have the hillside next to our house, and we'd pretend we were mining. We'd dig a little hole and stick one of the firecrackers in there and light it off. We used to spend a lot of our time swimming, too. There is a place up where the Northstar Preserve is now. It was called Dead Waters 'cause the water would circle around a couple of deep holes that had sand in them.

You didn't dare get into trouble when you were young. Trouble and mischief were two different things. There was a girl who I had a crush on. She had a ponytail and she always had her hair on my desk. After we had a fight, I told her to take her hair off my desk. She kept on, and I took her hair and stuck it in the inkwell. She had a white blouse on and it got all over. I had to pay for the blouse. I think it was six dollars — a lot of money back then. They had to take scissors and cut part of her hair off.

In high school — when D.R.C. Brown's home was converted into the high school — once we wanted to tease the girls. So we found a dead cat. On the third story, we had our laboratory and experiments. So anyway, we tied that cat out on a rope and dangled it by the assembly hall. The girl sitting by the window shrieked. Another time we had a professor, and he would go to ring the bell. So we'd get a wad of gum and stick it on the bell. When he went to ring it to change the class, he knew right away what we had done.

We used to go out on Halloween and swipe these big wagons from people that had horses around town and put them in the high school where nobody could get in.

We tipped over outhouses. One time there was a fellow in it. He was in there waiting with a shotgun. And we tipped it and he let a charge go off. Of course, he didn't hit anybody 'cause it went in the air, and boy did we take off! And another thing we did was take gates off the fences and climb up the trees and hang the gates. For every gate we took, my dad made us put it back. We paid for it. My dad made sure that we took every one back that we took off to the right place.

I used to ski and I was crazy. I had long skis and greased them up real good with candle wax. We would build a big jump. We heard over the radio that a fellow jumped a number of feet in the Olympics. We thought he was going straight up. So we built a ramp on the mountain, and I got to go first because I got the longest straw. I went way up, and it was a good thing there was a lot of soft snow. I went up and into about five feet of snow. It felt like my hips jumped out of their sockets. The skis that we used were just ordinary fifty-gallon barrel stays. All we did, when we found an old pair of shoes or something, was to take leather and nail it across the shoe. Then we would get some old innertube tires and cut them so we could put it at the end of our toes to hook onto our heels, so it would stretch. That was the only thing we had. Later on, when there was a lot of these old vacant houses, we used to get the door frames and would carve skis out of them. We would put them in hot water and get them all soaked up. We had to cut out the tips. Then we would put it in a vise and put a lot of weight on them so the tips would bend. After that, we would leave them to dry. Sometimes when we built them in a hurry, we got some ordinary tin and curved the tin so it wouldn't cut us if we happened to fall. Then we nailed it to the tip. That's how we used to make our skis.

When we were just getting out of high school, we used to go up and get on the river, ice-skating. We used to go after work around eight o'clock in the evening back where they called "Sparky's." All of us used to get together. We'd get wood and build a bonfire. We had a fellow by the name of Hannibal Brown, and he used to come there and make punch for us. He was the one that taught us how to skate. He taught me and my two brothers. Hannibal Brown was a very good skater. We used to go up to McLaughlin's Ranch where it was all ice, and we used to ski and skate all the way down the river.

We used to swim in Sullivan's Pond, just below the Crestahaus. The WPA, to get work for some of the elderly people (my dad was in charge of it), hauled sand and everything to put in Sullivan's Pond. Before it was cans and everything. That was supposed to be kind of like a public swimming pool. They didn't make a beach; they just put a sand bottom in it. They kind of cleaned it up. My dad did that. And then we used to swim there. Also, we used to swim down there in that pond below the old hospital. It's the old Ice Pond, they called it. Mostly the boys swam there — wouldn't allow the girls to go down there because the boys went nude swimming.

A while back, I used to mine in Lenado. Originally, the fellow that owned it gave it to my dad. He needed help and nobody had too much money. So Judge Shaw, his wife Dorothy, Liz Callahan, and my dad were partners. So that is why they call it the Four Friend Mine. They started mining there. Judge Shaw and Dorothy deeded their share to my two brothers and I, and Liz deeded her share to us also. My dad gave his share to us, too. At that time, there were quite a few people in Lenado. They had sawmills and I guess about thirty to forty families up there. They knew exactly when we were going to let off the charges. What we did was, we'd go clean up the tunnel. Then we would drill. I would fix up the powder and dynamite. When they were through drilling, I'd have all these sticks fixed up and they'd go load 'em and blast 'em. We'd wait to make sure all the charges

Roch Run,
Aspen Mountain, 1938.
Courtesy Del Gerbaz.

went off. If some of them didn't go off, we would write it on the blackboard. But most of them went off and sometimes both of 'em would go off together. We shook the whole town of Lenado. They almost could set their alarm clock by our charges, 'cause every day about 10:00 P.M. the charges would sound.

We found a trace of everything in our mine — zinc, molybdenum, a little gold, and platinum. Potash was something unusual up in there. No uranium.

Everybody knew us, and they was good to us. In the 1960s and 1970s was when the hippie stage was. A couple of them went off the road up in Difficult Campground. I was checking my rifle at that time — it was hunting season. We pulled them back on the road and the whole hippie tribe knew us. We went up to Lenado to work. They had barbecued for about two days. They had all kinds of food, and everybody came up to us. They had a big meal for us — fresh pork, beer, and everything that you would have at a barbecue.

Everything started to change when the Paepckes came. All the different people started coming and started buying. At that time, if you got a $45,000 home, you thought you had a lot of money. People came in with more money and started buying up homes. Paepcke bought a lot. He bought the Hotel Jerome and where Crossroads Drug used to be. He picked up all that, and across from Aspen Drug. And then the Goethe Bicentennial, when Dr. Schweitzer came. That was after the war. Then the music students. The opera house was fixed up, and all the music students practiced all around town. Music was continuous, and nobody minded — everyone loved it. In the evening they started singing outside. It was good for our business because we had a great big ice-cream freezer in Aspen Drug. They would flood in there for ice cream. We got to where we knew most of them, and that made it real nice. And every year we couldn't wait for them to come back. They would come visit us right away. Now it is different — they are out-of-towners.

I don't mind the change, but there are some things I don't like. I don't like how the city and the county are run. Things could be better there, but they have problems. Before, when we were here, it was nice and quiet; you hardly ever saw any cars around. Now this is like a highway running up and down.

What advice would I give to make Aspen a better place? I would say one thing — obligation and cooperation. At one time years ago, everybody helped, and now it's every man for himself. Everybody used to trust everybody. You never wrote anything down on a piece of paper — you shook hands.

To show you how friendly people were years ago, when we started building this house, most of us didn't make good money. I was only getting seventy-five dollars a month. I could only save so much, and whatever I could save, then I would buy material. Well, we had to dig the foundation. A fellow came up by the name of Red Rowland — came up with the bulldozer and dug out all my basement. Didn't cost me anything. So then we put the foundation down and were getting ready to pour the cement. There was John Litchfield, who owned the Red Onion. He and another friend were walking up the street. We just started pouring — we only had one wheelbarrow. We only had the four of us. We knew it was going to take us about two days, 'cause we couldn't do it all in one day. So John Litchfield came by and he knew me real well. He said, "What are you doing?" I said, "Getting ready to pour the walls." "Okay, I'll see you later." That was all. And then about thirty guys came back with him, with wheelbarrels going all around the block gathering rocks. I had around fifty sacks of cement, and I don't know how much sand there. He saved me almost half the cement. He had these guys pouring cement and guys behind them throwing rocks in. They had that all done by noon. I said, "I don't have any money to pay you. What can I do?" John says, "You don't pay them nothing. They owe me for their beer tabs. This is the day I am gonna make 'em pay." But that's how things were.

I started building the house, but I didn't have any experience in carpentry. We knew how to go about it all right. We had the blueprints. But the old lady living in the cabin next door was watching. She would watch and she would say, "Ah, ah, ah, not that way." She would come over and show us. It was her guidance that helped us put the house together. Don't remember her name. This was all in 1958. She would direct us how to do it, and then she would come in and show us how to cut the angles and would cut it for us. She was smart. That just goes to show you how people helped each other out. Now you can't get nobody unless you pay them ten to fifteen dollars an hour. It is a complete change. You'd take a kid and let him mow a lawn for somebody and give him two bits — that was fine. You take a kid now and you got to give him twenty dollars. That's how our boy got through college — lawn mowing.

All in all, I have no regrets about staying here. I was born here, and I'm going to die here. I have a lot of friends, and I get along with everybody. And you know, I cherish that.

◆

Photo by Kathy Daily

*Hazel seems to have taken
care of kids for a century.
She's very comfortable with
them. She is proud of her
past and of who she is.*

Hazel Anderson Loushin

I was born March 9, 1926, in Aspen in my folks' house, 34 West Hopkins. Dad was born in 1890 and his name was August Anderson. He came from Norway. Dad worked in the Midnight and Durant mines. Later he worked on the dynamite crew on Independence Pass. My mother was Swedish and her name was Anna Anderson, born in 1894. She was an excellent seamstress. I grew up and

The old hospital at the bottom of Red Mountain, 1905. Courtesy Peggy Rowland.

went to school here. I graduated from the red brick building, the high school, in a class of fourteen in 1944.

Although father came from Norway and my mother from Sweden, we didn't learn the Swedish language at all. The schools didn't encourage us in anything but English. My older cousins knew how to speak Swedish, but they were kind of ridiculed at school.

I left here after I graduated from high school for awhile and went through nurse's training at Presbyterian Hospital in Denver. I graduated in 1947. Then the war was over and I came back to Aspen.

My parents loved to dance, and at every opportunity they went to dances. They probably met at a dance. The Swedish people used to have big Swedish picnics and then, of course, there was always dancing at these affairs. Some of the picnics were up in the area where Hilder Anderson grew up — Snowmass, or Brush Creek, actually. It was up in the Brush Creek area where the Swedish people in my

304

parents' era held their big dances. Big dances were held at the dance pavilion at Hallam Lake for the community, too.

I was nursing and raising a family — two children — when my husband Frank was in the pharmacy. When I first started at the hospital, there were only three nurses in 1945. We would work twelve-hour shifts so we could have a day off. But there were only maybe four patients sometimes.

Women would come to the hospital to deliver babies, and we had a small nursery. When Frank and I had free time, we went to dances at the Armory Hall (City Hall). Christmas and New Years dances there were held there, and May Day dances and Valentines dances and the Flower Show.

Gardening was a pastime here and everybody competed with each other, like who would get the

Hotel Jerome, about 1948. Courtesy Ingrid Elisha.

biggest cabbages. At that time, there were different types of flowers and everybody had beautiful gardens. You had to have some real good flowers in order to compete. I won first prize on bachelor buttons one time.

I used to hike and climb for entertainment when I was young. I did a lot of climbing around Shadow Mountain. We used to ride up to the Midnight Mine with the miners in the morning and hike over the mountain coming down on the Aspen side.

I belonged to the school band, and we went to Grand Junction for competitions. Aspen always did very well.

The biggest town change came in 1947 when Walter Paepcke started remodeling buildings. If I had a favorite year, I'd stop Aspen in the 1960s, when everybody still knew everybody. Nowadays, there is too much government. They should let people think for themselves.

◆

*Angie has an
infectious laugh
that captures your soul.
She understands
a good time.*

Angie Maddalone Caparella

I was born February 4, 1921, in a little town called Erie, Colorado. My father's name was James Vioent Maddalone, and my mother's name was Ida Evelyn Puckett. My dad came from Italy. Seems to me like he was very very young when they brought him over to Leadville. Later on, he met my mother there. Then they got married and came here to Aspen. My brothers Joe, Tony, Jim, and Jess were all born here in Aspen. Then they moved around Boulder or Erie, Colorado — one of those little mining towns. And that's where I was born. I remember coming here when I was four years old.

There were ten children in our family, and I was the fifth. There were four boys ahead of me — Joe, Tony, Jim, and Jess — then me and Stogey, then my sister Frances. She died when she was twelve years old. After Frances was born, there was Mary, Ida, and Chuck.

When we came here, it was on the first of July, and we rode the train all the way up to the Glory Hole. It was the Rio Grande. I can remember when we got up to Aspen there was all these little bald-headed kids meeting the train. They were my brothers and neighbor kids. They had come to meet the train. My brothers had been here with some of my dad's relatives. My mother, Tommy, and I was coming back from over at Erie. I was four years old. On the Fourth of July, my sister Frances was born. On July 8 — I'll never forget it — we always had my mother's dad living with us, my grandfather Puckett, and he died that day. All this happened within the week. He'd had a heart attack. He would swell up. His legs would get real big, and his stomach, too, and they would pump water out of him. He had dropsy. He was old. I believe he was a miner in Leadville.

Mom was Irish, Scotch, and Cherokee Indian. Dad was a straight Italian, so I have a good mix. We lived down there by the post office. That's where Frances was born. My Aunt Frances lived by there, and my uncle, well, I called him Foo Foo. I don't know what his real name was. Then down there where Gene Frye used to live, that was my Uncle Sindoin's house. That was Tony Maddalone. Why was my father called Jimmy de Buck? I have no idea. Everybody called him Buckshot. He was a pretty keen little guy. Everybody knew him. If you didn't know him and he didn't know you, he'd go up and introduce himself. I really don't know how he got that nickname.

My first chores were helping with all of the other kids and trying to cook. The first thing I guess I learned how to cook was spaghetti. I still cook a mean spaghetti — spaghetti and fried potatoes. Dad used to grow a good garden and caught a lot of fish. Today I hate fish. I won't eat it. We ate a lot of buckskin and we made homemade wine and beer.

I had to sew when I was pretty young. Everything was hand-me-downs. Mom didn't sew. My aunt taught me. We had to wear a dress to school, yes — with those old flour-sack pants that had "flour" printed on the back of them and with those big elastics. Cute, with flour across your butt. I can remember those. How did we stay warm when we walked to school? I think my aunt knitted me

a pair of black socks. We never had decent boots or shoes or anything. We had our jackets, hats, and coats, but then us kids only had a little way to go. We walked up the back — Tin Can Hill.

I remember going to school the first year at the Washington School. I only went six months because my brother Tony hit me in the eye with an arrow. From then on I stayed in the closet. It was just a little bow and arrow that kids play with, but it had a point. He was just playing around. I was six years old. It wasn't his fault — it was an accident. Of course, it wasn't taken care of because I don't even think I said anything. One day I was standing out in the yard and I could hear the train but I couldn't see anything. I had gone blind in both eyes. After that, I remember being in a clothes closet with stuff around my eyes. I'd stay in the closet all day and sometimes at night, too, because they didn't want any light getting into those bandages. What did I do in the closet? Sit there and cry, I guess. It was terrible. I think I stayed in that closet for about four or five months. I never got to go back to school again, and then when I did get to go back it was the next year and I was behind. I was scared. I don't even go in the john and close the door. That's real terrifying for a young kid.

When we got sick and had an earache, Mom would warm olive oil and put it on an old piece of cotton in our ears. For colds, we put mustard oil on our chest — real burny stuff, real strong. It was in a little white jar like the Vicks comes in nowadays. I remember having that around the house a lot. Mom would rub it on us . . . and cough syrup. That's about all we did.

My brother, Jim, used to take some kind of a liver tonic that he hated. After that cod-liver oil, or whatever it was, he'd get to have a piece of orange. Well, I loved oranges, so instead of him taking his cod-liver oil, I'd take the oil for him if he'd give me a piece of his orange.

Mother was such a good lady. She was marvelous. She'd bake bread about every day, and anyone going by our house was always given hot homemade bread and butter.

My first chores were cooking and cleaning and helping with the kids — diapers. We boiled and hung them out on the line. In the wintertime, they'd freeze on the line. Your fingers would get so cold. I can remember the other kids used to get to go play baseball and basketball and do things after school. I had to come home.

Did I get in mischief a lot with my brothers? Yeah. Fighting all the time. We had boxing mitts.

There was another Italian family in town, the Crocks, who lived on Main Street just before you get to the clinic — one block up. I had to go to church every Sunday. We'd come home from church, take off our Sunday best, put on our old raggedy jeans, and go up to the Crocks. Then the Crocks would walk out to the Caparella's place and we'd spend Sunday like that.

I was four years old when I met Teleo. He was there at the depot meeting us when I came to town. He was with my brothers. He was born in 1916 and I grew up with him. Teleo was going to kick my butt one day. He had made this little wagon and thought it was such a keen thing. So he wanted me to go for a ride with him. We were out at their place (Caparella's). I told him I didn't want to ride in that thing. It had tin cans for headlights. I was sixteen when I got married. We went dancing for years together.

Teleo Caparella and I got married in 1938. For the last fifty years, we celebrated on April 14. Then after he passed away, I found my marriage certificate and it was April 12. We'd been celebrating April 14 for fifty years.

My first son's name was Jessie and then Jinx. Teleo worked for Mountain Utilities — the electric department. They supplied all the electricity to Aspen from Glenwood. We lived on Frances Street, right across from Louiva Stapleton.

Then I can remember when my sister Frances got sick. She had diabetes. What I really think happened was that she had polio. I was fourteen. Frances was twelve. She was lying in bed and I was holding her hand when she died. Mother had gone to lie down. I told Mom, "Mom, you go lie down. You've been up with her night and day. I'll stay with her." And I can remember Mom hadn't laid down I don't think a half-hour when Frances died. Kids nowadays don't realize what we had to go through to survive. You had to be tough. You had to take care of each other, too. You don't have that anymore.

Grandpa Cap (James Caparella) in his garden, 1950s. Courtesy daughters of Mable Tekoucich.

Dad loved to fish. He had a name for all the trout. He'd catch the same trout once in awhile and then he'd turn it loose. He'd name those things. He'd know who he was catching. The only time he'd really bring fish home was when we'd want to eat them or he'd bring them to somebody. Dad caught a lot of fish, but he threw his friends back. Once in awhile he'd bring a nice one or two home and Mom would bake 'em. But usually the trout weren't that big.

What was mother's favorite food? I think Mom loved to put on spaghetti and meatballs, homemade noodles, and homemade bread. Breakfast? Cereal, coffee, and crackers. That was about the size of it. Supper was the big meal. Sometimes Dad didn't work for months at a time, and it was rough going. We depended on the garden and the wildlife. And I'm a vegetarian. Even when I was a kid at home. I wouldn't eat it. They'd put a pork chop on my plate and I'd give it to my brother Tony. They'd put steak on my plate; I've never eaten a piece of steak. I've never had a hamburger in my life.

I think that about the year that Paepcke and them started buying everything, Aspen started to change. If we had $500 at that time, we could have bought the whole town of Aspen. When T. and I bought our house, we paid $500 for it — $25 a month.

I miss living up in Aspen and often wished I could still live there. But I guess I'm like the others who had lived there and moved away — what can you do? The town is too expensive for most of us.

◆

Chuck can tell a good
story. He is a kind man
and very honest. He is
devoted to his wife, Pat, and
I admire their relationship.

Chuck Maddalone

I was born September 13, 1932, in Aspen. My mother was born in Granite, Colorado, right over the hill by Leadville. Her name was Ida Puckett. My father's name was James Maddalone. He came from Santa Maria, Italy. It's about three miles from Naples. He came straight to Aspen, and I think he met mom here. He was a miner. He came over when he was seventeen years old. His sister

313

already lived here, and we had some relatives in Chicago and New York. I don't know what Aunt Frances (his sister) — we called her Seatacake — was doing in Aspen. There were quite a few Italians around here. And he had a brother here, too. We called him Foofoo. Tony was his real name.

I think my poppa's mother died when he was real young, and he was raised by, I think, one of his sisters, aunts, or somebody. I think his sister and his brother came over here first and then he decided to come over. I think he had another sister also.

My dad was a great gardener. He had to be, raising ten of us kids. They wondered why we could run and swim so good when we were kids. If you ate as many fish, jackrabbits, and buckskin (venison) as we did, you could, too. Everybody ate well in Aspen, but nobody had a dime. We were a very poor people.

I'm not sure when Poppa came. I know him and Mama were married when Mama was very young. Mama was quite a bit younger than my dad; I think she must have been about fifteen. Poppa must have been at least twenty-one or twenty-two. Poppa worked in Marble for awhile. He worked in all these mines — Durant, Smuggler, Midnight. He was a leaser. A leaser is like a good gambler. Boy, they're betting on what they run.

My brother-in-law and him mined up here in the Durant Mine. Teleo Caparella, my sister Angie's husband, and Poppa worked a month to get a carload of ore out and they ended up splitting fifty cents for the month's work. He never patented any of his mines. He just worked the Durant Mine. The Rolphings, I think, owned it and they leased under them.

Our house was down behind where the post office is now, down by the railroad tracks. We lived right next to them. We lived right as you go around the post office to get back on the road where the electrical outfit is — right across the street. There's still a house that used to be Jessies Caps', and our house was right next to him. That was my Aunt Frances' place. That real old little house there now was Mrs. Larson's. They tore ours down.

Grandpa Caparella, he wasn't really my grandfather, but we called him Grandpa. I never did see my real grandmothers or grandfathers. Cap used to keep care of the D.R.C. Brown Sr. place and the Shaw place. He was a gardener and everything. We used to fish in the Roaring Fork about every night and at Hallam Lake.

Pat's grandmother is the one that had the bull that was a mean son-of-a-gun. Fishing was always good up Conundrum for years because nobody went up that way. That's because her grandmother Crosby owned that one big jersey. Then she brought him with her when she moved into town. I know he tore off

Waterfall in lower Durant Mine. Courtesy Robert Zupancis.

Mabel Tekoucich's (Ed's wife) back porch. They lived right above where Pat's grandmother lived and that bull got out. She was the only one who could control him, but boy, I'll tell you, that bull had the fear into everybody else. That bull's name was Raleigh — he was mean.

I was the youngest of ten kids. My oldest brother's eighty years old — brother Joe. He's in Glenwood. He was a section foreman up through Glenwood Canyon for I don't know how many years.

After high school, I went to college for awhile at Denver University. I had different scholarships. I had one at Dartmouth, I had one at Western State, I had baseball and basketball scholarships, but I went skiing for DU because that was the best thing. I needed all the help I could, but I didn't finish. I didn't get along with my ski coach too good. And I didn't have the money because my folks didn't have any money, so . . . and I ran a sports shop afterwards for Magnifico Sports, down across from the Jerome Hotel, which is Ellie's now.

The baseball team was a town team. We had a ski team, too, which never had any part of the school. We had to make up our work and all. Basketball they did, but it was never played on school time. We played in the old Armory Hall.

315

But then baseball was a town team thing. We traveled all over, played different towns. We did have a good ball team. We had Newt Klusmyer, Gail Spence. We had a guy, Jack Bererman. In fact, he was a conductor in the music institute. He was going to school here. He played music and was a baseball player. You'd never believe it. Jack, I think, now is the head of a music thing in North Carolina. You would never know he was a baseball player. God, he was a big guy. We had a good ball team. We traveled all over to Cañon City and Leadville. They had a lot of baseball teams then, back in the fifties and even before then because I played center field for the town team when I was in the eighth grade. We played good ball for a small town.

I first started skiing when I was three years old. We had just had a pile of snow that we'd walk up and down from early in the morning until dark. My brother had an old pair of skis. I never had any toys myself; I was always borrowing somebody else's. But this one kid had a pair of old skis. He didn't like them so I just got them. And then we had the boat tow and the rope tow.

I remember when the army was here training the Tenth Mountain. Us kids would go up there and eat with them at night. They had pretty good food — hell, better than we were getting at home. We ate right at the bottom of No. One. There was a ski lodge there. The Aspen Ski Club had it. And we had a little rope tow and a boat tow. It went up part way and then we'd walk all the way up to where Midway is if you were going to race. You'd climb up in the morning. Those guys would have their bottles, and we'd go up and race at noon — no gates or anything. Us kids would go in and eat with the Tenth Mountain, and we'd ski. We could ski better than those guys.

I remember this little kid named Eddie Doe Phillips. His dad was a miner up here. He'd be lining up with them tin cans they gave us to eat out of. They had plenty for everybody. One of the men would see us kids, and he'd say — he kind of talked funny anyway — "I'll bet you'd really like to be home having some nice chicken and everything." Little Eddie Doe looked at him and says, "Like hell. I'd be eatin' buckskin, and I don't want to eat buckskin."

I ski raced all through school. That's the only way we got out of town. And I played basketball, but I'd miss a game or two a year. I thought of being an Olympic skier when I was young. I skied with Bud and Max Marolt every day. We had a good ski team, especially downhill and slalom. We were probably the best. I also jumped — my longest was probably about 270 feet. Never got hurt. I got sprained up a little but nothing serious. I sprained my knee one time but it wasn't because I fell, it was because I snapped too hard on the takeoff. That's how come Buddy Warner was such a good downhill racer. He was a heck of a great jumper, Buddy was. He could have made any Olympic team. But there was a lot of things that took money and we didn't have it. We worked all the time.

Speaking of venison, you've got to be particular about how game is handled from the first time you get it — how you shoot it, how you handle it. My mom and Grandma Caparella, I swear they could cook a hoof of a deer, elk, or rabbit, or something like that, and it would be good. They knew how to cook. They had to. A lot of people don't know how to handle game. It's ridiculous. I've watched people and said, "God, it's no wonder they can't eat it."

I used to spend a lot of time up with John Lamicq up Hunter Creek. He had 1,800 acres and ran his sheep up Hunter Creek. He also leased some stuff from Fritz Benedict. I spent a lot of time with John and his sheep men — the Eckhards and all those guys. I'd get three lambs a year and I love lamb. You never touch a lamb except at the start. Did it with their hands. Never let the wool or anything touch the meat — very particular. It's just the way you handle game.

Hunter Creek Dam picnic, 1901. Courtesy Peggy Rowland.

317

On Halloween, we pushed over johns — old toilets. I remember one time we pushed over one and old Ruby Bandey was sitting in it. She was really shocked. She was the judge here for awhile. Don't quote me on that for sure. Somebody was in there! But one time Ted Armstrong and some of us were pushing an outhouse over and Ted fell in one of them — fell in the hole. We didn't have anything to do with him the rest of the night. Then we was tipping this one over one time and we dropped it, I think it was on Teddy's legs that time. But we didn't really do a lot of damage . . . except to Teddy! We never really did much serious damage.

We weren't really very old when we started working. My first job was with Walt Atchison. He used to come down and pick up the mail off the train at the Rio Grande and I'd help him. I know old Walt; he used to give me a dollar a week. A dollar a week and then an ice-cream cone every time he went in and had a shot and a beer at the Jerome. He'd go through quite a few shots and beers a day; I got the ice cream. He was a great guy. He got the mail and the

Rio Grande Depot, now Rio Grande Park, 1947. Courtesy Del Gerbaz.

freight. I'd just drag the bags off. I really wasn't that much use to him — he took them to the post office. He'd pick up the freight and bring it back down.

But hell, I could run one of those engines when I was a kid as good as any. Old Coke Wathers used to be the night watchman. I'd go up there because I lived so close. Those guys would call me. They'd go to Woody Creek and I'd jump in that train and go down there with the men. I'd fire coming back. My leg would just fit perfect to shovel coal. I'd go up and Coke would be there. I couldn't have been over six or seven. I'd sit and back that train up and down that track until my mom would come up and get me about midnight. Old Coke would let me back that train — it was on a sidetrack where Clark's Market is. The track went by there because they had a sheep and cattle load. Hell, I could run that train back and forth. I'd go to Carbondale with them — shovel coal. Coke was a nice guy. When I drove the train, it wouldn't go very far but back and forth — hear that woof woof. . . . He'd take me for a ride to Glenwood. That was a big trip to go to Glenwood on the train. It would take about eight hours by the time you picked up the milk and the food. That's when you had to pick up sheep cars. They'd load up the train with the sheep or the cattle in the fall. I knew all of those guys pretty good — old Danny Murphy and old Reeves. Danny was a conductor of the train. I loved being the engineer.

My next job was probably with Grandpa Caparella at D.R.C. Brown's, cutting the lawn and digging dandelions — where Mrs. Paepcke lives now. Grandpa Caparella had a huge garden there. He had one by Mrs. Shaw's and one at home.

Good old Martin Healy used to have a stable right over the railroad tracks from us. He had a little Shetland pony. I used to ride that thing every day. He had it where my brother would run his stables a little bit. They didn't have many horses.

After working with Grandpa Caparella, the Jerome opened. Me, Paul Beck, and Ronnie Rolphing were bellhops at the Jerome when they first opened. That was in about 1945 or '46. I was so damn little — I wasn't very big. I only weighed about ninety pounds. They had that old elevator where you pulled the ropes. I'd carry the key, the people would carry their own luggage, and they'd tip me. But we'd run that old elevator up and down. They used to have some good parties. They had the Blue Room. We had uniforms. It seems to me they were green.

I worked for the Ski Corporation and I worked for the Mountain Utilities in the summer. I worked for the Ski Corporation cutting trails. In the early spring, I worked for Steve Marolt out there where the golf course is. We'd go

Hyman Avenue, 1923.
Courtesy Peggy Rowland.

and pick rocks. I worked at Johnny Hoaglund's, the Cowlings, Duroux, and Stapleton some. The Marolts had the best potatoes. We always picked where we had the best feed. Marolts fed us the best (and the Cowlings). The Newberrys were out there right close around Starwood. We also picked at Trentaz's. That was in the fall. In the fall we used to get two weeks off from school.

We picked rocks after school off the field and threw them in a truck. We had Bud Marolt, I, and Glen Beck. We'd go out there and we had an old '28 Chevy dump truck, and that's where we all learned to drive. Glen Beck was bigger than we were. He was older and bigger, so whenever we'd get a big rock, we'd bet Glen a nickel that he couldn't lift it — and he earned it. I think we were getting twenty-five cents or fifty cents an hour. I know I earned enough to buy a bicycle. That was when I was in the eighth grade, or a freshman. It took quite a bit. Bicycles weren't cheap in those days. Bought that from old Leroy Waterman. I think it cost fifty bucks. The first bike I ever had.

Well, I had one other bike that somebody gave me. It didn't have any brakes. I about knocked my head off coming down old Syndoine Hill. That's back of where the old elementary school is. There was a hill down there that used to come down to our house, and that's the way I'd go to school. We'd call it Tin Can Hill. We'd go down that trail and I didn't have any brakes. I went off the side of the road and hit my head on a tree. Didn't hurt me, though. The Syndoines were relatives of my father. They lived down there. You could drive down that with a car. That's the way you used to come down to those houses there. You never came across the railroad tracks, because they never had any railroad crossings at that time. They used to have that old railroad house up there. I could run those railroad tracks faster probably than anybody could because there was that old section house alongside there.

Hell, Aspen never had any streetlights or anything. When I'd go to a spooky movie that cost a nickel at the Isis Theater, man, would I peel rubber going home. I could run from the top of the Jerome down to the bottom to my house, and when I hit the door I could hardly stop. Oh yeah, I could run those rails at probably a full tilt. You could do it if you ran them long enough. We squished pennies on the railroad tracks if we had one.

When I was a kid, I loved to dance. Our whole family was that way, including Pat and her sister, Luetta. Her sister's only a couple of years older than I am. When I was a little kid, they'd always dance with me because I was little, especially Pat's mother, Maymie. Hell, I'd go to all those dances. My dad used to play accordion at some of the dances where they'd have them get-togethers.

On a Sunday morning, mom would make macaroni. We'd eat only twice on Sundays. We never really had a big breakfast or anything — just coffee. And then about two o'clock in the afternoon, we'd have spaghetti and maybe rabbit, meatballs, buckskin, or something. And then my mom and pop would go up to Kelleher's to have beer. They'd close at eight o'clock. I was just a little kid and my sister Mary and Ida were still at home then. Most of the kids had gone different places because we never had that much room in the house. I'd go in there looking for them. I figured it was good for a candy bar or something. I'd walk in the front door and Poppa would see me and he'd have a few beers in him already. He'd look at me and he'd say, "Here comes the last decroppa. Here comes Chucky, my last decroppa." He called me Chucky, especially when he wasn't mad at me. He was a great man. He worked awful hard. So did my mother. They had to raise ten kids. Poppa died when he was about seventy-five. Mom was eighty-five. It's amazing they lived to be old. Boy, the life they had to live. He was a hard-rock miner and then he worked for the county. When

Poppa couldn't work anymore, my mom worked in a restaurant, Loni's Cafe. They called it the Silver Grill, right across from the Elk's Building.

I'd listen to some of those guys at Tim Kelleher's while I was waiting for my mom and poppa, like Spike Stapleton and Erickson, old Alex Barrailler, and Tony Perk. Tony was always the one at the ballgames. He'd get the foul balls to little Tony. Those guys all knew how to work, though. Jesus, they could shovel muck all day. Everybody had a coffee break at this time and that. It's amazing how they could pace themselves and work, and they knew how to handle it.

My favorite teacher was Mrs. Twining. We had ten kids and we were very poor. My sister, Ida, and me are two years apart. I used to go to Dr. Twining, and he'd always give Mom a dime or something for me and he said, "I bought you today. How much are you worth?" I was a little kid, and boy, I'd get scared. He'd say, "How much you worth today?" And I said, "A million dollars." They were real nice people. My mom and dad did all right for us. They taught us how to work. A little slim at times, but I wouldn't have traded it. But Mrs. Twining, I think she really kept an eye on us going through school. She gave me an offer to go back to school at Notre Dame if I wanted to. She did help a lot of children go to college. She was a great person. We had some really good schoolteachers. Some tough ones, too. But they were good. I can sit back now and realize why they were tough. Mrs. Hoaglund was a good one, and Hilder Anderson. She never taught me, but she taught Pat. I'll tell you, you knew your ABCs when you got out. Not that it shows! I can't spell all those names. Pat and Marlene, my daughter, geez, they could spell anything.

I had one sister die when she was twelve, but it was from diabetes. Now there's my sister Angie, sister Ida, Stogie, brother Jess, brother Joe, and me — six of us. Pat and I got married on September 6, 1952. It was thirty-nine years on September 6, 1991. We have one daughter, Marlene.

Through all the years, I think the people that impressed me the most were the people I got to meet in my business. I got to ski with a lot of different people — different air force generals, test pilots. But I was always impressed with and always liked Darcy Brown. Another person that was a good friend of mine was Byron White. I used to ski with him about eight days a year. He was a Supreme Court judge. We'd ride up a lift. That guy was so intelligent that no matter what you talked about, he knew about it. I haven't seen Byron for a couple of years. Otherwise, I was never too impressed with any of those so-called famous people.

Poppa used to make a good chokecherry wine, rhubarb wine, and grape wine. Grandpa Caparella used to make a good Oregon grape wine, but you had to be something special before you even got a taste of that. Then he made

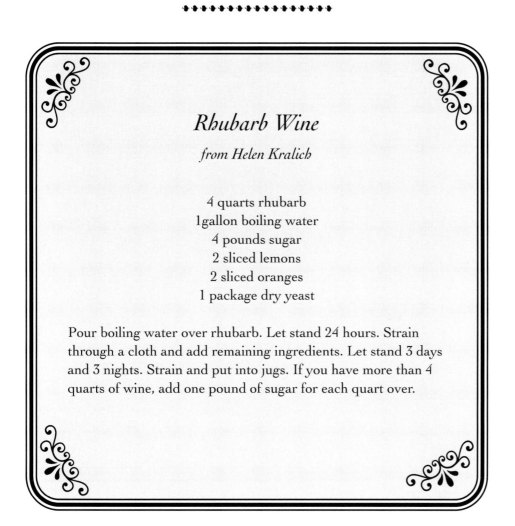

Rhubarb Wine

from Helen Kralich

4 quarts rhubarb
1 gallon boiling water
4 pounds sugar
2 sliced lemons
2 sliced oranges
1 package dry yeast

Pour boiling water over rhubarb. Let stand 24 hours. Strain through a cloth and add remaining ingredients. Let stand 3 days and 3 nights. Strain and put into jugs. If you have more than 4 quarts of wine, add one pound of sugar for each quart over.

grappa — that's a brandy, good stuff. And white lightning — good stuff. Put a little anisette in it and distilled water. Hell, you'd take a drink of that in the morning, you could run up over any hill you wanted hunting. Old Johnny Strong would come out, and he had one of them bottles and he'd have that full of grappa. By God, I'll tell you, you didn't want to light a match around John. Poppa always made good wine. But we were kids, you know. We'd be around the table and we always had a little belt of wine. He'd give us a little shot. We'd sit there, us kids, and say, "We want a little more." Pa would say, "Hey you kids, you keep it up you gonna be fighting pretty quick." Sure as hell, we'd all be fighting. I think we got that belt of wine in us and it would put us to sleep quicker at night. We always had a little taste of wine at dinner.

Bud Marolt and I, when we were kids, used to collect on the rope tow and the boat tow. It was fifteen cents, twenty-five cents, or whatever it was, and then we'd bring the cash down to the Jerome Hotel and give it to Laurence Elisha for the ski club. It was just on weekends, Saturday and Sunday, because we were going to school the rest of the time. Bud would bring Kilbasa (sausage) for our lunch. His dad and mother made it. And then at home, down at my house, we'd have spaghetti and maybe meatballs or something like that, so Bud would come down and eat with me. Poppa always had that jug of wine right by the table. He always knew how much was in it. Bud would tip us a glass. We were a little older then, at least eight or ten. And boy, Pa would come around and he'd look at that jug when he'd get home and he'd say, "You and that Marolt kid's been in it again, haven't you?" But Poppa would have wine in the basement. Old George Tekoucich, that's Buttons, he was a good friend of T's (Teleo) and them. Poppa had them barrels down in the basement. Boy, I'll tell you, to get in touch fast is to just suck on that hose. And Buttons and T. would go down there. We had a real tall fence in the back to protect the garden. When I was a little kid, I'd say, "You guys better get out of there. Pa's coming down Tin Can Hill." And they'd hit that fence, trying to crawl over that tall fence. Teleo Caparella was my brother-in-law, my sister Angie's husband. He just passed away here a year or so ago.

One time I was running the cat for my brother. He was in the excavating business. This must have been about '53 or '54, right after Pat and I were married. I did some bulldozing up in here some damn place. That was in the days when you didn't have many oil streets except maybe Main Street. I ran it down to my mother's; it was a D-7. We had to put new brake pads on it. It was the day of my birthday. Momma kept bringing out those little flasks of rhubarb wine, and my dad was sitting on the porch. He says, "You gonna get those two kids drunk." Boy, believe me, she got us, too. Three days later we got those brake pads finished. Pat had a party for us that night. That was the first birthday party I can ever remember anyone giving me. I must have been, well, I was married when I was twenty years old. Rhubarb wine was pretty potent. I remember old man Rolfing used to make such good dandelion wine. Mrs. Randall used to make some of the best dandelion wine you could get. Boy, it was good stuff.

My favorite years in Aspen were probably the 1950s, because that was the 1950 FIS. Us kids skied with a different team every year. We were going to get to forerun it and then something happened. God, we knew all of them — Pozzi, Zeno Colo, the whole works. We were so poor when I was a little kid, I decided in my mind I wasn't going to put up with that. I wasn't going to be poor.

◆ ◆ ◆ ◆ ◆ ◆ ◆ ◆ ◆ ◆ ◆ ◆ ◆ ◆ ◆ ◆ ◆ ◆

I worked for the Ski Corporation. If I included when I was on trails and everything, I was area manager for seventeen years on Aspen Mountain. I helped build lifts and did a lot of building in all the areas that we owned — Breckenridge, Snowmass. I started at Buttermilk; I was supervisor out there. That was a good duty. I like Buttermilk; it's a great hill. It really is a great mountain. As far as I'm concerned, people say, "Boy, it would be nice to be back in the old days," Not me. Forget that. And I remember back in '50 and '52 and '53 and into the Sixties. We were building ski lifts and everything in there and everybody said, "Aw, it's going to stop." I said, "No, you're all wrong." And right today I'll say the same thing. Aspen still is it, no matter what they think. People, you know, they sit back and say, "Geez, that's so expensive now." It's probably going to be a good buy five to ten years from now, whatever they buy in real estate, because there's only one Aspen.

This valley is special. It's not just the skiing. I love the summers. Last year was the first year in fifty-five years I didn't put on a pair of skis. I'm fifty-nine. I didn't miss it, as far as the skiing is concerned, because I had to spend many a day with ski boots on. There were a lot of days, years ago, when we didn't have snowmobiles and this and that. We ferried them on our back or hauled them places to work on the lifts. I love the summers as well as anything. There's a lot of people that don't give the credit to the Music Institute and all of that as much as they should, because it really helped put Aspen on the map as much as anything else.

Anything that was going to get something going around here was good. Otherwise none of us would have been here; we'd of had to go somewhere else. I knew Mrs. Paepcke and Walter, Herbert Buyers, and all of them when they came here. I knew them since I was a pretty young kid. I still think it was good. Look at all the building we've got around here. It's like I say, if anybody thinks Aspen's going to stop, they're nuts. There's no way. It's going to continue, as much as they fight their nongrowth and everything. There are some people in the area that are not my favorite people now that come in, but as far as the beauty, the area, the climate, and the snow — you can't beat the snow here. I don't care what anyone says. I never thought of leaving. I enjoyed my work. I was involved in different things. It's different in management now. It was getting that way when I decided that I was getting out of the business. I still do consulting with the Ski Company and help them out. I've been offered some other things to get back into the ski business in other places, but I haven't. We've worked our tail ends off long enough. I think it's time to stop, especially now. I want to make sure Pat relaxes more.

I hate to see some of the places get built up, but it's still beautiful here. What's missing from the stock in Aspen now — I think the trust and everything has changed. I remember our big trip. Once in awhile we'd go see my mother's sister in Denver. That was a big trip. You never locked the door or anything like that. You never worried about anybody breaking in your house. I think it's just become a faster society, and I disagree with the type of people that are running our politics. There are people that really could do a good job that are not running. It's not worth it. But see, it's hard to get people to do this. I remember the times back. They could have built a gymnasium for $17,000 when they built the school and they didn't. We had some hard-nosed people that wouldn't spend a dime. I thought that was a little too conservative. Now I really don't think we're getting our money's worth in a lot of things. I see a lot of mismanagement in our county and city. It starts not just from one person. It's the whole thing. That's what's hard, because I like to see us get a little more out of our tax dollar.

What would Dad think of Aspen now? Would he be laughing? Poppa, it probably wouldn't bother him too much. Poppa was a great fisherman. As long as he could fish the Roaring Fork, right below our house. He wouldn't care.

✦

Pat is a good-hearted,
hard-working woman.
I've known her for years.
I've always respected her
honesty and loved her
humor.

Pat Kearns Maddalone

I was born November 16, 1928, in Aspen. My father's name was Owen Kearns and my mother's name was Maymie Crosby. There were three kids in our family.

About 1879–1880, my mother's mother, Maria Steel, walked over Independence Pass from Leadville and spent the first winter in Aspen before there were buildings. They lived in a tent. There were very few white women in Aspen then — a few Indian women. My Grandmother Steel walked over the pass with her brother-in-law and her sister. She'd been sent by her parents to Leadville, Colorado, from Kansas because she had what they called consumption, which is tuberculosis. She was about eighteen years old when she went to Leadville where her sister lived. Ute Indians were in Aspen at that time. My mother's oldest sister, Bedelia Crosby, was born in Tourtelotte Park. My grandfather, Phillip Crosby, and my grandmother, Maria Steel Crosby, were up there because he was doing some kind of mining. Must have been in 1880-something.

Grandmother Crosby's maiden name was Steel and she married Phillip Crosby. He came here for the mining from New York. Later on, in the 1940s and 1950s, you found people here that were either skiers or construction people, but before that it was mining and ranching. Grandmother Crosby told me that Grandfather Crosby had ridden to put down the Meeker Massacre. He had ridden with the militia or something like that.

Grandfather Phillip Crosby, I think, came from New York to Aspen about 1880. He was a miner and owned a saloon on Cooper. He and my grandmother homesteaded up Conundrum and Castle creeks. He eventually owned property in town. He donated one-half block to St. Mary's Church on Main Street. That's where the church sits today. There were two sides of the family in this valley. I'm sure you'll find it of many of the early settlers. One side was farmers and ranchers and the other side was miners. So the Crosbys were the miners in our family and the Kearns were the farmers.

My father's father, Tom Kearns, and my father's mother, Margaret Mahoney Kearns, came here in the 1880s. My grandmother Mahoney came from New York to keep house for her two brothers. My Grandfather Kearns came from Wisconsin. They homesteaded out in what we call the Brush Creek Valley, which is now Snowmass. Their ranch was where the Snowmass Center is now.

My mother, Maymie Crosby, was the youngest of five children. She was born and raised in Aspen. My father, Owen Kearns, was one of seven children and was born and raised in Brush Creek and Aspen. They were married in 1926 and lived on a ranch in the Brush Creek Valley until 1954, when they sold the ranch and retired in Carbondale. My mother was a teacher and my father a rancher.

When we were young, we'd go to the Jerome Hotel after high school. It was called the Buffet. There was a big bar in the back. There wasn't any place where youngsters could congregate like the corner drugstore, or anything like that. The Jerome had a soda fountain like they did in most towns. We went to the Buffet in the Hotel Jerome and had our cherry Coke, the miners from the Midnight Mine came in and had their shot and a beer (a boilermaker), the Tenth Mountain soldiers came in and had their cruds (that was a milkshake with shots of brandy or shots of bourbon made with ice cream). I think it may have been named because it looked like spring skiing snow — they call it crud. The Jerome was the "town center" for all of us.

In the winter, I came to town and stayed with my grandmother because the Kearns were all ranching out in Brush Creek. In the first grade, I came to town and stayed with my Grandmother Crosby and went to the Washington School for a year. I was so homesick, that nobody else in my family had to do that. I went back to the ranch and went to school where the little red school is now.

One winter my dad rented a house on Main Street that belonged to Gertrude Stapleton for fifteen dollars a month. We stayed in that one winter and went to school from there. See, by the time I was twelve, I was a freshman in high school, and that meant that I was old enough to take care of my younger brother and sister. We did what we called baching, and I was the head of the household. Baching means when you are not keeping an acceptable kitchen and house. You know, the old men would go out in the hills and bach. They had a minimum housekeeping setup. We'd do our shopping and catch as catch can. We had some nice neighbors. We had aunts and uncles that lived in town, so we could call them. We could call our folks at the ranch on the telephone. We had a party line and that was another source of entertainment. Everybody listened on the party line. It was like the Oprah Winfrey Show or something.

In the summer, we'd take the cattle up Hunter Creek. That's where the summer range was. We used to ride from Snowmass (Brush Creek) to Hunter Creek. We'd drive them up, but during the war, no one could get cowboys to go up there and stay because they were all in the service. So we all had to take turns riding the range. They had a cattle pool — Stanley Natal, Trentaz, my dad, and a fellow named Wilson Popish that lived over on Wildcat. I can't remember how many other people. But all of the ranchers had to take turns providing somebody to keep the cattle out of larkspur and move them to different parts of the range. My brother, who was the youngest, would ride with me. I think we went up about three times a week. One day he'd ride with me from the ranch, where the Snowmass Stables are now, into Hunter Creek. Then we'd have a day off. The next day, he'd ride with my sister Luetta, up into Hunter Creek. I'm telling you, we were in good shape then. We'd go home the back way over Owl Creek Road to get to the ranch. We would get to the top of the hill where the Stapletons are and we'd start walking. Then we'd get back on and stand up in the saddle till we got home. That's a long ride. Left before the sun came up and got home way after dark. I suppose I left about four o'clock in the morning and probably got back about nine or ten. That's a long ride. I was fourteen or fifteen years old then. We raised cattle on our ranch. Also, we sold cream. Yes, they used to ship cream. They were probably ten- to fifteen-gallon cans, I can't remember what the size.

I remember the Hyman Street fire as being about the worst thing that happened in Aspen. That was in 1941, and it was a really awful fire. In the corner building, there was a blind man named Huey McCabe, and he sold cigars and tobacco — things like that. Next to him was one of my uncles, Ed Tiederman, who had lost his leg — he had a wooden one. He had a little shoe-shine chair and sold candy and hamburgers, anything to make a living. He even had a room in the back where the men played cards.

There were special events that would happen in Aspen. There would be a New Years or Christmas dance. It would be down at the Armory Hall. They had a little orchestra, and that was "the" event and everybody went to those kind of things. And then there would be the Valentine's dance and there'd be something at Easter time, and big 4th of July fireworks, dance, parties, and picnics. When there was anything, whether it was the 4th of July rodeo and dance, or whether the flower show, it was wonderful.

One of the things that was particularly nice about Aspen was, as you came into town, as you looked down Main Street, there were big old cotton trees. The ditches were running down the side and the yards had lilacs. In the summertime everybody's yard looked nice. The house may not ever have been painted, or may have been painted so long ago that you couldn't tell what color it was, but almost everybody had sweet peas on their fence and the yard looked well kept. There were very few people that didn't have a nice yard as poor as the town was. And in August, they had a flower show. There would be barrels of flowers all the way around the Armory Hall. In the summertime when they weren't busy with that, they had roller-skating there. They would roller-skate on those hard-wood floors.

After they dug the ditches, there used to be a little bit of a ceremony. They opened up the Salvation and run the water. Work was a social event, too. You'd get together to brand, you'd get together to thresh the grain. In the spring, everybody had to send somebody to help open up or clean the ditches with a shovel. I guess sometimes in really difficult places, they had some piece of equipment with a horse. All the neighbors got together to help each other. There would be great dinners and story-telling when the work was done.

There wasn't much crime in Aspen. In the West, you had a particularly self-enforcing way of handling things. It was very rare to see a stranger in town. If you saw a stranger and something went haywire, everybody figured it was him. And in a community where everybody knows everybody else, you really must be responsible to your neighbors, because if you aren't, you're gonna face the consequences. I think that's a very good system. They used to tell a story about somebody that stole some irrigation water over on Capitol Creek. Somebody killed him with an irrigation shovel. You irrigate with a shovel, and it's sharp.

I think we were very fortunate to have the Paepckes come to Aspen and all the people that followed them. It made it possible for us to live here and to enjoy absolutely marvelous things, like the Aspen Institute. You could go to the Institute and audit the courses. You could go out and listen to the lectures, and the same for the music school.

The missing ingredient in so many of our lives now is the continuity of families living here and the common history. Where once you knew your neighbors, their children, parents, and often their grandparents; now, your neighbors change twice a year.

♦

*Jim is laid back
and speaks real easy
— a friendly guy.*

Jim Markalunas

I was born May 3, 1930, but unfortunately I was not born in Aspen. I was born in San Diego and came to Aspen at the age of six weeks.

My mother was born on April 2, 1907, in Aspen. Her full name was Elsie Irene Warkentine. My grandfather, John Warkentine, came to Aspen in 1880 from Leadville. He was born in Germany and was a mining surveyor. He walked over to Aspen from Leadville in the spring of 1880 on snowshoes. They walked on the crust at night — woven cat-gut snowshoes. I believe he was single then, and he went back and married my grandmother, Mary Mirendorf, in Leadville. She also was from Germany, but they met in Leadville.

Grandmother came over to Aspen later on the stage. When Grandfather first came over, he was primarily prospecting. He bought a piece of property from J.R. Williams and built one of the first houses in Aspen, over on Spruce and Vine streets. The white house is still there — one of the oldest homes in Aspen. I think he built it right after they married, which was about 1885.

My grandfather, John Warkentine, died in 1915. He caught pneumonia. I never knew my grandfather or my grandmother. My grandmother died in 1928. They're both buried out in Red Butte Cemetery. Their children were Mamie, Alice, Irene, and Sophie. Some of them died of scarlet fever. One of the little children was accidentally shot playing with a gun when they were homesteading out at Wild Cat. This was sometime around 1890. My grandmother would never go out to Wild Cat again. She would have nothing to do with that place. Grandfather got rid of it. I don't know if he let it go back for taxes or didn't prove up on it. In those days, in the Homestead Act, you had to prove up on it.

My father, John Markalunas, was not from Aspen. He was a baseball player for the Pittsburgh minor league. He moved to Colorado Springs because he had contracted tuberculosis. At that time, my mother, Elsie Warkentine, was a nurse at St. Francis Hospital in Colorado Springs. That's where she met my dad.

Mother grew up in Aspen and then in 1926 or 1927 went to Colorado Springs to take nurse's training. The nuns ran the hospital there. I was born in San Diego because my mother, being a nurse, wanted me delivered in a hospital. My Aunt Freda had moved out to California. The Depression was taking place, and mining had pretty much dropped off in Aspen. There was no employment here to speak of. There was a great exodus of Aspen people, particularly to California and to the Denver area.

My mom and dad were married in Colorado Springs. Dad had to recuperate from tuberculosis. Dad was trying to get into the minor leagues playing baseball, but Mom had to make a living as a nurse in Colorado Springs. Then she went out to California to visit my Aunt Freda. I think she had planned to come back, but I came on the scene. She then came immediately back to Aspen to see her family and show me off.

My father died from tuberculosis in 1932. I was two, and he died when he was only twenty-seven. Mother became a widow at the age of twenty-five. She worked off and on and would bring me to Aspen to see the family. My Uncle

Duke Warkentine, known as The Duke of Aspen, inherited the household. He lived at the old homestead. His sister, Alberta, married Art Mikkelsen. My mother, being a widow, was between Aspen, Colorado Springs, and sometimes Denver. She worked in the hospitals. There was no work here in Aspen. When I was very young, I was up here primarily for visits. Then she would board me and I would stay with my aunt and uncle. In the late Thirties and Forties, I stayed with my Uncle Art Mikkelsen. My mother never remarried.

My mom would come to Aspen and we'd go fishing on the Roaring Fork. My mother was a great fisherwoman and loved to fish. She'd fish along the river. We'd have great times. And we'd fish up towards Ashcroft and below Independence. I remember that my Uncle Art's house was right by the railroad tracks. The trains would come in — the Rio Grande — the Midland had ceased to operate in 1918. The tracks were right behind Art's house and on over to the Cowenhovens. My Uncle Duke, who was an electrician, worked in the mines — he worked in the Cowenhoven Tunnel and for the Roaring Fork Light and Power Company. We would go back and forth on the railroad track between Art's and Duke's.

My Uncle Duke was a real genius. He had the first radio in Aspen. Everybody would go over to his house and listen. This was probably about 1923. He was hard of hearing so he had a big alarm clock that had an automobile horn on it. When the alarm would go off, it would also set off the horn so that it would wake him and the whole neighborhood. One time they had problems down at the power house in Glenwood, so they sent Duke down to see if he could help. They called Aspen and asked for Duke because they had heard of his reputation. Duke got on the train and went down to Glenwood. Later they called up and said, "Where's this guy that you sent down?" And the Aspen people said, "Well, wasn't he on the train?" They said, "No, there was just some old farmer." It was Duke. They expected someone dressed up and looking like the engineering type. Duke just wore an old hat and a pair of overalls.

As a boy, I shoveled snow for Liz Callahan. She always reminded me of this. I couldn't afford a wrist watch. I didn't own one, but I had a small alarm clock and would take it with me. I would wind it up and charge by the fraction of an hour so when I shoveled snow I would keep track of how much time it took. I would charge her about twenty or thirty cents to shovel her walks. She remembered how I used to pack that little clock with me.

I also had a little service called Jimmy's Coal and Wood Service. My customers were Mary McKinna and Lena VanLoon. I would empty the ashes out and split some kindling and bring in the coal. That's how I made some extra money.

Tough People, Hard Times

♦♦♦♦♦♦♦♦♦♦♦♦♦♦♦♦♦♦♦

I remember the big fire on Hyman Avenue in 1941. It burned down one night before Halloween. Us kids ran down to the Silver Grill because rumor had it, or at least the kids said, there was a whole bunch of silver dollars in the saloon. We went there to see if we could find melted silver dollars and coins. The town marshall chased us out.

I also remember that times were hard. Tony Caparella was a good friend of my Uncle Duke. They worked for the power company and the Browns. Duke worked in the power house and Tony was a lineman. Teleo Caparella also worked for the power company. He was quite a guy. He was short and tough. So was Tony. Tony was a boxer. Teleo was born in Marble and Tony was born in Aspen. They all chummed around. Tony and I would drag large timbers from the old smelter and cut them up into short blocks. Then the blocks were split into kindling wood for the kitchen stoves. Tony went with my Uncle Art's sister, Elenor (Susie) Mikkelsen. They had a little white house which is now up by the No. One lift.

When I was in high school, I got a job with the Mountain Utilities Corporation. We worked on the flumes. In the summertime they would hire on extra help. A lot of kids went to cutting trails for the Ski Company. I liked working on the flume gang. Tony and Riley Peterson were there, and Henry Sievers was the foreman. Some of the happiest times I had were in the summertime working on the flume — working outdoors. The flumes supplied water. They were big boxes that carried the water down to the power house. We would report to work at the warehouse (Visual Arts Center) which at that time was owned and operated by the Mountain Utilities Company. Mountain Utilities bought it from the Roaring Fork Light and Power Company. Earl Jenkensen worked for the power company in the office. My Uncle Art did service work, and some work on the lines. So did Tony. Teleo was also a lineman. Some of the Marolt boys and I would hire on. I think when I first went to work for them, I got something like forty-four cents an hour. We had to load up our truck and go up either Maroon Creek or Castle Creek. They would float the lumber down to the work site and shut the water off for a period of three or four hours. We had to work on the flumes and the power house would run on the other flume. We would cut lumber and stuff. Ikey Mogan worked up there, too.

Ikey Mogan was something else. He was really a character. He was a real live wire. He loved to play with powder and stuff. Once when we were working up on Maroon Creek, the water came down and went into a siphon. One year Mountain Utilities decided they would eliminate the siphon because it kept blowing out the bottom. They decided to put this pipeline across and cut a trench across the rocks. Ikey was the powder man. He loved to play with powder and dynamite and stuff. One day he set a charge and blew some rock out and the rocks went sailing. Well, Riley Peterson had this nice car with a canvas top on it. Here comes this big rock. It went right through the roof of Riley's car and put a big old hole in the floor board. Boy, was Riley mad! Riley chased Ikey down. That was the only time I saw Riley mad. *Really mad!*

Nubbs (Albert Sandstrom) worked for a while at the power house, too. Nubbs had this place under the turbine where he used to hide his whiskey down in the tailrace. They called it a tailrace when the water came from the turbine and went down into the river. There was a trap door that you went down under to pull the caps off the turbine nozzles. Old Nubbs used to have a string down there and had his bottle hanging. He didn't want Gene to catch him drinking on the job. One day we saw the bottle there, dumped out the whiskey, and put in some coal oil. Nubbs was really mad about that.

There was a big snowstorm in 1961. When I shut the power house down in 1958, I thought it was a lack of foresight not to keep it going somehow. In fact, I wrote a letter to the paper about it at one time. Well anyway, they kept it in mothballs and one of my jobs was to go down once in awhile to exercise and keep it going. In 1961 we had this big snowstorm on Labor Day weekend. The snow kept coming and coming and coming. The leaves were still on the trees and they fell down on the power lines. At that time, Avril Stardup was working for Holy Cross Electric as their lineman. They had no section line fuses and everything was "crowbarred" all the way back to Basalt. The trees shorted the lines out and there was no power. We went one day and night without any power. Pretty soon they were beginning to worry, because the locker at Beck and Bishop's Grocery was starting to thaw out. Mike Garrish happened to be on the utility board, and he came to me and said, "Marky, can you start up that power house?" So I went down and I started the power house and we got power going for the town. I ran the generators for that last time on Labor Day weekend. Finally the power was restored. The city took those generators out in 1962 or 1963. Thought it would make a great garage. The city could have kept it running. Those turbines had babbitt bearings, and they operated at a very slow speed. All they needed to do was just replace the flumes with pipes, which they did ultimately. I came back to work for the city in 1966 and I ran the city water plant until 1990.

I met my wife, Ramona Conner, in Denver. We were married in 1953. I was working for Western Electric at the time in Denver. In 1954, I quit my job and we drove up to Aspen. I talked to Gene Robinson and asked, "Can I get a job in the power house?" He said, "Yeah, we happen to have an opening." So I got a job working nights in the power house and I helped my Uncle Art. We did electrical work and wired places like the Glory Hole Motel and I did electrical work on the side at the St. Moritz and places like that. In those days, everybody in the lodge business put in brown tubs. Do you know why they put in brown tubs and brown fixtures? Because during the spring runoff you wouldn't notice the dirty water so much. The tourists wouldn't notice. It was the rage.

We had four children, all born and raised in Aspen. They were all born in the same hospital — practically in the same room. Julie Marie was born in 1962, Lisa Ann in 1964, John in 1967, and Tom in 1969. My mother was born here and my kids were born here, but I wasn't. I missed out.

A lot of people migrated out of Aspen and then came back later. It was hard times in the Twenties. They used to have picnics in Denver and in San Diego. They would always have an annual Aspen Day picnic. Aspen people would get together in Denver and have a big picnic. This was mostly in the Thirties. But the big migration occurred here in the twenties. They left by the carload because there was no work. During World War II, the menfolk worked at Pando (Camp Hale). My mother went to Denver and worked in the ammunitions factory. A lot of people left Aspen during the war to work jobs in Denver or other places.

If I could stop the time in Aspen, I would probably stop it in the late Forties, early Fifties. One of my favorite haunts was Bluebell Island, or Gobler's Knob, which was a little island where Ms. Munroe Lyeth has her home now. There was a little island where Hunter Creek branched out. I used to hang out and fish along Hunter Creek. I used to go fishing down in the willows on the forks behind the courthouse, or where the depot was.

One of my favorite times was when I used to hang out at the train station. I was the telegraph boy for Dave Maltsberger. Dave Maltsberger was the station agent for the Rio Grande. They lived over on Third and Bleeker. Dave operated a telegraph key. Telegrams would come in on the wire and he would sit there at the typewriter and type up the telegrams as they came in. He would put them in the envelope and address them and give them to me to deliver. I enjoyed that. I had a bicycle. This was in 1946 and 1947. I did this after school and in the summertime. I would go down once a day and pick up the telegrams. I worked for Western Union, actually.

Everybody with any influence or name always stayed at the Hotel Jerome. Most of my telegrams were delivered there. There was a water-operated hydraulic elevator there. I would go in the back and go down to the basement to get on the elevator and go up to the second floor. I would get by the front desk that way. If I could deliver the telegrams directly to the room, hopefully someone would come to the door and I most always got a tip. I would try it several times if they weren't there. Finally, if I couldn't reach them, I would take it to the front desk.

When did I notice Aspen changing? I think right after Snowmass came on line — in the mid-Sixties, early Seventies. I think that's when the change started to occur. My favorite years were probably the Forties. I guess I'm glad that I was sort of what they call the bridge generation. I came on the scene soon enough to remember some of the old-timers, some of the old prospectors, and I remember some of their stories. Times were tough here in the Forties. We used to go down by the railroad tracks near the sampler works. We would go down there and take old timbers out, cut them, and bring them to the house to split for wood. I used to go down along the railroad tracks and pick up extra coal that would fall off of the coal cars.

What does Aspen lack now that it had in the forties? I would say the camaraderie — knowing everybody. Everybody was poor, but everybody was very friendly. You knew everybody and everybody knew you. Everybody spoke to one another. And the smiles. The slow way of life. Nobody was in a big hurry, and everybody had time to visit with one another. A lot of times people played pranks on one another, but they were good pranks. It was just an easy way of life. They were hard times and people had to work hard because nobody had anything to speak of.

If I could give Aspen some advice today, I would say to slow down. Take time to enjoy the beauty that we still have. The mountains and the beauty are still around here. It's just that you don't know anybody anymore. I guess that's the problem. Then, everybody knew everyone. If someone was having a tough time, people pitched in to help out. It was a real community feeling. A lot of times people felt that you knew too much of their business or people knew too much of your business. But we had some good times. You could go down just out of town a little ways and go fishing along the creek. Nobody hassled you about anything. There were no "No Trespassing" signs around to speak of. You could go most anyplace you wanted. You didn't have to worry about whether you were on someone's private property. You never had to worry about crime or anything like that. You could leave your house and your car unlocked. Nobody had anything worth stealing anyway. I would say I liked the late Forties when the town was just beginning to awaken from the long sleep, or early Fifties when things were coming back to life.

♦

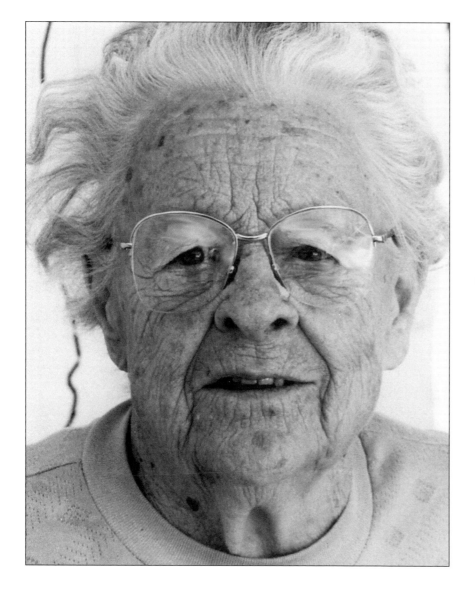

Photo by Kathy Daily

Polly will greet you at the door with a full-length apron and explain that she just put it on and, "Pardon the mess,"...

Polly Nyman Marolt

I was born September 3, 1902, in Winsted, Connecticut. My parents' names were Carl and Elin Nyman. I'm Swedish — my folks were both born in Sweden. My father was eight when he came to the United States, and my mother was four. Me and Ralph Nader are from the same town. In Connecticut, we moved into the country. My folks bought a house with about fifteen acres of land, although my dad always worked in town.

339

◆◆◆◆◆◆◆◆◆◆◆◆◆◆◆◆◆

My name is not really Polly; my name is Olive. Now, how did I get Polly from Olive? That's another story. When we were kids, we lived out in the country, as I said. And there were families who lived a quarter of a mile along this country road. One of them had a little boy about the age of my sister and me, and he would come down and play with us. I don't know why, but he always called me Polly, and it stuck — probably because he couldn't say Olive. I never thought very much about it, but I was always Polly, and of course, it stuck through all these years.

My sister, I, and my mother did the ranch business. My mother had a cow — hated to milk the cow but had to. She was so glad to get rid of it finally. These were the times when everybody in the street did the same business — everybody did. We had our own milk, cream, butter, and our own vegetables that we grew. We got a pig at least every spring, and in the fall it was butchered. So there was salt — before the days of common ordinary refrigeration, you know. There wasn't anything like that. Well, anyway, everybody got along just fine and you helped yourself the best you could and you weren't any worse off than anybody else. My mother had learned to sew from a dressmaker and so she kept her two kids looking very nice. My sister was three and one-half years younger than me.

On this country road that I speak of was a man called Frank L. Wentworth. His book has been advertised in the bookstores. He wrote a compilation of all these articles that appeared in the *Aspen Times* and made them into a book called *Aspen On The Roaring Fork*. Now, he lived on the same country road as we did in Connecticut. He had five children. The girls that my sister and me knew were the same age, and we all went to school together. Mr. Wentworth was our rural mail carrier, with a horse and a little wagon. He delivered the mail every day. He had been in Aspen before the silver panic of 1893. Then, of course, he had to leave. There was no way you could earn a living, you know. The bottom went out of silver and the bottom went out of everything else.

Several years later, he went back to Aspen, bought a furnished house for $500, and it's all been redone now. That was probably in the late Twenties. His girls were grown by then and used to go to Aspen in the summers to visit him. The Wentworth girls wrote to my sister and me and said, "Wouldn't you like to come to Colorado?" They said, "Of course there aren't any men, but we have beautiful scenery." That was in 1932 and I was twenty-nine. That's when I first met my husband, Steve Marolt, never dreaming that I would marry him eventually and come and spend all the rest of my life here. But that's what I did. I met him because my sister is a nut about riding horses. The other friends of the

Wentworths told her, "I know the guy who has the best horse in town." That was Steve, with his beautiful white horse, Snake. Well, you know they say if a horse is a little afraid, maybe steps aside a little, they say he's snakey. That was just an adjective they used, and of course Snake was kind of that way. So Steve came at the invitation, and two other young fellows who he knew came with their horses. We all went to Maroon Lake. There was no paved road. It was just a gravel road, and that was great. I spent four summers here before Steve and I were married. But Steve was always around when I came for the summer.

We had come in from a ride, and I'm not made to ride a horse. I ain't built that way. My sister and Helen Wentworth would go riding. And I suffered the tortures of the damned, I'll tell you. Mr. Wentworth said once, "Polly, I'll meet you with a stretcher and bring you to the house." I was so sore I couldn't turn over in bed. It's not funny. I still did a little riding with Steve. The country around here is something else, really. And thank God that the town and the rich people around here can't mess with it. They have to let it alone. Except for what skiing has done. So, Steve and I spent time together, and he asked me to marry him. I thought, well, I guess that might not be a bad idea. Steve was twenty-nine and I was thirty-four. I was five years older than he. He died in 1990. And I'm still here. Well, he lived to be eighty-two, which is older than any of his brothers, who died ahead of him. There's just one left of that big family, and she was a nurse in Denver. Of course, she retired some years ago. Steve lived to be eighty-two, and that was unheard of among the Marolt boys. We call them boys, you know. Steve died June 8, 1990.

The year 1918 was the big flu thing. It was awful. The Marolts lost three in very short order. One of the oldest sisters had come home to help the mother take care of the sick ones, and she got sick and died. And of course they missed her terribly. She was the oldest of the Marolt children — his sister, Mary, of whom we all spoke so very well. They thought the world of Mary.

Steve and I bought this house the year we got married. It's now over a hundred years old. I wanted to be in the West End because the ranch was right out where the golf course is and Steve wouldn't have to travel very far back and forth. It was just a little house, didn't amount to much, but it was in terrible condition. The first thing the guys did was put a roof on it.

We were married in New York City, city hall. I was from Connecticut, and I asked Steve to come and stay in the East for awhile. My folks didn't know him, and I thought, well, I had quit teaching so we could go visit and look at things. I didn't want any fuss. When you get to be as old as I was and you get married, all this beautiful stuff is fine when you're twenty, but we needed the

*Marolt Saloon,
about 1893.
Courtesy
Aspen Historical
Society.*

money. And another thing, Steve and his family were all Catholic and my mother was not a Catholic in any way, shape, or form. And I didn't want any fuss. We had a civil ceremony, and it was over in nothing flat and cost a couple of bucks. We were just as married as if we had the whole business.

Steve's father, Frank Marolt, came to Aspen in 1900 from Slovenia. He migrated from Yugoslavia to Cleveland, Ohio. He and a few of his friends walked from Cleveland to Leadville to work in the mines. They lived in String-town, just outside of Leadville, which was the factory town for the smelter. After awhile, his wife, Frances Rupert Marolt, came over. They had their first child, Frank Jr., in Leadville and the next ten children were born in Aspen. Frank Sr. had the Marolt Saloon and Boardinghouse. After silver went down, they bought the ranch.

After I was married and settled in Aspen, sometimes I would walk to town. We didn't have a car in those days either. I'd walk to town and do the shopping and look around me as I walked down and say, "What in God's name am I doing in this desolation?" I mean it. That's exactly what happened — the empty houses, the yards unattended, the long blocks of empty buildings. It was like a ghost town. Of course, after Walter Paepcke discovered it, that ended that performance. It was the tag end of nothing, I'll tell you.

I worked on the ranch a little bit when the hay was ready to be stacked. I would pull the stacker. I didn't very often pull it with a horse, but with a jeep. You see, we attached the jeep to the stacker. That would pull the stacker up. I would pull it so far and then stop, and then it would unload. The poor guy on top — if he was in the way, that's too bad. 'Cuz all that dry stuff, you know, you'd get hot and sweaty and it would go down your neck. It tickles. I did it to Steve every once in awhile and he'd be so mad at me.

Later on the ranch was divided. Steve got more land because his brother Frank got the house. The house the Marolt boys fixed over was the office for the elexiviation works that had to do with mining ore. The boys didn't call it elex-iviation — they called it the Lexavator. Steve got the lower part, the big part, plus the Maroon Creek River bottom. Now, his brother Mike got the upper part of that flat out there (the golf course) plus the land along Castle Creek, and the land that surrounded their house. There are two or three quite large, open fields that are close to the house, and that was Mike's. I say Mike because Frank died and Mike took over that part of the ranch. I don't know how many acres. Who pays attention to the amount of acres? All you know is you gotta work 'em.

It's hard to say which were my favorite years in Aspen. I certainly liked it after we got plumbing and paved streets.

Today, I wish people would not build such big houses and spoil their neighbor's view. Houses don't seem to fit into the landscape — one-story houses would be nice.

◆

Ethel will slap her leg and say, "You're damn right." What a character. She has a sense of humor, zest for life, and a lot of determination. Ethel took life by the tail and ran with it.

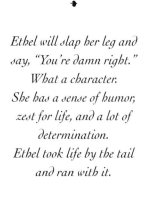

Photo by Kathy Daily

Ethel Smith McCabe

I was born June 10, 1910, on Cooper Street in my parents' home. My parents, Tony and Mary Smith, came from Yugoslavia. Dad used to work in the Smuggler. I think their original names might have been Kastelic. They had five children. I was the fourth child. As a child, I went to the Washington and Lincoln schools. I walked every day. God yes, it was a long way — ya damn right. As a kid, my first chores were rocks, the garden, and sheep.

344

Edward D. Pearce, my first husband, was in mining; his father was, too. He was born in Aspen. His folks came here in the 1880s. I was sixteen years old when I married Edward. I had Fred one year later. Edward died young, in 1933. Fred was only five. After that, I took care of Fred and made things work — ya damn right. My second husband, Elbert McCabe, was born in Emma about the turn of the century. But he was basically like so many of the people in Emma. If you see it on the marriage certificate or something, it would say occupation was miner, that was it. He was in the navy during World War I and served overseas, and as he tells it, he worked around Ouray and Telluride. His middle name was Gillespie, one of the original founders of Aspen. His mother was a Gillespie. She started a bible class or something in the church. I married Elbert McCabe about seven years later. I met him at the Hotel Jerome. I worked there for fifteen years, waiting tables. Elbert worked in the Midnight Mine. I had a second child, Jim, in 1938. Elbert died in 1963 of miner's "con" —consumption. My salary at the Hotel Jerome was one dollar a day. Elsie Snyder worked with me at the same time.

Neighbors of Edward D. Pearce, top of Mill Street, 1880s. Future Little Nell in the background. Courtesy Fred Pearce.

✦

Photo by Kathy Daily

*Fred has a way of speaking
that is quite different than
anyone else. His choice of
words, the way he sees
things — it's almost as if
I'm listening to a poet.*

Fred Pearce

I was born February 20, 1928, in Aspen. We lived up on Mill Street. My folks owned some of that area. Grandmother's side had a lot of mining claims and her folks sold them. My Grandma Pearce kept chickens, I think. My mom, Ethel McCabe, had a nice camera — a Kodak. She got a lot of snapshots of that area and family. My Grandmother Pearce was born in a little place called Gold Hill around

Richard Wadge Pearce
(front row center
with beard), 1880s.
Possibly the
Durant Mine.
Courtesy Fred Pearce.

the Central City/Boulder area in the late 1870s. I don't know when they first came to Aspen. They were English miners. I think they first stopped in Michigan and then came on. She was born in Gold Hill, and then they moved to Aspen. They owned several lots up at the top of Mill Street. My dad, Edward Pearce, had miner's "con" — consumption. He died young. I was five when my dad died.

Well, early in my life, down at the Washington School, we had a game that was dryland hockey, but we called it shinny — where you pick up any old two-by-four or maybe a tree branch and bat some object back and forth and score a goal. It was called shinny because you got barked on the shins. For fun, when we were kids, we would play sandlot baseball from the east side of our house. There was nothing between here and the *Aspen Times* — nothing but weeds, broken glass, and rocks.

Ed Tiederman had a little store in town. He imported coal — shipped it in from Silt, New Castle, wherever they mine it around here. Part of my job was to

Mrs. Swearengin and Bessie Pearce, 1930s, top of Mill Street. Opera house in the background. Photo by Ethel McCabe. Courtesy Fred Pearce.

bring in coal and take all the ashes out. My first paying job was at the hotel for Laurence Elisha. I was young, like about thirteen or fourteen, when I got my first social security card from Laurence Elisha, so I hustled up beer — rolled the beer kegs in. I remember some of those people in the bar. I can't think of the names, but I called them the twenty- or thirty-beer-a-day guys. That's where they would start their day and that's where they spent it. On Halloween, there was maybe some outhouse tipping and cabbage pilfering, and maybe a little soaping of windows — that kind of mischief.

One thing I remember about Aspen is that it takes time to build up a nickname. This town was replete with nicknames. My dad's name was Spud — came from potatoes. My nickname was the diminutive Fritz. It takes time to build up a nickname, and that's all we had in Aspen at that time. Wasn't a lot going on. We saw a lot of each other. You almost hate to even say anything, because everybody was so related or nearly related that it was just a given. I miss that sense of community intimacy that seems to be gone. Yet I can sense that if a town starts to inbreed that way — it can fossilize. It can stop. We have an influx now with young people about. I think it revitalizes. You ask my mom if in her day did you look out to the outer world much — no.

Well, we kids did, but we were just kind of insulated and now it seems all roads lead to Aspen. In those days, we hankered to go out in the world. Our venue was maybe the sports pages, Joe Louis. That was about the time Joe DiMaggio was hitting for fifty-six straight games. We would wait for the newsreel which might

*Skyler Swearengin and
Fred Pearce (boy),
about 1938.
Courtesy Fred Pearce.*

be six weeks late. We would be watching the Rose Bowl football game clip maybe in the spring because of the gap.

Speaking of which, I've had people of late vintage say that when they came through Aspen in the late '40s, early '50s, Aspen was a dump, with apologies to me. I accepted that, but to me, Aspen was never a dump. It was down in the dumps — mine dumps. It was like a prize fighter — down, but it wasn't out. Like Jack Dempsey said, "The champion is one who gets up when he can't." I don't think Aspen was ever out. It was down. It was down in the dumps, but not out.

Long ago, I had aspirations that I wanted to leave. I don't know — it would come about when you would hear that train whistle. That was to me the key to the great outer world away from Aspen. I would envision traveling. I rode the train — never hitched. And like I said, the aspen trees were growing back and you could almost reach out and touch the leaves from the train car. I

349

think with the many languages and influences of various cultures and nationalities that you had here that change was good for the town. It caused problems somewhat, but it gave new vitality instead of a clogged kind of feeling that sometimes comes out of the dumps a lot of the time.

On Aspen today, I have an anecdote. I took a relative of mine to the opera house to see a movie, maybe ten years ago or more. Of course, me being of Aspen vintage, I knew about the time that the opera house burned. But he saw that modern movie where things were thrown at you so blatantly and said, "Somebody ought to burn this place again." I don't know if that's wisdom or not, but that was his comment.

I think history does repeat. The wheels go around for the ski lift over the same trails that the ore cars used to wheel and deal.

When I grew up, there was kind of a presence in the whole town. It was so ramshackley. I kind of want to emphasize that. As latercomers to Aspen uttered things like Aspen was a dump, I never had that feeling. In those worst so-called hard times, with ramshackle houses and vacant lots, it was always kind of there — a presence or resurging of the aspen trees coming back. Growth came back. Nature sort of took over, and where there was a cabin, there might be an aspen tree starting up through the floor, and you'd see an old rat-eaten shoe in the corner, maybe an old *Police Gazette* cover. It kind of gave you the idea that people left here in a hurry. They just wanted to get away from Aspen because there was nothing to do, with the work and mining gone.

◆

Photo by Kathy Daily

Jerry collects old bottles —
all different colors.
She keeps them in
her window so when
the sun comes up
in the morning,
they all light up.

Agnes (Jerry) Jurick McLaren

I was born in Snowmass on January 4, 1918. My mother was born in Italy (1889-1952) and she came at the age of five to the United States. Her name was Lucile Guerin. She came from Florence, Italy. Actually, their real name was Guerino, but they dropped the "O". She was seventeen when she came to Colorado.

Aspen: The Quiet Years

❧❧❧❧❧❧❧❧❧❧❧❧❧❧❧

My dad, John Louis Jurick (1889-1972), came from Yugoslavia — Croatia — at the age of fifteen. His father was already here. These people in Aspen are different; they came from a different section than my dad did. We don't even speak the same language. My grandfather, John Jurick (1865-1941), had a ranch up by Windstar, up in that general area. My dad came with his mother, Theresa; my grandfather came first. He worked in the mines in Leadville and he also worked in Missouri. I don't know what he was doing in Missouri. Mining was not for my grandfather, and so he looked around for a small ranch. He came to Aspen around 1886, whenever the mining in Aspen was still going gung ho. He found this ranch, and my daddy came with his mother. My grandmother did not speak a word of English and she wouldn't learn.

My mother's family came to Milwaukee, Wisconsin. My grandfather on that side had a saloon. Mother helped with the dirty work, such as cleaning stools and scrubbing floors — I mean the really dirty work. You know, the old Italians believed in their women doing the work. The men didn't have to work so hard, they just made the money, the big deals. It was not that way in my family, no. No, my dad wasn't that way. My mother worked side by side with my daddy, but it wasn't because she was forced to. You just had to. It took everybody's effort to make a little fun work.

Grandfather didn't homestead the farm — he bought it. He didn't own all of Windstar, he just owned a section back further up in the little gulch — up that road and back, Snowmass Creek side. There was a valley. You go up to Windstar where it is now and keep going straight to the left. The Pabst family bought it from my parents and from my grandfather, or my uncle. My grandparents were already deceased. My grandfather had cattle, potatoes, hay, and oats. He sold some feed. He sold some cattle. He didn't sell much hay because he needed the hay for his own livestock. My father grew up there at the age of twenty, maybe twenty-four. He was a farmer cowboy. He had to take care of the livestock and take them to the range, so I suppose he was a cowboy in a small way.

Then my daddy went to St. Paul, Minnesota, to work in the wheat fields. He was getting to the age where he wanted to put some money in his pocket besides just working at home. And somehow or another, he met my mother in Milwaukee. She was a telephone operator at the age of seventeen. They were married. Daddy came back to Colorado to find a place to live. He came back to Snowmass. Mom followed him in 1917 on the Colorado Midland, down the Frying Pan, over Hagerman Pass. She had never been in the mountains. She looked at the rear end of the train and she said if she could have turned around and gone back, she would have. Oh yes, she would have left him, but she learned to love these mountains. You could not have taken her away from them. Well, for someone who has never been in the mountains, it must have been horrifying for her. Mom was seventeen. And I was born in 1918. Dad was twenty-eight. Mom was eighteen. He moved in with his father for just a very short time, and then he went to work for a man who lived close by — Harry Williams. Dad used to ranch hand.

Dad and Mom moved down into a little two-room cabin. And that's where I was born — in the cabin, right on Snowmass Creek. And of course the doctor gets there too late, but he does get there. You go after him because there was no telephone service. You just go after him, and in our case, they had to go to Basalt, which is roughly only eight miles, but taking a horse or buggy or whatever, it's an hour or more. There was five of us kids, three sisters and one brother. Mom wanted another boy and she got a girl.

I went to Capitol Creek School and to Upper Capitol Creek School. I knew the Wiebens and went to school with some of them. I was eleven when Sonny was born, and Ann Wieben wanted me to come up and help take care of him. She was a polio victim and needed help. I went up there one day and the house burned down that my folks were living in, so we had to find another place to live. We moved at that point back to my grandpa's house, but we didn't stay there long. We went on to Aspen in 1929 and lived near the Smuggler Mine Tunnel in a rental house.

There's only three of us left living in this area that were born and raised in Sopris Creek, and that's Bubby Light, Walter Wieben, and myself.

Dad homesteaded on Sopris Creek in 1922. To get there, we would have gone past Bubby Light's — up that canyon and clear up. You can't get up there anymore. That was my favorite place. I was five years old when we moved there. I went to school over on McCartney Mesa and down into Capitol Creek.

I rode horseback. I was born on a horse. We were on the homestead — 160 acres. Probably all we paid is $160. We didn't stay there too terribly long. Too many children were coming along. It was too difficult to get back and forth. We probably lived there for four years. He sold it to George Maurin.

We moved back to Snowmass, where my father was working as a tenant farmer. After that us kids moved to Aspen, and my daddy went to work at Woody Creek, which was the Albert Grange Ranch. It's all houses in there now. Do you know where the little red schoolhouse in Woody Creek is? Well, it was all that land right there on the river, from Gerbaz's clear up to the Woody Creek River. That's all subdivided now. You see, we lived there. Have you seen the house with the finger painted on it? Pat Fox's? Well, that's where we lived.

Daddy built that little cabin. I graduated from the Woody Creek School at the age of thirteen. Albert Grange's ranch was big; the whole thing went from the first Woody Creek turnoff to the Woody Creek that runs from Lenado. On the ranch, when I wasn't in school, we gathered the eggs, milked the cows, and went out and got the cows every night. We probably had eight or ten milk cows. We sold cream and chickens and turkeys. There was always something to do. The dishes had to be washed, and being there were three of us girls, we took turns — one wash, one wipe, and one put the food away. Mother did the cooking. Us kids would help peel potatoes and go out and get the vegetables in the garden.

I was Dad's favorite. I trailed along with daddy wherever he went. I was a tomboy. And I rode my horse like some of you drive your cars — hell bent for election. I got the best out of the horse. My favorite horse was a little old mare we had. All five of us could ride her. Her name was Red. We could do anything — we could slide off the rear end, go under her belly, go under her chest. She was just a faithful plug. But she had some feisty in her. She would take off on us and head for home.

When we were still on the homestead, I forgot to cinch up my saddle or have my saddle tight when I left school. I got to this place where they had a generator. She did not like the sound of that machine, and I had to get off and open a gate. So I got her angled. I was real little, so I had her standing so I could climb on her. Well, the saddle turned and away she went. I had to walk home. By the time I got home, here was my dad and mother coming to look for me. They just knew something had happened to me. She went home.

I don't remember ever having a hat, unless it must have been a straw hat that somebody passed down to me. And we couldn't afford cowboy boots. You were lucky to have two pair of shoes a year. Now the real cowboys, that's all they wore. They didn't wear tennies or shoes, unless it would be a pair of dress shoes, and then they wore cowboy boots again. I was pretty shy, more or less afraid of men. I'd hide behind my mother's skirt. I didn't cotton to them at all.

Dad liked to go up to Thomas Lake, Williams Lake, Capitol Lake, and Snowmass Lake to fish. The rest of the family didn't care to go much. He would have a horse and I would have a horse. One of the work horses would carry our stuff. At that time, we didn't have sleeping bags and we didn't have tents, just a tarp. And we carried our own skillet, potatoes, bacon, and eggs. We raised everything that one could want. We had our own meat, and we had access to lots of fish. I remember Daddy getting wet weeds and wrapping the fish. They were fine and fresh. We used worms and a safety pin. We'd use safety pins, a willow stick, and a heavy line. No good filaments. I think maybe Daddy had a reel, one of these little cheapy ones that you can buy now for three or four dollars — nothing fancy.

From the Grange Ranch, my dad wanted to buy a particular ranch which was known as the Walk Place. It is now known as the Burlingame Place. It is part of Buttermilk and the airport. It was a nice little 300-and-some-acre ranch. This was getting close to the Depression, the '30s. No one would loan you $3,000. You would have been a millionaire by the time you retired. But anyway, I went to high school from this ranch. It was just three miles to Aspen. And I rode my horse for three years. The school was the old D.R.C. Brown place. We moved to this ranch that Daddy wanted, but he couldn't buy it, so we just rented it in 1931.

I enjoyed riding to high school. My dad bought me a nice frisky little horse by the name of Charlie. Now Charlie did not like Maroon Creek and Castle Creek bridges, but I was stronger than he. He would get to school and put on a show for all the kids. He loved to rear up. But they antagonized him, too, and I didn't care 'cuz I could handle him. We had our own private little rodeo. But that's as far as my fun in high school. The kids in Aspen at that time were very clicky. Well, they still are. You know, schools are very clicky, and so, my being a country girl, I didn't have the smarts. They were cruel. And I didn't get to participate in everything that went on in school because it was too much of a chore. And I had to get back home. If there was something like a class play, we went to town in the wagon or the sled, whatever. The bridges were wood surface then. That drove the horses crazy. There was a lot of space between a lot of the boards. You could look down and see daylight. Anyway, I didn't find high school much fun. Socially, the best part was my horse. Of course I was in some class plays, and I did the junior and senior prom and banquets.

For my junior prom, my mother got a pretty little dress for me — it was a long one. And I got dressed at home. I hiked my dress up and wore my jeans. I rode the horse to the prom and put the horse in the same place that I did every day. My senior year, Mom decided that was too much. She let me stay at a lady's house overnight that lived only a block from the Hotel Jerome where we had our banquet and dance.

My favorite teacher was probably my Spanish teacher. I just liked her. She took special time with me, and of course she was our typing, spelling, and Spanish teacher. I was very good in those subjects, so I just worked harder for her than I did for anyone else. I had two years of Spanish. We had physics and chemistry, algebra and geometry, which I sneaked by.

Aspen: The Quiet Years

After I graduated, when I was seventeen, my father had a truckload of potatoes that he had sold to a trucker. This man was a good friend of my daddy's and he was taking the potatoes to Pueblo. Well, I wanted to go to Denver to school; I wanted to go on. I didn't want to stay home. I did and I didn't. I was very homesick for several years while I was away. So we took that truckload of potatoes and left Aspen over Independence Pass to Pueblo. It took us all day and all night to get to Pueblo. Then he put me on the train from Pueblo to Denver. And I was met by aunts and cousins — first time away from home. Oh, what an experience. I cried and I cried. I didn't know what to expect, and my aunts and cousins had lived there for quite awhile. They were constantly trying to do me over. I mean, I'm a country girl. But I soon learned. I worked in a beauty shop for a little while. I attended Barnes Business College, and I had to find a place to live, so I worked for my room and board — three dollars a week. I went into the business end of it. Barnes Business College was downtown. They were just barely getting started when I moved there. Because I had to work, I didn't get as far advanced as I wanted to, because I couldn't finish my courses. Everything you needed to do in nine months.

Then I went off to Milwaukee, Wisconsin, to visit my Guerin grandparents. I stayed with them two or three weeks, and my grandpa, as I told you, was stern. You do this and you do that. So I was lucky enough to work for my board and room with a sister of the lady that I worked for in Denver. Then I went to Spencerian Business College in Milwaukee for nine more months. I finally got my degree. It took me eighteen months. Then I came back to Snowmass.

At that point, my dad had left Aspen and had bought the Mary Frank Ranch. McCabe Ranch is what they call it now.

I went to work in Glenwood, and that's where I met my first husband. His name was Larry Stubbings. We worked at the Colorado Hotel. He was a wanderer. He liked to stay for six months and move on. We lived in Washington and Oregon. He just couldn't stand to stay in one place. I was probably twenty. At the Colorado Hotel, he was a bellboy and I was a waitress and we were sent to Mobile, Alabama, to work in a big hotel chain down there. My oldest son was born near Mobile. So after that, we came back to Colorado. By then I had two children and was working all the time. We ended up in Denver. We didn't stay here very long. World War II came along and he joined the marines. By this time, we were divorced.

He joined the marines, and I went to work at Fort Logan in Denver for four years and my mother took care of my children. There was no way I could keep them in Denver. I thought I had a nice place. It was a nice boarding place

Elk shipment from Wyoming sponsored by Aspen Elk Lodge and brought in by John McLaren, supervisor of Sopris National Forest. Courtesy Jerry McLaren.

for the kids and me on Grant Street. It turned out to be a prostitute house. Didn't take me long to figure that out. I called my mother, and I said, "I've got this good job in Denver and there is no place for me and the children." She said to bring the children home. They had the ranch up there. Daddy had bought this ranch up Elk Creek, and he finally had a ranch of his own. He had 320 acres, I guess. They raised pigs, sheep, and they paid for the ranch that way. So I brought my children home to my mother and daddy and they raised them for four years. I would come over about every two weeks from Denver.

During the war, you could have a C-Card for guests if you could show that you were commuting or taking passengers in your car to work. I took six people to work, and I could have their gas money. So I could afford to come to Aspen. I had an old beat-up Buick, and it didn't last very long. Then I was able to buy this nice little Oldsmobile. It was a one-owner car and had an automatic shift in it — an overdrive type of thing, so it was almost a modern car. You could just kick into second without shifting. I came over here every two weeks, winter or summer. It was tough, but I was young. I didn't think anything about it.

We had to come over Loveland. There was no tunnel then. I spun out a couple of times without my chains on. On that one turn before you get to the

Another photo of the elk shipment. Brought in on the Colorado Midland Railroad from Denver. Part of this shipment unloaded at Meredith. Aspen, April 16, 1914. Courtesy Jerry McLaren.

top, I did a 360. I stayed on the road. I ended up going where I wanted to. All my life, I think the Lord was looking over me. I came back home and lived with my parents for a year in 1946. I worked at the Bill Finley Ranch. There was a family living there with two children. I could just hop-skip over the hill, and I worked for her for a year. I babysat. You know, I still had children and I had to support them somehow. At that time, Patty was six and Mickey was four.

Then, in 1947, my dad decided that I should buy the Snowmass grocery store down here, so he helped me buy it. He was well on his way to having his own, so he bought the Snowmass store. I was postmaster there for seven years and ran the grocery store. Well, while I was working at this lady's house over the hill, I met my second husband, because he was doing some remodeling for her. He was a carpenter at that time. His name was John McLaren. We were married that same year in 1947. I had already bought the store. John was from Thomasville. He was born in Grand Junction, but his parents had interest in little ranches up the Frying Pan.

My son, John, was born in 1952. In the meantime, my husband, John, was looking for some property to buy. This place right here was just used as a picnic ground, so we got to snooping around. He was the son of a self-made surveyor. We walked up in the snow and found stakes. He found out that this piece of property was BLM land — government land — and where that apartment building is now was deeded property. So we proved up on this.

That's why this house is where it is. We built right here in 1953. We proved further towards the river up that way a little bit. We proved up on it for three years. You had to build a house, and it had to consist of a kitchen, bedroom, and a bathroom. That's all they said. So we built the bathroom, the utility room, and the kitchen. We lived in the utility room. We rented it for three years. You have three years in which to build what you want, then you can buy it. They put a price on the property that was sixty dollars per year. That was $180. We bought it for $160. We bought the deeded piece of land from Justin Cerise, who lived across the river. They had lots of Cerises here. I don't think he was related to Martin. You know, there's lots of Cerises that aren't really related.

When we came up here, there was an old cabin sitting where the trailer house is, and we lived in that while we were building the house. But it was primarily used before for a stop station for the men and the highway crew that were working on this Highway 82. They took out the Colorado Midland Railroad, and they didn't have anything but horses and rough equipment. So this was used as a cook house and a place for the men to rest their horses. The walls were all papered with newspaper. We built in 1954, and we borrowed $2,000 to build the bedrooms. My advice to anyone is, don't build bedrooms first. Build them last. You can sleep anywhere. The BLM didn't care about a living room, right? They wanted a kitchen — a kitchen and a bathroom. You could not build a bathroom outside — no outside plumbing.

I sold the store in 1954, but I did not give up my job. I gave up postmastership, but I didn't give up my rights as a postal clerk. I've been down there twenty-seven years. When I was there as postmaster the first time, there were thirty customers. See, everything up above there was all ranches. And they were big ranches — they weren't little ranches. You know, something like thousands of acres. We sold bread, flour, sugar, coffee, tea, beans, tomatoes. I didn't sell any produce. We couldn't keep produce until later. I finally got a deep-freeze, and we could buy meat. I think everything came out of Grand Junction. I sold a lot of Prince Albert — chewing tobacco — Bull Durham, Lucky Strikes, Chesterfields, Camels, no filters. I had to pay my bills once a month, every month, and if you came in and spent $2,000 or $3,000 per year, then I had to carry you somehow. So it became very difficult to try to keep ends going and still pay my mortgage and the principal.

In 1954 when we came here, I had to have something to do, or I was going to go crazy. I put in the dibs for school-bus driving. I did that for twelve years. My route was from here down to Snowmass and over. Later, I had to go to Phillips' and back. At one point, I had to drive up to Gerbaz and pick up kids along there at Silver Smith. I had scoundrels, sure. They would throw spitwads and I would say, "Now I can see you." They'd say, "How can you see; you are not even looking." I'd reply, "I have eyes right in back of my head." And then, I had one or two children that liked to be a little ornery and wouldn't pay any attention to me or mind me. I'd only tell them once, "Be quiet and behave or you're going to have to walk." Well, that didn't work, so one time coming home, when they were being unusually naughty, I just slammed on the brakes and they all came forward. "Mrs. McLaren, what is the matter?" I said, "I'm not telling you again; you are going to get off and walk right now." They said, "Oh no, please no!" At that time, I was driving contract. I owned my own car. I had nine to twelve kids. I had the weekly run, which amounted to twelve kids. That was enough. I'd leave home at 7:00 and get them to school by 8:15. Well, the route was not a paved road and in the spring of the year, it was a mess. My car would sink eighteen inches, clear down, and drag many a time. Bill Punkoney, Tom Lamb, or whoever happened to live over there would come with their tractor and pull me out. I'd tell the kids to get out and walk on the railroad track. As soon as they would get me through this, I'd pick them up. They didn't mind, you know. They were high school kids going to Basalt. My young son, who was eighteen months old when I started, went with me, and he rode to school with me every day until he was sixteen and was able to drive his own car. That's the way the high school kids were. I mean, they didn't ride with me after they got their own vehicles — except the Stewart girls.

At the time I was there, this company had a lot of sheep — Christiansen Brothers. Christiansen Brothers, George Annis, and Burton Tuttle, I guess they were the only really big ones. All the sheep were driven from Utah, which was their winter pasture. They were herded along the highway. It just took them days and days to get here, because they would go as far as they could one day and find somebody's mountain to bed them down for the night. One of my experiences in the grocery business was with David Christiansen. At that point, he was probably eighteen or twenty years old. It was his job to get the groceries, pick up the mail, and pick up the groceries for the sheep camps. And it was nothing unusual to come and knock on our door or not even knock, just walk in the house at three in the morning. I had many an argument with my husband. David just came in and walked right into our bedroom. I'd have to get up and go to the store and open up for him. It meant money in my pocket, you know, so I'd have to get up.

We always looked forward to fishing season. At that time in my life, about May 17 or 18, I used to get lures and hooks and various things for sale and special items that I knew fishermen might want to buy. We always looked forward to opening season, which was May 17. It was open from May 17 to after hunting season, sometime in November or the end of October. And so we took advantage of all the tourists and all the people who came. They didn't come with campers and supplies — they came with tents and camped out. And so they relied on the locals. The opening of fishing season would be a really big event.

We looked forward to hunting season, too. Because in those early days, hunters swarmed this country, but they were more respected then. I mean, they came to hunt. They didn't come to party. They came to hunt, and so you would look forward to taking care of those guys. And your house was open to them.

One time, when they had the Bicentennial in Aspen, there was a little cabin across from the Snowmass store. And there was someone living there or had moved in there. No one knew who he was or what he was, but the FBI came and very quietly asked us if an agent could live in the upstairs room in the store and watch this cabin. The guy was a suspect. They got him. I never did know what he did. They wouldn't tell us anything. They just said if we would be kind enough to not let anybody know they were up there watching this cabin.

I pumped many a gallon of gas. I got my gas from Phillips 66. They have gone self-service, and I say, no way. "We'll pump yours, Mrs. McLaren." I pumped a lot of gas in my day — in the cold.

Nowadays, I'm frustrated with Aspen. They've fouled up the building of this Highway 82 so many times. They are trying to back out of it now again. Twenty years ago, they started this. They'll either build a four-lane highway here, or they'll do an upper level, or they'll go across the river. I'd prefer they go across the river. I mean, it's more sensible to me; this is a slick piece of road. I've seen so many people in my yard. I've seen some pretty serious accidents here. They've ended up mostly in between two trees, and over behind the little shed where the dumpster sits. I've seen them upside-down. I've got pictures of them. Not last year, but the year before, we were all sitting here at Christmastime, and cars were just spinning over like nothing. And my older son — we had just got through talking about the one before — they just got it cleared out and I said, "Well, maybe it's time for another one." I barely got it out of my mouth, when three cars were right on the road — my access road. So, I've seen enough of them. I'm beginning to notice the highway noise, more than ever before. It's terrible now. There is a lot of nighttime noise — big service trucks, big trucks. And where they are going and what they are doing, I don't know. Normally, the traffic will stop around 2:00 or 2:30 and then not start up again until 4:30 or 5:00, but now it's constant. No place for them to stay up here; they have to go downvalley.

I don't want to change anything about Aspen at this point in my life; it doesn't matter to me. And it's not going to go backwards, it's going to go forward, and it's not going to get any better. There just isn't going to be any room. They are talking about environmentalists and preserving open space — it's not going to happen. People are closing roads that have been open for people to go through. I'd bet my last bottom dollar that in the next ten years, there will be a development in the Sopris Creek area, and that is supposed to be open space. We used to leave our doors wide open. Now they are locked.

❖

Photo by Kathy Daily

*Martin Mishmash is quiet
and reserved and chuckles
under his breath.*

Martin Mishmash

I was born April 13, 1920, in Aspen on East Cooper in the second house from
Cooper Bridge. There's a big condominium there now — on the left when
you're going toward Independence. My parents' names were Rose and Martin
Mishmash. My dad came from Yugoslavia, and my mother was born in Leadville, Colorado. Her maiden name was Rose Stibernick.

Rose and Martin
Mishmash, Sr.,
with Martin, Jr.,
May 1923.
Courtesy Helen Kralich.

My dad first went to Kansas from the old country. He had an uncle and some relatives there. He worked for awhile in the mines and then went to Leadville; I don't recall what year. He probably came to Aspen about 1918, over Independence Pass in a car. He and my mother met in Leadville. She worked as a sales clerk in Frank Zaitz's Mercantile. Zaitz was a relative, an aunt. My dad was a miner in Leadville.

In Aspen, dad went to work in the mines. He worked over in the Smuggler and Durant mines. He also leased up on top of Aspen Mountain. He worked in the mine that Billy Zaugg took over long afterwards. I was the first child. There are just two. Helen was born eight years after me, over on Cooper Avenue. Both my parents lived to be in their late seventies.

When I was growing up in Aspen, I used to bring in the wood, help feed the chickens, and help with the garden. Dad took me hunting when I was a boy. I was probably about fourteen when I first shot something. I don't hunt anymore. I did until about six years ago.

We lived up on Cooper, and most of the kids up on that end would rather take a lunch to school than run all the way back home to have lunch and then go back to school. The Washington School used to be where the old yellow brick elementary school is. We were always outside. If we got cold, we dealt with it. When we woke up in the morning, the house was freezing cold in the winter. Dad or mom got the wood and started the fire. They started the stove about six o'clock. They left it stoked all night — it never went out. Some of the blankets on the bed were store bought, and then we made down comforters.

Later on we moved to Oak Creek. At that time, Oak Creek had I'd say eight hundred to twelve hundred people. I was about seven. I started first grade in Aspen, and then we moved when I started the second grade. I came back and finished high school here. I really wanted to come back because I had more friends here and there was more to do. Wasn't much to do in Oak Creek. Dad was working in the coal mines. When we came back, he worked up on Tourtelotte Park.

*Frances Miklich, Martin Mishmash, Sr., a neighbor, Martin Jr., and Rose Mishmash, 1020 E. Cooper Avenue, 1924.
Courtesy Helen Kralich.*

●●●●●●●●●●●●●●●●

I left here in 1941 and came back in the early part of 1945. I left because there was no work in Aspen. At that time, I decided to go back in the service and try it for two more years. By that time, I had about eight or nine years in the air force. I was a flight engineer, aircraft maintenance supervisor, and NCOIC of Air Base SAC Inspection Team.

Louise and I started dating in 1947. We knew each other prior to that time. Everyone in Aspen knew each other. I went back in the service, but I would come back on weekends. I retired from the service in 1963. After retiring from the service, I went to work for the State of Colorado in the Workmen's Compensation Division as a supervisor of the records unit. We got married in 1949 in Denver. We've been married forty-three years. The same priest who married us married my dad and mother up at Leadville. He'd moved to Denver, down in Globeville.

I noticed a change happening in Aspen when I first came back from the service in 1945. I was offered the Red Onion to buy in early 1945. At the time, I didn't see no future in it. I figured at that time that I had about nine years in the service, and I thought I would go ahead and finish up my career. I wish I had bought the Red Onion. At that time, I wouldn't have only got the Red Onion, I'd have had that whole lot all the way across the street — cabins and all. That was $500, which in them days would equal probably millions today.

●

*Louise was funny. She had a way of laughing with people and blessing them at the same time.
You can tell that life was a wonder to her, and she gave herself to people.*

Photo by Kathy Daily

Louise Bradshaw Mishmash
(June 17, 1910 – March 1, 1994)

I never tell my birthdate to anybody. Anybody who would tell their own birthdate is silly. I have to? Well, my birthdate is June 17, 1910. I was born in Monte Vista — the San Luis Valley.

I had a great beginning. My dad was the only one who ever crossed the line from Monte Vista into this part of the country. My father's name was

Thomas D. Bradshaw. My mother's name was Elizabeth Mueler Bradshaw. They never lived right in Aspen. I'm the only one. They eventually settled down by Rifle, Colorado. They liked the farming country by Monte Vista. I was barely thirteen when I came here. My parents lived in Aspen seven years. I went to high school in Aspen. I wanted to stay when they moved. We lived out on the ranch — we moved up into Capitol Creek on a big ranch up there. They tore down my little home to build the monastery. We didn't sell it to anyone. It was leased to a big company. I don't know who lived there after we did. My dad was a rancher.

When I was young, I didn't have any chores. There were three kids in my family, one sister and one brother. My brother did very little, if anything at all, on the ranch. He was too young at that time. He was a very good horseman, and we were rodeo people. My brother made the navy his career later on. Me — I loved to cook. I still love to cook.

My mother was a nurse; that's how I remember her. Because of the many, many people on that ranch, during the flu epidemic of 1918, she took care of thirty-two of us. That was what you called a cattle ranch. There were at least thirty cowhands and thousands of head of cattle. That was in the cattle days. We're talking now about the ranch above Rifle, down by Grand Junction. That was my folks' type of living. Lots of people got sick during the flu epidemic. It was the middle of winter, and they would stack the bodies in the sheds, waiting for the spring to come so they could dig the ground. My mother, of course, being a nurse, would say to me, "You have to help me." I'm a nurse inside. Mother just went ahead and did it. She didn't make a big deal about it. Everybody got sick, but nobody died on our ranch. I was the first one to get sick from the flu. I was sick from the day before Christmas until June — my birthday. I could barely get out of bed. My lungs were affected so badly I would have died, but my mother was so strong-willed and such a good person. She could pull you together whether you wanted to or not. She had a knowledge that was beyond her.

I saw her amputate a leg once on the kitchen table. One of the cowboys had been kicked so bad it shattered the whole bone over the thigh. I watched her. She used knives — put him out with whiskey. Her father was a doctor, and so was his father before him. She had all kinds of beautiful medical instruments, because he brought them all from Boston — came right straight into Colorado by wagon train. My dad was a real cowboy and a pioneer. The guy whose leg was amputated lived. He was a very young boy — a cowboy. Just trying to do work on this big ranch.

I didn't like horses that well when I was little. My sister did, and my brother. My brother and sister did not watch the amputation. Nobody but me

*Hotel Jerome,
early 1900s.
Courtesy
Dorothy Portner.*

and my mother. We had the stomach for it. I still work at Fitzsimmons Hospital; I'm a volunteer there. I've worked there a long time. I picked up practical nursing, and I went to special schools for it.

When we were young, we went to the little school down Capitol Creek with Gladyce Christiansen. Then we lived right across from the Hotel Jerome, across Main Street. My parents moved in there. Then my dad leased a ranch. Later he was a sheriff in Rifle, New Castle, and Grand Junction — different years.

I married very young. I was barely sixteen. I married Ted Sandstrom. I had my first child one year later. The next one came nine years later. I was married to Ted Sandstrom for eighteen years, then divorced. I married Martin Mishmash in 1949. Ted was a mining engineer, so he took in quite a lot of places, even into California. I was scared he would never come back sometimes. We had nothing in common. We were just too young. He was about twenty-five when we married.

369

Ethel McCabe was married real young, too. She is the same age as me. We lived right next door; had babies about the same time, too. Her son Fritz is a bit older by months. And he walked first. We hated each other over that. When I got divorced, I was working for the Hotel Jerome and the Paepckes. I was kept very beautifully. They were very nice to me. Ethel and I worked at the Jerome together. She worked the dining room. I worked upstairs. My tips were good. With her tips, it should have been a little better than a dollar a day. In those days, there was a hole in the roof where the skylight was in the Jerome.

I worked for the Paepckes until I married Martin, and then we moved away. That was in 1950. I worked at the Jerome before that. That was a good job. I was in charge of all the guest homes and the apartments. I was in charge of all the housekeepers that kept them. I saw that everything was done and ready.

I loved Aspen from the time I saw Aspen Mountain. My dad and mom took me up for the first time. My dad said, "Wait until you see this mountain. That's going to be your mountain forever." My ashes are to be put up there, and I don't care how many thousands are ahead of me. I'll still be there, on top of that peak.

❖

Photo by Kathy Daily

When I first met Helen,
she seemed private.
After I got to know her,
she had much more of a
crazy little girl inside
than she first let on.

Helen Mishmash Kralich

I was born February 12, 1928, in Aspen. My mother's maiden name was Rose Stibernick (born June 22, 1898; died December 7, 1971). She was born in Leadville, Colorado. My father's name was Martin J. Mishmash. He was born in what is now known as Slovenia. In those days it was Yugoslavia. He was born in the little village of Visnje, which is about thirty miles from the capital city of

*Martin Mishmash, Sr.,
Martin Jr., a neighbor,
and Rose Mishmash, at
125 East Cooper Avenue,
1924.
Courtesy Helen Kralich.*

Lubjana. The house that he was born in is still there. He left his home at the age of seventeen and first went to Kansas City, Kansas, where his uncles sponsored him. He then went to Aspen, where there were other uncles living. I don't know how he met my mother in Leadville — if he just visited there from Aspen, or if he worked in Leadville for awhile and then married her. They were probably driven to Aspen by my uncle, who either had his own car or used a car loaned to him by the Zaitz family. My mother's mother was Mrs. Zaitz's sister. The Zaitzs were a prominent family and owned the Zaitz Mercantile and Clothing Store in Leadville.

Dad worked as a miner up on Tourtelotte Park. He would stay up there and board and then come home on weekends. My mother was a housewife. They first lived in a house somewhere in the neighborhood of what is now Neal or Gibson streets. They later moved to 1023 East Cooper, where my brother and I were born. There were just the two of us. My parents both spoke Slovenian,

372

and as a child growing up, I learned to understand it and speak it somewhat, although English was our main language and was always spoken if there were not Slovenian people present.

My parents were Catholic, and we were reared in that faith. My fondest memories are those of attending midnight Christmas mass, even when we were very little. We would always go to midnight mass and then come home to find that Santa Claus had paid us a visit while we were at church. We would open what few gifts we might have. After my husband and I were married and had our children, we carried on the same tradition. Christmas for most of us, at the time I was growing up, consisted of going to the Armory Hall for a bag of candy and perhaps an apple or orange that had been organized by the Eagles Club or some community organization.

In later years, a group of us young people formed a church group called the Sodality. It was mostly a social function, and we held our meetings in the old Convent Hall. On one particular night, we had a waffle supper, and since the wiring wasn't sufficient to carry the load, we kept blowing fuses and ended up eating by candlelight. The statue of Our Lady of the Snows was erected by this group and still stands at the corner of the Catholic Church rectory in Aspen.

On Halloween in Aspen we would go around to the neighbors and the rectory. When we would say, "Trick or treat" to the priest, he would say, "Earn your treat," and we would have to sing a little song before getting it. Mainly the younger children went to houses and got candy. The older boys would turn over outhouses and take gates off and move them from one end of the town to the other. Most people would try to take the precaution of removing their gates before Halloween night came around.

My first chores at home were helping in the garden and feeding the pigs, chickens, and rabbits. We would cook the vegetables for the pigs in a big iron bucket. I always had a pet chicken or rabbit and would refuse to eat if one of them "mysteriously" disappeared. I always had a dog for a pet. As I grew older, in the wintertime, the water in our house, as in many others, would freeze, and we would have to go down to the Roaring Fork River and carry buckets. Fortunately, we didn't live too far from the river. Sometimes you would get almost to the top of the hill and slip on a rock, the water would spill, and down you would have to go again.

When we were going to school, we couldn't wear pants. We kept warm by wearing black leggings and snowsuits. We stuffed our skirts down inside the snowsuit. We would walk to school and usually come home for lunch. In the wintertime, the snowbanks were piled high, and we would walk across the top of the bank until we came to the intersections, where you would jump down, come back up, and go down again. We thought that was a lot of fun. I lived better than a mile from the Washington Grade School (back of the old Mesa Store). Our recesses were always fun. We would play pump-pull-away and other such games. We always passed a lot of notes in class. There was one particular girl that was a snoop and always read your note before passing it on to the intended person, so we decided to pull a trick on her. We wrote the note and threw it so it would land at her desk. Unfortunately, the principal, Paul Smith, intercepted it before she got it. He didn't say a word, just put it in his desk. Mr. Smith was a very handsome man — very tall, dark complected, with real thick, bushy eyebrows. At the end of the school year he said, "These are some of my prize mementos." He pulled out our note and read it — "Boo! Did you get your eyes full?" I can still see those bushy eyebrows and eyes lighting up!

Our first year of high school was in the two-story [Brown] home that was converted to the high school, and we were the first class [second year] in the new high school that was built [old red brick building — long one still standing]. I put myself through high school by picking potatoes in the fall. The ranches I picked on were Marolts, Stanley Natal, Cowlings, and Skiff. Jennie Cowling

Washington School, 1940, located at 5th and Bleeker. Built in the 1880s, but torn down. The stones were used to build the Catholic church in Glenwood Springs. Courtesy Louiva Stapleton.

had the best food, and then the Natals. The Marolts didn't have to feed us. If we picked by contract, we got paid two to four cents a sack, depending upon the year. The first year I worked at the Marolts. We got paid two dollars a day, starting at 7 A.M. and working until 5 P.M. I was twelve years old. It was not fun. It was a very, very tedious job, and we worked hard, because we knew we were there for a day's work. It was a back-breaking job, as you can well imagine, being bent over all day. The third day was the worst. If you made it past the third day, you were okay. We only worked two weeks at the end of September into October. The school would excuse us until the harvest was picked. I used my money for my books and clothes in school.

Growing up in Aspen in those days was a lot of fun, even with the hardships. We were a tight-knit community with close family and neighborly ties. We mostly entertained ourselves by our school, playing after school long into the evening hours with games like run-sheep-run, kick-the-can, tag, ball, and card games. We played on the Durant mines and tramways, walking the tracks over the railroad trestles, with an ear and eye open for the trains. We hiked and roamed over the mountains. One of our favorite and most rewarding pastimes was to go to the Glory Hole, which was the town's dumping ground. There we would find dresses, shoes, etc., which we would carry home and play dress up in. There were always all kinds of things there to intrigue us. In the summer, my brother and I would hike up to Bell Mountain to pick wild raspberries. We would tie a lard bucket around our waist, enabling us to use both hands to pick the berries. Many times you would slip, and the berries would fall out and we would have to start all over again. There was swimming in Sully's pond in the summer and ice skating in the winter. We would usually have our feud in the wintertime with the West End kids, who always seemed to show up after we had shoveled the skating rink but never seemed to be there to help.

One of my favorite things was an outing to Warren's Lake. Our neighbors were the Warrens, so we were allowed to go there. We would hike up about ten miles and stay for a couple of days in the cabins, fishing, etc. There were always a lot of elk and deer to enjoy as well as the scenery. Then there were the dances at the Armory Hall, a trip to the Hotel Jerome to the soda fountain, Louise Berg's candy store, and many other fun things.

Skiing in those days consisted of cutting up an old innertube and strapping your overshoes onto a pair of skis and sliding down some small hill. The first boat tow was an adventure in itself, where you sat in this small sledlike structure, shifting your weight as you went over a small gully and arriving at what

Frank and Mrs. Warren
(Warren Lake),
early 1920s,
East Cooper Avenue
Bridge.
Courtesy Helen Kralich.

we called the Second Road on Ajax. By the time the boat tow had arrived, we had graduated to lace boots and metal bindings.

Bootlegging in Aspen was not an uncommon thing. Most people did it for their own use and a few engaged in selling it. Sheriff Bruin would usually alert the people when he knew the federal agents were coming to town, and most of the time he was aware of the bootlegging but did nothing about it. Dad used to make chokecherry and dandelion wine and we always had rootbeer. We would pick the dandelions — bucketsful.

What clothes we needed would be bought either at Kobey's or the catalogs. Dad would always fix our shoes by repairing the heels and soles. I still have the shoe stand that he would use. Mother also sewed a lot of our clothes. Our under-clothes were usually made from flour sacks when we were small.

We moved to Oak Creek in about 1929. It was a very small mining town, but I remember the house we lived in and the school. I attended the first grade there. Dad got hurt in the mine in 1934. There was a cave-in, and his ribs had punctured so close to the lungs and heart that he was never able to do heavy work after that. We returned to Aspen and mother went to work, sewing for the WPA project at the courthouse. In later years, Dad worked as a maintenance person for the Aspen Company — Mrs. Mitchell and Mrs. Paepcke.

I was valedictorian in my class, so I got a scholarship to go to college and went to Western State at Gunnison because it was small. When I came home from college, I started to work in Social Services (then called the Welfare Department). I worked for them for twelve years, from 1947 to 1959, and was acting director for two years. Social Services at that time handled old-age pensions, aid to dependent children, adoptions, and transients.

I was twenty-two when I got married. We adopted two children, Andrea and Mark. My husband, Frank, died in 1981 of lung cancer. My husband and I had the Conoco station and sold it to Jesse Maddalone. My husband went back to work at carpentry. We had a terrific business, but his idea of work was not pumping gas. He was a carpenter and his idea was creation — doing things with his hands. We would stay open until nine or ten each night and then spent another hour or more doing the bookwork. He had to wear the Conoco uniforms, and we could not afford more than two at a time, so each night one set had to be washed and ironed for the next day. One time a man from out of town was out of gas late at night, and the cops came and got us to open up the station so the man could get gas and be on his way. We didn't think anything of it.

I think kids today have it too easy. I don't think they appreciate the value of money or are satisfied with what they have. They seem to always want more. They seem bored quickly with what they are doing and have to have activities planned for them rather than thinking for themselves. I don't think they have the family ties that we did. Kids today take their money and do whatever they want with it. We weren't allowed that luxury, not because we were forced to by our parents — but it was just something that was instilled. It was a family situation. It was survival. You knew they needed help, so there was never a question of what to do. Go spend the money on yourself — it never occurred to us to do that.

I noticed the big change in Aspen in the Sixties. I think that greed and jealousy brought it on. People changed and were no longer content with what they had. It seemed like Aspen had lost the touch of people and caring for each other. People became more interested in making more money. We lived at 125 East Hyman and had a yard where our kids could play. It ended up that we had a continual flow of neighborhood kids because everybody else was building on their property to put in another addition or lodging. No one had time for their

Dandelion Wine
(from Helen Kralich)

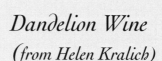

15 quarts dandelion blossoms
3 gallons cold water
15 pounds sugar
1 yeast cake
juice of one dozen oranges
juice of one-half dozen lemons
2 1/2 pounds raisins

Place the blossoms in cold water and simmer for 3 hours. Then strain the liquid. Mix it with the sugar. Boil up, then strain through a cheesecloth. When lukewarm, add the yeast cake, and let the mixture stand for 2 or 3 days, skimming it each day. Add the juice of the oranges and lemons with the thinly peeled rings of both oranges and lemons simmered for half an hour in a little water. There should be 5 gallons in all by measure. Put into a cask, and add the raisins. Leave the cask open for a day; then seal it tightly, and let it stand for 6 months before bottling. The wine improves with aging.

friends and neighbors, and the closeness and friendliness were gone. Because we were close to Lift No. 1, we would find garbage in our yard and even had one skier throwing snowballs at our picture window and climbing up on our balcony. People coming in were different and seemed to have no respect. An air of permissiveness began taking over the town, and when it took over in the school system at that time, it helped for us to make a change. In 1968 we moved to Emma.

I don't think it is possible for Aspen to handle the people today. Even in the Fifties and Sixties, when some of the people would complain of different people coming, we'd say, "Well, we should have locked the gates before *you* came in." I don't think you can lock the gates. Aspen is what it is, and I don't think there's any stopping it. I think that was the thing that made us leave. The trust was gone.

I have encouraged some of the younger people who come to Aspen and who talk with me. I say, "Go ahead and stay in Aspen for a year or two. Have fun, kick up your heels, do what you want to — skiing and things that you really enjoy — and then leave. It's just too expensive to ever have a place of your own, and that's sad. This is my own hometown. It just crushes me to think that they can't stay, and neither can the old-timers afford to remain. And then, looking back on the years, Aspen had its own characters. No one in town today could imagine what it was like.

♦

Nasie has a mischievous twinkle in her eyes and is always smiling. She welcomed me in her door and made me feel right at home.

Nasie Natal Pecjak

 I was born March 30, 1916, in Woody Creek on our ranch. My mother's maiden name was Valerie Betemps. My dad's name was Victor Natal and came from Aosta, Italy. Dad came to Aspen first. I don't know what year, in the 1880s. I think there was a whole bunch of them that came over here at that time to find work.

My mother's brother was already here, so she came over to be with him and later she married dad. They were farmers. Dad never did work in mines. I imagine he was a friend of my mother's brother and that's how they met. They were married and moved on our ranch up Woody Creek in the old log house. There was five children in our family — my two brothers, Arthur and Stanley, and I am the next to the last. I have a half-sister, Pierina. I had a sister, Rosina, but she was killed in a car accident. She died when she was twenty-three.

My first chores on the ranch were to wash clothes and peel potatoes and all those goodies. We rode horseback to the Woody Creek School — three kids on a horse. The horse didn't have a name — she was just Pony to us. The only time that I was ever afraid on a horse was to cross the river if the water was high because a horse swims and I don't. I was always afraid of that. And then down there by our place, there was always that ditch that leaked. In the winter-time, the horse was afraid of the ice and I was afraid of the horse — you know, a horse on ice. So we would go across hanging on white-knuckled. I would say it

Woody Creek School, 1903. Auzel Gerbaz in second row from front, fifth from left. Courtesy Del Gerbaz.

took us forty-five minutes to an hour to get to school. We didn't freeze in the winter, because we were always wrapped up real good. We wore overalls down to the schoolhouse and then we had to take them off. We couldn't go into the schoolhouse with them. We had our skirts tucked down inside. We had to do our own ironing.

I lost my mother when I was eleven years old, so we had to take care of ourselves. I couldn't tell you really what mother died of. In those days, they didn't call it cancer, but it might have been.

The Woody Creek School was just a one-room schoolhouse, and we had a little stove in the middle to keep it warm — just one of those little potbelly stoves. There were eight grades. I went through the eighth grade. Then I went to school in Basalt. I stayed with my sister in Basalt for the winter. I came home on weekends on the train.

We had dances in Woody Creek. Just the neighbors came — the Arlians and the Trentazs. Then there were the Mautzs. In Aspen, in those days they lived up above Aspen. And they used to come down and play accordions. We had an old organ. My sister played. Oh, it was just an old organ, just something that somebody must have given us.

In 1940, I married Matthew Pecjak. He was born and raised in Aspen. His dad Matt (1883–1943), was a miner — worked in the Midnight Mine. When I was little, his dad came down on the ranch during the Depression and rented some ground. So I went to school with him. This is when I met him, but we didn't get along in school. And then we started going to dances in Aspen. He was a good dancer. We both finished high school, he finished high school in Aspen and I did in Basalt. We both graduated in 1934. I was about twenty-three when we married. He was a year older. He was working at the Midnight. He didn't work down in the mines; he worked on the hoist. They took the men up and down in the mine. There was no work for women in Aspen. I had one little girl, she died the day after she was born.

Then I went to work. I worked always. I worked at the Hotel Jerome. That was about in 1945. We bought a house, and that house was $300, so we had to borrow the money. Matt was getting $60 every two weeks or something like that. You couldn't borrow money, because nobody wanted to loan it to you. We really wanted it, because the house we were living in was just an old thing. So Laurence Elisha said to us, "I'll give you board and room at the Hotel Jerome and give Matt his board, too. And I'll put up the $300 for your house and you can kick in some of Matt's paycheck until you have the $300." It took us one sea-son. So I worked tables, worked the laundry, and I did maid work for our board

Hotel Jerome, 1930s.
Courtesy Aspen
Historical Society.

and room. It was just a big dining room then and they had the bar. You went in the first door and walked right straight up to the bar. Very few women, if any, sat at the bar, but we would go in and have ice cream there. We thought nothing of it. Once in awhile we would go to a dance. If they had a dance in town, we always went. They had nice dances.

At Christmas we stayed in town. My brothers were married, too, at that time. Stanley was living on the ranch then. Stanley has been on the ranch all the time. It was just him and dad. But we get together more now because everybody is married and older. But in those days, we spent more time with Matt's family. He came from a large family. They were from Austria, but I don't know what town. It's awfully hard for you to get any history from anybody around here, because everybody's history is basically the same. If we went to dances or certain places, that is where all the rest of them were. Matt mined up until, oh, into his fifties or sixties. Then the Midnight closed down, so he went to carpenter work, then to butcher at Tom's Market. I worked at the Hotel Jerome for awhile, and then I worked for Hod Nicholson in dry cleaning. Later I worked for Tom's

Market. Matt died in 1971, and in 1973, I sold everything out and moved down to Carbondale.

My favorite years I would say were the '50's. That was about the best. What I liked about Aspen was everybody knew everybody. You could just see a car come up and you knew who it was. Everybody was so friendly. Now you can go to Aspen and know no one.

◆

*I'll always remember
Ellamae tying flies for fly
fishing and telling me her
flies would catch me
a big one.
She has had a
very productive and
bountiful life.*

Ellamae Huffine Phillips

I was born in Maryville, Missouri, June 25, 1909. I'm eighty-four. I was about eighteen when I moved to Aspen the second time. I was married by that time, about 1927. I got married when I was seventeen. I had my first baby right off the bat. Yes, I had all three, Jim, Dean, and Harriette, in six years. My husband's name was Concer H. Phillips. Con and I lived in St. Louis and couldn't find

385

work, so we came out to Aspen. We just bundled up the one child. I was expecting the next.

Before that, my dad, James Huffine, and mother, Francie McGuire, separated when I was twelve in 1921. We were with my grandmother at that time in St. Louis. My dad was a carpenter, and you know how carpenters had to leave home to get a job. At that time, my sister, Alta Spaulding, lived here in Aspen. She and her husband Bob had promised us a job, so my dad just bundled me and my brother up and brought us to Aspen after his divorce. That was about 1922. So I first moved to Aspen in the spring of 1922.

When my aunt's husband died in St. Louis, my dad and I went back to help her with her store. We were helping her get over her husband's death and all. Now Con was a friend of my aunt. He had done some work for her. I was in the setting room, don't you see, and my aunt came in and says to me, "Ellamae, I want you to come out here and meet somebody." I didn't know who I was going to meet or anything else. So I walked out with her, and when we got to the door, she says to Con, "Here is your pay." I looked at him, he looked at me, and I didn't know what to say. And he says, "I accept." He never did get paid for that job.

When Con and I came back to Aspen about 1927, we worked for the Vagneurs. They were all together at that time — don't cha see, they hadn't broke up the Vagneur clan. My husband worked on the ranch and I took care of the children. I had two children at that time. Con was a ranch hand. Anything that needed to be done, he would do. Handyman all the way around — it didn't matter what it was, he could finish up. The Vagneurs liked it because Con could take hold. They could go away and say, "Con, take care of things," and they liked him. I would say maybe we was on there for seven years. The Vagneurs all spoke Italian. They didn't want you to know what they were saying.

After seven years, Louis Vagneur became county commissioner. He says to me one day, "Ellamae, why don't you and Con buy the old Diemoz Ranch; it's up for sale." He didn't tell me what it was or anything else. And so when Con came in I said, "Let's go down and see the old Joe Diemoz place." He was a bachelor and had a little old one-room shack. We went and Joe said, "Yes," but that's all we could make out. We couldn't talk to him because he spoke Italian. He couldn't understand us, so we had to go back and get Louis to come down and be the interpreter. When Louis got through talking to him, he says, "I didn't know that ranch was that big, or I would have bought it for one of my kids." And I says, "Louis, if you undermine me, I'll kill you." He says, "Oh, I wouldn't do that." It was eighty-two acres. I still have seventy-five. We paid $500 in 1934.

After we bought the land, it was really nip and tuck. We worked like nobody's business trying to pay it off. I don't know how many years it took. The first thing we did was tell old Joe he could stay as long as he wanted in his cabin. But the kids worried him. You know how kids will do. So we borrowed the money and paid him off. Mr. Paige took the mortgage on it. He was a groceryman. Then he had the mortgage. We couldn't get any credit from the banks. They didn't have any money. We bought groceries at Paige's store.

The first winter we lived in a tent. We just sat a tent over our beds. The next thing we did was dig a basement. We bought Joe's horses and used them to scoop it out — just the two of us and the kids, but they weren't big enough to do any heavy work. We had to watch the kids by the river. We let them play in the ditch. We would bring them out until they got cold and then make them go back in the tent and stay until they got warm.

After that, we went to the hills and got the logs. I peeled every one of them. I peeled logs during the day and took care of the kids. I had a regular log knife. Con was working for the Vagneurs at the same time. We were trying to build a home. I'll tell ya, when I look back, I say, "How in the world did I do it?" It took all summer to dig the basement. I covered it with a tarp. We had a stove. The next summer we built it in sections. It has been a long time, but I have enjoyed every bit of it. While we were building, I wanted to put glass brick in. They were just starting to make that glass brick. Con says, "No, no, you are not going to." So I wondered what in the world I could do, because in those days we didn't have any money. I was canning fruit, and all at once it dawned on me, why can't I make glass brick out of these jars? It was my idea. So I went outside and climbed up on the ladder and poked one in between the logs. Con came around the house, and I says, "This jar, it will take the place of the glass brick." Con says, "No, you ain't going to put that in; I won't let you." So I said to my oldest son, "You bring those jars out and put them in the windows. If your dad won't chink them, I will."

My son came out with three or four jars. Instead of going up the stairway, he climbed the ladder with those jars, and here comes Jim and jars falling down! I ran out the door, and Con came around, and Jim was picking himself up and brushing himself off. Jim says, "Dad, you just as well better chink them in — not a one of them broke." That's how I got the jars in there. It worked just fine.

A long time ago, down by Shale Bluffs, there used to be a tunnel. That was the railroad. The Midland was running and the Rio Grande was running, too. I have to tell you why they call it the Cozy Point. There was a tunnel along that shale. The boys would get their girlfriends and buggies — we didn't have anything but wagons. If you had a car, you were rich. So, they would get together and a bunch of them would go in that tunnel and smooch. They would drive their buggies in. That is how it got the name Cozy Point. The train didn't run at night.

They had just pulled up the ties from the Midland Railroad when we bought this place. We had hay and cattle and about five or six cows that we milked. We had a garden and we had raspberries, strawberries, everything. We sold the garden stuff. Con was a jack-of-all-trades and master of half of them. I'll have to tell you what my dad said. He came to me after I was married, after this home had been built, and said, "Mae, I did you an unjust," and I looked at him so funny and I said, "Well, what did you do that was unjust?" He said, "I wouldn't teach you the carpenter trade and you are the only one that really used it."

I got run over by a horse once. I was out in the yard and here come a horse and ran right into me. It knocked me for a loop. They were driving the horse and it got loose. I was out in the yard. I didn't see him coming and didn't have time to get out of the way. I broke my cheekbone. I spent about three months in the hospital.

When the train came through here, my kids, no matter where they were, came to wave at the engineers. Those engineers would throw off candy.

My two boys were so inquisitive about everything. They always wanted a chemistry set. Well, we put it off as long as we could and finally we scraped together enough to get them one. You never knew what was going to come out of that chemistry set. I got four chemists out of it — my two sons and their friends. They all turned out to be chemists.

My favorite years in Aspen were in the Thirties and Forties, because everyone was in the same class — we were all poor. As for Aspen now, I would like to see it turn into a friendlier community. I'd like to see the politicians have more compassion. That's what I miss from the earlier days.

♦

Photo by Kathy Daily

Jennie Vedic Popish and Lillian Popish Dalton

Jennie:

I was born in Aspen March 29, 1905, in our home on Riverside down by the
river. My father's name was Anton Vedic and my mother's name was Antonia
Gregorich. They came from Yugoslavia. My mother was born in 1872, came to
Aspen in 1895, and died here in 1966 at ninety-four. My dad came to the United
States first and then got Mama to come over. Then they were married in the
1880s. First he came to Cleveland, Ohio, and I guess he rode the train to Aspen.

389

My father was an ore sampler and worked for the railroad. He fixed ties and nails and all that on the Rio Grande. They had him shoveling snow off the track. There were eight children in our family. Mother took care of the children. Then my dad got so sick that my mom had to take in boarders. When my father died, I was eleven. They think to this day that it might have been cancer of the stomach, because he had stomach problems. They didn't know about cancer at that time. Then my mother had all these kids to raise, and so she took in boarders, mostly miners. She had a place on Riverside Drive where they slept and she fed them. She raised all her own chickens and rabbits and had a cow for milk. She had her pork and goats — she was self-sufficient. She also raised gardens, and that is what she fed her miner boarders. She didn't have to buy too much. This is also how she managed to raise our family. She lived to be ninety-four.

My first chore around our place was milking cows. I was the sixth child. Frank, Tony, Mike, Grace, Joe, Mary, and Elizabeth were my brothers and sisters. The first school I went to was Lincoln School in about 1910. I went there through sixth grade, because we moved to Washington School and then I quit school when Dad died. When I was in seventh grade, I had to work. I walked to school from Riverside Drive. I wore overshoes. I never froze my feet because I walked too fast. We had an hour's walk. Mama always had lunch for us. We

Popish children: Louis, Lillian, Martin, Ed, Joe, and Bernie, 1932. Courtesy Jennie Popish.

walked home for lunch. They had coal stoves in Lincoln School. I still know my first-grade teacher and her name was Frolic. She was good.

I got married when I was seventeen. My husband, Primosh Popish, came from Yugoslavia. He first married a Zupancis, but she died. Then I took care of his mother and baby [Bernie] a little while. I got married when I was seventeen and Primosh was about thirty-five. I married in 1922. I had six children, five of my own. Bernie was a baby when his mom died. I raised him, too. I always call Bernie my own. I had all my babies at home with a midwife. We knew her for a long time. She helped with my first baby, and then I didn't have any help. I had them alone. I had a woman — she wasn't a midwife — she was just around.

I worked at farms when I was fourteen, before I even married. I worked at the Glendale for Jens Christiansen. I worked for Fred Light. Bubby is still living there. I helped the cook. I stayed at the big white house. I remember taking the horse and buggy and coming down to the store in Emma to get groceries. That big brick building is still there on the highway. I left home when I was thirteen to work on the ranches to help out my family. I got paid one dollar a day. I stayed up there and went home on weekends.

Jennie Vedic's house on Hyman Avenue, 1930s. Smuggler Mountain in the background. Courtesy Jennie Popish.

Primosh was a miner. He worked the Smuggler and Midnight. When he worked in the Midnight during the winter, he stayed up there a couple weeks at a time. We used to call up there and talk to him, I think when the snowslides were so bad. When the slides on that road were real bad, they stayed in a bunkhouse — not for long, just until the slides were down.

After we were married, I made my own bread. You could buy a bushel of peaches for a buck. I used to get a bunch of fruit from peddlers. We bought bushels of fruit and I used to can for our winter supply. Our house was up

Lillian Popish Dalton is a universal mother. She has written a cookbook on Slovenian recipes.

Photo by Kathy Daily.

where the ski run is near the 1A lift, up there by Dolinseks near Koch Lumber. That's where I lived when I got married. Then we moved to the 900 block of Hyman Street. That house cost seventy-five dollars in back taxes. Then we moved to the 800 block where the kids were born. That house cost fifty-one dollars. We sold our old house to some bachelors. We moved out of the house on 800 Hyman four years ago, in 1988. We sold that for a couple hundred thousand. And I got cash for it.

Lillian:

Dad had a lease over at the Smuggler Mine where he had men under him. Then the mine got so full of water that they couldn't pump it out. That's when dad had to get out of the Smuggler. Then he went to the Midnight.

Jennie:

There is a lot of silver left in the Smuggler, if you could get the water out. He told my son, Joe, where to look for the silver. They hired a diver one time to go down and try to operate the pumps. Actually, they were trying to get that water out. My husband said there was a lot of silver. The kids used to go in the mine with him. They loved to ride the cars and play around there. And then the kids would go way in where my husband would be working. He would say he was going to start loading the dynamite. That's when those kids would shoot out of that mine. They would blast at the end of the day, and the next day they would go and see what it did. The next day, they'd ride in there and would work all day, and then at the end of the day they would dynamite some more down, go home, and clean it up the next day.

Lillian:

Mom never went anywhere. The women in those days, their place was at home. Mom didn't even go to town shopping. She didn't do any of her own shopping. Dad did.

Jennie:

My dad, Anton Vedic, died during the flu epidemic in 1920. It was pretty bad in Aspen. Three of our neighbors died right there — three women. I guess I took care of my family pretty well. Some people died of the flu, and some people never got it. There were people that had the flu in our family, but not too bad because they lived through it.

    I think they used bourbon as medicine. If kids were catching the measles, my husband used to give them bourbon over rock candy to bring the spots out so they wouldn't suffer too much. You're sick until you break out, so in order for it to peak, we had this rock candy with bourbon in it. I still have recipes. For earaches, they would melt mutton tallow or beeswax down. They used to make kind of a candle from it, and then if you needed it, they would chunk it off, melt it, and rub it — not up and down, only down. You rubbed it on the outside of the ear and it would take the earache away. Also, they would take cheesecloth and dip it in the same stuff and dry it. Then they would roll it in dark brown paper. If we had a cut or something, we used to snip off a little piece and heat it over the stove. We'd stick it on the wound and wrap it up. That would take all the pus out of it. That's all we used for medicine.

    Did I tell you about the dance floor that was up by our house? We had an outdoor pavilion out there where I lived, up by Fritz and Fabi Benedict's, about 1915.

Lillian:

Mom used to tell about how these women would come in the horse and carriage wearing these big dresses to go to the dances. And then they had a great big swing across the river up there. They would swing these women all the way across the river and back with their big hoop skirts on. That has always stuck in my head. They had a dance hall up there, too. Well, they quit that dance down at Mama's. There were too many of them that started fighting, just because they had too much to drink. So they stopped having dances. I can just imagine in that big old field. . . .

Jennie:

It was kind of nice, you know. And then the next day, they would bottle stomp. That's where they put clogs on. No music. It was a Slovenian lodge, I think.

Lillian:

They used to have Slovenian lodges, like the SNPJ which is still back in Minnesota. I still belong to it — the Slovenian National Benefit Society. Mom used to be in the American Legion in the auxiliary. There still is an American Legion in Aspen, but they are not active. My brother takes care of membership dues. My two brothers go to the cemetery and raise flags every Memorial Day. Bernie and Louis and I belong to the American Legion Auxiliary, Basalt, but it is not active either. Seemed like after the Vietnam veterans took over, it went out. As long as the First World War veterans were there, they took care of it. And then after the Vietnam veterans came in and they kind of turned it over to them, well we have no active chapter. I still collect dues for the auxiliary. But we have no meetings. I have forty-six women in it, but they are all scattered from Alaska to West Virginia; they are charter members and have been in there for forty-some years. Aspen American Legion met in the Armory Hall. And then upstairs they had a big horseshoe table where they used to serve dinners. They had some fabulous dinners over there. The St. Mary's Parish used to serve St. Patrick's Day dinner over there and then they danced down below. They had a lot of dances — roller-skating and dances.

I used to wind the maypole when I was a little girl at the Armory Hall. They had what they called the winding of the maypole on the first of May. I wound the maypole once. That was quite a tradition up there. On May Day, us kids used to make May baskets. We made them out of tincans and old wallpaper. We would decorate the cans with wallpaper and put a handle on them. We would go out and pick May flowers. And we used to go, put a can by some of the old people's doors, knock, and run. We'd hide behind the big cottonwood trees that used to line the streets. That was a big deal for us. We had a symphony band with Mary McHugh. The band used to be all kitchen utensils. And we hit the milk bottle and it would cling. And the symbols were the pot covers. I was about eight. Bernie used to play the wood block. And they had the washboard. They also had pokers — you know, what you used to poke your fires with. We'd play at get-togethers, and if they had something going, maybe she would have us play for them. I played a milk bottle. There were quite a few bottles, and we filled them to different levels.

I was born November 24, 1927, on Thanksgiving Day. My fondest memory when I was little in Aspen was sleigh riding. We used to go up by the Crestahaus. Across from the Crestahaus, there used to be a little house, and they would all turn on their lights for us and we would start sleighing. We would turn down the highway and sleigh all the way to town in wooden sleds — the same ones they have now, like the Red Flyers. Dad bought me a six-man sled. We would pull our sled up and we would get on and we would go down. That hill was so slick!

There were very few cars in those days. I never learned to drive until my husband died a few years ago. I still don't drive very much. I just drive to town and back. Every place I went, my husband took me. We never had automobiles; we could walk everywhere. We would even walk at night. Walked way out of town just to walk.

Lillian Popish on the Cooper Street Bridge, about 1942. Harrington house in the background. Courtesy Jennie Popish.

On Halloween, I don't think the girls were as bad as the boys. The boys used to swipe gates. We used to just have the spools of thread where we would go to windows and make noise.

When we were young, we always had enough to eat. We had plenty of food. We had all kinds of things. We had meat, vegetables, chicken, and rabbit. We made sausage — Kalbasi. We never starved. When we were little, we all drank coffee, but we had cream and sugar in it. We started drinking coffee, I imagine, as soon as we got off the nursing bottle. As far as I know, that was our breakfast — coffee and bread. Mom made white bread and we would dip it. Mom always made good lunches. We always had macaroni and cheese, rice cooked in milk — that was our meal. Mom said the other day, "We'll have to have some of that milk rice." Instead of water, she used milk and raisins. You don't need so much sugar that way. Dad had to work in the mine, and five o'clock was dinner. We all had to be there, bar none. That's the trouble with kids nowadays — they never have one meal together. I think it's great when they do. And on Sunday we had to be there at twelve o'clock. During the week it was five.

Mom made bread three times a week. I was going to bake bread the other day and I told Mom, "I eat too much of it." So I don't bake too much anymore because we don't need it. We'll sit and eat a whole loaf of bread when it's fresh. She used to make these round loaves, and we used to chunk off the slices. We liked the crust.

Mom used to fry bread. Bernie and I worked at Sardy's Hardware Store when we were still at home, and Mom used to make bread. In the morning, she would take some of this bread for lunch and fry it in grease. It was so good. It was like a raised doughnut. Now my sister-in-law and I are writing a cookbook, and its all going to be in the book. We make a poticia, and that's our favorite. It's a raisin nut bread. Mom used to make cottage cheese.

My husband, Walter Dalton, was born at Palmer Lake, Colorado. His mother lived in Aspen for a long time. Way back, I think they were out of Illinois, and there is a book that is a history about the Dalton gang. One of Walter's friends had it, but we never read it. He wouldn't let us take it home and said if we wanted to read it, we would have to sit at his house. It told about the Dalton gang. They were bank robbers. They were all brothers. Walter had an uncle that had a bar in Cripple Creek, and his dad was Harry Dalton. He came to Aspen in the 1930s with his parents. I was going to school when I first met him.

Walter married and I married. I married Srechko Delost. They called him Lucky. That was a nickname. I think Srechko means Lucky. I got married in my twenties. I was only married a couple of years. I got a divorce because he was an alcoholic. I had one boy, Michael, from him. I knew Walter when I was still in school. We used to go to dances together. His sister was Edith Rader, and his brother-in-law used to own Mountain Electric, which was the electric company in Aspen at that time. And Edie used to have her restaurant and Walt used to come over when he was real young. I saw him after he was divorced, and I married him. He was eight years older than I.

Poticia

from Lillian Dalton

Dough:
2 cakes or pkgs. yeast
1/4 cup melted shortening
1-1/2 cups lukewarm water
1/3 cup sugar
2 eggs beaten
5 to 5-1/4 cups flour
1-3/4 tsp. salt

Filling:
1-1/2 # finely ground walnuts
2 eggs beaten
1 # sugar
1 stick melted margarine
Cinnamon – I use about 1/4 cup

Dough: Soften yeast in water. Add sugar, salt, shortening and egg. Add flour slowly, beating thoroughly after each additon until dough is stiff enough to knead. Knead until smooth and elastic. Place in a bowl, cover with warm damp cloth until double in bulk. Work down lightly and cover to allow double second time. Turn out on slightly floured cloth. Roll thin, approximately 1/4″ thick. Brush with melted butter then spread beaten egg over butter. Sprinkle with sugar, ground walnuts and cinnamon. You may also sprinkle raisins (optional). Roll up jelly roll fashion. Place in well-greased pan. Raise again before baking. Double in size. You can make one big loaf or cut roll into loaf sizes, pinching ends. Bake at 350 degrees for 45 minutes to one hour. Depending on size. Brush with beaten egg yolk just before taking out of the oven.

I worked at the Aspen Sanitation District for twenty-four years. When I first started, there were about 500 accounts. Now there's about 3,000. I retired just last year. I started in 1968. They didn't even have the metro district at that time. They just did the vicinity of Aspen. They didn't have all those condos and houses. Now, of course, the sanitation district is consolidated.

When I first got out of school, I went to business school. And then I didn't quite finish. Mom got real sick, and so I had to come home and help take care of the house and do cooking for my brothers. And then Sardy got me into the supply company and I started working there. So Alice Rachel and Doris Willoughby taught me. Later, I found this job at the sanitation district. (Mom worked at the Prospector Lodge for seventeen years as the maid.)

We had some prejudice in Aspen among the children when we were young — not the folks, but the kids did. They had the West End and the East End. The attitudes changed probably in the late 1930s and 1940s. And then when all the boys went to service, there was no one around. We didn't really notice the Depression. My dad was a provider, and my dad was a person that didn't waste. I can still remember our soup spoons. They were so sharp, because they were so old. But my dad figured that as long as they were spoons, we could still use them. Dad wasn't one to go out and spend money. He liked to conserve. Of course, he would throw a lot of money back in the mines. And my mom, she always had a nice good dress. She wore aprons. She never had a lot of clothes. Now she has. But, in fact, he provided through the Depression for a lot of my uncles and my grandmother. In fact, Uncle Louis, my mom's youngest brother, said, "If it wasn't for your dad, we never would have made it," so my dad, I think, provided for most of my family. Mom used to buy clothes for her mother. Instead of buying us clothes, she bought them for her mother.

I don't think we felt the Depression. Mom doesn't remember the Depression much. We were raising our own vegetables. We had a pig, because I scrubbed that pig barn outside after we got rid of that pig. I used it for a playhouse. The pig weighed about 500 pounds. We had rabbits and chickens. It was cold enough where you didn't need a deep-freeze. The meat would stay frozen all winter. Mom had a big table out in the shed, and if she wanted a piece of steak or something, she could take the hanging meat down and saw it off. It wasn't packaged meat — you sawed your own off. But my dad always made sure we had pork, beef, and venison. We always had plenty to eat. And then we had some farmers down the valley that brought us cream and butter. We had potatoes and we made sauerkraut. When ours ran out, we would go to my grandma's and get hers. We were pretty self-sufficient.

Looking toward Cooper Avenue; Ute Trail in the background, 1930s. Courtesy Jennie Popish.

Jennie:

I now have eighteen grandchildren and twenty-one great-grandchildren. I've seen Aspen change a couple of times. I noticed the mining going down. When the mining went down, my husband kept mining. He had his own lease up Smuggler. They called it the block, and he hired men to work it. He mined until he died. My oldest brother mined with him. But the rest of them worked out on the farm. My son, Joe, was a miner for a long time; he worked at Midnight until he went to the service. He worked with my husband. Primosh was foreman at Midnight. The Midnight continued to operate into the 1960s. The Smuggler operated until fairly late, but there was a lot of lease mining.

Lillian:

I think Aspen changed gradually. When you live in it, you don't notice as much as someone from the outside. If I had a wish for Aspen, I'd wish for the kids. I think my grandchildren have it so much different now. Everything you have to pay for. They don't know how to make their own fun because there is no place to make it. We had all these empty lots. We had streets, and we could go out in the middle of the street. I feel that kids are not getting what we had. I don't know what to do to remedy that, either. We had Sullivan's Pond, called Sully's. Then we had Hallam Lake, and the West Enders weren't allowed to skate on the East Enders' Pond because we used to groom it.

✦

Photo by Kathy Daily

*Bernie Popish has this
impish quality and great
sense of humor. He is a
very hard-working man.*

Bernie Popish

I was born April 4, 1921, up by the No. One lift on Aspen Mountain. My father's name was Primosh Popish, and he came to this country when he was twenty-two years old. He had two brothers and one sister; the sister was the oldest. The sister never came here. She lived in Illinois. My grandmother on my father's side died in 1921, the year I was born. My mother's name was Mary

Zupancis. She died in 1921, and I didn't know her. She died four months after I was born. They called it dropsy, but it was a heart condition, I'm sure. That's the old terminology. Primosh is my first name, and my middle name is Bernard. I never knew this until much later in my life when I got my passport. I was going on a trip to China with some people and I had a hard time getting a birth certificate because I didn't know that my first name was Primosh. They always called me Bernie. I found out about five years ago.

My mother, Mary Zupancis, was twenty-nine when she died. She was born and raised in Aspen and met my father here. She was born in 1892. She was Liz Callahan's sister. After my mother died, he married Joe's mother, my step-mother, Jennie Vedic. Jennie was born in 1905 and raised in Aspen on Riverside.

When we were kids, for jobs we'd shovel snow most of the time and cut wood for the Strong Lumber Company. They had a sawmill, and we used to cut cord wood for fifty cents a face cord. We cut that by hand with one of those big double saws and stacked it up. We were about twelve or thirteen and would do that because we wanted to go to the movie on Saturday. The movie cost ten cents for kids, so all the brothers could go, too. There were no pop concessions or nothing at the movie then. You couldn't eat in there — they wouldn't let you. No smoke or anything — no way.

When I was in school, you never had sports during school hours, you had that after school. We went to practice basketball at four in the afternoon at city hall (the Armory). That was our gymnasium at the time, and our dance hall and roller rink.

My step-grandmother, Antonia Vedic, up there on Riverside, used to have about four cows all the time, a hundred chickens, fifty rabbits. She had all that ground near the Aspen Club. She used to graze her cattle up there. The Cresta-haus, down below there, used to be Sullivan's Pond. That was our swimming hole. Once there was a dairy up there at Mountain Valley.

Mrs. Gallagher had a mean bull. We would get in there and he wouldn't let us out. When he would break loose, they said, "The bull's loose," and them guys would really scatter to stay inside. That bull came right downtown. Mrs. Gallagher would run you out when you were fishing there.

There was a lot of old-timers around here, and then they had the big fire in Aspen, I think in 1941. I worked for Sardy at that time, at the hardware store. Tom and I worked twenty years together. I worked as an apprentice mortician. When I came out of the service, I went to San Francisco to mortuary school in 1948. I was county coroner in Aspen for eighteen years. Tom Sardy was county commissioner, and he says I'm going to put you up for county coroner because he had the ambulance service at the time, too, and I worked for him.

Bernie Popish and Breezy Zordel in the Red Onion, 1947. Courtesy Jennie Popish.

I was coming home from church one day and Sardy drove up with his wife's Plymouth coupe. He stopped and asked me what my name was. That's when I first met him. I told him, and he said, "Would you like to go to work for me?" I was so happy to hear that, because I couldn't get a job when I got out of high school. I worked for the NYA for fifteen dollars a month, three days a month. Tom asked me if I could pick up a dead man without "turning my liver over" — that's the way he put it. Then he says, "Did you ever do it?" Well, I had never in all my life, and I said, "No," but I was willing. I did OK. I was seventeen or eighteen when I went with Tom. I apprenticed as a mortician — didn't have no problem.

I had to laugh at Tom one time when he still owned the hardware store. Beck & Bishop Grocery Store used to be on the Wheeler corner. Pigeons used to be on top and inside, and of course, the opera house was all dilapidated. Tom had one of these Benjamin pistols — BB guns. Mr. John Beck used to always feed the pigeons with wheat. One day he was out there feeding them wheat.

403

Tom went to the far door. He was pretty good with that damn BB gun and shot one of the pigeons. It fell right in front of Mr. Beck, and he looked straight up and didn't know what happened. He didn't see Tom. He stayed at the corner of the building. That pigeon plunked right down in front of him.

Years ago, we used to raise our own chickens and rabbits. We would get a pig in the spring of the year and raise it throughout the summer. We had a hog that was about 500 pounds once. Everybody up east of Aspen would pitch in and butcher it. We'd cure our own hams and bacon. There was a lot of barter going on during the Depression. We would go down where the Stein Ranch is now — that was the Skiff Ranch — and gather potatoes. We would get enough potatoes for the winter. We were good friends of theirs. Dad would buy a half of beef from them and then butcher it. Beef was running about five cents a pound then. I remember my dad bitching when he paid six cents a pound.

We had an aunt on my dad's side. She would have been one hundred years old if she would have lived another six months. There were a lot of tough people in Aspen. The cemetery is full of tough people! Liz Callahan is ninety-six. The eleventh of November, my grandfather was ninety-four, and my grandmother on my mother's side was ninety-two.

We used to go skiing at night up there on the main lift up to the second road. They had lights and that old toboggan. We skied down, and at 10 P.M. we would go to the hotel and whiskey for awhile. That was before the lifts, when that boat tow was there. There was no lifts at all then. The first lift went into operation in 1947. The boat was there until 1939.

If I could stop Aspen in a year, I'd pick the middle '40s. I think because everybody liked one another, even the people that came from foreign countries. We got acquainted with them — the Slovenians. We had dinner with them, they had dinner with us, and there was just good harmony here.

The memories I have, they can't take away from me, but to reminisce on all the memories, I don't know how I would sum it all up. But it's the congestion in Aspen I don't like now. There are all these buildings that are not conformed to the environment. I really think they got out of hand when they started building those big buildings all around town. I think they should have smaller buildings and then probably downvalley they could make bigger buildings.

They are taking a lot of your freedom away anymore. You can't do anything you want to do. And you pay taxes for what? You can't do what you want with your property anymore.

Photo by Kathy Daily

Joe Popish

I was born July 11, 1924, in Aspen in the 900 block of East Aspen. My dad, Primosh Popish, was from Yugoslavia. He first came to Cleveland, Ohio. He heard all about big money and the mines up in Aspen, so he came up and started mining in 1905. Before I was born, my mother, Jennie Vedic, worked for my dad taking care of his mother and baby Bernie. Dad was first married to Mary Zupancis. She died after Bernie was born.

I have a brother Louis who lives up the Frying Pan. He has Popish Electric. We had a brother Ed that was in between Bernie and me. There were five of us in the World War II navy. Actually, four of us were in World War II, and then the youngest brother was in Korea. He was on a destroyer. Bernie is the oldest, and I'm the third. Martin was a college professor in California. He's retired now. Then Lillian and Louis.

When we were kids, the Gillespy house, right close to the red brick school, was a haunted house to us. In fact, they tore it down to build a gymnasium. It was empty. It looked like a haunted house. The setting was like something on TV, like the old *Munsters,* you know.

I worked for Jens Christiansen in 1938 when I was in high school. School let us off for two weeks to pick potatoes. I made two dollars a day with room and board. They had a big barn that had a second deck and we stayed up there. We ate in the house. Gladyce cooked for us. Gladyce is a good cook. Then we worked for the Strong brothers for two dollars a day, cutting props for the coal mines.

Our class was just full of hell and the gals were meaner than the boys. One time in school, the girls rubbed Limburger cheese over these old steam radiators. When they kicked on, I thought we were going to have to close school. We had a professor that had a bald head — Old Coffee — and he would be leaning over his desk grading papers or something like that, and all of a sudden, one of the girls would go up and kiss him on his bald head and leave lipstick. So every time he looked down we would start laughing.

One time, Hubert Chisholm and I got drunk up at the Four Seasons Club in the afternoon, and we decided to come to Aspen to get us something to eat. We were with Buck Parsons, and we couldn't find any restaurants open so we decided to go to Glenwood. We got to going to Glenwood, and Buck bet me ten dollars that I would never see San Francisco again since I got out of the navy. I bet him ten dollars that if the train was sitting in the station in Glenwood, I would be on it. Hubert said if you are going, I'm going with you, and so — where did we end up that night? San Francisco. I sent Buck a telegram from San Francisco so I would win my ten dollars. The trip cost me $350. We ended up in Oakland and Hubert said, "Well, son, pick up your luggage." We had a quart of whiskey and each a toothbrush. We came back a week later. The funny part of it, when we came back, Hubert says, "Boy, my mom will be really mad," and I said, "I know mine will," because we never told anybody we were leaving. We didn't even have a suitcase. I didn't even have a jacket with me. So Hubert says, "Well, let's go to your house and see what happens." So we went up there and my mom wasn't home. I said, "Let's go down to your house, throw our hats

*Tramway from
Smuggler Mine
down to mill.
Red Mountain in the
background.
Courtesy Helen Kralich.*

in the door, and if they come out, then let's not go in." So we went into his house and the first thing she asked us was, "Are you guys hungry?"

You know, Aspen in them days, they never plowed any roads. They used to just deliver groceries with a sleigh and drag a chain behind it and pack it down. In the spring, the ruts would be two or three feet deep.

We went to school at the Washington School right behind the Mesa Store. We would all run for the Mesa Store and wait for Mike Garrish to come out so we could get a ride home with the groceries he delivered. He lived in the same neighborhood. If they didn't have a hitching post for the horse, they used to have a weight and a lead from the horse's halter with a weight on the end, just like an anchor.

Dad worked in the mines. He mined forty years in Aspen. He was one of the biggest leasing companies after the Smuggler Mine closed down. He leased part of the Smuggler and had about eight men working for him. When he went to the service, those men took care of his leases until he got back. The minerals ran out, so he shut it down. This was about 1918. That's when my dad was a big leaser. A lot of people, at least in certain sections of the mines, just dug out what they could. He made good money at it.

407

Later he invested money in another mine on Aspen Mountain and went broke — the Great Western. The Hyman Company out of New York owned the Smuggler Mine at the time. He leased a certain section of the mine, and if he got any silver and made some money, he paid a certain percentage of that to the company and he kept the rest. Whatever he made, he paid a percentage. I think it was 10 percent or something like that. I remember when there was about half a dozen men in the Smuggler No. One Tunnel leasing at the same time. The Smuggler Mine was laid out in what they call blocks — everything one hundred feet. You would take a certain block, like 14 block, 15 block, and lease it. The next guy would take maybe 10 block, 11 block, and lease it. My dad hit a big body of ore, and he mined it for about three years.

During the Depression, there was no work at all. Dad went back into the Smuggler Mine and started prospecting around. This one fella gave him so much a month to live on, and if he hit any ore or anything, he would pay this guy back, plus half of what he made.

I went in the mine with my dad when I was fourteen years old — the Smuggler Mine — used to work on weekends. There was no five days a week then, it was either six or seven. I remember when we used to tram that ore out by hand. There was a big bin in Smuggler. You dumped it into the bin by the railroad track. Most of it was shipped to Leadville. The Midnight Mine wasn't really scary, but one time we were drilling in there about 1,200 feet down in the shafts and we hit an underground lake. The water started flying around, and I took out of there and went up top. I wasn't sticking around. I was about twenty-four years old. I went to work in the Midnight Mine right after I came out of the navy in 1946. The Willoughby brothers owned the Midnight at that time.

We used to haul a lot of skiers up Castle Creek on our bus when we were going up to the mine in the morning. Then they would climb to the top where the Sundeck is now. Of course, the Sundeck wasn't there then. There must have been about fifteen or twenty of us working in that mine. During the war, they had pretty good silver ore up there, and there were about sixty men working. It's an interesting trade; I liked it. It would be just like one fella in Aspen said: "If God had intended for man to be underground, he would have put a tail on him." Them was good years. I worked in the Midnight Mine from 1946 to 1951.

My father died in 1947 when he was fifty-nine years old from kidney failure. He used to patronize the Marolt Saloon. It was sort of a battleground down there, right about where City Market is, on the corner — that's where the saloon was. We used to get those lard buckets with the ten-pound cans and would go down and buy the beer for our folks. They would give us so much money and would have parties at home. They would send a note, and the bartender would fill a bucket with beer for us to bring home.

When I went to work in the Midnight Mine, we were making $5.50 a day for eight hours underground. My father was making $2.50 a day when he worked for the Smuggler. See, money then was money. In fact, when I got laid off in 1951, I think my wages were $9.60 a day. The times were hard. Even Tom Sardy would close the hardware store and go work at the Midnight Mine. That was a good time to live here in the '40s. Everybody knew one another and helped each other.

I think today Aspen needs a good mine going. I would like to see 300 or 400 miners in Aspen. That was the basis of the whole thing. There must still be silver in those mines.

I never thought about moving from Aspen. There was too much fun to be had. And it didn't take that much to live either. I just love this valley. You used to be able to fish pretty near most every place in the valley in the old days. I miss that.

◆

Photo by Kathy Daily

Peggy Cooper Rowland

I was born April 8, 1915, in Aspen. My mother's father came here first in about 1880 from Indiana. He was Al S. Lamb. He had a drugstore on Hyman Avenue. Around the corner on Galena — the Wheeler Block — my father, Ed Cooper, had a bookstore called Cooper Book and Stationery. That was way back in the 1880s. Dad was Edward Cooper; my mom was Fleeta Lamb.

My grandfather, Al S. Lamb, was interested in grubstaking miners. He was a pharmacist. He was first in San Francisco, then came to Leadville and had a drugstore. Al S. Lamb came very early and then returned to Illinois to get his wife, Susan. They were married at the old Windsor Hotel in Denver. They spent their honeymoon at Manitou Springs, then came on the train to Granite and then on a stagecoach over to Aspen. He went a long ways. That was odd in those days. Came over Independence. He lived in the house on the corner of Second and Lake Avenue. It's still there by Triangle Park. I don't know who owns it now. That's where I spent my summers because I visited my grandfather Lamb.

Dad's family lived on Hallam between Second and Third street. His parents were retired. One of the Coopers was a bridge

*Al S. Lamb
(1885 – 1940°
Courtesy Peggy Rowland.*

builder and engineer who stayed in New York early on. Part of the family came to Kansas. That's where my dad was born. And then his family came here. You know the painted sign on the side of the Crystal Palace Building? That used to be the Commission Building, and my dad was on the board there. I have a picture of him by that sign because that sign was there way back. It wasn't like a

*Al S. Lamb and Bud
Cooper in front of
pharmacy, Hyman
Avenue, 1938.
Courtesy
Peggy Rowland.*

county commissioner. It was a commission for the food and supplies they brought in and then distributed. That's what they called them —the commissioners. They ordered the groceries and the cigars and all that stuff, and then they sold it back out. That was sort of like being a merchant, I guess — middle man. That's what it was.

I spent summers with my grandfather, Al S. Lamb, and my grandparents, the Fred Coopers. Dad couldn't make a living with the bookstore here. So we moved to Denver in 1919. I was four. I was born in Aspen, but I never went to school here. I was born in the old hospital up here. It had a big veranda around it. It was lovely. We left here, but we came back every summer because my Grandfather Lamb and the Coopers stayed here. I came back every summer to see the Coopers. They

died when I was twelve. From four years old on, we came back. I had a horse. I rode and I didn't care what happened. I rode every day from home anywhere. I always stopped at the drugstore to see my Grandfather Lamb. I could tie the horse to the post over in front of Beck & Bishops, which is now Bentleys. They had a big watering trough for horses. My horse loved that because it was high —

Al S. Lamb house, 1939,
2nd and Lake Avenue.
Courtesy Peggy Rowland.

he didn't have to lean over. I could have walked right in with the horse. There wasn't much going on.

The drugstore had a soda fountain originally with ice cream from Baur's in Denver. Baur's is gone now, too. My favorite ride was up into Hunter Creek Valley, simply because you can go so many places from up there. You can go up to the dam and then up to Thimble Rock. You can go over the hill and go up to Baldy. I went all around Red Mountain. I'd go down and come out at Trentaz's, back and around. You can go to Lenado — and on to the Frying Pan. What a ride!

I wasn't allowed to ride too far out of town when I was five but later on I rode a long ways. I kept a horse where my Grandfather Lamb lived. Triangle Park was in front of us. It was empty. It wasn't a park. There was a vacant lot on every single side of us. We kept the horse there. People ran cows in this town. They just let them loose. So we thought we had to beat it to the pasture by having a horse. We had a big barn where we put the horse at night.

*Ed M. Cooper and
"Strappie," in a 1906
Buick touring car.
Courtesy Peggy Rowland.*

I had all kinds of horses. My first was called Blue. What we did in those days, when people didn't pay their bills at the drugstore, was I got a horse in return for bills. We got butter that way, we got chickens that way, we got eggs that way. It was kind of a bartering system. That's how I always had a horse but they weren't mine.

I used to get Wootisie, the Stallard's horse, in the summer. I think it always bothered her. I thought that was the greatest horse. It was half Shetland and half horse. Orneriest thing on God's green earth. She'd dump me off. She'd do anything. She'd slip the bridle. Bite. I'd have big bruises on the back of my arm.

I got hurt riding lots of times. The worst accident I never told my husband Red about. I was married. I was up East Maroon. I had trailered the horse up there. At that time you couldn't ride from town. I trailered the horse up and unloaded. I saddled him, and apparently, I don't remember any of this, but after I got on, a lot of people came out of the brush and spooked my horse. I was way up East Maroon and I thought I'd had a stroke. I was in my sixties at the time. I just thought, "I think I've had a stroke. I guess I'd better turn around," and then

Ed Cooper's bookstore, with Peggy Rowland's Uncle Ted in the photo. Located on Galena Street, across from the Elk's. Courtesy Peggy Rowland.

I thought, "Well, I feel okay." So I rode on a little bit. Then I looked down and I was covered with dirt. I had been knocked off and knocked out. I had a big cowboy hat on, so I really didn't get hurt too bad, but I was filthy, so I knew I was thrown from my horse. I sure didn't tell Red, because I knew he wouldn't let me ride alone. I loved to ride. After that, I was more cautious riding. I don't ride alone anymore. I still ride, but I don't have a horse. I rode up at Wood's Lake the other day — one of Art Pfister's horses. Oh, I love to ride.

I married Red (Harold) Rowland at Maroon Lake in 1939. Red's parents were Patrick (1871–1918) and Mary Rowland (1876–1954). They came to Aspen in about 1900. His father was an engineer in the mines. He had an older brother, Leo "Pope", a sister, Kathleen, and a younger brother, Edward. Red was born here in 1908 and lived most of his life at 201 West Francis. His father died in 1918, and from then on he tried to bring in money to help his mother. He always had a horse. He made a V-plow and pulled it behind the horse to plow sidewalks in winter. They also had cows and sold milk in the summers. The three

Hunter Creek Bridge, South Trail, 1901. Courtesy Peggy Rowland.

boys worked on ranches for board and room — maybe a little money. As he grew older, he got a dollar a day. Later he worked in Midnight Mine, on the county road crew, and helped the Elishas at the Jerome Hotel. Red was a foreman for Maggofin Construction Company and worked on Grizzly Reservoir and the Twin Lakes Tunnel. He went on to work on Wolf Creek Pass, the Big Thompson Water Diversion Tunnel, and then back to Aspen, where he started with the Ski Corporation in the fall of 1946. Red worked for them until he retired in 1977. Harold always had one or more horses. He died in 1987.

The sad thing about Aspen now is people don't put down roots. They put a lot of money in, but not part of themselves. My favorite years were when I was riding my horse in Aspen and later raising a family. We had four children — Fleeta, Roine, and Jack and Jill are twins.

I first started to notice change in the 1970s. I wish there was more caring today — then we were a town. We used to gossip about each other, but when someone needed help, we were all there to help them. We really cared.   ✦

*Alice Rachael always has a
smile and a warm hello.
Anyone would want her as
a neighbor.*

Photo by Kathy Daily

Alice Rachael Sardy

My husband Tom Sardy and I came to Aspen in 1938 from Monte Vista, Colorado. We'd been married a year and a half. Gunnison was my hometown. Tom was born in Ouray. I taught in Ouray, and I met Tom there when he was home on vacation.

T.J. Sardy home, built in 1892 by Jack Atkinson. Courtesy Aspen Historical Society.

My background is early American. My parents' names were J. Francis and Osa Peck. I was born in Ohio. We moved to Colorado when I was two years old. Tom was of South Tyrolean descent. His parents came to this country when South Tyrol was part of Austria. After the First World War, South Tyrol became a part of Italy.

The Aspen Supply and Mortuary brought us here in March 1938. According to the latest 1930 census, the population was 707 in Aspen. It went down from about 14,000 in 1893. Tom was a mortician. Half of the downstairs of the Collin's Block building was mortuary, and half was hardware supply, with apartments upstairs. We lived in one of the apartments upstairs for seven years. We bought the mortuary from L.L. Wilks. He retired and moved to Denver. It was a combination mortuary and hardware.

We bought the big house on Main Street, across from Paepcke Park now, and moved in 1945. We bought it from Dr. Twining. But it was built by a man named Jack Atkinson. Now it's a hotel — the Sardy House.

❧❧❧❧❧❧❧❧❧❧❧❧❧❧❧❧❧❧❧❧

We moved the mortuary downstairs in the Sardy house, then sold it ten years before we sold the house. I remember when we bought the house, people thought, "Oh my goodness, they are paying too much for that house." We also remodeled the carriage house in the back. It became a guesthouse.

It was a well-built house. We had to do a lot of work. We installed a new furnace and added a new roof and painted the exterior wood trim. We had completely new interior decorations. Didn't change it much, just painting and wallpapering. We had only one fireplace in the big house and one in the carriage house. There was not a fireplace in every room, as in some old houses. The house was built in 1892. We are very pleased with what the new owners have done with it.

Jack Atkinson built the house. He had something to do with mining. The house was later sold to a man by the name of Manfred Smith, who was an attorney and later moved to San Francisco. They left when times were bad, and the house then was taken over by the county. Dr. Twining acquired it from the county. His wife, Maude Twining, was a fine old lady.

Galena Street, about 1944. Courtesy Martin Garfinkel.

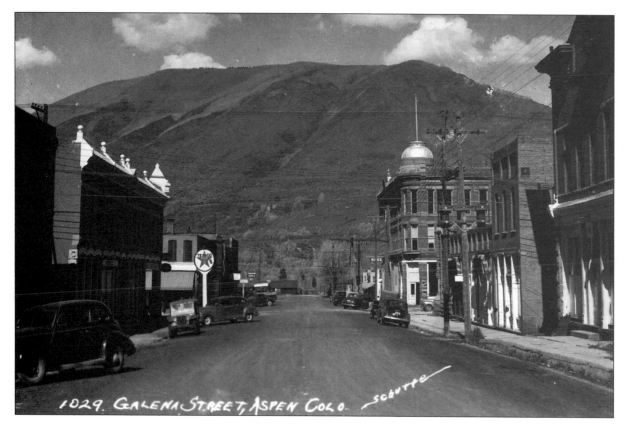

1029. GALENA STREET, ASPEN COLO.

Hyman Avenue, about 1954. Courtesy Martin Garfinkel.

We were married in 1936 and came here around the end of the Depression, March 19, 1938. I was twenty-nine. It was, of course, a quiet little town then. It was good for us to get started in our own business. After we moved here, a daughter, Sylvia, and son, T.J., were born. It was a good town in which to bring up the children. It was quite a move for me. The town didn't look too good then, especially in the middle of March. There were no paved streets, and there were many, many vacant houses and buildings. At first I was a little sad, but the summer was nice and the fall was beautiful. By that time I was pregnant with my daughter, and so life took on a different glow.

I am now reminded of something interesting about Aspen in the Thirties and how it changed. Some twenty years later, an article appeared in the "Empire Magazine" of the *Denver Post*. The information came from the Bureau of Vital Statistics in Denver. According to the article, in the Thirties, Pitkin County had the largest percentage of old-age pensioners in the state. Just twenty years later, the county had the largest percentage of young people.

When we came here, most of the East End was occupied by Austrians. They had come, not in the boom days of mining, but right around the turn of the century. There were many vacant houses after the demonetization of silver in 1893. Slowly, not immediately, but slowly the population decreased until it got down to around 700.

In the spring of 1938, we had been here just two or three weeks. The German Olympic team came here to ski, not because there was any special event, but some of them knew Andre Roch. Perhaps they had heard about Aspen and the new ski area here, so they came. I think they spent about a week. They stayed at the Jerome Hotel. They were served in the dining room of the hotel and before each meal, they would stand up and "Heil Hitler." The United States was not involved in the war at that time. It was long enough ahead of time so that most people were more or less amused, with the exception of a few old veterans of World War I who were very much disturbed about it.

In the Thirties, Forties, and Fifties, we entertained one another. We had dinner with different friends, and there was a lot of bridge and canasta playing. Sometimes the men were involved. We played a lot of bridge in those days. And, of course, there was skiing. Mike and Maggie Magnifico were good friends of ours. They had a shop, later Sabbatini Sports, next to the Collin's Block.

We were delighted when the Institute came. I think that the people in town as a whole were also. The Goethe Bicentennial was in the summer of 1949, and that was the first big event. It was thrilling for us. That's when Dr. Albert Schweitzer came and we met him. The town was still small, and the local people, many of them, met these wonderful, wonderful people who were just as gracious and pleased to meet us as we were to meet them.

I can tell you something else interesting that few people mention or think about anymore. Isaac Stern was scheduled to come in the fall. It was the first year of the Music Festival, 1949. They didn't realize that early in the fall, many people left town and there was a different feeling. It was too late to hold the concert in the amphitheater, so they had it in the opera house. I think maybe it was in October. A friend of mine who was a cellist had lived in San Francisco as a child and was quite an accomplished musician. We went to the concert, but there couldn't have been more than twenty or thirty people there. It was so beautiful. People in Aspen really hadn't been acquainted enough with that sort of thing. My friend had been in a recital with Isaac Stern in San Francisco when she was a child. She wouldn't go up and say anything to him. She was so embarrassed because so few people were present — so few that the whole place looked empty. Isaac Stern did not seem to be bothered by it. He was wonderful. It was beautiful. They scheduled those concerts too late. They didn't realize it was off season and, of course, off season then was really off! In those days we had a kind of a busy tourist season, but not that time of year.

The town had dances at Armory Hall and then there was the flower show. That was the big event of the year. We lived upstairs in one of the apartments over the store. Our back yard was between the Brand Building and the Aspen Supply. When we first came here, Tom planted a lawn there so we'd have a place for the children to play. It was fenced in with sweet peas all along one side.

Today, I don't like the traffic. But there's good and there's bad. It has grown very fast, almost too fast, and there are things that I miss. But I wouldn't want it like it was when I first came here. There have been a lot of wonderful things happen to Aspen, like the Institute and the Music Festival.

As far as Aspen is right now, you can't change it. It isn't going to be changed. I love Aspen. That's why I stay here. My main objection is the traffic.

✦

Photo by Kathy Daily

Elizabeth has a big friendly smile and a good sense of humor. I love to bump into her at the grocery store and have a chat.

Elizabeth Oblock Sinclair

I was born December 2, 1927, in Aspen at home — at 820 East Durant. My father's name was Matt Oblock and my mother's name was Ivana. My parents were from the Austria-Hungary Empire. My father came to the United States in 1900, and my mother came in 1903. They met over here. He came to Aspen first. I'm pretty sure he came here first because he was related to the Marolts and Mrs. Frances Marolt was here. She was married to Frank Marolt, Sr. Her

Mill Street looking toward Ajax Mountain, 1905. Courtesy Peggy Rowland.

maiden name was Rupert — her mother and my grandmother were sisters. Frances was the mother of the Marolt clan. My father and Mrs. Marolt were first cousins, so I don't know if that makes us first cousins, once removed, to Steve and Mike and the clan.

In Europe, Dad grew up on a farm. He was in the Austrian army. After he did his tour of duty, he came to the United States and started working in the mines. I think he worked in every mine around here — the Smuggler, Molly Gibson, Upper Durant. He worked in all of them except the Midnight, I think. At that time, the Marolts didn't have the ranch. They had a boardinghouse and saloon. The saloon was right across the street from City Market, where the Bell Mountain Lodge is now.

When my mother was nineteen, she got upset with her father. He was not just strict, but more like a miser. I think it runs in our family. Anyway, she got very upset with him because she had worked out in the fields along with the men since she was twelve years old. One day she worked at a brother's house,

424

and the second day they finished up. When she came home, her father said, "Why didn't you stay to have lunch?" because they were supposed to have lunch where they worked. And she was very upset because she felt she had worked all these years on their own farm, and here she didn't earn a lunch that day because she didn't work that morning at home. So she told her mother she was going to America. She already had an older sister who was in Brazil. At the time when her sister Frances left — she was quite a bit older than my mother — everybody was going to South America. Then they started to come to the United States. I take after her, I think. Her father paid for her passage. She met a girl on the train in Europe who was also coming to the United States. This girl had relatives and was going to Cleveland, so my mother said, "Fine, I'll go to Cleveland with you."

They landed in New York. She had no idea where she was going, and she couldn't speak a word of English. She had forty American dollars from her father. Her father was a tightwad, but he paid her passage. She went to Cleveland and worked in a sweatshop for thirty-five cents per day for a couple of years and didn't like it. She hated it. She was actually, you know, a farm girl. So then she heard about some girls who were going to Pueblo, Colorado, so she said, "I'll go with you." They traveled to Pueblo and worked. Then something happened where they wouldn't allow the young women to work where they had bars and saloons. There were dance hall fights or something, and she was working in one of those. So she came to Aspen to work for the Marolts. She heard they needed people in Trinidad and they needed women to work in Aspen. Everyone told her that in Trinidad, they had all coal mines and it was dirty and everything. So she said, well she wasn't going there. So she came to Aspen and got a job working at the Marolts. She took care of the children, helped cook, clean, and stuff like that. Father was boarding there. When they got married, my mother was twenty-three, I think, so my father was thirty-two. Mom never told us anything about their courtship. You never think about that, or you are afraid to ask. They married in 1906 in St. Mary's Church in Aspen.

I think they rented a house for awhile. The house was around the hill where the Tekoucichs used to live — somewhere in that area. After she married, mother stayed home. My mother had ten children. Matt was the oldest, and he was born in Leadville. They went to Leadville and lived there for seven years. I have no idea why they moved there — I think probably my father wanted to go. She had my oldest brother, Matt, then she had three children that died in Leadville. They all had pneumonia — a boy and two girls, all babies, and they were all buried over there in Leadville. After seven years, they came

STREET SCENE IN ASPEN, COLO.

*Galena Street
about 1952.
Courtesy Martin
Garfinkel.*

back here. Then my oldest sister, Mary, was born here, then Josephine. I'm the next to the youngest. My brother, Louis, is the baby. My mother also had two boys that died as infants in Aspen.

After they returned, they lived not too far from where we grew up, across the street. Originally, they bought one lot. And then they bought the lots to the east. I don't remember whether people didn't really own them or they went back and paid the taxes on them. Then there were these lots across the alley from us. I think I was a baby. My mother said that the man who owned them died and the neighbors started pasturing their cows there. They would tie up a cow in the back yard, and my mother said that the cow mooed all day long and she couldn't stand it. So she went down and found out whether the taxes were paid up on the lots. And so we bought them. Some of the neighbors got really upset, so they wrote to Europe to this man's relatives and told them that they could reclaim the property. His relatives wrote to the courthouse to find out what they had to pay. When they found out what they had to pay in American dollars, they weren't interested.

Tough People, Hard Times
◆◆◆◆◆◆◆◆◆◆◆◆◆◆◆◆◆◆

My parents paid seventy-five dollars for the house I grew up in on Durant Street. It was furnished, even with cooking pots and pans. It was owned by the Jaminson family. Mrs. Jaminson came to Aspen over Taylor Pass in a covered wagon and settled in Aspen. She had maybe three or four children. We owned the house until about two or three years ago when my brother died and I sold it.

I started skiing when I was seven or eight. My sister got a pair of skis and then I inherited hers. I skied at the bottom of Roch Run, and then Mike Garrish and Jimmy Snyder went out and cut a trail which is now part of Little Nell. It used to be pasture, and they made a trail down and I used to go and ski on their trail. I used to ski on the mine dumps and across the road from the house. I am still skiing. In 1946, my brother, Louis, and I raced in the first Rock Cup Ski Race. It was a miserable weekend with a lot of heavy, wet snow. Coming down the Cork Screw part of the course was something else! Back in the old days, they didn't manicure the race courses as they do now for the World Cup.

When I look back on the years I was a child, I realize that they were really special. We didn't have much money and all had to work hard, but we also enjoyed living outdoors. My brother and I spent hours fishing in the Roaring Fork. It was wonderful to be able to walk anywhere alongside the river. We had several great fishing holes. We used to fish a lot up Still Water, which is now part of The Preserve, or at Whirly Pool, which now belongs to Fritz and Fabi Benedict.

I also did a lot of hiking with my brothers Matthew and Louis. We had the lakes and mountains to ourselves, something that doesn't happen anymore. One time we were at Scott Lake up near Independence Pass. We had the place to ourselves except for a flock of sheep and the herder. The herder gave us letters to mail for him, which we did the next day.

I met my husband, Bob Sinclair, in 1948. The Hotel Jerome was just remodeled and I was going to college. I worked there as a waitress in the summer. And he came in to eat. I went to Western State — studied education. I never finished. My mother was very pro-education. My brother had been to college, and I had a scholarship and I liked to study.

Bob and I courted, not very long, about four or five months. I was twenty-one years old, and Bob and I married in 1948.

I was never much of a cowgirl. Our ranch was about 1,400 acres. We had close to 300 cows. We had dairy cows just for ourselves and chickens. We had four children.

Our ranch house was down in the middle of the golf course in Snowmass. We sold that land for the golf course. We had one full-time hired man. In the summer when we stacked bales, we used to get extra help and when we drove the cows to the railroad in Woody Creek. We used to all ship about the same time — Jens Christiansen, Meltons, Kearns — we'd all take them down to Woody Creek. We didn't do that very long, though, because we started trucking them. And we started to have the trucks come right to the ranch and load them. We stopped doing ranching in 1965. We miss it. I did not get on a horse a lot. I wasn't particularly crazy about horses, but I got on a few times.

A lot of the houses and buildings in Aspen were abandoned and falling down. I remember daydreaming that I wanted to make tons of money, come back to Aspen, and fix it all up. Aspen did get all fixed up by a lot of other people, and I was always happy to see the new houses and buildings. The only problem now is that I know very few people anymore. All the people that kept the place going during the Depression and World War II have either died or moved away. Rather sad, I think.

✦

Photo by Kathy Daily

Katie Popish Skiff

I was born September 13, 1914, on a little ranch which is now in the Buttermilk area. It was called the Columbine, and I don't know who owns it now. Polly and Steve Marolt owned it for years. Then my folks moved over to Wildcat, where I was raised in that log house which is Sandra Mosbacher's. It is an old one; in fact, it was my mother's homestead.

Mother's name was Jennie McKenzie. My maiden name was Popish, but no relation to the Popishes here. My father's name was Fred Popish. Mamma was born in Kewanee, Illinois. Her folks married in Scotland — one was a highlander and one was a lowlander. They married in Scotland and came directly to the United States and ended up in Kewanee, Illinois, after the big Chicago fire. Grandpa McKenzie was a stonemason, so he had a lot of work there.

Well, it was building up around Aspen, and Grandma had a sister who lived here. Grandpa had a cousin, the McLains, who lived on McLain Flats. But they ended up in Leadville, because Leadville was booming, and it was much older. That was about 1881. There were three different booms over in Leadville. Grandma had her a little boardinghouse for the miners there. My mother had two older brothers, and they were born in Illinois, too. Her sister, Katie McKenzie, was the youngest, born in Leadville. Grandpa was a stonemason and worked around all these towns that were building — Gunnison and Aspen — any town that was building then. It became so lucrative over here that they came to Aspen.

My aunt (my mother's sister) told a story once that in May of 1884, their family moved on a stage to Aspen. They came over Independence Pass through three- or four-foot snowdrifts. They bought a ranch about fifteen miles west of Aspen on the Snowmass Creek — paid $100 for 160 acres of land, and part of the payment was a horse. Their father, Walter, James, and Mr. Surprise were going to the ranch on a covered wagon and had to ford the Roaring Fork River. The water was very high and swift. One of the horses drowned and was washed away in the swift water. The other horse stayed on his feet. The wagon began to float in the deep water but caught up on some rocks in midstream. A neighbor, Walter Waltham, working in his field nearby, came over and brought a horse. He got the two boys to the bank and then hitched a horse to the wagon. The remaining horse pulled the wagon across. They finally got settled at the ranch. My grandmother walked to Aspen and carried her groceries home on her back most of the time. Roads were practically nonexistent, and travel was mostly by foot or horseback.

The first years at the ranch they cut wild hay with a scythe — raked by hand and stacked to feed the stock. Later they acquired more land. They got machinery to work it, and things were going pretty good for the family. Then in 1893, their father (my grandfather) passed on. They then had to control 2,220 acres, but most of it was dry land. They had to have irrigation brought to it before the government would issue deed. They made a ditch nine miles long to get water to the land. It was a hard, long task, but they received the deed and the ditch is now known as the Wildcat Ditch.

Tough People, Hard Times

✦✦✦✦✦✦✦✦✦✦✦✦✦✦✦✦✦✦✦

Times were hard and money was scarce and hard to come by. The Indians had been driven out of the country a few years before, and as they went, they burned the forests off — drove out a lot of the game. Wild raspberries came up where the timber had been, and the people came from all over to camp in tents and pick the berries. The McKenzie girls camped in an old cabin and spent the entire season picking raspberries. The McKenzie boys went to where the girls were camped twice each week. They carried the berries on long poles and ten-pound pails two or three miles to get them to the wagon to take them out to sell. They sold seventy-five dollars worth of berries that year — 1893 depression. The berries were sold for seventy-five cents per gallon.

In Aspen, most families had their own cemetery. When a person passed away, they were lowered into a grave. A dove was put in the grave, and when the graveside service was over, the dove was freed. It flew up and away. That symbolized the departing spirit of the deceased. When pioneer children outgrew their clothing, it was passed on from family to family until it was worn out.

Grandpa worked on the Wheeler Opera House, the Community Church, and I don't know what other buildings. When his health started failing, he got interested in farming. He was a farmer in Scotland; they were a farming family. They homesteaded out on Snowmass Creek. It's above the big slide. There is a tremendous slide in there. About forty years ago, I think, that came down. That used to be all a level field. Where the slide came down, their homestead cabin would have been in that area. Grandpa's health failed and he died.

Grandma had these two little girls (my mother included) about ten years younger than her sons. Grandma had the two boys, then two girls. The boys could work and do things like that. She stayed and proved up on the homestead. The boys would help her in the summer months, and then they would go and look for jobs in the winter to make a few dollars for food.

There were no public schools in those days, and Grandpa, when he was alive, always hired or boarded a man to teach reading, writing, and arithmetic. I don't know which year it was when the public schools started in the rural areas. My mother and my aunt were in the same grade. They entered at the same time. My mother and aunt were only about eighteen months apart.

When they were homesteading out there, the boys went out to look for jobs on different ranches, and the girls would drive a team of horses on a sled to school. They'd go home after school and load up the sled to feed the cattle the next morning, then ride to school. And that's the way they got their education. Grandpa died when the girls were very young, and they had to learn how to drive the horses and plows. They didn't have a riding plow — they had walking

Wheeler Opera House, about 1946. Courtesy Martin Garfinkel.

plows. My mother and aunt weren't allowed to dress in pants. They had to wear those big long skirts behind plows. One of the boys, Walter, married, then there was the other one, James. Grandma lived with him part of the time. He never married. Down here where the Maroon Creek Club is, that's where she died — my aunt's home. Grandma lived until I was about four years old. Mamma married when she was thirty-two. She was seventy-six when she passed away.

My dad, Fred Popish, was born in Pfeichurch, Germany. His mother was Theresa Mayerfelds. She was a German lady. Her husband was Popish — Austrian Hungarian — that's where the Popish name comes in. When they came to this country, he must have been about eighteen months old. He remembers being in his mother's arms, and there was some great big holes. So that must have been the portholes of the ship, as near as we can figure. In about 1893, they ended up in Leadville, and Grandpa Popish was trying to work in the mines. Later on they moved over to Aspen. Grandpa Popish, my dad's parents, came in on the Midland Railroad from Leadville — made the loop. Grandpa Popish was working around mines and doing odd jobs. It didn't take long after they got here that the price dropped out from under silver. They had to look wherever they could for work. My dad had three younger sisters. They lived where the forest service is now. They had a big house, and they would take in boarders and roomers. It was just a big house with extra rooms. The kids can remember sitting around the coal stove, and all the boarders would come in and visit them.

Dad had to go to work when he was ten or twelve years old because his dad wasn't supporting the family. His mother had to have something to eat and keep the girls going. So he was about twelve years old when he went to Cripple Creek and worked in a restaurant for a few dollars. He sent that money back home. As he got bigger, he worked cutting timber and on ranches. He also had a homestead. That's where I was born, on his homestead, and I grew up where Mamma homesteaded.

Homesteading was hard, but it was hard for everybody in those times. The first place that Grandpa McKenzie plotted out his homestead was jumped. He started out on Brush Creek, and by the time spring came, it had been jumped. He had to go to Snowmass. My parents were the same age, you might say. My dad was born in February, and my mamma was born in September of the same year. They were both rural people — every farmer knew everybody else.

There were five of us, and we came along in eight years. My parents moved over there on Wildcat. And that's where I was raised, until I moved. I was born on Columbine, raised on Wildcat.

We had to ride to school on our horses about two and one-half miles when we were six. There was four of us kids in school at the same time, and we had two horses. One rode in the front and one in the back. Whoever rode in the front had to tie up the horse and open the gates. We rode at least two and one-half miles and it was down a steep hill — on the Old Snowmass Creek. The schoolhouse is long gone now. I can remember getting bucked off a horse once. I was only about eleven. All eight grades were in one room. Once attendance got up to fourteen. But that was just as the farming help would come in and work.

My first chore on the ranch as a little girl was washing dishes. I was about four. Then, I took care of the chickens and the pigs. I learned to milk a cow by the time I was five or six, and I thought I got a whole lot done by then. As I got bigger, I did a lot more. We had some potatoes to sell but not a lot. We had pigs and a few sheep plus cattle to ship on the train to Denver, where they went to meat market. Also we milked enough cows for expenses and sent the cream to the creameries.

We came to town. The folks always made an effort that we got to see the special on Christmas Day at the Isis Theater. It was a long drive — about twelve

433

miles. We always came to town in the summer months for groceries and things like that, but our post office was in Snowmass.

My husband was John Skiff. He was born in Pueblo, and he came here when he was about a year old — about eighty-five years ago. He was Edith Chisholm's brother. His home was where the Stein Ranch is now. I met John at a dance. They used to bring the orchestra here. Some people used to come from Rifle, Glenwood, and over what is Bigelow on the Frying Pan. The girls would ride horseback, put their horses in a barn, and dance all night, then get on the horses and go home the next day. They had what they called dividing skirts.

John and I kind of knew each other — knew our families. Mamma says the first time she ever saw John and his brother, Tony, they were little boys. Grandpa Skiff was going to the ranch above the Columbine for some seed potatoes and had these two little boys. I was twenty when we married. He was seven years older. Got married in Glenwood Springs. Then we moved directly to town here. He was working for the county and highway department. They worked Highway 82 from Aspen to El Jebel. He worked with Jim Snyder's father. We lived in an apartment above the Brand Building. It used to be Brand's Garage. We had an apartment there for a month, and then we bought the house here at 920 W. Hallam and been here for fifty-eight years. Course, he's been dead twenty-five years. We paid $400 for this place.

My son was born when I was about twenty-one, and I didn't have a second child until ten and a half years later. The war came in between times. So ten and a half years later, my daughter was born. We just had the two.

Change comes on so gradually, you never notice it. Well, gosh, I've lived here for a long time. I liked Aspen before anybody came in. But I mean, I like it now as it is, because I grew up with it. The people that have been gone even six years, lots of times, they'll come in and they'll say, "How can you stand what they are doing to the old town?" But if I'm here, it was gradual. I miss not knowing anybody. In fact, I get real excited if I find somebody I know.

◆

Photo by Kathy Daily

Anita Roberts Smades

I was born November 16, 1934, at my home in Aspen on Maroon Creek — the ranch that Art Pfister has now. I can't say which of my grandparents came first. I rather suspect that my grandfather on my dad's side probably did — Robert Roberts. His family was originally from Wisconsin. He came to Aspen from Leadville in about 1887, or somewhere in the 1880s. He had a sawmill in

Lazy Chair Ranch on Maroon Creek, about 1910. Courtesy Anita Smades.

Leadville and brought it over Independence Pass in the winter — all of the equipment. They moved it in the winter because it was easier to move on the snow. It probably took a couple of days. They chained the sleds to slow them down on the other side going down. There were fatalities in some moves because of snowslides, but not in his one.

Robert Roberts was married at that time. His wife was Anna Sanborn. She was English. They married in Leadville. We sort of figured out that she was about fifteen years old when she married my grandfather. She homesteaded a ranch on Brush Creek while he ran the sawmill in Aspen. It was out on Brush Creek where Burnt Mountain is. His lumber was being used for the mines. He homesteaded straight up from Leo Kearns. It was right where the Y in the road is — where you go down the Highline Road. There's a big pine tree that stands where the yard used to be, but there's nothing else there now. They tore it all down. It was on the left side of the road going west — east of the Anderson Ranch. The Sinclairs live on part of that old ranch.

The Roberts had eight children. One girl died as a young child. My father was born to that family. His name was Arthur Bernie Roberts, and he grew up on that ranch. He worked some on the sawmill as a child but left home very young. He ran away when he was about ten years old. They thought he had tuberculosis and wasn't going to live, so they thought they would just let him do what he wanted. What my dad wanted to do was run away, so he did. He went down on the Frying Pan to another sawmill up the valley from Basalt. He hung around the sawmill camps and did chores. One year he said he had diphtheria, and a little old lady in Basalt took

John Sterner and daughter Barbara, 1920, with their team of horses, Edith and Lady. Courtesy Anita Smades.

him in and kept him until he was well. He was ten or twelve then. I don't know when he eventually worked his way back home. He lived to be eighty-four years old.

My grandfather's name on my mother's side was John Sterner and grandmother's name was Florence Corbitt from her first husband. She married twice. Her maiden name was Lockwood. She married my grandfather in Aspen. The ranch that my mother was born on on Maroon Creek was a dairy farm. My mother was their only child, but she had a half-sister and two half-brothers. Sterner Ski Run on Tiehack was named after her father. My mother's name was Barbara Lockwood Sterner. I'm not sure how my mother and father met. I

Art Roberts on Two Lazy Chair Ranch (Tiehack), about 1934. Courtesy Anita Smades.

imagine at a dance. My grandfather, John Sterner, was injured by a dairy bull, and if it hadn't been for his dog, I think the bull might have killed him. His health deteriorated after that. After my grandfather died, the ranch went to my mother and her mother. In 1922, my mother married my father (Arthur Roberts), and he took over running the ranch. She was twenty-one when she married my dad and he was thirty-seven. My mother taught school over on Capitol Creek. In the winter, they came into town from the Maroon Creek ranch by horse sled. My mother always rode a horse to school. She had nice horses and was a very good horsewoman.

Jennie Ferguson was my dad's sister. Her husband's name was Bob Ferguson. She was twenty when she got married. Their ranch was right across where the Buttermilk parking lot is off Highway 82. I think they homesteaded that place. Her original house still stands on the right-hand side of the road as you're coming out of Aspen. It's the little bitty red box house that sits way back across from Buttermilk. I would spend the night with Aunt Jennie a lot, because it would save me walking so far to Owl Creek School. Sometimes she would go out to milk the cows and she would say, "You come with me when I milk, but you can't go in the loft because there's a hobo sleeping up there." That was during the Depression. She didn't mind that, and she wasn't afraid. She always fed them.

*Sterner Ranch on
Maroon Creek
after sale to W. E. Morse,
about 1949.
Courtesy
Anita Smades.*

Aunt Jennie's the one that turned me in for walking the Maroon Creek Bridge rail. Her son had a dairy, Hoaglund's, in Aspen up where the old ski jump was on Little Nell. She would go in early to help in the dairy. She saw my brothers' and my footprints in the snow on the Maroon Creek Bridge railing, because we were walking the railing waiting for the teacher to come from Aspen and take us to Owl Creek. My granddad wouldn't even let me walk on the edge of the bridge when we took the sheep across, because he was afraid they'd push me through the sides. And we were walking on top of the railing. Jennie Ferguson had her two kids on the ranch. She was ninety-two when she died and her son is still alive. She raised those kids by herself and never remarried. She lived there until forty-something, and then she moved into Aspen. She cooked at the Aspen Hospital for years. She lived down catty-corner from the old high school.

My first chores on the ranch were to feed the chickens and gather the eggs. I still love to gather eggs. I was a tomboy cowgirl mostly. I grew up on horses.

439

Ray, Keith, and Anita Roberts on old paint, 1940, Two Lazy Chair Ranch (now Racer's Edge) in background. Courtesy Anita Smades.

The dairy farm went to sheep and cattle, mainly sheep. We had some cattle, but it was mainly sheep because we had a forest permit to run them up Independence Pass. I remember the time when I was quite small. I gathered the eggs and dropped the whole bucketful. My mother spanked me and my dad gave me a nickel. This reveals a lot about my dad. He was a character and loved kids.

I did a lot of sheepherding. I was kind of a shepherd. That's what I told a doctor one time. He said, "My, you have well-developed leg muscles." And I said, "You would too if you had been a sheep dog all of your life." My parents trusted me to take the sheep by myself when I was eight years old, and I drove the sheep down Bleeker Street behind the Jerome. We drove them up on Smuggler Mountain — up Smuggler Road and up the face of the mountain. They stayed on the south side and went up to Lost Man Dam. We always took a camp — a tent and such. There was always a paid herder for the summer. His job was to stay with the sheep all summer. We kids did our sheep-herding out on the ranch. Once a week, my dad would have to take horses up Independence and pack supplies in to the sheepherder. I never went up there, but my older brother did. I would go with the sheep until they got to Warren Lake and then come back. We always fished in Warren Lake.

I was twenty-two when I got married in 1956. I married Roger Smades. He was on the Denver University ski team when I first knew him. When he came back, he was in the Tenth Mountain Division. That's when our relationship sort of developed. He was from Watertown, New York. When we were dating, we set in the Red Onion a lot, in Beer Gulch. We skied; I skied a lot, too. He liked Aspen. They had a ski team in the high school, but I was never on it. We all skied on Wednesday afternoons for nothing. John Litchfield had the Red Onion then, and then John Siler took it on. Then Werner Kuster. I can remember as a little kid being in the Red Onion with my dad when it was Tim Kelleher's. I remember sitting at the end of the bar eating candy bars while my dad sat at the other end and drank beer. Actually, the front end of the Red Onion never changed that much. It was such a landmark.

How come those families stayed in the valley when everybody left? Because they were making a living on the ranches. They liked it. Like everybody likes Aspen. It's beautiful. The miners couldn't hack it, but the people that had land and were ranchers, their lives went on the same. Nothing really changed. Everybody was in the same boat. Nobody had money. Oh, there were a few that had a little bit more, but basically the ranchers were struggling and everybody was kind of gasping along.

I left Aspen in 1956. There were four kids in my family. Everybody left. My parents sold that ranch to Wendy Morse in about 1947 and then moved down on Brush Creek Road. They were the second ranch up on your left, and the little white house is still there. It was originally the Christopher place. They built that house. I don't know if they homesteaded or what. My dad cussed the rocks on Maroon Creek for so many years. It was a rocky place and bad for hay. When Wendy Morse came along and offered him the place for $30,000 he took it. I lived on Brush Creek until I was out of high school. I lived there probably four years, then my folks sold that ranch and moved to Capitol Creek. They were up on the mesa on the Jurick Ranch. Then they sold that to Mrs. Frank. After that they retired down to Delta. My dad died in Delta and my mother died in Denver. My dad was eighty-four and my mother was seventy-five. My dad and mother had a bad car accident and he didn't survive it.

What were my fondest memories of growing up in Aspen? I guess I just liked the general atmosphere. The ranch life and the people were very friendly.

You knew them all and they knew you. My least fond memory was that you couldn't get by with anything because everybody knew you.

If I could stop Aspen in any year, I would stop it in the Fifties. It was comfortable. The people were still very friendly. The new people that came in were very agreeable to get along with the people that were still here. There was no social division like you have now.

I wish for Aspen today that they hadn't built a house on every overhanging cliff in the valley. What did we have in the Fifties that Aspen doesn't have today? Everything. We still had a small town. We had a community. We had a good social atmosphere. It was a normal atmosphere. I don't think that's what you could call Aspen anymore.

I did have wishes of moving back after I married and moved to Denver. Aspen will always be home, and home's always home. However, when I get really realistic, there is no way that I would probably want to if I could do it, because it has changed so much. When I go up to Aspen, I don't see it as it is. I see it as it was. If I were to go up there as somebody brand new would see it, I don't know what I would think. It would be just a resort town.

Do I think Aspen could do anything now to save itself? No. They've made an image for themselves, and I don't see how they could ever undo that. I think if you stayed in Aspen and never left — kind of adjusted with those changes — you probably would have been alright. But to come back to it. . . . They've tried every which way in the world to spoil the beauty but so far haven't succeeded. They're well on their way. That was such a beautiful valley. It's still beautiful, but not in the pastoral sense of the word. It's changed so much. I hear how people are broken down into classes. When it was first developing, there was never any of this. Everybody was in the same class.

◆

Photo by Kathy Daily

Junior Smith is an outdoorsman and is close to his brother, Puppy. They are good friends.

"Junior" Nelson Smith

I was born October 19, 1922, in Akron, Colorado. My parents' names are Nelson and Pearl Louise. They were married in Missouri and moved to Aspen in 1923 for the mining. My dad worked in the Smuggler and the Durant. He didn't make much money leasing. Enough to buy a loaf of bread maybe.

We had twelve kids in our family so we usually had two houses. The main house and then a bunk house where part of the boys stayed. I don't think there was over two of us in any bed. We had lots of beds. I have two brothers and a sister older than I am. Puppy is three years younger than I am and his twin is Hazel. We had a few nicknames in our clan. There was Puppy and Schnook. I was always called Junior.

My first job as a little boy was leading a stacker horse in the hay fields. The first house we lived in was on Main Street about where the old library was. Then we moved out where Starwood is now for a year or two in about 1929 or 1930. When I was young we went hunting for rabbit, weasel, and muskrat. Whatever we could find. We sold the pelts to Sears Roebuck. We mailed them to Denver and I think we got 20 or 30 cents apiece. That was a lot of money. I don't remember anybody teaching me to shoot a gun, we just went out target practicing. We sold pelts so we could buy ammunition so we could shoot more pelts! We never made enough to put any money in our pockets.

My mom died when she was seventy-five. My dad died before her. He was 87. On our ranch all of the boys learned how to cook. Mom raised us all to do everything.

We moved out to Capitol Creek in 1931, on Stillwater in 1936, then back to Aspen in 1937. The Barraillers lived right next to us. Martin Healy had the place when we moved up there. He had the butcher shop in there in town for several years. Right across the street from Beck and Bishops. From Stillwater we went up to Red Mountain. We lived on Pitkin Green on that first little ranch with the red brick house on the right. That belonged to Jack McBay. We had a small dairy there. We milked a lot of cows and sold milk in town. We delivered it with a team and wagon — once a day. We had a dozen cows to milk. We would get up before we went to school to milk. And then in the evening around 5:30 P.M. we would milk again. Then we moved to the East End in about 1938. We didn't have cows there. I was working for the Herron brothers in the Smuggler mine for a while and then I went to work for Had Deane up on the T-Lazy 7 ranch for five years.

Had and Lou Deane had a dude ranch up Maroon Creek. Louie Sparovic and I worked up there. Later on Had started taking people into Snowmass Lake for horseback rides and that kind of stuff. That was fun. The tourists were really neat. More low-key than they are today. I left home when I was about sixteen. I was working out on ranches. They had a little bunkhouse up at the T-Lazy 7 down near the barn.

In 1943 I went in the service. World War II. I was in the army. I was twenty-two. I was stationed in the Philippine Islands. I came back in 1946 and then I worked for Anaconda Copper in about 1950. They were in here mining the Smuggler and the Durant. After that I worked on the Stein Ranch for three years as a foreman. We had about forty head of cattle and a few horses out there.

I really liked mining. Smuggler Mine over there is real warm. In the winter time too. The Durant was cold. There was a cold draft going through there all the time. I think it was because it was open at both ends. The kids used to go into both mines, the Smuggler and the Durant and play in there after they shut down.

I married Shirley Beck. We knew each other since we were kids. We went to school together. After I come back from the service we started dating and we got married in 1947. Our children are Donald, Tony, and Bonnie.

My favorite years in Aspen were back in 1939 and the 1940s. There were hardly any people around. There was a lot of fishing and you could do what you wanted. We'd go to square dances and country dances. They used to have them purt-near every Saturday night in the summer time and sometimes in the winter time in the old school houses around the country.

I don't think I'd ever want to move back to Aspen. I don't think so. Not the way it is now. I don't go up there so I don't really know what's going on any more. I think the four lane highway should come in. I left Aspen in 1969 and I haven't been back much since. I worked for several years up in Aspen right after I moved down here. I did plumbing and heating for Grant and Company for quite a while and then for Esco. I worked with Fred Willoughby for four or five years and I had some pretty funny times with him.

✦

Photo by Kathy Daily

Puppy — what a prankster. It doesn't seem like too much bothers Puppy. He is a good ol' boy.

"Puppy" Harold Smith

 I was born July 23, 1925, in Aspen. My dad's name was Nelson Smith, Jr. Mom's full maiden name was Pearl Louise Barker. They came to Aspen in about 1923, from Missouri. That's where they were born, raised, and lived. They also lived in Oklahoma and eastern Colorado for awhile. My parents came here for the mining. Dad worked over in the Smuggler at first. He worked in all of the mines.

There were twelve kids in our family. Our first job was to go out and pull weeds out of potato patches. They let school out so children could go pick potatoes and stuff. I think we got about three cents a sack. I remember my dad making beer. When we were out on the ranch, he used to make beer. We drank it cold — well, not too cold, because we didn't have any refrigerators. We kept it in running water.

For breakfast when we were kids we always had bacon, eggs, sausage, ham. It was one of the main meals. Then maybe just a sandwich for lunch. Dinner time was big, too — a lot of venison. Out on our ranch on Capitol Creek, we raised hay, grain, and potatoes. We had a good milk cow. We were just below the Wiebens. When I was little, there was not a lot of prejudice in town, not really. That was mainly between the kids. I was in the West End for awhile. When I moved up in the East End, I changed sides. Who was usually the toughest end of town? Well, there was more of us in the West End. When the ranch kids came into town, they didn't get to town that often, so they weren't really on any side. At night a bunch of us would get together and go to the other end. Basically, we all got along in the long run.

I believe there was nine kids in the Capitol Creek School, and most of them were us. There were twelve kids in our family. Wiebens went to school the same time as us, and the Scotts. There was one class, one room, one teacher — grades one through eight. Later we moved in town and went to the Washington School.

For mischief on Halloween, we used to turn over outhouses and stretch clotheslines across the sidewalks. The 4th of July we used to do stuff, too.

There used to be a train going downvalley. I rode it a lot of times. It seemed like forever to get to Glenwood Springs. We just sat there and looked around. We sat in an old car with wooden seats and a pot-belly stove in the center of it. There was a conductor. I didn't know him personally; I used to use the train to come into town. The conductors would walk from the depot up to the Hotel Jerome and have lunch there. They would have lunch, and the same engineers would go back and take it back. I don't know, it seemed to me like the Rio Grande went up there about noon or one. The Midland went out first. It made one trip a day. Of course, all the farmers would take their cream cans. There were a bunch of stops along the way. The train would stop and pick up the cans and then stop to drop them off, and it took a long time. They just left them with their names on them. They had a creamer in Glenwood.

Before I went into the service, there was no work there at all. When Paepcke came and first bought the Hotel Jerome, things started happening. I worked for the Ski Corporation the winters of 1949 and 1950. I hauled water up to the Sun Deck. They built a big water cistern up there, and my brother Joe and I hauled water for the Midnight Mine. We had a bulldozer with a sled and a tank and hauled water up to the water cistern. We made two trips a day, seven days a week. And then in the fall before we got any snow, me and somebody else, I can't remember his name, hauled water from the Tourtelotte Park up to the Sun Deck. There was a spring there. It used to come across under the road and we put a pipe in. That could be maybe where the Ski Company gets a lot of their water now, I don't know. Well, that cistern they had, I forget how big it was — 10,000 gallons. They didn't use any more water than they had to. In the winter, we hauled water up there in that bulldozer and sled. It took a whole day to take two trips. We got paid $1.25 an hour.

Phyllis and I married in 1948. We had two children. Jim and Harold. How did I get the name Puppy? Well when we moved back into Aspen off the ranch and were over on Pitkin Green we went down to what they call the Ice Pond to learn how to swim. A bunch of kids from town were there swimming and a bigger kid picked me up. He carried me out in the water and let me go. They said I came swimming in like a puppy dog, and that's where it started. My son Harold is nicknamed Spot and we used to call his wife Speck and their son Speckle. I was superintendent of the street department for thirty-eight years. The city designated a street to me on my twenty-fifth anniversary. It never had a name before that.

How many mayors did I work under? Oh, there were a lot of them. And Mike Garrish was on the city council when I started working there. There was Dean Robinson, Mike Garrish, Shorty Pabst, Eve Homeyer, and Stacy Standley.

*Elsie still has a lot of
spunk and a delightful
sense of humor.
She is very calm and
seems to take life
on life's terms.*

Elsie Garrish Snyder

I was born in Aspen on January 7, 1905, and raised here. I'm going into my eighty-eighth year. My dad's name was Nicholas Garrish and my mom's name was Agnus Baltazar. Dad was Croatian and Mother was Slovenian. They got married in Aspen. I couldn't tell you what brought my father here — mining, I guess. He done leasing more than anything else. He worked in the Smuggler.

He was never on the Durant. He'd take a lease from the mining company and have a certain area to work in. A couple times he struck it pretty good, but then a lot of times he didn't. My dad came in the late 1890s, and Mother came in 1900. America was more to their liking. Living in Austria wasn't that good at that time. They were from the mountains of Austria. It was Austria at one time, but after World War I they chopped it all up.

I was born right about in the middle of the block where City Market is. My dad and mother owned the whole half block. My dad bought two houses. He had a log house. We moved in that later. Next to us there was another little white house, and then there was a big hotel called the Rex Hotel. On our block, there was a big roominghouse, and on the corner there was a blacksmith shop. I think the blacksmith was Jim Harrington. On the other side there was a big yellow house, but it was set back farther and we tried to get Dad to buy that. We wanted to move in it. It was bigger. But he had different ideas. They finally tore the house down, and my parents acquired the lots clear to the corner.

There were a lot of haunted houses when I was growing up. The older kids wouldn't let us go in the street and play with them when they played Run Sheep Run because they thought we were too little. Mike Marolt, the oldest of the family, put on a sheet and just scared the living daylights out of us younger kids one night so we wouldn't bother them anymore. Our dad wouldn't let us play outside after nine o'clock. He'd come out of the house and whistle just once, and kids scattered. Right behind where I used to live, they called it the Holland Store. They always said that was haunted. It was on the corner of Cooper and Original, where that big house is. It was a grocery store at one time, I think. It was just sitting there empty. They had a few haunted houses out on the West End, but we didn't go out there very much. I'll tell you what I also heard a lot of times. When the old-timers would sit and chat, they said that there was a lot of silver ore buried up on Aspen Mountain. An old miner buried it. I've heard that there have been other people going up to hunt for it.

The Marolts paid my mother's way to the United States, and my mother worked in Marolt's Saloon for the grandfather of Max Marolt. It was right across the corner from our place. The bottom was saloon, the top a rooming house. The living quarters were in the back. They had a big kitchen and a big wine room, where the women would go with their men. That's where they were served if they came in with their women, because women were not to be in a bar. It had chairs and tables and looked like a restaurant. They served their food in there, too.

Tough People, Hard Times
◆◆◆◆◆◆◆◆◆◆◆◆◆◆◆◆◆

On the corner next door was Barne's Bakery. Next door to that was an American Express bar, that they kept their horse and buggy in, where Bell Mountain Lodge is now. I remember that my dad could get a five-pound bucket of beer at the Marolt Saloon. When he'd come home from work, I'd have to go across and get the ten-cent bucket of beer, and he'd sit and drink it. I carried quite a few of them in my day.

Mom worked in the kitchen. They had a big family. She had to help care for them, too. Frank Jr. was the oldest and there was two other girls. There was Pauline and there was Mary, and she was a schoolteacher. The reason I remember her is because she used to get so scared at night that she'd come over and sit with my mother so she wouldn't be so scared. They both died during the flu epidemic in 1918. Four Marolts died. Louis died, and then Rudolph Marolt. I got the flu and was pretty sick, too. Must have been sick at least two weeks. Other people in our family got sick but not as heavy as Dad and I did. I don't know if Mother got it. She was pretty tough. She probably did but couldn't afford to get sick with the rest of us ill. There was a lot of people lost in that epidemic. There weren't any antibiotics and they didn't have the right medicine.

My parents got married right about 1901, because my oldest sister was born in 1902. There was ten kids in our family. I had two brothers living, but three of them died in infancy. Mother had all her babies at home. So did I. I had all my children at home. I have four — two girls and two boys. Our house was on the corner of Original and Hyman Street.

After the children, my mother did garden work and raised her family. My sister came first, and then there was a boy who died. I was the third. After I got a little bigger, I helped raise the children. I had to work in the garden, you bet your boots. Well, I'll tell you, when my dad bought those empty lots, he would dig a big hole. We'd bury the rocks in it so all the boulders were under the ground, then we'd put the top soil on top again. That's the way we grew vegetables. My mother used to raise hogs. She'd raise three — they'd be 300-pounders. We'd have sausage, ham, and smoked meat. We smoked our own meat at home, and we made our own smoked sausages. We also used to make blood pudding.

When I was small, I remember the blacksmith. He pounded the anvil and you could hear it all over town. I used to walk over to my aunt's across the river where my brother Mike lives now, and I could hear it as I used to come from her house to mine. He's over on Gibson Avenue. Some of the boys hung around the blacksmith, but the girls didn't. Our parents were strict. We didn't get to go.

On Halloween when we were small, we didn't go trick-or-treating like they do now. One time there was a group of boys that brought a chicken crate

The Glory Hole, which fell in 1919. Courtesy Aspen Historical Society.

from Ed Grastos's store. They were going to drop it on our porch. My mother and father opened the door, and boy, did those kids scatter with that chicken crate. The boys used to go around and they'd turn over the outhouses and cut the clotheslines — anything they could do to get into mischief.

I remember it was about 1919 that the Glory Hole fell in. We were all standing up there. There was one lady, Carrie Dramer, that lived close by. She said, "Oh, it's the end of the world!" There was a big cloud of smoke. See, it was a stope in the mine where they took out ore and stuff. It made a big hole underground. When that caved in, the top had to go in, too. There were other tunnels under there, too. They used to tell us that there's a tunnel all the way from Smuggler Mountain to the Durant. I don't know if it's true, but there are people that said they heard the miners working in certain places across town. The whole thing just dropped. It even took railroad cars down, and everything went with it. For a long time, that was just one great big hole over there until they finally filled it up. For a long time it was the town dump. I was just a girl when it happened. There was quite a group of us standing there. Our house was real close by.

We walked to the Washington School. The Lincoln School was where the yellow brick school is in the West End. The Washington School was on the same street but up maybe four or five blocks. It would be right behind where the Mesa Store was. We had several little grocery stores in the East End. One was Ed Groster's. One was Wrigler's and then afterwards I always traded with Beck and Bishop. I stayed with Beck and Bishop until they went out of business.

In our teenage years, we didn't mix around much. When we went to school, the West Enders were kind of down on the East Enders. I don't know why. I guess they thought we were foreigners and weren't up to them. There were the Irish, the Slovenians, and some Italians up in the east of town. The other end was more, what would you say, English or what? My mother lots of times could speak English pretty good. She sold cabbage and things like that and she got so she could talk pretty well.

I started school when I was six. I lived with my aunt and uncle for awhile, to kind of get away from home. That's why I can't figure out this EPA. I lived with them across the river and they were almost at the foot of the Molly Gibson Mine. Here I am, eighty-eight years old, and I'm still living. At first, Aspen had a pretty good population because there was a lot of miners. I can still remember when they used to come off shift from the Smuggler and the Durant. They'd go opposite ways, each to their own home. But you'd see their lights in the night and early in the morning because it was still dark in the wintertime. It was beautiful.

I worked at the Hotel Jerome at one time waiting tables. We worked for Laurence Elisha's father, Mansor. I think I was high-school age. But I can't remember the year, because one year I went to work up at the Little Annie Mine. At the hotel, we were paid a dollar a day. We had different hours. Some would wait in the morning and some in the evening. Morning shift would be seven to noon. Sometimes we got a tip, but the biggest part of the customers were working people. They didn't have much more than we did when we were working. Mrs. Elisha, Mansor's wife, was the cook. She was a Healy by birth. The restaurant was on the first floor, straight back — where the big dining room is now. They had a big pantry and dishwasher on the one side, toward the east end.

I worked at the Little Annie Mine when I was about fourteen years old. I went up the mine in the winter. There was a certain area up there where the snowslides would come down. The man that drove the sled would really whip the team up to going fast, because sometimes the least little jar would start a slide down. I worked up there, helping in the cookhouse. I washed dishes and anything else. I remember the cook had a fight with somebody and she left. There was nobody to cook and there was a bunch of hungry men. I just helped wait tables and stuff. There was Mr. and Mrs. Valesca up there working. They had a couple of children, too. She tried to put a meal together and didn't know how to make bread. Well, my mother at one time, when she was working in the yard, happened to hurt her hand. She always figured she had cut her finger with poison grass or something. It could have been something else, but she couldn't use it for a long time. I was ten years old at that time and pitched in and made bread. I baked bread all my life. We loved it. So I made bread up at Little Annie's. I don't think I got over ten dollars a month at that time.

Midland Depot, with Glory Hole in the back. Courtesy Robert Zupancis.

When I lived with my aunt and uncle, I was about maybe seven or eight. We lived in a miners' apartment house. My uncle had company coming from Aspen and he said to me, "You go down and I'll come halfway to meet you. Bring half a gallon of wine." He didn't show up. I put that jug down and I set on top of it until he come to meet me — stubborn little Elsie. I don't know how many hours I waited, sitting on my wine. I can't remember that part of it, but I think it was a long time. I think, "Oh god, how ornery I was." Nothing wrong with being ornery. Nothing wrong with sticking up for what I think and say.

When I was growing up on the East End of town there was a big sampler at the times when the mine was still going. I think it was called the Russ Sampler. I was maybe ten years old. There was a fire that burned the whole building. Part of my home has still got some of the lumber in it that we salvaged afterwards. A sampler was where they sampled ore, crushed it, and shipped it out to different places. It was like a separator. And then they'd sample what was coming out. No one was hurt in that fire. It happened at night.

Blood Pudding
from Elsie Snyder

1 1/2 pounds white white
1 quart hog's blood
one tablespoon crushed mint
a little salt to taste

Boil white rice, set aside. Add hog's blood to rice and knead with hands. Add the crushed mint and the salt to taste.

Rinse medium-size sausage casings (buy at grocery store). Wash well to get salt off. Stuff sausages, but not too tightly. Tie casings fin circles with string so that stuffing will not fall out. Light boil sausages in water 30 minutes or so (poke with a toothpick, and when juice runs clear, it's done). Lay out sausages to cool on table. Next day, put them in refrigerator. Cook them in frying pan or oven before eating. Serve with fried potatoes and vegetables.

My husband John Snyder and I got married in 1922, the last day of the year. John was born in 1899 in Aspen. His dad was a miner and his mom was a housewife. When he was young, he worked on ranches. He worked on the Vagneur Ranch, haying and everything else. We bought our house for taxes for forty dollars. I sold it for $750,000 in 1989. The house is still standing. See, I have four lots. I was asking in the millions, but the damn city council, excuse my French, put a moratorium on it and none of us could sell it. Ray Bates and all of them have it, you know. They put a moratorium on it so the people that bought it couldn't build and we couldn't get the money.

Blood Sausage
from Helen Kralich

1/2 pork head or 5 pounds pork snouts or jowls or both
1/2 beef lung
1 lb. pork liver
1 lb. pork hearts
1 lb. leaf lard or cracklings
4 lb. rice
1 teaspoon ground cloves
1 teaspoon marjoram
1/2 teaspoon ground pepper
1 T. salt
1 T. ground cinnamon
1 lb. casing
1 quart of beef or pork blood

Cook snouts, jowls, lung, liver, and hearts. Coarsely grind or chop all meat along with the rendered leaf lard or cracklings. Cook rice using directions on box; drain and cool. (Don't use Minute Rice.) In large bowl, mix well with your hands, the ground ingredients, rice, and spices. Mix with blood before starting to fill casings.

Thoroughly rinse casings in cold water to remove salt in which casings were packed. With sausage machine, fill casings to about 4/5 desired length. Cut. Tie ends with string. Refrigerate. If not cooked to serve in 1-2 days, freeze and use within 6 months.

To cook: Roast 1 hour at 325 on broiler or uncovered in roasting pan with rack; turn sausage after 30 minutes of roasting.

Pork trimmings are an excellent substitute for snouts or jowls. Use trimmings uncooked and grind.

Anyway, it was funny how I met John. I was visiting my older sister, Mary, in Leadville. She was married over there. Her husband was working at the Little Johnny Mine and I went in the shoe shop. I'd lost a heel off my shoe and I met John there. He was in there with a fellow by the name of McDonald. We talked for a minute and I never paid any attention afterwards. Then when he come back to Aspen, he started courting me. We didn't go to dances. He never danced. I guess we went to a movie or something like that at the Isis. I used to go to dances, but not too often. He wouldn't dance, so what was the use of going alone?

Once in awhile, the whole family would get together and roast a hog. That's when I had a good time. We'd go up the river. There was lots of places. Now you can't do that because there are too many people around. We got married in 1922. Our wedding lasted three days. We got married at St. Mary's Church. We bought bootleg whiskey for one dollar a gallon from Bob (I had the name on the tip of my tongue, but I forgot it). Our family made raisin wine. There used to be a lot of people would make grape wine, but my parents never got into it. There was just too many kids. Instead of buying grapes, we bought other essentials we needed. At the wedding, we danced and had a big table full of food and a lot to drink. My mother and a bunch of the ladies helped with the food. We went out and invited each one personally. There was no invitation stuff. We went and done it personally, house to house. And I think there was more people at our wedding than there was at the mass. We went to mass in the morning and to communion, then at high noon we got married.

Jimmy was born in 1923. Jimmy is sixty-eight, Lucille will be sixty-four, Donny will be sixty, and Pat, my youngest one, will be fifty-four. My baby will be fifty-four. She works at the animal clinic down in Carbondale. I have sixteen great-grandchildren and fourteen grandchildren.

I had all my babies at home. Either my mother or my sister helped me — and the doctor usually, but sometimes they were too late. Let's see, the Eagles had a doctor at that time and it didn't cost us that much. I'm trying to think of his name. He was a big, heavyset man, and one time he was in our outhouse when the baby came. I think that was Lucille. My sister had everything taken care of, but of course he had to retie and everything. It cost me fifteen dollars anyway.

My husband John was by trade a horseshoer — a blacksmith. He learned the trade. You know where the Aspen Block is? Right on the corner there was a big blacksmith shop, and that's where he learned his trade. I'm trying to think of the blacksmith's name. Denny Hughes. He taught John the blacksmith trade. He used to do horseshoes and everything like that.

❖❖❖❖❖❖❖❖❖❖❖❖❖❖❖

Later on, in 1936, I think, or before, Louis Vagneur was a commissioner, and John got a job as road overseer. He was road overseer for Pitkin County for thirty-six years. A road overseer does everything — the hiring and the firing and doing the maintenance work. He had to work just like the rest of them. He was the supervisor of the whole road department.

There was never a time when I wanted to leave the valley. Nope. And you know, when I sold my house on Hyman Street, I had lived there sixty-six and one-half years. We were married fifty-seven years, one month, and five days when John died. At one time there were lots of houses, but not these big structures they're putting in town now. They were small homes.

The big change in Aspen came after 1950. The last three or four years have been the worst. You see, they built all these houses for speculation. A working man can't afford them. No way. That's why they're all going to Glenwood and on. They work from Rifle on up. Well, I wish it had been left alone like the 1950s were. It was still half decent. Right now when I go downvalley, when I hit Aspen, it's tacky looking to me. It's not like the way it was before. Aspen wasn't build for that. All those big townhouses don't belong in Aspen. A lot of people might think I'm against it, but I'm not. It just doesn't go here. We had a nice little ski area and it was wonderful. Now it's too glitzy. If I had a wish for Aspen, I'd wish it right back to where it was before 1950, before the movie stars started coming — the real rich people.

❖

Photo by Kathy Daily

*Jim has age, time, wisdom,
and soul in his eyes.
He has a twinkle
in there, too.
And he knows he's funny.*

Jim Snyder

I was born November 2, 1923, at 801 East Hyman. My grandparents' names were Anton and Agnes Snyder, and my other grandparents were Nick and Agnes Baltazar Garrish. My parents' names are John and Elsie Snyder.

All four of us children were born in the old house. In those days, very few went to the hospital. There were all the midwives in the neighborhood, and they were good at taking care of each other. As a boy, I spaded gardens for different

459

people to earn money. When I was in grade school, out in the old George Washington School, I used to take care of five houses in the evening. I'd get their coal and wood and carry out their ashes two days a week. So at the end of the week I had $1.25 to spend. That was a fair amount of money in those days. I dumped those ashes in the alley. They were cold coals and were just left and spread out in the springtime in the gardens — just scattered. A lot of times where the church was and Armory Hall, they had an old coal furnace. They had piles of ashes five or six feet high in wintertime. At the Catholic church, I used to rent a team and wagon for five dollars a day from John Strong, one of the old-timers that was a logger. Another kid and I, we'd contract to haul the whole pile away for twenty-five dollars. That was big bucks then. I was in the sixth grade. All the money went for clothes.

Dad was usually gone early in the morning and home about five o'clock at night. When I was a real young boy, his trade was a blacksmith. He'd be down at his shop shoeing horses. I used to watch him beat on the old anvil, and I'd get to pull the bellows once in awhile or wrestle an ornery horse. Dad never got kicked. He was very good with horses. Just one other kid hung out there, too. The other blacksmith there, they were kind of neighborly friends. Dad was heck for training saddle horses. He'd trade them about every third or fourth day of every week. He'd have five or six and he'd train 'em. If Dad would drop the reins, that horse just stood there and walked around them reins. He never ventured. It was just an art he had. Of course, everybody wanted a horse like that. He didn't have a hard time getting rid of them. Quarter horses were unknown in those days. He had just plain old broncs. He never taught me the trade, but I seen enough of it that it still hangs in my memory today. I can sharpen a pick, bar, and put handles on shovels and picks.

When we were young, a lot of us kids used to go around the old buildings, and we'd rustle copper and sell it to the secondhand store for about three or four cents a pound. All the old buildings had copper leads into them. We'd find some old copper boilers, lead, and babbitt. Babbitt's a part of a lead. It's got some ingredients to make it harder and was used a lot in bearings and shafts. So we'd go up and hound the old mine — anywhere there was a mantle that had those saddles, where we could break the babbitt out of it and melt it down to sell. There were dealers with a few other companies, out-of-town ones, that would come out once a month or something like that to pick up scrap goods. Old Man Sweeney, John Sweeney, had the main one in town here.

There was a local guy that was engineer on the train, and every time he got the run up here, why we'd wait over in this area for him. See, the tracks come right down below the road. As a matter of fact, Midland Avenue was the D&RG road. Right across my culvert, that was the Midland track. We'd hang around there, and he'd slow down and finally kind of stop. We'd get on, and he'd give us a ride over to the Glory Hole — went over to pick up ore cars. It took him awhile to switch them from the tracks. He'd get them on and then we'd hitch a ride back. He'd slow down and we'd jump off and wait for the next time he'd come up. We rode in the engine. I guess I was about seven or eight at the time.

We used to occasionally skip school and hitch downvalley on the train and then come home and get our butt whipped. Kind of learn a lesson until we decided to do it again. We'd just kind of hang around in Carbondale. It was about like Aspen with the old buildings and old-timers — farmers in town. We'd just kind of browse around and then start back home about 1:30 or 2:00. Depended upon what time we went down there. We very seldom came back on the train. See, the train only made one trip a day, and it usually came through that area real early. We'd just hitch rides with different people that had old Model Ts and Model As. Sometimes it was a wagon, slow and steady.

Of course, everybody's family then had a storyteller because they had their own doings. Whenever there was a get-together, stories would be told amongst the different families — what their dad or uncle or granddad did. The only story that really kept me interested was my grandfather's on the Garrish side. I guess he was living in Aspen in about 1920, and he walked from here to Leadville several times. It took him about two days. He'd spend overnight up there on the pass. There were wolves here at that time. I guess a band of them give him a bad time one night around his campfire. He had to keep the fire going to keep them backed off. He worked between the two towns. Leadville would be kind of up and spurring a little bit, and then Aspen would be down, and back and forth. He died when I was a year old.

When I was a kid, the American Legion used to sponsor a baseball team all over the country. They had one here and, of course, they had two different groups — the old ones and the young kids. We used to go down as far as Grand Valley and play. The first one we'd go to would be over at Red Cliff and Minturn. We never did play at Leadville. I was center field. A couple of times, I made some of them flys where you stumble and roll and get that hand out as you're going down. You'd grab it and everybody'd roar. It kind of gave out right after I was a senior in high school. The town started getting separated a little bit then.

Hannibal Brown used to be one that drove us on our American Legion baseball trips. He stuck the whole baseball team in his car. He was a volunteer. He had a green Hudson. It was him and Bill McCugh had a Model A, and

Jim Snyder's lynx and house cat. Courtesy Jim Snyder.

they'd haul us. Han worked there at the bank — tended it all those years. He was a janitor for the Aspen State Bank. I liked old Hannibal.

We also had, in the basement of the Elk's building, a gym outfit — the bars and the rings. One of the Caparella boys, Tony, was a pretty good little boxer — handy with the mitts. He'd always offer the boxing classes. He'd get in there and take advantage of those guys if he had a little grudge against them. He'd kind of rough them up a little bit.

Every Saturday night there used to be a dance at the Armory Hall — just a local one. Sis Richie was a fiddle player. Jimmy McCugh played the drums, I guess. Sis's daughter Vivian played in it when she got older. There was about six of them. They created a lively little affair down there — polkas and waltzes.

Back in those days, Dad pastured our horses at any vacant lot, just like all the women that had a milk cow. They'd turn it out in the morning and let it roam from lot to lot in town. The women would keep an eye on them once in awhile. Some of us had city water. For others there were irrigation ditches through town in just about every block. My grandfather's house didn't have water in it until 1946. I got out of the service and dug across the street — put city water into it. They had the ditch running in the summertime and barrels set off to the side with a little pipe running into them. That's where they'd get a

462

bucket of water. A lot of times they'd have it piped across the sidewalk and a barrel inside the yard. To water the lawn, they used to take a lid off a lard bucket and nail it on a lath, like flashing on a broom. They'd nail it on the end of the stick, and then they'd stand there and sprinkle the lawn.

I was eighteen years old in 1941 when I went into the army. They didn't give you time to get scared. In the Pacific, it was full of killing. We ended up where most of them were. You leave a boy, you come back a boy with a man's experience. War grows on you so fast you don't have time. You kind of run into a time you can see where you missed part of life — of growing up. There were quite a few Aspen kids that didn't come back from the war. There were four of them that I knew. At that time, Aspen did not have a memorial — not until years later. They kind of got together and put up a program for them.

After I returned, Dad was county road overseer. He started in '35 and he did it for thirty-seven years. I ran all kinds of equipment, even before I went into the service. That's what I was in — the engineers. Anybody needed a cat-skinner or grader operator, I'd go do it for them. I did that, and then I worked on the state highway department — five years with them. I got to seeing the daylight about that — same chuckhole, same pothole, same broken-down guardrail. You'd spend your life doing that. My boss was on there for thirty-eight years. I just couldn't see growing up with that. I worked for the county on and off whenever they needed help. I'd do it for Dad's sake. On the state highway department, I got to plow on the pass. We started oiling the first stretch of it the last year I worked for them. We did four miles out of town. That was 1959.

We had a couple of slides that just missed us one spring as we were up working on the very top. They'd start from their side, and we'd start from ours, and then we'd punch a hole through the top and kind of get together. One afternoon, the third water hole up, there was a heavy spot. You couldn't see it until it started kicking down over the side. We were just lucky. We were gazing up and backing up at the time, side by side, and we saw the dribble start in. So we kicked the throttle open and it was our day — we got out in time from the avalanche. We were on the uphill side where we had easy pushing to open it back up again. It was easy on the downhill leg. Uphill was much harder.

I lost a pickup up there one spring. We were opening the pass and I had parked my equipment for the night. It was about a quarter to four, and my friend Gene was still working from the Leadville side. He motioned me to get in his pickup and take it up on the other side. We liked to keep a cat on each side in case a slide came in overnight, because we wouldn't have to walk when we started working. So I got in the truck and started up. I spun out. I never drove it before. He never did mention the emergency brake. I pulled it hard but never did lock the wheels. I put it in neutral and left the engine running. The dump trucks were below me. As I turned around, here's the pickup backing down the road. It hit the edge. I don't know why — I jumped in as it was going over the bank. I thought again and jumped back out. It tumbled down, burned up — tires come off.

On Independence Pass, there's a little cabin by Linkin Lake. We used to call that Jakey's cabin. That's where an old prospector used to live. He was one of the early-time prospectors. He had a couple of mules. I was little when my dad used to go up and see him on weekends. Dad and an uncle of mine, Louis Popish, worked together at times up there on the pass. They'd open it by hand, when they used to get together — hand shovel it. They used to have big old Coleman trucks. There were a lot of places there they'd have to hand shovel it in the spring of the year — May or June. It was all more or less kind of volunteer work. If you just let the pass melt, what month could you possibly drive through there? July? God, if you're lucky! I've seen that pass close on a blue day with the sun out. The wind comes up and brings all the snow to the bottom of the valley, then brings it up and it just sits right in there. A lot of times when we kept it open until late in February, I'd just have to go up there and park. As soon as the snow was eighteen to twenty inches high, I'd knock them down. That was our biggest worry when we kept it open late — somebody getting stuck up there at night. A lot of them come over and did not have a full tank of gas and winter clothes.

Years ago, Mrs. Linkin was fishing at the lake up there and lightning hit and killed her. It's now called Linkin Lake. It was before my time. I think her husband was a prospector and they lived there in that area. That's always been a good fishing lake. I guess she was there in a storm. When she didn't show up, he went up and there she was, lying at the shore. I think that happened in the early 1920s.

Aspen used to have some adult bullies around — kind of drunks that would mix, more amongst themselves. We had a lot of local fellows and some of them were drifters. They just liked their drink. Where they hung out, we'd call it the jungles. They'd name it the jungle they were living in. They were all good jolly characters.

Timmy Sullivan always used to wrestle a bull when the dairy was up there on the end of Galena Street, on Aspen Mountain. There was an old roan bull that come into the milk cows every night and would come down by the Glory Hole area. Timmy was a big brawny. The old bull got to where he would look for him, too, as they come by to have their little set-to. The bull would hunch up and put his head down. Timmy Sullivan, he'd hunch up, too. He'd reach up and grab the bull and they'd push back and forth. It'd be a draw. Timmy was so looped up on fifty-cent wine that he had no control over himself at all. Self-exertion and just built damn strong did him in. The bull was pretty good sized but nothing heavy. Us kids would all gather around to see it.

I killed a bear when I was nineteen, on my birthday on November 2. I was working on the pass then. I ran the dozer. We had a snowfall the night before. I was by Difficult Campground, and I was cleaning it up, making it a little wider, pushing the snow over the edge. Of course, the whole road then was only twelve or fourteen feet wide. As I was rolling some of the heavy stuff down, I saw this black thing running and I figured it was a bear. So I killed the piece of equipment and climbed down. Sure enough, there were bear tracks in the slushy snow, and as he ran, it splattered out and made them look real big. Of course, he had a pretty good paw anyhow. I climbed back up and parked the cat.

Jim Snyder and bear, 1942.
Courtesy Jim Snyder.

I figured that was enough for the day and I went down and got my buddy Adolph Miklich out of school. We got our guns and went up there and rousted the old bear out of its cave. He was a pretty cinnamon color — weighed about 260 pounds. I was trapping at the time and I had what they called a muskrat bomb. It's a little smoke bomb that you throw in a muskrat hole to bring him out. I threw one of them in there, and that's all it took. There was a big roar and he come out right straight where we were standing peeking in. Our guns were back a few feet leaning against the quakies. As he come out, we ran for our guns. Mine was a couple trees further beyond where Adolph's was. Adolph got the first shot, and he hit the bear in the left shoulder. That turned the bear, and then I got a shot in the brisket crossways. As he was running away, one of us nailed him right underneath the top of the head, and one of us got him right above the tail. It lodged right in his spine, and that brought him down. So we loaded him and brought him into town. We drove all over town with him on the fender of the car, then finally hung him up to skin him out.

Hannibal Brown had to come up and see the doings, and he wouldn't come inside — just stayed at the door. He was scared of bears. Course, when he seen the bear, he jumped back. Finally he says, "You know, I'm going to leave you guys. You're teasing me too much. But I'd sure like to have some of that

*Hyman Avenue Fire,
October 30, 1941.
Courtesy Helen Kralich.*

lard. That I can render out." (That's when you cook the fat on the stove and squeeze it and it separates. After that you squeeze the fat to get the liquid out of it.) Han said, "That's good for chilblains and stuff like that." So my mother rendered some, too. Me and the Miklich kids had chilblains something terrible. It's worse than frostbite. It burns and it tingles. We used to go run in crusted snow barefoot. We'd take the good old Dutch brushes and rub each other's feet, put ice on them — it was terrible. You don't even hear of them anymore. I'll tell you, we put some of the bear grease on them, and that stopped it. Put it on in the morning and then put our socks on. Of course, those colored people, they had a lot of ideas us whites never even heard of.

Oh god, everybody wanted a chunk of the bear meat. It's just like pork, only it's real sweet. The bear was kind of a tan and cream color. You very seldom see them. In those years, you saw either brown or black.

In 1941, when the Hyman Street fire started, I ran down the street with Dad and there was two others that come up from the other end of town. We were the first ones on the scene. As we hit where Aspen Drug was, Dad told me to run on down and make sure. There was a hairdresser right above Huey McCabe's store — Mrs. Anderson was her name — to see if she was awake. She wasn't. I had to go around the Mill Street side and up the stairway — you know, the old-time stairs. I was hitting it so hard with my shoes it woke her up and she was right there at the door. I told her, "You look out the window and see the fire — that's why Dad sent me down here." She and her daughter got out.

Boy, that sure went up in flames. I think I was a freshman in high school. I still have some coins that melted in Charlie Gavin's wild bar in there. They used to call it the Cow Shed. When it cooled down, they opened the safe to see how much was there. Where the cash register was, all the quarters had melted together. I got a few of them left around here. The town took it pretty calm. They just saw this was it and watched. That's all they could do, because they didn't have the equipment to fight something that big — it was dry. They had a volunteer fire department back then. Dad was on it. But it was just too damn hot to get to. Quite a few little businesses were lost; Sweeney had his secondhand store there, and Charlie Gavin had the cafe bar. Then there was a little cigar store on the east end down there by the Loushin's house. Atkison was his name. He had a little section about twelve-foot wide with cigars and chewing tobacco. Then in the back he had a couple of poker tables. Aspen Drug got protected.

I was in the first ski club that we had in 1935 and 1936 — the Aspen Ski Club. There were seventeen or eighteen of us. But I skied before that. The neighborhood bunch used to make their own skis. We'd get in one of these old

Hyman Avenue and Mill Street, day after Hyman fire, 1941. Courtesy Francis Kalmes.

buildings and rip up the hardwood floor. Of course, in the East End, a lot of us had pigs, and we had a big old feeding tub that they used to cook food for the pigs. My grandmother had a good one. So we'd get these boards and fill that with water, put a fire under it, and steam-curl the end of the board. Then we'd take an old router plane and run a groove down the center of it. We used to put a leather strap from side to side — a loop — and we used to cut a car innertube about an inch wide and put that over our ankle. We put our foot in the loop and then stretched it down. It was very simple and inexpensive. In the spot of the ski where the boot would fit, we would drill a couple of small holes through the sides of the skis. Then about an inch and a half, two inches apart, we would take a small saw and saw that piece out and put the strap through with a hook on it. We'd make our loop on top and put our foot in. And then with an old rubber innertube, we used to cut about a one-inch piece off, which is a solid loop. We'd put it over our foot and put our foot into the loop of the ski and stretch the innertube loop from the back of our ankle down to the point of our shoe. That acted as our harness.

My first pair of bindings were the leather ones with a clamp snap for the heel. The toe piece was metal. A strap came over the top of the shoe and a strap came behind with a double snap to fold over and lock it in. They held up real good.

Andre Roch come in 1936 and gave everybody an idea what to do on Aspen Mountain. So we banded together and cut out the Roch Run and Corkscrew. Roch got us started and then there was an average from eighteen to thirty that worked on and off. It was all free. Some of the Glenwood people started coming up and helped us, too.

We built the boat tow. It was two sleds going up and down. They called them boats. It went up the second road. The guy that concocted the whole thing was Blaine Bray. He was in charge of a government program that they used to work for the young kids — WPA. He also built the Willoughby jump. It was a ski jump that sat on the left-hand side where the mine dump is. He could halfway engineer, just tinker around himself. For a motor, he bought an old Studebaker motor from my dad. Dad had an old Studebaker that had the pull-down curtains — the roll-up type. He wasn't using it, so Blaine made a deal with Dad to buy that big old engine from him to use for the motor. I think Dad just gave it to him. For our top skiing up where the Sun Deck is, every weekend the Midnight Mine would ride us up in their trucks. At the mine, they had a little cat with a big sled toboggan behind it. We'd get on it, and they'd ride us up where the Sun Deck is, and we'd ski down. They'd make two trips a Sunday.

When Andre Roch started giving lessons, he picked two spots. One of them was out there where the Highlands is now. That used to be the old Strong Ranch. In those days the hills weren't as loaded with trees as they are now. They were pretty sparse in places. I had a pair of full 7-foot skis — maple, from Sears, Roebuck. When we put them into the van to go up to the Midnight Mine, you couldn't close the door in back because they stuck out. That used to gripe everybody to have that door cracked with a draft coming in. But they put up with it. I tell you, when I turned them loose, I was gone. They weighed more than I did. That was it.

We had some good skiers. George and Leo Tekoucich — god, they were good. Shirts open, maybe a scarf around their necks, Levi pants. They used to come down that hill! Mike Manifico just thought the world of them. He'd furnish their skis and everything else. He had Magnifico Sports. He was real good that way. I won a buckle one year on one of the races up Maroon Creek. It's a plated buckle with a set of skis on it. I think I came in third. There was thirteen of us that knew each other real well, and the others were kind of the West Enders that we didn't mix too much with.

The last year I skied was 1952. I quit because of the influx of people. I just got griped. I couldn't believe the normality of skiing had left for me. We wouldn't stop a second. Goddamn, we'd just race up and down.

One time, Tony Kastelick and I were skiing and we had actually quit for the day on a Sunday. He said, "Let's make one more run." We were going up, and I unloaded all the stuff for him when the first lift come in. We decided to make one more run. Right above Zaugg Park, the tow was only about twelve feet off the ground. I made up my mind that I was going to make my last run and jump off. I had it all figured out as I come up, but I forgot one thing. When my weight left the chair, it was going to bounce. And it did. They had to rope the rest of the people off. You see, the cable jumped the bogey wheel, and that made it stop. Laurence Elisha had the Hotel Jerome. He was running the lift. About two and a half years later, he finally figured out who jumped. He caught me and he said, "Goddamn you, you jumped off that tow." Back then, they had a portable pulley. They'd lash it on and lower the chair down. I dropped and skied off. I was crouched, and as soon as I hit the snow, I took off. After I got down, I happened to look up and, "Holy God, what happened?" Never told anyone. I kept quiet about it. Laurence Elisha finally figured it. Tony was the only one that knew.

The Glory Hole Park — that used to be a big hole. It was about three hundred foot across and about a hundred ninety foot deep. It was where they stoped in the early days — a body of ore in there. See, there's two tunnels running across town from hillside to hillside, and as they stoped ore out and brought it out to mine, it finally gave in. My mother was standing on the corner. She was a little girl when that caved in. It never got anybody, but it took two cars. I think one had ore in it. You could even see part of the railroad tracks sticking up when I was a kid. It used to be the trash collector for years. Everything went in there — dead pigs, scrapings — threw it in the Glory Hole.

I had a pet elk awhile back. Nimnon was his name. It was a heavy winter when he was born up Capitol Creek right by the city waterworks. The whole herd was down in the trees there, and he got on the road. The dogs and cars were running him, and somebody told my brother about it. So we drove up and found him. We picked him up and took him up the river. There used to be an old log cabin off to the right-hand side — the old Jordan Ranch. The old barn was still there. We boarded up the holes, and I took some hay and rolled oats up to him. He stayed in there three days. Finally, he got healthy enough to jump out of a four-foot window. Then he got right back down on the road again. So I kind of kept a check on him, and one day I went up and couldn't find him.

Right there as you turn into the hospital, there used to be a deep pool of runoff water. He was in up to his neck. He was stuck. He jumped off the road. I got my brother, and we pulled him out with the jeep. Put a rope around him. We tried by hand, but every time we'd get him, he'd fall, so we tied it on the jeep. When I got him in the middle of the road, you ought to have seen him. Just as we were wrestling him to hogtie him, here come a couple of cars around the corner. They just

*Jim Snyder and pet elk
Nimnon, 1957.
Courtesy Jim Snyder.*

kind of drove off the road. So when the ruckus was over, they were standing there looking at us like a couple of idiots. I says, "You help me throw him in the back of my jeep, I'll pull you out and we'll get out of here." So they did. I kept him in a horse barn for a week. Told the sheriff I had him. He come up, looked at him, and seen what shape he was in. Later, I turned him loose, and he just hung around. He was that way for five years. Hell, he grazed along the river up there at Fred Iselin's. He was hanging around up at Jim Smith's. Anybody'd feed him goodies, and he'd hang around.

One time they were teasing him and were going to have Fred Iselin do a bullfight with him. Yet, in the meantime, Nancy's calling me up about the elk being in her raspberries. She kept it up so persistently. I didn't know this about Fred. He was keeping him up there so they could have this movie with Fred playing toro with him. One afternoon, I ran into somebody that says, "I see where your elk's going to be famous." And I said, "What do you mean?" And he said, "Well, Fred Iselin's going to fight him this coming Sunday up at Jim

Smith's. They're going to make a movie." That was a Thursday night. I went up that night with some firecrackers and caught him in her strawberry garden and I let them go. Hell, I might as well have shot a cannon over his head. It didn't phase him at all. He just looked at me. Of course, he knew every vehicle I had. So, it come down to Saturday night. It just burned me up, them hollering because Nimnon was in the garden, yet they were keeping him around for this damn movie. So I took a single-shot shotgun and loaded it with rock salt and went up and give him a light blast. It hurt me more than it hurt him. Anyhow, he got out and come home. And they didn't get their movie, believe me.

Another time, old Louis Trentaz owned a ranch out there where Starwood is. Louis called up one evening and said, "Jim, I like you and I like your dad. I think a lot of both of you." He said, "I like your elk, too." He says, "Right now the goddamn thing is out here. He's got the bulls up in the trees, he's got the heifers to himself." I says, "What do you mean, Louis?" He says, "Just what I say. He's got the heifers out here. The bulls he run off." Evidently there was some lovin' going on. I told him I'd be out and get him. I drove out, and just as you go into Starwood, at that first little meadow, that's where he was, having a hell of a time. So I went out and looked the case over, and sure enough, he was proud as hell.

The next day, I loaded up my saddle horse, took some rope, and went out there. Got the horse out, saddled up, and got in running the elk around. Every throw with the lariat was just three feet short. He'd move his head or something. I was getting perturbed, so finally I took two nylon ropes — lariats — and made some Indian snares. I got to running him around and nailed him with one. He slipped enough to get in the other one, so I had him pretty well stretched out. I lashed him together with the nylon lariats. Anyway, I got it done, but I had one chore. "Well, how am I going to get him in this horse trailer?"

The trailer had a drawring up in front, so I just dropped the tailgate and lined him up. I drug him up the line and put the rope through. I skidded him there head-first. Closed the door and come to town. I brought him home and chained him up. I didn't know what the hell to do. I hated to see him keep that up.

I was telling Red Rowland about it, and he says, "I got a pair of masculators; let's gild him." That sounded good to me. So he, Joe Miklich, Mick Strong, and Tommy Zordel came down one night. I had him in a corral — fed him molasses oats and he hung around. They showed up and we were kind of shooting the bull instead of starting right in. Red finally says, "Well, let's get the job done." He grabbed a rope and he started swinging it over his head. The old elk was over the fence in two seconds flat — gone. I had a hell of a time trying to get him back in where we could get him. I finally coaxed Nimnon in. I told Red, "Forget your cowboy stuff. Let me handle this." So I got to petting him and finally got my rope over his neck. I reached up and grabbed his two spike horns and started to lean on him. Elk are real easy. By pressing on the back, they'll go right to the ground. We had him. Red handled the masculators and we got the job done. He was one mad elk for a week. He laid right over here and wouldn't come down or nothing. That took it out of him.

Then Colorado College, CU — their biology class got ahold of the story, so they started sending kids over. The way they explained it to me, when you do something like that to an animal, each testicle has a certain side of the body that governs something. If you do the right one, the right horn will be funny and everything like that. When you do both of the testicles, both of the horns will. So they took movies of him and everything, and I took one, too. The outer shape was unproportionate and everything. The antlers don't come out nice and uniform. One would have a big ball and then sprout out. They were like a moose. That's what his horns were like after I did that. And then they finally started coming out pretty normal again. That last picture I got of him as a three-point, they were back pretty normal. That was hard to do to the old character, but I was in hot water and it was either that or shoot him. Why did I name him Nimnon? One night it just come to me. Don't ask me what it means. I should have called him Numb Nuts — that would have been a good one. Afterwards.

✦

Photo by Kathy Daily

Sam Stapleton

 I was born January 9, 1927, in Aspen at my home on Owl Creek. My father's name was William Emmett Stapleton. My dad was married twice. His first wife was Beda Holstrom. Later she died in childbirth with her second child. Then my father married Sally Lewis. There were nine children in our family:

On right, William E.
"Bill" Stapleton.
Courtesy Aspen
Historical Society.

William, Bernice, Bernard, Francis, Elmer, Dora, E. Sam Pete, Hazel, and Lurleen. Dad met Mom here in Aspen. Her parents were ranchers. Some of the land they owned was where the nature preserve is now up the pass.

My grandfather was Timothy Stapleton. He came from Tipperary County, Ireland. There were three Stapleton brothers that came to the United States. They split up on the East Coast. From then on, I don't know if they ever saw each other again. Grandpa was seventeen. He ended up in Leadville in 1879. He mined two years in Leadville and in 1881 homesteaded in Aspen. He married Ellen Kilker and had nine children. She was his second wife. His first wife died in childbirth in Black Hawk, Colorado.

In Aspen, he decided he didn't want any more mining. He wanted to be a rancher. So he went back to Leadville, and the next summer he moved the family over in a wagon. My father, Bill, was five years old. His job was to walk behind the wagon, and whenever the horses would need a rest, he'd put a rock behind the wheel so the wagon would stay put and the horses wouldn't have to be straining to hold it. My grandparents homesteaded where the airport is. They had cattle.

My first chores on the ranch were to chase the chickens and get an egg for my grandmother (on my mother's side) to make a cake or bread. I'd also pack in wood and coal and chop wood. We had about seven rooms in our house. There were usually three kids in our bed. I had to sleep at the foot. We had a bunkhouse we slept in most of the time. It was bigger.

Dad's income was livestock — he probably had 100 head. He drove them to the railroad livestock pens at Woody Creek. All the ranchers that had cattle were driving at the same time. Jens Christiansen was a really good friend. I remember when he was courting his wife, Gladyce. His was a smaller ranch. Altogether, we had probably 1,200 acres. We had cows and sheep both. I wasn't too old when I first was on a horse. I'm not a real cowboy. I can ride, but I can't do much roping off a horse. I can rope a cow off the ground, but I never did try to rope off the horse, because I didn't need to. I used to go up to get the milk cows on a horse. I was six or seven — wasn't very big. My dad would show you how to do something once and you knew what to do.

My dad had a heart attack when I was nine, in 1936. He was sixty years old. Mother was left with eight children. After that, we kids ran the ranch. We had a couple of hired men for a couple of years, and then pretty soon World War II came and two older brothers and a sister went in the service. I was in high school. Between my brother and I, we did all the work.

We went to Owl Creek School. While I was going there, Martha Waterman, Leona Hatch, and Marsha Shermann taught. It was a one-room schoolhouse. There were seven or eight kids. It went up to eighth grade. When I was in the eighth grade, there were four first-graders, four eighth-graders, and two or three in between. We walked to school; it was just at the foot of the hill down here. In the wintertime, we would jump on our sleds, and down the hill we would go. We got chilblains when we were little. We'd go out and stand in the snow without our shoes on. Tickled like hell. You want to itch it, but it don't do no good, you can't itch it. Just go out in the snow and it would help.

At night, to stay warm, we usually had one of the old flat irons, a brick, or a rock we would put in the oven of a coal or wood stove. We'd get it hot and then wrap it in a towel and put it at our feet. For meals, we always had eggs. We butchered our own pigs, lamb, chicken, sausage, or bacon. We had a good breakfast. Lunch would be a pretty good meal because everybody was working. The biggest meal was probably supper. But they were all pretty good-sized.

Serviceberry Wine

3 lbs. Berries
7 pts. Water
2 1/4 cups Sugar
3 tsp. Acid Blend
1/2 tsp. Pectic Enzymes
1/2 tsp. Energizer
1 Campden crush
1 pkg. Wine yeast

Starting S.G. 1.095-1.100

METHOD: The best time to pick these berries is after the 1st frost. Remove stems, leaves, and foreign matter. Wash and drain. Using nylon straining bag mash and strain out juice into primary fermentor. Keeping all pulp in straining bag, tie top, and place in primary. Stir in all other ingredients EXCEPT yeast. Cover primary. After 24 hours, add yeast. Cover primary. Stir daily, check S.G. and press pulp lightly to aid extraction. When ferment reaches S.G. 1.030 (about 5 days) strain juice from bag. Syphon wine off sediment into glass secondary. Attach airlock. When fement is complete (S.G. has dropped to 1.000—about 3 weeks) syphon off sediment into clean secondary. Reattach lock. To aid clearing syphon again in 2 months and again if necessary before bottling. To sweeten: Before bottling add 1/2 tsp. Stabilizer, then, add 1/4 lb. dissolved sugar per gallon.

VARIETIES: Serviceberries (Amelanchier L.) commonly called Juneberry also Shadbush and Sarvisberry. An attractive shrub anywhere from 5'-25', white flowers, 1/4" bluish-black small crab-apple like fruit. Saskatoon Serviceberry (A. alnifolia) is a common variety. Oblong-Leaf Juneberry (A. canadenis) can be found as tree also. Some are available from nursery.

We got up anytime after daylight. We milked the cows before school. We had two or three — never had very many. My favorite thing that mom made when she would make something really good was kolach in the summertime. It's a pastry with dried berries and stuff in it.

I met my wife, Elizabeth Hammerich, down at the schoolhouse when she was teaching at Owl Creek School. She was about nineteen; I was twenty. I was asked by the school board to keep the wood supplied at the schoolhouse. Liz moved up from Glenwood Springs to teach. She lived in a cabin at the airport ranch. We dated a year. After we were married, we lived in the Stapleton cabin for twenty years.

My brothers and sisters eventually moved away, and Bernard and I stayed. We had cattle and sheep. We sold the ranch in 1967 — sold the whole thing. I kept twenty acres and Bernard kept four acres. We built this house and moved in at Christmastime in 1968. We had three girls — Connie, Shannon, and Sydney, all cowgirls. After we sold the ranch, I leased the whole thing — what Jens Christiansen sold and what we sold — for five years and then leased 1,000 acres for seventeen years. I had sixty head of cows. East Owl Creek Subdivision took all the cow pastures. I don't have cows now, but I still like to ride.

Aspen started to change about 1958 and continued through the early 1960s. I can't really put my finger on what I'd want for Aspen today, except I wish it would slow down.

◆

Photo by Kathy Daily

Louiva Wilcox Stapleton

I was born in 1913 in Colbran, Colorado. My parents were farmers. I guess farming brought them to Aspen. Years ago, my grandparents, Charles and Cornelia Wilcox, came with their son (my father) to Aspen. At one time they owned what is now Starwood. That's where my mother and father were married in 1911. Farming brought my grandfather, Charles Wilcox, to Aspen from Wisconsin. That's where my father, Glen Lee Wilcox, was born. My grandfather died before I was very old, and I didn't get to ask him many questions. The Wilcox side of my family were English and came to the United States from Canada.

On my mother's side, William and Prometcha Bennett also came from Canada. They originally came from London and Ireland and settled in New York on the St. Lawrence River. My great-aunt Mary Ella Pattison (married a Stallard) came to Aspen. Her sister followed her, and then another sister. She came with a friend. The friend didn't want to come to Aspen alone in 1890, so my great-aunt Pattison came with her, as just a bodyguard. She eventually married Edgar Stallard. He was from Virginia.

My grandmother Prometcha Bennett married while here in Aspen. She lived right across the street here at one time. My great-aunt Mary Ella Pattison Stallard lived here in the valley, where the Aspen Historical Society is now. That's where I grew up — the Stallard House.

My mother died when I was only five and left three children. The youngest one was fifteen days old when she died in the 1918 flu epidemic. That was a terrible flu epidemic — terrible. People died like flies. The cemetery is just full of people who died in that. My father remarried. I didn't get along with my stepmother, evidently. Father finally wrote to Mrs. Stallard and said, "If you want Louiva, come and get her." We were living in Grand Junction at the time. Mrs. Stallard saw the conditions and she took all three of us home. That's how come I came to Aspen, in 1921.

My husband, Bill Stapleton, was born here in 1907, and the Stapleton family originally came to Aspen in 1881. And in 1991, we had a great big 100th celebration for the family, and I mean it was a big one, too. It was great. A lot of family came for it.

Mr. Stallard was working in the courthouse. I think he was assistant treasurer or something like that. Growing up with Mrs. Stallard was okay, but she was very strict. It was a home. Had to work hard. Oh, good heavens, there were a lot of chores to do — cutting and chopping wood. She had some acreage out on Highway 82 and used to ranch and farm it. Just a little spot out there. I can remember riding the horse, and she would be behind the plow digging the potatoes. Oh gosh, and then we would get off and pick up the potatoes. It was hard work. I worked hard all my life. I had two sisters and they were both younger. I'm the oldest.

There was the Washington School and then there was the Lincoln School right where the old elementary school is — the yellow brick building. I walked to school. We had a lot of fun playing at recess, and the old Lincoln School was

*The Stallard House,
1907. Built in 1888 by
J. B. Wheeler. Edgar
Stallard on the lawn.
Courtesy
Louiva Stapleton.*

quite a building — an old wooden building. The high school was an old home that was catty-corner from where the upper elementary school sits. I went there, too; I graduated in 1932. It will be sixty years this coming year.

I played basketball in school in 1932. It was the only thing we had. We had to fight for it tooth and nail. We traveled. The traveling was hard because it was all dirt roads and the tires were terrible. It was awful. We were good, but not state champions. We beat Glenwood and all those teams. Oh boy, those days we played in the zones, too. We had three zones. You didn't run back and forth across the floor like they do now. I played center.

I knew Bill right after high school. Dancing is where I met him. We used to have a lot of dances in Aspen at what is now City Hall — the Armory. That was the best hard-wood floor this side of the Mississippi. After our high school basketball games and everything, we would have dances and entertain the other team — things like that. It was really nice. We courted about a year and a half.

Marie, Ruth, and Louiva Wilcox Stallard in Stallard House, Christmas 1924. Courtesy Louiva Stapleton.

We went to the minister's house and got married forty-four years ago on his birthday. I was nineteen. I always said that was one birthday present he would never get rid of. He's been gone fourteen years in November now, but we had a nice life.

When we got married, he was ranching where the airport is. We lived next door to my house now. We bought that house when taxes were $35 in 1933. We sold it years ago. We got $250 for it. We paid $450 for this house partly furnished when we bought it in 1937 — $35 in 1933 around Aspen was quite a bit of money. It was a lot.

Bill worked for the county and then worked for the county road crew. He worked with Mr. Neihardt at the county clerk's office. When Mr. Neihardt quit, he ran for office and was elected county clerk and recorder. He bought several little insurance agencies and went into the insurance business where Stapleton Insurance Agency is now. It was 1955 when he bought the insurance business, so he was clerk and recorder in 1953 or 1954.

I worked practically for nothing. I went up and helped my husband. I helped with the insurance business and the county clerk's business, too. He would bring stuff home to me and I would do it at home lots of times. I was not on the county payroll. He finally turned in a bill for me, but they didn't want to pay anything. They finally did.

I was twenty when I had my first child. I loved it. I had three boys and one girl — David, Darrell, then Billee Lou, and Don. I was a mother first, then I used to do all the bookwork for the insurance agency.

Where the yellow school sits now, where the playground is, that half-block — a group of the men including my husband, Jimmy Snyder, and several more that are dead I could name — they all got together and flooded that whole half-block to make an ice-skating rink. They built a warming shack, somebody donated an old stove, and somebody donated wood and coal. Seems like there were a lot of skates that turned up all of a sudden, and record players. We would have music. It was absolutely wonderful. The men would go down at night, especially when it got cold, and they would spray that ice and make it smooth. Somebody brought a scraper pulled by horses, and we would smooth that ice off. We put on programs and plays and everything on that ice. The community skated — the older people, the younger people. Anybody that wanted to skate, free to everybody.

There were more places to skate. Sparky (Sparovik) used to live up there at Stillwater. You could skate on Stillwater. There used to be a dance hall up there, too. The farmers used to cut ice over on the ice pond below Red Mountain. There used to be a big pond. The farmers used to cut their ice every winter and store it in an ice house. They'd store their ice in sawdust and it would keep all summer. That's how they kept their meat.

How did the Slaughter House Bridge get its name? There used to be a slaughterhouse down there. There was a slaughterhouse down in the bottom of Castle Creek, too, by the name of Wurtz — almost down to the junction where the Castle goes into the Roaring Fork. My great-aunt had cows, and I had to herd the cows down to the bottom of Castle Creek every day all summer long. I was not very old. I played down there all day long with the cows. We had an old black and white cow that wasn't any good, and I used to ride her all the time — an authentic cowgirl. She didn't mind. She was old and she didn't care. I had a horse, too, and had a cart. In those days it was the only way to get around. You would hitch up your horse, cart, or buggy and go to town.

I was very busy in school things, helping with the kids and when they had parties or things. I wore out three cars taking them here and there because they were in the band, in basketball, football. Billee Lou was a cheerleader for four years. I was room mother for I don't know how many years. And it was, "Mom, will you go with us?" and, "Mom will you take us?" I went. I miss it. That was one thing I really did miss when they got out of school. And then the grandkids came along and I've been busy with them, which has been absolutely wonderful.

I didn't have any grandparents, and my kids didn't have any grandparents. I guess I just went overboard with my grandkids. I have twelve, and they are all very special. I'm getting over a heart attack, a real bad one, and for two days in Grand Junction, they didn't know whether I was going to make it or not. One day I woke up out of a sleep, and here were two grandchildren standing there, and I thought, "Now, that's funny, why are they coming down to see me?" They came. And the doctor even said I was a tough one. My oldest grandchild is thirty-three. I have four great-grandchildren.

What is special about this valley? I don't know, I always thought years ago it was the people. I still have a terrific amount of friends. The cards I got when I was sick were just unbelievable. And the flowers — I was in intensive care, and down there they let you have your flowers, and my room was banked. I still have a lot of friends.

Why do people come here? I don't know whether it is the beauty of the valley or some of these people like the night life, which I don't — never did. Only with my own group. I don't know what attracts them. It was very special to raise my children here. In those days it was really wonderful, and parents took so much of a part in everything. We had a PTA that was really active in everything. There was a big band going. It was just something all the time — church, too. I went to the community church. I sang in the choir for about twenty-five years. I enjoyed it.

I never wanted to leave this valley and move somewhere else. I really love this place. Why would I? My family and my friends and everything is here. I wouldn't change that for anything in the world. Now I'm too old. I'm not going to start over.

I only wish that my town were not quite so busy. There are too many people. It is just too busy. There are too many people that don't even live here. They build those homes — those great big million-dollar homes — and come here maybe two or three weeks a year. I don't think they are doing the town any good.

I really noticed a big change in Aspen when they started paving the streets. You knew then something was happening. They paved this street out here twenty-nine years ago. The side streets got paved. Main Street got paved just a few years before that. You just have to go along with change. My whole makeup is not to fight it. I have fought a couple of things, but I've tried to go along with it. The change brought people jobs. Insurance got better. You had things to insure at least.

I had a nice life. Part of it was really hard times. You don't want to go back, but there are no regrets. People were helpful — a lot of concern for the community. And nowadays they don't care. You know, I've never been to my neighbor's house.

◆

Photo by Kathy Daily

"Bud" John Ernest Strong

I was born in Park City, Utah, on January 3, 1929. I was the second child in my family. The first was Barbara Jeanne. After me came Bud, then George (Mick), Irene, Kenneth, Emma Lou, and Walter. The reason I was born in Park City, and not Aspen, is because Dad took, in the summer of 1928, an old Dodge truck with a camper, to Park City to work in the mines. He worked in Park City that

485

John Henry Strong
(1864 – 1953)
Courtesy Bud Strong.

winter and I was born in January. That spring we come back to Aspen. At that time there just wasn't any work in Aspen.

My grandfather, John Henry Strong (1864-1953), came to Aspen between 1884 and 1886. He was born in Ireland in 1864 and left when he was eighteen because of the potato famine. He came to the United States, stopped in Pennsylvania for a couple of years, and then came to Aspen. I guess he heard that there was work in the mines. Later he lost one eye in a mine accident. When he married my grandmother, Ester Jane (1865-1941), she was already here in Aspen. She was married to George Alford first. My grandmother came from England. I think her husband, George Alford, come from England also. He got killed in a mine accident sometime in the late 1880s. Then my grandfather married her. She was older. She had been married and had one son, George Alford — that's my uncle. After she married my grandfather, they had two more children. Uncle Ernest was born in 1894 and my dad was born in 1896. My dad's name was John Henry (1896-1976), just like my grandfather. I was named John Ernest. I went by John Ernest all my life, but my birth certificate says my name is John Henry, too. I asked my mother, "How come it says that?" She said, "Oh, they're wrong."

My mother's maiden name was Emma Luther. She was born in 1908 in Aspen. Her parents come from Leadville on the stagecoach in the early 1880s. Her father's name was Martin Luther and her mother's name was Martha (1883-1952). My grandfather came from Illinois or Ohio. He was a miner in Leadville and then they come to Aspen. My family on the Luther side had four boys and one girl. My mother was the only girl. A couple of her brothers worked in the mines. One of them, Uncle Bill, he's been crippled all of his life. He's still alive.

My grandfather, John Henry Strong, bought a ranch on Maroon Creek. It stretched from the school clear up to the T-Lazy 7. Actually, there were three ranches. Right below the T-Lazy 7, where that open flat is, that's what we always called the Home Place. That's where my dad worked when he was little. He bought that in about 1912. Sievers was up above Dad's place. Dad owned on the side of the river where the ski area is — that flat in there. The first ranch was on the left, then you crossed the river — all of that on the other side. There were three ranches and Grandpa bought each one of my uncles — George and Ernie — and Dad a small ranch. This was about 1912 or 1910. Then my grandfather and grandmother Strong got divorced and he went back to Ireland for a year. She stayed on the ranch. Dad helped her run it. They raised cattle, hay, and potatoes. Later on in the twenties, they even raised lettuce. One year they made a lot of money and the next year they couldn't even pay for the freight. They shipped the lettuce out to California. It was kind of a comic story. Dad got a check for ten cents. That was all that was left over after the freight — a whole year's work. Dad told a story that one year they run cattle and they had them up in East Maroon. That's where they run the summer cattle. It was kind of a dry year and they didn't have snow. St. Patty's Day it started snowing and it snowed three or four feet and it took them three days with horses to break trail to get the cattle back down. They brought them back down to the Marolt Ranch. My dad and uncles were about the same age as Teddy Marolt.

Ester Jane Strong
(1865 – 1941)
Courtesy Bud Strong.

My grandfather Strong spent a lot of time in Park City. He was a mine promoter. He'd buy claims. My dad, from the time he got big enough, ran the ranch until he was about thirty years old. Then he moved around 1926. He and my mother moved to Park City. My dad was thirty and my mother was eighteen. That's where they got married. He dated her in Aspen, and my mother's brothers worked for my dad on the ranch. They'd help him put up hay. Uncle Charlie used to help him make peach brandy in the bootleg days. They got the peaches in Grand Junction. One time somebody was shipping peaches from Grand Junction to Denver and they run off the pass road. They dumped a bunch of peaches, so he got all of his peaches for nothing that year.

Dad had a truck and he used to haul potatoes for the farmers and coal up the valley clear down to the coal mines for all the people in town. Then he got into the log business. He did a little bit of logging when he lived up on the ranch.

Martin Luther, William Luther (Martin's brother), Martha Luther, (1883–1952), Charlie Luther (baby). Courtesy Bud Strong.

He would cut some over on the hillside and haul them down with a team of horses to the Koch sawmill. That lumber was used in Aspen — it wasn't shipped out. He cut a lot of logs for Harry Koch, who had the sawmill on the back of Castle Creek. At that time Dad didn't have a sawmill. He just logged.

One summer he sold the logs to the sawmill, but Harry Koch went back to Europe for the summer. Dad piled up about 180,000 feet of timber at the yards. He couldn't get paid until Harry Koch come back from Europe. This had to be in the 1920s. The Koch sawmill was right on the edge of Castle Creek, right across from the old lixiviation works. Dad logged and sold a lot to Koch, and he also sold timber to Dorothy Shaw and Bill Shaw. They were all in the same grade at school together. I think my dad got into the sawmill business in about 1936 — Strong Lumber Company. Dorothy Shaw sold coal out of her dad's lumber company in the 1930s.

Dad had a lot of stories. He ran bootleg clear up to Wyoming and Grand Junction and to all parts of the Western Slope. He made all kinds of different hooch out of all sorts of things — potatoes, peaches, and such.

I went to Washington School when we lived in town. The whole family was born in Aspen. My dad and mom lived on Riverside past the Cooper Bridge for quite a few years. The Sullivans and Harringtons lived there. They were all good friends of my dad — all Riverside Irishmen. That's where my dad and uncle were born.

When I was growing up in the 1930s and 1940s, there were still a lot of old-timers around there — Billy Zaugg, Shaw, Koch, Old Man Caparella, Jimmy Buckshot. They all spent a lot of time at the Eagles — get together and play cards and all that kind of stuff. They'd talk about the old mining days. It was just so great being able to know everybody. I've always regretted that I didn't talk to my grandfather more about his life. My grandfather liked to talk, too. That was the problem. He'd get you in the corner and we didn't like that — we'd run away.

John Strong hauling lumber, 1947. Courtesy Bud Strong.

After high school I started logging. I started at the sawmill — Strong Lumber. I just gave it to my kid George here a year ago. My children's names are Peggy, Becky, Tina, George, and Bonnie. It's still Strong Lumber, down here in Carbondale. In the Thirties, I was skidding logs when I was fourteen years old up in Lincoln Gulch. The first sawmill Dad had was in 1936 when the Twin Lakes tunnel went in. He had a sawmill up there to cut timbers when they put in the tunnel. Actually, the sawmill belonged to Emery Arbaney, Bucky Arbaney's dad. When they got through the tunnel in 1936, the horses run away with a load of logs on Dad. The wagon run over his back and broke his tailbone. He was laid up for quite awhile. He was forty years old. When they got through with that job, Dad bought that sawmill and set it up in Lincoln Gulch. He had it up there from 1936 to 1940. When he moved it out of there, he moved it to town to 900 Hopkins, right where Mom and Dad's house was. He had a sawmill in town for a long time.

When I got out of the service, Ed Tekoucich (Peanuts) had a sawmill over on Basalt Mountain. I bought that sawmill off of him and I set it up on the Marolt's ranch. I kept it there until about 1953 or 1954 and then moved it over on Smuggler, where the Smuggler trailer court is now. Me and my brother Mick had it until 1960. Then we moved the sawmill from there to Meredith up the Frying Pan before they put in the dam in the early sixties. We logged up there for a couple of years. Then I moved it to Carbondale. I sawmilled for forty-five years.

We started the fire district in 1952. I was a fireman long before they started the district. I was a fireman twenty-one years. I retired in 1973. We just had an old army truck to start with, and then we finally got the old FWD. We started a district and acquired some tax money, firetrucks, and a firehouse. I'm number-one badge in the Aspen Fire Department.

What did we have that Aspen doesn't have now? Everybody knew everybody, and they were friendly. They were concerned. If somebody would get down, they'd help. The town took care of its own. Midnight Mine was probably the only payroll at the time in the town to speak of. There were a lot of old-age pensioners.

Would I ever want to move back? Never. If they'd clear the town I would. I don't mind it so much anymore. But my version of Aspen is it's just a bucket of worms. Let them have it, if that's what they want. They're the ones doing it. My favorite years in Aspen were all the way through, clear up to 1950. You knew everybody and then people started coming. Even in 1950 you still knew most of the people.

When I was a kid, Aspen had 300 or 400 people. We knew everybody in town. Everybody knew everybody — the Loushins, the Maddalones. If I could pick a favorite year it would be probably before I even got there. It wasn't until World War II that Aspen really started to change. My dad bought a half block for taxes right across from where City Market is now. There was an old house that he tore down for the hardwood floors and the windows. He bought it for fifteen dollars. After that he let the taxes go — never paid any more. When we lived in Aspen, we lived at 800 Hyman for a long time before we moved over to 900 Hopkins and built a house in 1947 — that old log house they tried to preserve. It sold a couple of years ago. They moved it down by the Slaughterhouse Bridge.

Aspen right now? I don't like the direction they're going. They're getting so exclusive. Everybody wants a part of Aspen, and nobody wants anybody else to have any. There are getting to be so many homeowners that don't live there. They're not concerned with how it's going and could care less. What's the attraction to Aspen? God, it's beautiful. You can never look back, but we thought we were in hog heaven. We had everything. We had nothing, but we thought we had everything. We always had plenty to eat. We lived on buckskin and potatoes. We were seven kids plus Dad and Mom, and always had a couple of saw hands eat at our table. Dad always traded lumber and slabs to the farmers for a case of eggs or half a beef, pork, or whatever. Nobody had any money, so you had to trade.

✦

Ed enjoyed talking about a lot of the old scoundrels in town. I think Ed was a bit of a scamp himself. I really liked him, and I was sad at his passing.

Ed Tekoucich
(January 1, 1910 – December 21, 1991)

I was born January 1, 1910, in Aspen. My father's name was Joseph Tekoucich, and my mother's name was Lena Skriner. I was born in a house in the East End. I was the third child of eight children. My brother George (Buttons) was the youngest. My sister Frances died when she was nine of appendicitis. My mother was born in Aspen too. Her dad was a miner like all the rest of them — my dad, too. She was a housekeeper. I imagine my folks met in Aspen.

Dad was born in Yugoslavia. Gosh, he must have come around the early 1900s. He was in his twenties. But he wasn't really a hardrock miner — he was a coal miner. He worked in the coal mines in Austria and Yugoslavia. He worked in all of the mines here — the Smuggler, Durant and that was just one big conglomeration. He worked everywhere. Dad must have been about twenty-five when he married my mother. She was about ten years younger than my dad. She was around fifteen or sixteen years old.

Up Castle Creek Road on the right was my family's homestead. There are still some coke ovens up there hidden in the Aspen trees. Way back then, they were trying to make coke for fuel. What the heck. They turned that coal into coke. You could go down to the lumber yard and get that coal. All they do is take the ash out of it and it's darn near straight gas, you know. It comes in chunks. Some outfit thought they were going to get rich up there. That grove was nothing but aspen trees, and this outfit was going to build ovens, and they were going to roast the moisture out of those green trees. They called it charcoal. It was really good if you'd throw it in a fire. It would burn for a long, long time and put out a lot of heat. They never got rich. Some guys would come up there and fire those ovens up, but they never did get anything out of it. Later on we kept animals in the coke ovens in the winter.

My dad, Joseph Tekoucich, all he ever done was mine. He started in the coal mines down at Redstone. My parents homesteaded and I grew up in Castle Creek. We used to move to town in the fall when it was time to go to school, and then we would move back up in the summertime. We had an old broken-down saddle horse and a team of horses. Mother had a big vegetable garden. We had pigs. That was the first thing we'd do in the springtime — get a couple of pigs. We'd feed them all summer long. I'd go out and chop alfalfa for them. We would always have plenty of oats and potatoes. We'd cook them up and feed them to the hogs. Oh, we had a pretty good life. The only thing that was rough was walking miles to school every day and back at night. But I don't know, I was young then — I would run most of the way.

When we were kids, on Halloween I was one of the worst ones. Oh, we would go around ringing doorbells and then hide. When they would come out, we'd scare them. They used to call the cops on us. But they never did catch us. A guy by the name of Charlie Wagner was the city marshall, and he was an ornery old son of a gun. He didn't hesitate a bit to grab you and take you to jail. We were mischief to destruction.

John Litchfield's
Red Onion, 1947.
Courtesy Jennie Popish.

As I got older, my first job was working in a sawmill — Harry Koch's Lumber Company in them days, but it's out of business now. I went to work there when I was fourteen. I worked in the sawmill carrying lumber and stacking it. I didn't get too close to the saw. After I worked there a couple of years, I got promoted to shaving off logs — you know, riding that carriage back and forth. Dangerous job. I had a lever. I had to pull it in order to push the log over into the saw whatever thickness was ordered. People got hurt sometimes. They had a pit down under the saw for the sawdust. They had a blower in there that blew the sawdust out in a pile. I don't know what happened to this one guy — he forgot what he was doing, I guess. He had this long stick and he was poking those chips out of the blower. The saw hooked the stick and it hit him alongside the head. Gawd, he was unconscious for a week. He lived, but he lost his hearing over it. Broke his ear-drums, you know.

At one time, I had my own sawmill. Didn't have any name. It was just a sawmill. I had it up on the flat tops. Forest service built a road in there and it wasn't much of a road. It was pretty expensive hauling that lumber out of there. I had a contract with some guys that had a finishing outfit, to finish the lumber. I starved to death on that deal.

When I got married, I was old enough to know better. I was pretty old when I got married. I was pushing forty. I married Mable Caparella. She was born in Aspen, too.

I owned the Red Onion for awhile. I bought it about 1940 from Tim Kelleher. I paid $2,000 for it, I think. I didn't own it very long — about six months. Nearly killed me. For one thing, all I could sell was beer and wine. So I applied for a hard liquor license and they turned me down. I says, "That's it." So I sold it to Johnny Lichfield. He went broke. I got my money before I'd let him move in. I hated having the Red Onion. It was the most demanding job I have ever seen. I had to be there all the time and listen to that old crap, over and over and over. I was the bartender. Oh, I seen a lot of fights. After they'd break up the bar, we had to fix it.

I also worked for the Ski Company, damn near fifty years. I worked with Ray Bates. That was a nightmare putting in those first lifts. There was dozens of them — Buttermilk, Snowmass, Aspen. Anytime they wanted a lift built, here they would come-a-running. But it was good money. Anything can happen when you are building lifts if you got a bunch of dingbats working for you.

I've seen Aspen change, but if I could pick a year that I would stop Aspen from changing, I don't know. That's a hard one. I think it is better now than it was fifty years ago. That's about all I can say for it.

◆

George is just full of the devil. I could tell that if I had known him when he was younger, he probably would have broken my heart.

George Tekoucich

 I was born February 22, 1919. They say I was born up by the coke ovens, up Castle Creek. People were making coke at those coke ovens. I really don't know who was doing it. It must have been around the time I was born or before. I think they were all finished when my dad homesteaded. Made the coke out of the trees around there. Later they got to making the coke out of coal. I think that's when they went out of business.

Mother's name was Lena Skriner and my father was Joe. I didn't know him. I was only six months old when he died. I was the last child. He died from that flu. A lot of people died at that time. There was another sister, I think, that died. She wasn't very old. She would have been the oldest child. There were eight kids altogether in the family. That includes the girl that died.

After my father died, the family moved to town from Castle Creek down by old grandma and grandpa's place. It was right at the foot of the hill by the Koch Lumber Company. Jimmy Gerbaz is living there now. They had a house right across the tracks from the Koch Lumber Company.

Mother was born in Leadville, and I believe Dad came from Yugoslavia. I don't know where they met. I think my mother's parents were in Leadville when Aspen was booming. They come from the old country. My mother's maiden name was Skriner.

I think my first job in Aspen as a kid was working at the Koch sawmill. I wasn't very old — about fourteen or fifteen. We just had to go across the tracks to go to work. There wasn't much mining around there then when we were growing up. All the mines were down. That was about the only work available. We worked on the farms over at Marolts. Picked potatoes and everything. I think that was about the only time we ever worked on a ranch. Later on I messed around, and then just before the war I worked in Leadville. We built a mill up there, up in California Gulch. They used to have a bunch of mines around there and were building a mill to run those dumps through for gold and silver. They had gold up there at one time.

On Halloween when we were little we went around and marked the windows up and turned over outhouses. There was no trick-or-treat then. Nobody had nothing to give you.

When I first went in the service, I was at Camp Roberts, California. Then I went up to Fort Lewis, Washington. That's where they started up the fighting Tenth Mountain Division. I was in the Tenth Mountain Division. We were trained as mountain infantry. Then we went to Italy, and I never did see any snow over there. I guess some of them did. We were mostly down in the Pyrenees, before you went into the Po Valley. Then we crossed the Po Valley and then went into the Alps.

We went up to the Aleutian Islands first — Kiska Cat. There was Japs on the other island the year before that. Japs gave them an awful beating because you couldn't see anything, couldn't hear anything. The fog came in so thick. Some of us landed up in the northern part of the island, some in the southern part, and we figured there was ten thousand Japs on the island and we were

*Tenth Mountain
Division on Main Street,
Aspen, 1943.
Courtesy
Robert Zupancis.*

going to push them in and get them. We got there and there were no Japs on the island. They took off in submarines. All their stuff was there. But they threw all their guns and everything in there and burned them up before they left. We were unloading these boats after we seen there was no Japs there. They brought all this food in, and the alcohol was for the medics — five-gallon cans of grain alcohol. That's pure alcohol, one-hundred and eighty proof. They would bring the ships in as far as they could, then they had the barges. These flat bottoms would come right up to shore. They told us to unload the barges. And the alcohol. Needless to say, they were missing a lot of alcohol.

I wound up in Butte, Montana, for two months before I came back to Aspen. I come back to Aspen in 1946. I was about twenty-eight. I got married to Pepper, and we had three children. Aspen started changing just after the war. That's when they started the skiing up. They just had Roch Run first. After the war, they started making more trails, put up the lift, and the Sun Deck. I worked on the Sun Deck. I helped build it. I worked for the Aspen Skiing Company. After that we cut trails. Then I left there, and that's when we went into the sawmill. My brother Ed had a sawmill up on Basalt Mountain. We went up in trucks and stuff. Ed and Russell Holmes had it. We all worked there — me, Leo, Ed, and Russell. Had them coming and going all the time. We worked up there about two years. Pepper was there, too. She was cooking for a while. She left and then I left. We left because there was nothing to eat! They went to town for a few hours and didn't come back for a week and left our eldest daughter, Pepper, and I together up there with nothing to eat — macaroni, canned milk, and cheese. I don't know exactly whatever happened to the business. We couldn't get any help there towards the end. We'd get them guys around there that were mostly drunks. They stayed a few days and then they would take off and wouldn't come back. I think old Joe Sawyer was up there for a little one summer. We had the sawmill in 1947 and 1948. I got out of the army just before that in 1945. I never went back to Aspen Mountain.

I never wore a coat all winter because I didn't have one. Did I wear gloves? I don't think so. The most fun years skiing for me were the early times. I never did go up on the lift or any of them after they was built. I skied the old boat tow and we used to walk up. I used skis from some outfit in Denver called Griswald.

I never hurt myself, not really. I hit a tree up there one day and tore the boot right off my foot. I saw that I was going to hit it so I started to fall the other way. My right foot caught the quakies, and when it caught the tree, why I kept going and the ski and boot stayed there. Sock was still in there, too. I landed down the hill about fifty feet. I just went straight through the air. Didn't break my leg. I don't know how. The old skis we had then had just binders — the old spring in the back and the deals in the front. They called them Bear Paw. No way of getting out of them. You just stayed with them. I went back up. Old Charley Grover was there. He was on patrol. All there was then of the ski patrol was two guys. Old Charley come down and he said, "What happened?" I said, "I don't know what happened." We looked around and I didn't see the ski or the boot. I thought I pulled my foot off. I reached down and grabbed it to make sure. Then I saw my boot up there, and Charley went up and got it. I just put it back on — stuck my foot in there. I skied back down the road. You understand I was a good racer? Yeah. I skied on my head more than I did my feet. Yeah, they had some races. Leo and I won a few — won a few and lost a few. When did I quit racing? After they put the lift in — too many people.

Later on, we went over to Lenado. The streets of Lenado. That must have been around 1950. We stayed up there about three years. They brought the school bus up there. They plowed out the road, then the bus came as far as the sawmill. We lived above the sawmill about half a mile. I was cutting timber. There was quite a bit of game up there at that time. I never seen no wolves around. Once in awhile you might see a bear. Mostly all the people at Lenado worked at the mill. I liked living up in Lenado. After three years, we moved to Glenwood. Never did go back to Aspen. Just didn't really care about it when it started building up.

I think I would have stopped Aspen from growing just before they started building it up. The Thirties were the best time. If I could give any advice to Aspen now? There are too many people there now, too much activity. It's too fast. I used to work and stay up there during the week — me and another fellow. We had some cabins up on top of Larkspur and up in there. Stayed in some old two-by-four cabins. Like to froze to death. Am I a real lumberjack? Oh yeah. That's about all I ever did — that and the mines. I worked around Aspen at the Smuggler and the Durant. That was after the war. Did I like mining? It was just about as good as anything.

✦

Photo by Kathy Daily

Sina May "Pepper" Tekoucich

I was born January 14, 1925, at St. Mary's in Grand Junction. My mother's name was Sina Eliza Parsons. She was born in Cripple Creek. My father, William E. Pepper, was born in Denver. We moved to Aspen in 1938 from Los Angeles when I was eleven. Aspen was very different for me. Most of the Aspen children had never seen an elevator, or an escalator, and I'd never seen cows. Saw only one cow that the Pet Milk Company brought around to the school in California.

Opening Independence Pass, avalanche clearing, June 1, 1926. Courtesy Warren Conner.

They milked the cow so we could watch. None of us kids would drink milk for at least a year after that.

I had seen snow before at Bear Lake in California. My father was a chef and apprenticed at the Brown Palace in Denver for thirteen years. He was also a CPA. He worked for Morey Mercantile for many years. My Grandpa Pepper was a Methodist minister in Glenwood for a long time and he rode the circuit clear to Parachute.

When my stepfather, Roy Curry, died in Los Angeles, my Uncle John Parsons came out to California from Aspen to get us and helped Momma sell the property and stuff. He lived in Aspen right at the foot of the pass, and that's where we ended up. John I. Parsons was a brick mason. He built most all of the fireplaces as far away as Norrie — some even over in Denver. My mother sometime later married Ole Miller Mikkelsen.

Uncle John built the parapets up on Independence Pass. He came to Aspen when he was very young. He and Aunt Jane were born in Muncie, Kansas. My grandfather was a stonemason also. Two of my uncles apprenticed to Uncle John. He traveled the whole state and got his own stone. He and Aunt Kate had no children. He leased from the railroad what we used to call Sully's Pond (by Crestahaus Lodge now) right below our house for my friends and I to swim in.

Tough People, Hard Times

Pepper was my maiden name. My given name is Sina May. People started calling me Pepper when we came here. It was easier than Sina May. When George and I got married, I got four "Monkey" Ward catalogs, all in a different name. Did they spell Tekoucich right? Very seldom; even now they don't.

My school days in Aspen were great. We had a good time. It was fun. Lots of the kids were allowed to work, go pick spuds, and babysit. Uncle John bought me a pinto pony. I can't remember what I called him. I only had him about ten days. He bucked me off in front of the Isis Theater, so my uncle took him back to the rancher.

My first real job was at the Jerome Hotel. I wasn't quite eighteen. I think I went in the summer that I graduated. Anyway, Connie — I don't remember his last name, but he was an old Irishman — he was the liquor inspector. I was back of the bar when he came in, and the first thing he asked me was, "Would you give me a drink, please?" I said, "No, but I'll sell you one." That was my first job in 1942. I dearly loved it. Women bartenders? Oh yes. There's one over here in Glenwood at the nursing home from Aspen. She's been there about a month. You didn't see them all over then like you do now.

Bartending? Well, it seemed at times that it was just like a big living room at home. The funniest thing — well, it wasn't really funny, but everybody in town laughed but me. Laurence Elisha was good about checks. This gentleman came in all cleaned up nice and everything and gave me a check for five dollars. That was a lot of money in those days. I gave him the change and he thanked me politely and left. I had the morning shift, and when I got to work, Laurence came in and said, "You've got five dollars, do you?" And I said, "Not right now; I'll have it pay day. Why?" He said, "You owe me five dollars." And he just laughed and laughed. Laurence read the signature. The man was a known forger, and Laurence didn't even take the check to the bank.

People would come in to the Jerome for a sandwich or such around 1:30 or 2:00. When the miners came off shift it was lively, but they were all good men. We had no trouble. I worked there, I can't remember just how long, but they were very good to me. As I recall, I lived there for several months.

I met George, my husband, the day his grandfather was buried in 1938. When my mother and I went into Aspen, our car broke down. We had a flat tire right at the end of Maroon Creek Bridge. Billy Mautz was sitting on one of the abutments on the bridge and so he came over; we didn't have to go and ask. He came over and he said, "Can I help you?" Momma told him that she was John I. Parson's niece and this was his grand-niece and we were going to live in Aspen. Mautz's cabins were right kittywompas from Uncle John's house. Jenkinsons

503

lived in the house across the way. He got the tire, got us into town, and that's how we arrived.

In the course of all this, there was a real good-looking guy walking across the street. This was down by Magnifico's. I said, "Who's that in that black suit? What's he wearing that suit for this time of day?"

"Well, that's George Tekoucich. He's coming from his grandfather's funeral."

That's the first time I ever saw him. When Uncle John finally allowed me to go roller skating at the Armory Hall, there was this beautiful skater — George. He skated just like he skied.

Did I ever call George Buttons? I did then. I can't recall when I stopped. His family didn't call him that. His brother Ed would call him that but his other brother Leo didn't. Leo called him George. When I asked people why they called him Buttons, everybody told me something different. The only one that I came to believe was Eddie Gregorich. They played baseball together. George would pitch. Eddie told me that the reason George was called that was it's because when he pitched ball, he would pull back and all the buttons would pop off his shirt.

George and I married in 1945. We had three daughters, Linda, Suzy Joe, and Jorgeann. My first child, Laurie Lee, was by my first marriage. She died when she was eleven of cerebral palsy.

Aspen started changing somewhere around 1945. My favorite years were the early ones. Svea and Laurence Elisha, all through the Depression, still had the best of everything — the whiskey and all that. I don't know who it was who developed the "Cruds," but we could use all the drop shipments. The cruds were a mixture of ice cream and brandy. You had to get so much brandy and rum before you could get a case of whiskey. Those were the days we had to stamp it by hand. George and I left Aspen in 1953.

It seems to me that Aspen now needs an influx of working people — some people with their feet on the ground. The town would benefit from this.

◆

Photo by Kathy Daily

*Arthur is a big Italian
cowboy — very friendly.
He's a good fisherman.*

Arthur Trentaz

I was born October 10, 1911, in Aspen. My dad came to Aspen from Italy in 1907. He had lived in the Aosta Valley in Italy. Dad liked this area, went back to Italy, and married my mother. Then they came to Aspen in 1910. My father's name was Severin Trentaz, and my mother's name was Sesarine Trentaz. Her maiden name was also Trentaz — I guess that was a common name in Italy. I think this Aspen area is very similar to the Aosta Valley near the Swiss border.

Nino Trentaz with a
bull stacker,
in Starwood, 1928.
Courtesy Arthur
Trentaz.

My dad bought Starwood in 1927 for $11,000 (Dad had worked in the mines until then and didn't want my brother and me to work in them, too). There were nearly 1,000 acres. Of course, it wasn't called Starwood then. We bought the original place where the Bandar house is now for $10,000, and then $3,000 was a later buy. That area is where a lot of the houses are on Starwood now. That was a separate ranch. It used to be the Gavin Ranch.

My dad built that irrigation ditch on Red Mountain. One of those ditches on Red Mountain is called the Trentaz Ditch, and one is the Red Mountain Ditch. He dug it with a pick and shovel. In those days, they didn't have backhoes and things like that. It was a steep hillside with scrub oak on it, and it was all hand work — they worked hard.

We saw some hard times in Aspen. We went through the Depression. We bought Starwood during those times. We raised potatoes and sold them for twenty-five and thirty cents a hundred, and it was hard going.

Arthur Trentaz with a grain binder, on Trentaz Ranch, Starwood, 1952. Courtesy Arthur Trentaz.

I'll have to tell you the little Christmas story. We were at Starwood, and we didn't have any money with Christmas coming soon. We had an old horse and there was what they called a fox farm right before you climb the hill up Independence. They bought old horses to feed to the foxes. My dad said, "Well, let's bring this old horse up there." They were paying ten dollars for the horses, so I led this horse up. When I got there, they didn't have any money to pay me. They took the horse, and I came home without the ten dollars — two days before Christmas.

I didn't go in the service during the war. We were running the ranch at the time and there was an agricultural exemption. I was supposed to raise more hogs than we had been raising. We had to build new pens and went into the hog business. Then, of course, they had rationing. I was on the rationing board and rationed gas to all these people in the valley, and you made a lot of friends doing that. I can still remember some ranchers used to use so much gas, and we didn't let them have any more. They got their name in a black book.

507

Garfield School on Aspen and Durant Street, East End, 1905. Courtesy Peggy Rowland.

I went to all those schools — they were wooden. There was one school over in the East End (Durant Street and West End Street) they called the Garfield School. That was empty when we came, and then of course the Lincoln School, which is there by what they call the yellow brick now. That was the first one I went to. The other one was just across the street east from the historical museum — the Washington School. That's the one I went to. I lived in the East End, and in those days the kids used to like to play marbles in the spring. That was quite a ways to go for lunch from Washington School. You always had to have a few games of marbles and always got to school late. I played marbles a lot with the former mayor, Mike Garrish.

My dad always made wine. The whole group that came from Aosta, Italy, practically owned every ranch between here and Glenwood at the time. They used to ship in a couple of railroad carloads from California, and these guys would go down and pick up their grapes. They all had stills and made brandy. Grappa is made by using the pulp residue left after making grape wine. The "mash" is run through a still. When making grape wine, nothing is added. The grappa is just another name for brandy. It has a very high alcoholic content.

Once in awhile, the revenue agents would raid, and they'd hide their stills. You'd find stills hidden in the old Salvation Ditch. Gosh, us kids looked under there and saw two or three stills that they used to make their brandy (grappa) with. Every once in awhile they would come and raid the place. We had quite a few bootleggers here that made stuff to sell. It was awful stuff, too.

Things got so bad for awhile, I bought a grocery store on Cooper Street which was almost a full block in length. There was a twelve-room brick apartment in the back of

Arthur Trentaz on Trigger, 1950. Two quarter circle bar brand of the Trentaz Ranch. Courtesy Arthur Trentaz.

it. I bought the whole thing and the land for only fifty dollars. Then we tore it down and hauled the lumber and stuff to our ranch to build cattle sheds. I tore down several houses in Aspen. We never paid more than fifteen or twenty dollars for the land and the house. Things were pretty bad during that one stretch of time.

As for me, the biggest change in Aspen was going from no cars — when we used to come in once a week to get the mail — to now when you can't even find a place to park.

Aspen has changed a lot, and now I'd like the government to get along a little better than they do. It seems like every little thing that comes up has to be a controversy of some kind or another. I think that I'd also like to see Aspen the way it was probably in the 1960s. It has changed quite a lot since then.

✦

Photo by Kathy Daily

Amelia Cullet Trentaz

I was born February 18, 1919, in Aspen in a house on East Hopkins Street. At that time, most women giving birth did not go to the hospital. Arthur (my husband) Trentaz's mother was present and assisted at my birth.

My parents' names were Mary and Fred Cullet. Fred Cullet came to Colorado in the early 1900s from the Aosta Valley in Italy. He farmed in the Roaring

Chokecherry Wine

Pick dark, red, ripe chokecherries and wash.
Measure 1 quart berries and 3 lbs. sugar per gallon of water. Boil water and dissolve sugar in it. Cool to lukewarm. Force berries through a colander to separate from pits — then add to water and sugar. Put in a 50 – 60 degree room to begin fermenting. If it doesn't start fermenting in two days — add some dissolved yeast. After 6 days begin to taste test each day for sweetness. When it has desired taste, then bottle. After bottled, don't seal or cork too tightly for a few days or it will explode.

Fork Valley and near New Castle. Mary Guistat came from the Piedmont Valley in Italy when she was a very young woman — perhaps at age eighteen or so. She was sponsored by an aunt and uncle, Mr. & Mrs. Vidano, at New Castle. She worked for them in a boardinghouse near the Vulcan Mine.

My parents were married May 9, 1918, in Glenwood Springs and immediately went to Maroon Lake to live. Fred was pasturing cattle there for the summer. When the snow and cold came, they moved into Aspen.

I started to school when I was five and one-half years old. My family spoke no English, so I, as many of the children of immigrant families, learned to speak English when we started school.

My life as a child was very simple. We didn't have any toys, and none were expected. We played games with friends such as hide-and-seek and kick-the-can.

In 1927 when I was in second grade, we moved to Glenwood Springs from Aspen, to a ranch at Canyon Creek, eight miles from Glenwood and four miles from New Castle. My father didn't have an automobile. Our belongings were put in a freight car, and the train hauled everything.

Tough People, Hard Times

◆◆◆◆◆◆◆◆◆◆◆◆◆◆◆◆◆◆◆

In 1927, my father bought his first automobile — an open touring car, a Chevrolet. It didn't have glass windows. He didn't know how to drive, and I remember the salesman from the garage spending a couple of hours teaching him.

We went to a one-room country school at Canyon Creek — walked one mile each way. There was one teacher for all eight grades, and she taught each grade all the subjects — reading, penmanship, spelling, arithmetic, geography, English, and history. If we didn't have too much homework to do, we listened to the teacher teaching the other grades and picked up all sorts of information.

Because we lived in the country, a trip to Glenwood Springs once a week for groceries was a treat. We were each given a nickel, and we usually had an ice cream cone. We raised almost all our own food. We only bought flour and sugar.

Even though my father had an automobile, we walked everywhere we wanted to go. I joined 4-H when I was nine years old. My first project was sewing. Later projects were foods and home furnishings. I was ten or eleven when I won a trip to the state fair in Pueblo.

Radios were invented in the 1920s. I probably heard my first radio in 1930. Our neighbor had one — you could only hear with use of headphones. If my father wanted to hear a prize fight or something, we drove to a garage in New Castle, where the only radio was located.

My father had several milk cows. He received a large portion of his income from selling milk and cream to the creamery in Glenwood. He got up at five o'clock every morning to milk the cows. The truck that picked up the milk came by around six o'clock. The cows had to be milked again at five o'clock in the evening. Consequently, there was never an overnight trip anywhere. I never learned to milk cows. My father tried to get me to learn, but I was never very good at it — the cows kicked the milk bucket over. Besides that, I was too slow and the cows quit giving milk. The cows didn't like it if the same person didn't milk them all the time.

I worked in the fields. Shocking hay was not a hard job but was really tiresome. We also had to weed the potato fields and weed the garden. We helped pick the vegetables and fruit and helped with the canning.

When I was ready for high school, I either had to go to Glenwood Springs, nine miles away, or to New Castle, four miles away. There was no transportation. My parents had friends in Glenwood that would let me have a room during the school week. My dad drove me in on Monday morning and picked me up after school on Friday. The room was probably very inexpensive, but I had to fix my own meals. My mother sent food with me — some things prepared and others that I had to prepare.

Klabasa

Add about 2/3 fresh pork to 1/3 lean beef. Grind in coarse meat grinder. Add salt, pepper and garlic to taste. Let meat stand overnight in very cool room. Stuff into pork casings. Let stand overnight. Smoke sausage (65 deg. F) Meat will be pink. To serve, boil in water 45 minutes. Serve with potatoes.

Other ingredients may have been used, such as dandelion water.

When we stayed in town, we kept up our homework and had good grades. Sometimes we'd stay up until all hours playing Monopoly. The game came out around 1935. I remember that I read a lot. I checked out library books and would sometimes read a book each evening.

When I got older, I went to college to become a pharmacist, but I didn't finish. After three years, I married Arthur in 1940, moved back to Aspen, and started ranching. We had two children, Fred and Mary Lou.

After the war, when Paepcke came, the skiing started, and you knew things were going to be different. The biggest change is the growth. You have to have growth or you die, but I think the growth could have stopped in at least the mid '70s. It wouldn't have been so bad then. I'd like to see everyone in Aspen have a home — an affordable place to live to help the parents have more time for their children. Children are just being cared for by other people a lot of the time instead of by the parents. They can't afford *not* to work.

◆

Photo by Kathy Daily

*I feel at home in
Barney's kitchen and know
I'm in for a good
chat and a laugh.*

Bernice Vagneur Morrison

I was born December 26, 1927, in the Aspen Hospital. My father's name was
Benjamin Vagneur and my mother was Grace Prindle. We had four children in
our family, Clifford, Eileen, Lucy, and me. My mother's parents came here
probably from Michigan. That's where there was an old settlement. I don't
know much about them. My mother was born and raised in Aspen. I'm a little

in doubt about what her father did. I don't think he was a miner. They lived in town up Mill Street about two or three blocks beyond the Wheeler Opera House. That little house was there until three or four years ago. They built up all around it. It's gone now.

I suppose my mom and dad met at a dance. There was a lot of dancing up and down the valley. My mother was an in-town person, and actually my dad didn't go to high school because the Vagneur sons all were sent to Fort Collins to go to a prep school instead of high school. It included high school and just about a two-year college education. All of the Vagneur sons were sent there instead of going to Aspen High School. My father, Ben, was born 1891. He was born out on the ranch in Woody Creek.

My grandfather, Jeremie Vagneur, was born in 1860. He came over here from Aosta, Italy, in early 1887. He and Estephanie Clavel were married at Doues in 1882. Grandpa Vagneur came over here with a little bit of money he had saved. He came to Woody Creek. Mr. Fred Clavel was a cousin of my grandmother (Clavel came to Aspen in 1884). He wrote my grandfather inviting him to Woody Creek. Grandpa worked for Mr. Clavel for $200 a year plus room, board, and tobacco. After one year, he bought the homestead of Pat Monohan. Later he sent for Grandma and their children. They had five boys, James, Louis, Dellore, Benjamin, my father, and Sullivan.

I grew up on the ranch which is now owned by Carol Craig. Grandpa Vagneur acquired that in 1895 from Charles Hamilton. He built a farmhouse that was essentially two bedrooms — two rooms with two stories. Grandpa was construction superintendent on the Salvation Ditch at that time. When my parents took the ranch over, they added onto the house and made it the size it is now. That must have come about 1923. I think they must have lived early on in something like a homestead cabin.

The order of Vagneur ranches from the top of the valley all the way down? Louis, Dellore, and James bought the Bourg Ranch in 1908. They call it Aspen Valley Ranch now. That was the old Louis Bourg place. Sullivan and my dad (Ben) sort of were in business together. Part of our ranch was on McLain Flats, along with the original on Woody Creek. Grandpa consumed a couple of homesteads to make the ranch as big as it was in my day. But I'm sure that Jim and Louis started off by themselves on what is now Aspen Valley Ranch, undoubtedly funded somewhat by my grandpa.

Then as the other men were married and established, they finally divvied up. Grandpa wanted to retire and get off the ranch. So they decided that my dad was to get the home place. He and Sullivan were in partnership for awhile, but when they decided my dad needed that ranch, Sullivan took the other one and they all got their own at that time.

We raised cattle, potatoes, grain, and of course hay for winter feed. My sister Eileen, by the time I was aware, was sort of forced by custom into the kitchen to cook and help Mama. Well, it stands to reason, she was the oldest. We fed the chickens and picked the eggs. Eileen was excused from the hen house because she was afraid of the feathers. She was a good helper for my mother. The oldest child just automatically took over. I was definitely a tomboy. My sister, Lucy, she was a little bit frail, certainly compared to me, and she was more a housekeeper, too. I was quite a tomboy, and I always liked to be outside on my horse (which wasn't allowed all the time). I had to put forth some effort. Daily chores included chopping firewood and hauling coal for the heating and cooking stoves.

By the time I was twelve, World War II was on and I was a field hand, working every day in the fields. I liked it. I would rather be doing that than what Eileen was doing. It had its perks, you know. Sometimes we drove cattle on the range and I got to ride my horse. The horse part I really liked. I didn't mind raking the hay. The men would harness the horses and have them ready for us. I would hop on back of the work horse and ride clear up on the mesa, hitch my team up, and rake hay all day long. I was about eleven years old then.

We all rode our horse to school. Three of us rode one horse a lot of the time. We never got bucked off. We got thrown off, I mean due to our own inattention or a car coming around the corner, scaring the horse — he would just shy to the right. Our horse would just stand and wait till we got back on.

At that time, I think there were fourteen or fifteen kids in the Woody Creek School. It was a large number because sometimes the people who came to work on the ranches for the summer would be there from September to the middle of October and put their kids in school.

I wore a starched dress to school. My mother would wash it and hang it out on the line to dry. When we brought the dresses in off the line, they were stiff with starch, so my mother would dampen and roll them up so they would get the right consistency. Then she would stand there with hot irons off the coal stove and iron dresses. We had to have two for each of us. We had to wear one every three days. This is the idiotic part of it — we would put a pair of Levis over the dress to ride the horse to school. Here was the dress all wrinkled up after she had spent hours and hours and hours on it. Well, you know, if you were riding on the back with no saddle, your skirt would rub on the sweaty horse. We wore plain black oxfords, or brown. Our feet were freezing by the time we got to school. We had overshoes, just rubber.

There was a shed behind the Woody Creek School for horses. We'd tie the horses in there, and they had no food or water all day long. So when you took the horse out at about 3:30, he was raring to go. We would really have to hold that horse tight until we all got on, then we flew. Eileen had to sit in front so she could hold the horse back. I don't know if you remember that road up to Carol Craig's house, but there is sort of a short corner and then the road is pretty straight from there on out about a half a mile. Sometimes we would let the horse go. Boy, if my dad caught us doing that, he was really mad.

My dad's favorite horse was old Spades until the time he died. Spades was just newly being broke when I was at home. I became attached to him because I wanted to ride the horse that was the latest one broke. No one ever gave me a horse. I never had anything of my own; nobody did. The horse I rode to school was Stardust; he was completely reliable. We had Brownie and a Bill at one time. My father was very much against any horse's names that would portray a bucking bronco. He also wouldn't put up with any kind of wildness in his horses. This was not typical thinking among his peers.

I married George Morrison in 1947. George and his whole family moved out here in 1945. They were going to buy Dellore Vagneur's ranch. They wanted to move to Colorado because George had bad hay fever and asthma in Oklahoma. By the time they planned this move and got it executed, his father was very sick and they thought they would come on out to see if he felt better here. He didn't. He had cancer and died. They got to Aspen at Dellore Vagneur's ranch in December, I think, and by May, his father had died of cancer, so they didn't follow up on their contract to buy that ranch. George went into the army at eighteen. After his father died, his family all went on to Oklahoma and stayed there while George was in the service. In about a year and a half, World War II was over and George was out of the service. The family all moved back here, and that is when they bought the Senator Taylor house in Glenwood and started apartments. George's mother went to work at J.C. Penney.

I met George at a dance at the Armory Hall, probably near Christmas. Was it love at first sight? Yes. We were getting pretty serious by the time he went in the service in May. It was probably in December or January when I met him and he was really pressing his case, so to speak. He had to go to the army, so he said he would be back. He came back two or three times during the year and a half. We got married in 1947.

During World War II, we all grew potatoes for the war, you bet. Every girl was out in the field. We had to work hard. My brother was there because the draft board gave him a farm deferment. They figured if they sent everybody to the service, who was going to raise the crops? It wasn't working. We got three or four dollars for a sack of potatoes. It got that good during the war. It hadn't been that good up until then. Aspen was pretty scarce of men. There was nobody around at that time. There were lots of fellows who weren't able to go to the service who were still there. And boys were coming home on furlough quite a bit. In our family, Clifford was married and then I. He married Kathleen Sloss. Then Eileen married Vic Goodhard. We all appreciated Vic for being jolly and easy to get along with.

How did Eileen get her name, Butch? I don't know. The only thing I ever knew was that Carl Pecjak turned around to her at school one day. He had some nickname he wanted to be called and he said, "You call me that and I'm gonna call you Butch." She had a crush on him so she thought that was real special to be called Butch. My dad just had a fit about that "Butch." All his life that bugged him.

My nickname is Barney. I didn't mind it. I never say anything about it to anybody anymore. About once every six months I run into somebody, "Well hi, Barney," and I think, "Who is that? That's got to be somebody from Aspen." I kind of liked the name. I had an uncle, Jim McKeever, who is my mother's brother-in-law in Grand Junction, and he used to like me for some reason — maybe because I was the youngest of all the kids, cousins, and everybody. I was the baby, and he called me Barney Google, with the goo-goo-googly eyes. He was an Irishman and he liked to sing Irish songs and drink. I suppose I laughed at him and so I became Barney.

If I could stop Aspen in a year, it would probably be just right after World War II, around 1945. The boys came home from the service and it became an upbeat place again.

•

Wayne has the appearance of a tough cowboy, but he has a boy's shy smile.

Wayne Vagneur

I was born October 31, 1929. I was born either on the Woody Creek ranch or in Aspen, but I couldn't really tell you. My first relative to come to Aspen was my Grandad Greener on my mother's side. He came here on a wagon train from Illinois to mine. They tried to come in 1879, but that was the year of the Meeker Massacre. The Indians ran them out. So they actually came in 1880. They didn't like the East because they had the plague and tornadoes back there, so the people all wanted to come West. Most of them came looking for ore. He didn't work in the mines very long. He was the marshall in Aspen in the early days, and then he was the road boss gang when they built Independence Pass. He's buried in Aspen in Red Butte Cemetery. They had three kids, and my mother was the youngest. Her maiden name was Clarice Greener (1898 – 1979).

The first Vagneur to come here was Jeremie Vagneur (1861 – 1950). He came here in the 1880s from D'Aosta Valley. He came here to mine. He was already married and had two of the oldest boys. He came over here to make enough money to send back and bring his wife Estephanie over. He worked up on Aspen Mountain and several different mines. He didn't mine very long and then he took up a homestead where Carol Craig lives up Woody Creek and started farming. He built the house where Carol lives. Two of his children died and are buried up there. There were five children left. He was Catholic.

There are two stories told in my family about my grandfather's brother. Grandpa Jeremie Vagneur had two brothers that helped him develop the homestead way back. The one brother named Battista returned to Aosta and Alcide stayed in Aspen and worked on other ranches. When Alcide had not returned to the ranch, Jeremie heard that a man had been murdered in Basalt. Jeremie was able to identify the belongings of the man as his brother's. They say that Alcide had been camping two miles below Basalt on the Roaring Fork River. The murderer was there also, and they were joined by a third man from a nearby ranch who came there to wash some clothes. After he washed his clothes, he hung them in the trees and sat down to swap stories. The third man returned to his ranch leaving his clothes in the trees. He returned early the next morning and found his clothes missing and a dead man lying there. The night before, Alcide had mentioned that he had some money in his belt. The man from the ranch notified the authorities and the murderer was picked up in Leadville, tried, and got a life sentence.

Now the second story tells an altogether different tale. My grandfather told me that his brother had won a lot of money in a poker game in Basalt. Alcide was going to return to Italy with his winnings. The next morning, he was found dead in bed. They found the murderer with Alcide's clothes and money and hung the guy in the streets of Basalt. That's the story I've always heard.

My father's name was Sullivan (1893 – 1971). In my family, there were Clayton, Glen, Clyde, myself, Leroy, and one sister, Claire. There were seven, but Jack died. He had a ruptured appendix when he was about fourteen. Dad had all brothers. My uncles' names were Jim, Dellore, Louis, Sullivan, and Ben. They all stayed in farming.

The Home Place was Craig's ranch, and they owned part of the mesa on McLain Flats. That was originally a different ranch called the McCormick Ranch. Jim and Louis and Dellore owned all that together. When they made the big shuffle, Jim and Louis moved off and bought out the Bergs, where Mary Jane Underwood is now. Then my dad bought the Little Woody Creek place from a man named Al Gray, and he took a little piece of the Berg place to go with his own ranch. They split it up where they all had equal acreage. Vagneurs owned from where Mary Jane Underwood is all the way up, except the Little Woody Creek was owned by the Arlians. All the Vagneur boys got along when they had ranches all next to each other. They pooled cattle. They took the cattle to Woody Creek. There was a store and a stockyard-loading station there. They just ran them down and loaded them out when they got ready to ship them.

On our ranch we raised potatoes, cows, and pigs. We sold some. My fondest memories of growing up on the ranch were the fishing and hunting. My first chores were milking cows, and I started around the age of six. It takes a couple of years to learn how. We used what milk we could and the rest we separated into cream. All the farmers shipped cream to a creamery for their butter and egg money.

I went to the Woody Creek School until the eighth grade and then to Aspen for high school. I walked to school. It was only half a mile. The kids that were farther away rode horses. In the winter, we wore shoes and overshoes. The Woody Creek School had kids from the first to the eighth grade and one teacher to teach them all. We had different teachers almost every year. Some of them stayed on about two years. Some of them were real good, and some of them were real poor. We had about fifteen to thirty-five kids in the school at different times. The Arlians were there, the Cerises, and the Granges. The school was just a frame building. It had one long room with seats in it, and then it had another little room on the side that had a little library cupboard, coat racks, and a place to put your lunches and stuff.

Did we ever skip school? Of course! When we skipped school, we went fishing and picnicking. We never hopped the train to Glenwood, because the conductor on the railroad knew better than that. He was already wised up.

The houses weren't big enough for all the Vagneurs to get together at Christmas time. Usually we would go to one house or another. Two families would get together sometimes. Christmas was a big deal. Getting a new sled was a big deal — sometimes a .22 rifle. That was the big event of the year. I was the next to the youngest boy. Leroy was the youngest. We had a big house. When we were little, there were usually two boys to a bed. There was lots of fighting going on. My dad was a boxer, so he'd try to teach us how to box. We started

*Jeremie and Estephanie
Clavel Vagneur,
about 1910,
with Dellore, Ben, Jim,
Louis, and Sullivan.
Courtesy Wayne
Vagneur.*

sparring with different ones and somebody always got mad and then the fight was on. Dad learned how to box in college. He went to college at Colorado A&M in Fort Collins. He studied agriculture.

Growing up on the ranch, we never went to Aspen very much in those days. My mother did the shopping. I had an aunt and uncle on my mother's side that lived in Aspen. She was a Greener and she married Charlie Gavin. His boy's name was Wilbur Gavin. We'd go to town and we'd play with him and the kids that were around.

My family was on the ranch we bought from Al Gray. My dad died there. He never moved off the ranch. I sold our ranch five or six years ago, in 1988. I was sad in a way to leave.

I met Lois in the Red Onion. We went dancing. I have two girls, and she has one girl. Mine are Laurie and Julie, and her daughter's name is Belinda. We didn't have any kids together.

✦✦✦✦✦✦✦✦✦✦✦✦✦✦✦

I team rope at the Snowmass Rodeo grounds now. Team roping is two on a cow. One ropes the horns and turns them, and the other one ropes the heels. You just turn, face, and stretch them. Everybody ropes with everybody else.

I noticed Aspen changing when they put in the lift in 1947. Then, in the Fifties, it started changing. It was still a pretty nice, friendly town until the late 1970s. Aspen is just not a real friendly place anymore.

✦

Photo by Kathy Daily

When I was with Ann, I felt as if I were in the presence of grace. Her maiden name was Devine and that she certainly was.

Ann Devine Wieben
(May 18, 1905 – January 31, 1993)

I was born May 18, 1905, in Aspen. My aunt, Teresa Lundy, and my uncle, Felix Kinney, came to Aspen first in my family. My Uncle Felix came from Ireland in about 1883. He lived in Ashcroft before Aspen. He ran the post office and the grocery store in Ashcroft when it was a good town, years and years ago; it was

525

*Cooper Avenue looking
west, about 1905.
Courtesy Peggy Rowland.*

booming then. I think there were about 3,500 people up there at one time. You wouldn't hardly believe it, but I guess that's right. I don't know — that was before my time.

My aunt, Teresa Lundy, came from Ireland to Colorado when she was thirteen. She came all by herself to Iowa because she had an uncle that lived there. Her uncle had a daughter who had tuberculosis. They heard about this sanitarium in Colorado Springs and wanted to send their daughter. They got my aunt to go with her, and so she came and stayed in Colorado Springs for a short time. She soon got acquainted with some other young people that were going to go to Aspen to get work. It was before 1900 when she came. She came over to Aspen and worked here for a long time. She kept house and she cooked. She was a super cook. She met and married Felix Kinney in Aspen.

My mother, Catherine Lundy, stayed with her own mother and father in Ireland until they both passed away. She and my aunt were probably the only girls. There were nine in the family, but I only knew one uncle. So when my mother came over to live with my aunt, I don't know whether she worked or not. She stayed with my aunt and uncle.

People proved on the mines before they could obtain a patent. My Uncle Kinney had one close to town that wasn't patented yet. I can remember we went up about a month every year and he worked on it. He had to do what he called assessment work, just like he had patented the other ones. He had three or four others that were already patented.

My uncle had people work for him in Ashcroft. He had men that brought his groceries and supplies over from Crested Butte. He had the grocery store, and in March, when there was lots of snow — when it had gotten hard and crusted — he sent two men with a jack train. He had thirty-six jacks [donkeys] and he sent them over Pearl Pass on the crust to Crested Butte. There they got all his supplies for his store on those donkeys and then brought them back over. They went in March because it was easier on the donkeys' feet than it would be in rocky summertime. He generally sent two men with thirty-six donkeys. Of course, they followed one another — they're no problem. But it was a hazardous trip. Once in awhile he'd lose a man. He'd freeze to death or something. Some came back with a frozen foot or a frozen hand. He had a hard time finding people that would go. Of course, they were all tough and rugged people in those days. They had to camp along the way one night, I know. It isn't too terribly far from Ashcroft up to Pearl Pass. When Ashcroft was dying down, he moved to Aspen. He just left his property in Ashcroft.

I don't know when my uncle came down to Aspen, but he bought up quite a bit of real estate. My uncle and aunt had several houses that they rented out. He was a miner. I was born up there where they had that Aspen Inn, kind of up on that hill — now the Ritz. Our family had a whole block of five houses. We called it Lawn Street, but I think on the maps it's called Juan. He also had two houses down on Cooper Avenue and another one on Hopkins. He rented those out for fifteen dollars a month furnished. My father, Daniel Devine, came from Ohio, and his family were all educators. My grandfather and grandmother Devine were both teachers. My father's brother was superintendent of schools for years and one of his sisters was a teacher. My Aunt Rose (my father's sister) wanted to get away from her home town. She came out here and got into Woody Creek, and that's where she was teaching — the old Woody Creek

Ashcroft, 1905.
Courtesy Peggy Rowland.

Road to Maroon Bells, 1905.
Courtesy Peggy Rowland.

School. Her name was Rose Devine. And so then my father decided he'd come out and visit her. Now that old Woody Creek School had an extra room on it for a teacher. She could live right in the schoolhouse in the little apartment next to it. This must have been before 1900. My father just had a fit because she was living there by herself and there wasn't too much population around then. Of course, people from back East thought the Indians were running around loose here and fighting. He was thinking maybe his sister should get a replacement for herself and come home.

Then my father heard about the boom in Aspen. I don't really know what he did, but he helped put his brothers and sisters through school — through college and so forth — and so he was less educated than his brothers and sisters. Anyway, he came to Aspen and got in the mines, too. That was in the vicinity of 1895 to 1900.

My mother and father met in church, I think — St. Mary's Catholic Church. My Uncle Kinney helped build the Catholic church in 1889. I don't

Ice-skating at Maroon Lake, December 8, 1938. Courtesy Warren Conner.

know how old my parents were when they got married. I don't think either of them was very young. They probably had children right away. I was the third. Mother was pregnant with another when I was a baby, but she got uranic poisoning and died. It's a kidney disease. She was pregnant, but she wasn't far enough along for the baby to live.

Dad worked, and we lived up close by my Aunt Kinney in one of their houses. My brother, sister, and I all got scarlet fever. Of course, in those days everybody got it. All three of us had it at once, and we were quarantined. Even my father couldn't go to work. He hired a nurse. I don't think she was a trained nurse but a practical nurse to come in and kind of keep house and care for us kids.

The doctor came every day. We had a shed where we kept coal and wood, and the doctor kept a big old coat in there. He put it on over his street clothes before he would come in the house to see us kids because of the germs. My sister and I got over the scarlet fever, but my brother didn't get better. He wasn't too well. I was two and a half and my sister was a little older. I think my brother was eight at the time. He turned up sick with sugar diabetes and, of course, in those days they didn't have insulin. We had a horrible diet — flour and bread (gluten flour) and nothing sweet. He was ten years old when he died.

Then my father was back to work and my sister and myself stayed during the day with my aunt. When my father would come home from work, we would go to our own house. We stayed there overnight and stayed with my aunt during the day. My sister, she had some problems, too. She died when she was fifteen. She got pneumonia. Of course, my father never got over that emphysema or black lung. Dad died when I was ten years old. From then on I lived with my Aunt and Uncle Kinney.

On Halloween when we were young, sometimes we had a pumpkin, sometimes we didn't. We'd have a shoebox and we'd make a face out of it. We'd put a candle up through it and put string on the top to carry, or we'd just carry it as it was. Then we had an empty spool about as big as an apple. On the edge we cut notches to make it all rough around the edge. We would get a string and wind it around the body of the spool and put a nail through the hole. Finally, we'd go up to somebody's window and jerk that string. Oh, it made the terriblest noise you ever heard!

There was an ice cream parlour in the Jerome called the Buffet. It was pretty. They had a nice counter and several little tables. You could get ice cream or ice cream sundaes and set at a table and eat, or you could get ice cream cones. One time there was a man and a woman that got married there across from Conner's station — middle-aged people. All us kids knew them forever, which is why we decided to chivery them. Whenever anybody got married, they expected this. All the kids would get together — go out and make all kinds of racket on their windows and stuff like that. The longer it took them to come out of the house, the worse the kids got. They'd do one thing after another. We was ornery, all of us kids together. It was kind of a tradition. And if they didn't come out (they knew it was coming, because everybody was prepared for it), some of the kids would climb up on the roof and put a gunnysack or something down through the chimney and smoke them out. So then they'd finally come out with a big sack of apples or something for the kids. That's what we used to do. But anyway, that couple, when we did finally get them out, the man was an old family friend of ours. He took all ten or twenty of us up to the Buffet and we could have anything we wanted. Wasn't that nice? Most kids had ice cream cones.

I met my husband, Chris Wieben, when I was in high school. He went to school down here in the country. He was born in Denver and his family moved over here on a ranch in 1912. I met him at a dance. Chris was going with a girl that was teaching country school down at the Lower Capitol Creek School. She was from Aspen, so on Saturdays they would oftentimes go to the dance. The train ran to Aspen, and sometimes he'd come down on the train and meet her. I

Ashcroft, 1920s.
Courtesy
Robert Zupancis.

was sixteen or so. He had a sister in my class in school and we were all friends, and I met him but I didn't pay too much attention.

I really didn't date him until I was teaching school over on Snowmass in about 1925. I taught the Snowmass School — all ages. He come over every once in awhile. He'd ride his horse over sometimes and visit me. We started courting. We courted not quite a year. I was twenty. He was twenty-seven.

I had three children. I lost my first baby. In September, the very first year we were married, I got polio, and I was pregnant. I lost the baby before it was born. There was not a lot of polio in the valley, not really. There were three people that I knew of — three women.

I was bedridden until January. I was in the hospital a couple of weeks and then went home. I thought it would be okay for the baby if I had a wheelchair and had a little girl who could help me, because my hands and arms were fine.

When I first got polio, I had bulbar, but that didn't last too long. Bulbar is when you get polio set right in your neck and sometimes it's fatal. And in your lungs. You can't move. But that only lasted a few hours. When I first realized there was something wrong with me, I couldn't move my arms or anything.

I hired a little German girl. The family had just come over from Germany and they were living over here. They wanted their little girl to go to school; she was ten years old. I said, "Chris, why don't you go over and talk to those people and ask them if we could maybe get that little girl to live with us. We'd send her to school from here." The school was just down the road, you know. So I talked to the county superintendent about it and he said, "Sure, that would be fine". So that's what we did.

I went on pregnant clear until March. I thought maybe if I could carry it a little longer, but . . . . Nowadays, if I had been in a hospital, maybe they could have saved the baby, but I lost it. 'Course, I didn't baby myself after I lost the child, and afterward I thought, "Well, now I'm going to see what I can really do." I got so I could get out of bed and get myself dressed between the bed and the wheelchair. Then after I got in the wheelchair, I'd go out in the kitchen to help. That fall, Chris wanted to go to the stock show in Denver, and so he said, "Why don't you come along?" I said, "Well, I would love to see our old family doctor and he's gone to Denver. Maybe we could talk to him and see what he thinks." So Chris said, "Yeah, I thought of that too." He was over selling cattle once before and he talked to some doctor about me and the doc told him, "I don't think there's much hope for her. She'll probably spend the rest of her life in bed." So I thought, "Well, brother." By then I was sitting up in a chair.

So we went to Denver and I had an appointment with this family doctor. He gave me a good examination and I asked if it was safe for me to try to have any more children. He said, "There's not a thing in the world wrong with you for havin' babies." I could feel my legs alright, but they just wouldn't work. For a while I got so I could walk, but not real good; it settled in my spine a lot. Later I could finally walk around.

My first child, Sonny, was born in 1927. I was in my middle twenties. The girl that lived with us — her father, in Germany, was a cabinet maker, a good carpenter, and he made me a baby cradle. He made me a table that had nice shelves on the bottom and the top. I was always afraid of lying the baby down someplace and he'd roll off. He made a little ledge around the top. I put a blanket in it, and that's what I used to bathe and dress him. I've still got that old thing.

I didn't teach again until my middle daughter, Shirley, was in the eighth grade. They couldn't find a teacher for the Upper Capitol Creek School. So the superintendent called me and she said, "Ann, is there any way that you would teach at that school?" So I talked it over with Chris. Shirley didn't like the idea very well. She didn't want her mother teaching her class. So I took the job.

We had cattle and my husband raised grain and hay. We raised chickens. I had a big garden and planted potatoes. When we went to get coffee and sugar, we went up to Aspen, generally at Becks. We didn't trade with Becks, but when we got to going to Glenwood, we had a man down there that we traded with. He bought lambs from us sometimes on trade. He said he got lambs from somebody else, but he said they tasted from the wool. You have to be so careful butchering a lamb. You have to make sure that the wool doesn't touch the meat or it will make it taste bad. It takes two to get the skin off and hold it away from the meat. You just keep rolling it back so that it doesn't touch the meat.

You know they say they now restored Ashcroft? Well, they didn't restore it, because if you move something you're not restoring it, I don't think. They moved our cabin down; you know how they're in a row now down there? With a boardwalk? Well, Ashcroft never had a boardwalk. My Uncle Kinney's cabin is still in there. It's still there, but it's down with that row of cabins. They moved it. I think they put new roofs on some of them. The jail is still there across the road.

I never get to Aspen now, not if I can help it. Oh my stars, it's been changing. After Mr. Paepcke got to Aspen, why it went downhill ever since to my notion. It isn't Aspen to me at all, the way they've built up everything. There's just no town to it. It's just a — I don't know what you'd call it. I don't go up there if I can help it. I go to the doctor's office. I go that far and no further.

What would I wish for the town now? Less people. Now don't get me wrong. There are some very nice people up there. Sometimes when we have people visit, we like to take them out to a nice place to eat. There are some nice places up there. But I don't think it could ever be the same. I don't think I'd want it quite as down as it was, but I'd just like to see that element that started this all out.

It used to be that you'd go downtown to the grocery store and you'd meet people on the street. There was very rarely a time that you didn't meet people. There was very rarely a time that you didn't know somebody, and you spoke to everybody. Now, if you speak to some people, they act like you're going to rob them or something. Everybody knew everybody else. Sundays we'd go and visit neighbors. My uncle loved to go fishing and my aunt would fix a lunch and we'd all go. He used to fish up at Stillwater, but mostly up Castle Creek. We'd go with him and sometimes take an extra bucket along because my aunt liked all kinds of wild berries. We'd find some gooseberries and make jelly. Serviceberries — we picked them, too. But they're so seedy inside. My aunt used to cook and strain them. Get just the juice and then put apple with them to make them gel. She used to put some apple to make it like a pectin. Those were good times.

◆

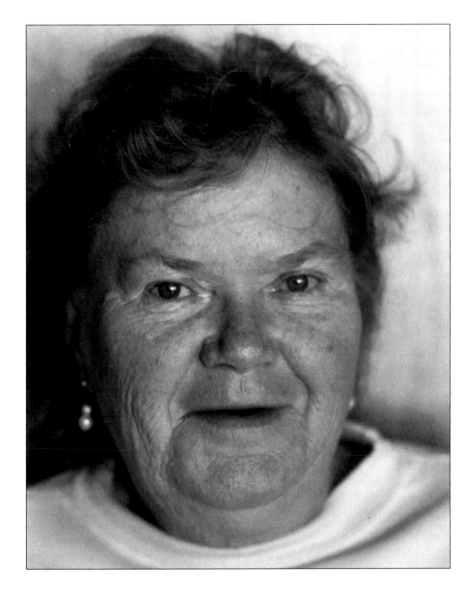

Photo by Kathy Daily

Helen is a hard-working woman and a good grandma. She is a friendly neighbor.

Helen Zelnick Zordel

I was born in Aspen on April 14, 1927. I was born in the house that we all lived in until my mother died — 923 East Cooper Avenue. It was right across the street from Loushin's — right across from that big rock there. In the old days, on the 4th of July, they used to have drilling contests on that big rock.

My mother was born and raised here. Her name was Mary Agnus Oberster. She was born at 816 West Main Street under the trestle bridge on Maroon Creek.

535

Her family came to Aspen from Austria in 1889. Her father, James, worked at the Smuggler Mine and purchased at least two statues in the Catholic Church.

Her mother, Mary Agnes Hochever Oberster, died at age thirty-five from childbirth. The baby twins died a few months later.

Her father later married Agnes Luba, who came from Austria to help the family. They were married December 31, 1901, and had eight children. My mother, Mary, quit school at ten to help out.

Her father, James Oberster, died in early 1913 (age sixty-one), and Agnes Luba Oberster married Anton Kralich later in 1913. This marriage produced five children. From three marriages, mother had twenty-one half-brothers and sisters. Those were hard times. My maiden name was Zelnick. My father's name was Louis Zelnick. His parents died, and then he came over from Austria when he was very young — sixteen — in about 1900. He came on a boat to Ellis Island. From there he went to Pueblo. He knew some friends in Leadville. Afterwards, his older brother came over to help take care of Louis. His brother died shortly after he arrived here. He got sick.

I don't know how my parents met, but they got married when she was sixteen in 1909. He was about eight or nine years older than she was. We had ten children in our family. Baby Gwenivere, the youngest, died when she was just a few months old. They called it "blue babies" then. My mother and dad lived at 923 Cooper Street. They bought the house for taxes. In those days, if there was an empty house, you just moved in. There were ten children in a three-room house. Three of us slept at the top of the bed, a couple at the bottom. There was this empty house next door, so some of them slept over there. Mom was always afraid of fire and would not build a fire in the stove over there. My brothers and sisters got hot tea with a bit of whiskey just before bed along with a hot iron or brick.

I was twenty-four when my dad died — that was in 1951. He was about sixty-seven. He had miner's consumption. In the mine he broke his leg and he had a terrible time. Dr. Twining was his doctor, and it kind of stuck out, so he set it. Later he had to reset it, and he ended up with gangrene. He didn't want his leg off. I'm sure that's how he died. By that time, my mother was on old-age pension. I was still home. My brother and I helped to pay expenses.

For my first job, I worked for the Ski Corporation at the Sun Deck. I was about eighteen or twenty. I didn't ski; I rode the lift up and down the hill. Then I got to know Joan Wright. They owned the Country Store. She and another friend, Maude, we all rode up the lift together. I helped cook and different things. I ended up staying up there to work — came down on weekends. So I slept up there.

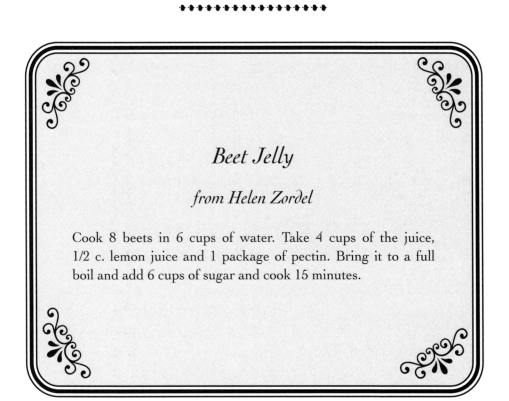

Beet Jelly

from Helen Zordel

Cook 8 beets in 6 cups of water. Take 4 cups of the juice, 1/2 c. lemon juice and 1 package of pectin. Bring it to a full boil and add 6 cups of sugar and cook 15 minutes.

After that, I worked for Joella and Herbert Bayer. He was an abstract painter and worked for the Container Corporation. I did housework for them, and from there, I worked other household jobs and babysat. In 1953, I went to the County and worked in the Treasurer's office. I retired in 1978. I was in there twenty-five years.

My husband's name was Delford. I met him around 1955 at the bowling alley here. I was about twenty-eight. I knew Breezy and Sally Zordel. They lived close to where I lived, and I got to be well acquainted with Sally and we were on the bowling teams together. Delford came from Concha, Oklahoma. His dad worked for the railroad and then they were farmers.

After we were married, we rented a little white house with a picket fence around it. It's that white house on the opposite corner from the Bank of Aspen. We rented it from Mary Vagneur for fifty dollars per month. She was the mother of George and Alice Vagneur. Anyway, we rented from her for awhile, and we asked her later if she would sell it to us, so she did. We bought it for $7,500. There was all this beautiful antique furniture in there.

In fact, we had a fire the first year we were married, on Christmas Eve. We had this little stove in the kitchen. We used it to heat up our water mostly. Del was home that day and made a fire. Then he came over to the courthouse.

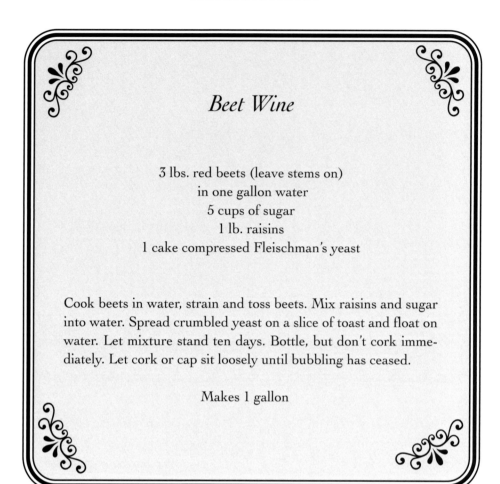

Beet Wine

3 lbs. red beets (leave stems on)
in one gallon water
5 cups of sugar
1 lb. raisins
1 cake compressed Fleischman's yeast

Cook beets in water, strain and toss beets. Mix raisins and sugar into water. Spread crumbled yeast on a slice of toast and float on water. Let mixture stand ten days. Bottle, but don't cork immediately. Let cork or cap sit loosely until bubbling has ceased.

Makes 1 gallon

We had a little party over there. Pretty soon the fire siren rang, and Peggy Coble came running down the hall and she says, "Helen, your house is on fire." And I went, "Oh my God." Here I was pregnant with my first daughter. This was about 1956. Anyway, he forgot to turn the flue down or something. There was water damage more than anything. Kurt Bresnitz, who owned the jewelry store, saw it. We never locked our doors in those days, you know. He saw the fire and called the fire department. The doors were open, so they got in. It wasn't a very good Christmas. Here we had our tree and presents and everything under there. So it mostly had water damage. Anyway, Mary Vagneur had it all fixed up and later on we decided to buy the house. We sold it for $18,500.

Later Del dug up the basement all by hand. Can you imagine? Well, he was supposed to have somebody come and help dig it out. Anyway, they backed out, so we went ahead and started doing it on our own. It took quite awhile. His dad came later and helped pour cement in the basement. I canned and we wanted to put a furnace in — a coal stoker at that time. Did you ever eat beet jelly? It's great; it's delicious.

Del worked for Sardy at the lumberyard. In fact, his brother, Breezy, worked there, too. Del came to Aspen I think in 1949. He lived with Breezy and Sally. We had two girls, Roxanne and Tina.

We used to make blood sausage. You would think it sounds terrible. It is out of the blood from the pig. We would cook the head, and my brother would clean it — that was his job. He would clean it all up, and then we would boil it, and my mother would put some of the skins in from the lard. Then we cooked rice and let it cool, then put our seasonings in. She put a lot of mint in, which would be like peppermint. After all that, we added the pork blood. They would stuff them with the sausage maker. Then Mom would boil them until they were done. You wouldn't believe how good blood sausage is. It just sounds horrible. It was black, after it was cooked. It was black from the blood. My dad would say, "Now you kids watch so you will know how to make this when we're gone, cuz we're not going to be here all the time. You watch how we make this." So we did.

We also made potica. It's kind of a walnut bread. It's wonderful. It's a Slovenian recipe. We usually make that on holidays. It's kind of tradition. It was expensive. But you know, my mother was the best cook there ever was. She used lard in a lot of her frying of meats. It wasn't good for cholesterol, as we know today.

I noticed Aspen changing in the early Fifties after skiing got started. My favorite years were my childhood in Aspen — the 1930s and 1940s. They were hard times, but they were good times, too. Aspen now? Oh, I don't mind it. My kids can't live here because they can't afford homes. Change Aspen now? I guess I'd have less people and cars. I'd hate to leave here. I was born and raised in Aspen, and I'll probably die here.

✦

*Molly is quiet and a bit
shy. It seems as though she
has taken care of people
since she was born.*

Mollie Zelnick Maurin

I was born October 25, 1910, in Aspen. My mother's name was Mary Oberster. She had ten children, and the youngest one died in infancy, so there was nine of us. I was the oldest. Mother was born in Aspen on April 9, 1893. Dad was born in the old country in Austria, close to Ublana.

As a child, my first chores were taking care of kids. To begin with, there were only three rooms in the house. Later there was an addition put on and an upstairs put in. There were four or five kids in each bed, and the oldest boy generally always slept in a bed by himself. The general rule was that one child slept at the foot of the bed. At least we kept warm. Mama made several quilts. She filled them with cotton batting. She actually made the little squares and then made quilts. I don't know how she had time to make all this stuff, because she also raised a big garden with vegetables and potatoes and raised a couple of hogs to butcher. She also made her own grease and made and smoked her own sausage. Mother died September 14, 1978, at the age of eighty-five in Aspen.

I went to the Lincoln School up to the sixth grade and then I went to the Washington School. After you passed the fifth grade, you went to the Washington School. We lived on the East End of town and had to go to Washington School. It was quite a ways to walk. We had to go home, and I'll tell you, we never wasted any time going home, because we had to get back there by one o'clock. At Christmas, we used to put pans under the Christmas tree for Santa Claus to bring us a treat, and the general rule it was candy and nuts.

Dad was one of the last men that worked in the Smuggler. He worked for the company for awhile until it quit, and then he went leasing. Never got much money leasing. He left in the morning and took a little lunch with him and stayed part of the afternoon.

My husband, Kenneth John Maurin, was born October 23, 1910, in Aspen, and I was born on October 25, 1910. So he was only two days older than I. His father was a farmer. We were married December 29, 1935. I was around twenty-five when we got married. We started going together when I was working at the hospital. His appendix ruptured and he was staying there. I helped the nurses, looking after the patients. Some of the old-timers stayed there at the hospital, too. They let them stay there because they didn't have any place to go. It was kind of like a caretaking facility for the older people. That is how come we got started going together. But as far as going together when we were in school, we didn't.

We went to dances. They had the dance hall in the Armory Hall. We had just one boy. John was born September 20, 1937. Kenneth worked on the railroad for awhile and worked for the plumbers, then he worked at the Red Butte Cemetery for a long time — about twenty-two years. He was caretaker out there.

Kenneth's grandfather was John Maurin and came to Pitkin County in 1888. He went up to Woody Creek and worked on the Bourg Ranch, which later became the Jim Vagneur Ranch. He went from the Vagneur Ranch up to Capitol Creek, and there was an old man on a homestead that was willing to trade the whole homestead for one of John Maurin's shotguns. The trade was

Aspen, Colo. from Red Butte.

Cemetery Lane, with cemetery in clump of trees. Courtesy Robert Zupancis.

made, and the family moved to Capitol Creek and remained there. They built a large log house of hand-stripped logs and shingled roof — quite a nice-looking place.

His grandfather died in 1900 and his grandmother and the boys ran the ranch. His grandmother died in 1905. The boys (Albert and John) took over the ranch, with Albert taking full control of the ranch. He also bought the ranch next to them to the north. This new ranch had a better location for the buildings, and the family moved to the new place. Not long before Albert died in 1953, he sold the old home place and the Salsberg homestead to the St. Benedict Monastery. His wife, Lillian, sold the home and ground to some stranger.

John (Kenneth's father) and his brother, Edward Maurin, left their home ranch as young bachelors and bought a ranch about two and one-half miles southeast of the old homestead place. Shortly after they bought the ranch, Ed died.

John Maurin married Sylvia Remseyer and kept the ranch until 1911, when he sold it. He then moved the family to a ranch on Maroon Creek, two and one-half miles southwest of Aspen, now known as the Highland Ski Area. He stayed at this place until 1920, when he sold to the owner of the ranch next-door, rented a house in Aspen for one year, and then bought a house on 300 South 7th Street.

My grandparents (the Obersters) lived in that house, and the Maurins bought it from them. That puts that house in my family and in the Maurins, I suppose. The Maurins worked on ranches and mines around Aspen and Victor, Colorado. They came back to Aspen, went to Park City, worked in the mines, went to Leadville, worked in the mines, and came back to Aspen. John Maurin died at 300 South 7th in 1955. Sylvia kept the home and lived there until she died in 1976. They had one son, Kenneth (my husband). I had the old place and sold it in 1971. So that is his side of the family.

Kenneth went to Lincoln and Washington schools, and he quit school after the eighth grade and went to work on the railroad. He was working for a farmer on December 7, and the Second World War started. The boss's wife came down to the field to tell them that Pearl Harbor was bombed. He then worked for the Forest Service in 1940 planting pine trees on Independence. The seedlings were about three to four inches tall; now they are taller than a man. We planted thousands of them. And he always said that he would sit under the shade of one of those pine trees one day, and he did. He worked in the mines in Aspen and also in Leadville in 1941. He leased in Victor, Colorado, in 1946. He came back to Aspen and worked for the carpenters doing remodeling and was a caretaker of the Red Butte Cemetery for twenty-two years, from 1948 to 1971. He did janitor work for the post office and city hall. He retired in 1974 and moved to Carbondale in the fall of 1981. Kenneth died June 21, 1991, of a heart attack here at home. I still live in Carbondale.

◆

Fritz Benedict and Elizabeth Paepcke
represent the end of the Quiet Years
and the beginning of the age of skiing.
This transition involved many other people
who were also in Aspen at that time,
but this is another book in itself.
The Aspenites who helped build a ski town
were newcomers and old-time locals alike.
Once again, the Aspen community came together
in order to bring economic relief
to their beloved town . . .

Photo by Kathy Daily

*Fritz has kind
and honest eyes
to match his soul.
He really cares
about people.*

Fritz Benedict

I was born in 1914 in Medford, a little town in northern Wisconsin. My father was of English extraction and my mother of German.

The first time I came to Aspen? It's sort of crazy. I won a ski race — I was Arizona's 1941 downhill champion! Because I had won that race, I qualified for the Nationals being held in Aspen in March. I had heard of Aspen from Frank

545

Mechau, an artist living in Redstone who had come to Frank Lloyd Wright's Taliesin West where I was an apprentice. It was crazy for me to enter that race. I wasn't that good, and I had never been on big, high, steep mountains. It took me three days to get up here, by train and hitchhiking. I carried my skis on my back the whole way. I reached Glenwood at night and slept under the bridge.

As is turned out, I broke both of my skis practicing, so I had an excuse to drop out of the race. But Aspen was so great to me those three or four days. I was sort of an imposter, really. I've been trying to get even with Aspen ever since — helping with civic things.

While I was in Aspen in 1941, I stayed at the Waterman cabins. The only other cabins were Sparky Sparovic's east of town, up where Knollwood is. Blaine Bray had built them. The Waterman cabins, no longer there, were on the west end of town where the highway makes the first turn coming into town. Now, there are some big fake Victorians on that block. I ate at the Hotel Jerome — one of two or three places to eat in town. Back then, the Hotel Jerome was just struggling to keep alive. Laurence Elisha and his wife, Svea, were doing most of the work at the hotel, and they only hired four or five people to help run everything. While I was there, Aspen had one of those beautiful March weekends — warm weather, blue sky, and marvelous powder snow everyday. I thought I was in heaven. I knew then that this was where I wanted to live.

As soon as I got back to Wisconsin, I was drafted into the army. I was sent to Camp Hale in 1943, and I came over to Aspen every chance I had. We would check into the Jerome Hotel for a dollar a night. There wasn't any charge to ski because you had to climb up. So in one day we would get just one run down Roch Run, the race course. To ride the boat tow cost about ten cents. That would get you 500 vertical and then you had to climb the rest of the way to the top. Buddies came over with me from Camp Hale to ski, and at night we went to the bars for a drink and singing. There wasn't much wenching. There weren't that many girls.

Camp Hale had the ski school and typical infantry training. We had maneuvers in the mountains and would camp out. In a way, life was easier when we got to Europe, because it was so cold on the maneuvers at Camp Hale. Of course, in northern Italy there were the bullets, but at least we got to stay in farmhouses before we went into action. Although everybody had skis at Camp Hale — all 14,000 of us — they sent very few skis over to Europe. I took one reconnaissance on skis, and there were a few patrols. The war for us was only three or four months, but we saw a lot of action. Our division spearheaded the drive to the Po Valley. People were killed. We sailed to Italy at Christmastime and didn't go into action until February. The war was over in April.

Tough People, Hard Times
✦✦✦✦✦✦✦✦✦✦✦✦✦✦✦✦✦✦✦

After the war, I came to Aspen. When I was at Camp Hale I discovered a small ranch up on Red Mountain and fell in love with it. The owner was Fred Gagnon. I had to sell my car to put a deposit on the ranch, so the first winter I had to walk or ski up and down Red Mountain — my only transportation was a horse-drawn sleigh.

I met my wife, Fabi, in 1948 when she was in Aspen visiting her sister Joella Bayer. I was a bachelor up on Red Mountain. There were guys helping me ranch; I was trying to be a subsistence farmer. Of course, I had a milk cow. I had milked cows as a kid on a dairy farm in Wisconsin. When I bought the ranch, I acquired six horses, a cow, chickens, and a pig. I raised my own grain for the chickens. They didn't lay a lot of eggs and one night, someone stole my pullets.

I was trying to build a dude ranch. The first winter I tore down an old barn that had some good logs. I hitched up the team of horses to drag those logs across the meadow and build a cabin. That was the start of this dude ranch! I actually had tourists come for a couple of years. I fixed up the barn. The loft space was for square dances. We housed the Richard Dyer Bennett School in the barn in 1949. Fabi cooked for the students in return for singing lessons — she had a beautiful voice. The dude ranch operation lost money. We did better renting the two cabins for thirty dollars a month.

The next winter, in 1950, the FIS races were held. Fabi cooked for more than thirty people, so she didn't get to go to the races. After Red Mountain and the dude ranch venture, I built up my architectural office. Fabi steered me into that. She was a big help in my practice. From Red Mountain, we moved into the old Bowman Building where Le Chefs is today. That building was a wreck. People had been stealing windows and doors from it and the back part had fallen in from the weight of snow. We turned the thirty-five rooms into apartments and rented them out to locals. There were seven apartments in the building and the rent was seventy-five dollars a month. Then we rented the space down below, but that wasn't profitable. My office was down there. One of the tenants was Dave Laurence, who was in partnership with Bob Oden. They tried to make the first plastic ski boot. Bob Colen had a bookstore there, and Burt Bidwell had his first ski shop on the corner. After we moved out, we built our own house where the Aspen Club is now. Then we sold the Bowman Building and bought 160 acres on Stillwater from Roger Dixon. It was his second home. Roger had paid $10,000 for 160 acres.

I loved everything about Aspen. I liked the mystique of the West — horses, cowboys, and all that kind of stuff. I loved to climb. I was passionate about the mountains. I loved everything about them. Aspen had wonderful people. It was so tough economically here that a lot of people left, but those that stayed on really

Stuart and Elaine Chisholm, about 1947. Courtesy Bert Chisholm.

loved the place. So many of them were characters. The majority really weren't interested in the idea of this becoming a tourist resort. They wanted mining to come back. But there was a hard-core group of people like the Willoughbys, Laurence Elisha, and Mike Magnifico who loved skiing and realized that skiing instead of mining could be the future of Aspen. They did not envision it being the glamorous resort it is now.

The difference between then and now in Aspen is like the difference between night and day. Then, everybody knew everybody else. There was no social strata. Lots of people who came to live here were struggling to make a living. There were a few retirees and very few tourists — very few second homeowners. The people who came really wanted to be a part of the community and didn't flaunt their wealth at all. Even the very rich built modest houses. There was an incredible period when there were interesting people coming to town who had been in the service and didn't want to go back to their old lives. They were intrigued by what Paepcke and Friedl wanted to do here. It was a very unique place — the kind of social life there was and the simplicity of everything. There were few diversions then — no music, no ballet, no health clubs. The change in Aspen was such a creeping thing. I noticed the change when the condominium law emerged in the Sixties. I designed the first luxury condominium — the Aspen Alps. George Mitchell was the developer. When we started, it was going to be a co-op because the condominium law didn't exist. Then it became a condo. That's kind of the turning point. At about the same time, wooden skis were replaced by synthetic skis, which made it a lot easier to learn to ski, and Bogner ski pants replaced Levis and baggy pants.

There's nothing like Aspen. It was so unique fifty years ago, and in its own way, it's still the best place in the world to live. However, there is too much dissension here now. That bothers me tremendously. It puts a sour note on life here. There's so much controversy and negativism in the papers. I wish people would relax and realize that we have such a paradise. Why fight all the time? There was a period where there weren't enough controls and too much development too fast. For instance, there should be more control over those huge houses going in on the West End. We should be preserving the small scale that existed. ✦

Photo by Kathy Daily

Elizabeth Paepcke

I was born August 28, 1902, in Baltimore, but we traveled a lot because my father was a university professor. He was head of the romance language department at the University of Chicago. The year 1938 was the first time I came to Aspen. I came from our ranch, Perry Park.

Perry Park is an historical ranch that we owned at that time. It had 7,000 acres on the Eastern Slope between Denver and Colorado Springs. It was absolutely beautiful. Isabella Bird, who wrote a famous book called *A Ladies Life in the Rockies* (published in 1862), tried to find a way to Estes Park, about which she'd heard in England from Lord Dunraven. Isabella Bird was a famous world traveler, as many women of her circumstances in the Victorian age were — women of great courage and tremendous curiosity about the world. She went to the Hawaiian Islands and visited Queen Liliokalani. On her way back from the Hawaiian Islands, she wrote a famous book called *Six Months in the Sandwich Islands*. After that, when she came back to the United States, she took the Union Pacific Railroad to Denver. She described Denver and her journey to Estes Park. Every way she tried was wrong. She finally found a way up to Estes Park through Lyons Canyon. Subsequently, she stayed in Estes Park, where she climbed Long's Peak with a man called Rocky Mountain Jim, who had only one eye. With him, she fell in love. Now mind you, she was riding alone the entire time on her cross-saddle and had on what she called her Hawaiian riding outfit (which were pantalettes and a hoop skirt). The hoop was thrown away, and she threw her dress over the saddle. She slept out at night on the bare ground with her saddle blanket as her blanket. After several months in Estes Park, she rode to Denver via Fort Lyons, Longmont, and then Perry Park Ranch, where she stayed several days. She described Perry Park Ranch in *A Ladies Life in the Rockies*. It was an existing ranch and was the only place that she found that had a house with a roof on it. The Perrys lived there. So when we bought the ranch in 1936, the old ranch house was still there with its old Franklin stove and everything, just as she had described it in her book. We bought it from Bob Lamont. His father was Secretary of the Treasury.

Getting back to why I came to Aspen — the pipes burst in our ranch house. We had guests who had brought their skis from Washington, D.C., with them as they were top skiers. They mistakenly thought Rocky Mountain skiing was on the Eastern Slope. Anyway, they arrived with their skis, which I was absolutely horrified to see. Walter and I drove them out to our ranch and opened the back door. The kitchen ceiling looked like the underside of a bathtub. With the jar of the door, the stretched canvas of the ceiling suddenly burst. All the water that had gathered within its folds fell on the kitchen stove and the kitchen table and inundated the whole kitchen with everything in it. And here were two guests behind us from Washington, D.C., with their skis. Disaster, sheer disaster.

It was disaster all over the house. The foreman of our ranch had come out, and without checking the temperature of the house, had set it very low in order to save heat when we weren't there. Then before we came, he wanted us to find it nice and warm on arrival, so he turned the heat up. All the pipes had frozen on the second floor, then burst. We obviously couldn't put our guests up there. They stayed one night, and poor Curtis came down the stairs the next morning coughing and I said, "What's wrong, Curtis?" and he said, "Plaster sinus."

I'd heard from a drunken friend of mine that the best skiing in Colorado was up in Aspen, but I'd never been there. So we took a train from Denver to Glenwood Springs and arrived in Glenwood around ten at night. Anyway, it was pitch black. We had to drive up to Aspen in a snowstorm with drifts all over the road. A dark-haired man met us in Glenwood with an old trashy car. We piled all of our luggage and skis into this car and started out into the dark, with no lights anywhere. All that the headlights of the car revealed were the fence posts and huge drifts of snow that we occasionally had to dig our way through. We would go for a stretch, and then we had to dig some more.

We finally got up to Aspen around midnight. The town was dark, and not an electric light was burning — it was late. There was one light under the Jerome porte-cochere. A bare electric light bulb on a wire was blowing back and forth. You can imagine the blowing snow and that light swinging in the wind. We walked into the lobby and saw the safe of the hotel standing in the otherwise empty fireplace. Near that was a big black board, and on it were keys and rings of the hotel rooms. The man who drove us up here through the snow and drifts, then hauled our luggage into the hotel. Suddenly he sprang behind the desk and said, "Do you have a reservation?" Yes, we have a reservation. And he said, "All right, follow me." We started up the main staircase and there was snow on the very top of it. The snow had drifted down from the third floor to the second because the roof was missing a few stained glass panels. Anyway, the Munsons were looking at this and that, all around, not understanding any of it. Laurence Elisha took us into what was Parlour C or Parlour B in those days, and we said we wanted a double bed for the Munsons and I wanted a single room. Parlour B had a room with a double bed, but the double bed was an in-a-door bed. Now, do you know what an in-a-door bed is? It had beautiful glass and all handcarved casing. It looked like beveled glass, a regular mirror, which it was. When pulled down, legs came out which reached the floor. Laurence proudly pulled it down and said, "This is the bed." Well, Edith Munson gave a shriek and said that she wouldn't sleep in it because she'd just read some detective story about a person in Paris being closed up and smothered to death in a bed just like the present one. She just refused. So poor Laurence led them into another room in back that had two iron bedsteads. It did have a bathroom attached. He led me into my room, which had a great big double brass bed —

Parlour A. So I went to bed there. Breakfast was at six in the morning and lunch at noon, when the miner's whistles went off. We paid $3.50 for our room, which included three meals.

At six in the morning, we woke up for breakfast and looked outside. Nice day. In order to go skiing, we had to get into the miner's truck with the miners. There was one mine still operating and that was the Midnight Mine. We got into the miner's truck and were herded like cattle. We stood there with our skis with the miners. They were without skis, of course. They all stood with us. There were sixteen men working the Midnight Mine, including one of the Willoughbys. He was the foreman. Thus herded in, we stood up all the way up the road to the Midnight Mine. Halfway up the mountain, we got out, put seal skins on our skis, then herringboned up Little Annie Basin. Luckily, we had (because I couldn't ski) a top skier who had been raised in Denver. Bob Balsch, I think, was a member of the Tenth Mountain Division. He was a top skier because he had been raised in Switzerland. He'd skied since he was young. He led us up the back of Ajax Mountain. There wasn't a track anywhere. Not a deer, not an animal, nor a man in that pristine snow. We would cross a snow-bank. I didn't know how to traverse it. I knew how to snowplow, but I didn't know a thing about traversing. Bob Balsch would whisper for fear of starting an avalanche, and so we'd cross and follow him. We finally reached the top of Richmond Hill. When we reached the top, we found a huge fir tree where a building now stands. We dove under the fir tree for shelter, where there was no snow, out of the snow and wind. We ate our lunch while looking out over the landscape. As far as we could see, the world was newly made, and it was as though the world had first begun. We felt that somehow, we were the first human beings. We could look across the range of mountains where the snow was blowing veils off of the peaks. It was the most beautiful sight I've ever seen. That's when I really fell in love with Aspen.

I had to go down the way we came. My friends were such good skiers, they came down the face of Aspen Mountain, which wasn't packed or anything. I went back down Little Annie Basin with the help of Bob Balsch.

We stayed in Aspen three days. When I went back, I said, "Walter, we have to go up there some summer when it's terribly hot on our ranch." I said Aspen would be a marvelous place to camp. Well, that was the wrong thing to say. First of all, Walter loathed camping — just detested it. Secondly, World War II broke out and we couldn't come back for awhile even if we had so desired.

When the war was practically over, with our friends, the Eugene Lillys from Colorado Springs, we put our gas-ration tickets together. Otherwise we couldn't have come here. Between the Lillys and ourselves, and our ration tickets, we were able to drive from the Springs to Aspen. Eugene said, "Well, let's go up to Aspen. It is a wonderful place, Walter. Walter started grumbling a little and added, "It's a lovely place I hear from Pussy, who can tell you so because she's been there." We were stir-crazy. During the war, we couldn't travel or go anywhere. We Paepckes got out of Chicago by going to our ranch in Colorado, which was wonderful. We weren't too bad off, I mean, we ate off of our ranch — all the butter we wanted, eggs, and meat. We didn't suffer during the war in the least, because we lived off the produce of the ranch. So we put our ration tickets together, and then I had an afterthought: "Gene, how do we get back?" He said, "Oh Elizabeth, don't worry. After we've been three days in Aspen, the town will be so anxious to get rid of us they'll give us the gas." I said, "Are you sure, Gene?" and he said, "Just mark my words." So we came up here.

The second day we were in Aspen, Walter announced at breakfast with a grin on his face that he had a birthday present for me, and I said, "What?" because there was nothing for sale in Aspen. He said, "Oh, I bought you a house." With that, I could have shot him, literally shot him. A house. I didn't need a house up here. All I wanted to do was to bring him up here and show him this wonderful place we could escape to, and I didn't want another house. We had an apartment in Chicago. We had a farm outside of Chicago, and we had this beautiful ranch on the outskirts of Denver and Colorado Springs. The last thing in the world I needed was another house. Certainly not one up in Aspen that I'd have to run, take care of, worry about, and rebuild — although I loved to rebuild. I was educated as a designer and architect. I knew perfectly well the minute Walter had a vision, he would never leave anything well enough alone. He would strive to complete it.

He didn't buy it because he wanted a house. He bought it because he saw that in Aspen almost everyone was out of work and that the only jobs they once had were now nonexistent. They could dig ditches or they could run farms. There were sixteen men employed at Midnight Mine, but no more, and Laurence Elisha was trying to run the hotel. He saw people without jobs, a town that was becoming a ghost town, and he saw a need to rebuild. This was a beautiful town that had stopped completely developing in 1893 after the devaluation of silver, and people left — just moved out, leaving houses standing and furniture in the houses, papers, everything. And they just fled with whatever they could carry off. Walter had a vision. He always had a vision. I was filled with horror, because it meant work for me.

Walter bought Al Lamb's house. He had Lamb's Pharmacy here. That's one of the old, old houses. In our new home, standing there was a stuffed dog whom we called Max. We heard that he was originally the hunting dog of Mr. Lamb. When the house was shown to us by Judge Shaw, who had a key, he opened the door and here was this dog, you know, bright eyes, right in the front hall, pointing. The dog was there at alert, with these beady eyes looking at us, and I got freaked when I saw it. This was Max. Now, whether that was the original name or not, I don't know. We kept him in the front hall. Oh, he was just wonderful. Eventually someone stole him.

I opened one of the closet doors upstairs, and it was filled with the most beautiful dresses I have ever seen of that period — 1819 to 1900. They were magnificent. You've never seen such dresses — velvet, taffeta, pleats, underskirts, hats, gloves, everything you can imagine, and they were all marked Poiret and French houses.

Walter wanted to make Aspen come alive, which meant giving people jobs. The Hotel Jerome needed renovating. So he started rebuilding the Jerome. Walter had no vision about skiing. Walter wasn't the least bit interested in skiing. We heard suddenly that there was a man who had been up here looking into the possibilities of skiing and that he was interested in forming a ski association or something like that. He had come from Sun Valley — Friedl Pfeifer — and had just been mustered out of the army. Walter heard about him, so we invited Friedl to come to our ranch in Perry Park. Walter wanted to consult him about the possibilities of starting a ski thing up here, because it was quite obvious that skiing would be great. We heard from our friends in Denver, who had come up here and skied for years, that this was the best skiing anywhere. So Walter thought he should get ahold of this man who wanted to organize skiing in Aspen. Walter, not knowing anything about doing skiing, and I not being interested in skiing, invited him to come to our ranch in Perry Park.

That is a funny story in itself, because at the same time that we invited Friedl to come to our ranch, we were expecting a turkey herder from Mexico whom we needed to care for our turkeys. We were running turkeys on our ranch, and this was another scheme of Walter's which didn't exactly work out; suffered a great loss. But anyway, Walter got in touch with Ralston, who sells things cheap, such as turkey food, and we ran 2,000 to 4,000 turkeys at Perry Park. This I never want to go through again. Friedl was supposed to arrive on the bus in Larkspur. A man from our ranch went into Larkspur to meet the turkey herder. He saw a man in a used army uniform who was dark and who couldn't speak English very well, with a strong German accent. Our man didn't know German from Spanish, and so he picked up this man at the bus station thinking it was the needed turkey herder. While driving ten miles from Lark-spur into our ranch, he questioned the man, "Do you like turkeys?" Friedl said, "Sure, I like turkeys at certain times of the year." He also asked, "How do you like the West, living here, and the outdoors?" Friedl replied, "Oh, I love the West, I love outdoors."

"Oh, that's good. How long have you been associated with turkeys?"

"With vat?"

"With turkeys."

Well, they drove on for awhile and the conversation sort of lapsed. Finally, they drove into the entrance of our ranch, which is actually three miles from the house, and our man said, "You're sure you like to herd turkeys?"

"Vat?"

"Well, aren't you coming to take care of our turkeys?"

Friedl said, "I don't know what you mean. I've been invited to the Paepckes for dinner and to spend the night."

"You mean you're going up to the Paepckes?"

And Friedl said, "Yah."

So the man drove him up to our house and Friedl got out and he was laughing and laughing. We couldn't understand what it was about. Finally he told us the story — that he was taken for the turkey herder.

It was not a good business deal. Although Walter was grateful to get ahold of Friedl, and Friedl said he would raise all of the money for building the lifts, he never raised a cent. He was the first director of the ski corp. He laid out a lot of the skiing on Ajax, but it was so tough that beginners had difficulty. Then Friedl conceived of the idea of Buttermilk. That was Friedl's idea.

In 1948 Walter and Robert Hutchins had already been talking about having a Goethe Festival. Walter decided to have the Goethe Bicentennial Convocation in Aspen to celebrate the bicentennial of Goethe's birth. Walter was on the board of the University of Chicago, and he was also vice-president of the Chicago Symphony. He was on the board of the Art Institute, so we had a background. Now Walter had great business sense.

It's a funny story how we got Albert Schweitzer to come here for the Bicentennial. We were in Hawaii with our children that summer of 1948, I think it was. I walked down the boardwalk, interested always in what book-stores sell. I was looking in the windows of a bookstore and I saw two books by Albert Schweitzer, *In Search of Historical Christ* and *The Edge of the Primeval Forest*. Because our family all swam like mad and spent the whole day on the beach like slugs in front of the Royal Hawaiian Hotel, I wanted to have something to read during the hot hours of the day. I wasn't interested in just swimming, so I read these two books of Albert Schweitzer. As I read *The Primeval Forest*, I read how he had gone down to Lambarene in Africa and started the hospital there for the black people, and I became fascinated.

So when Walter came out of the waves of the Pacific, I said, "Walter, you know this is the man you should have in Aspen. The one thing we lack is somebody to speak out for the black races in this country or the black races in the world. Albert Schweitzer is the one person that we still need in order to pull the whole thing together." Walter went to Robert Hutchins and said, "Pussy has a crazy idea that we have to get this man, Schweitzer, from Africa to come to the Goethe Festival, and have you heard of him? Hutchins said, "Dear Walter, Albert Schweitzer is world famous. We could never get him here; I've tried," said Bob Hutchins. Walter said, "Well, let me try." So what he did was, he cabled Albert Schweitzer and said that he would not give him $5,000 if he'd come and all expenses paid, but he would give that amount in medicines to his hospital. Walter had a connection with Abbot Laboratories in Chicago, and he would send free medicines to Lambarene, Albert Schweitzer's hospital, in lieu of honorarium if he would come to Aspen.

When the cable came from Aspen to Albert Schweitzer, naturally he looked Aspen up in his atlas. His atlas was dated 1913, so it made no mention of Aspen. I found this out later from Albert Schweitzer himself. Since he couldn't find it, he decided it must be a suburb of Chicago. He was delighted to come to Chicago, get an honorary degree from the University of Chicago, and go right back to Africa. He would never have come to Aspen because he was allergic to altitudes. Mrs. Schweitzer and he were suddenly, to their horror, put on a train to come out here. Later, since there was a wreck on the tracks going to Glenwood Springs, they had to come all the way around through Colorado Springs and the Royal Gorge. They didn't get into Glenwood Springs until two in the morning. Walter went to Glenwood to meet the Schweitzers during the first concert of the evening with Erika Morini singing.

In the meantime, I had to handle the whole thing with the dinner after the concert. Suddenly, there was a fight in our house between the cook and the maid we had brought from Chicago. I went into the kitchen, and dishes, pots, and pans were flying, and I stopped and said, "Now stop it immediately. I'll come back the minute the concert is over and we'll decide the fight at that time." After that, I walked out and met Anne Lindberg. We walked over to the Meadows from Pioneer Park. I was shaking like a leaf, and I said to Anne,

"Walter isn't here. He's meeting Albert Schweitzer down in Glenwood and I'm having to go after the first concert and arrange the dinner afterwards, my nerves are on edge!" Anne looked and me at she said, "Yes, and it's so catching!"

So when Dr. Schweitzer and his wife arrived in the middle of the night, he asked Walter very solemnly, "What time is breakfast?" Walter said eight in the morning. So the next day, there I was, eight A.M., still in my nightgown. I wore a frowner at night — you know, a paper patch on my forehead. You can buy them in the drugstore. I pasted it on my forehead because I frown so at night when I sleep. So I put the frowner on and that was pasted on my forehead. My hair was out like a fright. I had a nylon nightgown on that was a little Greek thing that had machine pleating that I loved. Suddenly, at eight in the morning, there was a shriek from the bathroom from Walter. He was trying to take a shower, and he said, "Pussy" and he always said, "Pussy, do something!" because he never handled even a hammer in his life. As I walked in, he was standing in the middle of the bathroom floor and the water had risen two inches. It was pouring out of the toilet. It was pouring out of the shower drain, and pouring out of the washtub, when he said, "Do something!" So of course, I had to see that the water was turned off. That meant running by the front door with my frowner, my wild hair, and my nylon gown. I ran by the front door to the kitchen to tell them to get hold of Pete Rosset, because he knew where the water turnoff was. Then I seized a mop and pail, rushed back through the dining room, past the open front door, and there stood Dr. Schweitzer in a morning coat and a little tie, with Mrs. Schweitzer in a pale gray gown with a garnet pin, looking at me — mop, pail, frowner, hair, everything. I said, "Oh, Dr. Schweitzer, I'm terribly sorry. There's been an awful problem. My husband is standing in the bathroom and water is coming from everywhere. I have to mop and clean up. Breakfast will be ready right away. Just go into the living room." When I said the water was pouring and I had to mop up, he said, "Oh, I see I'm just in time for the second world flood." Ten or twelve years later, when I visited him in Africa, he told me, "You know, Elizabeth, I looked you up and down that morning and you revealed everything!"

Oh, there were all kinds of people and stories. Stories about Ortega Gasset — you know, the great Spanish philosopher. Ortega was wonderful. He had a partially bald head, and he loved the kind of cold cuts I had. I got them from the German delicatessen in Chicago. I had all of this shipped from Chicago. Ortega would come to our house and he'd say, "Oh, you know, Elizabeth, I do love your hors d'oeuvres. I can't get them at the Jerome Hotel where I'm staying; where did you get this?" I said, "I have it sent from Chicago." And he said, "Oh, how

I'd love some for my patrons." I said, "Well, we'll have some wrapped up for you. What do you want?" He said, "That's alright." He immediately scooped it up from the plate, put the pieces on his bald head, and put his straw hat on top before walking back to the Jerome.

Artur Rubinstein stayed at the Jerome, along with Arthur Piatigorsky, and Nathan Milstein. We put them up at various places. But anyway, Artur came to me one day and he said, "Pussy, at the Jerome Hotel we've learned that there is no valet over there and I don't know where to get these suits pressed before appearing in the tent in order to play at concerts. They get wrinkled, so I have to get them pressed." And he added, "I have Piatigorsky, Nathan Milstein's, and mine. Do you mind seeing that your valet or whomever you have can press our trousers?" And I said, "You've come to the right place. I'll see that it is all done." After ten days, when the festival was over, Artur was in the house and said, "Pussy, I'm so grateful for the pressing you had done for us and everything. I want to leave ten dollars for the man who's been doing it." And he handed me the ten or twenty dollars — I've forgotten how much it was. And I stuffed the money in my pocket. He looked at me, and I said, "Well, Artur, it's come to the right place." He was shocked and asked, "What do you mean?" I said, "Well, all I'm saying is, that I thank you, it came to the right place." And Artur said, "I still don't understand." And then he suddenly said, "You didn't do it, did you?" I said, "Yes."

Leo Szilard. He was a famous professor and physicist. Oh, he did all kinds of naughty things. He wrote a famous book called *The Song of the Doves*. It was really well known. Everybody read it. It was mainly a very witty book about peace. The book made him very famous because it was a sort of a novelette which had a world message and a purpose. He came to my husband, at just about the time in '49 or so, when there was the world scare with polio. He said, "Walter, you give me some money, and we'll put it into a kitty and we will make a medicine that we will say cures polio and it won't be anything but sugar water. Because people want to believe things. If they do, these panaceas that people believe in are nothing but hoax anyway, and nothing has been found to cure polio." Well, he said, "So we'll sell this and people will buy it and be cured." With Leo Szilard, you never knew if he was pulling your leg. I thought this one about Leo Szilard is a funny story — in a wicked, wicked way.

Now Walter had a great business sense. He founded the Container Corporation of America, and he brought it to its height again. It only went downhill after he died. Just as Aspen has. Had Walter lived longer, as I see it, what has happened now with the Aspen Institute and the land out there would not have happened. But Walter was a kind, generous, courageous, visionary person, and he gave all the land we owned — the Meadows — to the Aspen Institute without any strings attached. He didn't think of writing down that it could never be sold or that it had to remain in the Aspen Institute forever. He trusted others to do as he would himself.

The Container Corporation was founded in 1926 entirely by my husband, and he put together a lot of small paper companies. When we married in 1922, his father was a wooden-box manufacturer. Mr. Paepcke was in a lumber company, and it was called the Chicago Mill and Lumber Company. Mr. Paepcke was dying of cancer, and Walter went to him, his only son. He didn't say much. He didn't want to give his father too much of a body blow, but he said he could see that paper was going to be the new way of crating oranges and milk and all the other things that had been contained in wooden crates. I used to make dollhouses out of wooden crates. Walter put together various small paper companies in many states, including California. Put together these container corporations became the Container Corporation of America. Of course, when Walter died, the whole thing folded. Everything folded. That was the end, because the company was merged first to Montgomery Ward, which was a fatal mistake. Then from there, Montgomery Ward sold out to Mobil Oil. In the end, Mobil Oil sold to an Irish company. That was the end of that.

What I would want for people in Aspen today? Fight hard for the things they believe in. But that means a constant fight, and it doesn't mean only Aspen — it means wherever you live, here, or anywhere.

When you're in a certain position, you always have people for and against you. You're going to be judged. People either like you or they don't. It doesn't really matter. After Walter died, suddenly he became a saint. I'm left to be the witch.

◆

Scamps, Tramps, and Socialites

The Folks About Town

The Quiet Years blessed Aspen with wonderful characters who also had nick-names to match. The town took care of its own. The community adopted those who could not take care of themselves, and no one went hungry. The stories that evolved from these delightful characters kept later generations smiling and fascinated. The tales became bigger than the personalities themselves.

As stories are passed down through families, a modest life can become a legend. Memory may change the truth forever. What is the truth? Everyone has his or her own personal realities and memories. Time, too, changes both. In the telling and retelling of stories, superheroes and myths are created. Maybe our lives are only as real as the stories people tell about us after we are gone.

The following people leave us their stories and their myths.

POPE ROWLAND
Leo Rowland
(1904-1984)

I don't know how Pope Rowland got that name. I called him Pope a lot because I had quite a bit to do with him. I don't know, I suppose that was a name that they hung on somebody like that. Maybe it was because he was a Catholic.

◆

His real name was Leo. I knew Pope well for a long time. He went to church all the time — almost every day. I think the funniest story was when he had the bar across from the Armory Hall. They had dances and a liquor store in the bar. Everybody was trying to buy stuff and drink. One night he closed the bar down early and said, "I have to save what I have left for tomorrow." And he walked real fast. Somebody stopped and asked him if he wanted a ride once and he said, "No, I'm in a hurry." Pope was a nice guy. He was Red's brother.

◆

The only story I have about Pope is that everybody used to say he always walked so fast. They would stop and offer him a ride and he would say, "No, I'm in a hurry." So that was one thing that everybody used to laugh about.

◆

Somebody gave him that name when he started his beer joint across from the Armory Hall where the Thrift Shop is now — the way he was preaching to them when they were putting up the cinder block. Somebody gave him the name of Pope.

◆

Pope? Well, he didn't have much to do, so he went to church every day. So then they started calling him Pope Rowland. Well, he was a big chatterbox is all I ever knew about him. He'd stop you on the street and you couldn't get rid of him.

◆

Pope Rowland. I think a lot of those nicknames came around 'cause somebody would point a finger in a history textbook and say, "Oh, Pope Leo — Pope Leo did this," and his name was Leo, you know. That's the way with a lot of those nicknames. People had a lot of time on their hands. You could get whimsical with your nicknames. Pope was a very fast walker. He was lean and walked fast with his head down and talked fast. You might see him dart out of an alley, at almost sprinter speed. Ask him if he wanted a ride and he would say, "No thanks, I'm in a hurry." He always said things twice.

◆

Pope Rowland used to come in the White Kitchen. He'd always walk real fast. I had a counter and stools. He'd just come running in there and he'd say, "Couple Navajos, couple Navajos. No hurry, no hurry." Navajo blankets — he named 'em that. I called them a short stack. Then in deer season in October, I had deer hunters out the door, up the sidewalk. And of course everybody had a red hat. So old Pope was trying to get in to get his couple of Navajos in the morning and couldn't because there were too many hunters. So he waited 'til Bullocks opened up and went over and bought a red hat. He thought he had to have a red hat to get in. I don't know how Pope Rowland got his name. I knew him for a long time. He was Red's brother. His name was Leo. And they called him Pope.

◆

How did Pope Rowland get his name? No idea. He used to have that old place right across from the Armory Hall. During church on Sunday, he had that nickelodeon. He would turn it up, and god, the music was so loud. I drank a lot of beer over there.

◆

I don't know how Pope Rowland got that name. I imagine, just making a guess, the way he talked. He would talk in a real short spurt. You would see him on the street and you would say, "Hello, Pope." "Hello, good day, I'm in a hurry, so long." I mean, this was the way he talked. He was always in a hurry.

◆

"The funniest story I ever heard, that ever stuck with me about Pope Rowland, was that somebody stopped their car and asked him if he wanted a ride and he said, 'No, I'm in too much of a hurry.'"

How did Pope Rowland get his name? Probably from the Pope. Maybe they thought he was going to be a priest.

✦

Pope Rowland? It was because he picked up every damn thing — was nothing but a regular packrat. After church for awhile, we were having whatever the ladies brought and coffee. I think that he'd eat the most. He sure helped himself, that's true. Pope was something else.

✦

The funniest story I ever heard, that ever stuck with me about Pope Rowland, was that somebody stopped their car and asked him if he wanted a ride and he said, "No, I'm in too much of a hurry." He was also quite a drinker and funny, funny, funny. His brother, Red, was a funny man, too.

✦

The only thing I remember about Pope was I'd walk from home into work, and when I'd meet him, he'd say, "Hi, hi, hi." He'd come around you, "Hi, hi, hi." He ran around all the time and he never looked up. That's how he got killed you know — a car hit him. A car run into him in Grand Junction. Never looked up — always head down. "Hi, hi, hi."

✦

Pope Rowland? Probably the nickname was religious. He was a good Catholic. You'd always stop and ask him if he wanted a ride and he would say, "Nope, I'm in a hurry."

✦

I remember Pope Rowland when he had the lot across the street from the post office on Spring Street. He had a silver trailer sittin' there. The city condemned it. They said, "you'll have to move that; there are no trailers allowed. It's zoned. We're going to haul it away." "Okay," Pope said. "Okay, you can do that. I'll have it filled full of concrete tomorrow." And he would have. I'm sure he would.

> *"*
>
> *Pope used to be quite a character. Early in the morning he would go out and pick up everything. He was one of those scavengers. I don't care what it was, he would be packing it home. Then he had a liquor store right across from city hall. He didn't last long in that. I think he was his own best customer*
>
> *"*

•

I wouldn't want to tell you about Pope. I didn't like him. We didn't get along at all. When he was fixing that building up for his liquor store, he was doing a lot of the work himself and it had gotten so crummy. All the old sacks and everything would blow around. I'd be cleaning them up every morning when I went to work. He and I just about came to blows. He shouldn't have been in business in the first place.

•

I can tell you a cute story about him. In the early days they had what they call a duff wagon. That was a wagon that was drawn by horses that you would fill with dirt and haul it. When you wanted to dump it, you would pull the lever and the bottom would drop out. Pope and two other guys were loading these wagons up near Stillwater. The boss was there, and these guys were busy loading it as long as the boss was around. The boss says, "I've got to go down the road and I'll be back in a few minutes." The minute he left, they slowed down and the wagon wasn't full when the boss came back. He got after Pope about it. He jumped on Pope about it and Pope said, "Gee, what can you expect when you have a washer between two nuts?"

•

Everybody called him Pope as far as I know. I don't even remember what his real name was. We would be walking by, and he always tipped his hat at you. He would say, "Nice day, isn't it?" even if it was raining cats and dogs.

> *" Everybody called him Pope as far as I know. I don't even remember what his real name was. We would be walking by, and he always tipped his hat at you. He would say, 'Nice day, isn't it?' even if it was raining cats and dogs. "*

•

Pope used to cut a rug around with one of the Caparellas — I think Mike. I seen them walking up and down the street, both of them, staggering, barely able to stand up, trying to hold each other up. They done a lot of drinking together. That's about all I remember.

•

Pope used to be quite a character. Early in the morning he would go out and pick up everything. He was one of those scavengers. I don't care what it was, he would be packing it home. He walked real fast, too — he would really go. You would stop by with a car and say, "Pope, do you want a ride?" and he said, "No, I'm in a hurry." Then he had a liquor store right across from city hall where Little Cliff's Bakery was. He didn't last long in that. I think he was his own best customer. That liquor store was going on during the time the tunnel was being driven up there in Lincoln Gulch and Lost Man. I always knew him as Pope. In fact, it was years before I knew his right name, Leo.

*
* *

Pope always ran a little faster than a car around town. He owned a house out there in the West End and had a nice trailer in town. He always said everything twice — "In a hurry, in a hurry." I think he was named after Pope Leo. His name was Leo Rowland. When he was born, Pope Leo was Pope in Rome.

*
* *

Pope Rowland always walked very fast down the street and you'd say, "Hey, Pope, do you want a ride?" And he'd say, "Nope, nope. Haven't got the time." Pope had that little liquor store across from city hall. One time they had a school thing where they made up a dummy — a nice one. My cousin, Neil, went by and thought it would be a good trick. They saw Pope there and threw this dummy out in the street, hollered, and acted like they ran over it. They went down by the corner and watched. Pope come out. He saw this body there and he couldn't tell. It was dark. He got a stick and he poked at the thing and fiddled around for the longest time. He was afraid to get too close. I don't know if he ever did actually find out.

*
* *

Pope Rowland had a liquor store right across the street from the Armory Hall. He was open all day. The only thing he served was beer, but he had a liquor license, too, to sell liquor out. And then he delivered on foot. He was fast service. He would come around about noon. The old folks got stuff from him. He would deliver the stuff and help them drink the wine and then got to eat with them, too. Good deal.

*
* *

I remember Pope Rowland when he had the lot across the street from the post office. He had a silver trailer. The city condemned it. They said, 'You'll have to move that; we're going to haul it away.' 'Okay,' Pope said. 'You can do that. I'll have it filled full of concrete tomorrow.' And he would have. I'm sure he would.

Pope Rowland looked like a Pope, but I forget which Pope it was. I think he looked like a Pope from the 1930s and 1940s. Now there was a character and a half. He used to have that liquor store across from Armory Hall and we would be in the Eagles or something for a dance on Sunday night. Of course, the bars closed at 8 P.M., and believe it or not, there were cars parked in front of his place and across the street. He was running in and out with whatever anybody wanted. And I suppose on the weekends he would sell after hours. During the week, there just wasn't anything that would really stay open that much.

✦

SLIM AND LONI WILLIS

Slim Willis was a thin guy. He used to wander around town, and I understand he was pretty heavy in the gambling ring — a little circuit around town, kind of undercover stuff. They played poker mostly, I would guess.

✦

Slim and Loni Willis bought the Silver Grill from Jackie and Slim Marshall. They were characters. Loni was quite a drinker. I worked for them for awhile for breakfast. I was nineteen or twenty. I should not have been serving liquor. Anyway, they weren't watching too close then. She'd come down about 10:00 A.M. and have herself a double shot to get her going. And then she'd have a little coffee. But she'd hurry, 'cuz Slim was trying to keep her from drinking in the bar.

✦

I knew Slim and Loni Willis real well. Loni was a welder in World War II, and a very good one, too. She was on the coast in the shipyards. And Slim was just a regular old barfly, easygoing, cordial as hell, and that's about all. No rush to get into the world and no rush to get out of it.

✦

"Loni was a welder in World War II, and a very good one. She was on the coast in the shipyards. And Slim was just a regular old barfly, easy going, cordial as hell, and that's about all. No rush to get into the world and no rush to get out of it."

*Silver Grill Cafe,
Hyman Avenue,
1936.
Tony Kastelik and
Louis Vedic.
Courtesy
Ed Gregorich.*

Saloonkeepers. She liked her booze, that's about all I can remember about her. Gawd, every time you went in there she was drunk. Slim was skinny.

◆

Loni and Slim Willis had the Silver Grill Cafe. Loni was a tough gal. She was little — tougher than heck, but a nice person. My mother worked in the restaurant.

◆

Loni was one of the tough ones. Boy, she could handle the drunks, I'll tell ya. I don't think she ever stopped drinking. She found out the formula for not having a hangover — stay drunk. They used to take the beer and dump those shots, glass and all, right into a beer — a boilermaker. They dumped the glass and all.

◆

Slim and Loni, sure I remember them. They had the Silver Grill Bar. Slim was noted as kind of a Texas gangster. Nobody ever messed around with him — they were always afraid of him. He was slim and kind of quiet. He'd get a little mad at her, but, you know, I think there was an occasional toot that she would go on. It was a good bar, and people liked to go there. You know, people liked her. Well, they liked Slim, too, but he just didn't have much to say. Everybody suspected that Slim was some kind of a gangster. I guess he carried a pistol around in his coat and stuff. But I never saw the pistol.

◆

Slim and Loni Willis. Well, she was colorful. I wouldn't go to any extent to say how far she went with anything. She could outdrink any man in town, things like that. Not very feminine but kind of pretty.

◆

The Silver Grill days. Loni was quite a character. She could outdrink any man and she could outswear any of them, too. That was a fun place to go because they had an accordion player. His name was Vic Sarson. This was in the late 1940s, early 1950s. Jap Mogan would go in and Vic would start playing his favorite, and he would start singing "Does Your Mother Know You're Out, Cecilia?" Hoofy would sing "My Wild Irish Rose." The two of them would try to outdo each other, singing those two songs.

◆

Loni hit the jug a little bit, but she was a nice lady. She really was.

◆

"

Slim was noted as kind of a Texas gangster. Nobody ever messed around with him — they were always afraid of him. I guess he carried a pistol around in his coat and stuff. But I never saw the pistol. Loni was quite a character. She could outdrink any man and she could outswear any of them, too.

"

PANHANDLE PETE
George Stringer
(1877 – 1964)

"

Don't know how he got his name. But Panhandle I think you could find in the dictionary. Panhandlers were people who could work a scam. Had their hand out in tough times. But there is also a Panhandle of Idaho. I think it was the Oklahoma Panhandle.

"

Panhandle Pete was real tough, but he had a pretty soft heart whenever it broke down on him. He pulled a good one on me when I was a boy. He burnt the irrigation ditches in town. In the spring when they burned the grass around them, I would help. He would go down two or three blocks and be burning. He would watch the flame, and then he would send me to bring his pickup down to him. Then that night, or several nights later, he would show up down at my house — call my dad out and give him hell for me driving without a license, saying I wasn't old enough. I was about twelve. It used to bug me. I didn't know whether, the next weekend, to go up and fool around with him or not. He'd do it to egg us on.

◆

I think Pete came from Oklahoma — the Panhandle. Some people used to call him Pistol Pete. I don't know whether he liked it or not. Most everybody just called him Pan. He was pretty fair. He kept the law. Kind of tough, especially when they were doing the tunnel. He kept the town in line pretty well on Saturday nights when the tunnel shift would come to town. He was a tough one.

◆

Panhandle Pete was marshall at one time and had some kind of police capacity. Everybody knew him. He would get around the schools warning kids about the traffic. There wasn't any traffic in those days. The dogs could lie in the middle of Main Street — Highway 82 — most of the time. We had only one that was killed. Don't know how he got his name. But Panhandle I think you could probably find in the dictionary. Panhandlers were people who could work a scam. Had their hand out in tough times. But there is also a Panhandle of Idaho. I think it was the Oklahoma Panhandle, which is a very interesting story in itself. One of the Sunday supplements in the *Denver Post* had a feature story about the Oklahoma Panhandle — how they used to feel left out of every state. Some of the rest of Oklahoma regards them in that way, too. They're nowhere.

◆

Oh yeah, I knew old Panhandle. He was tough. Oh hell, I heard how he got that name one time and now I can't remember. But he was a tough son-of-a-gun. We called him Pickhandle Pete. We'd say, "Here comes Pickhandle Pete," and by God, he put the run on us kids. Old Brice Arlian's wife was Panhandle Pete's daughter.

Panhandle Pete (George Stringer). Courtesy Aspen Historical Society.

◆

Panhandle Pete. Do I know George Stringer? I remember Panhandle George. Darned if I know how he got that name. Well, he wasn't a bad sort of fellow. I think he was a marshall at one time. He did a lot of jobs and was a good friend of Bill Tagert. He was kind of lame in one ankle — must have had a broken ankle or something. He kind of walked on the side of his foot.

◆

Panhandle Pete? Yes, I got kicked in the butt by him a few times when he was marshall. He was a pretty big person and, you know, I won't say that he was mean, but he was very stern. If he thought you were doing something you shouldn't have been doing, he'd give you a good kick in the butt.

◆

I knew Pan well. He was quite an old guy. In his early days, he drove horses; they called him a teamster. He hauled ore from the mines. He was a tough old character who later became sheriff, and I wouldn't want to cross paths if he ever got his temper up. He knew how to handle these bad men — didn't coddle them in those days. But I liked old Pan. When we got together, we generally had a nip or two. I don't know why they called him that. His name was George Stringer. I don't know how the hell they hung that name on him.

◆

Panhandle Pete was a strange person. He was a big tall fella. I think he'd been married and his wife left him and also left the daughter with him. He raised that daughter. He sort of kept her in the background, sort of protective-like. I talked to him all the time. He would always stop and say hi to the kids and come in and have something to drink in the summertime. I can't put too much on him. How did he get the name Panhandle? He was a panhandler when he first came to town. I guess maybe he just borrowed and borrowed. That's all he ever did. Just odd jobs and begging sort of.

◆

Panhandle Pete. Yes, I used to know him. He used to run around in a pickup all the time. When I was a kid, we used to walk to the Washington School which was clear at the West End. I grew up in the East End. It was almost a mile walk to school. And in the wintertime, they used to plow the snowbanks up. Instead of walking on the sidewalks, we walked on the snowbanks. Pan

"

Pan was quite an old guy. In his early days, he drove horses; they called him a teamster. He hauled ore from the mines. He was a tough old character who later became sheriff, and I wouldn't want to cross paths if he ever got his temper up.

"

would come by about that time of the day and chase us off to the sidewalk. When he was gone, we would go right back. I don't know why he did that — there wasn't no traffic.

◆

I knew Panhandle Pete. He came from the Panhandle of Texas. They had him as a marshall in town, and he was typical of the old generation about that time. He was a rather big guy, big and muscular. You had to be at that time to control some of those guys around town, when they got into the bar, you know. He was real adaptive for that. He was pretty mean and pretty tough. And the people respected him. When he asked people to behave, they took notice.

◆

Yeah, Pete was married to my mother's sister. How did he get the name Panhandle? He was probably off panhandling all the time. He wasn't very industrious.

◆

His daughter and I were pretty good friends. How he got the name Panhandle? No, unless he came from that part of the country — Texas or Oklahoma. Anne Slavins and I picked potatoes for his daughter. Her husband told us he was raised in Oklahoma. I figured that's where he got the name.

◆

Panhandle Pete was sheriff. We almost ran into him one time. We had a wagon we made — salvaged, you know. We put a board between a couple of sets of axles and braced the back ones so they couldn't turn, and we guided the front with our hands. A whole bunch of us kids would sit on it. We would go down Aspen Street. The brakes were to drag our feet. Well, the railroad track went across there. We sailed across that hill and the board broke. Good thing the board broke or we would have hit Panhandle Pete. He was coming down Durant Street. We come right at the corner about the same time that board broke. He was in a car.

◆

"

Panhandle Pete used to pay us kids to go turn the cows out at the Williams Ranch. The cows would come to town, and then Pan would pay us to put them in the impound lot. Mrs. Williams would come and pay Pan to bail the cows out. Then she would pay us to take them back home again.

"

They used to take the water from the Roaring Fork and run it down along Durant Street for irrigation. Panhandle Pete would go along the ditches where we kids would make paddlewheels. We cut slits in coffee cans, punched a hole, and put a piece of wire or nail in it. Then we'd dam up the ditch and stick the paddlewheel in. Of course, it would overflow and he'd come along, take all our paddlewheels, and break the dam.

❖

Panhandle Pete used to pay us kids to go turn the cows out at the Williams Ranch. It was over by the old hospital. The cows would come to town, and then Pan would pay us to put them in the impound lot. Mrs. Williams would come and pay Pan to bail the cows out. Then she would pay us to take them back home again.

❖

"

Oh, that renegade should have been hung. There are all kinds of reasons. He was dirty, that's all.

"

How did he get the name Panhandle Pete? Well, I guess he lived up the Frying Pan at one time. When I was a kid, Pan was always trying to get me. He had me confused with another kid. He used to say, "I'm going to get that Wheatley kid." There was a Wheatley Ranch near us. My older brother, Stuart, every once in awhile let me drive. Finally I got in the car myself. We had an old Star — they were a darn good automobile. And I drove around the block. But still, I didn't know how to park very good. I was backing out at the end of Main Street, which was gravel then, and here came Panhandle Pete in his vehicle or whatever he was driving. I almost hit him. He jumped out and he says, "I ought to arrest you, boy." Boy, was he mad — he was as mad as could be. "Next time I'm going to get you; you are going to jail." Well, it wasn't too long and Laurence Elisha's car was sitting there and darned if I didn't just get my bumper close enough to catch under his bumper. Oh, Laurence was a great guy and a good friend of my family. He said, "Yes, I think I'll call Panhandle Pete." But, of course, he was kidding. He got a jack and jacked me up and I got out of there.

❖

Ol' Panhandle. They were having an air show and planes were flying over and ol' Pan came down there suspicious, watching everybody. You weren't supposed to bring any liquor or drink out around the airport. He didn't want any of those

"Wheatley" guys like me. I said, "Get out of here." I said, "They ought to take you up there and drop you off and see if you'll fly," or something like that. He got so darned mad.

◆

Oh, that renegade should have been hung. There are all kinds of reasons. He was dirty, that's all. Loni Willis owned a bar here; she was a great gal. I'd get drunk in there. She had rooms upstairs, and she knew I was a Scotsman, and she'd say, "You damn Scotsman," and we'd kid back and forth. She'd always get me upstairs and give me a room. But one night I was so drunk I got in one bed and on to another. I didn't know where I was. I thought I was down in the Jerome Hotel. And boy, I came down in the morning and she says, "You son of a gun, I'm going to charge you for three rooms." Well, one day later she was back to herself again. But that Panhandle Pete — Loni didn't like him and nobody else did. He'd see a drunk that was obviously drunk. All he had to do was grab him from the back and twist his arm to bounce him out. Any of the bouncers at a good hotel know how to bounce a guy out of a bar. Instead of that, he'd pull out this leather, filled full of shots, and give them a concussion if he hit hard enough. Just knock 'em out. Yes. And boy, Loni jumped up at that and she said, "You son of a bitch, you get out of here." He was the law, but he got out when Loni said it. Then she said, "Don't you come back in here and hit some drunk in the back of the head!"

◆

His name was George Stringer. He was the city marshall. He arrested me one time for speeding down Main Street. Actually, a friend of mine had a Buick and I had a Chevrolet. We were racing. Pan walked with a limp and lived two doors west of the Mesa Store. I don't know how he got his name. They used to always call him Pan. I never heard anybody call him George — just Pan. He was ornery alright. We didn't get thrown in jail, but we were fined — I think ten dollars or something — but we were able to pay it off at two dollars per week.

◆

I don't know how he got his name. He was kind of what you call an outfitter. He used to haul stuff from the mines and that. He was a sheriff later on.

His name was George Stringer. He was the city marshall. He arrested me one time for speeding down Main Street. Pan walked with a limp and lived two doors west of the Mesa Store. He was ornery alright. We didn't get thrown in jail, but we were fined.

577

◆

Panhandle Pete was marshall in Aspen. He was crippled up pretty much. His name was George Stringer. They called him Panhandle and Pistol Pete. I don't know why.

◆

Panhandle Pete was kind of a big old grumpy guy, but he's really basically the reason there is no mine machinery around here. In World War II he went up and gathered everything. They sold it to the government.

◆

OLD MAN SWEENEY
(1893-1944)

Old man Sweeney, he had a secondhand store. We went around to the liquor stores and would gather up these beer bottles and take them in. He would give us a penny a piece for them. He stored them out in the alley. Then we would go around back and pick those bottles up again and take them back in and sell them for another penny. We never did get caught.

◆

JENNY ADAIR

Jenny Adair. I was real little when she was going on — about five, six, seven — and she had a sawmill. At that time it was rented by a guy named Joe Ferguson. I used to go down with him. I had an uncle that used to help him out sawing, and I would help carry trimmings off the log. She would be around a lot, telling him to be careful, cutting it too thin, and all this and that. She was a hard old gal. She came out full boar, I'll tell you.

> "
> *Old man Sweeney had a secondhand store. We gathered up beer bottles and took them in. He would give us a penny a piece for them. He stored them out in the alley. Then we would go around back and pick those bottles up again and take them back in and sell them for another penny. We never did get caught.*
> "

✦

She was quite a character. We had cows, you know. Well, everybody did, and boy if they got over on her property! It was alright for her cows, though — they could go anywhere they wanted.

✦

Jenny Adair? You know we would be standing around the fire while we were out at Sullivan's Pond. We younger ones would just listen to the older guys. Jenny Adair's name would come up like so many others, but I don't really remember.

✦

Jenny Adair used to live near Hallam Lake. There was Mrs. Guestin and Mrs. Jenny Adair. Geez, them two would fight. They'd throw sheep manure, cow manure, goat manure, and everything else at each other. I remember when I was a little kid, Mrs. Adair used to have a big ram. She used to run a sawmill and had some property up Hunter Creek — a couple of claims or something. That ram, he was a mean son-of-a-gun. He kept us all at bay. He'd get out and run the hell out of every one of us. He'd walk up and down the railroad track, and us kids would sit around and look. We was afraid to go out. We were quite a neighborhood.

✦

Did anybody ever tell ya — in sixth grade, they gave us the afternoon off to go to the courthouse. They were having court that day and somebody had sold Jenny Adair a bull. She was suing this guy because he sold her a bull that had a broken prick.

✦

Jenny Adair used to come to my house and bring me milk and cream. She was always very good to me and my children. She said, "If I could have been pretty like you and had stayed in the middle of the road. But I was a beautiful young girl. I just got carried away with all the praise." And the men, when they got a real young girl like that, there was no protection. She came from a very good beginning and she had a very nice streak.

✦

"

Jenny Adair used to live near Hallam Lake. There was Mrs. Guestin and Mrs. Jenny Adair. Geez, them two would fight. They'd throw sheep manure, cow manure, goat manure, and everything else at each other.

"

Jenny Adair. They say she used to strain the milk through a dirty old pillowcase covered with cat hair. She owned a lot of cats. In fact, I heard that she used to eat them. Oh yes, thirty or forty cats. I knew her and seen cats all around her place. They lived right down there on Puppy Smith Street. She had a sawmill right there and a place up Hunter Creek.

✦

The only thing I remember is that she had a bunch of goats and a sawmill. She always wore a long black dress.

✦

> "
>
> *In sixth grade, they gave us the afternoon off to go to the courthouse. They were having court that day and somebody had sold Jenny Adair a bull. She was suing this guy because he sold her a bull that had a broken prick.*
>
> "

Jenny Adair — I've heard a lot about her. Jenny Adair, after she died, came back as a ghost. She used to be slammin' doors and opening windows all over town. Well, I don't know how they figured out it was Jenny Adair, but Jenny Adair is Jack Dalton's wife's aunt. Eloise's mother somehow figured out that it was Jenny slammin' those doors. I haven't heard about Jenny for a long time, but I did when I was a kid all the time. It was scary then. It could be that she was just trying to lay one on the kids — I don't know. She used to scare the hell out of me with those spooky stories about Jenny Adair. In town there were always vacant houses and the kids used to play in them. Probably she told those stories to keep the kids out of there. I think there were a lot of ghost stories told. Jenny Adair was the only one I heard about. There were a couple of houses in town that were supposed to be haunted, like the Koch house. That was about Fifth and Main. Mrs. Koch lived there — Dorothy Shaw's mother. Mrs. Koch had a mental disease and lost her marbles. They moved her out and left everything intact — the towels, everything. The house stayed that way for years. Mrs. Koch went to live with Mrs. Shaw. Everybody always thought something happened to her to make her lose her mind. I'm not sure if it was a death in the house or what happened, but anyway, that house was haunted. We lived close to it, and I never did worry about that one. But Jenny Adair used to scare the hell out of me.

✦

She just had her cows down there, right behind the post office now, where Red Rowland's house is. She would herd them cows up the hillside. She was secluded, by herself — would never go out into public. She had a real mean bull. It would run us out of the pasture when we went down there fishing.

✦

We bought the rights to the Red Mountain Ditch from Jenny Adair. She owned the land up there in Hunter Creek. That is who we had to buy the right-of-way from to build the new upper Red Mountain Ditch. She used to have a little sawmill down where the post office is now. She sawed logs and lumber.

✦

I remember Jenny driving around town delivering the milk in the evenings. In the summer, she had a wagon, and in the winter, she was on a sled.

✦

Jenny Adair could not keep house very well. It was the dirtiest place you ever went into. She was very nice. She had cows and separated her own milk. She had a big patch of raspberries and she would give me raspberries and fresh cream. Sam ran the sawmill for her. I think she had a little ranch up Hunter Creek.

✦

Jenny Adair was my good old friend. She lived behind my family down behind the post office. She used to make me and Stogey tend to her cows and then she'd try to feed us. Stogey would sit there and eat and I'd gag. I don't know what she fed us, but the only time I remember sitting there watching Stogey eat, I told him, "You can't eat that." She said it was dumplings and stew, but it looked like a pot of coffee with some old sloppy dough thrown in. I wouldn't eat it. She had a lot of cats. And she lived up Hunter Creek years ago. Then she moved to town behind us. Why didn't she ever marry? Because she was having too much fun with all these old men like that Schwartz. She'd wear overalls under her skirt. When she'd go to town to buy anything, she'd lift up her dress so that she could get her pocketbook out of her overalls. She was something else.

✦

"

Why didn't she ever marry? Because she was having too much fun with all these old men. She'd wear overalls under her skirt. When she'd go to town to buy anything, she'd lift up her dress so that she could get her pocketbook out of her overalls. She was something else.

"

581

RASPUTIN
Russell Holmes

Russell Holmes was Rasputin. He fiddled in the mine. He worked with the Ski Corporation and was a good friend of Ed Tekoucich. I remember his dad, Harry — he couldn't hear too well. I remember him and Leo Tekoucich. They'd go to Tim's — a Sunday deal and then a movie at eight. They'd move out and go to the movie. Harry used to be hard of hearing. Harry and Leo would come in the movie, and we kids would sit in front of them. I think Ted Marolt would go with him once in awhile, too. But it would be mainly Leo. They already had had a few. A good-looking young gal come in and old Harry, he thought everybody couldn't hear him. He said, "Hey, Leo. How'd you like to have some of that?" Punch him in the ribs! They'd talk. They'd think that they were being quiet. Everybody in the place could hear them and laugh. Harry was a big man — a hard worker. He did a lot in the mines, and logging and stuff.

◆

Russell Holmes was called Rasputin. He got that name in the seventh grade and don't ask me what went on to get it, but that is where he picked it up. Our teacher was Paul Smith. He was the principal, and Rasputin was a rough boy. He always had something going up his sleeve. He had a brother by the name of Douglas that was just the opposite. He was kind of quiet. His old man, Harry, was sure a character, I tell you. He was deaf, you know, and he would talk real loud — tall fella, really tall. There was a girl in the family, too, and I can remember when they separated. It was kind of a sad feeling. His wife was a real nice person.

◆

Russell Holmes was called Rasputin, probably because he was always some kind of philosopher. Russell always would analyze, talk, and emphasize everything.

◆

Russell Holmes was old Rasputin. He was a good friend of Peanuts (Ed) and George Tekoucich. I don't know how he got that name. Ed and them all called him that. Peanuts is what we called Ed. Don't ask me how to spell Rasputin either.

HARRY HOLMES

I knew old Harry. He worked for my granddad when he was a young man. Harry was quite a bronc rider when he was young. He was long legged, and Harry had no fear of anything. As long as he had a gut full of tobacco, Harry was happy. He was one of these men that probably looked old at middle age. I think he had a hard life. His folks died young, or he didn't have a family or something. Harry was a good old honest man, I'll tell you that.

✦

I knew Harry Holmes. He homesteaded the property that we later bought up on Owl Creek. Harry Holmes had homesteaded part of that property, and there was a log barn there. Now whether he built it, I don't know. But I'm sure it was there when he lived there. There are the remains of an old spud cellar, and you can see where somebody had tried to farm it. Of course, they went broke. After that he moved into town. He and his wife lived in town as long as they were together.

✦

Harry Holmes was kind of the same cut as Hod Nicholson and those guys. I can picture them yet with their arms around each other — maybe the blind leading the blind coming out of the Hotel Jerome.

✦

He worked up in the Midnight Mine when I was up there. When they had the water-diversion tunnel in Lincoln Gulch, my dad, Harry Holmes, and all of them worked up there.

✦

Harry had a homestead up on East Owl Creek. His family lived there with him — his wife and three sons. I think he worked for Jens up at the ranch. He was a blacksmith by trade.

✦

They were walking along and Harry kept limping. Harry said, 'I don't know what's the matter. I have something in my shoe.' So finally they stopped and he took his boot off and found his knife. He'd been walking on it all morning.

Harry Holmes used to run around with old Tom Stapleton, and this is funny as hell. They were in Guidos one night eating. Old Tom said something to Harry, and Harry kept saying, "Eh, eh," because he couldn't hear. Tom yelled, "I'd like to screw that blonde over there." I happened to be at the bar and I just about fell over. That was something else.

•

Harry dug my cesspool one time, before the sewer system was in. He was a big fellow — very tall. The only thing I remember about him is he went with Parsons, who was in charge of the telephone company. Harry went because he needed the help to take care of the phone line. They were walking along and Harry kept limping. Harry said, "I don't know what's the matter. I have something in my shoe." So finally they stopped and he took his boot off and found his knife. He'd been walking on it all morning.

•

Harry was hard of hearing. He and my husband at the time were very good friends. They'd go out to beer joints, hollering and yelling up the street. I never will forget the time he says, "Yes, Jesus Christ, every time I hung my pants on the foot of the bed, my wife got pregnant."

•

MABEL

Well, Mabel lived where the Apen Clinic is now. She liked her beer. She liked to nip every now and then. Anyway, one time my husband and I had been downtown having dinner. We were on our way home, and right in back of the Bank of Aspen, along that block, here was somebody in the snowbank. It was wintertime. Low and behold, it was Mabel. She'd been to the bars. She was in her seventies. And so Tom said, "Mabel, what are you doing here?" And he picked her up, stood her up, and he said, "Well, now we'll walk you home." So we walked her home. So when he let her in her house and she went in, she said, "Oh, thank you Tom. I'll do the same for you sometime."

"

Harry was hard of hearing. He and my husband were very good friends. They'd go out to beer joints, hollering and yelling up the street. I never will forget the time he says, 'Yes, Jesus Christ, every time I hung my pants on the foot of the bed, my wife got pregnant.'

"

RATTLESNAKE BILLY
Bill Anderson
(1863-1931)

Rattlesnake Billy. I don't know how he got that name, but he was kind of a funny old character. He wasn't much for having kids around, but about twice a summer, why he would have a couple of old donkeys up there he would let us ride. He was kind of like a real lonesome guy — a roustabout. He used to bootleg real heavy from what I can remember back when Dad talked about him. But he never mixed with anybody. He lived back at the end of Waters Avenue. The only two guys that used to get along with him was the two Swedes. His name was Bill Anderson.

❖

Rattlesnake Billy? Yes, he had a little shack where the old Koch Lumber Company was — right above that, right close to the railroad tracks. And I never did see him. He stayed by himself there. I know he had some kind of a deal with the groceryman. The groceryman would come on a certain day, and Bill had a little box out in front of his house, like a mailbox, and the groceryman would put his few groceries in there and that was it. I never did see him come out.

❖

Rattlesnake Billy? Yes, he used to live right over here. He used to sell whiskey. I don't think he liked kids. I think the revenuers came in one time, and where did he hide his whiskey, but in the horse manure! It was in bottles. He had a cabin and it burned down when he was making whiskey. Boy, the powder was going off. It was quite an explosion. I was just a kid. He lived right next-door to Maggie Early.

❖

He was an old miner. I remember the old-timers talking about how he sort of rattled like a rattlesnake when he talked.

❖

"Rattlesnake Billy used to sell whiskey. I think the revenuers came in one time, and where did he hide his whiskey, but in the horse manure! It was in bottles. He had a cabin and it burned down when he was making whiskey. Boy, the powder was going off. It was quite an explosion."

Rhubarb Wine
From Helen Kralich

4 quarts rhubarb
1 gallon boiling water
4 pounds sugar
2 sliced lemons
2 sliced oranges
1 package dry yeast

Pour boiling water over rhubarb. Let stand 24 hours. Strain through a cloth and add remaining ingredients. Let stand 3 days and 3 nights. Strain and put into jugs. If you have more than 4 quarts of wine, add one pound of sugar for each quart over.

"

He was kind of a funny old character. He wasn't much for having kids around, but about twice a summer, why he would have a couple of old donkeys up there he would let us ride. He was kind of like a real lonesome guy — a roustabout.

"

He lived up here in this end of town. He died in a fire. His house burned down. They said he was cooking hooch. You have to watch it, because the boiler can blow up. If it starts burning, it will blow. His real name was Billy Anderson. I think he got that name because he had a temper like a rattlesnake.

✦

Rattlesnake Bill. As far as I know he had some claims or something up Independence Pass. He had the cabin up in the West End somewhere and it burned down. He had a bunch of powder in there. He used it to mine. I know somebody said that he was a hollering for the people to stay away from the cabin because he had the powder in there.

✦

ONE-EYED JOE
Joe Sawyer
(1872-1960)

One-Eyed-Joe used to play cards in Tiederman's Store. If I remember right, I think he was splitting wood and a piece popped up and hit him in the eye. Real nice gentleman. He had a cabin on the bank of Castle Creek up there by the old town of Ashcroft. Never any excitement or anything, just plain old Joe.

✦

Old Joe Sawyer, he always worked around these sawmills, when he would get a job. I think he lost his eye on the damn sawmill — got a splinter in it, or something like that. He was a pretty good guy. That's all he ever done was work around sawmills.

✦

I knew Joe. I don't know how he lost his eye. I knew he and his brother. I can't remember what his brother's name was. Every once in awhile, we'd drive up to Ashcroft and we'd stop and see him and have a cup of coffee. One-room cabins was all anybody ever got into — kitchen/loft — typical Ashcroft cabin. They would live up there in the summertime, and then they'd move back to his house somewhere up near Shadow Mountain in the winter.

✦

Joe Sawyer. I think he worked for my uncle, Harry Koch. I can remember him. He had a sleigh. He would take the front bob of a sled and go up in Sawyer's Gulch (it was named after him) and putter around all day long in the snow. The snow was deep, too. He'd bring down an old jag of timber on this one bob. He was a pretty nice guy.

✦

I knew Joe Sawyer. He worked up at the mine with us. He worked the Midnight Mine, too. I don't know how he lost his eye. He was mostly in the logging

" Old Joe Sawyer was kind of deaf. He cupped his ear all the time. This other fella was partially deaf, too, and they used to get to talking together and one would say, 'You going fishing?' And the other would say, 'No, I'm going fishing.' 'Oh, I thought you said you were going fishing . . .' "

587

Main Street in Ashcroft, 1926. Courtesy Robert Zupancis.

business and more or less a loner. There was a lot of them old fellas working up there cutting timber for the Midnight Mine. They didn't work inside; they were outside cutting timber for us to use in the mine and stuff like that. He was kind of deaf. He cupped his ear all the time. This other fella was partially deaf, too, and they used to get talking together and one would say, "You going fishing?" And the other would say, "No, I'm going fishing." "Oh, I thought you said you were going fishing . . ."

❧

One-Eyed Joe? I just remember him on the street. He had a patch on his eye. It seems to me he had a patch on his eye and he wore a black hat. And that's all I can remember.

❧

One-Eyed Joe? Oh my God, yes. I haven't heard about Sawyer for a long time. He had a crush on my sister for one thing. He was nice, and he was a gentleman, really. He always dressed nicely and he looked clean and well kept. I think he lived up in Ashcroft at one time. He must have fixed up one of the old houses.

❧

Joe Sawyer lived up at Ashcroft. He had mining claims. He was on the north side as you cross Express Creek — that log house. I don't know whether it's still there or not.

❧

Joe Sawyer lived in Ashcroft. He was a fixture. He was a nice man. He had a cabin in town on Main Street. He loved to be out in the hills. I think by rights he was involved in timbering — you know, the sawmill business. He just had one eye. I don't know how he lost it. When we first got our jeep and were jeeping around the country, we always stopped in Joe Sawyer's and visited him.

❧

Joe Sawyer on his ninetieth birthday. Taken on Hyman Avenue, 1952. Courtesy Helen Kralich.

589

Aspen, 1905, from Ajax. Courtesy Peggy Rowland.

One-Eyed Joe Sawyer was just kind of an old prospector as far as I know. He never married. I don't think any of them ever married. There were three of them that I knew. There was Joe and Scott. He run the sawmill for Kochs out there. He was like a foreman. He run the carriage and everything.

●

One-Eyed Joe Sawyer had the little house up from the house that Cactus Gold and Ruby bought. He was always pleasant. We went to the sawmill. Russell and Ed set up a sawmill on Basalt Mountain. I went up to cook. I had the girls. Lindy was just little. Mike, Cap, Russ, George, and I — I guess there were about nine of us. There's some great stories from there. Anyway, Joe Sawyer come along. He was a good worker. One time I had just got

Lindy to sleep and went into the kitchen to do the dishes. Joe went out for his walk around to pick his teeth. Uncle Harry Holmes would tip his chair back and take a piece off the wall for his toothpick at his house. He was like Grandpa to all of us. He'd babysit my girls and everything. If he got tired of their bickering, he'd just turn off his hearing aid. Oh, George would be so mad. Anyway, Joe was out there walking around. He had a horrible cough. Lindy had just gone to sleep. She sat straight up in her crib. Scared her to death. He did this all the time. We'd just get to sleep and here he'd be, coughing. Did he lose his eye in the mill? I think so. A chip flew into it. I had seen him with a patch, but as a general rule I don't recall his wearing one all the time. But it wasn't messy looking.

◆

DEWFLICKER MOGAN
Joe Mogan
(1888 - 1934)

I knew Dewflicker. I knew the old man and the kid. Old man Dewflicker used to ride the train — hitch a train. I don't know where the hell he'd go, but he'd always stop by and my mom would give him a loaf of bread. He'd jump on that train and away he'd go. Young Dewflicker, I didn't know him too good. He got killed in the war, I think. I really don't know how he got that name. He was a good athlete, I know that. Boy, he knew baseball and he knew all of them. The senior Dewflicker — he knew his sports. He used to take us kids and go fishing. He used to tell us some great stories about some guys he used to play ball with or something like that.

◆

His name was Joe Mogan. I don't know whether Dewflicker came from the amateur boxing days. They used to box in the Elk's Club, and I can imagine Dewflicker being somebody that was fast with his dukes.

His name was Joe Mogan. I don't know whether Dewflicker came from the amateur boxing days. They used to box in the Elk's Club, and I can imagine Dewflicker being somebody that was fast with his dukes.

◆

He worked for the electrical company when Browns had the electrical. How did he get the name Dewflicker? I remember dad saying something, something with the light bulb — the lights or something, but I can't remember all of it. He was a small little fella.

◆

Now Dewflicker is a name that I use still. For everybody that I can't remember their name, I call them Dewflicker. Dewflicker always rode the electric light truck when we went to the top of Brush Creek Line. It was a Model T. I always thought Dewflicker was a name that the Browns dreamed up (he worked for the Browns).

◆

Dewflicker Mogan. Oh, he was another drunk. Yes, he was a moocher. He'd follow you around if he thought you had some booze or was going to get some. He'd follow you all over town.

◆

Dewflicker used to be an electrician. He was a very good baseball player — a pitcher. Maybe Dewflicker came from that. I couldn't say.

◆

His son, Dewflicker Jr., was an electrician, too. He was on the power pole. Flicker might be pertaining to the lights and stuff. He was Ikey Mogan's brother and he got killed in the service. Dewflicker Sr. got his name when he was working on electric lights. He was turning the electricity on and off and kept yelling, "Do 'dey' flicker?" to his partner. That's when they started calling him Dewflicker.

◆

I don't know how he got that name. He was a little man. His wife was little. She always looked like she just came out of a beauty shop. His son was called Dewflicker. His other son, Ikey, was the one that was a fire bug.

◆

"

Dewflicker got his name when he was working on electric lights. He was turning the electricity on and off and kept yelling, 'Do dey flicker?' to his partner. That's when they started calling him Dewflicker.

"

IKEY MOGAN

Ikey Mogan. Yeah, he was off a little bit. When we hiked to Snowmass Lake, he wore a pair of tennis shoes with hardly any sole on them. He almost didn't walk back out of there. Have you ever walked to Snowmass Lake? There are a lot of rocks and stuff. He just had a light pair of tennis shoes and walked over them rocks all the way up. We used to walk up and out of there in a day.

✦

Ikey? Yeah, he started fires all over town and then was the first one there with a hose to put them out.

✦

Ikey Mogan was in my class at school. The teacher asked him to close one ear for a hearing test — stick a finger in one ear to see if he could hear her talk. He stuck his pencil in his ear and the eraser came off. Well, he had a temper, you know, so they took him to Denver. It went in his ear so far that they couldn't operate. They always felt that was the cause of his problems. Evidently they never did take that eraser out of his ear.

✦

There was a house on Main Street., half torn down. Ikey had this house all rigged up with props. He would pull wires, strings, and ropes, and curtains would close and open, and there was noise. He was creative without a doubt. Oh, he had an imagination like a trap. He would create all these effects to make this house really haunted. I remember once he took my brother Bud in there. He had a vise. Ikey took Bud in and he tied one hand to his belt loop in the back and put his other hand in the vise. He had some kind of a seance going there and painted my brother's face with silver paint. Bud was smart, but Ikey was a lot bigger — not huge, but he was big enough to take care of a twelve- or thirteen-year-old kid. Ikey was twenty-five. He just thought it was funny. He'd get a big kick out of that. Bud came home really scared. My mother was mad as a hornet.

✦

"

Ikey Mogan was in my class at school. The teacher asked him to close one ear for a hearing test. He stuck his pencil in his ear and the eraser came off. Well, he had a temper, so they took him to Denver. It went in his ear so far that they couldn't operate. They always felt that was the cause of his problems. Evidently they never did take that eraser out of his ear.

"

Ikey Mogan. One day when I working for the city, he was trying to dig up a water service. The ground was frozen right over across from City Hall by the Brand Building. He took a bunch of dynamite and set it on the ground. He was going to blow up the frost on the ground so they could dig it up. This other guy that was working for him took the front-end loader and put the bucket down on top of the dynamite. I was down in the basement of city hall and I thought the whole building was going to fall down. It made a U-shape out of the bucket of the front loader and broke a lot of windows in cars.

❖

"

Ikey Mogan had all his teeth pulled. I won't start to tell you why, but I can tell you that Ikey Mogan could open up a beer bottlecap with his gums.

"

Ikey Mogan was a young punk running round. He was just absolutely crazy. You didn't see a truck come into town very often, but one time a semi was coming down Main Street — Rolfing Hill — and Ikey lived down at the bottom. Ikey Mogan went out and sat in the middle of the street. This big semi came down and went around Ikey and on down the road. He was always doing things like that.

❖

I had a little submarine once that I ran in Sully's Pond when I was a little kid. I went up to the pond and Ikey Mogan took it away and threw it in without the little cork, so it sunk. Then later he brought it down to my dad and said, "I got your kid's submarine back for him" and wanted a reward. "I had to go out there and go underwater to get this for him." He didn't mention that he threw it. He was our boxing coach. We had a golden gloves tournament. Ikey Mogan and Teleo Caparella were the two best. Ikey was a great boxer — one of those guys that flitted around and could duck. He would come up to you and say, "Try and hit me." He burned down John Henry Stewart's house with all the stuff in it.

❖

My brother was sitting by Ikey Mogan in a bar one time and Ikey was trying to cut his wrists with a pocket knife. "Tired of living." I asked my brother why he didn't try and stop him and he said, "I didn't give a damn if he killed himself." I guess he didn't work hard enough at it with the pocket knife.

❖

Ikey Mogan had all his teeth pulled. I won't start to tell you why, but I can tell you that Ikey Mogan could open up a beer bottlecap with his gums.

◆

Ikey? That firebug. We went to school together. We knew all those kids. When Ikey was little he was the only kid that owned a tricycle and we'd beat the hell out of him so we could ride it. He had long blond curls. He looked like a llittle girl. His mother, Shermy Mogan, later married Mel Henricks. She was a pretty lady.

◆

BUCKSHOT MADDALONE
Jimmy Maddalone
(1882 - 1957)

Buckshot Maddalone was Charlie's dad. Jimmy Buckshot, yes. I don't know how he got his name. He acted the big-shot role, you know. It wasn't Big Shot, it was Buckshot.

◆

Jimmy Maddalone was just a little bitty guy, and I remember him very well during high school. His wife was blond. She wasn't Italian. She was pretty tall.

◆

Buckshot was kind of notorious for blasting at things and people with a shotgun filled with rock salt. People used to raid his garden and try to steal his wine and stuff. He would blast that shotgun at them. I don't know if he ever hit anybody. He would maneuver that shotgun around over heads a few times. That would clear them out. That's probably where the Buckshot came from.

◆

> *"*
>
> *Buckshot was kind of notorious for blasting at things and people with a shotgun filled with rock salt. People used to raid his garden and try to steal his wine and stuff. He would blast that shotgun at them. I don't know if he ever hit anybody. He would maneuver that shotgun round over heads a few times. That would clear them out. That's probably where the Buckshot came from.*
>
> *"*

Buckshot Maddalone, bless his heart. You know he was just about this high. He came to my house sometimes. Everybody came to my house because of the pies, cakes, and fresh bread. Little Buckshot, he'd always come up. He was a very good barber. Kept my boy's hair nice for school. I always liked him.

◆

Jimmy Maddalone was called Buckshot. I guess he got his name because he was little. I heard Buckshot used to go visit his mother every once in awhile. He'd walk into the yard and say, "Momma, you workin' too goddamn a hard in the yard." Jimmy Snyder and Mike built a lake over at Jimmy's house. Buckshot came to Mike's one day and said, "Mike, you sommabitch, you get a lake and you get a chickenshit" because they wouldn't let him fish in their lake. He was a little guy and used to come in and get fishing boots. They had to sell him boy's size irrigation boots — size four maybe. I don't know how he ever made it working as a gandy dancer for the railroad as little as he was. They called the section workers on the railroads "gandy dancers."

◆

He probably got his name from the terminology "buckshot." He lived down behind the post office. He used to have a bucket by the river where he would get water and bring it up to some of the animals. He had it always sitting on a post and somebody shot it full of holes. So old Jimmy would say my, "My bucket is shot, my bucket is shot." So they called him Buckshot. I worked with him up at the Midnight Mine. Little Jimmy — he was a real short guy. And he strutted around like a little bandy rooster. He was proud all the time. You couldn't see him when he was pushing one of the ore cars out of the mine, he was so short. One time we thought it was a runaway car, so we threw a log in front of it and it almost broke his neck. It really stopped him. He said, "I maka a mine outta you."

◆

Buckshot used to stop in the Red Onion and have a beer or two, and then his wife would send Chuckie to go get him for dinner. Little Chuckie was only about ten years old, and Jimmy would see him coming in the Red Onion and say, "This is my Chuckie, de last of de croppa."

◆

596

Teleo Caparella,
Bob Kopp, and
Buckshot Maddalone
at the Eagles.
Courtesy
Maddalone/Clapper
Family.

Buckshot? I don't know. I think because he was a pretty small man and in those days he didn't like it. They used to call my brother, once in awhile, Brother Jim Buckshot. Boy, he didn't like that. Dad didn't like being called Buckshot.

◆

He'd cut hair for everybody — old Babbick and different people. He cut mine, too, until I got enough money to earn my own and go. Christ, he pulled more hair. Well, you can see, there ain't much left! He'd put a little oil on the clippers and heat them up. "That's better." Like hell it was. Poppa was a pretty small man. He was about four eleven or five feet.

◆

597

Buckshot Maddalone. I asked a friend of Jimmy Maddalone, and Walt used to call him Buckshot, and I says, "How did he get that name?" And he says, "I guess because he's so short."

✦

What about Buckshot Maddalone? They used to call him Jimmy de Buck. He was a miner. I think he got his name because it was a slang term for dollar.

✦

"

Dorothy Shaw was a gant old lady, shrewd — too shrewd for her own good as far as I'm concerned. Tight? You could squeeze her and get nothing.

"

JUDGE WILLIAM SHAW
(1894 - 1974)

DOROTHY SHAW
(1894 - 1979)

Dorothy Shaw was a gant old lady, shrewd — too shrewd for her own good as far as I'm concerned. Tight? You could squeeze her and get nothing. When I was a young kid, a couple of my friends used to work down there on weekends for a few bucks. I would go down for an hour or two and she was always putting a buck or two, or a ten-dollar bill, out somewhere in the open, tempting us to find out what kind of guys we were. We found copper and brass and got our money that way. We didn't have to steal it. But it was just her way of finding out what kind of guys we were. The judge chain-smoked; he would mooch cigarettes left and right. Dorothy wouldn't give him pocket change.

✦

Dorothy Shaw, the old skinflint? That's what we called her. Yes, boy, she wouldn't spend a nickel to see the finest circus in the world. Oh, Judge Shaw was a pretty good guy. I don't think he ever done anything wrong to get a story told on him.

✦

I remember Dorothy. She was interested in the thrift shop and would buy up all kinds of stuff and store it in her house. They said one of her rooms was just stuffed. She saved everything. She and her husband, Judge, would never sell their cars. They would buy a new car maybe every four or five years, but they would keep the old one. They had cars all over the place. I don't know whatever happened to them. I suppose the grandson finally got rid of them. They always bought good cars when the Judge was able to get around. He had a big Cadillac. Judge Shaw was always bumming cigarettes. Back then, the lawyer represented both the buyer and seller. I think that was exactly the role that Judge Shaw filled. He was the only lawyer probably in Pitkin County.

❧

Judge Shaw was a big man. I think he was about six feet, and he was bulky. I remember him saying to me, "When you sell your house, remember me." He was a good wheeler-dealer. He got rich real quick, but not from us. He died before we did.

Dorothy Koch Shaw and Judge Shaw, June 4, 1950.

❧

Judge Shaw had a system. People would die and he would be the administrator for their estates. That would go on and on for years, and then he'd finally present the family with a bill. The bill was worth more than the property was worth. So naturally they would say, "Well, you can take the property." Never spent any money. Never gave any away.

◆

The Judge and Dorothy Shaw had that house next-door. She was the worst miser I have ever met in my life outside of Silas Marner. Much worse than anything you have ever read about, was Dorothy. She hoarded everything. They owned most of the gasoline stations and the Koch Lumber Company. Now imagine this woman, Dorothy, was a relative of Robert Koch, the man who we must thank for discovering the bacillus for T.B. and anthrax. She was related to this doctor, this wonderful man whom Germany has written books about. During the war, she hoarded every piece of iron up here. Everybody was supposed to turn in anything that was metal. Well, Dorothy decided if the government thought it was worth something, why wasn't it worth something to her? She collected everything metal and she hid it. She had old houses here that she owned that were full of everything you can imagine — extra furniture she picked up in old houses, papers, metal, and anything that she could find.

◆

Oh Lord, I knew Dorothy Shaw for a long time. She collected antiques. She figured that nobody would take charge of anything, so she grabbed onto everything that she could. But she was one of those rather well-educated women in town. She married Judge Shaw, and he was county judge for years and years.

◆

Dorothy Shaw. When she was a girl going to high school, she was real athletic. We were playing basketball and boy, she picked me up like nobody's business. She was strong. We wore bloomers and black stockings — they were hot.

◆

"

Judge Shaw was a big man. I think he was about six feet, and he was bulky. I remember him saying to me, 'When you sell your house, remember me.' He was a good wheeler-dealer. He got rich real quick, but not from us. He died before we did.

"

What about Dorothy Shaw? They were all wealthy when they died. I don't know how much good it done any of them.

Harry Koch and family, McClain Flats Road. Courtesy Aspen Historical Society.

✦

I remember Dorothy. Well, Dorothy was a Koch, and they were a very prominent family with a legal background in the area. So they were kind of high-society folks. Then she married Bill Shaw, who was a pretty brilliant lawyer actually. There was kind of a common knowledge around town that she was tighter than a tick. She would invest every penny in property — you know, buy up the back taxes. Her husband was the county judge, and he had access to all the records. Their grandson sold it all in about two days. Through all those years, they gathered up all his property, millions of dollars worth, and their grandson unloaded it so fast that they were probably both turning over in their graves.

✦

Dorothy Shaw was my neighbor. I lived here, she lived there. I tell you, the Judge was very unloving. Very. She wheeled her boy in the baby carriage until he was in the first grade. Terrible. He was sick all the time. They always had a nurse. It was sort of pitiful, because she gave her love like that. She didn't have anything else. I'm glad she enjoyed him. His son was a chemist — absolutely brilliant. There was no other name for him. He married. He had children, too. The Judge smoked incessantly and always bummed cigarettes. I think he was too dumb to be smart.

◆

What about Dorothy Shaw? They tried to steal everything. They would steal anything they could get their hands on. They might not steal it — they would give you a dollar for something that was worth five hundred.

◆

Dorothy Shaw was a pretty good friend. She told me one time — she admitted it — "I had to make everything count when we were first married." She said, "My dad had money and he wouldn't help us, and so Bill and I just made everything count." And she says, "I admit it — I'm very tight."

◆

The Judge would come in the treasurer's office, bumming cigarettes from Phil Crosby because Dorothy wouldn't give him any money for cigarettes. He would say, "Phil, can I have a cigarette?" Then he would take about four or five out of the package.

◆

He was the only judge in Aspen for years and years. During the Depression, he was the only one that had money. He married Dorothy Koch. The Judge always bummed cigarettes off everybody because Dorothy wouldn't let him buy any.

◆

Dorothy Shaw was a rich lady. I remember the Shaws had that big red car. She was big and tall. He was, too. She was always very nice. I remember her all during

"

He was the only judge in Aspen for years and years. During the Depression, he was the only one that had money. He married Dorothy Koch. The Judge always bummed cigarettes off everybody because Dorothy wouldn't let him buy any.

"

those years. The Shaw's kid never did live here. But they owned that big house on Main Street with the pillars. After Dorothy's mother died, nobody ever lived in that house. They had old antique cars out in the shed. There were lots of characters around here then.

◆

Dorothy Shaw never threw anything away. She was cleaning out her attic and we had us an old truck. We hauled I don't know how many truckloads of newspapers and magazines and moved them into one of those buildings over by Koch Lumber. We just baled them up and stored them. I have no idea what happened to all that stuff.

◆

I'll tell you a good one. When she died, her grandson told us we could have all the stuff in the attic. I was with the historical society at the time. What a job! We finally sent somebody up to the store to get some masks to put over our noses and mouths because it was so dusty. She never threw out one magazine. She never threw out a paper. Rags — her son's tiny underwear — all in rags. And old bills, shirts, clothes. Never threw out a thing. Unbelievable. I'll never clean out anybody else's attic again.

◆

I knew Dorothy Shaw. She seemed nice enough, but the way she raised that boy of hers, I felt sorry for the kid. She babied him so and protected him so much that after he did leave home it was rough on him.

◆

I worked for Judge Shaw for awhile. That was one geek and a half. I had never seen an office that was more disorganized in my whole life. He spent all of his time trying to bum a cigarette. When he dictated to me, he dictated the whole legal form — the Where Is's and the Here To's and the This Is's — and then hand me the form. I had to take the whole damn form down in shorthand.

◆

> *" I worked for Judge Shaw for awhile. That was one geek and a half. I had never seen an office that was more disorganized in my whole life. He spent all of his time trying to bum a cigarette. When he dictated to me, he dictated the whole legal form — the Where Is's and the Here To's and the This Is's — and then hand me the form. I had to take the whole damn form down in shorthand. "*

DEACON JONES

Deacon Jones. When I was growing up about 1910, he was an old black shoe-maker. His shop was south from the opera house if you were going up Mill Street. He repaired shoes. If he wasn't busy, why you'd see him sitting outside in a chair with somebody visiting with him. He had a strange voice. When he talked, it squeaked real funny. I couldn't even describe it to you. I know when my father was still living, I said to him, "Why does Deacon Jones' voice do that?" And so my father said, "I don't know. I think he puts too much lard on his bread."

✦

Deacon Jones had a boot shop right in there by the Bank of Aspen. I was with him in the old, old hospital when he died. I was nursing at the time. And you know he said he was a preacher. You never heard anybody give such a sermon. And you know, he was short. He was really black with a real wide nose. He was pretty old. I think he got pneumonia or something like that. When he passed away, he was by himself — no family. He had a funny voice.

✦

HORSE THIEF KELLEY
James H. Kelley
(1850-1928)

I didn't know much about Horse Thief Kelley. I know he always had a bunch of starving horses. Couldn't make enough money to feed them, so he just throwed them out in the countryside and let them fend for themselves. Hell, he had so damn many horses he couldn't keep them in the wintertime, so he just let them run wild anyplace they wanted to go. He was always in jail for letting his horses run in the streets of Aspen. That was against the law.

✦

> *"Deacon Jones was a black shoemaker. He had a strange voice. When he talked, it squeaked real funny. When my father was still living, I said to him, 'Why does Deacon Jones' voice do that?' And my father said, 'I don't know. I think he puts too much lard on his bread.'"*

Horse Thief and his daughter lived about four blocks from us. They used to have a lot of goats and raised honeybees. They sold honey and milk. He was pretty old when I remember him. He was all stooped over from my recollection. But his daughter, Bertha, took care of the goats and the bees. She was a learned person, but very odd. She used to work with the bees without any kind of netting.

●

Horse Thief Kelley wasn't in the country when I was young. I knew his daughter, Bertha, and she lived where the Original Curve Apartments are. She ran a herd of goats up on Aspen Mountain every day. She had bees. She would always go pick the honey and never put a net on. She used to travel with Horse Thief when he ran his horses. He would travel from town to town. He traded, raced, and everything else. He would send her to Aspen, and when his dealings was over, it was her job to start them over the pass. Then he would show up four or five hours later, drunker than hell.

●

I heard about Horse Thief Kelley. It could be that Horse Thief Kelley lived on that ranch that my grandfather bought. It could be that Horse Thief Kelley lived there, and if he did, he was the guy that had the chickens live in the house with him. I guess it was easier to put them in the house than building a coop.

●

Horse Thief Kelley? It just meant what it says. He was a horse thief. He'd gather up all the horses he could and take them to his place and sell them later. He'd maybe alter them a little bit and sell them again and again and again — as far down as the horse would let him, I guess.

●

He was a real photographer and used to take family portraits. We called him Horse Thief Kelley "with a buckskin belly." Kids would say a few more things with a few more added onto that.

●

" *Horse Thief Kelley? It just meant what it says. He was a horse thief. He'd gather up all the horses he could and take them to his place and sell them later. He'd maybe alter them a little bit and sell them again and again and again — as far down as the horse would let him, I guess.* "

Kelley did have a good stallion, and he'd come by our place. What my dad didn't like was that Kelley'd go immediately to our grainery. Boy, he had nags — we called them broom tails. His darn horses, they weren't worth anything. He'd go feed them on our good expensive grain. Even then it was one dollar for fifty pounds for his broom tails. But then he'd go right into the bunkhouse with my grandfather. My grandfather probably had the equivalent of a college education, because he studied everything. Kelley was also a great student and, of course, his religion — he was a convert actually. Boy, he studied science, mathematics, and architecture.

We called lunch our dinner at noon. Horse Thief would go right into the house and sit down at the big long table. There was always extra people. It was loaded, especially on weekends. Kelley would sit up and eat. Anybody coming along the road, they'd stop. It was automatic that they were invited to sit down for supper. Kelley had free board and room. Then he'd leave our place and travel on up over Capitol Creek, all around, and take family portraits. I still have some old photos.

Horse Thief Kelley lived in Aspen up on Cooper Avenue. His daughter had goats, and every morning she'd take the goats up Aspen Mountain to graze. He'd ride along on an old pinto stallion. One time, he stopped at our place. He had a washtub dragging behind his horse and had a heck of a time getting out of it. He was sitting in this washtub, pulled by the horse, like a two-wheel deal. But I remember him having a black stallion that he toured the whole neighborhood with. This was a big black Percheron. When he used to stop at our place, Mother, when she saw him coming, would pull the blinds down. He was dirty. Actually, he was really a pretty smart man. He wrote poetry and stuff. He had some horses running loose. He let them graze where they could.

I don't know how he got his name. He used to tour the country to different farms for breeding purposes. He rode around the ranches and the barns in search of stud fees.

*Cowboys up Woody
Creek, about 1900.
Photo by
Horse Thief Kelley.*

Horse Thief Kelley? I didn't know too much about him, but they say he got
more horses by doing it the wrong way than the right way. He was an old horse
trader. I don't know that he ever stole any, but they called him that. And he got
around a long time.

•

I don't remember Horse Thief Kelley, but I do remember his daughter that had
the goats. She used to live where the Original Curve is. She was a well-educated
person, too, but you wouldn't know it. She had an old hat, and for an apron she
had a burlap bag. She looked like a rag lady, I'll tell you. They said she had a
Stradivarius violin that was worth some money.

•

607

TIM KELLEHER
(1874 - 1945)

NORA KELLEHER
(1879 - 1954)

"

Tim was kind of a solemn old character. He had a jaw that kind of hung down. In the morning when he woke up, he punched the cash register drawer open and it stayed that way until he closed at night. He just left it wide open. He never rang up a sale or anything.

"

Nora and Tim Kelleher, I knew them well. They had a saloon where the Red Onion is now. When I was little, I used to have to go down and get a pail of beer five times a Sunday for the folks at home. We'd just use the old blue-and-white lard pail that usually come out in those days — nickname was Puritan. And of course with every bucket of beer, you got a sack of pretzels. The pretzels were free, and the beer was ten cents for a five-pound pail and twenty-five cents for a ten-pound pail.

❦

Tim was kind of a solemn old character. He had a jaw that kind of hung down. He held his pipe in the same manner; it would hang loose in his mouth. In the morning when he woke up, he punched the cash register drawer open and it stayed that way until he closed at night. He just left it wide open, and all he would have to do is turn around and make his change. He never rang up a sale or anything. Tim's was also a restaurant. It stayed open until about nine or ten at night — that is, after the mining slowed off.

❦

Where the Red Onion is now, it was old Tim Kelleher's. Old Tim was an ex-boxer. He had a lot of boxing pictures. They are still in there, I think. He had them lined up. Used to get a schooner of beer. Tivoli was probably the popular beer at that time. They used to have them for ten cents, or something like that. They owned a bunch of log cabins across the street.

❦

I can visualize Tim. Irish — almost gray when I remember him. Kind of ruddy-faced. Kind of apple-cheeked and a pipe stuck in the front of his face.

❦

Tim always wore a copper bracelet. It wasn't a flat bracelet — it was one of those big wires, twelve-inch or better, about a quarter-inch thick. He said it was good for the arthritis or rheumatism. He never took it off. Nora used to help out. They had a small kitchen there. You could get a sandwich or two. I don't remember her too well. I remember Tim pretty good. Tim was a pretty good size. He was a stocky fellow, heavyset. He still had that Irish brogue. Him and his wife were both Irish.

❖

Tim Kelleher and Nora. They just got along like nice Irish people. Cussed each other good. Certainly. They had to make known their ifs, ands, and whatnots.

❖

Nora was short and stocky. Both of them had heavy Irish accents. When my brother came home from the service, Tim wanted to sell him the Red Onion for something like $150. My brother said, "What am I going to do with that?" Tim said, "You make a few nightmares."

Judge John Leahy and Tim and Nora Kelleher. Courtesy Aspen Historical Society.

❖

609

JUDGE JACK LEAHY
John M. Leahy
(1858-1939)

Old Hotel, Main Street, Ashcroft, 1926. Courtesy Robert Zupanics.

Judge Leahy was a very educated, dear man. Was he really a judge? Yes, he was. He was educated way back East someplace. He was a very learned, dear person. We could always talk. I'm a talker. We would talk at no length about everything and anything. I loved him. He was very eccentric. He didn't give one damn whether he was married or not. He didn't need anyone else. He lived up at Ashcroft. He was a very dear gentleman but a little on the eccentric side. He had quite an extraordinary cabin in Ashcroft with junk hanging on the walls — all kinds of tea kettles, pots, and pans.

Judge Leahy was a self-taught judge. Judge Shaw wasn't real popular, and of course a lot of people would go up to Ashcroft and have Leahy draw up legal papers. If somebody wanted to loan somebody money, he would fill out whatever papers it took. When there was nobody left, he had all the town's papers. The only thing I can remember well about Leahy is that he had a cabin in Ashcroft where the stove and the door lined up. This was probably in late fall or early winter. He didn't want to bother to cut the wood, so he would go out and cut a big tree. This was a pretty big wood stove, and the tree was too long to leave inside the cabin, so he left the door open. When the end of it burned down, he would just keep shoving the wood along into the stove, with the door wide open. That's what stood out in my mind. I don't know whatever happened to him. In those days, there was probably very little put into the papers, and a lot of people didn't get the papers. People just faded away as far as I'm concerned.

◆

FLOYD CALLAHAN

One time Had Deane went into Callahan's Hardware Store to buy a saw. Old Floyd said it was a certain price and Had said, "I could get it cheaper at Montgomery Ward." So Callahan said, "I'll sell it to ya at the same price as Montgomery Ward then." So he paid for it and Floyd hung the saw back up on the rack. Then Floyd said, "It will take you three days to get it from Montgomery Ward. Come back in three days and you can have your saw."

◆

Floyd didn't take no crap from nobody. Another guy was working for him, and Floyd was in the office. A customer came in and the door was open. Floyd heard the conversation. This guy wanted something and said, "How much?" And the help told him, and he said, "For how many?" That irritated Floyd, and he came right up to the customer and said, "You come here on your own free will, and if you want this you buy it and if you don't, the door is still open, you can go."

◆

"

Judge Leahy had a cabin in Ashcroft where the stove and door lined up. He didn't bother to cut the wood. He had a pretty big wood stove, and the tree was too long to leave inside the cabin, so he left the door open. When the end of it burned down, he would just keep shoving the wood along into the stove, with the door wide open.

"

This fellow I worked with named Callahan, at the hardware store, had a thing about a certain group of people. They were what he called "leading citizens." They would wander around from place to place with no means of livelihood, but yet they always had money for cigarettes and such.

◆

SLIM AND JACKIE MARSHALL

There was a restaurant called the Silver Grill. Now there was a couple you should have met — Jackie Marshall and Slim. She was a statuesque woman. She painted her fingernails black. She wore a black uniform with a white starched collar that came up in a ruff behind her head. Slim was the cook, and he was anything but slim. The two of them must of run that place from early in the morning until two in the morning. And the after-dinner crowd was quite a crowd in those days.

◆

Slim Marshall and Jackie, they ran a restaurant here. I guess they had quite a brawl at one time, and I think she threatened to shoot him. She was tough — part Cherokee. Yes, she ran the show.

◆

Slim and Jackie Marshall? Yes, I remember. It's kind of hard to bring these people all back to life again. Let's see — she drank more than she sold.

◆

You probably heard that Jackie was under suspicion that she'd killed her former husband. People didn't think that highly of her. But when you knew her, she was quite a nice gal. Yes, she was a good-looking gal, too. She was very nice and very business-like.

◆

"

There was a restaurant called the Silver Grill. Now there was a couple you should have met — Jackie Marshall and Slim. She was a statuesque woman. She painted her fingernails black. She wore a black uniform with a white starched collar that came up in a ruff behind her head. Slim was the cook, and he was anything but slim.

"

Jackie Marshall had real black hair, and she was a big girl —not real heavy, just big, and very pretty. I think she dressed a lot in black and white.

✦

They were great dancers. They'd go to the Armory Hall and dance. Oh, she was quite a gal and was the waitress of all waitresses. I mean, she was really spiffy when they first came to town. I don't think they ever closed. He cooked and she waitressed. They were hard-working people.

✦

Slim Marshall was originally from Silverton. Did they tell you about Jackie? I used to go with her daughter, Rosalie. Jackie was part Cherokee. Did anybody ever tell you what happened to her in Montrose? Did anybody ever tell ya, she killed her husband over there? This was before she married Slim. Rosalie wasn't his daughter. She shot him. That's what they say, you know what I mean. A lot of people didn't know that, but I knew it. I think she was a very good friend of the D.A. She was a very attractive woman and could outdrink anybody.

✦

Jackie Marshall, you could say, was a character. But I wouldn't name it one way or the other — which kind of a character. She was very swank. She was flashy. I knew her well, but she was flashy. Everything had to be ultra-bright.

✦

Slim and Jackie were good people. Jackie wore the pants in that family. She was nice looking. She looked like one of those early-day queens. She could carry seven or eight breakfast platters on one arm. They were heavy. She was part Indian.

✦

Slim Marshall was "I can get it for you wholesul." He was always trying to sell Joyce a car. He would tell her, "I can get it for you wholesul."

✦

"

Slim and Jackie
Marshall?
Yes, I remember.
It's kind of hard
to bring these
people all back to
life again.
Let's see —
she drank more
than she sold.

"

BERT SCHWARTZ AND BESSIE

Bert Schwartz and his horse, Bessie. He used to ride her up to the old post office every day and tie her to the stop sign there. And, of course, a few of the kids tried to bug the horse trying to let her loose and run away on him.

✦

Bert lived down by the ice pond. I used to always wear a swimming suit or a pair of shorts in the summertime. I loved swimming, and anytime I was out, and there was water available, I'd take to it. I was over that way one afternoon. I guess there was some gals from Texas or something. I took a swim out in the pond and came back. As I got back, Bert confronted me and he says, "You are a dog to be swimming this time of the day," or something like that. And he kind of told me I was trespassing and everything, but actually he didn't own the land. He was just squatting there himself.

✦

I worked for some fellas that had the Texaco Garage right catty-corner from the Elks Building. In those days, Bert used to always come over and use the restroom. And so to get even with him one day, I put the hose in the men's restroom. The ceiling was all open inside the garage, you know. I just took the hose and put it up over the wall and left it. When he walked over, I heard the door slam. I gave him a shot of water. He never came back to use our restroom anymore. He didn't come inside to raise Cain or anything, but I think he had an idea who did it.

✦

Bert was fat — a little short guy — and so was his horse. They both waddled. He'd go after the mail and park his horse outside. He'd have to get Bessie near the curb so he could get on. I don't remember him ever doing anything. He was a bachelor and wasn't really that old. He must have had a pension of some sort.

✦

"

Bert was fat — a little short guy — and so was his horse. They both waddled. He'd go after the mail and park his horse outside. He'd have to get Bessie near the curb so he could get on. I don't remember him ever doing anything. He was a bachelor and wasn't really that old. He must have had a pension of some sort.

"

Bert Schwartz and his horse, Bessie? They used to come uptown, and he would come to Tiederman's in the afternoon. He'd get his supplies, visit with everybody, and play a few hands of cards. Tie Bessie up to the post.

◆

I knew Bert. He lived right below us, down around where Peggy Rowland lives now — in that area. He took that horse just about everywhere. Old Bert was tough, too. You didn't make any cracks about that horse. He was as bad as John Healy. You'd make a crack about that horse and you got problems. Geez, yes. Old Bessy. Healy's horse was really a good Palomino — beautiful horse, good looking, and old John was proud of him, too. You didn't make any smart remarks because old John Healy was a tough son-of-a.

◆

Bert Schwartz. I remember Bessie was swayback. Bert used to come riding on Bessie. He used to keep everybody in line. If something wasn't right, why he would be down your throat pretty quick about it, giving you hell.

◆

I didn't know Bert too well. He was quite an old guy when I knew him. He was getting some age on him, and I think he was probably an old miner that had retired. In his later years, he was old and couldn't work and didn't have too much to do. He was quite a figure around town, and I think he went over to Aspen every day and visited around and went back to his little cabin at night. I don't think Bert had any enemies. He would ride Bessie over to town every day. They built a new bridge over there that goes over to what was the old hospital. So when they decided to cut the ribbon, they thought they would wait until Bert rode up and he could cut it. But Bert was busy that day and he never got there, so someone else had to hack the ribbon. Bert missed it. He missed his big opportunity. That would have been a great day for Bert.

◆

Bert Schwartz and his horse Bessie — the old black swayback horse. They were a great couple. The horse would bring him to town, and he'd go to the bar, usually

"

Bert Schwartz and his horse Bessie — the old black swayback horse. They were a great couple. The horse would bring him to town, and he'd go to the bar, usually the Red Onion, drink up, get on Bessie, and she would take him home.

"

*Elks Building and
post office, 1950s.
Courtesy Aspen
Historical Society.*

the Red Onion, drink up, get Bessie, and she would take him home. He was pretty old when he died. All I remember is his riding Bessie.

◆

Bert Schwartz and Bessie? I remember the name. Schwartz — he used to make sausage — liverwurst. It was his wagon they hoisted up on Halloween.

◆

Bert used to ride old Bessie to the post office every day; there was a telephone outside. The post office was in the Elks Building, and he would tie old Bessie up to the telephone and get his mail. He'd stand around and talk to everybody and ride back home again. He lived down by the ice pond.

◆

GROUND HOG JOE

Ground Hog Joe. I was told he lived in a shack where the old Durant dump is up on Ute Avenue. Just to the right, there was a spring alongside the dump. I don't know how he ever got that name. Never did hear his real one. My uncle used to go and drink out of the spring when he was a boy.

✦

Ground Hog was a miner. As I understand it, he took over right where the Ute Springs were. That's where the Indians used to camp in the early days. Then Old Joe moved in after the Indians left. The last two Ute Indians were buried in the Ute Cemetery, I was told. When we were young, Ikey Mogan and I went up to the cemetery at midnight to dig them up and get the artifacts buried with them. We weren't very successful at that because an eerie feeling scared us right out of there. We never did go back.

✦

We used to have an avalanche that used to come down right where the Aspen Club is. There used to be an old bachelor there. We called him Ground Hog Joe, but that wasn't his name. I don't know what his name was. We thought his cabin went one time, but the avalanche went right by him.

✦

Ground Hog Joe. My mother said that one time when the snow was really heavy and they thought the avalanches were going to run, he moved to town to get away. And he stayed in town for a couple of weeks. He finally decided the avalanches hadn't come down, so he was going home. So I guess the night he came home, the avalanche ran that morning. He ran out the front door in his underwear. Never hurt him, though.

✦

A snowslide come down once over here, where you go up towards the Aspen Club. We didn't say "Ground Hog Joe." We always called him Holy Joe because

" One time when the snow was really heavy and they thought the avalanches were going to run, Ground Hog Joe moved to town to get away. He stayed in town for a couple of weeks. He finally decided the avalanches hadn't come down, so he was going home. So I guess the night he came home, the avalanche ran that morning. He ran out the front door in his underwear. "

he lived in a little cabin right on the crest of the hill — right under a slide area. The snowslide come right over him. He escaped it. We called him Holy Joe. Maybe he got the name Ground Hog Joe because he lived so close to the ground. I don't know.

◆

HOD NICHOLSON
(1882 - 1964)

Hod Nicholson was sheriff for a long time, and he always used to deputize my dad to help him out when he was in the East End of town and some of the old bootleggers would start fighting. He was a hard worker, real hard. He was honest as the day was long and had a faithful wife. When he worked up at the Midnight Mine, he would come to town for his weekend drunk. Hod would hit from bar to bar. She would drive the old pickup and stop where he went in. About 2:00 or 3:00 A.M., he would finally come out, stop in the liquor store, and get himself a quart. Then he'd get in the truck and drive back up Aspen Mountain to the Midnight Mine to their little cabin. He would be back to work the next day.

◆

What about Hod Sr.? I remember mainly a western kind of cowboy — a modified hat, plaid jacket, and a chaw of tobacco.

◆

Hod Nicholson — the old man? He was a tough little guy. He was a sheriff. I remember he could chew tobacco and drink a shot of whiskey at the same time. Old Hod was the blacksmith up at the Midnight Mine. When you go up by the Midnight Mine, in that one little log house, that used to be old man Hod's house. I know that it is still there. He did their blacksmithing — sharpened tools and stuff like that. He'd come into town and boy, he could put them away pretty good. He'd be in the Eagles Club and he'd have a roll of bills. He always had money. He'd bring 'er out and say, "I want a drink." That was even after I

" When Hod Nicholson worked up at the Midnight Mine, he would come to town for his weekend drunk. Hod would hit from bar to bar. His wife would drive the old pickup and stop where he went in. About 2:00 or 3:00 A.M., he would finally come out, stop in the liquor store and get himself a quart. Then he'd get in the truck and drive back up Aspen Mountain. He would be back to work the next day. "

Hod Nicholson's place, Capitol Creek, 1927. Courtesy Aspen Historical Society.

was older. He'd look at it and he'd buy you a drink and then he'd say, "Wait a minute — I'll skin 'er back here." He'd skin those bills back. He was a great little guy, a tough son-of-a-gun. He was sheriff here, too, for awhile. He was probably five–two or five–three. But he was a tough son-of-a-gun.

❧

Hod Nicholson was another alcoholic. He was the sheriff for a long time. He would go around and say he was going to make a raid on the bootleggers, and then he'd sit around there and drink all their booze.

❧

Hod Nicholson worked at the Midnight Mine, too. He was the blacksmith for years. Hod didn't draw a sober breath for a long time. His wife was always faithful. She would go to every bar and wait in the truck till she could take him home.

❧

"
I sat down with
him and he
drank this vodka
straight. He said,
'Get him one,' so
I drank it. Boy,
that was the only
one I ever
drank straight,
especially vodka
like that.
I couldn't do it.
All the miners
would stop after
work and have at
least one drink..
They would do
all their mining
in the barroom
and talk about
women in
the mine.
"

Hod was real short. And he always wore a hat, just a regular old rounded hat. One time up at the Midnight Mine, in the blacksmith shop, I was going to go in the tunnel. Somebody had left a cigarette burning on the bench and he got mad and said he was tired of tripping over them cigarettes all the time. He said he wished we would stay out of his shop. He loved his booze. I drank with him one time at a dance at Slim Willis' bar. I sat down with him and he drank this vodka straight. He said, "Get him one," so I drank it. Boy, that was the only one I ever drank straight, especially vodka like that. I couldn't do it. All the miners would stop after work and have at least one drink. They would do all their mining in the barroom and talk about women in the mine.

Hod ran a boy's tourist camp way up at the head of Capitol Creek for years. I think he was probably the first person to go into the tourist business in town. He had boys come out from, I think it was Cincinnati, Ohio, and they would camp out six weeks every summer. Went from lake to lake and rode in the mountains. When they were home, his wife, of course, would feed them. I don't know how many boys he would have — maybe five or six. But every summer he would have them come out from wealthy families. It was very good for the kids.

Hod Nicholson Sr. was sheriff. He chewed tobacco a lot. He wasn't big, but he was stout and loved horses. They were an old ranching family. He had a big ranch and homesteaded out on Capitol Creek, right up above the monastery.

His wife had so much patience with him. You know, they lived up at the Midnight. She would sit all day and all night till the bars closed. He was up at the old Eagles a lot. She would sit there all day and all night waiting to drive him home. She never drank, you know. She just sat there.

I remember Hod. There were two Hods, father and son. Hod Sr. was a little guy, a miner and a cowboy and a blacksmith. He was big on horses, probably more than a miner. Hod was at the Midnight Mine for years. He was the caretaker and ran the mill, the blacksmith, and everything — they were big horsemen.

❦

Hod has been around this country a long time — an old-time character. He worked for my grandfather before I was ever born. He was a blacksmith for my grandfather, a good many years, and then he married Balina Gates. Hoddy, his boy, was my age. But when Hod was young, before he was married, he worked for my grandfather a lot, and he was quite a hunter and fisherman. They had a little homestead up on Capitol Creek. His father's name was, I think, Billy Nicholson.

❦

Hod Nicholson. He liked prestige. He loved to be sheriff. He liked to be the head of something because he couldn't do that at home.

❦

Of course, old Hod, he was more or less one of the old cowboys, too. He was one of the old teamsters. The only thing I knew about him is he loved to go to a bar and drink, and if anybody was looking for a fight, he was always accommodating. It took a good fellow to match him.

❦

Big Hod Sr. was a great guy. He worked at the Midnight Mine for years and years. Him and my dad worked for the forest service cleaning trails.

❦

Hod Nicholson was an alcoholic, but he was a pretty nice guy. He worked at the Midnight Mine. I guess at one time, he was the sheriff in Pitkin County. I understood that, but when I knew him he was more or less retired. He was a binge drinker. He'd go on a binge for a week or two weeks. He was more or less doing blacksmithing when I knew him. He wasn't very big, but he was strong.

❦

"

Hod Nicholson was another alcoholic. He was the sheriff for a long time. He would go around and say he was going to make a raid on the bootleggers, and then he'd sit around there and drink all their booze.

"

Hod Nicholson worked up at the Midnight Mine and ran the sawmill for the timber they put in the mine. I was probably about ten or twelve years old, and I used to go up there on the weekends when he ran the blacksmith shop. He'd give me an old hacksaw blade, and I'd be on the grinder and try to make a knife out of it. He'd show me what to do. Him and Dad was real good friends. He was a sheriff for quite awhile. He could shovel that booze down. He used to call me Blackbird and I'd call him Snowball. I don't know why he called me Blackbird. He give me a name, so I give him a name. He used to have a saying, "Goddamn you, you ain't even got sense enough to piss a hole in the snow." He had all kinds of good sayings. It was always something. He was a funny old guy.

◆

CLUBFOOT BROWN

Clubfoot Brown was kind of an old bird. He lived down on the corner of Hyman and Center Street, I think, in a little cabin. He was born with a club-foot. A nice fella — didn't move around too much. His wife died real early, as I remember.

◆

Clubfoot Brown didn't have a foot. When I was a kid, he lived down on Hyman. He worked in the Midnight and he'd shovel the concentrate. He'd dump it into the railroad car. When I was a little kid, I'd go up there. Had a big square point on his shovel. They'd dump it in the chute with a truck. He would shovel it back in the cars and do that all day. I'd go up there and fiddle around with him. He'd get dirtier than hell. Geez, he'd take that square point — I don't know how he did it. That stuff was heavy. Day after day. He was a nice old guy. At that time, he wasn't very young, I'll tell you — fifties, I would imagine. It's hard for me to figure out ages, because an "old guy" might have been in his thirties. But he was tough. He could shovel.

◆

> "
> *Hod Nicholson used to have a saying, 'Goddamn you, you ain't even got sense enough to piss a hole in the snow.' He had all kinds of good sayings. It was always something. He was a funny old guy.*
> "

Clubfoot, oh yes. Something was wrong with one of his legs and I think they cut it off at the ankle or something. Then they called him Clubfoot after that.

✦

Clubfoot Brown. Did he have a real clubfoot? Yeah, he did. I don't know how it happened. He was sort of a plumber around town. He was very neat and spiffy all the time, even when he was working. He was a big man, clean-shaven, and well dressed all the time. He lived in a little house across from where Frances Herron lived.

✦

Clubfoot was another one that worked in the Midnight Mine. He was a big, heavy-set guy. He looked like old Santa — he was just about as roly-poly. He was crippled. I don't know how he got his clubfoot. He worked up by the Midnight Mine, cutting timber. He was a nice person, very sociable. When they would ship the concentrate, when they milled it, he would shovel it out of the truck into the railroad car. That was one of his jobs up at the mine. Boy, he was good.

✦

I remember Clubfoot. I think his name was Charlie. He was a miner. I don't think he ever married, to my knowledge. Don't know whether he had an artificial foot or not. I remember every afternoon when he got off work, he would really dress up, put on a suit, white shirt, and a tie to go uptown.

✦

Clubfoot Brown — I don't know why he got that name. His injury probably came from a frozen limb. I remember he used to be a teamster, from the Midnight Mine, as I recall. He was strong.

✦

Did he have an actual clubfoot? Yes, he did. I don't think he was born with it. I think that it happened to him someplace along the way. He was a very secretive,

" Clubfoot Brown was a big, heavy-set guy. He looked like old Santa — he was just about as roly-poly. He was crippled. He worked up by the Midnight Mine, cutting timber. He was a nice person, very sociable. "

big man. He was not so tall, but he was big, and you would always hear him clomping around. I don't know much about his character except he was nice. Most men, if they weren't too nice, liked to paw little girls, and I was a little girl. You notice things like that. He wasn't that way and always dressed real nice — good shoes and good everything.

✦

HOOFY SANDSTROM
John Sandstrom
(1900 - 1962)

I don't know how he got Hoofy as a name, but I remember Hoofy real well. He was one of the best miners, they said, around this country. Drank quite a bit. He lived right below Ed and Mabel Tekoucich. We used to play baseball with a stick and tennis ball when we were kids. Antonia was his wife, and they had a daughter who was really a nice gal. He was a great miner, but he sure drank a lot. I think he was a singer. He would go in to Ed Tiederman's and sing "Wild Irish Rose." Old Ed hit him in the head with a cantaloupe one day. It was in Ed's store. Hoofy come and he started to sing. Old Ed told him to shut up and get out. Hoofy wouldn't, and old Ed had real ripe cantaloupes. Man, he pasted old Hoofy. Did he stop singing? No. Not for very long. But Hoofy was a nice man. He just drank quite a bit, I guess. He and Antonia were both really nice people.

✦

Hoofy used to live in the West End, and somehow he ended up in Oklahoma Flats. Hoofy was in his cups a lot of the time. One day he got annoyed at some ants 'cause there was an ant pile out in the front yard. So he got his powder supply out and loaded that ant pile up — I don't know how many sticks of dynamite — and set them off late one afternoon. It broke all the windows in Oklahoma Flats and brought all the neighbors to attention. Hoofy was perfectly satisfied that he got all of the ants.

✦

"

Hoofy would go in to Ed Tiederman's and sing 'Wild Irish Rose.' Old Ed hit him in the head with a cantaloupe one day. It was in Ed's store. Hoofy come and he started to sing. Ed told him to shut up and get out. Hoofy wouldn't, and old Ed had real ripe cantaloupes. Man, he pasted old Hoofy.

"

*Mine shaft near
Aspen.
Courtesy Ruth Perry.*

I worked with Hoofy in the Midnight Mine. But we don't know how he got the name. He was one of our partners. Used to come up half-boozed. He was a good, safe miner, though. If it wasn't for him, one night we would have all been killed. We walked in the mine and seen two little rocks fall down, and he said, "I don't think we better go in there for awhile. It might be a little dangerous." So we sat down and had a cigarette, and the whole back of the mine caved in and we would have been under it.

✦

Hoofy lived down there in Oklahoma Flats. That was about 1948. He used to get drunk and go swimming right in the Roaring Fork. That's where they found him dead. He could have fell in. I don't know, he was drunk.

✦

After pay day, Hoofy wouldn't show up to work for a couple of days. He used to go down to the Red Onion when nobody was in there and get on stage and sing. Hoofy was quite a character.

✦

Hoofy thought he was the maestro of town. He lived over in a little house. He and his wife would come home at all hours of the night, drunker than hell. You could hear him because he would start singing. Maybe he sang all the way from downtown. You could hear him coming two blocks away.

✦

Hoofy had an excellent voice. He had dynamite, too. But you know, all he had to do was get two belts of liquor under his belt and he would start singing. He used to sing down at the Red Onion and the Silver Grill (we called it the Greasy Spoon).

✦

"

One time, Hoofy wanted to get rid of the ants at his house. So he put several sticks of dynamite in the ant hill. He blew all the windows out of his house and most of Oklahoma Flats.

"

One time, Hoofy wanted to get rid of the ants at his house. So he put several sticks of dynamite in the ant hill. He blew all the windows out of his house and most of Oklahoma Flats. When he used to have too much to drink, he'd go in the Red Onion and sing "My Wild Irish Rose," and Kuster would pay him a dollar to go down to the Golden Horn. Steve Knowlton had the Horn then. He'd sing it there, and they'd send him back and forth to get rid of him.

✦

Poor old Hoofy. He was an alcoholic in the worst way. I don't think he ever had a name outside of Hoofy. He liked to dance, and gawd, he'd get out on the dance floor by himself. He'd go around and around. So they called him Hoofy.

✦

When Claude was little, I said, "You stay in the window and watch because this is groundhog day. Call me if you see a groundhog." Pretty soon he called, "Mamma, mamma. There goes a groundhog." It was Hoofy Sandstrom.

✦

Poor old Hoofy. He drank like a fish. This was a dirty, dirty shame, because his wife was a wonderful person. She was a great cook and housekeeper, then all of a sudden, she let everything go. I never knew him except when he drank, but her, it was altogether different. I don't know how Hoofy got that name. I don't know his real name for sure.

✦

I don't know how he got that name. He came into the White Kitchen. He would open up the door and sing an Irish song, any time of the day. He'd just open up the door and start singing. Did he have a good voice? Yes, I think it could have been. It was very high, you know.

✦

Old Hoofy lived in Oklahoma Flats, and he had a big ant pile by his house. He took a couple sticks of dynamite and blew up the ant pile, but he also blew windows out of everybody down in Oklahoma Flats. I don't think it did much damage to Hoofy. I don't know how he prevented that. He worked in the mines, so I guess he knew how to handle dynamite. Apparently he wanted to make sure the job was done. He was quite a guy.

✦

Hoofy lived down here by us. He would get so drunk you can't believe it, and of course his wife was right along with him. I tell you, they made a pair. He always was Hoofy, and that's what they called him.

✦

Hoofy Sandstrom — god, what a subject. There was no harm in him. He was always singing, and after he would get drunk, he'd just go from home to home and sing songs. He could sing. He had a darn good voice. Hoofy was born here. His father was a miner and contracted lung disease. He died when he was only thirty-three years old. Their mother raised six kids, four boys and two girls. Terrible. Hoofy went into the service real young, I guess to get away. I don't know how come he chose what he did, because I didn't know him at that time. When he came back from the service, he was in his late twenties, I suspect. He

"

When Claude was little, I said, 'Now you stay in the window and watch because this is groundhog day. Call me if you see a groundhog.' Pretty soon he called, 'Mamma, mamma. There goes a groundhog.' It was Hoofy Sandstrom.

"

worked in Aspen. There wasn't anything else to do except mine. They all died young. The Sandstroms were Norwegian and Finn. Did he have a bit of an accent? No. He had everything else but that, I think. He had a whiskey tenor — very high. What did Hoofy drink? Anything he could get his hands on.

✦

Yes, Hoofy and Antonia. They lived over in Oklahoma Flats. Pope in his last few years was over there, too — was kind of a wino. I remember one time they had a big row and Hoofy ended up with a black-and-blue mark. Pope whacked him with the broad side of an axe. They went to court, and I don't even know who was magistrate then. I guess it was old Ruby Bandy. That was Dirty Herwick's sister. Anyhow, she threw them all out. They were there at the bar again at nine in the morning, buddy-buddies and drunker than hell.

✦

" Hoofy thought he was the maestro of town. He lived over in a little house. He and his wife would come home at all hours of the night, drunker than hell. You could hear him because he would start singing. Maybe he sang all the way from downtown. You could hear him coming two blocks away. "

I don't know how he got his name, but he was married to a cousin of mine. She loved to drink it just as fast as he. That's what killed both of them. She was a nice girl. It's a shame that she turned out that way. Whenever he got a little bit tight, you could hear Hoofy. Everybody knew he was around.

✦

Oh, they used to fight. You could hear her hollering, "Help, help! He's killing me!" They lived down the block on the corner from me. My husband and I'd stand out there and listen to them. I'd go, "Honey, should I go help?" He'd say, "Don't you get into it. Don't you dare go down there and get into it." The first thing you'd know, they'd be walking up the street going like fury. She was always walking ahead of him. Either she was ahead of him or he was ahead of her. They never walked together.

✦

Hoofy took a bath in the Roaring Fork River. That's how he died. I think she was gone before him. She used to make the most wonderful raised doughnuts you ever ate in your life. Was she ever a cook! I tell you, I've never eaten anything like her raised doughnuts and her bread. She's the one that showed me how to make it.

✦

He used to sing the song "My Wild Irish Rose." They used to give him a bad time about it. Told him how good he was and tried to get him on the radio. Antonia left him to live with his brother. I don't know if they ever got married, but they were living together.

✦

THE REVEREND RAY or ITCHY RAY
David Ray

David Ray used to come up to our house; he always visited us. He would sit in a chair, and anything he touched would have to be scrubbed. He smelled. He had a limp and had a cane. I think he was in the service — World War I. He belonged to the Legion. One time, at a party, David Ray came in and they gave him black gloves to wear so he could eat. I guess nobody ever suggested that he take a bath. They just let him live like he wanted. His little old wife was really small, real short, and she was very quiet. Never heard anything out of her; she never went out of the house.

✦

He was our neighbor. There was never a funeral that went by that he didn't attend. He would reek from the smell of goats. I laughed at Tom Sardy. David used to come in the store and ask, "Tom, could I borrow your phone?" And Tom would sort of relent and let him use it. Afterwards, Tom would take Kleenex and clean it. It was terrible.

✦

I guess Dave was a preacher. He did have a church, but I don't think he was ever ordained or anything — just did it on his own. My high school graduating

> *"David Ray smelled. He had a limp and a cane. One time, at a party, he came in and they gave him black gloves to wear so he could eat. I guess nobody suggested that he take a bath. They just let him live like he wanted."*

class of '42 went down there to see what kind of church it was. When we got in there, he was praying on the pulpit. Suddenly, a black goat came in and looked through the door, and Dave said, "Get out of here, you black bastard," and went on with the praying again, right there in the house. It was on the 800 block of Hopkins where the Original Curve condo is now.

◆

Dave Ray — you've heard him called Itchy Ray, haven't you? Everybody called him Itchy Ray. They wouldn't call him that to his face, but that was the going term. He didn't take a bath. His wife was just as bad. She always came in behind him. Margie Jenkins' father ran the drugstore and carried a line of perfume called Evening in Paris which Margie used. One day she was in the drugstore, and Itchy Ray and his wife came in and bought a bottle. Margie went right home and threw out every bit she had.

◆

He was a preacher. He had a church of his own. Did anyone go to it? No. He and his wife was about all, I guess. The boy was crazy, you know. I don't know just what he did, but he had some horses and he would come out to our place to get hay and oats. You could hear him for three miles away hollering at his horses. He was a preacher. It was sort of his own religion. He would attend every funeral whether he knew the people or not. He and his wife would sit in the very front row.

◆

David Ray and his goats. He was kind of a comical old devil. He was a preacher and everything else. One Halloween, why, he had a big old billy goat that was in the shed in the block below him. A couple of guys and I took that billy that night, this was in 1946 or 1947, because the hotel was starting up. We took it in the lobby of the hotel and it got away from us. In order to get out of that mess, we left it alone. We finally got it outside. He didn't do any damage except run around trying to get out of the building. At about eleven at night, one of the fellas that was crossing the street seen a wheelbarrow laying there. I don't know how he knew the billy was in a fighting mood, but anyway, he grabbed the wheelbarrow and started thrashing toward the billy. The billy squared off and come after him, and they hit head on. The billy ended up in the old wheelbarrow, feet straight up. Knocked him out. And then later on that evening, somehow somebody put it in Hughy Chisholm's car and left it there all night. It made one hell of a mess in the car. We never did find out who the character was that did it.

◆

He went to everybody's funeral. He was there first, oh yes. Their house caught fire and my brother went down there so he could help them. And he walked in and said, "Let it burn."

◆

Dave Ray was a preacher, you know. We were having a party with the Snyders on a Sunday afternoon. We played a joke on Mike Garrish and this gal. Jim Snyder said, "Let's go down and get Dave Ray," and I said, "Okay, I'll go with you." It was only a block away, so we went down and said, "Dave, could you come? We got somebody that wants to get married." (Our friends didn't think we were going to do it.) He came with his book, Bible, and cane. Jim and I were snickering all the way ahead of him as we were walking up the street. About the time he hit the end of the block, our friends saw that we got Dave. That house just opened up and everybody flew, Garrish and all. And we said, "Oh, I guess they decided not to get married."

◆

Dave Ray's house was where he had the church. It wasn't real big. I don't remember a sign. I don't even know what Dave called his church. He had a son. I went to school with him. His wife wore curtains on her head for a veil. They were lace curtains that looked like a veil.

◆

Oh, Reverend Ray. I remember him wearing black — he was a preacher. He kind of wore black clothes, and he was lame on one side of his leg.

◆

"

That same night, about eleven, one of the fellas that was crossing the street seen a wheelbarrow. I don't know how he knew the billy was in a fighting mood, but he grabbed the wheelbarrow and started thrashing toward the billy. They hit head on. The billy ended up in the old wheelbarrow, feet straight up. Knocked him out.

"

"

There was just one David Ray, and there was nobody like him, I'll tell you. People said he smelled like a goat. And you know, he never missed a funeral — never, never, never. He went to all the funerals. His wife went, too. Her name was Ruthie. That was something else. Well, the poor gal — I really think that there were two or three buttons missing.

"

There was a marvelous old fellow here named Dave Ray. There must have been, even in those days, something you could clip out of a magazine and get a diploma that said you were a reverend. Anyway, he got himself a diploma that said he was a reverend, and he was called Reverend David Ray. He raised goats on East Hopkins. He was a very untidy man and smelled like goats and tobacco. He married this woman named Ruth Roberts, who I think was probably retarded or not very bright. One time, Reverend David Ray's wife had to have her appendix out, and her father was helping David pay the bills for the appendectomy. You know how you get a doctor bill, and then you get a bill from the anesthesiologist, and then one from the hospital, and one from the drugstore, etc. So Ruth's father met Hannibal Brown at the post office and he said, "Han, I got something serious to talk to you about. Do I owe you anything for Ruthie's operation?"

✦

David Ray lived up on Hopkins above us. I don't know what kind of a minister he was. He had goats and was a war veteran who had been injured in the war. I think he got an army pension, and so that is the way he lived. He had a son that was very, very brilliant. His name was Robert Ray, or Bobbie, we called him. He was a scientist, so I guess you never can judge them, can ya?

✦

There was just one David Ray, and there was nobody like him, I'll tell you. People said he smelled like a goat. And you know, he never missed a funeral — never, never, never. He went to all the funerals. His wife went, too. Her name was Ruthie. That was something else. Well, the poor gal — I really think that there were two or three buttons missing. He really knew what was going on, and I don't think his wife did. Dave Ray never missed a funeral. He just kind of went around healing a little bit like a minister. That's why he never missed a funeral, you know. Anything could have happened with that old guy.

✦

David Ray lived down on Hopkins. He was a self-professed preacher. He never missed a funeral in town, whether it was Catholic, Protestant, or what. Dave Ray was there. He buried everybody. I never went to his church. I knew David Ray. He was a goat man. I think he was kind of a holy roller.

◆

*In front of the
Hotel Jerome, 1923.
Courtesy
Robert Zupancis.*

David Ray had goats. All I remember is Dave Ray was sort of the town buffoon. His wife never left the property, I don't think. I don't know if he had any customers as a preacher or not.

◆

Dave Ray — that's a character. There wasn't a human in this town that couldn't come to my door and not have something to eat or to be greeted nicely, and here he came one stormy night. Oh god, he was dirty. He stunk. He came to the door and he said, "Do you have something left from supper?" I said, "Yes, I do. Do you want to come in?" Well, he came in. I had a beautiful big cocker dog. Dave Ray came in and started taking off layer after layer. The room was getting very close. My dog came out from behind the stove, and he started howling at him. He said, "Why is that dog acting like that?" And I said, "Oh, he's been acting funny all day." But I knew . . . there was a peculiar scent.

❧

Dave Ray didn't come to town with a wife. He advertised for a wife — mail-order type. She came in by train, and of course everybody wanted to see her. He was so proud. But he got somebody just like himself. Who else would answer? He said he wanted a good-looking woman for himself. But he also wanted someone who nobody else would look at. Well, he found her.

Dave Ray didn't come to town with a wife. I don't know if it was his parents or relatives he stayed with. You could smell them for blocks. And then he advertised for a wife — mail-order type. She came in by train, and of course everybody wanted to see her. He was so proud. But he got somebody just like himself. Who else would answer? He advertised for a wife to take care of his boy. He said he wanted a good-looking woman for himself. But he also wanted someone who nobody else would look at. Well, he found her. He used to say that to everybody. He said it and meant it. Everybody went to the train to see Ruthie get off. And she fell for him like a ton of bricks and vice versa. They were happy ever after, I guess. I never heard anything of conflict. She used to walk two feet behind him everywhere. And it wasn't because she was Japanese. He preached anyplace and everyplace. I think he was a very God-fearing person, a dear person. He wasn't mean. He thought he had this calling. Like in Denver, you'll hear them on the street corners. He preached anyplace that anybody would listen.

❧

Dave thought he was a preacher, and he'd go to every funeral. He didn't care what denomination or anything. He went anyway. He kind of smelled like a goat. Did I ever go to his church? God, no.

❧

He was in World War I. He was kind of crippled and limped. They were real hillbillies, he and his wife. She was short and stooped and walked like she was behind a plow all the time. She didn't say much, and he talked all the time.

❧

Dave's wife, Ruthie, had the goats. There was another lady who had a whole lot of goats. That was Horse Thief Kelley's daughter, Bertha — a very educated woman. They had nothing in common. Ruthie used to wear curtains around her head like veils — like a little girl dressing up. She wasn't all there. She was very much vacant. The town liked her. She was very kind. Everybody was tolerant and nice. That's one thing about Aspen — very tolerant of another person's weakness. They were always willing to listen to her or give her things. It was beautiful — a real genuine tenderness.

✦

David Ray was a veteran of World War I and had a bunch of goats along the river. He was getting disability from the government from World War I. He walked with a cane when somebody was looking. But when they wasn't looking, he would pick up his cane and step them off as good as anyone. He called himself a preacher. They would have church on Sunday, and one of them played a guitar. They would play "Red River Valley" and a few things like that at the church meetings. He was pretty unusual, he and his wife. His wife, I do remember one time — I mean I hate to say it — but he went down to Parsons, the pharmacy, and asked for something for his wife. He said his wife smelled so bad he couldn't get near her. Parsons said, "Well, you know, maybe just some soap and water would take care of the deal."

✦

He was quite a character. He thought he was a preacher. His church was something out of his house. Just Dave Ray — period. I couldn't tell you who went to the church either, because I never ventured down there. He wasn't a very clean man. Just ordinary, but not clean.

✦

Dave Ray used to go to all the funerals. He was at every one. That was the oddest couple. They had a horse and a cart, and he used to go out and scavenge. He was always scratching and itching. She usually wore an old black hat. They were strange.

✦

David Ray? Well, I don't know what kind of a preacher he was. I don't think he had anybody but his wife there. He milked them goats and sold the milk. I would see him delivering it around town. Never missed a funeral. They both sat in the front row. Her nose was flat as a pancake. He told me the way that happened was that she used to stand at the window, her nose up against the window

"

Ruthie used to wear curtains around her head like veils — like a little girl dressing up. She wasn't all there. The town liked her. She was very kind. Everybody was tolerant and nice. That's one thing about Aspen — very tolerant of another person's weakness. They were always willing to listen to her or give her things. It was beautiful — a real genuine tenderness.

"

watching for her dad to come home when she was little. And that's how her nose got that way. I never did believe him.

✦

David Ray had one son, Bob. I think he was a genius. I don't know what ever happened to him. Robert Ray died in Junction eight or nine years ago. The old man never bothered anybody or anything — he just wandered around. But he was intelligent, too. A lot of people thought he was a crackpot, but I didn't think so. He was very different. He was a real eccentric, and I think why people thought that way was because they were so very poor. He wasn't what you would call ambitious. But he had a little church. Did I ever go to this church? Yes. I think it was Jimmy Skiff, me, and Loretta (we called her Lovey because her last name was Love). There were four of us, and I can't remember the other one. I think it was Tommy Burback. His mom and dad worked for Ditty and Bob for many years on the ranch. We were in high school. I think it was around Easter. We'd gone to our church and were all dressed up. So off we went. Everything was nice enough, and the boys put stuff in the collections. Dave says, "Now we'll bow our head in prayer," which was a little loud. Pretty soon, I guess the others were deaf or else they didn't know, but I hear this tinkle, tinkle, tinkle. I thought, a cat with a bell on its collar at church? It was a goat with the bell around the neck. The goat was just walking down the aisle toward Mr. Ray. I tell you, I thought Jimmy Skiff was just going to have a stroke right there. Oh, we hooped and hollered — not until we got outside. But finally I said, "I think maybe we'd better go. I think this is not the place for us. I don't know about you people, but I'm going to have to laugh." Burback says, "Pepper's always polite." I said, "You better be, too." He replied, "How come?" And I said, "Because I'm with you." So we all went out and I thought old Skiffy was going to roll around on the ground. We never went back. His wife was very strange.

✦

David Ray was small and tattered looking. He walked with a cane. I never went to his church — Lord, no. People laughed because they always went to weddings and funerals. They never had an invitation, but they always went.

✦

> *"Her nose was flat as a pancake. He told me the way that happened was that she used to stand at the window, her nose up against the window watching for her dad to come home when she was little. And that's how her nose got that way. I never did believe him."*

636

ALEX BARRAILLER
(1881 - 1961)

Alex was a bachelor. He was one of the town characters. He was always pick-led, and all kinds of things happened to him — rolled in the creek, etc. He was just a neat guy. He lived forever. Pickled all the time and lived to be an old man. He was a brother to Emery Barrailler. He lived on King Street, right across the street from No Problem Joe. Sometimes they'd find him sleeping between mat-tresses. He had stacks of mattresses in his house.

✦

Alex Barrailler? Oh yes, the little drunk in town. He never did hurt anybody. I'll have to tell you, this is not even funny, but anyhow, he drank, and my uncle drank, too — my Uncle Alex (his name was Alex, too). Anyhow, Alex Barrailler would always go by the Catholic Church. He would see the priest, and he would always tell the priest, "I know, I don't come strict." He used to go to church every once in awhile, but then he would always be drunk. He would say, "I know I'm not too religious, but when I die, would you take me into the church?" He was drunk the day he was talking. And then my Uncle Alex died. My uncle was born in the old country as a Catholic, but he didn't go to church here. So we didn't feel like it was the thing to do, to have him go through the church for burial. So we asked the Father if he would come down to the mortu-ary to do the service. And he said, "Oh, you know, he can come into church. I promised him when he died he could come to church." That was so funny, because the Father wanted to take my Uncle Alex into church because Alex Barrailler had stopped and told him.

✦

He always had his dog with him — just a plain old shepherd dog. I think in the olden days he was a miner and bootlegged. As he got older, he just ended up being kind of a drunk around town. They lived across the road from the Smith property. There was a little old log cabin up there just across the road — just above Stillwater. It's still there.

✦

> "
> *Alex was a bachelor. He was one of the town characters. He was always pickled, and all kinds of things happened to him — rolled in the creek, etc. He was just a neat guy. He lived forever. Pickled all the time and lived to be an old man.*
> "

Red Onion crew,
about 1950.
Left to right:
Alex Barrailler,
Chuck Hannon,
Mathilda
Hendrickson, Frances
Zupancis, Johanna
Muhich, Roy Porter,
Tobey Thowbridge,
and Hod Nicholson.
Courtesy
Elsie Snyder.

Alex Barrailler used to live up there on the Smith Ranch in a little cabin. One time he came to town and got a big bag of groceries and left his sack by the door. He got pretty drunk, and Tony Caparella and I took all of his groceries out and put about six bricks in his bag. He carried that bag of bricks all the way home. Later Tony and I took his groceries up to him. That was on Saturday night. We never went up until the next morning. He already knew by that time, and he was really mad. He knew who did it when we got there.

✦

He was walking with his dog. He had a paper sack, weaving. All of a sudden, his hand opened and crashed his whole dozen eggs. He never even looked back.

✦

MRS. BARRAILLER
Theresa Barrailler
(1896 - 1992)

Mrs. Barrailler was a bootlegger. That's all I knew about her. She'd go around to the stores and gather up all the old fruit that they were throwing out and then take it home and make booze out of it. It was good enough to kill you. They threw everything in that booze them days. Did anyone ever die in Aspen of alcohol poisoning? Oh, I don't know. *I* damn near died from it!

✦

Mrs. Barrailler was a very good-looking woman. My dad liked her. My dad made his own wine, but I guess she had a little whiskey. They were good friends. See, they're all Italians. I have a comment I could tell you, but I better not. But old Emery used to say, "All I want is a little a bread, a little a soup, an' a little a fuckey." Those were basic Italian traits. He says, "That's all I want." She and her sister both were very beautiful, attractive women. I remember them when I was even older. They were around. They were always very good-looking women, and smart women. You betcha. Mrs. Barrailler used to make good cheese and ham.

✦

There was one woman — Mrs. Barrailler was her name. She lived up the Roaring Fork by what they called Stillwater. She bootlegged, and she'd get caught lots of times. Well, they fined her and then kind of broke up the still. Then she would find it and go at it again.

✦

Mrs. Barrailler was a pretty good bootlegger. La Queen, they used to call her. She was a very good-looking lady. A lot of the old boys had a crush on her even though she was married. During Prohibition, she was one of the renowned bootleggers. I understand she had good whiskey, too. I don't think she ever killed anyone with it.

✦

> "
> *Mrs. Barrailler was a pretty good bootlegger. La Queen, they used to call her. She was a very good-looking lady. A lot of the old boys had a crush on her even though she was married. During Prohibition, she was one of the renowned bootleggers. I understand she had good whiskey, too. I don't think she ever killed anyone with it.*
> "

Mrs. Barrailler was an absolute delight. They had a big party for her, and she said she just couldn't wait in order to dance at a party that had chow and cake. One party she served cake and jello. She worked when she was really old cleaning hotels, and she made good Italian booze.

✦

Mrs. Barrailler stories? Not much that I'd want to repeat, because she'd come get you. She'd slit your throat. She wouldn't hesitate. Beautiful lady. Emery Barrailler kind of laid back — pushed back, I'd say. "Out of the picture." She took charge. She was very strong willed. She was hither and thither. She saw that her wares were known about. She was very discreet. She wasn't open.

✦

I hardly knew Mrs. Barrailler for the simple reason that my mother and her — you put them together, and there was just no peace. That's where my mother first met my father — at her house. She owned a house and all that land around Stillwater. My mother didn't get along with her. The only way they got along was when they never saw one another.

✦

Mrs. Barrailler wouldn't ever get caught bootlegging. We had a sheriff about that time. Whenever they'd have a raid, they'd come and pick up the moonshiners. She wasn't the only one. There was a lot of moonshiners around Aspen. So the sheriff would get on the phone and tell all the moonshiners, "There's going to be a raid. The revenuers are going to be around tomorrow, so you'd better hide your still and all your booze." He would tip them off, so normally when the agents came, they'd never find booze. Anyway, Mrs. Barrailler would have what they called "runners" back in those days running the booze. The big center was Denver for selling. She would have people, and I think her son did it. They'd have a souped up V-8 Ford. Back in those days, bootleggers would go up to Glenwood Canyon and stick the booze in these culverts across the road. They put the whiskey in quart jars — Mason jars. They'd stash it then. The people from Denver would come pick them up. It was brandy made out of fruits. The Italians would call it grappa. As a matter of fact, in Aspen there was a still. I don't know who it belonged to, if it belonged to anybody, but it was a nice big

---

*Rowdy cowboys,
about 1910.
Courtesy
Bert Chisholm.*

still. Everybody moonshined, but not to the point of selling it. It was for your own family. So you'd go up into town and say, "Hey, where's the still?" "Well, so and so come down and picked it up." So you'd go to so and so and he'd say, "So and so picked it up from me." So anyway, you'd go to five or six people before you'd finally locate it. It was just kind of a community still. Mrs. Barrailler drank, you'd better believe. I saw her a few times. She could drink, and she could fight when she got drunk.

✦

Mrs. Barrailler remarried. She has a son and a daughter. That is a story of its own. You could write a book on her. She somewhat ran a brothel. I think before they really got down to business, the guys were too drunk and she'd roll them. Mrs. Barrailler was a woman before her time. I'll tell you one thing that more or less started this whole way of life. Back in those days, people had no relief or nothing to fall back on. If you had any property at all, you couldn't get any handouts. Her husband Emery wasn't a fireball — you know what I mean — he was pretty laid back. He had a brother, Alex, in town. He was the town clown. He was quite a character.

✦

To survive, people had to do whatever they could. Back in those days, there was no way that anybody'd help you. Nobody had anything to help you with. I think she was kind of forced into this. It was one way of making a living. She was a true survivor. I think she would have been a good businesswoman in any area. The husbands back in those days were the guys who were the fighters — get out there and make a success. Emery lacked that. This was her only way out. I don't think he would have done anything on the ranch if she didn't go out there and do it with him. They owned Stillwater. That's all the Smith Ranch — Northstar Preserve. But really, talk about the grappa, I think she was just kind of a come-on to get business. She'd feed them a lot of booze and get their money. She had some buildings down in town that burnt down during the early Forties. I remember Sheriff Bruin used to go up to her ranch quite a lot. I think the hooch she had was another thing. She was good looking.

✦

I remember Mrs. Barrailler's bull. Boy, he was mean. We would sneak up there on her property to fish, up at the dead waters. It was all calm from Still Waters back. The bull would chase anybody. He put Frank Loushin up on the shed. A wagon came along and he had to jump on a load of wood because the bull wouldn't let him off. The kids would climb on the shed until George Strong came down from Independence hauling a load of wood into town, what we call thick-and-thin lumber, down to the East End of town. The kids would holler and he would pull the wagon over to the shed so that they could get off on the load of wood. A lot of times, Mrs. Barrailler's bull would put you in the swamp. A lot of places were thick enough that he couldn't get through. So we would have to just stand in the water and wait until he left — sometimes half a day until after dark. That wasn't the only dang bull that was up in that area. Mrs. Gallagar had a dairy ranch with a bull. And Mrs. Early had a bull. Gallagar's was up by Benedict's place, and Mrs. Early had a bull right down there. They were pretty much calm until the cows came into heat. One bull would just walk down Deane Street, which was the old D&RG Railroad.

✦

> *I remember Mrs. Barrailler's bull. Boy, was he mean. We would sneak up there on her property to fish. The bull would chase anybody. He put Frank Loushin up on the shed. A wagon came along and he had to jump on a load of wood because the bull wouldn't let him off. A lot of times, Mrs. Barrailler's bull would put you in the swamp. So we would have to just stand in the water and wait until he left.*

TIMMY SULLIVAN

Timmy Sullivan always used to wrestle a bull when the dairy was up there on the end of Galena Street, on Aspen Mountain. There was an old roan bull that come into the milk cows every night. It would come down by the Glory Hole area. Timmy was a big brawny. The old bull got to where he would look for him, too, as Tim come by to have their little set-to. The bull would hunch up and put his head down. Timmy Sullivan would bunch up, too. He'd reach up and grab the bull, and they'd push back and forth. It'd be about a draw. Timmy was so looped up on fifty-cent wine that he had no control over himself at all — self-exertion and just built damn strong. It wasn't a real big heavy bull. He was pretty good sized, but nothing heavy. Us kids would all gather around to see it.

◆

Timmy Sullivan was a good strong miner. I remember him wrestling bulls and fighting. Once, they staged some fights here on the 4th of July, and I remember him fighting. I don't know who it was, but they had three or four different bouts. Tim was a wonderful, honest, good person, and he liked to have a swig or two now and then. A lot of people drank because they didn't have an awful lot to do. My gawd, they weren't afraid to work, though.

◆

Timmy Sullivan . . . my first beau. Lord, lord, lord. Oh, he was a macho, big, blond kid. You had to notice him because he couldn't stay hidden. I remember when my mom and dad used to bring me up to the dances at the Armory Hall. Here was Timmy Sullivan. "I love you." I thought that was just marvelous for somebody to profess they loved me. He didn't know me or nothing, and I was such a kid — about fifteen. But he did marry a pal of mine. She was a very strong woman. She ruled him. But he loved it and they got along nicely. They have twelve girls — an even dozen.

◆

" Timmy Sullivan always used to wrestle a bull. Timmy was a big brawny. The old bull got to where he would look for him, too, as Tim come by to have their little set-to. The bull would hunch up and put his head down. Timmy Sullivan would bunch up, too. He'd reach up and grab the bull, and they'd push back and forth. It'd be about a draw. "

Tim was one of the leasers in the Smuggler Mine at one time. He was a big Irishman. He always wore a cap cocked to one side and had that Irish brogue. He drank a lot. I never saw an Irishman that didn't.

◆

Tim Sullivan was a good friend of my dad. I got a story on Tim Sullivan. He used to booze pretty good — pretty heavy. He rolled his car down on Shale Bluffs clear to the creek. They asked Tim, "What the hell happened to you?" He said, "I seen two roads and I guess I took the wrong one."

◆

Tim Sullivan used to booze pretty good. He rolled his car down on Shale Bluffs clear to the creek. They asked Tim, 'What the hell happened to you?' He said, 'I seen two roads and I guess I took the wrong one.'

BUTTONS TEKOUCICH
George Tekoucich

Buttons would always button just the first three buttons down. Even when he was skiing, he would have his shirt wide open with only a scarf around his neck.

◆

I don't know who gave my brother that name. I guess it was because he never had any buttons on his shirt. I never seen him with a coat on, summer or winter.

◆

Peanuts, Buttons, and Leo were good skiers — great athletes. They could do about anything. They could fight, play baseball, ski, lumberjack. They were tough guys.

◆

I expect that Buttons got his nickname because he couldn't say anything else for awhile when he was little. He was a man's type — a good macho figure.

◆

I really don't know how Peanuts and Buttons Tekoucich got their nicknames. Buttons was a real good skier — well, both of them were good skiers. In the middle of the winter, Buttons wore an old Levis jacket unbuttoned, no gloves, a pair of shoes — not overshoes — unbuckled halfway.

◆

Buttons was by reputation quite a flashy guy around here before he went into the service. During his service years. I'm sure he was really coordinated; he was very popular.

◆

Buttons Tekoucich? That's George. Never had his shirt buttoned, even in the middle of winter. When he would race on Aspen Mountain, he would come flying down the hill, his ol' bare hairy chest and his shirt flying behind him. He was a great skier.

◆

The only story that I have in mind about George is when he fell on top of Cork-screw and tore his feet out of his ski boots. He was lying in the snow and looked up and said, "My God, I tore my feet off." His boots were in a tree. He was a great skier — couldn't seem to hurt himself. I remember him coming over to the bottom of the ski lift in the middle of the winter working with his shirt off.

◆

I worked part of one summer with George Tekoucich for the Aspen Company on a truck. He was something. George was an absolute barbarian. He never wore a shirt. He was very strong and well built. He was a good skier except that he had absolutely no judgment. He was in a race down Zaag Park, which was very straight down with a road at the bottom. You had to hit that road and go down to Dipsy Doodle. Well, naturally, he came down too fast and shot off the road into the trees. He landed down below and his ski and boot were still up in the tree. He married Pepper, a great gal.

◆

> *" Buttons Tekoucich? That's George. Never had his shirt buttoned, even in the middle of winter. When he would race on Aspen Mountain, he would come flying down the hill, his ol' bare hairy chest and his shirt flying behind him. He was a great skier. "*

645

PEANUTS TEKOUCICH
Ed Tekoucich
(1910 - 1991)

Peanuts Tekoucich? That was Ed Tekoucich. I guess he got his name because he was so long and lanky.

❖

Peanuts Tekoucich — I don't know how he got that name. I imagine somebody gave him that name up in the Midnight Mine. I know Joe Popish and him used to be pretty good buddies, and he always talked about Peanuts.

❖

> "
>
> *The way I hear it is that he got his name by eating a lot of peanuts when he went to the saloons and bars.*
>
> "

The way I hear it is that he got his name by eating a lot of peanuts when he went to the saloons and bars.

❖

I don't know how they hung that name on me. Some old-timer called me that one day and it stuck. Every kid had a nickname in them days.

❖

Ed was good company. We did ski with him a lot. He went with us to the top of Avon skiing — Ed, Leo, George, and Albina. This was a long time ago. They didn't have any money and didn't have any mittens. It was colder than the blazes. Somebody said to Leo, "Why, you need some mittens." He said, "Oh, they always thaw out anyway." One time we were packing on Roch Run — side-stepping up. Sometimes we would side-step the whole way to the top. But it made it nice coming down. It was pretty cold and Leo didn't have any gloves and I said, "Leo, aren't your hands cold?" They were probably frozen. He said, "Oh yeah, they are pretty cold." "Do you want some mittens?" "No. They'll thaw out again." Buttons was a good strong skier, slightly crazy. They carried Albina's lunch to the top. We got there a little later than the guys. Albina asked for her lunch and they'd already eaten it. Her own brothers.

✦

Peanuts Tekoucich — Ed. I never heard him called Peanuts. He was always Ed to me. The only thing I know about him is when he went skiing this one time. There was a group of us — my brother Donny, Frank Willoughby, myself, and Beck. Anyway, Ed was one of the group. We stayed in a cabin in Ashcroft and there was no chinking in the walls. You could stick your hand through the wall; it was cold. There was a pretty good little stove and we'd go down to the creek to get water. During the evening, we would hang our skivvies on a nail in the back to dry. On this particular night, Ed had put his boots on a nail slightly below the stove. The next morning I got up and started a fire. I put the water pail on the stove — there was thin ice on top. The heat from the stove melted that ice just a little bit. Somebody started to pour it into the tea kettle. That cake of ice floated right out and was just big enough to cover the top of the tea kettle. All the rest of the water shot right out and went into his boots. Ed got up and put his boots on and there was this ice. You should have heard the cussing.

✦

BILLY TAGERT
(1873 - 1966)

"

I don't know how they hung that name on me. Some old-timer called me that one day and it stuck. Every kid had a nickname in them days.

"

I remember him as kind of a small man, very neatly dressed with a modified ranching hat, not a big one. I thought he was pretty neat. He played fiddle and banjo at the country dances.

✦

I knew Billy Tagert. He was quite an independent gentleman, you know. He was a little guy. He was real short, but of course he was here for years and years. He had wild horses to break and broke his hip. Later on, in later life, he walked quite lame, but even so, he was always out among people and was busier than goodness knows what.

✦

DANCE

Gerbazdale Hall
~ WATSON ~
Saturday, June 12, '26
6-Piece Orchestra
SUPPER SERVED
Good Time Assured All
Admission, - - $1.00

From the Print Shop of C. P. Rice, Glenwood Springs, Colorado

I don't know whether I should tell you — if you want to hear the straight story or not. I don't know whether Billy was too honest a citizen. You get different stories. He had a livery stable and ran a few cattle. He acquired real estate. I don't know if he started from nothing. I guess he made it off the livery stable. I don't think he was ever wealthy or anything like that. It was easy to own things in those days. Like a lot of people back then, they would leave their property and not pay taxes on it, and he would go and pay a nickel on back taxes — a very nominal sum. Kind of like Judge Shaw.

◆

Billy Tagert was an old-timer, kind of salt of the earth. When they first started skiing in Aspen, I guess he used to haul them back up the hill. He had four horses on a sleigh. They would ski down and then he would haul them back up — I don't know how far. He was getting old then. In his younger years, he ran a livery barn and he was kind of the town pillar. I imagine he had his fingers in a lot of business.

◆

Billy Tagert was an old skin flint. I never heard of a good thing he ever did in his life as long as I knew him.

◆

I was his daughter's best friend — Wilma. He had a daughter, Nellie, too. I knew him as middle-aged and so on. He was very notorious for his womanizing. How do you think he got the limp that he got? He was a businessman and was very shrewd. He was shrewd in dealing with miners, trying to get out of them whatever he could — or anybody else for that matter.

◆

Billy had a blacksmith's shop where Mezzaluna is now and a ranch down by the Slaughter House Bridge. He had stuff going on all over the place. I called him Step and a Half. He was crippled.

◆

"

My friend and I swiped some polo mallets when we were kids from Tagert. We took our horses up to a vacant lot and tried to play and swing those things. We got to going and I swung so hard that I missed. I ended up hitting my horse right in the jaw. I knocked her out. I was so scared — I thought I killed her. That was our last polo game.

"

*Aspen, 1910,
where City Market
and Butchers Block
are located now.
Courtesy Del Gerbaz.*

Billy Tagert had a little dog. It was strange because everybody had mutts in town. Nobody ever saw anything in their lifetime but a mutt. He had this runty little thing that a little old lady would have.

❖

My friend and I swiped some polo mallets when we were kids from Tagert. We took our horses up to a vacant lot and tried to play and swing those things. We got to going and I swung so hard that I missed. I ended up hitting my horse right in the jaw. I knocked her out. I was so scared — I thought I killed her. That was our last polo game.

❖

I remember when he had the livery stable up by Mike Garrish (by City Market). He was a short fellow. He owned that Tagert's Lake up there. Wouldn't let anybody fish in it — it was a private deal.

◆

As I understand it, he came into Aspen as a boy and just worked in different places — saloons and so forth — and saved his money. He was quite a wealthy man. He walked with a slight limp, but I think he got that from being thrown off a horse one time and broke his hip or something. He was quite a bit older than we were.

◆

He used to go to the dances at the Armory Hall and loved to dance. He always had a limp. He had something wrong with one leg. I remember him running cattle up Hunter Creek way above the dam. He also owned what is now the Black Birch.

◆

I knew him all my life. He came to Aspen before I did, of course. He came over from Leadville barefooted. He was always a gentleman. Somebody took care of him when he was little. He ran away from home because his father was an alcoholic. After he grew up, he had a livery stable. He raised cattle down there by the Red Butte Cemetery. His house was down there. Then he ran the Midland Ranch for several years. Then the Marolts finally bought it. He also had his cabin up Independence. He made money. Later on, he broke his hip — horse fell with him. He always limped a little; he was a little short on one leg. Billy always went to the dances. He was a good dancer.

◆

Billy Tagert was an old mining type, like Johnny Williams, that always was sure that next week they were going to strike it rich and never quite did. He had the mine up Castle Creek at Montezuma Basin. Actually, Billy Tagert in a way is partially responsible for skiing getting started in Aspen. When Billy Fisk and Ted Ryan met this fella Tom Flynn who had been in Aspen (he was a pretty

"

I knew him all my life. He came to Aspen from Leadville barefooted. He was always a gentleman. Somebody took care of him when he was little. He ran away from home because his father was an alcoholic. Billy always went to the dances. He was a good dancer.

"

good talker), they mentioned they were interested in skiing. They met him out in California. Tom knew Billy Tagert and he talked them into coming to look in the Aspen area for skiing. And Billy, I think, took them up Castle Creek. That would have been 1940.

✦

Billy Tagert had a ranch down by Slaughter House Bridge, which is the Black Birch area now. He would also go put up the hay when they were farming on the Midland Ranch (which is the golf course now). He had a livery stable where the Aspen Square Building is now (Le Tub) and an indoor ring for training his horses about where the entrance is now.

✦

Tagert had the lake up Independence Pass — Tagert's Lake. He owned that. He wouldn't let nobody in. Only fishing for him. The only way we could sneak in was we'd go up above and come down by the lake, down the canyon.

✦

HUGHY MCCABE
(1871-1944)

Hughy McCabe was blind. He used to come to our school sometimes. I know he came out to the Washington School when I was in seventh grade. Our teacher invited him to talk to us kids, and we could ask him anything we wanted. The kids asked him how he knew how to walk uptown by himself — how he knew to cross the street. He said he had a cane and he'd walk to the edge of curbs, where he could feel his cane, and then he'd stand there. He said pretty soon someone would say, "It's all clear Hughy," and then he'd walk across. People would watch for him. The kids wanted to know how he could tell time, and he said he had a watch that had raised numbers on it. He showed it to all of us. He told us all about how he knew different money. The only thing he didn't know was paper money. I know a neighbor down here, he's dead now,

> *"*
>
> *Hugy McCabe had his little store and, do you know, nobody got away with anything without Hughy knowing it. He was a clever little man, even being blind.*
>
> *"*

too — Leo Light — well, he'd ride his horse up to Aspen sometimes. He'd come along, clippity clop, clippity clop up the street. Hughy used to sit outside of his place in a chair a lot. Leo would come along and he'd say, "Hi, Hughy." And Hughy'd say, "Hi, Leo." He knew his voice. He knew his horse, too.

♦

Hughy had his little store and, do you know, nobody got away with anything without Hughy knowing it. He was a clever little man, even being blind.

♦

I guess it was 1932; there was an old gal. Her name was Maggie Early, and she had a dairy up the pass. When I was a boy, I used to herd her cows up in the pasture. I'd bring them in and help her milk and then help her deliver at night. I'd crank the goddamned separator. She'd get it started for me, and then I'd get on that handle and hope it didn't flip me around like a dishrag. God, that thing used to get wound up. We used to deliver the milk to Hughy every evening at the corner store on Hyman and Mill. He knew every kid. All you had to do was walk normal and he could tell who you were. He had one of these small-voltage cigar lighters. When you pressed down, the machine made a little arch and the flame lit up. I'd always sneak up to go light it. He even got so he could tell when I was just about to reach up there. He'd say, "Now I told you," and that's all it took. He knew everybody. He could tell some people's horses coming down the street.

◆

Hughy McCabe was my husband's uncle. He was a nice gentleman and a musician. He played piano. Hughy was a blind man who used to sell cigars. You could not go in there and steal anything, 'cause he knew. Say if you give him a nickel for a candy, he would feel if it was a nickel. He knew all his coins. Or if you give him a quarter, he knew exactly what change to give you. He always stood back there and smoked a cigar outside the store. The shop burned down in 1941. He was Ethel McCabe's uncle. I remember when I was a kid, I was trying to get penny gum, and I didn't know the difference. A nickel wouldn't fit in the penny gum machine. He came out and said, "What's the matter, hon?" I said, "The coin won't go in." And he said, "You're using a nickel."

◆

Hughy McCabe was blind. He had a candy store and you'd go in and buy a jaw-breaker. You'd lay down a penny and try to fool him, but he never got fooled.

◆

All I remember about Hughy McCabe is that he had a store. He had hats, gloves, and a lot of things. As I remember, he didn't have them on shelves. He had them on tables and you'd give him a dollar or whatever — paper money — and if it was five dollars, he'd give you change. I think he depended on people to say, "Here's five." I think people were honest with him.

◆

Hughy McCabe was blind. We'd sell him lead and copper and stuff like that. He had a store. He used to make lead toys and also sold copper. There were all these old linesmen that used to work on the lines. Tony Caparella worked for

> "
>
> *You could not go into Hugh's store and steal anything, 'cause he knew. Say if you give him a nickel for a candy, he would feel if it was a nickel. He knew all his coins. He always stood back there and smoked a cigar outside the store. The shop burned down in 1941.*
>
> "

the electric outfit. In them days, Harry Brown still owned the electric company. Tony and Clarkson Brown would be working on putting in new lines. Those goddamned guys would have this copper and throw it down a hole. They'd take us kids by our feet and hold us down the hole so we could get that copper. They thought that was funny as hell, especially old Tony Cap. We'd take it down to Hughy's and sell the copper.

✦

MAGGIE EARLY

Maggie Early used to live up in the East End and had a dairy. Maggie's place was where the Gant is. She lived with her mother and had a son, Bill, and she ran a dairy up there for years and years. In fact, we used to buy milk from her when our milk cows were dry. When Maggie delivered milk, she would come by our house in a cart wagon with her son. It was pulled by a horse, and they had the milk in big metal cans. I would go out there with our milk pail, and she would pour it out with a dipper. She delivered milk over most of the East End.

✦

I think Maggie Early was a very stoic, dear lady. The first I can remember of her is delivering milk from door to door. She had a child, but she never married. They didn't have a nice name when I was a girl growing up. But I would sneak to see her.

> *Maggie Early was a very stoic, dear lady. The first I can remember of her is delivering milk from door to door. She had a child, but she never married.*

✦

TONY THE WEASEL
Antony Harvett

The Weasel was a bootlegger. He'd get caught every week. They'd catch him one week and he'd be in jail the next. Next week they'd catch him again.

✦

Elizabeth Obester, Paul Muhich, and Tony Harvett (the weasel). Seated: Annie Obester, Tony's new wife. Courtesy Richard Cowling.

Oh, Tony the Weasel? He was a bootlegger. He sold the cheapest booze in the county, and it was the rottenest booze in the county, too. I don't know what the hell he made it out of — old rotten potatoes, I guess. But it was sure awful to taste. Oh boy. He was always in jail, but his house was on 1006 East Cooper Avenue.

❧

My brother used to make whiskey for Weasel. He would go to Tony's and give him a hand. Then Weasel would share it with him. Tony was married. He had a daughter that they used to call Little Orphan Annie. Her mother passed away when she was young. It was a nickname. They made whiskey down at his house on Cooper Street. When we was kids, we used to get whiskey in bottles and sell them for a penny a piece. We would find them in the garbage over by the Glory Hole, and in some of these old houses.

❧

Tony the Weasel was a nincompoop. He was very illiterate. I knew his daughter very well — Little Annie. She was great. She was a nursemaid for the Browns. We had three nursemaids. There was two from Denver, and Annie and I oversaw them when the war was going on. I lived right across the street, and I stayed there most of the time with the children. I had about nine children I took care of.

•

Tony the Weasel — I think there's a story there. When the revenue agents used to come to Aspen, he'd want the whole town to inform him to evade the revenuers. I have a vivid recollection of Tony, with his still under his arm, running out and dumping all the mash in the chicken coop. The chickens would eat that mash. Gawd, they was all drunk. They'd be staggering around. The rooster would try to hop up on the fence to crow, and he'd fall off. That's the truth. Everybody used to dump their mash right away. Great eggs for the weasel.

WHISPERING SWEDES
John and Gus Nelson

The Whispering Swedes got their names because of their soft voices. Their liquor was really potent stuff. They had an old log cabin and it was rustic as hell. It was worse than a graveyard. I was trying to think, there was a fella down below them. He had a smaller log cabin and his name was Studebaker. He was a neat little German fella — everything washed down and whitewashed from rubbing so damn hard with a brush. He was a different liver altogether, but he used to mix with them. They got along real good.

•

Whispering Swedes — there were two of them, Gus and John Nelson. They were watch men. One of them fixed watches. I remember going there with my father to pick up a watch or something that they had fixed, and everything was all dusty, like something out of a Charles Dickens story. I remember Gus wiping off this very nice glass with his shirttail and pouring a drink for my dad. Then

"When the revenue agents came to Aspen, Tony'd want the whole town to inform him. I have a vivid recollection of Tony, with his still under his arm, running out and dumping all the mash in the chicken coop. The chickens would eat that mash. Gawd, they was all drunk. They'd be staggering around. The rooster would try to hop up on the fence to crow, and he'd fall off. That's the truth. Great eggs for the weasel."

657

he gave us some that was kind of watered down. I didn't know how I was going to handle that, because we had to drink out of that dirty glass.

◆

I remember a lot about the Whispering Swede. He had a brother, too. He had all these old guns he'd sell. He had an old second-hand gun. My pal would go in there and buy an old gun from him because it was a dollar or two and it would backfire. He had watches, too. Christ, he had more stuff in that place. He kind of whispered all the time he talked. That's why we called him the Whispering Swede.

◆

"

The Whispering Swedes got their names because of their soft voices. Their liquor was really potent stuff. They had an old log cabin and it was rustic as hell. It was worse than a graveyard.

"

Whispering Swede was down there by the Concept 600. They had that big two-story red house. I was never in, but I remember the outside. I remember the Harrington boys died from the Swedes' booze.

◆

Swede — I can remember him walking around town. He was short. You just saw these people. It's not that you confronted them or talked to them that much. They were just there, as you were there. All I can remember is him wearing tweedy suits. He was a shabby gentile, you might say, and wore a hat. Lots of guys wore hats in those days. People were joiners. They joined the Elks. So the Whispering Swede, among many, is probably one that wore the gold fobs and watch chains to the lodge. That's about all I remember about him. He was a prospector, kind of a loner.

◆

I don't remember them other than the fact that people used to tell about them. I knew the Swedes when I saw them. They always brought out in the spring of the year an old Model T Ford. I guess they would cover it up and put it in hibernation during the winter. In the spring, they would turn it upside-down and work on it to get ready for traveling around. One sat behind the steering wheel, and the other one sat on the opposite side in back.

◆

The Whispering Swede lived right where Concept 600 is, and he was mean. He'd come up the hill and cut our fence. He had a brother by the name of John who was older, and he wasn't too bad. They had some mining property somewhere, and they'd spend the summer there. But his older brother passed away before he did. The house caught fire, and he was in the fire. He was saved, but he was getting old. He died in the hospital after that fire. There was a fella next to the Whispering Swedes, in that two-story building, by the name of George Geisler. He was a shoemaker here. When he passed away, the Swedes acquired his house. I guess they just naturally took over. And then next to George Geisler was a log cabin, and it was owned by a man with the last name of Barney. I forgot his first name. He was a retired soldier. Well, the Swedes acquired that. They acquired everything on the block.

◆

The Swedes lived next to my Aunt Elizabeth, and they couldn't get along at all. My grandfather and the Swede really battled over water. They used to have an irrigation ditch there. The Swede used to stop the water above, and my grandpa needed to irrigate his garden. I guess they would meet once in awhile. He hit my grandfather with a hoe once. They had it out.

◆

I guess the Whispering Swede was a good watchmaker. There were two brothers. I knew they were bootleggers, because my dad used to go down there and the old Swede would say, "Would you like to have some punch today?" I was only in there once where he had the repair shop. He had a little table where he repaired all these watches and stuff. It wasn't long after that the house burnt down. It was dingy.

◆

In the summertime, the Swedes had some kind of mining claims up the mountain. They would disappear in the summer, and in the winter would come back. I had forgotten about the Whispering Swedes. They were pretty grumpy and hard to get along with. Their reputation was that. Everybody in Aspen during the Depression was making booze. They used to bring grapes by railroad carloads. People would order so many pounds of grapes. There would be two or

"

They had a Model A or Model T Ford. I don't know which it was. It was an old car anyway. And they'd take it out. Maybe they'd drive to the cemetery and back or down the highway and come back. Then they'd tear it all apart and work on it. Every time they'd take it out, they'd do that.

"

Garfield School, 1900.
Durant Street,
East End.
Courtesy
Peggy Rowland.

three railroad cars of grapes come into Basalt, and then they would distribute them and make wine. I drank plenty of that, too.

✦

The Swedes were brothers. One was a jeweler. They had a Model A Ford two-door. One time they got hit by a train down by those curves down below Gerbaz — Phillip's Curve, right there. They were hit by the train, but it didn't hurt them — it just pushed them off the road. They always had the driver sitting up front, and the other brother was sitting in the back seat on the opposite side, so, they said, the car would be balanced. They got burned out. One of them died from the fire. They pulled him out, but he died about three days later in the hospital.

✦

The Whispering Swede fixed watches. There were two of them. They always drank wine. You go there, you could get drunk with them. One time we went up to Gold Hill. Took the jeep up Taylor Pass, and one of the Swedes was up there walking. He had a mine up there. I guess his name was Gus. I don't remember what the other one's name was. I knew him, too. And the reason he got his name was because he whispered when he talked. He was a jeweler and fixed watches. In fact, I think I've got an old, old, old watch that he either gave me or that he worked on. I've still got it. It don't run anymore. It's an old thing, and I think it wound up with a key.

✦

They weren't very friendly, 'cuz I used to go by there to school. They had a Model A or Model T Ford. I don't know which it was. It was an old car anyway. And they'd take it out. Maybe they'd drive to the cemetery and back or down the highway and come back. Then they'd tear it all apart and work on it. Every time they'd take it out, they'd do that.

✦

I knew the Whispering Swede, John Nelson. He was pretty recent history. He lived up on the block from Elizabeth, on Main Street, in a big house there. He was the Whispering Swede. He was a Swede and he whispered. You know, he didn't have a voice; he kind of talked real quiet. And he had a brother, Gus, who died. They had a pawn shop — a junk shop. You would go in the house, and you couldn't wade through the place. There was junk everywhere. He was a big bootlegger. The story has it, you know, that he poisoned other people in town because of bad liquor — not on purpose.

✦

The Whispering Swedes were not a friend really of anyone. They were both Swedish brothers, and they were very, very abused at home. Every time they opened their mouths, "Shh." You know, "Be quiet." The only time they said they could laugh and talk would be out behind the cow shed. But not in the home. Their mother was sort of wishy-washy and let the father have his say with them. As far as they were concerned, it was a family thing, being quiet. "Shut your mouth." That's about all they ever heard. Well, what are you going

> *"*
>
> *They drank a whole lot until their vocal cords, I expect, maybe were affected, too. We had a lot of them whispering — not the whole town, but a whole lot of them.*
>
> *"*

661

to do when you're a little kid? It just went on and on and on. Are you kidding? They drank a whole lot until their vocal cords, I expect, maybe were affected, too. We had a lot of them whispering — not the whole town, but a whole lot of them.

◆

The Whispering Swedes were a pair of characters right on Main Street. They were a couple of very superstitious old-timers. They didn't trust the banks or people. I mean, they were very much loners. As I remember, they spent most of the time over in Gunnison. They supposedly had a gold mine up on Italian Mountain in Gunnison. When the snow would leave, they would go over the pass. They had a Model A sedan. They would tie all their belongings on the roof and sides. Someone was telling me they had a couple of mules and would hike up on Italian Mountain. I know they used to make a lot of beer and sell it. You could go to their place, and they had walls of railroad watches and all kinds of stuff. When they bulldozed that area out, of course the old-timers all figured that they kept their gold probably hid somewhere in their cabin. The people that had been in there knew that they had a little furnace — a melting furnace, like a forge furnace — in the basement. Firemen used the place for fire practice, and they burned it down. The old-timers like Bennie Smith said, "Well, chances are there was gold stashed away." Nobody ever found it. Before anything was known by the older people, they had already bulldozed the whole area and covered everything up.

◆

Whispering Swedes were the only guys that fixed watches and clocks in town. They were across from the Catholic Church. It was a real narrow little two-story place. My dad knew them well. As the postmaster he knew everybody. They knew him and liked him. At first you couldn't understand them because their accent was so strong. They had to like you or they wouldn't work on your clock or watch. It was scary to go in there for me as a little kid because it was really dark and dirty. They were nice friendly little guys, but the place itself was like a witch's house. These clocks were clanging, dinging, and going off. You would give them something to fix and it took weeks.

◆

"It was scary to go in their house for me as a little kid because it was really dark and dirty. They were nice friendly little guys, but the place itself was like a witch's house. These clocks were clanging, dinging, and going off."

BUCKSHOT PARSONS

Buckshot Parsons ran the pharmacy. I don't really know how he got his name, but the only thing he hunted with was a shotgun, so they called him Buckshot.

✦

I knew Buckshot well. Gees, I don't know how he got his name. He was just Buckshot. He was a big, flamboyant, overzealous type of guy — extroverted. He would play the trumpet with Louis at dances. He and Louis Spence were good friends. Between the two of them, they were both good musicians, and they could toot up a good storm. Buck's dad owned the drugstore. He always had access to money. He was just kind of the bigshot around town, so I guess they called him Buckshot. Bigshot is what they should have called him.

✦

Big Buck was a buddy of mine. I was a little one. I run around with Buck a lot when I was a kid. He was older, I would imagine — at least six or eight years older than I was. I don't know how he got his name. He was a big, tall guy. Buck stood about six feet, four. His dad owned the drugstore and the Isis Theater. We were on the fire department together for years.

✦

Damned if I know how Buckshot got his name. I won a bet from him one time. That was when the old train was still running and we all got drunk and went to Glenwood. Old Buckshot was along and several others. Anyway, we got to Glenwood, and Joe Popish and I were talking about riding the old Zephyr out to San Francisco. I said, "I'd like to go; I know some gals out there." We didn't have any clothes with us. I said, "What do you say we get on and ride out for a trip?" And so we did. And ol' Buckshot got down and said, "Ha ha. I'll bet ya, I'll bet ya twenty dollars you won't get on." First thing you know I took him up on the bet. I said, "Ok, we're taking off." We got on that train, and he laid alongside the rail and was laughing and kicking his heels.

✦

"

I knew Buckshot well. Gees, I don't know how he got his name. He was just Buckshot. He was a big, flamboyant, overzealous type of guy — extroverted. He would play the trumpet at dances. He and Louis Spence were good friends. Between the two of them, they were both good musicians, and they could toot up a good storm.

"

DIRTY HERWICK
Loren Herwick

> "*Dirty Herwick was a lineman for the electric company. He had a streak across the back of his neck where the wire had burned him. He fell from the post. When he hit the ground, the impact started his heart again. He was the sheriff here and had one eye.*"

Dirty Herwick was the sheriff. I don't know how he got his name, but I would assume because he always talked dirty.

I don't know how Dirty Herwick got his name either. We knew him pretty well. I remember when he was electrocuted. He was a lineman for the electric company. He had a streak across the back of his head where the wire had burned him. He fell from the post. When he hit the ground, the impact started his heart again. He was the sheriff here and had one eye.

Dirty Herwick. Oh yeah, Loren. He was the sheriff. My dad used to call him Duty Duty. Loren was a nice man.

I don't know how Dirty Herwick got his name, because if there was ever anyone that was a clean model of cleanliness, it was him. I never called him Dirty because he went to work for me in the office in about 1951 or thereabouts, before he was elected sheriff. He was always Loren to me. Maybe it was because when he was riding a horse, you know, he was a cowboy.

Oh, I knew Dirty. He was just a bad-talking son-of-a-gun. Just a dirty mouth is why — that's how he got his name. But Dirty was a pretty kind guy. He was a good sheriff and a good citizen, but he was a dirty-talking guy.

He got his nickname after he was electrocuted off a pole one time. He got knocked off. Dirty used to be an electrician. That's where the name got started.

He was sheriff. I worked with him as the county coroner over the years. He was not too tall, but pretty stocky. Oh yes, he was tough. Just like I say — the cemetery is full of tough people.

◆

Dirty was a good friend of ours. There used to be a comic in the funny papers, and one of the kid's names was Dirty and kind of resembled this kid. So everybody started calling him Dirty. His name was Loren Herwick. He was a heck of a good sheriff, I'll tell you. He didn't take monkey business from anybody. He lost an eye in some kind of accident. Before he was sheriff, he worked on power lines and got an electrical shock and lost quite a few fingers. He was on a pole, and he backed into a high-voltage line. He had a big scar across the back of his neck. It killed him, actually, but it knocked him off the pole and he came down and hit the ground. It started his heart beating again.

◆

Dirty got his name because he wore these dirty chaps when he was a kid. That's where he got the name. Dirty was from "Dirty Dalton," a cartoon character. They called him Dirty Herwick, 'cuz he wore these dirty chaps. He was sheriff in Aspen for many years.

◆

How did Dirty get his name? It was told to me that he could stand up straight, in a clean house, and still get dirty. That was some of the stories that were told — but they just called him Dirty Herwick. He was the sheriff, but his first work was electrical. They were working on the electrical poles and they weren't supposed to turn the power on for a certain length of time. Somebody turned the power on too soon, and he got caught right behind the neck. They turned the power off right away, but it knocked him down to the ground. It didn't kill him. That's what brought him back was the fall. They figured that the fall was enough to jar him back. He had a scar that went the full length of his neck. He was the sheriff. He had one more year and was trying to get that other year in so he would have twenty years as sheriff.

◆

> "
> *Dirty got his name because he wore these dirty chaps when he was a kid. Dirty was from 'Dirty Dalton,' a cartoon character. Dirty Herwick was sheriff in Aspen for many years.*
> "

665

Dirty was our neighbor when we was little tiny kids. He grew up in Aspen and later was elected sheriff and served for many years. He did it all by himself. He didn't have ten or fifteen deputies. Of course, Aspen was a smaller town then. How did he get the name? I think from a cartoon character, "Dirty Dalton." I think he resembled the cartoon.

♦

I knew all of the Herwicks. I don't know how he got that name, but I guess maybe because he was so clean. He was sheriff here for a long time and did a good job. Dirty was an awful name for him, because he was always so neat and spruced up.

♦

Dirty Herwick? I think he was riding a horse one time and he got piled in a bunch of horse shit, and so after that they called him Dirty. That's what I was told, anyway.

♦

Well, I don't know why they called him that. I knew Dirty well, and I liked him. His real name was Loren. I think in his younger days he liked a little prize fighting. They may have hung that name on him for awhile. I liked him, and he was a mild-mannered man when I knew him. He was sheriff for years. He was a good guy, and if you behaved, he was a good friend, but don't try and fool him.

♦

He used to tease my kids when they were little with that glass eye of his. He'd pop it out at them. My youngest had nightmares for a month after that.

♦

Dirty Herwick was a snotty-nosed, dirty little kid. That's the only thing I can remember about him. It must have stuck to him, because he was a good enough little kid — just dirty. One of these snotty-nosed little kids.

♦

> "
> *I knew all of the Herwicks. I don't know how he got that name, but I guess maybe because he was so clean. Dirty was an awful name for him, because he was always so neat and spruced up.*
> "

Dirty Herwick was a sheriff and he had one eye. He lost it. He used to be a lineman and was up working on a transformer and got electrocuted. I think the fall brought him back to life, but he lost an eye. It was burned. He had a glass eye, and he was sheriff for quite awhile here.

❖

He was the sheriff. How did he get the name Dirty? He cussed like a trooper.

❖

Dirty Herwick got his name from a comic strip back in the early 1900s. He was more or less a cowboy — he and Red Rowland. Most men were miners, but they were the cowboys. They were the guys that worked on ranches, and the comic strip was a cowboy character. That's where he got the name Dirty.

❖

Dirty Herwick used to ride in the rodeos. He was a little long on the list at this particular one up there by where the racetrack is now. He got a mean horse, I guess, and it bucked him off in some fresh manure. He was very very angry, and I guess he did go home and cleaned up.

❖

Dirty Herwick was an ornery, mean kid when he was young. I'm related to Dirty. He's married to my cousin Ester. My grandmother's name was Ester Jane. Wid was his dad. He was a character, too. He was a tough old man with a reputation of being that way. I think he might have worked with horse teams.

❖

I knew Loren real well. When I was working at the courthouse, Ester and Loren would watch my child for me. If something was happening he'd hand-cuff my kid and bring her up the steps. She thought that was the greatest thing.

❖

"

Dirty Herwick used to ride in the rodeos. He was a little long on the list at this particular one up there by where the racetrack is now. He got a mean horse, I guess, and it bucked him off in some fresh manure. He was very very angry, and I guess he did go home and cleaned up.

"

✦✦✦✦✦✦✦✦✦✦✦✦✦✦✦

MUGSY WILSON
Al Wilson

Yeah, I remember Mugsy. He reminded me of an actor — of *My Fair Lady* kind of stuff. He really had an English accent — no, I would say, almost Cockney. That's how it struck me when I heard him talk.

✦

Mugsy was our camp cook when we would go on a big camping trip. We'd take friends along and all. He sat around drinking beer at the Jerome soda fountain when he wasn't occupied elsewhere.

✦

I knew old Mugsy. He had a house right across from the police department. But young Mugsy Jr. is the one who taught me how to swim. Boy, that guy could swim. Jesus, he'd hold his head above water and never get a drop of water on his head. Old Mugs was a pretty good patron of the Tim Kellehers, too.

✦

Mugsy Wilson was the town gossip. If he didn't know it, nobody knew it.

✦

Mugsy used to raise pigeons in that little white building right next to our plumbing shop. What the heck was that? — Cheap Shots, behind that building on Hyman Avenue. He'd turn them loose. That's why they were all in the opera house before they remodeled it. That's where all them pigeons used to come from.

✦

I've heard a lot about Mugsy Wilson. He was a good friend of all my uncles. He died before I came along. Oh, they used to tell stories about Mugsy Wilson, and he was a tough hombre, too. He was a big sport back in those days. That was the

> "
> *Mugsy used to raise pigeons in that little white building right next to our plumbing shop. He'd turn them loose. That's why they were all in the opera house before they remodeled it. That's where all them pigeons used to come from.*
> "

way you measured your manhood, just like the animal kingdom. Beat up on all the neighbors, you were a big guy.

Hotel Jerome Bar and Soda Fountain, February 1946. Roy Porter seated at bar on right. Courtesy Aspen Historical Society.

◆

Mugsy Wilson had the house right where the Impressions Building is. Most of the time when I knew him he was a miner. He played in a band, too — oh, just a little get-together — the Harrington Boys and Jack Shafter.

◆

Mugsy Wilson wasn't very good looking. In a city you would call him a mug.

◆

SKYLER SWEARENGIN

When I was a toddler standing around the kitchen table or on some elder's knee, they'd talk. That's how I came to know a lot of this. At that time, he was Mr. Swearengin. People would not have presumed to have called him by his first name. He was of good stature. I remember him being one of gentlest fellows, most composed of people. He could let loose "expidus" on any given thing. He might be leafing through a magazine and something would strike him and he could turn the air blue. But he didn't do it for shock effect or to get people's attention. He just talked like that.

✦

Skyler Swearengin was a teamster, I think. He had a dog that used to ride on the wagon — just a plain old cur.

✦

I've been in the mine with Skyler Swearengin quite a few times, and he used to take me back to where he was working and show me the lead and zinc in the Smuggler No. 2 tunnel.

✦

He and his family were from Missouri originally. They had worked in the lead mines. In spite of the fact that his expletives could come out in a torrent, you took it, you know. It was just a part of him. He was still a gentleman, and about the time World War II broke out, you can imagine the expletives about the war that escaped his mouth. He was one that did what they call leasing — a kind of lone-wolf mining operation.

✦

Skyler worked over in the Smuggler. He pecked around in one of them old holes. He'd go up there and dig out a little bit of something.

✦

"

I remember Skyler Swearengin being one of the gentlest fellows, most composed of people. He could let loose expletives on any given thing. He might be leafing through a magazine and something would strike him and he could turn the air blue.

"

670

KATE LINDVIG

Kate Lindvig, "Snowmass Kate" — she was out there at Snowmass Ranch, right at the foot of the trail going to Snowmass Lake. Kate used to rent out horses to go up to the lake.

◆

Kate Lindvig used to have a stable in Snowmass Creek. During the summer, she had trips going into Snowmass. My buddies used to work for her. I think she was Jens' aunt. She chewed tobacco.

◆

Kate, the Queen of Snowmass? Damn, I can't remember her name now. I don't know if she was tough or not. She could have been. It's so darn long ago, I can hardly remember my own name.

◆

She was Jens Christiansen's aunt. Nobody got the best of her, either. She had a little money and would pick up the vouchers that we used to get for our grain off of Pitkin County. She'd hang onto them, and then when they got a high price, she'd make money on them.

◆

Kate Lindvig, the Queen of Snowmass. That's Jens' aunt — his mother's sister. I don't know much about her. I talked to her when she came in from the ranch and visited me. She was a very slender, very slight woman — a nice look.

◆

I remember Kate Lindvig. She would sit up there in her wagon and look down. To me she was sharp featured. She'd pull that old hat down over her eyes and sit up there with them reins. She had that whip right there. One time, Uncle John and I were going up there and she was coming down. Them horses didn't go

"

Kate Lindvig ran cattle. They just named her the Cattle Queen of Snowmass because she was the only single woman who homesteaded over there and all of that. She was a maiden lady. She ran a boardinghouse in Aspen first, for the miners.

"

671

*Miss Kate Lindvig,
with American flag,
homesteaded
Snowmass Falls
Ranch.
Courtesy Aspen
Historical Society.*

quite as much as she wanted, and boy, she pulled that whip out and smacked them. I don't know why she never married. I only met her that one time, but I saw her many times. Kate was related to Christiansen — she was Jens' aunt.

✦

Jens' aunt, Kate Lindvig, was known as the Cattle Queen of Snowmass. She ran cattle. They just named her that, I guess, because she was the only single woman who homesteaded up there and all of that. She was a maiden lady. She was a virgin, too, she said. She ran a boardinghouse in Aspen first, for the miners. I think it was called Kate's. When she came to this country, she loved it here. After she became an American citizen, she just worshipped the American flag. She didn't have any yen to go back to Denmark at all. In the photo, she is standing with the flag over her arm.

✦

I knew Kate very well. She was a character. She used to walk from Snowmass to Aspen to get her groceries in a day. She'd stop and see my grandmother on Brush Creek, and they would always plan a trip. My grandmother would say, "As soon as I get rid of the old man, you and I are going to take a trip."

✦

FRANK MOUSHARTS
D. Frank Kochevar
(1863 - 1937)

We owned the land up where the Gant is. We bought all that. And the Whispering Swedes owned land on the other side of the hill. We used to have some good water wars with them. They used to take our water from us, and we'd go take it back. I think they were deaf, weren't they? Those guys did drink a lot, but most Swedes do. The guy who lived right in front of him who was Slovenian — his name was Frank Kochevar or we used to call him Musharts, because that's the village he came from. They used to wash him out all the time — take so much water, you know, the water that should be going over the hill. They would really flood out his fields and Musharts' potatoes, his garden, and everything else. Musharts was always mad at them.

✦

There was a fella in there that they called D. Frank Mousharts, and I don't know how you spell it. He used to make flags out of the old George Washington tobacco bags. This was all in colors and everything. He used to make blankets out of them — sew them together. He was a pretty good sewer, too.

✦

JACK RAY
RAY THUMB

Jack Ray and his horse, Smokey — I knew him real well, as a matter of fact. When he got out of the horse business, I fixed him up. I rented him a room. As my family started, I bought a trailer to put over on this property for him. Ray Thumb was his actual name. He was a prize fighter, you know. He was pretty good. As a matter of fact, I ran into a couple of fellas that seen him in the ring. He was married, and I guess his wife slickered him out of about $40,000. He

> "
> *There was a fella in there that they called D. Frank Mousharts. He used to make flags out of the old George Washington tobacco bags. This was all in colors and everything. He used to make blankets out of them — sew them together. He was a pretty good sewer, too.*
> "

673

wouldn't ever talk too much about it. I split-shift with him. One night he got to singing the blues and gave me the story. That kind of surprised me; a lot of people didn't know. He used to be very defensive about all his horses. They were just like kids. I used to tell him, "Jack, you need some kids instead of these goddamn horses."

◆

Jack Ray — Ray Thumb, they called him. He was an ex-boxer. He ran the stables. One of them was down by the railroad track where Cap's Auto is. There was a barn down there and another one up by the dairy. He had a horse named Smokey — a really good horse.

◆

I knew Jack Ray well. He was marshall, along with John Loushin. He was the night marshall and John was daytime. He was a professional fighter, and a very nice guy. He ran the stables out at the Meadows for years. He worked for my mother-in-law for a long time. He was sort of the gardener for a few hours a day. My dad was getting Jack Ray once to coach me for boxing. I talked to him once about it, and all he said was, "Remember, always tape your hands right. That's what put me out of business." He had a bend in his hand. He said, "This stopped me and my career in fighting because I broke this hand. It wasn't taped right."

◆

WARREN CONNER

Warren Conner's nickname was Puj. I think the Miklich kids named him that. They were doing something one day down by the Catholic Church, and Warren has sometimes that special action he goes through. It's something we were doing and Warren was helping. I don't know if it was the way he was pushing or what.

◆

"

Ray Thumb, he was married, and I guess his wife slickered him out of about $40,000. He wouldn't ever talk too much about it. I split-shift with him. One night he got to singing the blues and gave me the story. He used to be defensive about all his horses. They were just like kids. I used to tell him, "Jack, you need some kids instead of these goddamn horses."

"

Puj was another high school nickname, I think. They called Warren "Kelly," too. A lot of them still call him Kelly.

＋

How did I get my nickname, Puj? That was clear back in high school. Puja is a name that was Austrian, and I don't know what it means in Slovenian. So I was interchangeable. I was Kelly more than I was Puj. I know some of the guys — Frank Loushin and Jimmy Snyder — they still call me Puj, but Albert Bishop calls me Kelly and never has called me anything else. A lot of other friends say, "Well, Kelly, what do you think?" It is a good Irish Catholic name, I guess.

＋

GARY COOPER

Gary Cooper came in the White Kitchen and he'd order breakfast. Then his wife would come. Rocky was her name. She'd wait till he got his, and then she'd look to see how it was. Then she'd order. So it must have looked pretty good. He came in quite regularly. I can remember someone said they all went down to the hotel to see Gary come in when they first came. This one guy was a character, Bradshaw. You know Rocky had this big holder on her cigarette. He went down to see if she was going to bring that cigarette holder to her lips or if her lips were going to jump towards it and take a puff. They used to go around holding it way out. So he went to see if she was going to jump up there.

＋

"

Gary Cooper came in the White Kitchen and he'd order breakfast. Then his wife would come. Rocky was her name. She'd wait till he got his, and then she'd look to see how it was. Then she'd order. So it must have looked pretty good.

"

He built a house in Aspen. He loved our town because people wouldn't hound him for autographs all the time. He'd go into the corner drug, Rexall Drug, and people wouldn't bother him. He was just like a real Aspenite. He used to sit outside the Hotel Jerome on the bench and talk to the old-timers. Nobody made over him.

＋

675

Hotel Jerome, 1905.
Courtesy
Peggy Rowland.

His wife was the celebrity. She was crazy. So was he — crazy about women. I loved him. That don't take anything away from it. He had plenty to spread around. He was a painter, too. Not landscapes — sort of very modernistic.

❖

Why did Gary Cooper like to hang out in Aspen? Because it was more like home to him. He was from a small town in Montana. He loved the countryside. He loved the rustic part of Aspen. He was a very simple man with simple tastes. I kept home for them. I saw to everything — serviced the home. Everything ran perfectly like she wanted it. Rocky (his wife) was the boss. She would come out on Sunday mornings with her fur coats and scarves and say, "You think they'll recognize me?" Going to church and all. I said, "I don't think so."

❖

676

For the Gary Coopers there had to be fresh flowers in every room, even the bathroom. He'd say, "What the hell you got them in here for, Rocky? Smells bad enough as it is, let alone putting roses in."

✦

Gary was so handsome. All the women thought so, too. They drove her crazy. Women was at his feet. He loved it. They deserved each other. You know what I mean. The minute he was out of town, she was with someone else.

✦

When Gary Cooper first started coming to Aspen, he loved to go in Sardy's Hardware Store. There weren't as many people here then. They didn't make over him or pay too much attention. He'd wander around in the store, just like everybody else. Everybody liked him.

✦

JUDGE TOURTELOTTE

I had ol' Judge Tourtelotte that I took care of in the hospital. Tourtelotte Park was named after him. He was kind of old and senile. We had six beds in the men's ward. Down at the entrance, there was Al Wilson, but we called him Mugsy. He had a broken leg. Judge used to roam around in the night. They put a cast on Mugsy's leg. They didn't operate on them in those days like they do now. So this one night, the judge got to wandering around. Mugsy had a flashlight, and he flashed the light at the judge. He was down at the far end in the last bed. I heard the commotion, went in there, and they were all laughing and having a good time. The judge had the blankets pulled over his head and I said, "What's the matter, Judge?" And he said, "Well, you know, I was shot at like that once before."

✦

"

Why did Gary Cooper hang out in Aspen? Because it was more like home to him. He was from a small town in Montana. He loved the countryside. He loved the rustic part of Aspen. He was a very simple man with simple tastes.

"

(Above): Wagon train, Tourtelotte Park, 1890s. Courtesy Robert Zupancis.

(Right): Judge Henry Tourtelotte's cabin, about 1910. Courtesy Ruth Perry.

GUS SWANSON

I knew Gus Swanson. He had a dog, Tootsa. He was a logger, which was pretty typical of the Swedes. Swedes were in the logging industry and drove the horses. Gus did a lot of logging around Independence, Lost Man, and all that area up there. He would bring his logs into town. He was quite a drinker and loved his booze.

✦

Gus was an old wagoner and an old Swede. He used to haul the ore and then hauled coal for the coal company. He had a dog that always followed him along, and several other dogs would follow the dog. That one dog he called Tootsa — mine Tootsa, he would call her. He had a team of horses and a big old wagon

*Tourtelotte Park,
on Aspen Mountain,
1905.
Courtesy
Peggy Rowland.*

and used to do all the freighting around. Another one that loved his grog. That was in the 1930s.

◆

I knew him quite well. He was another alcoholic. He had two horses and he used to haul logs. We used them to build my house. He was a logger — he cut logs and sold lumber.

◆

Gus Swanson was a great big, hard-working teamster. He worked with Al Frost, who was Mona's father-in-law. I can't remember all the names of a lot of the other ones, because in the wintertime they used to stay up there. They would only get to come down maybe on weekends or Saturday mornings. There wasn't any up and down, everyday business when they were working on the contracts widening the road and cutting. They were blasting the cliffs out and stuff like that.

◆

MAX MAROLT

I'll tell you something cute about Max Marolt. His mother was working at the Jerome. It was a soda fountain and bar for a long time. Maxy was just little, you know. He got so he could yodel. It was really nice. People would ask him to yodel. Then someone started to give him a dime or a nickel. So after that, he wouldn't yodel unless you paid him. He was about five or six years old.

◆

NEWT AND BOB KLUSMIRE

All I remember is the time Bob rode his horse into the Red Onion. He'd always go in and get his hat full of beer, take it out, and give it to the horse. He put everything in that hat. He was a real character. He would take the shirt off his back and give it to you, though. Good guy.

◆

All I remember is the time Bob rode his horse into the Red Onion. He'd always go in and get his hat full of beer, take it out, and give it to the horse. He put everything in that hat. He was a real character.

Bob rode his horse in the Red Onion all the time. And when the horse would poop, Bob would put his hat under the horse, pick it up, take it out, and dump it.

✦

Bob Klusmire usually rode his horse in the Onion and then got off. But they didn't let him keep it in there too long. Rita was the horse's name.

✦

Bob was a character. He was a roustabout at every kind of job there was. He worked for us in the plumbing shop. We contracted the five miles of new water line in Aspen at one time and he worked in the trenches — more of a short-term job. His dad told me one time, "Don't pay him because he won't come back." We paid him and he never came back. That was it when he got a pay-check. He thought that was it. He tried to court my aunt one time. He had a mule and used to come see her riding that mule.

✦

Newt and Bob Klusmire were notorious. They were descendants from the Dalton gang — Jessie James and the Daltons. And they acted just like them. They would come to town and had everything but the pistols. They used to come with their horses and get drunk.

✦

Newt and Bob Klusmire were priceless. I have never laughed at a family like I laughed at them. They were the most free-wheeling people. They had the funniest relationship with each other and their dad. Their dad was hilarious. He was a night watchman at the power plant. Once when the boys made his lunch, they put cardboard in his sandwich and put the top on his thermos with a pipe wrench. He came home the next morning and Newt and Bob were still at home. He walked in and he didn't say one word, just walked over and flattened both of them. He was as funny as the boys.

✦

> *Bob rode his horse in the Red Onion all the time. And when the horse would poop, Bob would put his hat under the horse, pick it up, take it out, and dump it.*

BREEZY ZORDEL

Breezy Zordel worked for Tom Sardy at the lumberyard and he was very good. He was wonderful to everybody and waited on them and did for them. How did he get the name Breezy? I don't know, except he had a manner that was sort of like that in a way. He was always ready to talk and laugh. Shoot the breeze.

◆

How did he get his name? He came to Aspen with it from Kansas.

◆

How did Breezy get his name? He loved to talk.

◆

I talked to Breezy's brother the other day, and he said he got that name when he was a kid playing baseball. He was so fast they called him Breezy.

◆

BUBBY LIGHT

I guess my dad was great to put a nickname on everybody. He always did. When I was born I was real fat and I couldn't get up. If I fell down, they'd have to set me up. I don't know whether that was why Dad called me Bubby, but he always had a nickname for every kid in the valley. I don't guess his brothers did, but some of their friends their age would come, and by God, when they left, they had a nickname of some kind.

◆

Gladyce Christiansen taught him in school in the fourth grade on Capitol Creek. Bubby was laughing all the time. He's got a real hearty laugh.

◆

"

When I was born I was real fat and I couldn't get up. If I fell down, they'd have to set me up. I don't know whether that was why Dad called me Bubby, but he always had a nickname for every kid in the valley. I don't guess his brothers did, but some of their friends their age would come, and by God, when they left, they had a nickname of some kind.

"

682

PUPPY SMITH

How did I get the name Puppy? We went down to what they call the ice pond and were going to learn how to swim. A bunch of kids from town were swimming, and a kid by the name of Bobbie picked me up and carried me out in the water and let me go. They said I came swimming in like a puppy dog, and that's where it started. My boy is called Spot. We used to call his wife Speck and their son Speckle.

◆

CHARLIE RAYMOND
(1876 - 1936)

Charlie Raymond lived right across the street from us. He used to come over on cold mornings. Charlie had an old Model T Ford. He jacked it up and would get in and pretend he was driving it. He had a garage next door. One day, the damn thing tipped off the blocks and crashed and went through the garage. Then he took it downtown and knocked down a telephone post. Those Model Ts had a habit of jackknifing. They'd just take off. Poor old Charlie had a helluva time with that Model T. He would come over. He would read the thermometer and would say, "It's ten zero below zero."

◆

FRED WILLOUGHBY
(1910-1975)

I worked for Fred Willoughby up in the mine, and then when we started the plumbing shop, he worked for us — Grant and Company. Fred was doing mostly service work, and we asked him one time if he would like to take work in the evenings. So we advertised his phone number and said if you have an emergency, call Fred Willoughby. So one day, he came over to the office and he said, "You haven't come over to the house for a long time, Joe. Come on over tonight." I said, "Well, if I get a minute, I will." So I went over there and we got to drinking and feeling pretty good. The phone rang and this woman said,

" Charlie Raymond had an old Model T Ford. He jacked it up and would get in and pretend he was driving it. He had a garage next door. One day, the damn thing tipped off the blocks, crashed, and went through the garage. Then he took it downtown and knocked down a telephone post. Those Model Ts had a habit of jackknifing. Poor ol' Charlie had a helluva time with that Model T.
"

"Fred, I got a leak in my kitchen sink," and Fred said, "Go ahead. It's your sink." And he went back to drinking.

✦

Fred Willoughby really deserves a lot of credit for Aspen becoming a ski area. Fred and Frank did a lot of physical work. Frank was a surveyor, too. He surveyed the property at the ranch in the 1940s. His dad was mayor of Aspen. Fred was the plumber. Frank was an engineer and a very quiet person. very studious and intelligent. Frances Willoughby is a twin sister of Frank Willoughby.

✦

The Willoughbys and my father and mother were very close. They were social with the Becks and the Magnificos. There were a considerable number of parties and these were always late-night parties because the Jerome Buffet Room would never close until 1:00 or 2:00 A.M. After that, they would have these huge spaghetti dinners with the Magnificos. I've never been able to find anything as good as that. I can remember Fred Willoughby one night wearing a shade off one of the lamps at our house across the street from the Jerome and my mother's nightie. He was double-jointed. He'd do the craziest contortions that you've ever seen in your life. Unbelievable. These parties went on to 3:00 to 5:00 A.M. And then my mother would go and open up the Buffet Room at 8:00 A.M.

✦

FREDDIE FISHER

He used to have that fix-it shop. Fred went down to do service work on this one house, and this woman had a big pot of beans on the stove. So after he got done with the service work, the woman said, "Well, Fred, you want to get paid in cash or take it out in trade?" Fred says, "It is against company rules to take it out in trade, but I'm going against the rules this time. I'll have a bowl of them beans." His wife was real Irish — big, heavyset Irish. So some woman asked Fred if he had a dishwasher at home and he said, "Yes, a heavyduty Irish."

✦

> "
> *I went over there and we got to drinking and feeling pretty good. The phone rang and this woman said, 'Fred, I got a leak in my kitchen sink,' and Fred said, 'Go ahead. It's your sink.' And he went back to drinking.*
> "

OLD MAN GROHAR
Louis Grohar

JOHANNA GROHAR

Old Man Grohar lived in Aspen a long time. They lived in that little Victorian house on the last block when you're going toward the pass. His wife was a character. She used to bootleg all the time in Leadville before she married him, and then they bootlegged together. He used to go fishing out at Snowmass. In those days, he came back with whole tubs full. We would go over there when I was little. She had a lean-to kitchen, and the stove was in the back. There were coffee cans with flowers in the window. In those days, when your window got cracked, you put a button on each side and sewed them together. Every one of her windows had a button. Grandma's windows had them, too. They would have buttons so that the glass wouldn't fall out. Old Man Grohar was a great character — a blacksmith. They were Slovenian. He had a blacksmith shop where City Market is. He had a great big red barn back there. We used to go there and have our plowshares sharpened.

◆

ED TIEDERMAN

I loved Ed Tiederman's store. It was right next to Angie's White Kitchen. It was one of those little narrow things. We used to go buy candy there all the time. He sold coal and everything else. We used to deliver grain to their house. Mrs. Tiederman was a delight.

◆

Ed Tiederman was a very good friend of mine. He had a wooden leg. I guess he broke it or something and they had to amputate it. He had Tiederman's store, and he used to sell coal all the time. All the old-timers used to play cards in the back — sluff or hearts.

◆

"

In those days, when your window got cracked, you put a button on each side and sewed them together. Every one of her windows had a button. Grandma's windows had them, too. They would have buttons so that the glass wouldn't fall out.

"

Ed Tiederman had a little grocery, cigar, and tobacco store. In the back room they used to have a cribbage game or something going on all the time, or poker. The place always reeked because they had an outdoor privy and it was attached to the building. He used to deliver coal, too. His wife sold eggs and chickens.

✦

CAP CAPARELLA
James Caparella
(1881-1957)

Cap Caparella was a beautiful, dear gentleman. He was a powerful man. He could stoop down and scoop up most any man. I loved Cappy, and I loved his wife. She was a darling. She had twelve children. And the one thing I remember about her so well is she loved *all* those kids. She took very good care of them. She was wide and fat, but darling. Gulio, her beloved child — she loved that boy the best of all. He was her last boy. I don't know if there was any daughters after that, but Gulio, mind you, she loved him. During the first part of the war, he came home for a visit with her. I knew that he was home, and I spoke to him several times. After he left, she called me. She said, "You've got to come quick. Please come." So I rushed over and she had a lovely plant — a big green plant. Gulio had given that to her when he was little. I rushed over and that plant had wilted. She knew Gulio was killed in the war. That hurt me so bad.

✦

James Caparella — Old Man Cap — was a wonderful man. I don't have any idea how he got hired, but he did some amazing things. He lived right across the street from us. He came from Marble as a marble cutter — he and Jim and then Teleo, Galleo, Tony, Jimmy, Mike, Victorio, and Gulio. Caparella was probably the best gardener in the country. He was wonderful. He had two unusual traits. The first one was the willow baskets. He made the most beautiful willow baskets you ever saw — big laundry baskets. Ours lasted a long time. Secondly, my dad imported pea seeds from Scotland. Cap got peas from him and kept the seeds every year. We had peas from Scotland every year from then on.

✦

"

Old Man Cap was a wonderful man. He had two unusual traits. He made the most beautiful willow baskets you ever saw — big laundry baskets. Secondly, my dad imported pea seeds from Scotland. Cap got peas from him and kept the seeds every year. We had peas from Scotland every year from then on.

"

The Caparella family: Jimmy, Mable, Tony, Mike, Carmen, Teleo, Vick, Galleo, Gulio. Parents Rosa and James. 1920s.

Cap Caparella could pick up a big kitchen table with his teeth. He had never gone to the dentist, and his teeth were pearly white. You had to persuade him to do it, but if you worked on him long enough, he would. I only saw him do it once. He'd get down and bite that table, then stand up and the table would come right up. His teeth were strong from pulling reeds when he made baskets.

Cap Caparella was a great basket weaver. He wove some of the finest baskets in town. In the spring of the year he would go down along the Forks and get the willows. He would sit there and weave baskets. That's where Cap learned his trade. He was quite an artist. Cap was also a marble worker.

JUDGE DEANE
(1853 – 1930)

Judge Deane was a darling. I just loved him. I was thirteen years old and Grampsy — that was his wife — was getting so she could not get up in the morning and get going. So she said, "Please come over and help Judge Deane." My mother said, "Do it for her." They were good friends. So I went over and I'd do little old things. I would fix coffee for them. My mother would tell me how to make so and so, and I'd make that. I was very close to them. He was old then.

✦

Had Deane came here to visit his grandpa and grandma one summer. I think that we were both fourteen or fifteen. We'd see each other over at the Hotel Jerome and have ice cream and so on, and then he'd come over to my house, right across the street, and we would play the Victrola. We never danced. We'd hold hands over the Victrola. It was cute. It was a sweet thing.

✦

RED ROWLAND
(1908-1987)

Red Rowland had his horses. Snort was one. He also had Prince, Snow King, and Carrie. He had quite a few horses. He always looked like he was riding a horse when he was walking down the street. Red could train a horse for a mountain horse probably better than anybody I've ever known. I was riding Prince one time, and the saddle spun. I had had my leg hurt when I was hunting. I slipped. I had bad knees anyway. I went underneath that horse, and that horse stopped right there. It was in the trees and everything. That's the kind of horse you want to ride.

✦

Red broke horses. Then he used to take hunters out — guide them, mainly — over Hunter Creek. He loved horses. He and Peggy were married on horseback at Maroon Lake. He was a pretty rugged character.

Red Rowland, 1954.
Courtesy
Peggy Rowland.

✦

Hunter Creek Dam, 1901. Courtesy Peggy Rowland.

This was told to me by Kathleen, who is Red Rowland's sister that lives in Grand Junction. She told me that when Red was a young man he used to take Lowell and Donny with him a lot around town when Red was going with some girl. She came to him and she said, "I wish you'd get rid of those two boys." They were just young kids. "They'll think they belong to us or something." And so he dumped her because he wasn't about to dump the two boys.

◆

TONY PERKO
(1882 - 1955)

Tony used to walk like Charlie Chaplin — kinda waddle. Tony was short and stocky — a real hard worker. I remember some guys teased him about the way he walked once. Tony got so mad. Later they found out he used to work in the Pueblo smelters. A bucket of molten ore tipped and flooded the floor area on him. He got caught and couldn't get out of it. A tough guy.

◆

JAKEY YECKEL
(1860 - 1946)

Jakey lived at the hotel when I knew him. He would stake claims, then go back East and sell people on the idea. He got their money and lived on it. He never dug a nickel's worth of metal, but he would go out maybe on a Monday and have somebody take him out to the mountain and set up there. He'd do a little assessment work and have somebody else with him — never any dirty work. He was in his fifties. He'd spend a couple days there and then come back and sit around the hotel. Had the money rolling in. Always lived at the hotel and was single.

❖

You could almost tell the day that Jakey Yeckel was going to arrive in Aspen. He stayed at the hotel during the day, but every afternoon around five he would come downstairs all dressed to the nines and sit down in a rocking chair and smoke a cigar. He was a big prospector, I guess. He had property up at Lenado.

❖

VIZA'S RESTAURANT

Viza's Restaurant was on Hyman Street. He used to fix the best steaks. That's all he'd fix. If you wanted anything else, if you wanted salad or anything, you brought your own. He had a great big stove — six feet — with a heavy cast-iron top two inches thick. When that got warm and heated up, it would stay hot until the next day. There was no place in town where you could get a better steak than at Viza's. He and his wife had a frilly carriage, and she would be decked out in jewelry all the time — rings on every finger.

❖

CAT KELLY

Cat Kelly. I just marveled at that woman. She fascinated me to no end. She lived here during the Depression. She had a mining claim way up in the Midnight. Ashcroft — up that way. Everybody would say, "Watch, she'll gather cats all summer." And she did. She gathered up kitty cats, and they're easy to gather, and put them in sacks. Then she'd make several trips to the mountain and carry big sacks of cats. I really watched her. I'm a very curious person. Anyway, when spring came, there was not *one* cat left. She did cook them. She did roast them.

> " *Cat Kelly. I just marveled at that woman. She lived here during the Depression. She had a mining claim way up in the Midnight. Everybody would say, 'Watch, she'll gather cats all summer.' And she did. She gathered up kitty cats and put them in sacks. Then she'd make several trips to the mountain and carry big sacks of cats. When spring came, there was not one cat left.* "

691

✦

She never did anything else unusual. She acted like a very calm, nice person. Did she ever marry? Oh, I hope not. I mean, I hope she didn't get him first. That woman used to fascinate me to no end. Here were all these cats, who I loved. I was sorry she was gathering them up. There was cats all over — litters of kittens. She was in middle life and mentally very off.

✦

CRAZY BILL OF ASHCROFT

Sure can — many's the time I've seen him passing the Hurricane, when I used to work steel there. He had a mighty comfortable cabin, too. He had it built against the side of the hill — they are easy to find. He had a big open fireplace and bin over it like an ore bin. He'd fill this with logs about once a week. He had a chute with a rope, so he could set in his chair and pull a string when he wanted another log on the fire. You fellows has seen these new fangled cigarette boxes. He had a pair of slippers nailed on the wall alongside the fireplace. He'd take off his boots in the evening and put his feet in his slippers. Didn't even have to hold his feet in place. He was a contriving cuss, even if he was crazy. As always, there's a fine drawn line between brilliance and craziness.

✦

WALT ATCHISON

Walt Atchison had the Conoco station. Then he was a mail carrier. He used to go down and bring the mail up from the train to the post office. He stopped at the Hotel Jerome all the time and had a shot or two. But I never saw him stagger or wobble or nothing. He could put away a lot of whiskey. He'd come by there and get a drink or two and then go on his business.

✦

> "
> *Crazy Bill had a big open fireplace and bin over it like an ore bin. He'd fill this with logs about once a week. He had a chute with a rope, so he could set in his chair and pull a string when he wanted another log on the fire. He had a pair of slippers nailed on the wall longside the fireplace. He'd take off his boots in the evening and put his feet in his slippers. Didn't even have to hold his feet in place.*
> "

JENKY
George Jenkinson

Jenky. George Jenkinson. He was the caretaker at the cemetery. He had a little donkey and a little cart. He wasn't born here. He was born on the Isle of Man. He and his brother came over together to mine, as far as I know. Frank was his brother. He was a janitor over at the old Washington School.

✦

Jenky. That was George Jenkinson. He was cute. He was Welsh — from the Isle of Man. He wore a little flat cap and had a donkey and little cart. He lived right across the street from me. He took care of the cemetery. In his cart he would have a shovel and a broom. He kept the cemetery nice. He looked old. His wife died three days before she was 100. Her daughter now is ninety-one. We called them Pop and Nana.

✦

Another funny story — I can't remember his first name, but he was a caretaker at the cemetery. He lived up there by the Crestahaus. His name was Jenkinson. I was just a child growing up. He had a donkey. The burro would come to the Cooper Avenue Bridge and would not cross the bridge. So he would be out there tugging and tugging on it. As a matter of fact, one time he built a fire under him and the donkey got away from him and ran up the hill.

✦

IRMA ROGERS

Irma Rogers was the one that put the car in the bank. I don't know why she did. Put it right up those stairs, right in the door. They have a photo of it.

✦

Irma Rogers backed her car up the bank steps. I think it was an accident. She was wild. She just lived to be happy.

> *"*
>
> *George Jenkinson had a donkey. The burro would come to the Cooper Avenue Bridge and would not cross the bridge. So he would be out ther tugging and tugging on it. As a matter of fact, one time he built a fire under him and the donkey got away from him and ran up the hill.*
>
> *"*

*Irma Rogers' car,
1930s.
Photo by
Francis Kalmes.
Courtesy Aspen
Historical Society.*

◆

Everybody knows the story about Irma Rogers backing into the bank. She was flea-brained. I think it was an accident. Nobody could have done it deliberately. She must have been going pretty fast to get up those stairs.

◆

I'm sure you have the story of Irma Rogers. She was a town character, too. She got drunk one night and, believe it or not, at the Bank of Aspen (Ute City Banque), she got her car up those steps all the way to the top. It was an amazing thing to see.

◆

TILLIE ROTHCHILD

Tillie Rothchild was a diminutive little lady who had been there from the early days. She always wore her 1800-period clothing. She was an old, old lady. She wore those little brooches and that little lace thing on her head like a doily. She lived down toward the West End. She was on the Aspen Mountain side of Main Street, straight down from Ruthie's Run — somewhere in there. She was kind of a precious little thing. It was sad because she was destitute. People tried to help her out, but those people didn't take kindly to alms. She was like something out of a picture book.

◆

I used to go to Mrs. Rothchild's house after work and bring in her coal buckets and everything. She used to tell me stories about how she used to write to the newspapers. She and the editor would have things going back and forth.

◆

Irma Rogers' car on the bank steps. Courtesy Aspen Historical Society.

695

Calvin Miller with William C. Stapleton at Calvin's cabin in Ashcroft, 1938. Courtesy Louiva Stapleton.

CALVIN MILLER

A little old prospector used to live behind me in the alley. He had one of those miners' shacks with all kinds of old stuff crammed in there. Calvin had a long, gray ponytail down his back and never cut his hair. Not long after he died, his shack burned down. He must have had a lot of sulphur in there because it stank to high heaven. They used sulphur in mining, ya know. That smell was in the neighborhood for the longest time — smelled like rotten eggs.

◆

CHICKEN BILL

Chicken Bill's last name was Lee. He developed the nickname Chicken Bill because he was arrested stealing chickens. He worked for my father when he was doing something special and needed a hand for a few days. I think the chickens were available and he thought he would like to have 'em.

◆

RUBY BANDY

Ruby Bandy had a horse out at the ranch that my dad was boarding for her and she wouldn't pay the bill. He asked her for the money and she hit him across the mouth with a quirt. He never did get the money. She got fired from Kalmes and Company because some lady tried on a hat and she laughed.

◆

CACTUS GOLD

How did Cactus get that name? From fighting. He was as tough as a cactus.

◆

THE BOYS AT THE POST OFFICE

All the old men used to hang out around the post office. Alex Barrailler, Alex Betemps, and Roy Porter all lived down in that area right where the Eagles Club is now. They used to go up there and sit on the benches. They were real old-timers and the gals would go by there when the short skirts come along. They had chewing tobacco and would spit on their legs as they went by.

◆

All the old fellows used to go up to the post office, where Esprit is now. They'd sit out there whether they got any mail or not. They'd always go down about noon. I know none of those old boys would get mail too often. They'd sit on the shady side in the morning and then when the sun come 'round, they'd sit over on the other side. Gary Cooper used to go over there and talk with them. They thought they were really popular. There was Alex Barrailler, Chuck Hannan, Jack Shafter, and Hoofy Sandstrom — the guys around the post office. You could always see the same guys sitting on the steel benches. When Gary Cooper came, he used to sit out there with them and shoot the breeze with all of them. They'd go to the Red Onion early in the morning and get a few beers and then go sit by the post office and wait for their mail, which they never got. It was always social, people coming and going. Everybody went to get their mail there, so they saw everybody.

◆

The old men around the post office — oh, hell, they were notorious — the Harrington brothers, Jap Morgan, Chickie Hannan, Alex Barrailler. They all were notorious for the Post Office Round Table meeting every day. Chickie was

> "
> *Gary Cooper used to go over there and talk with them. These guys would go to the Red Onion early in the morning and get a few beers and then go sit by the post office and wait for their mail, which they never got. It was always social, people coming and going.*
> "

Post Office,
Elks Building, 1931.
The gathering place.
Courtesy Aspen
Historical Society.

a miner and did everybody's labor. He was kind of all-around handy. August Erickson was always around there. You know you'd go down to the post office, and they were always there. Sometimes they would drink wine. It was kind of tough to get to know them. But in those days, Aspen's society here was so simple and so informal. Little kids six years old would walk down the street, and they could see Jap Morgan who was sixty years old, and the little kid would say, "Hello, Jap," and Jap would say, "Hello, son" If you wanted to talk to them, they would talk to you. That doesn't happen now in our society. That's the way it was then. If I was walking by there, I didn't have anything to do, either. So I would say, "Hello, Jap; hello, Chickie." They would say hello back. There would be forty years difference in age. If you wanted to sit and listen to them or talk to them, they would talk to you.

❖

There is a story that one of my uncles told me about this guy, Dick Myers. Dick lived by the Roaring Fork River. He was a proud old coot, but he never did learn to read — he was illiterate. Anyway, he would come down and sit in front of the post office, buy a paper, and pretend like he was reading. This one day he was reading the paper and it was upside-down, and there was a picture of a ship on it. Somebody looked over his shoulder. He looked up and said, "Ha, ha, a disaster at sea." They were always talking mining — mining and girls. They were frisky old buggers.

✦

Anton Kastelik lived up beyond my grandfather somewhere, and he used to walk downtown all the time. They called him Andy Gump. All the Slovenians and Italians walked downtown with a gimp — with their hands behind their back and hunched over. Often they walked around the house all winter, and their linoleums were always worn. They'd walk from window to window for exercise, I guess. They used to chew mail pouch — big-leaf tobacco, a great big jawful. My dad, he used to chew that tobacco. He had a spit can and spit into it. Betemps used to come to the post office. He was a little short fat guy. I remember those guys would be there all the time. I think they went down in the morning. Some of them went and had a beer and just hung around the post office and talked in foreign languages half the time.

✦

Old guys sitting around the post office? Gawd, they used to look the girls up and down. You felt like you were going through a gauntlet when you walked in. I think my father was one of those. All these old Aspenites used to go down and stand by the post office. Another place they used to stand is up by where Tompkin's Hardware used to be, and they'd stand and watch people ski. That's when they were starting to ski. You'd go in the post office, particularly on a winter day, and if they weren't working — I think it was more during the Depression — they used to stand around the post office all the time and just hang out there.

✦

We used to sit down there with the old-timers. When we were kids, and later after the war, it used to be the same way — people would socialize. They had a big bench on the south, so they were able to watch people ski sitting there. There were benches outside, too.

✦

"

All the old men used to hang out around the post office. Alex Barrailler, Alex Betemps, and Roy Porter all lived down in that area right where the Eagles Club is now. They used to go up there and sit on the benches. They were real old-timers and the gals would go by there when the short skirts come along. They had chewing tobacco and would spit on their legs as they went by.

"

On the corner by the old post office when it was in the Elk's building, Gary Cooper would sit there and chew tobacco with the old-timers. Shoot the breeze. Chew tobacco and have a cheap bottle of wine under their bench. Alex Barrailler and Tobey, Alex Betemps, Roy Porter, the Hannans. There were quite a bunch of them. You'd catch them in phases. There'd be one group and then the next.

✦

He would use that degree mark as a zero. A lot of them used to loaf around the post office. That was quite an old gang. I'll never forget the guys talking; they would laugh about it. The gals started wearing these short skirts and everything, and they would take a spit and put tobacco juice on their legs and the gals would look at them.

✦

"

They were always talking mining — mining and girls. They were frisky old buggers.

"

Roy Porter just hung out at the post office. I think he was an old miner. Those old guys used to sit around the post office. Sat on these wire benches. The thing I remember, in the summer months you would hear the train whistle about 11 in the morning. When you heard the whistle blow at the Butte, you knew that the train was coming in. That was the signal for people to head uptown, because they knew the mail would be coming in. Walt Atchison, who had the Federal Express, would go down and unload the packages and the mail to take it up to the post office. Alton Beck was the postmaster. All the old-timers would sit on these wire benches and people would come in and chat with them. They had all them old boxes with the combination numbers. I remember in the spring of the year, you would hear the baby chicks chirping in the back there. They came in boxes with little holes in them and you would see their heads sticking out of these holes. They were sticking them out and looking around. Can you imagine that today? That sterile post office down there? I think about how it used to be when you could go in and smell that oil that they mopped the wood floors with. Hannibal would hang out there. Next door to the post office was Paige's Grocery. One of the things I remember the most was the first of the month. People would pay their bills. It was all cash. Carry mostly, credit. When our folks would go in to pay the grocery bill, there would always be a sack of candy for the kids. We always looked forward to the first of the month because we would get some sweets.

✦

Ol' Bert Schwartz would ride Bessie to town everyday to the post office. After he was done with his doin's, why a couple of fellas would always hit Bessie in the rump with peashooters so she'd act up a bit. Then Bert would get her in line and couldn't figure out why she got so frisky. A frisky day at the post office!

✦

Old-timers talked about their horses, too. There were thousands of stories about different horses. I remember Steve Marolt's horse's name was Snake, but his notorious horse was Girly. This was before my time. He used to race this horse at the race track, and Girly won everything. Steve was kind of a little lightweight guy and used to get on that horse and beat the wind. Horses were everybody's life. Everybody loved them. Bob Klusmire's horse, Rita, followed Bob everywhere. Red Rowland loved horses — he always had a horse. If he had a choice between a horse and a car, he would always take a horse. In those days, everybody had a dog, and 80 percent of the people had a horse. Everybody had a good dog. They used to train their dogs. They followed the guys wherever they went. They would ride the tops of their pickups and their cars. The dogs were a jewel — an important part of life.

✦

Post office, Elks Building, about 1947. Courtesy Martin Garfinkel.

In an age of computers, fax machines, videos,
Xeroxes, and everything else
that enables us to do things faster,
we no longer have time to sit down and chat.
We no longer have time to meet our neighbor.

Aspen's population of people
born during the Quiet Years is dwindling.
Many have died.
Many have moved to slower towns.
Most of the stories are gone with the residents
and some remain to remind us
of what we have become.

Aspen has worked hard to save
the physical remains of a once-great mining town.
This book is dedicated to preserving
its spiritual heritage as well.

INDEX TO INTERVIEWS